EUROPEAN UNION LAW AND DEFENCE INTEGRATION

This new work examines the legal dimension of European defence integration from 1945 onwards, revealing the evolution of 'European defence and security law' in its legal, historical, and political context. The notion of 'defence law' describes the entire field of rules created to regulate the defence of a nation or alliance. Commencing with the earliest mutual defence treaties and the failure of the European Defence Community the book examines the disappearance of defence and security from the mainstream of European integration in the 1950s and its revitalisation in the Treaties of Maastricht, Amsterdam, and Nice. In the context of this evolutionary process, the book examines the function of Community Law and its impact on the composition of the armed forces, the procurement of armaments, or the regulation of the defence industries. The book concludes with an analysis of the Common Security and Defence Policy of the Constitutional Treaty, agreed in 2004, which aims to overcome the three-Pillar structure of the Union. Nevertheless, it leaves the intergovernmental character of the security and defence policy intact and introduces flexible frameworks for its mutual defence, crisis management, and armaments components. However, the author argues, the Union needs a coherent defence policy to ensure her security and to speak with one voice on the international scene.

Volume 7 in the series Modern Studies in European Law

Modern Studies in European Law

1 Soft Law in European Community Law *Linda Senden*

2 The Impact of European Rights on National Legal Cultures *Miriam Aziz*

3 Partnership Rights, Free Movement and EU Law *Helen Toner*

4 National Remedies Before the Court of Justice *Michael Dougan*

5 The National Courts Mandate in the European Constitution *Monica Claes*

6 EU Environmental Law *Maria Lee*

7 European Union Law and Defence Integration *Martin Trybus*

European Union Law and Defence Integration

Martin Trybus
University of Nottingham

·HART·
PUBLISHING
OXFORD AND PORTLAND OREGON
2005

Published in North America (US and Canada)
by Hart Publishing
c/o International Specialized Book Services
920 NE 58th Avenue, Suite 300
Portland, OR 97213-3786
USA
Tel: +1 503 287 3093 or toll-free: (1) 800 944 6190
Fax: +1 503 280 8832
E-mail: orders@isbs.com
Web Site: www.isbs.com

Hart Publishing, Salter's Boatyard, Folly Bridge, Abingdon Road,
Oxford, OX1 4LB
email: mail@hartpub.co.uk
Telephone: +44 (0)1865 245533 Fax: +44 (0)1865 794882
WEB SITE http//:www.hartpub.co.uk

British Library Cataloguing in Publication Data
Data Available
ISBN 1-84113-440-6 (hardback)

Typeset by Compuscript Ltd., Ireland in Minion 10/12 pt
Printed and bound in Great Britain by
Lightning Source UK Ltd

Meiner Schwester

'As a Union of 25 states with over 450 million people generating a quarter of the world's Gross National Product, and with a wide range of instruments at its disposal, the European Union is inevitably a global player [...] Europe should be ready to share the responsibility for global security and in building a better world.'

From the European Security Strategy

Preface

2004 HAS BEEN a momentous year for European defence integration. Enlargement to twenty-five member States has multiplied the defence and security issues facing the Union, while the Constitutional Treaty represents an attempt to address some of these concerns. The Union's military presence has grown from the small missions in Macedonia and the Congo in 2003, to a much larger force in Bosnia replacing the NATO-led force from December 2004. Member States' agreement to develop more effective legal mechanisms and powers to facilitate defence and to promote security under the so-called second pillar has only been achieved in more recent times. In contrast, as might be anticipated with an organisation based historically on economic integration, there exists a much more developed jurisprudence under the First Pillar of the Union.

Part I of this timely monograph traces the evolution of European defence integration from the failed European Defence Community initiative of the 1950s to the Common Foreign and Security Policy enshrined in the Maastricht Treaty of 1992 and developed further by subsequent treaty amendments. It also details the manifestation of a European Security and Defence Policy beginning with the Saint-Malo Summit of 1998, when the United Kingdom finally fully recognised the need for European security. While the legal mechanisms and norms in this area, essentially the external aspect of EU Defence Law, are still underdeveloped, Part II of the volume shows a high level of sophistication in its internal aspect, namely the development of Community law as an instrument of defence integration. Both primary and secondary legislation, as well as the case law of the European Court, are carefully analysed, as are the effects of security concerns on the application of fundamental principles governing free movement, competition, procurement, the defence industry and the armed forces. This Part shows that 2004 has also been a significant year for the First Pillar and defence integration, with the application of a new Public Procurement Directive analysed in chapter 7, while a New Merger Regulation is considered in chapter 8.

Part III brings the story of defence integration fully up-to-date, and beyond, with its discussion of the implications of the 2004 Constitutional Treaty. Whether or not this Treaty enters into force, the discussion that it has provoked, and will continue to provoke, shows the importance of defence and security matters to the Union. As the period of post Cold War instability continues well beyond the attacks of 11 September 2001 and their immediate aftermath, European defence and security will continue to occupy the minds of politicians, lawyers and citizens of the Union. Dr. Trybus' monograph provides a much needed, clear exposition of the whole range of key legal issues concerning European defence and security.

Professor Nigel D White
Centre for Conflict and Security Law
University of Nottingham School of Law

Acknowledgements

I WANT TO express my gratitude to the colleagues who supported me in writing this monograph. Anthony Arnull (Birmingham) and Steve Peers (Essex) acted as referees for the successful study leave application to the Arts and Humanities Research Board that made it possible to complete the book. Colleagues at the University of Nottingham, namely Sue Arrowsmith, Olympia Bekou, Aristides Georgopoulos, Matthew Happold, Tammara Hervey, Jeffrey Kenner, Thérèse Murphy, Franceso Seatzu, and last but not least Nigel White provided useful comments on the entire book project or on individual chapters. During my time as a visiting fellow at the University of Utrecht colleagues there did the same, namely Deidre Curtin, Ige Dekker, Filip Dorssemont, Kamiel Mortelmans, Ronald van Oijk, Sacha Prechal, and Ramses Wessel. Moreover, colleagues from various institutions similarly supported me, namely George Berman (Columbia), Panos Koutrakos (Durham), and Nanette Neuwahl (Montreal).

I would also like to thank Christopher Yukins from The George Washington University Law School, Washington, DC, USA, Hugh Corder from the Faculty of Law at the University of Cape Town, South Africa, and Ige Dekker from the University of Utrecht, The Netherlands and the staff and students at these establishments for welcoming me on my study visits when writing this book.

Moreover, I am grateful to the University of Nottingham School of Law and the Arts and Humanities Research Board for financing a full year study leave that made the completion of this book possible.

Finally, I want to thank Nigel White for writing the introduction to this book and his wife Gil White for helping with the proofs. The title of chapter 1 was inspired by Erich Maria Remargue's novel 'All Quiet on the Western Front'. The title of chapter 7 was inspired by Sun Tzu's book 'The Art of War' and the title of chapter 9 by William Shakespeare's 'Henry V'.

Supported by:

A·H·R·B

arts and humanities research board

The AHRB funds postgraduate training and research in the arts and humanities, from archaeology and English literature to design and dance. The quality and range of research supported not only provides social and cultural benefits but also contributes to the economic success of the UK. The importance of the arts and humanities has been recognised by the government's decision to make the AHRB a research council through the forthcoming Higher Education Bill. For further information on the AHRB, please see our website www.ahrb.ac.uk

Outline Table of Contents

Table of Contents

Table of Cases

EUROPEAN COURT OF JUSTICE
(Chronological order)

COURT OF FIRST INSTANCE

(Chronological order)

(Alphabetical order)

INTERNATIONAL COURT OF JUSTICE

NATIONAL CASES

Germany

Ireland

United Kingdom

Table of Legislation

INTERNATIONAL TREATIES

SECONDARY EUROPEAN LEGISLATION

EC Directives

EC Regulations

EU Decisions

National

AUSTRIA

BELGIUM

DENMARK

FINLAND

FRANCE

GERMANY

Basic Law

Abbreviations

CFSP	Common Foreign and Security Policy
CSDP	Common Security and Defence Policy
EAA	European Armaments Agency
EC	European Community
ECSC	European Coal and Steel Community
EEC	European Economic Community
EDA	European Defence Agency
EDC	European Defence Community
EDF	European Defence Forces
EPC	European Political Cooperation
ERRF	European Rapid Reaction Force
ESA	European Space Agency
ESDP	European Security and Defence Policy
ETD	Equal Treatment Directive
EU	European Union
EUMC	European Union Military Committee
EUMS	European Union Military Staff
EUPM	European Union Police Mission
OCCAR	Organisation for Joint Armaments Co-operation
LoI	Letter of Intend
NATO	Northern Atlantic Treaty Organisation
PSC	Political and Security Committee
QMV	Qualified Majority Voting
SEA	Single European Act
TEU	Treaty on European Union
UN	United Nations
WEAG	Western European Armaments Group
WEAO	Western European Armaments Orgnisation
WEU	Western European Union

Introduction

EUROPE IS NOT a peaceful continent. It has endured the Thirty Years' War, the Eighty Years' War, and even the Hundred Years' War. The 19th century saw *inter alia* the Napoleonic Wars, the Crimean War, and the wars leading to the unifications of Germany and Italy. World War I, World War II, and the Cold War followed a series of Balkan wars in the 20th century. Most recently the break up of the Soviet Union and most notably Yugoslavia led to a series of armed conflicts. The regular occurrence of war made it necessary for European governments to raise armed forces. Ever since such government institutions existed, the cabinet ministers responsible for the military were called 'secretaries of war' and their offices the 'departments of war'. This was a reflection of the dominant understanding that, as Clausewitz put it, war was a "continuation of politics by other means". After two devastating World Wars the prohibition of the use of force limited the legality of war, from a national perspective, to the right to self-defence. Consequently the ministers and departments of war gradually became ministers and departments of defence. Theoretically the sole task of these ministries was to organise the defence of their country, especially against the threat posed by the other military bloc during the Cold War.

After the end of the Cold War the military threat posed by NATO and the Warsaw Pact respectively vanished. As the extensive defence effort of the past was no longer necessary the armed forces of many countries had to find new reasons for their expensive existence in times of tight budgets. New security activities, from humanitarian action to peacemaking, had already developed into an additional *raison d'être* for the military. Moreover, recently the fight against terrorism was added to their tasks. Just as the focus shifted from 'war' to 'defence' after World War II, the emphasis has been shifting from 'defence' to 'security' after the Cold War. The notion of 'security' can also be understood as a wider term that also includes the classical function of 'defence'. It is possible that this shift of emphasis will be reflected in the name given to the responsible minister and department. Hence the ministries of defence, once the ministries of war, might become the ministries of security. Nevertheless, this book will use the term 'defence', as today the shift from defence to security is far from completed. In Europe the armed forces and the ministries responsible for them are mainly concerned with the traditional task of homeland defence. Only a small part of financial, technical, and human resources is dedicated to security policy as described above. Moreover, public opinion perceives the armed forces mainly as defence forces. Finally, the discussion will show that defence is the most sensitive field of integration, whereas security is generally subject to international co-operation.

Similar to most other policy fields, an important issue such as defence is necessarily subject to regulation. Hence, the notion of 'defence law' describes the entire field of rules created to regulate the defence of a nation or alliance. This covers provisions, customs, and judgments of constitutional law. Rules on the commander in chief, the role of the armed forces, powers of the executive, tasks of the minister of defence, parliamentary control, the defence budget, or the human rights of soldiers are provided in most legal orders. Defence law also includes administrative rules regarding the organisation of the armed forces. These cover the duties of soldiers, the regulation of their service, statutes regarding discipline, or rules of engagement. Related to these legal frameworks are provisions of social law which affect the armed forces. These regulate issues such as recruitment, vocational training, promotion, salaries, pensions, medical care, sick leave, maternity leave, and insurance. Moreover, many legal orders have a separate military criminal law. Furthermore, for the purposes of this book defence law is understood as a wide concept which goes beyond the military and includes the defence industrial sector as part of the national or common defence effort. The regulation of procurement for the armed forces and of competition in the defence industrial sector is therefore included in this notion.

Defence is at the heart of national sovereignty. The defence of the country was paramount when most European States were created, and in most cases, the very reason for their foundation. Without sovereignty over their national defence and security, many governments feel that they possess no sovereignty at all. This feeling contributed to the failure of many initiatives towards European defence integration and to the treatment of national security issues in European Community and Union law. In particular in the context of the European Communities any transfer over defence matters had to be avoided. European integration through the Community was to be mainly a commercial enterprise. Later other policies were added, excluding defence. While the notion of sovereignty is still a strong factor, the exclusion of defence from the integration process through the Community is not complete. Defence has commercial and social implications. Export, public procurement, and competition are substantial parts of the internal market established by the EC Treaty. They affect the defence sector just like any other part of industry. The automatic exemption of that sector for national security reasons would exclude a significant part of industry from the application of the Treaty and might be detrimental to the functioning of the internal market as a whole. Moreover, the armed forces are a part of the workforce and thus affected by the social rules of the Community. Therefore the founders of the EC had to strike a balance between the objectives of the common market and the national security interests of the Member States.

European defence integration has considerable advantages for the participating nations. First, whatever defence aims to achieve: deterrence, crisis management, independence, or political weight in international affairs, would be enhanced through a coherent European defence policy as a consistent part of a common foreign and security policy. The 25 medium size, small, and very small military powers which make up the European Union today are increasingly aware that only a common approach will enable them to conduct an independent security policy, ensure the survival of the defence industrial base, and give them a say on the international scene. Second, synergy effects, economies of scale, and rationalisation would allow to conduct an effective and credible defence and security policy in times of tight and ever decreasing defence budgets. In other words, one European Rapid Reaction Force, for example, would be cheaper and more effective than 25 national forces. Similarly, a single armaments market would allow economies of scale and synergy effects thereby ensuring better value for money. Third, public opinion wants European defence integration[1] for the reasons stated above and to benefit from a peace dividend after the end of the Cold War.

There are also potential losers. National governments lose through the transfer of sovereignty to common defence structures. However, they also gain through their participation in intergovernmental institutions of a common defence structure with a substantially increased international weight. The United States might lose influence over security in Europe. However, it would also win a more equal partner and ally able to shoulder more responsibility for its own defence in NATO. The taxpayer might have to pay more to increase military capabilities. However, this investment is subject to NATO requirements anyway and it is likely that defence will become cheaper through synergies, economies of scale, and rationalisation in the long run. Finally, the national armed forces, military administrations, and defence industries might lose through rationalisation. However, with regards to the defence industries, integration appears to be their only way of survival and the armed forces and military administrations have been and will be reduced with or without European defence integration.

The notions of 'defence', 'defence law', and 'defence integration' were explained above. The book will show that European defence integration was conducted through more supranational and more intergovernmental frameworks. The notion 'intergovernmental' is understood as referring to an institution or organisation dominated by the governments of the participating States. Decisions are taken by unanimity giving each government the right of *veto*. Moreover, an intergovernmental institution is composed of government representatives, answerable to the governments of the participating States. The United Nations, NATO, and most international organisations are more intergovernmental in nature. The notion 'supranational' is understood as referring to an institution or organisation with a degree of independence from the governments of the participating States. Decisions are taken by majority voting. Independent institutions have the power to take decisions, which are binding on the participating States even against the latter's will. The European Coal and Steel Community and her High Authority are the best examples for a more supranational organisation and institution. There are no purely intergovernmental or supranational organisations and institutions. The notions of 'supranational' and 'intergovernmental' are rather understood as opposite ends of a spectrum. This spectrum allows to classify organisations and

[1] 78% of Europeans are in favour of a common defence and security policy and 69% are in favour of a common foreign and security policy, see Eurobarometer 2004, Brussels, 10 December 2004, IP/04/1460.

institutions as 'more intergovernmental' or 'more supranational'. The European Community, for example, is a more supranational organisation, but the position of the Council, which is composed of representatives of the governments of the Member States and a main decision-making body, represents a considerable intergovernmental element. The Council is a more intergovernmental institution, but the dominance of qualified majority voting adds an important supranational element since individual Member State governments can be outvoted. The Commission is a more supranational institution as they are independent and able to take binding decisions. However, the considerable influence of the Member States on their appointments adds an intergovernmental aspect.

This book describes European defence integration conducted through legal frameworks created by European States and institutions. This framework consists of various legal and organisational structures forming part of the evolutionary process that is European integration.

Part I, consisting of three chapters, follows this evolutionary process from World War II to 2004. Chapter 1 covers the beginning of European defence integration. Starting with the early mutual defence treaties after World War II, the chapter will also discuss the ambitious project of a European Defence Community of the 1950s which envisaged the creation of a supranational organisation and is still an important benchmark and model for the future. The chapter ends with the separation of defence from the mainstream or main path of European integration through the foundation of the European Communities and the Western European Union. Chapter 2 provides an analysis of the Common Foreign and Security Policy of the Treaty on European Union in its Maastricht and Amsterdam versions. This more intergovernmental framework is kept separate from the more supranational framework of the Community and brought defence back on the European agenda, in the beginning only as a side product of foreign and security policy. Chapter 3 continues with a discussion of the emerging European Security and Defence Policy under the Treaty of Nice, after the Summit of Saint-Malo even including a plan for an autonomous military capability of the European Union.

Part II consists of six chapters and represents the central part of the book. It aims to examine the function of Community Law as an instrument of European defence integration. The defence-related exemptions in the EC Treaty and secondary Community instruments are analysed in order to determine the limits of Community law in relation to this function. Chapter 4 discusses the public security exemptions of the free movement regimes of the EC Treaty. This analysis facilitates the understanding of chapters 5 and 6 on the national security exemptions in the Treaty. Chapter 5 examines the armaments and secrecy exemptions in Article 296 EC and chapter 6 the extreme crisis exemption in Article 297 EC. The discussion is complemented by three chapters on the operation of both the EC Treaty and secondary legislation in specific fields of regulation affecting defence. Chapter 7 describes the effect of EC public procurement legislation on the purchasing activities for the armed forces of the Member States. Chapter 8 examines the effect of Community law on the regulation of competition in the European defence industries, including concerted practices, abuses of dominant positions, merger control, State aids, intra-Community transfers and the export of armaments and dual-use goods. Finally, chapter 9 shows the impact of EC sex equality legislation on the armed forces, as an example for the relevance of Community social law for defence. Part II presents Community law as a legal framework of European defence integration. This complements the discussion of the evolution of European defence integration in Part I thereby providing a relatively comprehensive analysis of the contribution of European Union law to the process. The analysis is only 'relatively comprehensive' since in the interest of a concise argument many aspects of defence law subject to European defence integration were not covered. These include national constitutional law, duties of soldiers, the power of command and the duty to obey, administrative appeals law, the law of institutional representation, military disciplinary law, and military criminal law.[2]

The final Part III, consisting of three chapters, continues the story told in Parts I and II. Chapters 10, 11 and 12 cover the Common Security and Defence Policy as part of the Treaty Establishing a Constitution for Europe proposed by the Convention on the Future of Europe in 2003 and agreed by the European Council in 2004. The new Treaty aims to overcome the three-Pillar structure of the European Union described in Part I, thereby *inter alia* uniting the more intergovernmental framework discussed in chapters 2 and 3 with the more supranational framework discussed in Part II. As this Constitutional Treaty had not entered into force by the time of completion of this book at the end of 2004, it actually forms part of a possible future. However, the European Council agreed on it in June 2004 and the Member States signed the final text in October 2004. Therefore the Constitutional Treaty might be part of a future that has already begun. During the proofreading stage of this book the French and Dutch people rejected the Constitutional Treaty in referenda held on 29 May 2005 and 1 June 2005 respectively. On 16 June 2005 the European Council in Brussels agreed on a 'pause for reflection' in response to these negative votes. Therefore the Constitutional Treaty will not enter into force on 1 November 2006 as planned; nor before 2007 or 2008, if at all. However, the innovations of the Constitutional Treaty relevant to defence and security are and will be introduced on the basis of the Treaty of Nice or alternative future frameworks. Thus Part III forms an essential element of this monograph. Chapter 10 discusses the objectives of the Common Security and Defence Policy, followed by a discussion of its scope in chapter 11 and an examination of its institutional structure in chapter 12.

This book describes European defence integration as an evolutionary process towards a common defence through law. The Member States and Community institutions conduct this process through supranational and intergovernmental frameworks inside and outside the legal order of the European Union. The discussion will show that the multitude of frameworks does not necessarily undermine coherence to an extent that would prevent the emergence of an independent European defence policy.

[2] On a comprehensive comparative analytical discussion of harmonisation in these fields see: G Nolte, (ed), *European Military Systems* (De Gruyter Recht, Berlin, 2003).

Part I

The Evolution of European Defence Integration

1

All Quiet on the Western Front: The Early Legal History of European Defence Integration 1944–1958

1. INTRODUCTION

THE CURRENT LEGAL framework of European defence integration cannot be analysed without an understanding of its origins. The treaties, legislation, and case law forming this legal framework are determined by their historical context, a context formed by political, social, economic, cultural, and strategic considerations. Moreover, the legal framework and its context are influenced by factors such as vision or fear. During the sixty years of European integration these factors changed the historical context leading to changes in the legal framework.

The first part of this book consists of three chapters. They will discuss the evolution of European defence integration from the end of World War II to 2004. The focus on 'evolution' is part of the methodological approach.[1] This involves "telling a story of evolution over time"[2] thereby allowing to put the current legislative framework of European defence integration into its historical context. The legal framework will be described and analysed as part of a development. It will be shown that this evolution has not necessarily been one of increasing or deepening defence integration. Seen as an evolution towards a common defence,[3] the process had 'it's ups and downs'. Chapter 1 will describe and analyse the evolution of European defence integration from the end of World War II to the foundations of the Western European Union in 1954 and the European Economic Community in 1957. Chapter 2 will describe and analyse the Common Foreign and Security Policy of the Treaty on European Union under the 1992 Maastricht and the 1997 Amsterdam versions. Moreover, it will cover European Political Co-operation

[1] The use of the notion of 'evolution' itself is inspired by P Craig and G de Búrca (eds), *The Evolution of EU Law* (OUP, Oxford, 1998).

[2] JHH Weiler (ed), 'The Transformation of Europe' (1991) 100 *Yale Law Journal* 2403, cited from *The Constitution of Europe: 'Do the New Clothes have an Emperor?' and other Essays on European Integration* (CUP, Cambridge, 2002), at 12.

[3] The notion of 'common defence' is used in the Treaty on European Union and shall be discussed in ch 2. It could be described as the 'final destination' of European defence integration, a state of close integration, possibly including supranational European armed forces, a European defence budget, and European military structures replacing those of the Member States.

leading to the Treaty on European Union from the late 1950s. These frameworks are both the continuation of the legal history of defence integration covered in chapter 1 and the foundation of the current state of affairs covered in chapter 3. Chapter 2 therefore analyses a subject matter separate but connected to the subject matters of its previous and subsequent chapters. Chapter 3 will describe and analyse the current state of defence integration starting from the 1998 Saint Malo innovations. The latter developments are discussed in a separate chapter because they represent the current law as opposed to the legal developments leading to it, which are described in chapters 1 and 2. All three chapters are necessary components to provide a comprehensive analysis of European defence and security law. Furthermore Part I is required to facilitate the understanding of the contribution of European Community law to the European defence integration process. This contribution is only briefly discussed in chapter 1, as it is the main subject matter of Part II of this book.

The discussion in this chapter will explain the links of defence with other fields of integration. Defence integration is at times separate and at times united or combined with economic and social integration. Moreover, as defence is at the heart of sovereignty, it is often closely linked to political integration. Consequently defence integration is pursued both through separate legal frameworks and combined with other aspects of integration, in particular economic integration.

The analysis will show that the evolution of European defence integration was influenced considerably by three fundamental questions. First, the early period was influenced by the question of German participation in Western defence against the Soviet Union and its allies. Second, the question of the contribution and commitment of the USA to the defence of Western Europe is of paramount importance until this day. Third, the question of whether European defence integration should be organised on a more supranational or on a more intergovernmental basis has not yet been answered conclusively.

As outlined above the discussion will cover the period from World War II to the late 1950s. Major events were the first mutual defence treaties and the foundation of NATO, the foundation of the first European Community, the failed European Defence Community, and the foundations of the Western European Union and the European Economic Community.

2. FROM WORLD WAR TO EUROPEAN INTEGRATION: THE 1940S

European defence integration in particular and European integration in general cannot be understood without understanding the historical context that existed at the very start of this process. The political, economic, social, and strategic situation immediately after World War II triggered and shaped the subsequent evolution of an integrated Europe. The experience of two world wars taught most European leaders the lesson that the traditional patterns of European relations based on national competition and antagonism had to change. Some politicians had already understood that after the carnage of 1914–1918.[4] Hence European integration was initiated with the impression of the casualties, wounds, starvation, destroyed infrastructure, and despair of World War II.[5] Unlike the situation after World War I, the hostilities were not followed by a hostile peace, with no 'Versailles II' to repeat the mistakes of 1919.[6] The Schuman Declaration of 1950[7] made the causal link between a lack of integration and war absolutely clear:

> "World peace cannot be safeguarded without the making of creative efforts proportionate to the dangers which threaten it. The contribution, which an organised and living Europe can bring to civilisation, is indispensable to the maintenance of peaceful relations. In taking upon herself for more than 20 years the role of champion of a united Europe, France has always had as her essential aim the service of peace. A united Europe was not achieved and we had war."

Therefore European integration was a direct reaction to World War II. It provided the advocates of integration with their most powerful argument. Moreover, a main objective of European integration, the European Community, and the European Union is the preservation of peace in Europe as a contribution to world peace.[8] The method to achieve peaceful integration was to establish common organisational structures for individual policy fields.

Economic factors also influenced the emerging integration process. First, substantial parts of the infrastructure had been destroyed during the war. Energy,

[4] For example, in 1929 the French politician Aristide Briand had proposed a European League of Nations, rejected by the British government under Ramsay MacDonald. For the development of ideas towards European unification before World War II see: D Urwin, *The Community of Europe: a History of European Integration*, 2nd edn, (Longman, London, 1995).

[5] Winston Churchill summarised the situation in his famous speech on the 19 September 1946 in Zurich as follows: 'What is the plight to which Europe has been reduced? [...] Over wide areas a vast shivering mass of tormented, hungry, care-worn and, bewildered human beings gape at the ruins of their cities and homes and scan the dark horizons for the approach of some peril, tyranny or horror.' 40 million were dead and in 1946 100 million were living near starvation levels. In Germany 3 million out of 5.5 million houses were destroyed, Frankfurt was destroyed by 45%, Cologne 66%, Düsseldorf 93%. All Rhine bridges, 75% of all other bridges and most of the railway track were destroyed. Belgium and Poland lost 60% of its locomotives and rolling stock. In France, Belgium, the Netherlands, Greece, Poland and Yugoslavia industrial production was only 20% of pre-war figures. Coal output in Europe was 42% of what it was before the war. Massive inflation forced a rapid devaluation in France, Italy, and Germany. Finally living in defiance of authority and without the law had led to moral disintegration in the formerly occupied countries. See A Nutting, *Europe will Not Wait: a Warning and a Way Out* (Hollis & Carter, London, 1960) 1–3.

[6] The comparable 'hostile' peace Treaties of Trianon for Hungary and Neuilly for Bulgaria (both countries had also sided with Germany and Austria–Hungary in World War I) were not an issue because these countries had come under Soviet influence, the comparable Treaty of Saint Germain for Austria was not an issue because the future of the allied-occupied country was not decided in favour of neutrality until 1955. The comparable Treaty of Sévrès was not an issue because Turkey had kept out of the war. See S Varosta, 'Peace Treaties after World War I' in R Bernardt, (ed), *Encyclopedia of International Law* (North Holland, Amsterdam, 1982) vol IV, 110, and also E von Puttkammer, 'Versailles Peace Treaty', at 276 and HF Köck, 'Trainon Peace Treaty', at 249; 'Neuilly Peace Treaty', at 3; and 'Saint–Germain Peace Treaty', at 198 of the same volume.

[7] Schuman Declaration of 9 May 1950, *Bulletin of the European Communities* 13 (1980), 14, 15; available at: http://www.cec.org.uk/whatsnew/schuman.htm.

[8] Weiler, above n 1, at 91.

housing, and food were short, agricultural and industrial production were far below their pre-war levels, and in parts of Europe starvation was a reality rather than only a danger.[9] Coal and steel were the most important industries to get the continent back on track. Coal was found mainly in the German Ruhr and Saar[10] regions, iron ore mainly in the French region of Lorraine. Hence a solution 'crossing borders' was needed to allow both countries and others to prosper again.

The emerging integration process was influenced by strategic and military factors as well. During the war a new antagonism that would soon replace the existing one emerged: the antagonism between the Western allies on the one side and the Soviet Union and its 'allies' on the other side. Towards the end of the war the Red Army had occupied most of Central and Eastern Europe and gradually established communist-led satellite States in Poland, Czechoslovakia, Hungary, Romania, Bulgaria, and East Germany. Moreover, the Soviet Union exercised great influence over the governments of Yugoslavia and Albania. The opposition was oppressed, politicians imprisoned or murdered, democratic structures gradually abolished. Countries and territories that had fallen to the Soviet Union after the Hitler-Stalin Pact: parts of Poland, Estonia, Latvia, and Lithuania were not given their independence or handed back to Poland. In Western Europe and in what was left of Central Europe the USSR was perceived as a serious political and military threat. It did not take much imagination to predict what would happen to a European country not able to defend itself. In Italy the conflict between Communists and Christian Democrats and their allies remained mainly peaceful. In Greece, however, there was civil war. The USA was the only nuclear superpower of the day but the Stalinist Soviet Union would catch up very soon. It was not clear whether Washington would commit itself to the reconstruction and defence of Europe or adopt an isolationist foreign policy approach leading to the withdrawal of its troops. This would have necessitated a Western European military alliance under the leadership of the United Kingdom. However, London seemed reluctant to assume this role.[11] Overall the world seemed close to yet another global conflict and the defence of the West was not yet organised. Once again peace in Europe was fragile.

The Soviet threat was connected to another strategic factor: the necessary rearmament of West Germany. In order to establish a credible defence effort against the Russians, the west of the country, soon the Federal Republic of Germany and its more than 60 million inhabitants, without armed forces since 1945, had to

[9] Nutting, above n 5.

[10] The Saar region was occupied by France until 1955 when in a referendum the population voted for re-accession to Germany and the Saarland became a state of the Federal Republic of Germany (founded in 1949).

[11] Nutting, above n 5, at 3 cites the then Foreign Secretary of Belgium, later Secretary-General of NATO and founding father of the European Community, Paul Henri Spaak:

> You had no idea just how much Britain meant to all of us—during the years immediately after the war. Our countries had suffered grievously, in the moral as well as the physical sense, from being occupied by the enemy. Great Britain had not had to undergo the demoralizing experience, where patriotism meant breaking laws and cheating and even killing one's compatriots. And so she represented something pure and untarnished and we looked to her–all of us–for moral leadership [...] but, alas, we looked in vain.

make a contribution to the defence of the West.[12] However, the peoples and political establishments of Western Europe opposed the emergence of new German armed forces so soon after the end of the war. This feeling was particularly strong in France.[13] The memory of German soldiers invading and occupying their countries was too fresh in their minds. Moreover, even after having lost a third of its territory, separated from Russian occupied East Germany, and struggling with the reconstruction of the country and 10 million refugees, it was clear that Germany would soon re-emerge as a considerable European power. France and the smaller Western European countries were very concerned not to re-arm their recent enemy too soon. An alternative to a sovereign German *Wehrmacht* was called for.

Hence the situation of the second half of the 1940s can be summarised as follows: a largely destroyed Europe tired of war faces a Soviet threat. This threat necessitates two measures. First, military alliances between the democratic Western European countries,[14] with a prominent role of the United States, have to be created. Second, Germany has to make a contribution without giving this recent enemy control over sovereign national armed forces.[15]

2.1. The First Step Towards European Integration: the Benelux 1944

The story of European integration started just before the end of the war. On 5 September 1944 the governments-in-exile of Belgium, the Netherlands, and Luxembourg in London agreed on a customs union between their countries.[16]

[12] R Aron, 'Historical Sketch of the Great Debate' in D Lerner and R Aron, *France Defeats EDC* (Praeger, New York, 1957), English version of *La Querelle de la CED* (Armand Colin, Paris, 1957) 2, at 4; A Philip, 'The Interplay of Interests and Passions', in Lerner and Aron, above, 24, at 37; A Grosser, 'Germany and France: A Confrontation' in Lerner and Aron, above, 54; J Stoetzel, 'The Evolution of French Opinion' in Lerner and Aron, above, 72, at 81–85; JJ Marchand, 'A Tableau of the French Press' in Lerner and Aron, above, 102; J Fauvet, 'Birth and Death of a Treaty' in Aron and Lerner, above, 128; S Hoffmann, 'The Postmortems' in Aron and Lerner, above, 164.

[13] Aron, above; Philip, above; Grosser above; Stoetzel, above; Marchand, above; Fauvet, above; Hoffmann, above.

[14] Portugal was isolated under the right-wing dictatorship of Salazar, Spain was isolated under the right-wing dictatorship of Franco. The Republic of Ireland, Sweden, Switzerland, and Finland were neutral. The allies governed Austria until 1955.

[15] At the same time it was advisable to avoid any offence of the Federal Republic by making Germany an unequal partner. Such a policy could also have had a destabilising effect on the new democratic government and system of the Federal Republic. The harsh terms of the Treaty of Versailles had made the establishment of a democratic Germany very difficult after World War I. Versailles is partly responsible for the failure of the Republic of Weimar.

[16] *Benelux Information*, General Secretariat of the Benelux Economic Union, Brussels, (no date of publication 1995?) at 7. This convention was preceded by a monetary agreement signed by the three countries in London in October 1943. The agreement set the exchange rate between the (Belgian and Luxembourg) franc and the Dutch guilder and established a mechanism for mutual financing should one of the partners show a deficit in the balance of payments. This followed earlier moves towards integration with the Convention of Oslo 1930 and the Convention of Ouchy 1932. Belgium and Luxembourg had started economic integration even earlier on with the Belgium–Luxembourg Economic Union signed in Brussels on 25 July 1921, 9 LNTS 223. This replaced the traditional economic attachment of Luxembourg to Germany through the German Zollverein since 1842. The Zollverein could be called the first example for European economic integration. The Belgium–Luxembourg Economic Union is recognised in Article 94 of the Benelux Treaty and Article 233 European Economic Community Treaty. The current text of the Treaty: 381 UNTS 165. See EDJ Kruijtbosch, entry on 'Benelux Economic Union' in R Bernardt, *Encyclopedia of Public International Law* (North Holland, Amsterdam, 1983) vol 6, at 36.

These three Western European states would charge the same tariffs on external borders and abolish any customs duties on trade among themselves. This agreement was supplemented on 14 March 1947 with the Protocol of The Hague and culminated in the Benelux Treaty of 3 March 1958, which entered into force in 1960. The Treaty has an economic focus and provides for the free movement of goods in Article 3, workers in Article 2, services in Article 5, and capital in Article 4, and other policies. The Benelux concept as outlined in the Protocol of The Hague was clearly a model for the European Economic Community of 1957 described below. Integration through the Benelux framework does not include defence. The organisation exists until this day, complementing other integration efforts. The three countries can still be called a crucial driving force behind European integration participating in all future integration projects and initiating the most important one: the European Economic Community.[17]

2.2. The International Framework for European Integration and the Foundations of the European Security Architecture: the United Nations 1945

The regional European defence integration process is founded on an international organisation comprising of almost all states of the world. The United Nations Organisation (hereinafter UN) was founded on 24 October 1945 to ensure world peace. Article 2 (4) of the UN Charter[18] prohibits military aggression against other states. Article 51 UN Charter[19] allows states to use military means in defence against military aggression of another state. The Security Council, an important institution of the UN comprising of the United States, France, United Kingdom, the Soviet Union, and China as permanent members can take action against military aggression under Chapters VI and VII of the UN Charter, including military means. The allies fighting Germany and Japan during World War II prepared the foundation of the UN. Hence Article 107 UN Charter[20] allowed military aggression against Germany and Japan.

[17] T Marauhn, *Building a European Security and Defence Identity, Bochumer Schriften zur Friedenssicherung und zum Humaniären Völkerrrecht 30* (Universitätsverlag Dr N Brockmeyer, Bochum, 1996) at 10.

[18] Treaty Series No 67 (1946), Cmd 7015. Article 2(4) UN Charter reads: 'All Members shall refrain in their international relations from the threat or use of force against the territorial integrity or political independence of any State, or in any other manner inconsistent with the Purposes of the United Nations.'

[19] Article 51 UN Charter reads:

> Nothing in the present Charter shall impair the inherent right of individual or collective self-defence if an armed attack occurs against a Member of the United Nations, until the Security Council has taken measures necessary to maintain international peace and security. Measures taken by Members in the exercise of this right of self-defence shall be immediately reported to the Security Council and shall not in any way affect the authority and responsibility of the Security Council under the present Charter to take at any time such action as it deems necessary in order to maintain or restore international peace and security.

[20] Article 107 UN Charter reads: 'Nothing in the present Charter shall invalidate or preclude action, in relation to any State which during the Second World War has been an enemy of any signatory to the present Charter, taken or authorised as a result of that war by the Governments having responsibility for that action.'

The UN forms the foundations of European defence integration. Most European countries participating in defence integration are founding members of the UN.[21] This means that they committed themselves to the preservation of peace and the prohibition of aggression enshrined in Article 2 (4) UN Charter before committing themselves to any project on European defence integration. Therefore any such project would necessarily have a defensive character to comply with the requirements of the UN Charter. An aggressive character was ruled out by the participation of most European countries in the UN. The commitment of European integration projects to the objectives of the UN is regularly spelt out in the preamble of the respective founding treaty.[22] These references make the objective of peace including the essential prohibition of aggression an integral part of all European organisations. The UN Charter forms the foundation on which is built the rest of the European security architecture.

2.3. The American Factor: Truman Doctrine and Marshall Plan 1947

A fundamental change in US American policy towards Europe determined the next phase of both the defence and economic integration of the continent. In relation to defence integration the Truman Doctrine introduced a clear commitment of the USA to the defence of those European countries not yet under Soviet dominance. The Doctrine was first expressed in a speech to Congress 12 March 1947 concerning substantial military aid and military missions to Greece and Turkey.[23] In this speech US President Harry S. Truman said, "it must be policy of the United States to support free people who are resisting attempted subjugation by armed minorities or by outside pressure". The Truman Doctrine would determine US policy concerning Europe and the Soviet Union until the end of the Cold War.
In relation to economic integration the Marshall Plan introduced a clear commitment by the USA to the reconstruction and economic recovery of Europe. The plan was first expressed in a speech at Harvard University on 5 June 1947.[24] In this speech US Secretary of State John Marshall suggested that Europe should agree on a programme of reconstruction supported by American financial aid. The Plan was open to all European countries willing to participate. However, under Soviet

[21] Germany is the most noticeable exception and did not join the world organisation before 1973.

[22] See: Preamble to the Treaty Establishing the European Community: 'Intending to confirm the solidarity which binds Europe and the overseas countries and desiring to ensure the development of their prosperity, in accordance with the principles of the Charter of the United Nations,' Preamble to the Treaty Establishing a European Defence Community: 'Determined in co-operation with the free nations and in the spirit of the Charter of the United Nations, to contribute to the maintenance of peace, more particularly by ensuring the defence of Western Europe against any aggression in close collaboration with organisations having the same purpose'; Preamble of the Brussels Treaty: 'To reaffirm their faith in fundamental human rights, in the dignity and worth of the human person and in the other ideals proclaimed in the Charter of the United Nations'; Preamble to the Washington Treaty: 'The Parties to this Treaty reaffirm their faith in the purposes and principles of the Charter of the United Nations and their desire to live in peace with all peoples and all governments.'

[23] Nutting, above n 5, at 13.

[24] Above, at 15. 1947 is also the year in which the General Agreement of Tariffs and Trade (GATT) was signed.

pressure all satellite states declined the offer.[25] The Marshall Plan would start and facilitate the fast economic recovery of Western Europe. The Organisation for European Economic Co-operation (OEEC) was founded in 1948 to organise the Marshall Plan.[26] All Western European countries were member States and the newly founded Federal Republic of Germany joined in 1949. Yugoslavia, Canada and the USA were associated members.[27] Moreover, the European Recovery Programme and the Intra-European Payments Scheme, the predecessor of the European Payments Union were established. The successful implementation of the Marshall Plan led to the quick economic recovery and reconstruction which was well on its way when plans for the integration of Europe were discussed in the 1950s.

2.4. The First Step Towards European Defence Integration and the Transatlantic Alliance: the Brussels Treaty on Western Union 1948

The story of European defence integration *strictu sensu* started with the Brussels Treaty for Collaboration in Economic, Social and Cultural Matters and for Collective Self-Defence. It was signed by the United Kingdom, France, the Netherlands, Belgium, and Luxembourg on 17 March 1948[28] and built on the Treaty of Dunkirk of 4 May 1947.[29] The Brussels Treaty established a collective self-defence and economic co-operation organisation, the Western Union (hereinafter WU) or Brussels Treaty Organisation, with a limited duration of 50 years.[30] The economic, social, and cultural objectives stipulated in Articles I, II, and III respectively were only broadly defined and did not amount to common market provisions comparable to those of the Benelux community emerging during the same period. The principle objective was to set up a joint defence system, which is combined with other policies. The crucial Article IV provided:

> "If any of the High Contracting Parties should be the object of an armed attack in Europe, the other High Contracting Parties will, in accordance with the provisions of Article 51 of the Charter of the United Nations, afford the Party so attacked all the military and other aid and assistance in their power."[31]

[25] Albania, Bulgaria, Finland, Hungary, Poland, Romania, and Yugoslavia. Czechoslovakia cancelled her original acceptance under Soviet pressure. Nutting, above n 5, at 16.

[26] See the Convention for European Economic Cooperation, signed on 16 April 1948, 888 UNTS 142.

[27] In 1960 the OEEC was succeeded by the Organisation for Economic Cooperation and Development, 888 UNTS 180.

[28] 19 UNTS 51.

[29] 9 UNTS 187. This rather rudimentary Treaty between the United Kingdom and France contained an obligation of mutual assistance as well as a general undertaking relating to economic integration, see P Macalister-Smith, entry on 'Western European Union' in Bernardt, above n 16, at 366.

[30] See Article X of the Brussels Treaty.

[31] The UNC context is also emphasised in Article V:

> All measures taken as a result of the preceding Article shall be immediately reported to the Security Council. They shall be terminated as soon as the Security Council has taken the measures necessary to maintain or restore international peace and security. The present Treaty does not prejudice in any way the obligations of the High Contracting Parties under the provisions of the Charter of the United Nations. It shall not be interpreted as affecting in any way the authority and responsibility of the Security Council under the Charter to take at any time such action as it deems necessary in order to maintain or restore international peace and security.

The WU was the first European intergovernmental organisation after the war and included institutions: a Permanent Consultative Council and a Defence Committee presiding over the WU Chiefs of Staff. However, there were only rudimentary rules on the Consultative Council; the Treaty did not lay down its structure and function and there was no permanent secretariat to implement its measures.[32] The accession of any other State was possible[33] and the WU was understood as a regional arrangement within the meaning of Chapter VIII of the UN Charter.[34] As Marauhn put it: "[the WU] was an important step [...] because it brought Western states together in a military alliance of unprecedented duration and automaticity."[35] It is submitted that the Brussels Treaty is also important as it represented a first step towards integration. The preamble speaks of a "common heritage", "social and cultural ties by which they [the signatory States] are already united", and of loyal co-operation. The creators of the WU were already aware of common ground which constitutes the base of European integration.

There are a few points to be made about the Brussels Treaty. First, the WU was yet directed against a possible German as well as a possible Soviet aggression[36] and therefore necessarily excluded Germany.[37] The anti-German provisions of the Treaty were omitted in 1954 when Germany and Italy joined the organisation, then renamed Western European Union (hereinafter WEU). Second, it was intended to organise the European component of a later transatlantic defence treaty and can be considered a reaction to the Truman Doctrine outlined above. Third, France joined the Benelux countries as the *avant-garde* of European integration. Fourth, the United Kingdom participated in this intergovernmental organisation. For Belgium, the Netherlands and Luxembourg economic integration through the Benelux framework was now separated from defence integration

32 Macalister-Smith, above n 29.

33 Article IX (1) of the Brussels Treaty reads: 'The High Contracting Parties may, by agreement, invite any other State to accede to the present Treaty on conditions to be agreed between them and the State so invited.' This would not have included Germany. First because Germany was not a sovereign State in 1948 and second because the Treaty was directed against a future German aggression.

34 Articles 52–54 UN Charter allow regional arrangements 'relating to the maintenance of international peace and security as are appropriate for regional action' (Article 52(1) UN Charter).

35 Marauhn, above n 17, at 7.

36 Macalister-Smith, above n 29. According to Article 53(1) UN Charter a regional security arrangement such as the WU could take enforcement action against Germany without the authorisation of the Security Council.

37 Marauhn, above n 17, citing the preamble to the Brussels Treaty: 'To take such steps as may be held to be necessary in the event of a renewal by Germany of a policy of aggression'. Article VIII (2) of the Treaty:

> At the request of any of the High Contracting Parties, the Council shall be immediately convened in order to permit the High Contracting Parties to consult with regard to any situation which may constitute a threat to peace, in whatever area this threat should arise; with regard to the attitude to be adopted and the steps to be taken in case of a renewal by Germany of an aggressive policy; or with regard to any situation constituting a danger to economic stability.

The preamble also speaks of the Treaty being directed against aggression in a wider sense: 'To afford assistance to each other, in accordance with the Charter of the United Nations, in maintaining international peace and security and in resisting any policy of aggression; [...]'. The notion of 'any [...] aggression' refers to the Soviet Union without mentioning her. However, this indirect notion is weaker than mentioning Germany twice, in the preamble and in Article VIII (2).

through the Brussels Treaty.[38] This early separation of the 1940s was the predecessor of the later separation into economic integration through the European Communities and defence integration through the WEU from 1958, which will be discussed in more detail below. The United Kingdom, suspicious of any more supranational arrangement, initially participated in the latter but not the former.

2.5. Council of Europe 1949

The Brussels Treaty became the nucleus for the next step towards integration: the Council of Europe.[39] The five Brussels Treaty powers and Italy, Norway, Sweden, Denmark and Ireland signed the Treaty establishing this intergovernmental organisation in London on 5 May 1949.[40] In order to protect its sovereignty the United Kingdom insisted on a more intergovernmental organisation.[41] A Committee of Ministers and a Consultative Assembly were established. However, the Council of Europe did not become the main instrument for European integration. The central activity of the Strasbourg organisation is the protection of human rights through the European Court of Human Rights on the basis of the European Convention of Human Rights.[42]

2.6. The Establishment of a Transatlantic Alliance: the Northern Atlantic Treaty Organisation 1949

The step that followed was the foundation of a military alliance comprising the WU countries, the European countries Norway, Denmark, and Portugal, and the USA and Canada. The Northern Atlantic Treaty or Washington Treaty[43] was signed on 4 April 1949. The main concern of the Northern Atlantic Treaty Organisation (hereinafter NATO) is the organisation of the defence of its member States. NATO is an intergovernmental international organisation. Article 5 Washington Treaty clarifies that an attack on one member State will be considered an attack on all of them.[44] The foundation of NATO answered one of the fundamental questions of European defence integration for a long time, the question on the contribution of the USA. NATO implemented the Truman Doctrine and sent a clear message to the Soviet Union about the commitment of the USA to the defence of its European allies. The organisation proved successful during the Cold

[38] The economic provisions of the Brussels Treaty were only very rudimentary.
[39] Nutting, above n 5, at 23.
[40] 87 UNTS 103; ETS 1.
[41] Craig and de Búrca, above n 1, at 8.
[42] 213 UNTS 221; ETS 5.
[43] 34 UNTS 243.
[44] JS Ignarski, entry on 'NATO' in Bernardt, (ed), above n 16, 264, at 269, considers this a qualified provision which 'compares unfavourably with the equivalent Article V of the Modified Brussels Treaty'. See also Marauhn, above n 17, at 7.

War and afterwards. An armed attack on the Western European NATO states never occurred,[45] the Warsaw Pact, an organisation founded as a military alliance against NATO between the Soviet Union and its satellites and the Soviet Union itself were ultimately dissolved, and many countries joined the Western alliance.[46]

Since the foundation of NATO the means of giving effect to the provisions of the Brussels Treaty are possessed and exercised by NATO institutions. Since the establishment of the NATO Supreme Allied Command in Europe in 1951 the defence functions of the WU have been largely absorbed into NATO.[47] It is submitted that these steps made the WU largely redundant.

3. THE GENESIS OF THE EUROPEAN COMMUNITY FOR COAL AND STEEL 1950–1953

Following the Benelux framework the economic integration of a wider Europe started with the important coal and steel industries. As outline above, these sectors were crucial to the reconstruction of Europe. Nevertheless, the European Coal and Steel Community (hereinafter ECSC) proposed in the Schuman Declaration of 1950 was also connected to defence:

> "The pooling of coal and steel production should immediately provide for the setting up of common foundations for economic development as a first step in the federation of Europe, and will change the destinies of those regions which have long been devoted to the manufacture of munitions of war, of which they have been the most constant victims."[48]

The 'underlying rationale' for the ECSC was strongly influenced by defence.[49] There is no modern warfare without weapons made of steel made with iron ore and coal. The internationalisation of the coal and steel production would take the major tool to fight a war out of the hands of the European nation-States.[50] At the same time the founders were aware of the connection between peace and economic policy, the failure of which can become the reason for war just like national antagonism. The preamble to the treaty establishing the organisation proposed in the Schuman Declaration, the European Coal and Steel Community Treaty of 1951, emphasises the connection between European integration and the

[45] Article 5 was invoked only once. The USA invoked it after the attacks on New York and Washington on 11 September 2001.

[46] The Czech Republic, Hungary, and Poland joined on 16 December 1997. Bulgaria, Romania, Slovenia, the Slovak Republic, Lithuania, Latvia, Estonia joined on 26 March 2003.

[47] Macalister-Smith, above n 29, at 367.

[48] Schuman Declaration, above n 7.

[49] Marauhn, above n 17, at 7, also citing D Arter, *The Politics of European Integration in the Twentieth Century* (Ashgate, Dartmouth, 1993), at 120: 'The ECSC offered first and foremost a means of providing security against a possible resurgence of German militarism [...]'.

[50] Marauhn, above, at 8.

preservation of peace by almost repeating the words of the then French Foreign Secretary.[51]

Following the proposal made in the Schuman Declaration, France, Germany, Italy, the Netherlands, Belgium, and Luxembourg signed the Treaty Establishing the European Community for Coal and Steel Community (hereinafter ECSC) in 1951 in Paris. All Member States ratified the Treaty, which entered into force on 1 January 1953. The Treaty established a common market for coal and steel and was to have a limited life span of fifty years, which expired in 2002.

The ECSC introduced an important innovation into the European integration process. The Community was the first more supranational (European) organisation in contrast to the more intergovernmental organisations of WU, UN, and NATO. As outlined in the introduction to this book, although a clear definition of a supranational organisation is difficult due to different interpretations, it is submitted that it is basically characterised by the combination of three factors. First, the decision-making machinery is at least partly independent from the member States and the decisions of this machinery are binding on them. Second, there is a legal system or order with its own judicial body and its decisions are binding on the member States. Third, there are direct legal relations between the international authority or institutions and individuals.[52]

The ECSC institutions had the power to bind the Member States. Nine independent appointees from the six Member States made up the High Authority, the main executive institution of the ECSC, responsible for implementing the aims of the Treaty. The High Authority was a supranational institution as it could make binding decisions by a majority. The ECSC was also self-financing through levies on coal and steel production, which enhanced its independence and supranational character. A classical international organisation such as the UN is financed exclusively through contributions of the participating states and donations. In 1952 binding decisions of an institution of an international organisation and an independent income were the crucial elements of supranationality.[53] The ECSC Council was made up of one representative of each Member State government and represented the intergovernmental element of the Community. Some decisions of the High Authority were not final, as they had to be approved by the Council. Nevertheless, the balance of power between High Authority and Council was not comparable to later organisations such as the European Economic Community as it had a stronger supranational and a weaker intergovernmental

[51] Treaty of Paris 1951, Community Information Service, *Treaties Establishing the European Communities* (1987): 'Considering that world peace can be safeguarded only by creative efforts commensurate with the dangers that threaten it.' The preservation of peace, however, was not the only motive behind the establishment of the ECSC. An important economic aspect was the fact that the iron ore was in French Lorraine and the coal to melt and work it in the German Rhine and Coal Area (Ruhr) and the soon German Saar.

[52] See interpretation of F Capotori, entry on 'Supranational Organisations' in Bernardt, above n 16, vol V, at 264 and the citations at the end of his entry.

[53] Supremacy and direct effect, which shall be explained briefly below, could also be considered elements of supranationality but were only developed in the early 1960s.

element.[54] However, this was also due to the greater level of detailed policy in the ECSC Treaty.[55] Moreover, with the Court of Justice the ECSC had its own judicial body and, as the Court of Justice of the European Economic Community later clarified in a seminal decision also applying to the ECSC, the Treaties established "a new legal order".[56] Finally, this Court also decided in the same judgment that there are direct relations between the international authority and individuals through the principle of direct effect which allows natural and legal persons in the Member States to enforce certain provisions of Community law in their national courts.[57] Hence the ECSC clearly fulfilled the requirements for a more supranational organisation.[58]

At the time the decision for the next more supranational organisation, the European Defence Community was made, this type of arrangement with a strong emphasis on the supranational element, was the only existing example of a supranational European organisation known to the decision makers in the Member States. The only alternative was a more intergovernmental organisation such as the WU. The ECSC represented the most important model for the next integration proposal attempted by the six Member States of the ECSC, which from now on would be the core of European integration. However, the discussion on whether to continue the European defence integration process by establishing more supranational or more intergovernmental organisations entered the European agenda with the foundation of the ECSC and has been there ever since.

The more supranational character of the ECSC was also the reason for the United Kingdom not to participate in the Community as it feared for its sovereignty and was concerned about its responsibilities in the Commonwealth.[59]

[54] P Craig and C de Búrca, *EU Law*, 3rd edn, (OUP, Oxford, 2003) 9; Capotori, above n 52, at 266.

[55] Above.

[56] Case C–26/62, *NV Algemene Transport- en Expeditie Onderneming van Gend en Loos v Nederlandse Administratie der Belastingen* [1963] ECR 1.

[57] Above.

[58] Hence the supranational organisation represents a more intense form of international co-operation than a traditional intergovernmental organisation. A federation can be distinguished from a supranational organisation, as RL Lane, entry on 'Federalism in the International Community' in Bernardt, above n 16, vol 5, at 179 put it: 'Once a system is recognised to satisfy federal criteria, the international legal personality of its component states is extinguished and a new State, a new primary member of the international community, possessed of all ensuing rights and obligations, is created.' The ECSC had authority only with regards to a limited subject matter, it did not possess of all ensuing rights and obligations. The international legal personality of its Member States was not extinguished; they kept their authority with regards to all subject matters not transferred to the ECSC. However, it should be emphasised that this distinction is subject to controversy. In the same entry Lane argues: 'transfer of sovereignty, with a reasonable degree of certainty that it is irreversible, is the hallmark of a federation'. According to the European Court of Justice in *Van Gend*, above n 56, with the Community Treaties the Member States have 'transferred their sovereignty, albeit within limited fields'. At least for some Member States this transfer is irreversible.

[59] Marauhn, above n 17, at 7–8 citing S Greenwood, *Britain and European Cooperation Since 1945* (Blackwell, Oxford, 1992) at 34 and 37: 'Above everything else, though the British could see the political advantages of the Schuman Plan in settling the Franco–German problem, they were not prepared to submerge aspect of their own sovereignty to bring this about [...] and [...] Britain [...] wished to maintain her links with the United States and the Commonwealth'.

4. THE FAILURE OF THE EUROPEAN DEFENCE COMMUNITY TREATY 1950–1954

The next step for integration directly concerned the sensitive defence area: the establishment of a more supranational European Defence Community (hereinafter EDC) with the participation of the six ECSC Member States. The EDC envisaged nothing less than the merger of the armed forces of the Member States into European Defence Forces (hereinafter EDF) including newly created German divisions. These forces were to be organised and supervised by a supranational EDC administration answerable to a European Assembly. During the New York and Washington conferences in September 1950 the French Prime Minister René Pléven made an unofficial proposal for an EDC. The war in Korea had started three months before the Pléven Proposal. Communist North Korea had invaded South Korea with the help of the Communist People's Republic of China. A military force of the UN under the leadership of the USA intervened. A first armed conflict between Communist states and the West had started and made the organisation of the defence of Europe with the inclusion of a substantial German contribution an urgent matter. All six governments signed the EDC Treaty resulting from the Proposal in May 1952. The German, Dutch, Belgian and Luxembourg legislatures had also ratified the Treaty by summer 1954. It was sent for ratification in the French parliament and Italian ratification was anticipated soon afterwards.[60]

The EDC project consisted of the Treaty itself[61] with a preamble and 132 articles,[62] a number of protocols,[63] and other instruments.[64] The discussion

[60] See the chronology of EDC, in Lerner and Aron, above n 12, at XV–XVI.

[61] *La Traité Instituant la Communauté Européene de Défense—La Documentation Française* was originally published by the *Ministère des Affaires Etrangères* in Paris [undated 1952?]. There are two English translations. One was presented to the United Kingdom Parliament in April 1954 as The European Defence Community Treaty Paris, 27 May 1952 (together with related documents), Cmd 9127 (HMSO, London, 1954). This excluded translation of the protocols on jurisdiction, military penal code, finance conditions of pay of the military and civil personnel and their pension rights, the status of the European Defence Forces and that of the commercial and fiscal regime of the EDC (see below). The Office of the United States Special Representative in Europe published a separate and slightly different unofficial translation of the EDC Treaty on 26 January 1953 based on the United States Senate publication 94118 (82nd Congress 2nd session), a NATO version published on 12 July 1952 and on translation of one of the agreements by the Allied High Commission's Secretariat.

[62] Part I: Fundamental Principles, Chapter I: The European Defence Community (Articles 1–8), Chapter II: European Defence Forces (Articles 9–18); Part II: The Institutions of the Community, Chapter I: The Board of Commissioners (Articles 19–32); Chapter II: The Assembly (Articles 33–38), Chapter III: The Council (Articles 39–50), Chapter IV: The Court (Articles 51–67); Part III: Military Provisions; Chapter I: Organisation and Administration of the European Defence Forces (Articles 68–79), Chapter II: Status of the European Defence Forces (Articles 80–82); Part IV: Financial Provisions (Articles 83–100); Part V: Economic Provisions (Articles 101–11); Part VI: General Provisions (Articles 112–32).

[63] The Military Protocol, the Jurisdictional Protocol, the Protocol relating to Military Penal Law, the Financial Protocol, the Protocol on the Conditions of the Remuneration of Military and Civilian Personnel within the Community and on their Pension Rights, the Protocol regarding the Grand Duchy of Luxembourg, the Protocol regarding the Relations between the EDC and NATO, the Protocol on Guarantees given by Member States of the EDC to Parties to the North Atlantic Treaty, the Protocol relating to the Status of the European Defence Forces and the Commercial and Fiscal Administration of the EDC, the Protocols of Signature and the Protocol on the Interim Committee.

[64] The Common Declaration of the Defence Ministers on the Duration of the Treaty, the Agreement envisaged in Article 107 (Paragraph 4 b), the Exchange of Letters between the Government of the

will be limited to the most important provisions of the Treaty and the protocols.

4.1. Supranationality

Article 1 EDC Treaty established the supranational character of the Community, comprising common institutions, common armed forces and a common budget.[65] This supranational character also manifested itself in the competencies and independence of the main executive organ and the common budget, as will be discussed below.

This general approach followed the example of the ECSC. Supranationality, also featuring prominently in the preamble to the Treaty,[66] was the most controversial aspect of the EDC and ultimately the reason for the failure of the project.[67] At a conference in Brussels in August 1954, a few weeks before the French Parliament rejected ratification, the French Government under Prime Minister Pierre Mendès-France put forward proposals that essentially deleted the supranational character of the EDC.[68] Until this day a supranational common defence organisation goes too far for many European States. This is not surprising, as establishing such an organisation would be equal to an almost total transfer of sovereignty over defence issues from the participating nations to the organisation. As defence and national security are at the heart of sovereignty, it is not easily acceptable for states to forfeit something they perceive to be such an essential part of their independence. Consequently, the European Economic Community Treaty, the next major integration project after the failed EDC, included defence exemptions to clarify that defence matters were largely outside the application of the Treaty.[69]

Federal Republic of Germany and the Governments of the Co-signatory States to the EDC Treaty concerning Article 107 of the Treaty, the Treaty between the United Kingdom and the member States of the EDC, the Protocol to the Atlantic Treaty on guarantees given by the Parties to the North Atlantic Treaty to the Members of the EDC, the Tripartite Declaration by the Foreign Ministers of the United States, France and the United Kingdom, and the Exchange of Letters between the Government of the Federal Republic of Germany and the Governments of France, the United States and the United Kingdom: one concerning the control of atomic energy and the other concerning civilian aircraft.

[65] Article 1 EDC Treaty: 'The High Contracting Parties, by the present Treaty, set up among themselves a European Defence Community, supra–national in character, comprising common institutions, common Armed Forces, and a common budget.' The EDC proposal has even been called 'supranational *par excellence*', see P Koutrakos, *Trade, Foreign Policy and Defence in EU Constitutional Law: The Legal Regulation of Sanctions Exports of Dual Use Goods and Armaments* (Hart Publishing, Oxford, 2001) 9.

[66] Paragraph 3 of the preamble reads: '[...] Considering the fullest possible integration to the extent compatible with military necessities, of the human and material elements of their Defence Forces assembled within an above-national European organisation to be the best means for the attainment of this aim with the necessary speed and efficiency'.

[67] E Fursdon, *The European Defence Community: A History* (Macmillan, London, 1980) ch 7, 'Prelude to failure', pp 227–65, and ch 8: 'La ronde est complète' pp 266–99. This section on the EDC is to a certain extent based on his chapter 5 on the EPC Treaty.

[68] *Projet de Protocole d'Application du Traité instituant la Communauté Européenne de Défense*, later published by the Belgian Government: *Textes et Documents*, Brussels, *Ministère des Affaires Etrangères et du Commerce Extérieur*, 24 August 1954. See in particular Chapter I Point 2 and Chapter II Point 6.

[69] See Part II (chs 4–6) of this book on these provisions.

These provisions will be discussed in detail in Part II of this book. In 1992 in Maastricht the Common Foreign and Security Policy was established as an intergovernmental Second Pillar of the Treaty on European Union, separate from the supranational First Pillar of the European Community.[70] This will be explained in more detail in chapter 2 and below under point 6.

Nevertheless, there are arguments for a supranational defence organisation. The preamble of the EDC Treaty calls this the "speed and efficiency"[71] to attain the objectives of the Community. An international or supranational organisation taking over the responsibility for defence and national security from its Member States needs the power to make binding decisions. Otherwise Member States can undermine the cohesion of the organisation to further a national agenda. For example, they can refuse to follow individual decisions, withdraw troops or other means from the Community without approval, or leave the Community all together, in the worst case during a crisis situation. Examples for such a scenario are the withdrawal of France and Greece from the military structure of NATO, in 1966 and 1981 respectively. Undermining the cohesion of the smallest military unit means compromising effectiveness: the unit cannot do its job.[72] Compromising effectiveness means compromising security. Similarly, it could be argued that undermining the cohesion of an organisation or Community in charge of defence means undermining efficiency thereby undermining national or Community security. Supranationality as a prerequisite for cohesion is therefore also a prerequisite for deterrence. Only a cohesive Community deters potential enemies. The deterrent effect of a Community of medium and small states as compared to the deterrent effect of an individual Member State is only enhanced through the cohesion of the Community. An incoherent or even divided Community will not be taken as a serious deterrent. For the EDC project, due to the Soviet threat, deterrence was the main objective. It is submitted that in a military Community which does not include a military superpower that can easily compensate for the withdrawal of any of the other participating states, the cohesion of the medium and small countries that make up such a Community is of even greater importance. NATO is the most successful military international organisation. However, the membership of the USA makes it essentially an organisation made up of a superpower plus a number of considerably smaller allies, essentially under the protection of the superpower. The US dominance ensures cohesion and makes it less important at the same time. As will be explained below, certain provisions of the EDC Treaty connected the Community to NATO thereby also aiming to use the impact of the involvement of the superpower USA to further the cohesion of the European security architecture. However, the EDC as a

[70] During the Dutch Presidency of the EC in 1991 the Hague Government proposed to integrate the CFSP into the EC legal order: see First Dutch Draft Treaty Proposal from the Dutch Presidency, 30 September 1991, in FS Laursen and S Vanhoonacker, (eds), *The Intergovernmental Conference on Political Union: Institutional Reforms, New Policies and International Identity of the European Community* (EIPA, Maastricht, 1992) 407–12.

[71] See para 3 of the preamble, above n 66.

[72] See chs 11 at 303 and ch 12 at 305–353 on this issue of cohesion.

strong European component of a transatlantic alliance and as the framework for a German contribution perceived to be crucial to ensure a sufficient defence effort, could not afford to remain intergovernmental. An intergovernmental Community would have required the establishment of sovereign German armed forces. The other thinkable alternative, a European defence for Germany and a national defence for everybody else, would have been discriminatory and hence unacceptable for Germany. Hence supranationality was essential for the EDC project.

4.2. The Defensive Character of the EDC

Article 2 (1) EDC Treaty provided that the objectives of the Community were exclusively defensive. On a literal interpretation this means that the EDC would not have participated in UN missions in the context of chapters VI and VII of the UN Charter, for example the war in Korea. Moreover, Article 2 (3) and (4) EDC Treaty provided:

> "3. Any armed attack against any of the Member States in Europe or against the European defence forces shall be considered an armed attack on all Member States.
>
> 4. The Member States and the European Defence Forces shall afford to the State or force so attacked all the military and other aid in their power."

This "all-important 'automatic action' commitment"[73] made the EDC a military alliance comparable to the WU,[74] NATO,[75] or later the Western European Union.[76]

[73] Fursdon, above n 67, at 153.

[74] See above.

[75] Article 5 Northern Atlantic Treaty. It reads:

> The Parties agree that an armed attack against one or more of them in Europe or North America shall be considered an attack against them all and consequently they agree that, if such an armed attack occurs, each of them, in exercise of the right of individual or collective self-defence recognised by Article 51 of the Charter of the United Nations, will assist the Party or Parties so attacked by taking forthwith, individually and in concert with the other Parties, such action as it deems necessary, including the use of armed force, to restore and maintain the security of the North Atlantic area. Any such armed attack and all measures taken as a result thereof shall immediately be reported to the Security Council. Such measures shall be terminated when the Security Council has taken the measures necessary to restore and maintain international peace and security.

See: http://www.nato.int/docu/basictxt/treaty.htm.

Article 51 of the UN Charter reads:

> Nothing in the present Charter shall impair the inherent right of individual or collective self-defence if an armed attack occurs against a Member of the United Nations, until the Security Council has taken measures necessary to maintain international peace and security. Measures taken by Members in the exercise of this right of self-defence shall be immediately reported to the Security Council and shall not in any way affect the authority and responsibility of the Security Council under the present Charter to take at any time such action as it deems necessary in order to maintain or restore international peace and security.

See: http://www.nato.int/docu/basictxt/bt–un51.htm.

[76] Article V WEU (Brussels) Treaty. Article V reads: 'If any of the High Contracting Parties should be the object of an armed attack in Europe, the other High Contracting Parties will, in accordance with the provisions of Article 51 of the Charter of the United Nations, afford the Party so attacked all the military and other aid and assistance in their power.' See: http://www.weu.int/Treaty.htm.

However, the comparison with the similar Article 5 Washington Treaty reveals that the commitment in Article 2 EDC went much further as it did not subject the action to be taken by the other Member States to reservations. Action was to be automatic, which could be considered another expression of the more supranational character of the EDC. Not only the Member States but also the supranational EDF are obliged to take unlimited military and other action to the aid of the attacked Member State. The Member States transferred sovereignty and therefore responsibility for defence to the supranational EDC. Hence, they had to be sure that in case of an attack, against which, due to the lack of armed forces of their own, they would not take individual action regarding their self-defence, the Community would commit all its power to their defence. Therefore, the supranational EDC merging the armed forces of its Member States into supranational armed forces had to assume the responsibility for the military security of the Member States. The automatic action commitment, in other words an action commitment without reservations, was therefore the necessary compensation for the transfer of sovereignty. Moreover, as the military apparatus now committed to their defence would be considerably more substantial than in the case of individual self-defence, the national security of the Member States was at least in theory enhanced. The influence of the individual Member States on their defence was to be more limited than before because action was ultimately determined by the institutions of the EDC. However, the more supranational character and the automatic action commitment would have made the EDC a mighty military power and a considerable deterrent. The enhanced military and political power would have deterred the Soviet Union from an invasion of Western Europe.

The segment "in Europe" clarified that the overseas territories of the Member States, such as the Dutch Antilles, Belgian Congo, or the French departments in Algeria, were excluded from this protection. This segment represented the only limitation of the automatic action commitment. Therefore the respective Member States had to ensure the defence of these territories on a national basis.[77] In other words, as they did not transfer the sovereignty and responsibility for these territories to the EDC, they would be allowed to keep national armed forces and to withdraw parts of their troops from the EDF[78] in case the security of one of these territories so required.

The fact that alongside the European Defence Forces, also the other Member States have to help an attacked Member State, refers to non-military aid, for

[77] The WEU Treaty, above, contains a similar limitation to Europe. The NATO Treaty, above n 76, has a different approach in Article 6 which reads:

> For the purpose of Article 5, an armed attack on one or more of the Parties is deemed to include an armed attack: on the territory of any of the Parties in Europe or North America, on the Algerian Departments of France, on the territory of or on the Islands under the jurisdiction of any of the Parties in the North Atlantic area north of the Tropic of Cancer; on the forces, vessels, or aircraft of any of the Parties, when in or over these territories or any other area in Europe in which occupation forces of any of the Parties were stationed on the date when the Treaty entered into force or the Mediterranean Sea or the North Atlantic area north of the Tropic of Cancer.

[78] Subject to an approval procedure, see below.

example civil supplies, money, and civil defence and possibly national armed units permanently or temporarily outside the EDF.

4.3. Non-discrimination

Article 6 EDC Treaty provided that there should be no discrimination between Member States.[79] This was a requirement important to Germany. As outlined above, a major motivation for the EDC project was to integrate the future German contribution to the defence of Western Europe into a European framework: independent German armed forces were to be avoided. This was also the German position.[80] The German government, however, also saw its contribution to the EDC as an instrument to gain full or partial sovereignty and wanted to avoid the status of a second class Member State.[81] The Bonn Convention,[82] which was to give the Federal Republic of Germany its sovereignty, was negotiated at the same time as the EDC, linked to the EDC, and could not come into effect separately.[83]

In its *Projet de Protocole d'Application du Traité instituant la Communauté Européenne de Défense*[84] of 19 August 1954 the French Government asked for changes in the military provisions of the EDC Treaty. Integration of forces would only apply to German forces and to forces of the other Member States stationed in Germany. This meant, as Nutting pointed out, that the French government "was asking for a European army for the Germans and a French army for the French."[85] It is submitted that this could not have been reconciled with Article 6 EDC Treaty as it discriminates against Germany. Moreover, it shows that such a provision is necessary, as non-discrimination cannot be taken for granted.

A similar provision to Article 6 EDC Treaty is implied in all European treaties, including the EC Treaty and can be called a basic rule of European integration. In the context of the EDC it emphasised that the different sizes of the Member States in relation to territory, population, and military would not lead to discriminatory treatment in relation to the other Member States and the EDC. Apart from the special case of Germany who had no sovereignty over defence to transfer, the non-discrimination rule is an important assurance for a Member State transferring sovereignty to a more supranational Community, which requires trust in the other Member States. This does not mean that different financial and military contributions would not be taken into account, for example in relation to defence procurement, as will be explained below. Moreover, it is generally doubtful that there is no discrimination between Member States in practice. A large Member

79 Article 6 EDC Treaty reads: 'The present Treaty shall in no way discriminate against its Member States.'

80 Nutting, above n 5, at 36.

81 See Fursdon, above n 67, at 96, 107–8, 116, 122, 153; Nutting, above n 5, at 38.

82 See on the Bonn and Paris Conventions: WA Kewenig, 'Bonn and Paris Agreements (1952 and 1954)' in Bernardt, (ed), above n 16, vol III, at 56.

83 Nutting, above n 5, at 42 and 69.

84 Above n 68.

85 Nutting, above n 5, at 67.

State will often throw her weight around to promote a national or their Community agenda. An example is the hefty reaction of the Member States of the EU against the inclusion of the right wing Freedom Party in the Federal Government of the small Member State Austria in 1999. The inclusion of the right wing National Alliance in the government of the large Member State Italy did not cause comparable reactions. However, these might also be isolated examples. Nevertheless in practice a large Member State such as France will exercise more influence in a Community like the EDC, than a small Member State such as Luxembourg, especially in the context of intergovernmental institutions such as the Council.

4.4. Institutions

Article 8 (1) EDC Treaty listed the institutions of the Community: the Board of Commissioners, the Assembly, the Council, and the Court. Article 8 (2) EDC noted that their organisation would be as described in Part II of the EDC Treaty unless and until replaced by a new organisation resulting from any federal or confederal structure. This structure was to be worked out later by the Assembly under the terms of Article 38 EDC Treaty, as will be explained below. Articles 19 to 67 EDC Treaty dealt with the details on the four institutions of the EDC.

4.4.1. The Board of Commissioners

Articles 19 to 32 EDC Treaty regulated the composition and powers of the Board of Commissioners, the executive institution of the Community. The nine Commissioners had to be nationals of a Member State, were appointed by agreement between the national governments, and would normally serve for six years. One third of the members would be replaced every two years and not more than two were to come from one Member State.[86] The Board was the most important element of the more supranational character of the EDC, since they were to be independent from the governments of the Member States and empowered to take binding decisions. An "important direction on their independence"[87] was stated in Article 20 EDC Treaty:

> "In the accomplishment of their duties, the members of the Board of Commissioners shall neither ask for or receive instructions from any government. They shall refrain from any action inconsistent with the supranational character of their duties."[88]

The Board would have a quorum of five and decisions were to be taken by majority of those present.[89] The governments of the Member States, after consulting the

[86] Article 21 EDC Treaty.
[87] Fursdon, above n 67, at 155.
[88] Article 20 EDC Treaty.
[89] Article 24(1) EDC Treaty.

Board, would appoint a Chairman of the Board of Commissioners from among its members by mutual agreement for four years.[90]

The Board of Commissioners was to have executive and supervisory powers.[91] According to Article 27 EDC Treaty, in the exercise of its powers it was to take Decisions, make Recommendations and express Opinions. Decisions were to be binding in all their aspects. Recommendations were to be binding in respect of the purposes which they lay down, but were to leave to whom they were addressed the choice of the means of achieving that purpose. Opinions were to have no binding force. According to Article 30 EDC Treaty the Board were to have at their disposal the civil and military personnel necessary to enable them to carry out all the tasks devolving on them under the Treaty. The military and civilian personnel in the services they were to form for this purpose were to be subordinate to them on the same footing and on the same basis. Article 31 EDC Treaty dealt with its powers in respect of EDF ranks and appointments.[92] Thus the Board of Commissioners would have been the EDC ministry of defence. Moreover, it would have had the power to pass secondary legislation in the form of binding decisions and recommendations. The latter follows the example of the powers of the High Authority of the ECSC. The European Commission has no general powers comparable to that of the Board under Article 30 EDC Treaty. Most general decisions are taken by the intergovernmental Council who are also the co-legislator with the European Parliament. The European Commission has only very limited legislative powers.[93] WU, NATO, or Western European Union did or do not have a comparable institution. At time of writing there is no plan to create an equally powerful supranational institution.

The independent Board of Commissioners was to be the institutional manifestation of the supranationality of the EDC. It was the crucial supranational institutional element in contrast to the intergovernmental element represented by the Council. The Board was to be the only institution the EDC was not to 'borrow' from the ECSC. Hence it was the only wholly separate EDC institution safeguarding the interests of the Community.

The far-reaching independence and powers of the Board of Commissioners were one of the reasons for the French opposition to the EDC Treaty. In Chapter II of its *Projet de Protocole d'Application du Traité instituant la Communauté Européenne de Défense*[94] of 19 August 1954 the French Government proposed to limit the task of the Board of Commissioners to the management, administration and equipment of the EDF. It would have no political prerogatives and be subordinate to the Council. Moreover, for eight years after the Treaty came into force, a Member State could suspend any decision of the Board of Commissioners, which

[90] Article 25 EDC Treaty.
[91] Article 19 EDC Treaty.
[92] Article 31 EDC Treaty.
[93] Under Articles 39(3)(d) and 86(3) EC and when legislation is delegated from the Council to the Commission (which means that the Council can also take these powers back), see Craig and de Búrca, *EU Law*, above n 55, at 140.
[94] Above n 68.

it considered as affecting its vital interests. For the same period, the latter's right of appeal would be equally suspended. This would have eroded the supranational character of the EDC enshrined mainly in the provisions on the Board of Commissioners. As Fursdon wrote, "the once-powerful Board of Commissioners would have been downgraded to a Board of Technical Management only."[95] It would have been harder for the Board to come to decisions and executive implementation of these decisions would have been very difficult. The French proposals would have "removed the whole supranational concept".[96]

4.4.2. The Assembly

Article 33 to 38 EDC Treaty dealt with the Assembly, which was the Assembly of the ECSC increased by three delegates each for Germany, France and Italy. The members were to be elected on the same terms as the other delegates by the national parliaments, not directly by the peoples of the Community. Hence the Assembly was one of the institutions the EDC "borrowed" from the ECSC.[97] They were to meet annually and members of the Council and the Board of Commissioners could attend and address them. The latter had to report to the Assembly, who would discuss the report, make suggestions and comment thereon. The Assembly could pass a censure motion forcing the entire Board of Commissioners to resign. It is submitted that for various reasons that go beyond the aim of this chapter, the EDC would have suffered from a democratic deficit. It Suffices to say that the similar provisions of assemblies and the European Parliament in other European treaties caused criticism of the democratic structure.[98] The EDC would not have had a directly elected institution, this at least indirectly elected institution would have had only a consultative function, could not elect the Board of Commissioners, and a Council made up of representatives of Member State governments and an executive Board would have produced legislation.

The "very important [...] 'let out' [A]rticle"[99] 38 EDC Treaty charged the Member States of the EDC Treaty to examine, within six months of signing the EDC Treaty, a new form of federal or con-federal structure for European unity. In this context, the Assembly was charged with studying the constitution of an Assembly of the EDC elected on a democratic basis and the powers which would devolve on such an Assembly. Moreover, it was charged with studying any changes

[95] Fursdon, above n 67, at 284.

[96] Nutting, above n 5, at 67.

[97] RA Wessels, *The European Union's Foreign and Security Policy: A Legal and Institutional Perspective* (Kluwer, The Hague, 2000) 2.

[98] See J Weiler, U Haltern and F Meyer, 'European Democracy and its Critique' in J Hayward, (ed), *The Crisis of Representation in Europe* (Frank Cass: London, 1995), at 32–33; J Weiler, 'European Models: Polity, People and System' in P Craig and C Harlow, *Lawmaking in the European Union* (Kluwer, London, 1998) ch 7; P Craig, 'The Nature of the Community: Integration, Democracy and Legitimacy' in Craig and de Búrca, *Evolution*, above n 1, at 1; G de Búrca, 'The Quest for Legitimacy in the European Union' (1996) 59 *Modern Law Review* 349; Craig and de Búrca, *EU Law*, above n 54, at 167, citations in n 107.

[99] Fursdon, above n 67, at 156.

which might eventually have to be made to the EDC Treaty concerning other institutions, particularly with a view of safeguarding an appropriate representation of the interests of the Member States. In carrying out its work, the Assembly was directed that the recommendation for a final organisation to replace the interim EDC should be so conceived as to allow it to constitute one of the elements in a subsequent federal or con-federal structure. This structure was to be based upon the principle of separation of powers and having a bicameral system of representation. The Assembly was to make a report within six months after its establishment to the governments of the Member States who would have to convene a conference for consideration of this report within an additional three months. According to Article 5 of the Draft Treaty the European Political Community was not designed as a particular community with specific functions but to provide the quasi-constitutional basis of a general supranational European Community merging the special communities EDC and ECSC.[100] Hence a more supranational political community would have followed the establishment of the EDC. In other words, the next step would have been the establishment of a federation or confederation as a roof for all existing and new communities.

4.4.3. The Council

The Council were to be composed of representatives from each Member State government, each becoming chairman by turn of alphabetical order. Hence the Council were the intergovernmental element in the institutional structure of the EDC. They were to meet as often as necessary but at least every three months and could be called into session on the initiative of the Chairman or a member of the Council or the Board of Commissioners. In order to function at any time, a Council Member could be represented by a deputy and also each Member State had to have a permanent representative nominated.

In broad terms their task was to harmonise the activities of the Board of Commissioners with the policies of the governments of the Member States.[101] Their main function was similar to that of the Councils of the ECSC or the later European Economic Community, Euratom and European Union: the Council was to be a legislator. They were to issue directives to guide the activities of the Board of Commissioners, to give approvals which the Board of Commissioners must obtain before taking decisions or making recommendations, and to take decisions.[102] However, in contrast to the role of the Council in the EC and EU, the EDC Treaty envisaged a strong legislative role of the Board of Commissioners, both as a legislator and as an initiator of legislation. This followed the example of the High Authority in the ECSC. Broadly

[100] G Rees, entry on 'European Political Community' in Bernardt, above n 16, vol 6, at 197. See also AH Robertson, 'The European Political Community' (1952) 29 *British Yearbook of International Law* 383–401; HW Briggs, 'The Proposed European Political Community' (1954) 48 *American Journal of International Law* 110–22.

[101] Article 39 (1) EDC Treaty.

[102] On the forms of EDC legislation, see below.

speaking the fundamental decisions were to be taken by the Council[103] but generally the Board of Commissioners took the decisions. For example, Articles 31 (1) EDC Treaty provides that ranks higher than those of Commander of a basic unit of homogeneous nationality shall be conferred by Decision of the Board of Commissioners on approval by the Council acting unanimously.[104] Article 31 (2) EDC Treaty provides decisions on ranks in homogeneous units shall be made by the respective Member State. According to Article 31 (3) (b) EDC Treaty "all other military appointments", in other words on lower ranks in heterogeneous units, were to be taken by the Board of Commissioners. This example illustrates the point made above: political decisions are taken by the Council. The less political and more administrative the decision the less the involvement of the Council.

Article 43 EDC Treaty dealt with the voting procedure to be followed in implementing the different types of decisions called for in the Treaty. There were three variations: a simple majority, a specified or qualified majority, and unanimity. A simple majority meant an absolute majority of representatives or, in the event of a tie, by a majority of representatives of Member States which together made available to the Community at least two thirds of the contribution of Member States. The term 'contributions', as used in the simple or specified majority voting procedure, was taken as meaning the percentage of financial contribution actually paid during the previous financial year and the percentage of manpower composing the EDF on the first day of the current half year. The voting procedure was thus, in certain circumstances subject to a 'weighting' dependent on the size of a nation's contributory defence effort towards the EDC. Obviously it would be some time before such contributions were formed into the echelons of the EDF and so an agreed scale was required to enable the Council to function over this interim period. Article 43 *bis* EDC Treaty gave this on a provisional basis as Germany, France and Italy three each, Belgium and Netherlands two each and Luxembourg one. A specified or qualified majority was to be achieved either by the proportion of votes so specified, provided that such a majority included the votes of Member States which together made available to the Community two thirds of the contribution of Member States, or by the vote of five Member States. According to Article 39 (4) EDC Treaty the decisions and approval of the Council were to be decided by simple majority unless the EDC Treaty provided otherwise. However, as the Treaty required qualified majorities or unanimity for most thinkable decisions, decision making by simple majority would have been of little importance in practice.

A qualified two-thirds majority was required with regards to matters of a lesser, managerial or administrative nature with regards to general principles, the

[103] See the list of decisions to be taken by the Council and the respective legal bases in n 106 and n 107.

[104] A similar procedure applies to other high appointments under Article 31(3)(a) EDC Treaty.

EDF, or finance and budget.[105] In broad terms the unanimous vote of the Council was required on important matters affecting the EDC generally, modifications to any arrangements relative to the EDF and their associated common equipment programmes, on financial arrangements and the common budget.[106] A unanimous decision was achieved if the votes in its favour included those of all Member States represented in the Council. Abstentions could not prevent the adoption of such a decision.

There are two remarks to be made about these voting procedures. First, the allocation of votes took the different contributions of the Member States into account. However, as the provisional allocation of votes indicates, this did not take the real differences in contribution into account but balanced them with the fact that every Member State had to have a vote. Second, the distribution between simple majority voting, qualified majority voting and unanimous vote indicates a fine balance between the intergovernmental and the supranational. The intergovernmental institution Council were to take decisions on the more important matters on an intergovernmental basis: unanimity means that there is no possibility to be outvoted, there is a national *veto*. All Member States are equal: one government one vote. Decisions on less important matters are taken on a more supranational

[105] A 2/3 majority Council decision was required for general matters in Article 46(1) EDC Treaty on inviting the Board of Commissioners to take any measure within its competence, Article 114(1)(2) EDC Treaty on laying down directives governing the transfer of information from the Member States to the Board of Commissioners considered necessary for the exercise of the latter's duties, Article 123 (2)(1) EDC Treaty regarding provisional measures taken in the context of this article, Article 126(1) EDC on convening a conference for the amendment of the EDC Treaty; for matters regarding the European Defence Forces in Articles 13(1), 14(1), 77(2)(1), 78 *bis* (4) point 2 EDC Treaty; and for finance and budget in Articles 85(2) EDC Treaty on the nomination of the members of the Board of Auditors and its Chairman, Article 87(2)(b) EDC Treaty on the allocation of expenditure, Article 89(4) EDC Treaty on the choice of a common accounting currency for the budget, Article 90(1) EDC Treaty regarding transfers of credits between the chapters of responsibility of the Board of Commissioners, Article 102(2) EDC Treaty on general instructions regarding common programmes for the armament, equipment, supply, and infrastructure of the EDF, Article 103(2) EDC Treaty on the Council approval of the seven-year programmes of the Board of Commissioners regarding common armaments programmes, Article 104(4) and (5)(3) EDC Treaty on the Council approval of regulations regarding public procurement and contract management of common armaments programmes submitted by the Board of Commissioners, and Article 107(2)(2) EDC Treaty regarding amendments to the list of armaments in Annex I to Article 107 EDC Treaty.

[106] A Unanimous Council decision was required for general matters in Articles 119 EDC Treaty regarding the linguistic system of the institutions of the Community, Article 123(1) EDC Treaty for decisions taken in the context of cases of grave and urgent necessity, Article 124(1) and (2) EDC Treaty for the approval of Board decisions to be taken in cases not provided in the Treaty, Article 125(1) EDC Treaty regarding adjustments of the rules relating to the exercise by the Board of Commissioners of the powers granted to it due to unforeseen difficulties, Article 129 EDC Treaty regarding accession to the EDC; for matters concerning the European Defence Forces in Articles 15(2) EDC Treaty regarding the organisation of the EDF, Article 39(2) EDC Treaty regarding the directives guiding the activities of the Board, Article 44 EDC Treaty regarding modifications to the text defining the status of the personnel and the texts governing the general organisation, recruitment, strength and officering of the forces, and modifications to the plan constituting the EDF, Article 48 EDC Treaty regarding relations between NATO and the EDC, Articles 68(2), 69(2), 77(1), and 78 *bis* (1) point 1 EDC Treaty on specific rules relating to the organisation and administration of the EDF; and for finance and budget in Articles 84, 85(2), 87(2), 95(1), 99(3), EDC Treaty and the economic provisions in Articles 104(7), 105(2), and 107(4)(d) EDC Treaty.

basis: a simple and a qualified majority imply that there is a possibility to be outvoted and the number of votes takes the 'size' of the Member State into account.

Lastly, the Council alone was responsible for decisions regarding any joint sessions with the NATO Council or in regard to the EDC-NATO Protocol. The joint sessions were essentially sessions of the EDC Council extended by the representatives of the USA, Canada, Portugal, Denmark and Norway. Any decisions taken unanimously during such joint meetings of the two Councils were to be automatically binding on the EDC institutions.[107] The joint sessions of the Councils were to be one of the links between NATO and the EDC as two interdependent elements of the European security architecture. The EDC was to be the first and only 'floor' based on the 'basement' of NATO in turn based on the 'foundations' of the UN.

According to Article 46 EDC Treaty, acting on a two-thirds majority, the Council could invite the Board of Commissioners to take any measure within its competence. The Board did not have to comply with this invitation. If they did not comply then the Council or any Member State could call the Assembly into session with a view to obtaining a motion of censure and hence the Board's resignation. This scenario would have involved a serious confrontation of the institutions and Member States amounting to a constitutional crisis. Such a crisis would have undermined the coherence of the EDC and the security of Western Europe and therefore it is unlikely it would ever have happened. As the Council would have had to jump over such a high hurdle to overcome their resistance to comply with their invitation, Article 46 EDC Treaty does not represent a significant limitation to the Board of Commissioners right to initiative.

4.4.4. The Court

Articles 51 to 57 EDC Treaty regulated the Court of the EDC, which was to be the existing ECSC Court of Justice.[108] They were to ensure respect for the law in the interpretation and application of the EDC Treaty and its regulations[109] and have jurisdiction to hear appeals by Member States, the Council, or the Assembly against decisions or recommendations of the Board of Commissioners.[110] Similarly, they were competent to give judgment on appeals brought against the proceedings of the Council by a Member State, by the Board of Commissioners or by the Assembly.[111] Appeals could be made on grounds of lack of legal competence, violation of procedure, violation of the Treaty or any legal rules concerning its application, or misuse of powers, as outlined in Articles 54 (1) and 57 (1) EDC Treaty. The Court could set aside the recommendations or decisions of the Board and at the request of a Member State or the Board of Commissioners, set aside the proceedings of the Assembly. However, according to Article 58 (1) subparagraph 2 EDC Treaty such an appeal could only be based on grounds of lack of legal

[107] Article 47(2) EDC Treaty.
[108] Article 52 EDC Treaty.
[109] Article 51 EDC Treaty.
[110] Article 54 EDC Treaty.
[111] Article 57 EDC Treaty.

competence or violation of requisite formalities. Action had to be brought within one month from the notification or publication of the act in question[112] for reasons of legal certainty. The EDC Treaty did not provide for individual action, in other words appeals of natural or legal persons. Under the ECSC Treaty this was possible within certain limits. However, Article 62 EDC Treaty provided for a procedure whereby only the Court was competent to rule on the validity of decisions taken by the Council or the Board of Commissioners. Therefore the Court had the function of a constitutional court in the framework of the EDC.

The strong position of a court of law in a defence organisation was and is unprecedented. Neither the WU, NATO, or later the Western European Union provide for judicial review. Moreover, chapter 2 will explain that the jurisdiction of the European Court of Justice is excluded from the Common Foreign and Security Policy of the European Union.[113] Chapter 12 will explain that even under the envisaged Constitutional Treaty foreign and security policy remains excluded from the jurisdiction of the Court.[114] The *nonchalance* with which the Member States provided for judicial review in the EDC Treaty can partly be explained by the fact that in the early 1950s they could not be aware of the pivotal role of the Court of Justice, a role that only became apparent with the Luxembourg jurisprudence of the 1960s, which will be discussed below. Suffice it to say at this point, that had the Member States known about *Van Gend* and *Costa/ENEL* at the time, it can be assumed judicial review would have been a more controversial matter. Another reason might be the desire of the Member States as the creators of the EDC Treaty to introduce some form of control over the powerful Board of Commissioners. Finally, in a Community largely replacing the defence efforts of the Member States rather than forming a military alliance of still independent national forces, administrative and legislative action has to be subjected to the same checks and balances as that of the Member States. This is necessary to meet minimum requirements of democracy, legitimacy, and accountability. In other words, when the State is replaced in a particular field, the replacing entity should be subjected to the same level of judicial control as previously was the State.

The absence of a possibility for individuals to bring an action for judicial review is not surprising considering the objectives of the EDC. However, the rules on limited standing for individuals in the EC Treaty[115] shows that it is possible to protect the functioning of a supranational community from frivolous claims without excluding individuals from judicial review altogether. It is not unlikely that this issue would have been subject to reform later on.[116] Finally, the Court would have given rulings by virtue of an arbitration clause contained in a public

[112] Articles 54(2) and 57(2) EDC Treaty.
[113] At 78–80.
[114] At 386–391.
[115] See Craig and de Búrca, *EU Law*, above n 54, at 482 *et seq.*
[116] See also Article 64(2) EDC Treaty: 'The Court shall be competent to give ruling on any other matters covered by an additional provision to the present Treaty.'

or private law contract passed by the EDC or on its behalf.[117] Hence at least private companies doing business with the EDC could seek remedies.

Finally, Article 62 EDC Treaty provided that the Court alone was to be competent to give rulings, of a prejudicial character, on the validity of the decisions and recommendations of the Board of Commissioners and on the proceedings of the Council, should a dispute referred to a national court call their validity into question. This provision was included to ensure the uniform interpretation of the EDC Treaty similar to the possibility of national courts to make a reference for a preliminary ruling to the European Court of Justice under Article 234 EC Treaty.[118] This would have given individuals an indirect possibility to challenge EDC acts through proceedings in a national court leading to a ruling of the EDC Court.

4.5. The Budget

Article 3 EDC Treaty laid the basis for national contributions to the EDC budget. According to Articles 86 to 96 EDC Treaty the Community was to have a common budget. The Board of Commissioners, in consultation with the governments of the Member States and in the light of their EDF plans, was to prepare it. Their common plans for armaments, equipment, supplies and infrastructure to which the budget was related would be annexed to it. The Council would decide by unanimous vote on the total size and the size of the contribution of each Member State. It would also decide, by a two-thirds majority, on the allocation of expenditures. The unanimity requirement gives every Member State control over its own contribution and the overall size of the budget. In contrast the allocation of expenditures is subject to a qualified majority preventing decisions being blocked. The Assembly could accept or reject the Council-approved budget as a whole or propose modifications. It could not increase the overall expenditure. Thus the Council was to decide on the common budget. The Assembly had mainly a consultative role on matters of detail. In contrast to the later European Community the EDC was to have no income of its own, it was to be financed exclusively through the national contributions of the Member States. These contributions were dependent on national budgets and therefore national parliamentary approval. Hence the EDC Treaty did not envisage a common budget independent from national interests, the existence of which might be considered essential for an effective defence community. However, sovereignty over defence would have been transferred to the EDC. In other words, the Member States would have had no defence but the EDC. As outlined under the next heading below, there would have been almost no national forces after the creation of the EDF. It is submitted that this fact would have ensured that individual Member States would not have abused the unanimity requirement to deliberately undermine the EDC through

[117] Article 63 EDC Treaty.
[118] See Craig and de Búrca, *EU Law*, above n 54, at 432 *et seq*.

the budgetary provisions because this would have undermined their national security.

4.6. The European Defence Forces

Articles 9 to 18 EDC Treaty laid down the principles for the constitution and organisation of the EDF. Units from the Member States were to be made available to the Community "with a view of their fusion". No Member State could recruit or maintain national armed forces other than those for which the EDC Treaty had made special provision.[119] Such circumstances were to apply only where the Member State would have assumed defence responsibilities for non-European territories or for the fulfilment of international missions in Berlin, Austria, or under United Nations' auspices. On completion of such missions, the troops were either to be disbanded or made available to the Community. Such forces could, with the agreement of the Supreme Commander NATO, be rotated with those assigned to the EDF. Troops intended for the personal protection of the Head of State could remain national. Navies, in addition to the general provision regarding territories outside Europe, could be used nationally to protect communications with and between overseas territories and for the fulfilment of NATO tasks accepted prior to entry into force of the EDC Treaty. The total size of national armed forces for non-European tasks was not to be so large as to prejudice contributions to the EDF. Article 11 EDC Treaty allowed Member States to recruit and maintain police and gendarmerie forces but stated that these should in size and nature not "exceed the requirements of their mission". Hence the EDF was to replace the armed forces of the Member States.

Articles 12, 13, and 14 EDC Treaty laid down the conditions under which a Member State might, with the authority of the Board of Commissioners temporarily withdraw part of its EDC force contribution to meet national contingencies. The situations envisaged were those of disorder or threatened disorder in the Member State's own territory, in the event of a major crisis affecting a non-European territory for which it has assumed responsibility, or to fulfil an international mission entrusted to it outside the EDC area. Whereas in the first case the requirement was for the Board of Commissioners merely to notify the Council, in the latter two cases the formal approval of the Council by a two-thirds majority and the agreement of the Supreme Commander NATO were required.

Article 15 EDC Treaty dealt with personnel. The EDF was to be made up of conscripts[120] or regular volunteers integrated as provided for in Part III of the Treaty and wearing a common uniform. In the 1950s all Member States of the EDC and the United Kingdom had conscript forces. Article 12 of the Military Protocol clarified that only nationals of the Member States of the male sex were subject to conscription.

[119] Article 9(2) EDC Treaty.
[120] On the impact of European Community law on conscription see ch 9 at 000–000.

Lastly, the Supreme Commander NATO was authorised to ensure that the EDF were organised, equipped, trained and prepared for duty in a "satisfactory manner". As soon as national contributions were ready they were to be placed at the disposal of the Supreme Commander who, in turn, would give the Community his requirements regarding the articulation and deployment of such forces.

Part III of the Treaty and the Military Protocol contained the military provisions. Articles 68, 69 and 70 EDC Treaty covered the basic structure of the Army, Air Force and Naval elements of the EDF. The basic operational unit of the Army was to be national. It was to be as small as was compatible with effectiveness, as free as possible of logistic functions and supported and maintained by higher integrated echelons. The Army Corps would be composed of basic units of different nationalities, other than in exceptional circumstances resulting from tactical or organisational situations proposed by the Supreme Commander NATO, determined by the Board of Commissioners and approved by the Council. The Corps' tactical and logistic support echelons would be integrated; the later made up of homogeneous national battalion-size units in the same proportions as in the Corps' basic unit structure. The Army Corps' Command and the General Staff were also to be integrated. There was to be freedom of grouping of basic and support service units as between NATO and EDF corps.

Air Force basic units, tailored to specific tactical tasks, equipped with homogeneous combat equipment and as free as possible from logistic functions, were to be national. "A certain number" of basic units of different nationalities would be grouped together under, and supported by, integrated higher echelons. The same logistic and interchangeability conditions applicable to Army units were to apply.

European naval forces would consist of what was required for the protection of the home waters of the Member States' European territories. Contingents were to form groups of the same nationality for single tactical tasks but have European status; they could be incorporated in part or whole, as an integrated force into NATO Commands.

The following provisions covered a number of essential yet diverse responsibilities and functions. Conscripts from Member States were to perform the same period of active service,[121] and the Board of Commissioners and the Council were to act quickly to standardise practice. The Board of Commissioners was to be responsible, as from an agreed date and within the framework of the common provisions set out in the Military Protocol, for recruiting for the EDF. It was also responsible for training and preparing them in accordance with a common system and standard method, taking into consideration the several official languages. It was to direct the Staff Colleges of the Member States, prepare mobilisation plans and carry out such inspections and supervision 'as may be necessary'. The deployment of the EDF in the framework of the Supreme Commander NATO's recommendations was also to be the Board's responsibility as was the administration of its personnel and equipment. Finally an agreed common code of general military discipline, applicable throughout the EDF, was to be prepared.

[121] According to Article 12 of the Military Protocol at least 18 months.

The second chapter of Part III of the EDC Treaty covered the status of the EDF and the rights and obligations to international law and conventions, and their conduct in relation to public international law. Article 80 EDC Treaty covered a significant point of Community collective vis-à-vis sovereignty over the EDF when it stated:

> "The Community shall have, in respect of the European Defence Forces and their members, the same rights and obligations as the states themselves in respect of their national forces and their members, under customary international law."

The 'social' regime of the EDC for military and civil personnel was not very developed. There are rules on recruitment and conscription but only with regards to the raising of forces and only a few provisions regarding promotions. There is nothing in the EDC Treaty or the Military Protocol on pensions, access to employment, vocational training, hospitals, 'veterans affairs', or military burials. Although this is not expressly mentioned in the Treaty, the limitation of conscription in Article 12 of the Military Protocol to men implies that at least armed service, if not service in general, is limited to men. However, the EDC is a project of the 1950s and this limitation would have probably been subject to changes later on.[122] It is submitted that the EDC Treaty implies that the social and labour standards of the personnel of the EDF had to be the same irrespective of the nationality of the unit or the individual soldier.[123] Moreover, the EDC Treaty implies a general principle of non-discrimination on grounds of nationality regarding personnel.[124] Only Article 16 of the Military Protocol contains a human right for soldiers regarding religious freedom.[125] Hence it could be said that the EDC Treaty did not see soldiers as workers with specific rights.

4.7. The Defence Economic Regime[126]

Part V of the EDC Treaty contains the envisaged defence economic regime of the Community. According to Article 101 to 111 EDC Treaty the Board of Commissioners was to prepare and execute common programmes for the

[122] On European Community law and equal treatment of men and women in the armed forces of the Member States see ch 9.

[123] See for example: Article 72(1) EDC Treaty: 'Personnel recruited by conscription to serve in the European Defence Forces shall perform the same period of active service.' Article 74 (1) EDC Treaty: '[...] shall carry out the training and preparation of the European Defence Forces in accordance with a common system and standard methods.' Article 79 EDC Treaty: 'A uniform code of general military discipline applicable to the members of the European Defence Forces shall be prepared [...].' Article 12(2)(2) of the Military Protocol: 'In all the Member States the minimum period of active service shall be eighteen months.'

[124] Above.

[125] Article 16(1)(3) Military Protocol reads: 'Suitable arrangements shall be made to enable members of the European Defence Forces to practice their religion.'

[126] On defence procurement under the current regime see ch 7.

armament, equipment, supply and infrastructure of the EDF. It was to simplify and standardise armaments, equipment, supplies and infrastructure "as much and as rapidly as possible", also with regards to compatibility with NATO requirements.[127] According to Article 102 (1) (b) EDC Treaty the Board had to take account of the contributions made by Member States. The Board was also responsible for the placing of contracts in support of the various programmes and for supervising and accounting for their execution.[128] Article 104 EDC Treaty set out the basic public procurement regime including the principles of competition and non-discrimination,[129] specified the procedures[130] and award criterion[131] to be used, and contained a legal base for passing regulations on public procurement.[132] It would go beyond the aims of this chapter to discuss the compatibility of this procurement regime with the requirement to take the contribution of the Member States into account.[133] Article 106 EDC Treaty complemented the procurement regime with a common programme of scientific and technical research in the military sphere. These provisions were to establish the Board of Commissioners as a European defence procurement agency conducting their activities on the basis of a common procurement code partly contained in the Treaty. The defence procurement regime of the European Community shall be discussed in detail in chapter 7.[134]

Moreover, Article 107 EDC Treaty established *inter alia* a common regime for defence exports and imports:

> "The production, import and export of war materials from or to third countries, measures directly concerning establishments intended for the production of war materials, and the manufacture of prototypes and technical research concerning war materials shall be forbidden except as [...]"

[127] Article 102(1)(c) EDC Treaty.

[128] Article 104 EDC Treaty.

[129] Article 104(3)(1) sentences 1 and 3 EDC Treaty: 'Contracts shall be placed after the widest possible tenders have been asked for, except in cases justified for reasons of military secrecy or for technical reasons or on the grounds of urgency [...] Exclusion based on nationality shall not be maintained in respect of the nationals of Member States.'

[130] Article 104(3)(1) sentence 2 EDC Treaty: 'Contracts shall be concluded after public or restricted tendering, or without tendering (by private contract) with contractors capable of carrying out the work, and who are not excluded in their own countries from public tendering.'

[131] Article 104(3)(2) EDC Treaty: '[...] contracts should be placed with the contractor submitting the most advantageous tender.'

[132] Article 104(4) EDC Treaty: 'The procedure relating to the placing of contracts and the supervision of the execution and receipts and settlement in respect of work and supplies shall be determined by regulations. [...]'.

[133] This is and was also a problem in relation to later regimes, see M Trybus, *European Defence Procurement Law: International and National Procurement Systems as Models for a Liberalised Defence Procurement Market in Europe* (Kluwer, The Hague, 1999) ch 2.

[134] See also the discussion of the European Defence Agency in ch 11 at 319–328.

Annexes I[135] and II[136] to this article provided a comprehensive list of war materials to which this rule was to be applied. This "very important and tough provision [...] with far-reaching implications for all [M]ember [S]tates"[137] represented a prohibition of independent national defence industrial activities. The Board of Commissioners replaced the economic defence authorities of the Member States. In order to enforce this position they were given the power to make direct requests to the firms in question for the information required to fulfil their function and to proceed to verify this information through their agents.[138] Moreover, the Board could ask the Court of Justice for a ruling and the Court could impose fines on persons and companies contravening the provisions of Article 107 EDC Treaty.

Article 104 (7) EDC Treaty complemented the basic procurement and exports regimes of the Community with a rudimentary defence State aids and competition law regime:

> "If the Board of Commissioners notes in the execution of the programmes that *official intervention or concerted agreements or practices among firms* tend to *falsify or seriously restrict the normal play of competition*, it shall seize the Council of the matters, which shall decide, acting unanimously, on the measures necessary to remedy this position. The Council can be seized under the same conditions by a Member State.[emphasis added]"

The term "official intervention" refers to State aids and the phrase "concerted agreements or practices among firms" refers to competition law. In contrast to the European Community, where the Commission has the power to police these activities, in the EDC the Council takes the necessary measures. Moreover, the Council has to act unanimously. This means that in cases of State aids the violating Member State could have vetoed any measure against it. Moreover, the Board of Commissioners would not have had the extensive powers under Article 107 and 108 EDC Treaty in relation to the State aids and competition law regimes. This

[135] Annex I to Article 107 EDC Treaty:

> 1. *Weapons.* Small arms, machine guns, anti-tank weapons, artillery and mortars, anti–aircraft weapons and equipment for artificial fog, gas and flame-throwing. 2. *Ammunition and Rockets for all military purposes.* Ammunition for the above weapons, grenades, self-propelled missiles, torpedoes, mines and bombs of all types. 3. *Propellants and Explosives for Military Purposes.* The exemptions for civil use were listed. 4. *Armoured Equipment.* Tanks, armoured vehicles and armoured trains. 5. *All types of warship.* 6. *All types of military aircraft.* 7. *Atomic weapons.* 8. *Biological weapons.* 9. *Chemical Weapons.* 10. *Component parts only suitable for the construction of one of the items listed in groups 1, 2, 4, 5, 6 above.* 11. *Machines parts only suitable for the construction of one of the items listed in groups 1, 2, 4, 5, 6 above.*

For the list according to Article 296(2) EC to which Article 296(1)(b) EC applies see ch 5 at 144–145.

[136] Annex II to Article 107 EDC Treaty contained an additional list of atomic weapons; chemical weapons; biological weapons; long range missiles, guided missiles and influence mines; naval vessels other than minor defensive craft; and military aircraft. According to Article 107(4)(a) and (b) EDC Treaty it was extremely difficult to obtain an export licence for any of these categories of weapons from the board of Commissioners.

[137] Fursdon, above n 67, at 164.

[138] Article 108(1) and (2) EDC Treaty.

weakened the rudimentary remedy system considerably and turned it essentially into a political rather than a legal process. The EC defence State aids and competition law regimes shall be discussed in more detail in chapter 8.[139]

There are three observations on these arrangements. First, Chapter V of the EDC Treaty shows that the creators of the Treaty understood defence as a comprehensive concept ranging from politics to economics. The production and procurement of weapons, what US Americans call the military industrial complex, is an essential part of defence that needed to be addressed in the EDC. Second, until this day defence procurement is understood as a defence or security rather than a commercial activity and the European Defence Agency was only established in July 2004.[140] Third, Article 107 EDC Treaty envisaged a transfer of sovereignty over weapons or hard defence material to the jurisdiction of the EDC. This would have entailed the replacement of the national defence industrial complexes of the Member States by a European defence industrial complex. There is no literature on the matter. However, it is submitted here that the abolition of national military complexes is likely to have caused fierce opposition of the national defence industries, behind the scenes, especially in France.[141] Moreover, Article 107 EDC Treaty would also have transferred the sovereignty over trade in arms to the EDC. This would have meant that Member States were prevented from buying weapons from third countries even for national troops outside the EDF.

4.8. The United Kingdom and the EDC

As outlined above the United Kingdom did not want to be a Member State of the EDC. However, her government signed a *Memorandum regarding United Kingdom Association with the European Defence Community*, an *Agreement regarding Co-operation between the United Kingdom and the European Defence Community*, a *Statement of Common Policy on Military Association between the Forces of the United Kingdom and the European Defence Community*, and a Declaration in which they committed themselves to the continuous stationing of troops on the European continent, most notably in Germany.[142] Moreover the government declared that it would consider a military attack on any of the Member States of the EDC an attack on the United Kingdom. Hence the United Kingdom aligned itself closely to the EDC, even partly integrating its armed forces with the EDF and making a defence guarantee. However, London did not join the more supranational structures of the Community as a full Member State.

[139] At 248–252 and 231–248 respectively.

[140] See ch 11 at 319–328 for details. The European Defence Agency is not comparable with the arrangements of the EDC Treaty.

[141] See J Vernant, 'European Politics Faces French Economics' in Lerner and Aron, above n 12, 39, at 51.

[142] (1952) Cmd. 9126.

4.9. The Failure of the EDC

As outlined above, by the summer of 1954 the six Member States had signed the EDC Treaty and only in France and Italy was ratification pending. However, on 30 August 1954 the French parliament, the *Assemblée Nationale*, effectively refused to ratify the EDC.[143] This put an end to the project, the Treaty never entered into force, and the Community it had envisaged never became reality. There were many reasons for this outcome. In 1954, after the end of the war in Korea and the death of Stalin uniting for strength seemed less urgent.[144] There were considerable concerns about the transfer of sovereignty and the loss of identity for France, particularly but not only for the Gaulists.[145] For many the new Community was to have too many supranational powers.[146] The Communist votes against the Treaty were ordered from Moscow.[147] Fear of Germany, its rearmament and its weight in the EDC, was another concern.[148] Many deputés misunderstood the situation as if they could vote against German rearmament.[149] Connected to this fear was the fact that the United Kingdom did not participate in the new supranational organisation.[150] Moreover, the EDC was considered unrealistic and inefficient from a military point of view.[151]

There are three important points to be made about the Community that was to be established by this Treaty. First, the EDC would have started a more supranational European defence integration process, until then governed by the intergovernmental 1948 Brussels Treaty. The supranational character of the Community was the main reason for its failure as it proved unacceptable to the United Kingdom and ultimately France. Second, the EDC would have paved the way for European political integration. As the EDC failed, the process towards a political Community, envisaged in Article 38 EDC Treaty and outlined above, died with it. Third, the as yet separate processes of European defence integration and European economic integration, the latter through the ECSC and a subsequent economic community, would have been merged under the roof of European political integration. The failure of the EDC would keep defence integration separate and more intergovernmental for a long time.

[143] Strictly speaking the Assembly did not reject the ratification of the Treaty. It voted on a motion under Article 46 of the Assembly's procedure, a *motion préalable*, that the occasion of the debate was not suitable for deliberation and that the matter under discussion be definitely rejected without being brought forward for proper deliberation.

[144] A Aron, 'Historical Sketch of the Great Debate' in Lerner and Aron, above n 12, at 3 and 8; Fauvet, above, at 146; Lerner, above, at 220.

[145] Philip, in Lerner and Aron, above n 12, at 26; Stoetzel on the basis of public opinion as reflected in *sondages* at the time, above, at 72; Marchand, above, at 108. Lerner, above, at 209 and 216.

[146] Grosser, above, at 54.

[147] Above.

[148] A Aron, 'Historical Sketch of the Great Debate' in Lerner and Aron, above n 12, at 11–13; Grosser, above, at 54; Stoetzel, above, at 82; Marchand, above, at 109; Fauvet, above, at 128; Hoffmann, above, at 166.

[149] A Aron, 'Introduction to the American Edition', Lerner and Aron, above n 12, at IX.

[150] A Aron, 'Historical Sketch of the Great Debate', above, at 12; Grosser, above, at 54; Stoetzel, above, at 84.

[151] (French) General Koenig, according to Fauvet, in Lerner and Aron above n 12, at 151.

5. DEFENCE DEVELOPING SEPARATELY FROM THE MAINSTREAM OF EUROPEAN INTEGRATION

The failure of the EDC did not grind the European defence integration process to a halt. On the contrary, the Western European states addressed the issue swiftly following the vote of the French Parliament. However, defence integration through a more supranational organisation was off the agenda. The establishment of an organisational structure based on the alternative intergovernmental model was the order of the day. This approach had at least one political advantage: the United Kingdom, traditionally opposed to any supranational solution, would participate in an intergovernmental organisation. The supranational model became the base for economic integration as the main next step, for the time being limited to the six Member States of the ECSC.[152] The result was that defence integration was separated from the mainstream of integration pursued through the European Communities.[153] As the plan for a political union had died with the EDC, there was no roof that could bridge the separation of defence from the rest.

5.1. The Intergovernmental Western European Union

After the failure of the EDC Europe had to adopt an alternative model to address the defence issues of the day, most notably the urgent German contribution to the defence of Western Europe. The London Conference of October 1954 decided that the inclusion of Germany and Italy in a revised Brussels Treaty would be the way forward.[154] The Paris Protocol I revised the Brussels Treaty and the member States of the former WU, Italy, and Germany established the Western European Union (hereinafter WEU).[155] Moreover, it admitted Germany into NATO. Three further protocols on military forces are an integral part of the Paris Protocol according to its Article I.[156] Protocol II committed the United Kingdom to maintain certain forces in Europe with their removal, except in an emergency, subject to the agreement of the majority of the other parties. In Protocol III on arms control the Federal Republic of Germany committed itself not to manufacture atomic,

[152] This does not mean that the 'struggle' between the supranational and the intergovernmental approach was not fought within the European Communities as well, as will be explained in more detail below. Moreover, it continued beyond the Communities when the Member States started to take measures to develop an international presence.

[153] Instead of 'integration stream' the term 'integration path' could be used, see R Bray, (ed), K Lenaerts and P van Nuffel, *Constitutional Law of the European Union* (Sweet & Maxwell, London, 1999) Part I.

[154] Final Act of the London Conference, 3 October 1954, (1954) Cmd. 9289.

[155] Protocol (with Exchange of Letters) Modifying and completing the Brussels Treaty, signed 23 October 1954, 211 UNTS 342.

[156] [Paris] Protocol II on military forces set limits on the maximum size of the land and air forces maintained by each member State. It also committed the United Kingdom to maintain certain forces in Europe with their removal, except in an emergency, subject to the concurrence of the majority of the other parties. In [Paris] Protocol III on arms control the Federal Republic of Germany committed itself not to manufacture atomic, chemical or biological weapons and equipment. Moreover, all member States accepted control of their stocks on certain weapons. [Paris] Protocol IV established the Agency of the Western European Union for the Control of Armaments.

chemical or biological weapons and equipment. This German commitment was an important French requirement.[157] The anti-German passage in the preamble was replaced by the words "to promote the unity and to encourage the progressive integration of Europe".[158] This constituted a claim by the WEU to be a part of European integration. The new Article IV of the Modified Brussels Treaty linked the new organisation to NATO.

The necessary German contribution to Western defence was achieved by rearming the Federal Republic of Germany on a national basis. What the opponents of the EDC wanted to avoid the most became inevitable: in 1955 West Germany established her own national armed forces. Nevertheless, to this day the greater part of the *Bundeswehr* is under the direct command of the NATO Supreme Allied Commander Europe rather than the Federal German Minister for Defence.

In contrast to the EDC Treaty, the Modified Brussels Treaty envisages an intergovernmental organisation. According to the new Article VIII the Council composed of the foreign ministers of the Member States is the central organ able to consider all matters relating to the implementation of the Treaty. Unanimity prevails in the absence of any other arrangement.[159] The new permanent Secretariat has merely managerial functions. The Assembly, composed of the representatives of the WEU member States to the Consultative Assembly of the Council of Europe, makes non-binding recommendations and transmits opinions to the Council.

The more forceful terms of Article V of the Brussels Treaty, which through the Paris Protocol I became Article V of the Modified Brussels Treaty, compared to Article 5 of the Washington Treaty, were explained above. The earlier represents an automatic commitment without reservations and individual Member State discretion whereas the latter is subject to reservations and discretion. Theoretically, this further reaching commitment establishes a more cohesive alliance and a more convincing deterrent to potential enemies thereby providing the individual member States with a higher level of security. However, as the WEU has always existed parallel to NATO, it is argued that the participation and commitment of the USA rather than the wording of Article V of the Modified Brussels Treaty provided the main necessary deterrent during the Cold War and beyond.

The WEU contributed to the integration and security of Europe. It helped to settle the German contribution to Western European defence and to ease relations with the other member States. Most notably it helped the Franco-German rapprochement over the question of the Saar soon after its foundation.[160] From the foundation of the European Economic Community in 1957-58 to the accession of the United Kingdom to the European Communities in 1973-74 the WEU provided

[157] Marauhn, above n 17, at 9.
[158] Article II Paris Protocol I.
[159] Macalister-Smith, above n 29, at 368.
[160] Macalister-Smith, above, at 369.

the institutional framework for the necessary liaison between London and the Six.[161] As enlargement has always been an important aspect of Community foreign policy, the WEU could therefore be called an instrument of such a policy. The Modified Brussels Treaty contains more extensive obligations of a predominantly technical character than the Washington Treaty, especially in relation to arms control and military resources. Moreover, the WEU stimulated the re-equipping and expansion of certain European defence industries and the post war rearmament effort in general.[162]

Despite the achievements outlined above, it is argued that with the foundation of NATO little more than a year after the Brussels Treaty the then WU became redundant. With the entering into force of the Washington Treaty and the establishment of the Northern Atlantic institutional and military structure including all WU Member States, NATO took charge of Western European defence issues. The WEU does not represent any added value. By the time the WEU was founded, "the idea of European co-operation and self-reliance [in defence] remained dormant."[163] Consequently it is argued, that the WEU was redundant and unnecessary. The crucial elements of the Modified Brussels Treaty could all have been regulated in the NATO framework: the rearmament of Germany, arms control, defence industrial policy, and the military commitment of the United Kingdom in mainland Europe. The solution of the Saar problem and Franco-German rapprochement could have been conducted within the framework of the ECSC. Furthermore, an alternative framework could have been found for Community-United Kingdom relations, a function the WEU lost after 1973 anyway.[164] Similarly the later WEU joint actions in the Gulf 1988-90,[165] the WEU operations in the context of the Yugoslav conflict 1992-96,[166] and the crisis management operations 1998-2001[167] could have been conducted in the framework of NATO. Moreover, they could often not be conducted without additional support from NATO anyway. WEU in addition to NATO seems a waste of resources. However, the foundation of the WEU is part of the European integration process and the direct reaction to the failure of the EDC. At the time it was the only positive alternative available, especially with regards to the inclusion of the United Kingdom. The only other alternative would have been to refrain from starting a European

[161] Macalister-Smith, above n 29, at 369.
[162] Macalister-Smith, above, at 369.
[163] Marauhn, above n 17, at 9.
[164] Even the WEU itself concedes that from 1973 to 1984 'WEU's activities as an intergovernmental organisation gradually slowed down.' Economic, cultural, and social areas of activity were covered by the OEEC/OECD and the Council of Europe and the political issues lost relevance with the development of European Political Co-operation of the European Communities. See under 'WEU History' at http://www.weu.int/.
[165] Co-ordinating mine-clearance operations in Gulf waters: 'Operation Cleansweep'. WEU also contributed to the humanitarian actions for Kurdish refugees in Northern Iraq.
[166] WEU/NATO Operation Sharp Guard in the Adriatic, the WEU Danube operation, and the police contingent in Mostar.
[167] (Police) mission in Albania, WEU de-mining assistance mission in Croatia, general security surveillance mission in Kosovo.

defence and security organisation all together. Moreover, some of the creators of the WEU hoped to develop it into more than it eventually became. Nevertheless, as argued above the foundation of the WEU separated defence integration from the mainstream of the European integration process. Broadly speaking, the earlier is more intergovernmental whereas the latter is more supranational. This separation is further emphasised by the different membership of the WEU and the Communities.[168]

5.2. The More Supranational European Economic Community

The European Economic Community Treaty (hereinafter EEC) as the main instrument of economic integration entered into force on 1 January 1958, more than three years after the failure of the EDC. However, the six Member States of the ECSC, which would also form the EEC and Euratom, reached agreement on the basic principles of economic integration as early as 1955 at a conference in Messina. The basic plan for the new Communities was published in 1956 and the EEC and Euratom Treaties were signed in Rome in 1957. The Treaties established two more supranational organisations with their own Commissions and Councils. The Assembly and Court were shared with the ECSC. In contrast to the latter and the EDC, however, the EEC and Euratom had a stronger Council and fewer powers for the Commission. Hence it can be said that the new organisations were more supranational but had stronger intergovernmental elements than the previous integration projects.

The more important EEC Treaty aimed at establishing a common market between the Member States. It establishes regimes for the free movement of all factors of production, regimes for competition law and state aids, a common agricultural policy and other policies. Immediately after the failure of the EDC, the fathers and mothers of the Treaty were aware of the fact that defence had to be excluded from the application of the EEC. The new Treaty was designed as an instrument of economic integration. Defence, however, has commercial implications. Trade in arms, defence procurement, competition in the defence industrial sector or state aids to the defence industries are examples. The EDC Treaty had addressed a number of these issues, mostly by expressly including them in its field of application. The authors of the EEC Treaty went the opposite way and addressed the problem by inserting a number of defence and security exemptions to balance the common market interests of the new Community with the national security

[168] In 1954 the United Kingdom was the only WEU Member State not also in the ECSC Spain and Portugal joined the European Communities in 1985–86 and the WEU in 1990. Greece joined the former in 1979–80 and the latter in 1995. Norway, Turkey, and Iceland have been Associate Members since 1992, Poland, Hungary and the Czech Republic since 1999. Denmark and Ireland joined the Communities in 1973–74 and are Observers with the WEU. Austria, Finland and Sweden joined the European Union in 1994–95 and also became Observers with the WEU. Bulgaria, Romania, Latvia, Estonia, Lithuania, and the Slovak Republic became Associate Partners in 1994, Slovenia in 1996. Romania and Bulgaria will join the European Union in 2007 or 2008, the other Associate Partners joined in 2004.

interests of the Member States. These exemptions have remained the same until this day. Their interpretation and their application determined the limits of the EEC and later the EC Treaty as an instrument of defence integration regarding the economic aspects of defence. Therefore they are crucial to understand the current law of European defence integration and are covered in chapters 4 to 6 of this book. Most detailed laws of European economic integration are not regulated in the EEC Treaty itself but in secondary or subsidiary instruments created by the institutions of the EEC and authorised by legal bases in the Treaty. In those areas of regulation which concern defence and security, the specific exemptions in the relevant secondary instruments reflect the defence and security exemptions in the Treaty. A selection of these provisions is covered in chapters 7, 8, and 9 of this book.

The decade that followed the EEC Treaty did neither see any major treaty projects towards European integration nor an enlargement of the three Communities. A treaty-based innovation worth mentioning was the Merger Treaty of 1965, which merged the separate ECSC and EEC institutions into one set of Community institutions.[169] The other important treaty-based innovation came through the First Budgetary Treaty and the Own-Resources Decision of 1970, which strengthened the supranationality of the Communities by giving them a certain degree of financial independence from the Member States.[170] Customs duties from third country imports, a maximum of 1 per cent Value Added Tax (VAT) as applied to an assessment basis determined uniformly for the Member States, and agricultural levies, added independent resources to the Community budget in addition to the Member State contributions.

Nevertheless this was a period of consolidation rather than stagnation. The European Court of Justice as the judiciary of the Communities rather than the Member States was the main actor in this consolidation process of the 1960s.[171] In a number of seminal judgments the Luxembourg Court defined the new legal order established by the Treaties, including the *sui generis* character of Community law as "a new legal order of international law",[172] its primacy over the national law of the Member States,[173] and its direct effect.[174] These judgments defined and enhanced the supranational character of the European Communities. Sovereignty had been transferred to the Communities; primacy and direct effect were just a consequence of this transfer. The six founding Member States ultimately accepted this case law and the Member States acceding from the 1970s were fully aware of these principles.

[169] [1965] OJ 1E/120. The Parliamentary Assembly and the Court of Justice were already shared (decided in the Convention on Certain Institutions Common to the European Communities, signed on the same day as the EEC and Euratom Treaties in 1957). The Merger Treaty merged the Commissions and Councils to one Commission and one Council for all three Communities. The Merger Treaty was later repealed and replaced, without any substantive amendments, by Article 9 of the Treaty of Amsterdam 1997.

[170] Craig and de Búrca, *EU Law*, above n 54, at 18.

[171] Craig and de Búrca, above, at 17.

[172] Case C–26/62, *van Gend en Loos*, above n 56.

[173] Case C–6/64, *Costa v ENEL* [1964] ECR 585, [1964] CMLR 425.

[174] Case C–26/62, *van Gend en Loos*, above n 56.

On the other hand the Luxembourg Accords[175] essentially abolished qualified majority voting in the Council in favour of unanimity. Through the unanimity requirement beyond the transitional period, the Council, intended as a supranational institution voting by qualified majority, in practice operated as an intergovernmental institution. This diminished the supranational character of the Communities[176] as the Council was the main legislative institution at the time. Moreover, the importance of the supranational institutions, the European Parliament and Commission, was reduced.

6. CONCLUSIONS

Many of the political, economic, and strategic factors that influenced the European integration process after World War II still prevail today. Many still see European integration as a welcome cage for the German tiger. However, today only few would see a problem serving in the same military unit with Germans and the German armed forces are not seen as a threat any more. The United Kingdom is still opposed to defence integration on a more supranational basis and France is still concerned about its sovereignty. This led to a central feature of the evolution of European defence integration that dominated the early years and still prevails today: the question whether European defence should be organised on a more supranational or a more intergovernmental basis. The supranational model, first introduced by the ECSC and later developed in the EEC and Euratom, disappeared from the European defence integration agenda with the failure of the EDC. The intergovernmental model, introduced to the process with the Dunkirk and Brussels Treaties, prevailed with the Modified Brussels Treaty. However, the supranational model failed to deliver European defence integration. Europe continued to have largely national armed forces using largely different equipment within largely independent organisational structures. The only cohesion was achieved through the leadership of the USA in NATO and the fear of Soviet aggression.

The EDC remains the only precedent for a more supranational European defence organisation to date. Civil servants, military officers, and politicians

[175] [1966] OJ 1E/71; [1966] OJ 2E/79. Unanimity was required in the Council(s) during the transitional period. After that period had expired in 1965, decisions were to be taken by qualified majority. A proposal made by the Commission suggested the Community raise its own resources from agricultural levies and external tariffs rather than from the national contributions of the Member States. Independent resources are a characteristic of a supranational or federal unit. The French government under President de Gaulle objected to this approach and for seven months adopted an 'empty chair' policy in the Council. The Luxembourg Compromise or Luxembourg Accords: the French opinion was that in cases where the Treaty provided for qualified majority voting negotiations had to continue until consensus was reached, while the view of the other five Member States was that in such circumstances the Council would 'endeavour within a reasonable time, to reach solutions which can be adopted by all'. In practice the French view and the unanimity requirement for voting in the Council prevailed.

[176] Craig and de Búrca, *EU Law*, above n 54, at 15 citing P Dankert, 'The EC–Past, Present, Future' in L Tsoukalis, *The EC—Past, Present, Future* (Basil Blackwell, London, 1983) at 7.

prepared it over many years. The representatives of six different countries reached agreement over the precise contents, which included issues such as institutional structure, military organisation, procurement, and finance. Therefore the provisions of the EDC are a benchmark for the current state of European defence integration and a source of inspiration for future defence integration projects.

2

A Pillar of Our Security: European Foreign and Security Law 1959–1998

1. INTRODUCTION

THE FOLLOWING CHAPTER builds on the previous one. Chapter 1 described the early legal history of European defence integration from World War II to the late 1950s. Chapter 2 continues the discussion of that evolutionary process. The actual subject matter of this chapter, the Common Foreign and Security Policy (hereinafter CFSP) was only introduced in 1992 by the Treaty on European Union (hereinafter TEU). Nevertheless, chapter 2 will also cover the period between 1959 and 1992. On the one hand this period was characterised by stagnation regarding defence integration. Matters remained settled in the mid-1950s, organised through the Western European Union (hereinafter WEU) and the European Communities. Defence was separated from the mainstream of European integration. On the other hand, this period saw the slow emergence of a framework that would eventually lead to the CFSP: European Political Co-operation. Then the CFSP put defence back on the European agenda, at least partly bridging the gap between defence integration and the mainstream of European integration conducted within the Communities.

This chapter has two functions. First, it continues the legal history of European defence integration into the late 1990s. It thereby almost completes the story told in chapter 1. The legal history of European defence integration provided in chapters 1 and 2 facilitates the understanding of the current state of affairs, which will be discussed in chapter 3. The latter will complete the legal history of European defence integration by covering the period between 1998 and 2004. Second, the CFSP under the Maastricht and Amsterdam Treaties represents the foundation of the current European Security and Defence Policy (hereinafter ESDP) analysed in chapter 3. The latter is structured according to the same principles and an integral part of the earlier. Therefore the CFSP forms 'a separate chapter' of the current state of European defence integration, which needs to be analysed separately from the 'early' legal history of this evolutionary process. Third, the CFSP is the most important more intergovernmental model of integration within the framework of the TEU. The contribution of the more supranational Community Pillar to

European defence integration described in Part II of this book is the antithesis to the more intergovernmental CFSP. An analysis of the CFSP facilitates the understanding of the Community contribution. The final part III of the book will discuss the future of European defence integration based to a large extent on the Constitutional Treaty signed on the 29 October 2004 in Rome, which proposes to reunite the pillars in one document. As this involves a comparison of supranational and intergovernmental forms of integration, the previous analysis of the CFSP will serve as a point of reference.

2. THE EMERGING EUROPEAN POLITICAL CO-OPERATION

The separation of defence from the mainstream of European integration continued for decades from the 1950s until the 1990s. While economic integration moved forward through EEC Treaty revisions, subsidiary Community law, and the jurisprudence of the European Court of Justice, the Western European defence focus was on NATO, with a largely dormant WEU.[1] Hence European defence integration as part of a general European integration movement was sent to sleep in the WEU, until the European leaders would decide to wake it and continue the process.

Defence integration would eventually get back on the European agenda with the CFSP of the 1992 TEU. The CFSP was the result of an attempt to co-ordinate the foreign policies of the Member States of the European Communities. This attempt, European Political Co-operation (hereinafter EPC), emerged over more than three decades. It gradually developed from regular meetings of the foreign ministers of the Member States, over regular and prepared consultations with their own institutional structure, to a treaty-based co-ordination of foreign policy. It should be emphasised that foreign policy and not defence was the subject of this emerging policy. However, it was through the process of intensifying EPC eventually leading to the CFSP, that the dormant process of European defence integration could finally re-continue. For the purpose of this chapter foreign policy is understood as a narrow concept, excluding important aspects of European foreign relations to which Community law applies, such as enlargement and the common commercial policy under what is now Title IX of the EC Treaty. The development of the EPC can be divided into three main phases.

The first informal phase of the EPC started slowly in Strasbourg on 23 November 1959 with an agreement by the foreign ministers of the six Member States of the Communities to meet every three months.[2] In contrast to the second phase the EPC of the 1960s was not formalised in reports and communiqués.

[1] Seeing Europe as a whole the focus depended on the country. For the NATO member States it was NATO, for the Warsaw Pact States it was that alliance. For neutral countries such as Switzerland, the Socialist Federal Republic of Yugoslavia, or Sweden, defence had a purely national focus.

[2] JA Frowein, entry on 'European Political Cooperation', in R Bernardt, *Encyclopedia of Public International Law* (North Holland, Amsterdam, 1983) vol 6, at 199. See also: O von der Gablentz, 'Luxembourg Revisited or the Importance of European Political Cooperation' (1979) 16 *Common Market Law Review* 685–99; D Hurd, 'Political Cooperation' (1981) 57 *International Affairs* 383–93.

However, the practices developed during the first phase would eventually become formalised in the second phase. In contrast to the third phase there was no treaty base. The agreement of Strasbourg set the framework for the first phase, which lasted over ten years. During this incremental period of the EPC, which at the time did not even have that name, the Communities began to find their voice in international politics and were increasingly perceived as one entity rather than six separate States.[3]

The second formalised phase started with the Luxembourg Report of 20 July 1970,[4] which set out the so-called Davignon System and largely formalised the practices which had developed during the 1960s. The main reason for the formalisation of the foreign policy system or mechanism was a perceived need to balance the international presence of the Communities with their economic power. The modest objective[5] was to co-ordinate national views. Foreign ministers would meet for consultations every six months. A Political Committee (hereinafter PC) of the directors general for political affairs of the foreign ministries of the Member States would prepare these meetings. According to Article V of the Luxembourg Report, the Commission of the European Communities would be asked to comment on the results of these consultations "should the work of the Ministers affect the activities of the European Communities". The PC and the Council of the European Communities as foreign ministers would discuss foreign policy with the Political Committee of the European Parliament[6] twice a year in order to meet the need for democratic legitimacy. The limited role of the more supranational institutions of the Communities reflected the distinction between EPC and the Communities:[7] foreign policy, later combined with security in the CFSP, was as yet separated and outside the mainstream of European integration conducted within the framework of the Communities. However, the modest involvement of two institutions of the Communities in the EPC was also the start of a slow rapprochement of the two streams that should continue during the following decades.

The Copenhagen Report of 23 July 1973[8] prescribed four meetings a year, delegated a number of tasks from the foreign ministers to the PC, and prescribed correspondents in the foreign ministries to keep in touch and working groups for specific tasks. Article 10 of the Report clarified that EPC:

> "[...] is *distinct from and additional to* the activities of the institutions of the Community which are based on the judicial commitments undertaken by the Member States under the Treaty of Rome. Both sets of machinery have the aim of contributing to the development of European unification [emphasis added]."

[3] P Craig and G de Búrca, *EU Law*, 3rd edn, (OUP, Oxford, 2003) at 14 mention the 1967 GATT negotiations and the signing of the Yaoundé Convention between the EEC and 18 African States in 1963 as examples.

[4] *Bulletin des Communautés européennes* (1970) No 11, at 9–14.

[5] P Koutrakos, *Trade, Foreign Policy and Defence in EU Constitutional Law: The Legal Regulation of Sanctions, Exports of Dual Use Goods and Armaments* (Hart Publishing, Oxford, 2001) 9.

[6] Article VI and Part III (4).

[7] Koutrakos, above n 5, at 10.

[8] *Bulletin des Communautés européennes* (1973) No 9, at 14–21.

This confirms the separation of the EPC from the Communities and preserves its intergovernmental character. On the other hand Article 12 (b) of the Report recognised that the EPC:

> " [...] keep[s] in mind [...] the implications for and the effects of, in the field of international politics, Community policies under construction."

The provision accepts that the two "sets of machinery" cannot operate in isolation[9] and that they necessarily have implications for each other. This touched upon a paradox: the Member States wanted to keep the two frameworks separate, which nevertheless had implications for each other. The paradox entailed an inherent danger of one system contradicting and thereby undermining the other, which would have to be addressed more clearly in an intensifying EPC and especially once it was enshrined in a legally binding Treaty.

The London Report of 13 October 1981[10] included a commitment of the then ten Member States to consult the other partners before adopting final positions or launching national initiatives on all important questions of foreign policy which are of concern to the Member States as a whole. The relationship between EPC and the Communities was addressed in a new way in the preamble by suggesting the use of Community instruments to promote EPC,[11] by upgrading the role of the Commission,[12] and by allocating responsibility for the co-ordination of the two frameworks to the Presidency.[13] The political and economic aspects of defence could be discussed subject to "a flexible and pragmatic approach",[14] thereby including them in EPC for the first time.[15]

The EPC of this phase was based on informal communiqués and reports and established only a loose system of practical co-ordination,[16] which was not legally binding. Moreover, the consultations were not always successful, for example the nuclear powers France and later the United Kingdom refused to discuss matters that concerned their *veto* power in the UN Security Council. Nevertheless, EPC often served its purpose.[17] Generally the Member States of the Communities were increasingly seen as one unit pursuing a single policy with regards to conferences

[9] Koutrakos, above n 5, at 10.
[10] *Bulletin of the European Communities* (1981) Supp 3, at 14–17.
[11] Above, at 14: '[...] the maintenance and development of Community policies in accordance with the Treaties will be beneficial to a more effective co-ordination in the field of foreign policy and will expand the range of instruments at the disposal of the Ten [Member States]'.
[12] Article 11: 'within the framework of the established rules and procedures the Ten attach importance to the Commission [...] being fully associated with Political Co-operation at all levels'.
[13] Article 11: '[t]he Presidency will ensure that the discussion of the Community and the political Co-operation aspects of certain questions is co-ordinated if the subject matter requires this'.
[14] Article 11.
[15] Koutrakos, above n 5, at 12.
[16] Frowein, above n 2, at 201.
[17] It had a prominent role in the preparation of the Helsinki Conference and Final Act on Security and Co-operation in Europe and activities within the UN were prepared in the EPC framework.

and third countries. In the political circumstances of the time EPC was the only "workable form of unification in the field of foreign policy".[18]

The third phase gave a treaty base to the practices developed during the first and second phases of EPC. The Genscher-Colombo proposals[19] led to the Solemn Declaration on European Union agreed at the Stuttgart Summit on 19 June 1983.[20] The supplemented contents of the Solemn Declaration and the Reports of the second phase got a treaty form in Title III of the Single European Act (hereinafter SEA).[21] From now on EPC had a legal basis and was legally binding.[22] According to Article 30 (5) SEA Member States had an obligation to consult each other on any "foreign policy matter of general interest". Moreover, security featured in the SEA. First, rhetorical mention[23] of the role of closer co-operation on European security issues was made in Article 30 (6) (a) SEA, which stated that the High Contracting Parties were "ready to co-ordinate their positions more closely on the political and economic sides of security". Second, the economic and political aspects of defence could be discussed in the EPC context and "opened the door for EC involvement in defence industrial affairs".[24] However, this did not question the general separation of defence integration from both the Community and EPC frameworks. Article 30 (6) SEA clarified that the envisaged closer co-ordination on the political and economic aspects of defence was not to impede security co-operation within the NATO and WEU frameworks. The aim of the SEA-based EPC was not to establish a common foreign policy. According to Article 30 (1) SEA, the aim was rather "jointly to formulate and implement a European foreign policy". EPC was placed outside the Community framework. Hence it did not share the supranational features of the Communities, but remained an intergovernmental system. EPC under the SEA was a treaty-based

[18] Frowein, above n 2, at 201.

[19] *Bulletin of the European Parliament* (1981) No 50, at 31–32.

[20] *Bulletin of the European Communities* (1983) No 6, at 18–29.

[21] [1986] OJ 2E/147. Generally the SEA had a clear market focus and 'represented the most important revision of the Treaties since they were first adopted', see Craig and de Búrca, above n 3, at 19. The central reforms were the inclusion of new legal bases for market legislation based on qualified majority voting in the Council and co-decision with the European Parliament and a new approach to the harmonisation of laws. The Communities committed themselves to achieving the internal market by 1992. With the SEA European integration in general regained momentum and has been progressing at a much greater pace since then.

[22] In *Crotty v An Taoiseach and Others* [1987] 2 CMLR 667, at para 37 the Irish Supreme Court ruled that under international law Article 30 SEA was binding on the Member States to engage actively in the procedures laid down therein. The Irish government had refused to ratify Title III of the SEA. Koutrakos, above n 5, at 14 citing D Freestone and S Davidson, 'Community Competence and Part III of the Single European Act' (1986) 23 *Common Market Law Review* 793, submits that Title III SEA is legally binding. The vague and ambiguous terms of an obligation 'may undermine its effective application but not its legal significance'.

[23] Koutrakos, above n 5, at 13, n 39. See also RA Wessel, 'The EU as Black Widow: Devouring the WEU to Give Birth to a European Security and Defence Policy' in V Kronenberger, (ed), *The European Union and the International Legal Order—Discord or Harmony?* (TMC Asser Press, The Hague, 2001) 405, at 414 (hereinafter 'Black Widow').

[24] T Marauhn, *Building a European Security and Defence Identity, Bochumer Schriften zur Friedenssicherung und zum Humaniären Völkerrecht 30* (Universitätsverlag Dr N Brockmeyer, Bochum, 1996) at 13.

but more intergovernmental mechanism based mainly on consultation, in which the commitment of the Member States remained phrased in vague and ambiguous terms.[25] Koutrakos has provided a comprehensive analysis of the passages in the SEA that prove the continued separation of the more supranational Communities from the intergovernmental EPC.[26]

Nevertheless, the external policies of the Community and EPC have to be consistent. According to Article 30 (5) SEA, consistency was entrusted to the Presidency of the Council in relation to EPC and to the Commission in relation to the Communities. Hence the consistency requirement governing the interdependence of the two frameworks, a principle developed during the second phase of EPC, also got a treaty base. It is submitted that the consistency requirement is a main reason for the limited inclusion of defence and security in the SEA. Only the interdependence of security issues with issues regulated within the Community framework, in particular the economic aspects of defence, made the Member States address the issue in the SEA at all. The consistency of the two frameworks necessitated addressing security in the context of the EPC.[27] The political and strategic situation at the time of the SEA has to be taken into account to understand the limitations of the SEA with regards to defence. The nuclear arms race between the West and the Soviet Union had entered its final phase and the first United States INF missiles were delivered to Germany and the United Kingdom in late 1983. This had caused strains in transatlantic relations creating uncertainty about the impact of European defence integration on NATO in a security environment dominated by the Soviet threat.[28]

The EPC had a dynamic and incremental character.[29] Third countries and international organisations perceived the Member States as a collective actor in international politics, within and beyond the limits of the Communities. This perception was not without its foundation, as the same Member States developed the EPC and even integrated it into the main treaty reforming the Communities: the SEA. The foreign policy system emerged from the informal co-ordination of the 1960s to the formalised framework of the 1970s to the treaty based EPC of the SEA, always consolidating and further developing the arrangements already in practice. This led to a new type of foreign policy framework, which was neither

[25] Koutrakos, above n 5, at 12–13.

[26] The preamble to the SEA says that European Union is to be implemented: 'on the basis firstly, of the European Communities operating in accordance with their own rules and, secondly, of European Political Co-operation among the Signatory States in the sphere of foreign policy'. Article 1 SEA: '[t]he European Communities and European Political Co-operation shall have as their objective to contribute together to make concrete progress towards European unity'. And distinguishes the former, which 'shall be founded on the Treaties [...] and on the subsequent Treaties and Acts modifying or supplementing them' from the latter which 'shall be governed by Title III [of the SEA]'. Title III made reference to the 'High Contracting Parties' as opposed to the 'Member States' in the Community context. Article 30 SEA is excluded from the jurisdiction of the Court according to Article 31 SEA.

[27] See chs 4–6 on how security is addressed in the EC Treaty.

[28] Marauhn, above n 24, at 14 citing MJ Hillenbrand, 'American Perceptions of NATO and the European Community' in C Coker, (ed), *Shifting into Neutral? Burden Sharing in the Western Alliance in the 1990s* (London: Brassey's, 1990) 103, at 110–14.

[29] Koutrakos, above n 5, at 14–15.

based on the national nor the international models of conducting foreign policy. The distinct character of the EPC included a paradox. On the one hand the EPC was based on procedures instead of policy and on declarations instead of means of action, lacking clear objectives. Therefore there was no erosion or even transfer of sovereignty over foreign policy matters; EPC did not hurt the Member States. On the other hand EPC was fashioned against the traditional models of sovereign foreign policy, it pretended to be a distinct and single foreign policy of the Member States of the Communities. Third countries expected from EPC a common foreign policy of the Member States. In other words the EPC was intended and perceived as a foreign policy comparable to that of a sovereign State without being given the means to implement it. This 'expectations-capabilities gap' showed itself in the failure of EPC in the conflicts resulting from the dissolution of Yugoslavia,[30] which will be discussed in more detail below.

Nevertheless, the first reference to defence in the SEA represents a first sign for a change in the basic pattern of integration. The intergovernmental EPC had the potential to develop into a bridge between the supranational European Communities as the mainstream of integration and the separated European defence integration process, until then lying dormant in the intergovernmental WEU. It also revealed a need to co-ordinate EPC and the Community to ensure the consistency or coherence of the two frameworks. The next steps towards integration would bring the separate streams even closer together again.

3. THE COMMON FOREIGN AND SECURITY POLICY OF THE TREATY ON EUROPEAN UNION

The momentum created by the SEA soon moved the Member States of the European Communities to a next step towards integration. The 1989 Jacques Delors Report on European Economic and Monetary Union suggested an intergovernmental conference on the subject matter of the report simultaneously with a second intergovernmental conference on political union. In 1991 the Luxembourg Presidency presented a Draft Treaty on European Union and in 1992 the Member States signed a substantially revised version in Maastricht.

According to the popular 'Greek temple' notion, the Treaty on European Union (hereinafter TEU) of Maastricht established a three-pillar structure of what from now on would be known as the European Union (hereinafter EU). The more supranational European Communities formed the First Pillar whereas the more intergovernmental CFSP formed the Second Pillar.[31] The latter represented the continuation and development of the EPC under the SEA and was introduced to balance economic integration under the First Pillar with political integration.[32]

[30] F Fink-Hooijer, 'The Common Foreign and Security Policy of the European Union' (1994) 3 *European Journal of International Law* 173, 194.

[31] The intergovernmental Co-operation on Justice and Home Affairs, in Amsterdam renamed 'Police and Judicial Cooperation in Criminal Matters' in Title VI TEU formed the Third Pillar.

[32] Craig and de Búrca, above n 3, at 22.

The 'roof' of the 'Greek temple'[33] was the EU, which formed an autonomous new international legal entity. A comprehensive discussion of the dispute regarding the legal personality of the EU[34] would go beyond the limits of this chapter. Suffice it to point out that the Union has at least one separate and autonomous institution, there is a clear distinction between the EU and its Member States, the EU is endowed with competencies to pass decisions on Second and Third Pillar issues, and has its own Treaty-making capacity. These characteristics will be further explained below.

The CFSP built on and covers the EPC *acquis.*[35] However, as the specific mentioning of security in the name of this second pillar indicates, the CFSP now also expressly included security and defence related matters. The TEU gave momentum to the dormant European defence integration process by putting it firmly back on the agenda.

European integration kept the pace introduced by the SEA and was continued with another intergovernmental conference as early as 1996. The latter resulted in the 1997 Treaty of Amsterdam, which entered into force in 1999. This treaty introduced changes to the CFSP. Therefore the following section describes Title V of the TEU containing the CFSP with reference to both the Maastricht and Amsterdam

[33] The alternative notion of a 'layered international organisation' describes the EU as a legal entity sheltering other legal entities, in particular the European Communities, see C Trüe, *Verleihung von Rechtspersönlichkeit an die Europäischen Union und Verschmelzung zu einer einzigen Organisation—deklaratorisch oder konstitutiv?* (Vorträge, Reden und Berichte aus dem Europa-Institut, No 357, Universität des Saarlandes, 1997); DM Curtin and IF Dekker, 'The European Union as a "Layered" International Organisation: Institutional Unity in Disguise' in P Craig and G de Búrca, (eds), *The Evolution of EU Law* (OUP: Oxford, 1999) 83–136; A Dashwood, 'The Council of the European Union in the Era of the Amsterdam Treaty' in T Heukels, N Blokker and M Brus, (eds), *The European Union after Amsterdam: a Legal Analysis* (Kluwer, The Hague, 1997) 117, at 126, also refers to the 'sub-orders' rather than the 'Pillars' of the EU. Other notions include the 'trinity structure': JHH Weiler, *The Constitution of Europe* (CUP, Cambridge, 1999) 137; the 'gothic cathedral': B de Witte, 'The Pillar Structure and the Nature of the European Union: Greek Temple or French Gothic Cathedral?' in T Heukels, N Blokker and M Brus, (eds), above, 51–68; and the 'Russian doll': Curtin and Dekker, above.

[34] RA Wessel, 'Revisiting the International Legal Status of the European Union' (2003) 5 *European Foreign Affairs Review* 507–37 (hereinafter 'Revisited'); RA Wessel, 'The international Legal Status of the European Union' (1997) 2 *European Foreign Affairs Review* 109–29; O Dörr, 'Zur Rechtsnatur der Europäischen Union' (1995) 30 *Europarecht* 334–48; Trüe, above; Curtin and Dekker, above; J Klabbers, 'Presumptive Personality: The European Union in International Law' in M Koskenniemi, (ed), *International Law Aspects of the European Union* (Kluwer, The Hague, 1998) 231–53; for a legal order which implies a fusion of the three pillars: A von Bogdandy and M Nettesheim, 'Ex pluribus unum: The Fusion of the European Communities into the European Union' (1996) 1 *European Law Journal* 267. Against a distinct legal personality of the EU: the German *Bundesverfassungsgericht* BverfGE 89, 195; German Federal Constitutional Court judgment of the Maastricht Treaty of 12 October 1993, (1994) 33 ILM 388; U Everling, 'Reflections on the Structure of the European Union' (1992) 28 *Common Market Law Review* 1053–77; MR Eaton, 'Common Foreign and Security Policy' in D O'Keefe and P Twomey, (eds), *Legal Issues of the Maastricht Treaty* (Wiley Chancery Law, London, 1994) 215–26, at 224; N Neuwahl, 'A Partner with a Troubled Personality: EU Treaty-Making in Matters of CFSP' (1998) 3 *European Foreign Affairs Review* 177–96; P Willaert and C Marqués-Ruiz, 'Vers une politique étrangère et de sécurité commun: état des lieux' (1995) *Revue du Marché Unique Européen* 35, at 38.

[35] Fink-Hooijer, above n 30, at 173; MR Eaton, 'Common Foreign and Security Policy' in O'Keefe and Twomey, above n 34, 251.

versions. In the Maastricht version the CFSP is regulated in Articles J.1–J.18 TEU and in the Amsterdam version in Articles 11-28 TEU. Differences between the two 'Dutch Treaties' shall be highlighted when appropriate. The CFSP provisions in Title V TEU have to be read together with a number of declarations adopted by the 1992 Intergovernmental Conference annexed to the Final Act of the Conference.[36] Moreover, they need to be read together with the common provisions of the TEU, in particular Articles 2 (ex Article B),[37] 3 (ex Article C),[38] and 4 (ex Article D)[39] TEU. Finally, there is substantial interaction between the Second and the Third Pillars of the TEU, in particular through Articles 20 (ex Article 8c),[40] 60 (ex Article 73g), 300 (ex Article 228),[41] and 301 (ex Article 228a)[42] EC Treaty. The latter allows the Community to interrupt or reduce trade with a third State.[43] The TEU in the version adopted during the next Intergovernmental Conference 2000 in Nice is part of both the current state of European defence integration and its history and shall be discussed in a separate chapter of this book.

Political integration in general and defence integration in particular became possible due to profound changes of the political landscape of Europe. In 1989

[36] Relevant to the CFSP are: Declaration No 27 on voting in the field of CFSP, Declaration No 28 on practical arrangements in the field of CFSP, Declaration No 29 on the use of languages, Declaration No 30 on Western European Union (WEU), European Council Decision concerning certain problems raised by Denmark on the Treaty on European Union.

[37] Listing the objectives of the Union, see below.

[38] Article 3 TEU read:

The Union shall be served by a single institutional framework which shall ensure the consistency and the continuity of the activities carried out in order to attain its objectives while respecting and building upon the acquis communautaire. The Union shall in particular ensure the consistency of its external activities as a whole in the context of its external relations, security, economic and development policies. The Council and the Commission shall be responsible for ensuring such consistency and shall cooperate to this end. They shall ensure the implementation of these policies, each in accordance with its respective powers.

[39] Article 4 TEU reads

The European Council shall provide the Union with the necessary impetus for its development and shall define the general political guidelines thereof. The European Council shall bring together the Heads of State or Government of the Member States and the President of the Commission. They shall be assisted by the Ministers for Foreign Affairs of the Member States and by a Member of the Commission. The European Council shall meet at least twice a year, under the chairmanship of the Head of State or Government of the Member State which holds the Presidency of the Council. The European Council shall submit to the European Parliament a report after each of its meetings and a yearly written report on the progress achieved by the Union.

[40] Article 20 EC reads:

Every citizen of the Union shall, in the territory of a third country in which the Member State of which he is a national is not represented, be entitled to protection by the diplomatic or consular authorities of any Member State, on the same conditions as the nationals of that State. Member States shall establish the necessary rules among themselves and start the international negotiations required to secure this protection.

[41] Article 300 EC provides for agreements with third states.

[42] Article 301 EC reads:

Where it is provided, in a common position or in a joint action adopted according to the provisions of the Treaty on European Union relating to the common foreign and security policy, for an action by the Community to interrupt or to reduce, in part or completely, economic relations with one or more third countries, the Council shall take the necessary urgent measures. The Council shall act by a qualified majority on a proposal from the Commission.

[43] Fink-Hooijer, above n 30, at 175–76.

and 1990 democratic governments took over in Hungary, Poland, Czechoslovakia, East Germany, Romania, and Bulgaria. The Federal Socialist Republic (SFR) of Yugoslavia and the Soviet Union started disintegrating in 1991. In 1990 East Germany was the first 'Central and Eastern European Country' to join the European Communities through unification with the founding Member State Federal Republic of Germany. The political and military threat posed by the Soviet Union and her satellites in the Warsaw Pact was considerably diminished. The demise of the Soviet threat constituted an increase in European 'independence' from both the Eastern Bloc and the USA. On the other hand the demise of the Soviet Union, the resulting security vacuum, and the changed social, political, and military realities of the early 1990s also caused and increased the risk of international and European instability, in particular through a revival of nationalist trends.[44] These nationalist trends manifested themselves in the break-up of the SFR Yugoslavia, and the Member States failed to respond as one voice within the EPC framework. Moreover, the Community concerns of economic integration and stability cannot be seen in isolation from political and security considerations. Political instability has an effect on economic stability thereby affecting Community interests. Conflicts disrupt trade, destroy markets, generate immigration through refugees, can cause environmental damage affecting Member States, and impede enlargement. Therefore, the CFSP also became a necessity as a means to safeguard the *acquis communautaire*. The events that ultimately triggered the establishment of the EU, however, were connected to the failure of the Communities to present a united front on the Gulf crisis in the framework of the EPC under the SEA.[45]

3.1. The Objectives of the European Union

In Article 2 (ex Article B) hyphen 2 TEU the EU sets itself one of five objectives:

> "to assert its identity on the international scene, in particular through the implementation of a common foreign and security policy, including the progressive framing of a common defence policy, which might lead to a common defence, in accordance with the provisions of Article 17."

The provision almost repeats paragraph 10 of the Preamble,[46] with the exceptions of the "independence" of the EU and the promotion of "peace, security, and progress in Europe and in the world", as additional objectives of the Treaty. The assertion of

[44] Fink-Hooijer, above, at 174.
[45] Marauhn, above n 24, at 84.
[46] See also the Preamble to the TEU: 'Resolved to implement a common foreign and security policy including the progressive framing of a common defence policy, which might lead to a common defence in accordance with the provisions of Article 17, thereby reinforcing the European identity and its independence in order to promote peace, security and progress in Europe and in the world.'

its identity on the international scene implies a presence that is more visible than EPC with regards to both the foreign and the security components of the CFSP. These components are already indicated by the name 'Common Foreign and Security Policy'. However, the objective goes beyond these CFSP components to be established by the Maastricht and Amsterdam Treaties right away by adding the notions of 'common defence policy' and 'common defence'. With regards to the common defence policy, the wording "progressive framing" indicates that the common defence policy is intended as an evolutionary process starting with the Maastricht Treaty. With regards to a common defence, the wording "which might lead to" indicates that a common defence is set in the future, is uncertain, and will not begin with the Maastricht Treaty. Nevertheless it is of great significance that for the first time since the EDC the possibility of a common defence is expressly mentioned in a European treaty.

To summarise, Article 2 TEU seems to differentiate four inter-connected component notions of the CFSP: (1) foreign policy, (2) security policy, (3) defence policy, and (4) common defence. The precise scope of these component notions requires a closer look at Title V of the TEU.

3.2. The Scope of the Common Foreign and Security Policy

The scope of the CFSP is defined by its objectives. According to Article 11 (1) TEU (ex Article J.1) "[t]he Union shall define and implement a common foreign and security policy covering *all* areas of foreign and security policy [emphasis added]". *Prima facie* this wording suggests a very broad if not unlimited competence.[47] On the other hand it does not provide a definition of the notion of foreign and security policy.[48] The following analysis will outline the general objectives of the CFSP with special emphasis on its defence and security dimension, before discussing the provision dealing specifically with a common defence policy.

3.2.1. The Objectives of the Common Foreign and Security Policy

The objectives of the CFSP were spelt out in broad terms[49] in Article 11 TEU (ex Article J.1). The wording of the 1992 Maastricht version of Article J.1 (1) TEU: "Member States shall inform and consult one another within the Council on any matter of foreign and security policy" still reflected the EPC approach where the focus was on information and consultation. In contrast, the 1997 Amsterdam version of Article 11 (1) TEU: "[t]he Union shall define and implement a common foreign and security policy covering all areas of foreign and security policy" indicates an increased detachment from the concepts of the 1970s and 1980s. The notion of "*all* areas of foreign [...] policy [emphasis added]", has to be read as

[47] Fink-Hooijer, above n 30, at 176. N Neuwahl, 'Foreign and Security Policy and the Implementation of the Requirement of "Consistency" under the Treaty on European Union' in O'Keefe and Twomey, above n 34, 227 at 228 calls this 'generously but vaguely described'.

[48] Neuwahl, above.

[49] Marauhn, above n 24, at 87 'fairly broad terms' and at 88 'open to a broad interpretation'; Koutrakos, above n 5, at 19 'very broad terms'.

excluding those areas of external relations within the competence of the Communities. The detachment from the EPC is emphasised by another detail. Articles 30 and 33 SEA referred to the "High Contracting Parties", a term used in international law, whereas Title V of the Maastricht Treaty referred to the "Member States", a term used in Community law.[50] Moreover, whereas Article J.1. (1) TEU (Maastricht) referred to "the Union and its Member States", Article 11 (1) TEU (Amsterdam) merely spoke of "[t]he Union". The earlier wording was introduced on the request of the United Kingdom who was concerned that the implementation of the CFSP would go beyond intergovernmental co-operation.[51] In order to counterbalance the notion "and its Member States" , Article J.1. (4) TEU was introduced, which requires Member States refrain from any action that would jeopardise the CFSP.[52] The fact that the notion was dropped in the Amsterdam Treaty shows at least that going beyond intergovernmental structures was not a concern any more.[53]

The first article of Title V TEU lists five broad objectives of the CFSP. First, it was "to safeguard the common values, fundamental interests, independence, and integrity of the Union in conformity with the United Nations Charter". Common values and fundamental interests are notions of foreign policy not directly related to defence. Independence of the Union includes *a maiore ad minus* the independence of an individual Member State in relation to third states.[54] The independence of the Union or a Member State can be compromised through a threat that leads to certain behaviour under duress, for example handing over resources, not conducted if the EU or the Member State would have had the liberty to act without such a threat. The Amsterdam Treaty added "integrity of the Union" to this objective. Koutrakos argues that this addition refers to the territorial integrity of the Union.[55] The territorial integrity of the Union includes *a maiore ad minus* the territorial integrity of an individual Member State. The territorial integrity of an alliance or state can be threatened by an armed attack or duress generated by a military threat leading to territorial loss. This means that the defence of the Union as a whole or of an individual Member State against an armed attack has been an objective of the EU since the Amsterdam Treaty. This enhances the security or defence component of the CFSP, outlined in detail below. It needs to be stressed that due to the absence of a military capacity the EU could not really take responsibility for integrity. However, this does not diminish the symbolic significance or

[50] CW Stoller, 'Europa nach Maastricht: Die Gemeinsame Außen—und Sicherheitspolitik' (1992) 33 *Neue Zeischrift für Wehrrecht* 221, at 223; Eaton, above n 34, at 220.

[51] Fink-Hooijer, above n 30, at 177.

[52] Marauhn, above n 24, at 89. Article J.1. (4) TEU supplemented the general loyalty clause in then Article 5 EC, now Article 10 EC, the crucial para 2 reads: 'They [the Member states] shall abstain from any measure which could jeopardise the attainment of the objectives of this Treaty.'

[53] Whether this was because after a few years under the TEU intergovernmentalism was considered to be sufficiently safeguarded or because it was no longer considered important is another question.

[54] The Member States of the EU are not 'independent' in relation to the Union and the other Member States.

[55] Koutrakos, above n 5, at 26 also citing J Monar, 'The European Union's Foreign Affairs System after the Treaty of Amsterdam: A Strengthened Capacity for External Action' (1997) 2 *European Foreign Affairs Review* 413, at 418.

the potential to facilitate the adoption of a common policy of the EU should integrity ever be at stake.[56]

Second, the purpose was "to strengthen the security of the Union in all ways". This is the main reference to security as far as the objectives of the CFSP are concerned, although the references to independence and integrity discussed above also refer to security. The Maastricht version of Article J.1 referred to the "security of the Union and its Member States". In the Amsterdam version the reference to the Member States, emphasising the intergovernmental nature of the CFSP, was omitted, as was explained above. The words "security of the Union" introduced a new notion into the law of the EU. So far only the notions of 'public security' and 'national security', always referring to the security of an individual Member State, featured in the Treaties and secondary Community law.[57] Although the notion of 'security of the Union' and its relation to the other notions of security is not yet well defined, the very use of these words represents the introduction of an important new concept. Potentially there could be a narrow interpretation referring to situations affecting the security of the Union as a whole. However, there could also be a wider interpretation including situations where the security of only one Member State is affected.

Third, another purpose was "to preserve peace and strengthen international security, in accordance with the principles of the United Nations Charter, as well as the principles of the Helsinki Final Act and the objectives of the Paris Charter, including those on external borders". This objective also has a direct relevance to defence. One important aspect of the EU is that it does not have any aggressive objectives. The use of force is only envisaged within the context of self-defence according to Article 51 of the United Nations Charter or when authorised by the UN Security Council. This interpretation is supported by the list of the security and defence tasks in Article 17 (2) TEU (ex Article J.7). It was not a contentious issue for any Western State when the Maastricht and Amsterdam Treaties were signed. However, unilateral action beyond the limits of the United Nations Charter has become an issue again since the US led invasion of Iraq in 2003, which was not authorised by a UN Security Council resolution, let alone justified by self-defence. This shall be discussed in more detail in chapter 3.

Fourth it was "to promote international cooperation". Fifth, the CFSP was "to develop and consolidate democracy and the rule of law, and respect for human rights and fundamental freedoms". These are mainly foreign policy rather than defence objectives.

Finally, the notions of 'common defence policy' and 'common defence' appearing in Article 2 TEU are not mentioned in Article 11 (1) TEU. The Draft prepared by the Luxembourg Presidency of 19 June 1991 had contained these notions as objectives in Article J.1, but this section was deleted in the final version of the Maastricht Treaty.[58] The Amsterdam Treaty did not change that. Moreover, the list

[56] Koutrakos, above, at 27.

[57] This will be discussed extensively in ch 4 to 9.

[58] F Laursen and S Vanhoonaker, (eds), *The Intergovernmental Conference on Political Union: Institutional Reforms, New Policies and International Identity of the European Community* (EIPA, Maastricht, 1992) 399, as cited by Wessel, 'Black Widow', above n 23, at 407–8.

of instruments in Article 12 TEU refers to Joint Actions (Article 14 ex J.4 TEU) and Common Positions (Article 15 ex J.4 TEU) and not Article 17 (ex J.7) TEU on the common defence policy. Therefore the instruments of the CFSP regulated in Article 12 (ex J.2) TEU which are only related to the objectives in Article 11 (ex J.3) TEU cannot be used for a common defence policy because that is not one of the objectives in the latter provision.[59] Hence it could be argued that defence policy is not a part of the CFSP. However, a common defence policy and possibly a common defence are objectives of the EU according to Article 2 TEU and with Article 17 TEU the provisions of the CFSP contain a separate legal base. Wessel attributes this confusion of objectives and instruments to the carelessness of the drafters of the Treaty.[60]

The use of the words "all areas of foreign and security policy" indicates that the list of objectives is not exhaustive. Moreover, the objectives are open to a broad interpretation. Nevertheless, an aggressive and expansionist policy or a policy that would include the unilateral use of force would contradict many of the objectives and can be excluded. Therefore the capacity of the EU to act in the field of foreign and security policy under the Maastricht and Amsterdam Treaties is very broadly defined but not unlimited. The scope of the CFSP as defined in Article 11 TEU shows the political will of the Member States to actively respond to the challenges posed by the political and strategic situation after 1989.[61]

3.2.2. A Common Defence Policy

The security or defence component of the CFSP was addressed mainly in Article 17 TEU (ex Article J.7). Article 17 (1) TEU stipulated:

> "The common foreign and security policy shall include all questions relating to the security of the Union, including the progressive framing of a common defence policy, [...] which might lead to a common defence, should the European Council so decide."

This reference to a common defence policy goes beyond the contents of the EPC and has been called an "important difference"[62] or "the major innovation"[63] of the CFSP. Moreover, Article 17 (1) TEU clearly abolished the old differentiation between the political and economic aspects of security covered by the EPC on the one hand and the military aspects of security excluded from the EPC on the other hand.[64] "Common defence policy" and "common defence"

[59] Wessel, 'Black Widow', above.
[60] Wessel, 'Black Widow', above, at 408.
[61] Fink-Hooijer, above n 30, at 174 calls this 'to no longer react but act' on the basis of the Maastricht version of the TEU.
[62] Marauhn, above n 24, at 94; Eaton, above n 34, at 219–20 calls it 'a main difference' and at 216 a 'significant change'.
[63] Fink-Hooijer, above n 30, at 194.
[64] Neuwahl, above n 34, at 232.

necessarily require aspects that add to the security element of foreign policy outlined in the context of the objectives above. Possible additional aspects that amount to a defence policy would involve the co-ordination of national defence capabilities or even the creation of European capabilities. Defence capabilities could include *inter alia* troops, military intelligence, logistic support, and military training. However, the issue of capabilities is not mentioned in the Maastricht and Amsterdam versions of the TEU. The wording of Article 17 (1) shows that due to the sensibility of the subject a careful approach was chosen, which started or continued a process of defence integration without really committing the Member States to any tangible steps in the immediate future. The use of words such as "might" and "eventual" in the Maastricht version of the provision reveals that the advocates of defence integration had to reach a compromise with its opponents.[65] The word "might" was still there after Amsterdam, whereas the more determined "progressive" replaced the Maastricht "eventual". The compromise thesis is supported by the fact that according to Article 23 (2) subparagraph 3 last sentence TEU (ex Article J.13) issues having defence implications were expressly excluded from qualified majority voting. However, the reference in Article 17 TEU was a beginning that might well allow the new Union to eventually assert a European security and defence identity on the international stage. Hence this first reference confirmed in Amsterdam can be seen as the beginning of a dynamic process. The notion of 'capabilities' is addressed indirectly in the provisions in Article 17 TEU referring to the WEU. These will be discussed separately below.

The wide notion of security is somehow qualified but also clarified in Article 17 (2) TEU which stipulated:

> "Questions referred to in this Article shall include humanitarian and rescue tasks, peacekeeping tasks and tasks of combat forces in crisis management, including peacemaking."

These were the 'Petersberg Tasks' developed in the framework of the WEU and discussed in chapter 1. Another possible field of activity was mentioned in Article 17 (1) subparagraph 4 TEU: co-operation in the field of armaments. This field of co-operation was to support the "progressive framing of a common defence policy" but only as and if Member States consider appropriate. Hence the importance of armaments was recognised but not yet addressed in the TEU. It is submitted that these references to the Petersberg Tasks and to armaments co-operation limited the progressive framing of a common defence

[65] Eaton, above n 34, at 218: 'The compromise is that it is there but a long way off'. Neuwahl, above, at 232: 'No great steps forward can therefore be expected to be taken in the near future'.

policy to these fields of activity and that the Member States were not able to agree on activities that go beyond these. An activity beyond these tasks is for example mutual defence. This shall be discussed in more detail in chapter 3.[66]

Article 17 (5) TEU stipulated that the provisions of Article 17 TEU would be reviewed in accordance with Article 48 TEU,[67] "with a view of furthering the objectives of this Article". This put the subject matter of the CFSP on the agenda of the next intergovernmental conference and kept the momentum of integration, also with regards to defence.

3.3. The EU institutions as Parts of the Single Institutional Framework

The TEU does not explicitly refer to EU institutions.[68] However, institutions involved in the CFSP were the European Council, the Council, the Presidency, the High Representative for the Common Foreign and Security Policy, the Commission, and the European Parliament. Apart from the European Council these are the institutions of the EC[69] for which the concept of a single institutional framework enshrined in Articles 3 (ex Article C)[70] and 5 (ex Article E)[71] TEU applies. The concept of the single institutional framework is an important component of the principles of unity, consistency, and coherence between the Pillars

[66] At 103–104.

[67] Article 48 TEU reads

The government of any Member State or the Commission may submit to the Council proposals for the amendment of the Treaties on which the Union is founded. If the Council, after consulting the European Parliament and, where appropriate, the Commission, delivers an opinion in favour of calling a conference of representatives of the governments of the Member States, the conference shall be convened by the President of the Council for the purpose of determining by common accord the amendments to be made to those Treaties. The European Central Bank shall also be consulted in the case of institutional changes in the monetary area. The amendments shall enter into force after being ratified by all the Member States in accordance with their respective constitutional requirements.

[68] With the exception of Article 4 TEU, see below.

[69] The Political Committee is not an institution and the High Representative is also the General Secretary of the Council, see below.

[70] Article 3 TEU reads:

The Union shall be served by a single institutional framework which shall ensure the consistency and the continuity of the activities carried out in order to attain its objectives while respecting and building upon the acquis communautaire. The Union shall in particular ensure the consistency of its external activities as a whole in the context of its external relations, security, economic and development policies. The Council and the Commission shall be responsible for ensuring such consistency and shall cooperate to this end. They shall ensure the implementation of these policies, each in accordance with its respective powers.

[71] Article 5 TEU reads:

The European Parliament, the Council, the Commission, the Court of Justice and the Court of Auditors shall exercise their powers under the conditions and for the purposes provided for, on the one hand, by the provisions of the Treaties establishing the European Communities and of the subsequent Treaties and Acts modifying and supplementing them and, on the other hand, by the other provisions of this Treaty.

of the TEU.[72] The purpose of this principle is to avoid the fragmentation of the EU legal order, which could undermine the uniform applicability and enforcement of EU law and even threaten *the acquis communautaire*.[73] The establishment of separate EU institutions for each Pillar would be incompatible with the principle of a single institutional framework and undermine the coherence of the Union. Therefore Article 5 TEU provides that Parliament, Council, Commission, and the Courts of Justice and Auditors shall exercise their powers under the Community Treaties on the one hand and the TEU on the other hand. The notion of "other provisions" in Article 5 TEU included Title V on the CFSP of the TEU. Although these institutions already existed as EC institutions before the TEU, the EU does not just "borrow" them from the Community.[74] They have to be considered EU institutions.[75] The borrowing theory[76] contradicts the principle of a single institutional framework and would undermine the coherence of the Pillars.[77] Nevertheless, according to the latter provision the institutions operated on the basis of different rules in the context of the more intergovernmental CFSP. This shall be explained in the context of the individual institutions below.

3.3.1. The (European) Council

According to Article 4 TEU (ex Article D) the European Council, which is an institution composed of the heads of State or government and the President of the Commission, is the highest political authority in the EU[78] between intergovernmental conferences, superior to the Council, and the "cornerstone" of the EU institutional structure.[79] Moreover, it is the only distinct organ of EU[80] as opposed to the other organs, which are also Community institutions. The European Council has to be differentiated from the Council meeting in the composition of the heads of State or government, which is still the Council.[81] Article 7 EC only

[72] Jacques Delors: 'A unitary approach implies a logically structured entity absorbing (or expanding) the existing Communities and all its achievements and building further on the basis of that solid foundation.' Bulletin of the European Communities, Supp 1/88, at 17.

[73] It has been argued that the TEU failed to establish a true single institutional structure safeguarding that principle. In particular by D Curtin, 'The Constitutional Structure of the Union: A Europe of Bits and Pieces' (1993) 30 *Common Market Law Review* 17, at 28: 'by a single institutional framework can, in the light of the substantive provisions of the Treaty, be described, not too unkindly, a mere lip-service to an ideal'; Neuwahl, above n 34.

[74] Trüe, above n 33, at 16–17; G Ress, 'Die Europäische Union und die neue Qualität der Beziehungen zu den Europäischen Gemeinschaften' [1992] *Juristische Schulung* 985.

[75] RA Wessel, *The European Union's Foreign and Security Policy: A Legal Institutional Perspective* (Kluwer, The Hague, 1999) 74–75 (hereinafter '*Foreign and Security Policy*'); Wessel, 'Revisited', above n 34, at 22; Curtin and Dekker, above n 33.

[76] Curtin, above n 72, at 26; Everling, above n 34, at 1061; Dörr, above n 34, at 337.

[77] Trüe, above n 33, at 16–17.

[78] Fink-Hooijer, above n 30, at 178.

[79] Curtin, above n 73, at 26.

[80] Wessel, *Foreign and Security Policy*, above n 74, at 76; 'Revisited', above n 34, at 21; Trüe, above n 33, at 15; Curtin, above, at 27; Dörr, above n 34, at 337; H Lecheler, 'Der Rechtscharakter der Europäischen Union' in J Ipsen, *et al*, (eds), *Verfassungsrecht im Wandel* (Carl Heyermanns Verlag, Cologne, 1995) 383, at 388.

[81] Thanks to Ramses A Wessel (University of Twente, Enschede) for bringing this point to my attention.

lists the European Parliament, the Council, the Commission, the Court of Justice, and the Court of Auditors as EC institutions. The existence of a distinct EU organ is an important condition for the international legal personality of the Union.

According to Article 13 (1) TEU (ex Article J.3) the European Council had to define the principles and general guidelines for the CFSP, including for matters with defence implications. According to Article 13 (2) TEU (ex Article J.3.) it was to decide on Common Strategies to be implemented by the EU where the Member States have important interests in common. It was to set out its objectives, duration and the means to be made available to the Union and the Member States. Therefore it has indirect competences when implementing the CFSP in that it makes possible or facilitates the decision making of the Council.[82] According to Article 23 (2) subparagraph 2 sentence 2 TEU (ex Article J.13) the European Council would take decisions by unanimity when one of its members opposed the adoption to be taken by qualified majority, as will be explained below. The powers of the European Council for cases in which the EU would avail itself of the WEU will be discussed below.

The European Council's "very prominent and powerful position in the institutional landscape of the Union"[83] is a crucial element of the more intergovernmental character of the CFSP and the EU as the roof construction for the three Pillars of the TEU. It has no supranational features.[84] An organ composed of the highest representatives of the Member State governments takes unanimous decisions. It does not get more intergovernmental than that. Moreover, as will be outlined in the context of the other institutions below, the strong position of the European Council is not counterbalanced by significant powers of the more supranational institutions: the Commission, Parliament, and European Court of Justice.

In the context of decisions having defence implications under Article 17 TEU (ex Article J.7) the European Council and not the Council was the main decision making body.

3.3.2. The Council of the European Union

In the context of the First Pillar the Council is the main legislator. Since the Maastricht Treaty, however, the co-decision procedure of Article 251 EC makes the European Parliament an important second player in the Community legislative process.[85] Moreover, the Commission has an exclusive right to initiative for new legislation, which is subject to review by the European Court of Justice.[86] This institutional system is not equal but close to the checks and balances and the separation of powers of a modern democracy. In the context of the CFSP the role of the more intergovernmental Council is increased compared to the Community, while the role of the other more supranational institutions is substantially reduced.

[82] Wessel, *Foreign and Security Policy*, above n 75, at 77.
[83] Curtin, above n 73, at 26: 'the intergovernmental organ par exellence'.
[84] Above.
[85] See Craig and de Búrca, above n 3, ch 4.
[86] Above, ch 11.

The Council of the European Union[87] (hereinafter the Council) is the main decision-making body of the CFSP.[88] According to Article 13 (3) TEU (ex Article J.3.) it takes the necessary decisions to define and implement the CFSP on the basis of the general guidelines defined by the European Council.[89] The earlier would also recommend Common Strategies to the latter and implement them by adopting Joint Actions and Common Positions, as will be discussed in more detail below. This procedure represents a considerable deviation from the decision-making procedures developed in the context of the Community Pillar. This deviation is an element of the more intergovernmental character of the CFSP. First, the more intergovernmental Council rather than the more supranational Commission exercises the right to initiative. Second, the more intergovernmental European Council and Council of Ministers takes the decisions without any significant involvement of the more supranational and directly elected European Parliament. Third, the more supranational European Court of Justice does not review these decisions, as will be explained below. The Council in the context of the Communities and the Council in the context of the CFSP are the same only in name. Due to their different position in the decision-making process of the Community on the one hand and the CFSP on the other, they can be seen as two different organs. With respect to the Council the TEU merely continues the arrangements of the EPC. These institutional elements of the intergovernmental character of the CFSP contradict the notion of a single institutional framework as part of the notions of unity and consistency. The contradictions are so significant that they pose the question whether the requirement of unity and consistency can actually be achieved between a supranational framework such as the Communities and an intergovernmental framework such as the CFSP.

3.3.2.1. Common Positions One important instrument,[90] according to Article 15 TEU (ex Article J.5.) to be adopted by the Council, was the 'Common Position'. Common Positions shall define the approach of the Union to a particular matter of a geographical or thematic nature. Member States had an obligation to ensure that their national policies conform to Common Positions. This is an instrument of classical diplomacy and the traditional instrument to achieve co-operation and consultation during the EPC periods.

[87] Due to the extension of competences beyond the Community Pillar and because political Declarations are adopted in the name of the Union, the Council of Ministers formally adopted this name after the entry into force of the TEU: Décision du Conseil du 8 Novembre 1993 relative a sa dénomination suite a l'entrée en vigueur du Traité sur L'Union Européenne, Decision 93/591, [1993] OJ L–218/16.

[88] For a discussion of the role of the Council see: A Dashwood, 'The Role of the Council of the European Communities' in D Curtin and T Heukels, *Institutional Dynamics of European Integration, Essays in Honour of Henry G Schermers*, vol II (Martinus Nijhoff Publishers, Dordrecht, 1994) 117–34; A Dashwood, 'The Council of the European Union in the Era of the Amsterdam Treaty' in T Heuekls, N Blokker and M Brus, (eds), *The European Union after Amsterdam: A Legal Analysis* (Kluwer, The Hague, 1998) 117–29.

[89] CFSP decisions are normally taken by the General Affairs Council in the composition of the Ministers for Foreign Affairs.

[90] Fink-Hooijer, above n 30, at 180, calls it 'one of the most important assets' of the CFSP.

3.3.2.2. Joint Action The most important instrument of the CFSP, according to Articles 13 (3) and 14 (1) TEU (ex Articles J.3. and J.4.) to be adopted by the Council, was the 'Joint Action'. According to Article 14 (1) TEU "joint actions shall address specific situations where operational action by the Union is deemed to be required. They shall lay down their objectives, scope, the means to be made available to the Union, if necessary their duration, and the conditions for their implementation". According to Article 14 (3) TEU Joint Actions committed the Member States in the positions they adopt and in the conduct of their activity. The Council could alter the contents of Joint Actions in cases of a change in circumstances. National action pursuant to a Joint Action obliged Member States to provide prior information to allow for possible prior consultation within the Council. The Member States could deviate from a Joint Action only by taking urgent action in cases of imperative need arising from changes in the situation and failing a Council decision.

The concept of Joint Action is a crucial innovation introduced by the TEU. In contrast to the notion of the same name mentioned in Article 30 SEA, it is not merely a joint policy but represents an operational, well-defined, and legally binding instrument for a specific action.[91] Political or commercial measures agreed by the Member States under the EPC framework, for example through declarations, *démarches*, missions, political dialogue with third states, or the adoption of Common Positions in international organisations were not legally binding. They had to be implemented on the national level and there was no control or enforcement by a judicial or political authority.[92] There still is no judicial enforcement mechanism but through the binding character of Joint Actions the Council becomes a political authority to remind Member States of their obligations under the TEU in case they should deviate from positions they agreed to. The binding character is necessary to prevent the unity, effectiveness, and consistency of the CFSP to be undermined by sudden unilateral Member State action contradicting a Joint Action.

However, the binding character is balanced with Member State sovereignty by an element of flexibility. This element of flexibility has three aspects. First, according to Article 14 (6) TEU (ex Article J.4.) Member States may act unilaterally in cases of urgency. Second, according to Article 14 (2) TEU there is a review procedure for joint actions in cases where circumstances have changed in a way that has a substantial effect on a question subject to a Joint Action. Third, Article 14 (7) TEU allows the adoption of special solutions for particular Member States having major difficulties in implementing a joint action. However, it is submitted that all these safeguards for Member State sovereignty have to be interpreted narrowly as a wide interpretation would undermine the "unity, consistency, and effectiveness" of the CFSP. Moreover, the sovereignty of the Member States is accommodated by the unanimity requirements for most joint actions, as will be discussed in more detail below.

[91] Marauhn, above n 24, at 90.
[92] Fink-Hooijer, above n 30, at 181 and 183.

In 1992 in Lisbon the European Council adopted general guidelines as envisaged by Article 13 TEU (ex Article J.3) on the areas for which Joint Actions should be used.[93] With regards to the security dimension of the CFSP these should be: the CSCE[94] process; the policy of disarmament and arms control in Europe, including confidence-building measures; nuclear non-proliferation issues; and the economic aspects of security, in particular control of transfer of military technology to third countries and control of arms exports.[95] The Lisbon Report also identified areas in which Joint Action should be used with respect to individual countries that would appear to be particularly beneficial for the attainment of the objectives of the EU. These included Central and Eastern Europe, the former Yugoslavia, the Maghreb, the Middle East,[96] North-South relations, the continuation of relations with the United States, Japan, and Canada, and the co-ordination of action in international organisations or conferences. Generally the geographical proximity of a given region or country, the existence of an important interest in the political or economic stability of a region or country, and the existence of threats to the security interests of the Union should be taken into account.

3.3.2.3. International Agreements The Treaty of Amsterdam introduced the conclusion of international agreements as a new competence of the Council. According to Article 24 TEU the Council can authorise the Presidency to open negotiations in view of an agreement with one or more states or an international organisation.

3.3.2.4. Voting Depending on the matter the Council decided by unanimity, qualified, or simple majority. According to Article 23 (1) TEU (ex Article J.13) the Council had to act unanimously when taking decisions on the CFSP. It would act unanimously when authorising the Presidency to open negotiations towards agreements with third countries and international organisations and when eventually concluding these agreements under Article 24 TEU.

In derogation from the unanimity rule Article 23 (2) TEU required only a qualified majority "when adopting Joint Actions, Common Positions or taking any other decision on the basis of a Common Strategy or when adopting any decision implementing a joint action or a common position". If a member of the Council intended to oppose a decision to be adopted by a qualified majority for "important and stated reasons of national policy", a vote was not to be taken and the matter could be

[93] Paragraph 10 of the Lisbon Report: Strengthening democratic principles and institutions and respect for human and minority rights; promoting regional political stability and contributing to the creation of political and/or economic frameworks that encourage regional co-operation or moves towards regional or sub-regional integration; contributing to the prevention and settlement of conflicts; contributing to more effective international co-ordination in dealing with emergency situations; strengthening existing co-operation on issues of international interest such as the fight against firearms proliferation, terrorism and traffic in illicit drugs; promoting and supporting good government. The Lisbon Report has been published in EUROPE, No 5761 (new series) of 29/30 June 1992, Annex.

[94] Conference on Security and Cooperation in Europe, now Organisation for Security and Cooperation in Europe.

[95] Paragraph 35 of the Lisbon Report, above n 93.

[96] Paragraphs 20–33 of the Lisbon Report, above.

referred to the European Council to decide unanimously. The votes would be weighed according to the procedures for qualified majority voting in the EC Treaty. However, qualified majority voting would not apply to decisions having military or defence implications. This shows a lack of consensus concerning defence integration during the lifetime of the Maastricht and Amsterdam Treaties. According to Article 23 (3) TEU the Council decided by a simple majority on procedural questions.

The unanimity requirement is an intergovernmental feature since it gives the Member State governments a right to *veto*. The importance of unanimity voting in the CFSP differs considerably to the mixture of unanimity, qualified, and simple majority voting in the Council of the EDC discussed in chapter 1 and represents an important part of the CFSP's intergovernmental nature.

3.3.2.5. The Political Committee According to Article 25 TEU (ex Article J.15) a Political Committee was to monitor the international situation in the areas covered by the CFSP and contribute to the definition of policies by delivering opinions to the Council at the request of the Council or on its own initiative. It also had to monitor the implementation of agreed policies, without prejudice to the responsibility of the Presidency and the Commission.

3.3.2.6. The Presidency Article 203 EC, which according to Article 28 (1) TEU (ex Article J.18) applied to the CFSP, provided that the Presidency of the Council was held in turn by each Member State for six months.[97] According to Article 18 (1) TEU (ex Article J. 8) the Presidency was to represent the EU in matters covered by the CFSP, according to Article 18 (2) TEU also by expressing the position of the EU in international organisations and international conferences. It was responsible for the implementation of CFSP decisions. According to Article 21 TEU (ex Article J.11) it had to consult the European Parliament "on the main aspects and the basic choices of the common foreign and security policy and [has to] ensure that the views of the European Parliament [were] duly taken into consideration". The Presidency was also the representative to open negotiations to conclude agreements with third States and international organisations according to Article 24 TEU (ex Article J.14). The Presidency would be authorised by a unanimous decision of the Council and when appropriate assisted by the Commission.

Although Article 22 (1) TEU (ex J.12) did not give the Presidency a right to initiative, it qualified as a Member State under this provision, and thus proved to be the initiator of most Common Positions and Joint Actions.[98] Member States took the role very seriously and used their six months and the pivotal position that

[97] The Treaties do not contain a basis for the assertion that the Presidency was a separate institution. The Council used this argument in the context of refusing an individual and the Ombudsman access to documentation. See Reply of the Council to the Ombudsman concerning a series of complaints made by Mr Tony Bunyan regarding several requests for access to documents, Report of the Ombudsman for 1997, as cited by Wessel, *Foreign and Security Policy*, above n 75, at 88.

[98] D Galloway, 'Common Foreign and Security Policy: Intergovernmentalism Donning the Mantle of the Community Method' in M Westlake, *The Council of the European Union* (Cartermill, London, 1995) at 222; Wessel, *Foreign and Security Policy*, above, at 98; Willlaert and Marqués-Ruiz, above n 34, at 53.

came with it to make an impression on their electorate and the other Member States. This *de facto* 'custom' of initiative and the autonomous competences outlined above, gave the Presidency a role in the context of the CFSP that is comparable to that of the Commission in the context of the First Pillar.[99] A couple of critical points can be raised in the context of this strong role of the Presidency. First, the rather short period of six months and the fact that the Presidencies worked almost exclusively with their national civil services while holding office, could lead to a series of different and even contradictory policies rather than to a consistent CFSP that has an impact. Second, the pivotal position could mislead certain Presidencies into following narrow national agendas rather than the interests of the Union, thereby undermining the development of a consistent CFSP.[100] Finally, having two initiators, the Commission for the Community and the Presidency for the CFSP, requires clearly separable policy fields. Additional coordination would be required if competencies overlap, potentially undermining coherence. Moreover, the concept of two initiators for different pillars is difficult to reconcile with the principle of a single institutional structure.

3.3.2.7. The High Representative for the Common Foreign and Security Policy Article 207 (2) EC, which according to Article 28 (1) TEU (ex Article J.18) applied to the CFSP, provided that the General Secretariat of the Council led by the Secretary-General was to assist the Presidency.[101] According to Article 18 (3) TEU (ex Article J.8) the Secretary of the Council was to exercise the function of High Representative for the Common Foreign and Security Policy. He or she had to assist the Presidency and, according to Article 26 TEU (ex Article J.16), the Council in matters within the scope of the CFSP.[102] The High Representative could contribute to the formulation, preparation and implementation of policy decisions. This function inevitably had implications for decision-making. Moreover, when appropriate and whilst acting on behalf of the Council at the request of the Presidency, the High Representative could conduct political dialogue with third parties. The Amsterdam Treaty introduced the office of the High Representative

[99] Galloway, above; Wessel, *Foreign and Security Policy*, above n 75, at 88.

[100] An example is provided by Wessel, *Foreign and Security Policy*, above, at 89, citing S Keukeleire, *Het Buitenlandse beleid van de Europese Unie* (Kluwer, Deventer, 1998): '[...] the attempts of the Netherlands Presidency in the UN Human Rights Commission in Geneva 1997 to organise a clear condemnation of the human rights situation in China led to a visible division within the EU which was not too helpful in portraying the EU as a serious global player. It was however, a way of the Dutch Government to satisfy its own national Parliament.'

[101] In Case T–14/98, *Heidi Hautala v Council of the European Union* [1999] ECR II–2489, the Council argued that it was a single body including all its compositions and all of its working parties and committees. This argument supported the Council's refusal of access to a report from the Working Group on Conventional Arms Exports approved by the Political Committee. At the same time it refused access to a Third Pillar document on the grounds that the Secretariat must be considered a separate institution to the Council, see Curtin and Dekker, above n 33, at 36.

[102] In practice the Secretariat provides important support to the Presidency by advising them on procedures, drawing up minutes and other reports of meetings and for functions such as arranging the production, translation and circulation of Council Documents, see Curtin and Dekker, above, at 39.

in an attempt to increase the visibility of the CFSP and to remedy certain shortcomings of the CFSP.[103] The personal union with the office of Secretary-General of the Council was a compromise between those who favoured the *status quo ante* and those who wanted a separate new organ.[104]

Establishing the office of a 'Mr or Mrs CFSP' helped to improve the visibility of the CFSP simply by personalising the policy. Furthermore, the High Representative component of the office was partly detached from the interests of any individual Member State. This put the new office in a better position to lay down guidelines that transcend national interest. Moreover, the establishment of a Policy Planning and Early Warning Unit[105] was an adequate step towards addressing the lack of forward planning and the inadequate ability to react quickly to current political events. The High Representative needed able staff to support his or her office. Finally, the office could also emphasise the instruments available to the Union thereby possibly increasing their use.

3.3.3. The European Commission

In the context of the First Pillar the Commission is the most important and more supranational institution having the exclusive right of initiative for new legislation,[106] important competencies in the area of external relations,[107] a 'watchdog' function regarding compliance with Community law,[108] an individual decision

[103] According to a Report by the Secretary-General *Setting the CFSP Policy Planning and Early Warning Unit*, Brussels, 6 November 1997, at para 8 these shortcomings were the external invisibility of the CFSP, its inadequate ability to react quickly to current political events, the difficulty of laying down guidelines that transcend national interests, the insufficient use of the instruments available to the Union, and the lack of forward planning.

[104] Wessel, *Foreign and Security Policy*, above n 75, at 87.

[105] The establishment of the Policy Planning and Early Warning Unit (PPEWU) is a reflection of the implications of the new office for decision making. The PPEWU was established by Declaration No 6 adopted by the closing conference of the 1997 Intergovernmental Conference. It falls under the responsibility of the Secretary-General and is situated in the Council Secretariat. The tasks of the PPEWU are: monitoring and analysing developments in areas relevant to CFSP, providing assessment of the Union's foreign and security policy interests and identifying areas where CFSP could focus in future, providing timely assessments and early warning of events or situations which may have significant repercussions for the Union's foreign and security policy, including potential political crises; producing at the request of either the Council or the Presidency or on its own initiative, argued policy opinion papers to be presented under the responsibility of the Presidency as a contribution to policy formulation in the Council, and which may contain analyses, recommendations and strategies for the CFSP.

[106] In particular Article 251(2) EC reads: 'The Commission shall submit a proposal to the European Parliament and the Council.'

[107] The Community has exclusive competence for agreements with third states regarding the common commercial policy according to Article 133(3) EC. The Community and the Member States have shared competence for cooperation with third countries and international organisations in the context of environmental policy according to Article 174(4) EC, education according to Article 149(3) EC, vocational training according to Article 150(3) EC, culture according to Article 151(3) EC, public health according to Article 152(3) EC, and development cooperation according to Article 177 EC. In the context of the latter EC policy is even complimentary to the policy of the Member States.

[108] In particular Article 211 EC which reads: 'In order to ensure the proper functioning and development of the market, the Commission shall: – ensure that the provisions of this Treaty and the measures taken by the institutions thereto are applied; [...]'.

making capacity,[109] and a crucial role in the implementation of Community law.[110] In the context of the Community Pillar the Commission holds a position comparable to that of the EDC Board of Commissioners discussed in chapter 1, although the latter was to have an even stronger position as a co-legislator. This powerful position is a crucial component of the more supranational character of the Community.

In the context of the CFSP the role of the Commission was considerably reduced compared to the pivotal position it occupies in the Community. First, Article 28 TEU did not refer to Article 211 EC thus depriving the Commission of its 'watchdog' function and its individual decision making capacity. Second, according to Article 22 (1) TEU (ex Article J.12) any Member State or the Commission may refer to the Council any question relating to the CFSP and submit proposals to the Council. Hence the Commission did not have an exclusive right to initiative. In the context of the Community the Commission effectively proposes draft decisions because there is no Council decision without a prior Commission proposal and unanimity is required in the Council to alter the proposal. Moreover, the Commission is an important actor in the negotiations because it may alter the proposal any time before the Council has reached a decision. Therefore the Commission was not the stimulator of decisions in the context of the CFSP. The European Council occupied this role. Third, although according to Article 27 TEU (ex Article J.17) "the Commission shall be fully associated with the work carried out in the [CFSP]", this full association was not clearly defined thereby allowing the Member States to give or not give further meaning to it. Finally, the fact that Article 202 EC[111] was not applicable to the CFSP prevented the delegation of executive competences from the Council to the Commission.

However, the role of the Commission in the CFSP was still significant. First, Article 18 (4) TEU (ex Article J.8) allowed the Commission to be "fully associated" with the work of the Presidency making it the fourth and only permanent member of the Presidency 'Troika', made up of the previous, current, and next Presidency of the EU. This allowed a certain degree of consistency of all aspects of

[109] In particular Article 211 EC which reads: 'In order to ensure the proper functioning and development of the market, the Commission shall: [...]—have its own power of decision and participate in the shaping of measures taken by the Council and by the European Parliament in the manner provided for in this Treaty; [...].'

[110] In particular Article 211 EC which reads: 'In order to ensure the proper functioning and development of the market, the Commission shall: [...]—exercise the power conferred on it by the Council for the implementation of the rules laid down by the latter.'

[111] Article 202 EC reads:

> To ensure that the objectives set out in this Treaty are attained the Council shall, in accordance with the provisions of this Treaty: [...]—confer on the Commission, in the acts which the Council adopts, powers for the implementation of the rules which the Council lays down. The Council may impose certain requirements in respect of the exercise of these powers. The Council may also reserve the right, in specific cases, to exercise directly implementing powers itself. The procedures referred to above must be consonant with principles and rules to be laid down in advance by the Council, acting unanimously on a proposal from the Commission and after obtaining the Opinion of the European Parliament.

external policy and accommodated up to a point the wish of third countries to enter into a comprehensive dialogue with the EU, encompassing CFSP and economic concerns.[112] Second, the Commission was represented in the CFSP at all levels and was a full negotiating partner in all working parties and committees. The President of the Commission was a member of the European Council. The Commission was in many ways the '16th or 26th Member State' on any CFSP negotiating table safeguarding the Community interest and *acquis*.

The comparatively weak position of the supranational Commission in the context of the CFSP is a reflection of the intergovernmental nature of the Second Pillar. The intergovernmental Council, including the European Council, is the only important institution of the CFSP. To reduce the role of the 'European civil service', in particular regarding foreign and security policy, has been a policy of many Member States since they realised the strong position of the High Authority of the ECSC under Jean Monnet. As explained in chapter 1,[113] the strong position of the supranational Board of Commissioners in the EDC Treaty was an important reason for its rejection in the French Parliament. A role for the Commission comparable to their role in the Community would come close to the introduction of a more supranational CFSP.

3.3.4. The European Parliament

The European Parliament is the only directly elected institution and therefore the cornerstone of the democratic legitimacy of the Community. Moreover, it is one of the three central more supranational institutions of the EU, together with the European Commission discussed above and the European Court of Justice discussed below. Regarding its powers, Parliament has come a long way since its early years as Assembly of the European Coal and Steel Community, developing from a consultative body towards a veritable legislature. The Maastricht Treaty reformed the legislative procedures, thereby not solving but considerably improving a situation commonly referred to as the 'democratic deficit' of the Communities. In particular the co-decision procedure stipulated in Article 251 EC brought the Strasbourg institution close to a European Parliament that deserves the name.[114]

In the context of the CFSP the role of the European Parliament is reduced to the bare minimum. In fact, it could be said that the CFSP merely recognises its existence. This situation follows the tradition of EPC and the SEA.[115] According to Article 21 TEU (ex Article J.11):

[112] M Cremona, 'The European Union as an International Actor: The Issues of Flexibility and Linkage' [1998] 3 *European Foreign Affairs Review* 67, at 71.

[113] At 28–30 and 43.

[114] See Craig and de Búrca, above n 3, ch 4.

[115] Marauhn, above n 24, at 93–94, compared this to the role under Article 30(4) SEA which provided: 'The High Contracting Parties shall ensure that the European Parliament is closely associated with European Political Cooperation.' *Prima facie*, to Marauhn, the TEU seems to give a lesser role to the Parliament than the SEA. However, Title V cannot be read in isolation and Article 300 EC (ex Article 228) gives Parliament a greater role with respect to agreements with third States and through the administrative expenditure of the CFSP which is charged to the budget of the Community. Parliament also has the power to exercise some control.

> "The Presidency shall consult the European Parliament on the main aspects and the basic choices of the common foreign and security policy and shall ensure that the views of the European Parliament are duly taken into consideration. The European Parliament shall be kept regularly informed by the Presidency and the Commission of the development of the Union's foreign and security policy.
>
> The European Parliament may ask questions of the Council or make recommendations to it. It shall hold an annual debate on progress in implementing the common foreign and security policy."

The terms "main aspects", "basic choices", "taken into consideration" and "regularly" are all sufficiently vague to allow the Presidency discretion to define and reduce them to a marginal right of information. Parliament had to hold an annual debate on progress in implementing the CFSP. Since the Treaty of Amsterdam the Council has prepared an annual report on the main aspects and basic choices of the CFSP, including the financial implications. However, the wording of Article 21 TEU does not suggest that there is an obligation to present such annual reports. The European Parliament presents its own annual report in which it regularly criticises Council and Commission. The role of the European Parliament with regards to the budget shall be discussed under a separate heading below.

Title V TEU does not guarantee any influence of the European Parliament over the CFSP. This 'influence' is only directed at vaguely defined basic policy lines and not at a concrete decision.[116] Moreover, the Council seems to more or less ignore Parliament in the context of the CFSP.[117] Furthermore, the consultation procedure has proven to be inadequate as the Council informs Parliament too late for the latter to share its views with the earlier and the annual debate is limited to an exchange of statements. Control of the European Council can only take place *ex post facto* on the basis of its reports communicated to the Council.[118] Finally, the power to ask questions and to make recommendations does not make the Council accountable to the Parliament.[119] Therefore it could be suggested that the CFSP suffers from a democratic deficit.[120] However, three considerations have to be mentioned that put this suggestion into perspective. First, not only the role of the European Parliament but that of all more supranational institutions is reduced in the CFSP context compared to the First Pillar context.[121] Therefore, the minimal

[116] Wessel, *Foreign and Security Policy*, above n 75, at 95.

[117] See for example the Working Document of the Committee on Institutional Affairs on the functioning of the Treaty on European Union with a view to the 1996 Intergovernmental Conference—implementation and development of the Union, 23 May 1995, Doc A4 0102/95, as cited by Wessel, *Foreign and Security Policy*, above, at 96.

[118] In the Report of the Committee on Foreign Affairs, Security and Defence Policy of 20 April 1995 (A4–0083/95) at 17, Parliament complained that it had never been consulted on the main aspects and basic choices of the CFSP or on any concrete proposals for Joint Actions.

[119] The possibility to make recommendations has been used modestly, see the recommendations of the European Parliament concerning regions in crisis failing a strong policy of the Council, for instance in Chechnya in 1995 and in Kosovo in 1996, see European Parliament Document PE 216.369/def of 30 May 1996 (the Fernández–Albor Report) and Document 220.788/def of 28 May 1997 (the Spencer Report), as cited by Wessel, above, at 216.

[120] Wessel, *Foreign and Security Policy*, above n 75, at 213.

[121] See on the European Commission above and on the European Court of Justice below.

role of Strasbourg is partly due to the more intergovernmental nature of the CFSP making the European Council and the Council dominate the decision-making process. Second, in many otherwise democratic countries parliaments have a limited influence over foreign affairs and security policy.[122] Therefore Strasbourg's reduced role in foreign and security policy is not unique to the EU. Even the Assembly of the European Defence Community discussed in chapter 1[123] would have had a relatively weak role, although this precedent also shows that the role of the Parliament can be considerably stronger than it is in the CFSP. Third, it took the European Parliament a long time to gain its current position in the Community decision-making process.[124] Therefore it might be just a question of time before Strasbourg increases its influence to remedy fully or in part a situation that could be called the democratic deficit of the CFSP.[125]

3.3.5. The European Court of Justice of the European Communities and Union

In the context of the First Pillar the European Court of Justice (hereinafter the Court) represents the judicial branch of governance. A Court of First Instance is attached to it.[126] According to Article 220 EC the Court ensures that the interpretation and application of the EC Treaty is observed. According to Article 226 and 227 EC Community law can be enforced against Member States, according to Article 230 and 231 EC Community acts can be reviewed and annulled, and according to Article 234 EC the national courts of the Member States may ask Luxembourg for a preliminary reference to ensure the uniform interpretation of Community law. Moreover, the Court has developed most of the doctrines of Community law, such as supremacy and direct effect, thereby creating a body of Community law through judicial activism. The European Court of Justice is the cornerstone of the rule of law of the Community, just as the European Parliament is its cornerstone of democracy. As outlined in chapter 1,[127] the Court of Justice had a comparably strong role in the European Defence Community.

[122] T Grunert, 'The Association of the European Parliament: No Longer the Underdog in EPC?' in E Regelsberger, P de Schoutheete de Tervarent, W Wessels, (eds), *Foreign Policy of the European Union: From EPC to CFSP and Beyond* (Lynne Rienner, Boulder, 1997) 109, at 112: 'In the individual states, foreign and security policy is traditionally the exclusive competence of governments. Parliaments can monitor government action through questions, motion of non-confidence, the adoption or rejection of international treaties, and by means of ratification procedures.' See also A Cassese, (ed), *Parliamentary Control over Foreign Policy: Legal Essays* (Sijthoff & Noordhoff: Alphen aan den Rijn, 1980).

[123] At 30–31.

[124] See Wessel, *Foreign and Security Policy*, above n 75, at 213–23.

[125] Similar to the situation in the First Pillar context, the European Parliament has been fighting for its rights since the creation of EPC, although Parliament's interest in foreign policy had been very limited before 1973, see G Gaja, 'European Parliament and Foreign Affairs: (1) Political Cooperation among the Nine' in Cassese, above n 120, p 191, 193; see also European Parliament Resolutions of 6 April 1973 [1973] OJ C–26/26; of 19 January 1978 [1978] OJ C–36/33; later A3–0189/92 of 20 January 1993 [1993] OJ C–42/129; A3–0322/92 of 18 December 1993 [1993] OJ C–21/503; on the European Council Report Towards European Union of 11 March 1993 [1993] OJ C–115/175.

[126] See Article 225 EC.

[127] At 34–36.

In the context of the CFSP the role of the European Court of Justice is considerably reduced. According to Article 46 TEU (ex Article L) the jurisdiction of the European Court of Justice does not include the provisions on the CFSP.[128] There is no alternative enforcement mechanism. While the Draft Treaty proposed by the Dutch Presidency suggested a certain role for the Court,[129] Article 46 TEU reflected the position of most Member States[130] and even the Commission.[131] Member States were concerned about a body of EU law being created by judicial activism comparable to the developments in the context of Community law.[132]

However, as Wessel put it, the European Court of Justice is the "ultimate arbiter to decide where the line of demarcation between the Union's issue-areas lies".[133] This became clear through judgments concerning sanctions,[134] the withdrawal of privileges from Yugoslavia (Serbia and Montenegro),[135] and access to information.[136] The Court would annul a CFSP decision according to Articles 230 and 231 EC if a Community legal base should have been used.[137] A national court can make reference for a preliminary ruling under Article 234 EC concerning a national measure implementing a CFSP instrument.[138] This authority of the Court derives from Article 47 TEU, which provides that "[...] nothing in [the TEU] shall affect the Treaties establishing the European Communities [...]". Article 47 TEU is covered by Article 46 TEU and safeguards the Community *acquis*.[139] The Court could,

[128] Article 46 TEU as amended by the Treaty of Nice reads: 'The provisions of the Treaty establishing the European Community, the Treaty establishing the European Coal and Steel Community and the Treaty establishing the European Atomic Energy Community concerning the powers of the Court of Justice of the European Communities and the exercise of those powers shall apply only to the following provisions of this Treaty: [...]', then the provision lists the Community provisions, provisions on Police and Judicial Cooperation (Title VI TEU), provisions on closer cooperation (Title VII TEU), fundamental rights and freedoms with regards to the institutions (Article 6(2) TEU), and the final provisions (Articles 46–53 TEU) only.

[129] The Dutch Draft Treaty wanted to allow the Court to 'review [...] the legality of the application of the procedures for deciding upon the joint action referred to in this Title of the Treaty', see F Laursen and S Vanhoonacker, *The Intergovernmental Conference on Political Union: Institutional Reforms, New Policies and International Identity of the European Community* (EIPA, Maastricht, 1994).

[130] Wessel, *Foreign and Security Policy*, above n 75, at 224; U Everling, 'L'avenir de l'organisation jurisdictionelle de l'Union européenne' in G Versanden, (ed), *La Réforme du Système Jurisdictionel Communautaire* (Éditons de l Université de Bruxelles, Brussels, 1994) 1, at 19.

[131] Working Document of the Commission SEC (91) 500, of 15 May 1991, at 41 cited by Wessel, above.

[132] Neuwahl, above n 34, at 244.

[133] Wessel, *Foreign and Security Policy*, above n 75, at 225.

[134] Case C–84/95, *Bosphorus Hava Turizim ve Ticaret AS v Minister for Transport, Energy and Communications Ireland and Attorney General* [1996] ECR I–3953; [1996] CMLR 257; Case C–124/95, *The Queen v HM Treasury and Bank of England, ex parte Centro–Com Srl* [1997] ECR I–81; Case C–177/95, *Ebony Maritime SA and Loten Navigation Ltd v Prefetto della Provinzia die Brindisi and Ministero dell'Interno* [1997] ECR I–1111; [1997] 2 CMLR 24.

[135] Case C–162/96, *A Racke GmbH v Hauptzollamt Mainz* [1998] ECR I–3655.

[136] Case C–174/95, *Svenska Jornalistförbundet v Council* [1998] ECR II–2289; Case T–194/94, *John Carvel and The Guardian Newspaper Ltd v European Council* [1995] ECR II–2765.

[137] Case C–170/96, *Commission v Council (the 'Airport Transit Visa Case')* [1998] ECR I–2763.

[138] Case C–314/85, *Firma Foto–Frost v Hauptzollamt Lübeck–Ost* [1987] ECR 4199, [1988] CMLR 57.

[139] Wessel, *Foreign and Security Policy*, above n 74, at 224.

for example, annul parts of a CFSP decision that could harm the *acquis communautaire.*[140] Within these limits the Kirchberg could be called the Court of Justice of the EU.[141] Moreover, the Court decides on the borderlines of Community law by the scrutiny exercised over the public security exemptions, for example Article 30 EC,[142] the national security exemptions Article 296 and 297 EC,[143] and similar exemptions in secondary Community law which will be discussed in detail in Part II of this book.

Nevertheless, the jurisdiction of the European Court of Justice is limited: most importantly it does not extend to decision making within the CFSP, there is no judicial scrutiny over the legal basis or the procedure for CFSP decisions, no Member State or EU institution can bring proceedings against these decisions, and the consistency requirement in Article 3 TEU is excluded from judicial scrutiny. This means that the rule of law does not apply to the CFSP as no judicial body has the power to scrutinise measures taken within the scope of the CFSP. This follows tradition, since Article 31 SEA also excluded EPC matters from the jurisdiction of the Court. Therefore it could be said that, in addition to the 'democratic deficit' discussed above, the CFSP suffers form a 'rule of law deficit'. The development and consolidation of the rule of law is one of the objectives of the CFSP according to Article 11 TEU. This amounts to a considerable contradiction: one of the three basic values of the EU, the rule of law, is to be promoted by the CFSP without applying to it.

Apart from the aim of the Member States to avoid the development of a body of EU law through judicial activism, the reduced role of the Court as a supranational institution is also a reflection of the intergovernmental character of the CFSP. Moreover, in the context of many democracies judicial scrutiny over foreign affairs and security is often reduced up to the point of judicial deference.[144] Moreover, as the 1991 Dutch Draft Treaty and the scrutiny of the borderlines outlined above show, the exclusion of CFSP from the jurisdiction of the Maastricht and Amsterdam Treaties might not be the last word.

3.4. The Western European Union

The WEU features prominently in the Maastricht and Amsterdam Treaties. Article 17 (1) subparagraph 2 TEU (ex Article J.7) recognises the WEU as "an integral part of the development of the Union providing the Union with access to an operational capability, notably in the context of" the Petersberg Tasks stipulated in

[140] Eaton, above n 34, at 221 and S Peers, 'National Security and European Law' (1996) 15 *Yearbook of European Law* 363, at 398–99.

[141] Curtin and Dekker, above n 33, at 27; DM Curtin and RH van Ooik, 'Denmark and the Edinburgh Summit: Maastricht without Tears' in O'Keefe and Twomey, above n 34, 349.

[142] For example: Case C–72/83, *Campus Oil Limited v Minister for Industry and Energy* [1984] *ECR* 2727, see ch 4 for details.

[143] In particular: Case C–414/97, *Commission v Spain* [1999] ECR I–5585, see ch 5 for details.

[144] See in particular TM Franck, *Political Questions/Juridical Answers: Does the Rule of Law Apply to Foreign Affairs?* (Princeton University Press, Princeton, 1992) discussing the USA, the United Kingdom, and Germany.

Article 17 (2) TEU. It was to support the EU in "framing the defence aspects of the [CFSP] as set out in [Article 17 TEU]". The importance of the WEU was further emphasised in the defining Article 17 (1) subparagraph 1 TEU which stipulated that the security component of the CFSP would be "in accordance with the second subparagraph" on the WEU. Moreover, this is emphasised in the Declaration on Western European Union annexed to the Final Act of the Maastricht Intergovernmental Conference.[145] Close institutional relations with the WEU were envisaged[146] and the possibility of the future integration of the WEU into the EU was expressly stipulated. The WEU was to develop into the defence arm of the EU. In this context the WEU was to support the EU in framing the defence aspects of the common foreign and security policy.

According to Article 17 (3) TEU the EU would "avail itself of the WEU to elaborate and implement decisions and actions of the [EU] which have defence implications". The European Council would have the competence to establish guidelines in the sense of Article 13 TEU with respect to matters in which the EU would avail itself of the WEU. In such cases all Member States would have the right to participate fully in the task in question. The Council in agreement with the respective institutions of the WEU would adopt the necessary practical arrangements to allow all Member States contributing to the task in question to participate fully and on an equal footing in planning and decision-making in the WEU. Hence the question of European defence capabilities, as the most important aspect of what a common defence or common defence policy would add to the security aspects of foreign policy, would take place in the framework of the WEU. This arrangement, and in particular the complex formula in Article J.4 (1) TEU, was a solution suggested by the Belgian delegation to reconcile the positions of the Member States which advocated a common defence, such as France, with those who opposed it, such as the United Kingdom.[147]

The reaction of the WEU is contained in the Declaration on the role of the WEU, adopted in Maastricht and annexed to the 1991 Final Act.[148] According to this Declaration it "is prepared, at the request of the [EU], to elaborate and implement decisions and actions of the [EU] which have defence implications". Moreover the Declaration contains the objective to build up the WEU in stages as the defence arm of the EU. This represents a commitment to respond positively to an EU "avail", although it would do so only on a case-by-case basis[149] and the Maastricht and Amsterdam versions of the TEU did not contain a formal legal

[145] (1992) 31 ILM 370.

[146] Co-operation between the presidencies of the EU and the WEU, the General-Secretariats of the Council and the WEU, and the synchronisation of dates and places of meetings.

[147] E Remacle, 'La politique étrangère et de sécurité commun de l'Union européenne après Maastricht' in M Thelò, (ed), *Vers une nouvelle Europe?* (Edites Européennes, Brussels, 1992) 239, at 242, as cited by Wessel, 'Black Widow', above n 13, at 414.

[148] *Declaration on the Role of the WEU*, Maastricht, December 1991, in A Bloed and RA Wessel, *The Changing Functions of the Western European Union: Introduction and Basic Documents* (Kluwer, The Hague, 1994) Doc 28.

[149] Wessel, 'Black Widow', above n 13, at 406; *Foreign and Security Policy*, above n 75, at 132.

obligation on the WEU to react positively.[150] However, it has been argued that the Declaration in conjunction with Article 17 (1) 2 and (3) TEU established an obligation on the WEU to react positively to an EU request.[151] The practice seems to confirm this interpretation as the WEU always responded positively to requests made by the EU.[152] Moreover, most WEU member States are also Member States of the EU. This made a negative reaction very unlikely.

Read together, Article 17 TEU and the Declaration of the WEU attached to it formed an agreement between the two organisations, the EU and WEU. This relationship is further regulated by a document entitled *Relations between the Union and the WEU*, which was adopted by the General Affairs Council on 26 October 1993 and accepted by the WEU Council on 22 November of the same year.[153] The two organisations were under a clear obligation to co-operate in clearly identified fields on the basis of this document. Therefore, the document can be considered as an international agreement,[154] although this interpretation is controversial.[155]

Theoretically, the EU-WEU arrangement was unreliable. The EU Council had to rely on another organisation for the implementation of the CFSP with regards to matters having defence implications. After a decision was taken in the EU Council and a request was made to the WEU, the autonomous decision-making procedures of the autonomous WEU had to be followed before the practical implementation of the EU policy could go ahead. Moreover, it was not possible to link the decision-making processes of the two organisations.[156] Crucial elements of the policy, parts of the decision-making process and the actual implementation, had to be conducted outside the EU. These elements were linked to but not integrated in the Union. Disruptions of the link were thinkable. In theory, the mere possibility of disruptions already questions the coherence and effectiveness of the policy. Furthermore, it was not purely an EU policy but a combined EU and WEU policy and therefore only of limited utility to help the EU to assert its place on the

[150] Wessel, above; L Münch, 'Die Gemeinsame Außen—und Sicherheitspolitik (GASP): ein Schaf im Wolfspelz?' (1997) 57 *Zeitschrift für Ausländisches Öffentliches Recht und Völkerrecht* 389, at 410; Th. Jürgens, *Die Gemeinsame Außen– und Sicherheitspolitik* (Carl Heyermanns Verlag, Cologne, 1994) 369.

[151] Wessel, 'Black Widow', above, at 407; *The European Union's Foreign and Security Policy*, above, at 285.

[152] For example by contributing the police contingent to the EU administration of Mostar.

[153] Annex IV of Chapter IV of the document on the implementation of the Maastricht Treaty, Brussels European Council, 29 October 1993, Conclusions of the Presidency. Also published as Document 1412 of the WEU Assembly, 8 April 1994.

[154] See Article 2 of the Vienna Convention on the Law of Treaties between States and International Organisations or between International Organisations, 1155 UNTS 331: 'Treaty [is...] an international agreement governed by international law and concluded in written form [...] whether that agreement is embodied in a single instrument or in two or more related instruments and whatever its particular designation.' Supporting this interpretation: Trüe, above n 33, at 55; JA Frowein, 'Die Europäische Union mit WEU als Sicherheitssystem' in O Due, *et al*, (eds), *Festschrift für Ulrich Everling* (Nomos Verlagsgesellschaft, Baden-Baden, 1995) 313, at 323; Wessel, 'Black Widow', above n 13, at 409.

[155] N Neuwahl, 'A Partner with a Troubled Personality: EU Treaty-Making in Matters of CFSP and CJA after Amsterdam' (1999) 2 *European Foreign Affairs Review* 177, at 180.

[156] According to Annex I to Council-Decision 1999/404/CFSP this is due to the 'specific features of each crisis situation' and 'the need to facilitate very rapid reaction'.

international scene. However, all of the then ten WEU member States were represented in the EU Council and therefore involved in making the request in the first place.[157] This made a negative reaction unlikely. Moreover, in case the request was made on the basis of a unanimous decision in the EU Council, a vote against it in the WEU Council might have amounted to a violation of international law in the form of estoppel. As the use of the WEU for the implementation of the CFSP in practice remained rather limited, there is no long list of successful missions that could prove the success of the EU-WEU arrangements under Maastricht and Amsterdam.[158] The co-operation of the two organisations regarding the administration of Mostar in Bosnia and Herzegovina in 1994 was not based on the then Article J.4 TEU since no defence issues were involved. The WEU contribution concerned police work. Council-Decision 1996/670/CFSP on the Joint Action of the Union in the African Great Lakes Region was based on Article J.4 TEU. However, it contained merely a request to the EU "to examine [...] how it can [...] contribute to the optimum use of the operational resources available", in other words, how it could contribute to the Joint Action.[159] In 1998, the EU Council requested the WEU to implement a Council-Decision on mine clearance in Croatia on the basis of Article 17 (3) TEU.[160] This indicates the will of the EU to use the provision in a more substantial way. Generally it seems appropriate to 'test' a still new mechanism with modest requests before using the WEU to the full. Nevertheless, Article 17 (3) TEU and the WEU Maastricht Declaration were never used to an extent that would prove them as a sufficient mechanism for an EU defence policy.

The EU-WEU rapprochement[161] can be interpreted as a first step towards overcoming the separation of defence integration from the mainstream of European integration discussed in chapter 1.[162] The WEU and the CFSP would be combined and developed together. Moreover, through the single institutional structure and more generally through the requirement of consistency the WEU as part of the CFSP was drawn even closer to the mainstream of integration within the Community. However, the envisaged integration of the WEU into the Second more intergovernmental Pillar of the TEU can also be seen as the continuation of the separation of mainstream and defence, as the CFSP stayed separate from the more supranational Community pillar. Hence Maastricht and Amsterdam were only first steps towards 're-unification'. It seems that the Article 17 (1) TEU mechanism was intended as a provisional solution. Article 17 (1) TEU introduced "the progressive framing of a

[157] Wessel, 'Black Widow', above n 13, at 410.

[158] The following examples are based on Wessel, 'Black Widow', above.

[159] See also Joint Action 96/588/CFSP of 1 October 1996 and Joint Action 97/817/CFSP of 28 November 1997 on anti-personnel landmines, where the Council states that the Union 'shall retain the option of having recourse to the [WEU]' Common Position 97/356/CFSP of 2 June 1997 on conflict prevention and resolution in Africa, where the Union only announced that it will forward a request to the WEU when defence implications become apparent.

[160] Council-Decision 98/547/CFSP of 22 September 1998.

[161] Wessel, 'Black Widow', above n 13, at 410.

[162] At 44–49.

common defence policy" in accordance with Article 17 (2) subparagraph 2 TEU which made the WEU an integral part of the development of the Union. Hence the arrangement in Article 17 (3) TEU was only a stage in an evolutionary process, which is outlined in Article 17 (1) TEU. The future evolution of European defence integration was enshrined in the Treaties of Maastricht and Amsterdam. It was envisaged that the paragraph 3-arrangement may evolve into another arrangement within the evolving defence policy. The possible final stage of this evolutionary process was also stipulated in Article 17 (1) TEU: as it "might lead to a common defence". A common defence would probably include an autonomous military capability that would make arrangements with the WEU unnecessary. Therefore it is submitted that the Article 17 (3) TEU arrangement was intended as a provisional solution. Nevertheless, it should be emphasised that the Maastricht and Amsterdam versions of the TEU did not envisage an independent EU military capability.

3.5. The Requirement of NATO and UN Compatibility

According to Article 17 (1) subparagraph 3 part 2 TEU the EU "shall respect the obligations of certain Member States, which see their common defence realised in [NATO]". The CFSP had to "be compatible with the common security and defence policy established within the NATO framework." This requirement of compatibility with the Washington Treaty and NATO obligations in general amounts to a priority of established NATO policy over the CFSP in the event of a conflict between norms.[163] This rule was reinforced in Article 17 (3) subparagraph 4 TEU according to which decisions having defence implications dealt with under this Article had to be taken without prejudice to the policies and obligations under NATO. There never was a conflict between NATO policies and the CFSP during the lifetime of the Maastricht and Amsterdam Treaties.

According to Article 103 UN Charter "in the event of a conflict between the obligations of the members of the United Nations under the present Charter and their obligations under any other international agreement, their obligations under the present Charter shall prevail". The TEU recognises the principles of the UN Charter in Article 11 (1) hyphen 3 (ex Article J.1.) TEU. Therefore there is also a requirement of UN Charter compatibility. The TEU needs to be compatible with NATO and both need to be compatible with the UN Charter. NATO and UN compatibility are not new requirements: the European Defence Community Treaty discussed in chapter 1 also adhered to these principles. The European security and defence architecture has always been built on the United Nations and NATO.

3.6. Neutral Member States, Nuclear Powers, Denmark, and Closer Co-operation

The Maastricht and Amsterdam versions of the TEU also provided a number of special arrangements with respect to some Member States. According to Article 17

[163] Münch, above n 150, at 404; Wessel, *Foreign and Security Policy*, above n 75, at 137 and 290.

(1) subparagraph 3 part 1 TEU the policy of the EU shall not prejudice the specific character of the security and defence policy of certain Member States. This provision, originally included to accommodate Ireland's traditional policy of neutrality,[164] gained in importance with the accession of the neutral Member States Austria, Finland, and Sweden in 1995.[165] However, the provision did not mention neutrality and was not restricted to it.[166] The United Kingdom and France could also have invoked it in their capacity as nuclear powers[167] or as permanent members of the UN Security Council.

Section C of the *Decision of the Heads of State and Government meeting within the European Council, concerning certain problems raised by Denmark on the Treaty on European Union* provides "Denmark does not participate in the elaboration and the implementation of decisions and actions of the Union which have defence implications, but will not prevent the development of closer cooperation between Member States in this area."[168] The legal nature of this Decision was disputed[169] and the Member States denied that it had Treaty status.[170] The effect of this arrangement, which is a reaction to the rejection of the Maastricht Treaty by the Danes in a referendum, held on 2 June 1992, is that Denmark remained outside the CFSP with regards to decisions having defence implications. It would not take part in decision-making and would not contribute to the financing of operations in cases where the EU would avail itself of the WEU.

Article 17 (4) TEU (ex Article J.7) declared 'closer co-operation' in the field covered by the defence component of the CFSP between two or more Member States as generally compatible with the TEU. This could happen on a bilateral level or within the NATO or WEU frameworks. However, the paragraph also included the reservation that this kind of closer co-operation was not to run counter to or impede the CFSP. Examples for such closer co-operation between two or more Member States on a bilateral level during the lifetime of the Maastricht and Amsterdam Treaties were the multilateral defence co-operation frameworks like the Dutch-German Corps in Münster, the Euro Corps in Strasbourg,[171] or the Organisation for Joint Armaments Co-operation (OCCAR) in Bonn.[172]

[164] Wessel, *Foreign and Security Policy*, above n 75, at 136.

[165] Declaration of Austria, Finland and Sweden annexed to the Final Act adopted on the occasion of their Accession, see Fink-Hooijer, above n 30, at 197.

[166] Münch, above n 150, at 403–4; Wessel, above n 75, at 136.

[167] Above.

[168] Part B of the Presidency Conclusions at the European Council at Edinburgh, 11–12 December 1992, [1992] OJ C–348/1.

[169] For a clarification agreement and agreement in the sense of Article 31 of the Vienna Convention on the Law of Treaties (VCLT): the United Kingdom Government according to D Howarth, 'The Compromise on Denmark and the Treaty on European Union: A Legal and Political Analysis' (1994) 31 *Common Market Law Review* 765, at 772; for an international agreement in simplified form: Curtin and van Ooik, above n 141, at 356; for a reservation in the sense of Article 19 VCLT: Münch, above n 150, at 405; for a subsequent agreement between the parties regarding the interpretation of the treaty or the application of its provisions according to Article 31(2)(a) VCLT: Wessel, *Foreign and Security Policy*, above n 75, at 139.

[170] Howarth, above, at 778.

[171] Wessel, *Foreign and Security Policy*, above n 75, at 140.

[172] See ch 7 at 224 for details.

3.7. The Budget

The budgetary provisions of the TEU relating to the CFSP distinguished between administrative expenditure and operational expenditure on the one hand and operational expenditure for defence operations on the other hand. According to Article 28 (2) and (3) TEU (ex Article J.18) the administrative and operational expenditure of the institutions would be charged to the budget of the EC, which necessitated the establishment and specific and permanent line for this purpose in the Community budget.[173] Hence Article 28 TEU establishes an incremental 'EU defence budget' which is actually a 'Community defence budget'. This is the first time since the EDC that such a budget, in whatever form, was on the agenda.

The TEU gave the European Parliament at least some control over the implementation of the CFSP as it had the competence to adopt the Community budget and could amend or even reject CFSP expenses.[174] However, it could also be argued that the Parliament implicitly agreed to the budgetary implications of the CFSP when it was consulted and informed by the Presidency in advance. As discussed above, the CFSP did not attribute a prominent role to the European Parliament and therefore arguably suffers from a democratic deficit. Nevertheless, it would go too far to attribute to Parliament a decisive influence over the decision making process with regards to the CFSP through the backdoor of a competence attributed to it in the context of the Community Pillar of the TEU.[175]

According to Article 28 (3) TEU operational expenditure arising from operations having military or defence implications and in cases where the Council unanimously decided accordingly, would be charged to the Member States. Member States who made a formal declaration on qualified abstention in the Council under Article 23 (1) TEU (ex Article J.13),[176] would not be obliged to contribute to the financing of expenditure arising from operations having military or defence implications. This special treatment of defence and military operations was necessary, as the Community did not have the resources to fund such operations. However, it also reinforces the more intergovernmental character of operations conducted in the framework of the CFSP.

Together with the legally binding character of decisions and the operational capability to implement them, the financing of the CFSP was a crucial aspect for its success. The financing through the more supranational Community budget rather than intergovernmental individual Member States' contributions added to the new identity on the international scene the CFSP aimed to establish. However, adding to the tasks to be financed through the Community budget without adding to the size of the same budget had considerable negative potential. Problems finding the funds in the Community budget for CFSP action could undermine the effectiveness of the CFSP. Over-stretching the Community budget

[173] Fink-Hooijer, above n 30, at 184.
[174] Marauhn, above n 24, at 94; Fink-Hooijer, above.
[175] Fink-Hooijer, above n 30, at 185.
[176] With the effect that the decision of the Council commits the EU but not the abstaining Member State.

to finance CFSP could undermine the Community Pillar. Ultimately it will be unavoidable to increase the Community budget except by increasing the income of the Community. A veritable 'Union defence budget' will become necessary should the EU develop its own military capability. This can be achieved through a new source of independent income or through higher Member State contributions. Higher Member State contributions do not necessarily mean higher defence budgets as the higher contributions can be financed through cuts in the individual defence budgets of the Member States.

3.8. The Requirement of Coherence

In the Treaties of Maastricht and Amsterdam the principle of consistency[177] was enshrined in Articles 1 (ex A),[178] 3 (ex C), and 13 paragraph 3 (ex J.3)[179] TEU. According to Article 3 (1) TEU "a single institutional framework shall ensure the consistency and the continuity of the activities carried out in order to attain the objectives while respecting and building on the *acquis communautaire*". According to Article 3 (2) TEU this is particularly important with regards to external activities where external relations, security, economic- and development policies have to be co-ordinated to form a consistent approach. Council and Commission shall co-operate to fulfil their responsibility to ensure this consistency and the implementation of these policies, in accordance with their respective powers. In addition, a number of other provisions in the TEU were aimed at ruling out inconsistency.[180] Articles 11 (2),[181] 14 (3)[182] and (7),[183] 15,[184] and 19[185] TEU concerned the relations between the EU and its Member States and tried to anticipate or rule out inconsistencies.

Krenzler and Schneider define consistency in relation to the CFSP as "coordinated, coherent behaviour based on agreement among the Union and its Member

[177] See on the discussion in general: C Tietje, 'The Concept of Coherence in the Treaty on European Union and the CFSP' (1997) 2 *European Foreign Affairs Review* 211; U Schmalz, 'The Amsterdam Provisions on External Coherence: Bridging the Union's Foreign Policy Dualism?' (1998) 3 *European Foreign Affairs Review* 421.

[178] Article 1(3) sentence 2 TEU reads: '[The Union's] task shall be to organise, in a manner demonstrating consistency and solidarity, relations between the Member States and between their peoples.'

[179] Article 13(3) subpara 3 TEU reads: 'The Council shall ensure the unity, consistency and effectiveness of action by the Union.'

[180] N Neuwahl, above n 34, 227, at 124; Wessel, *Foreign and Security Policy*, above n 75, at 297.

[181] Article 11(2)(ex J1) TEU reads: 'The Member States shall support the Union's external and security policy {and they] shall refrain from any action which is contrary to the interests of the Union or likely to impair its effectiveness as a cohesive force in international relations.'

[182] Article 14(3)(ex J4) TEU reads: 'Joint actions shall commit the Member States in the positions they adopt and in the conduct of their activity.'

[183] Article 14(7)(ex J4) TEU reads: 'Should there be any major difficulties in implementing a joint action, a Member State shall refer them to the Council which shall discuss them and seek appropriate solutions.'

[184] Article 15(ex J5) TEU reads: 'Member States shall ensure that their national policies conform to the common positions.'

[185] Article 19(ex J9) TEU reads: 'Member States shall coordinate their action in international organisations and international conferences.'

States, where comparable and compatible methods are used in pursuit of a single objective and result in an uncontradictory (foreign) policy".[186] According to Nuttall the principle of consistency has three elements or layers.[187] First, there is a requirement of non-contradiction: the various policies on a similar matter should not contradict each other. This refers to the substance of different actions. For example, economic sanctions and development aid for the same country will normally contradict each other. Second, there is a requirement for interaction between services for a common and overriding purpose. This refers to organisational consistency and includes co-ordination, transparency and communication.[188] For example, the administration and decision makers for sanctions have to know what their counterparts in charge of development aid are doing. Third, there is a requirement for a bureaucratic and political hierarchy. To continue the example on sanctions and economic aid, there should be an administrative and political layer above the decision makers on sanctions and aid. This layer should be in charge of the overall external policy definition, should co-ordinate the different aspects of external policy, and have the power to override decisions of the hierarchically lower sanctions and aid layers. Ideally all aspects of external policy are based on the same legal document, authorising one organisation, with one single executive body to oversee all external action. Sanctions and aid, for example, are only departments of that single executive body. Most States, including the Member States, have organised their foreign policy on this basis.

Consistency is related to coherence.[189] However, as Missiroli pointed out, there are differences between the two terms: consistency only means absence of contradiction whereas coherence should also lead to synergy and added value.[190] This leads to another related notion: a coherent EU external policy is assumed to be more efficient and effective than 15 or 25 separate Member States' external policies. An inconsistent and incoherent EU will not add any value to 25 separate Member State policies. *Prima facie* this seems convincing. In 2001 the United States Department of State, for example, had 15,000 staff and less than 300 missions compared to 40,000 staff and 1,500 missions of the foreign ministries of the then 15 Member States and the EU external action services taken together. Nevertheless, the USA exerts more influence in international affairs than the EU and its then 15 Member States.[191] The concept of coherence allows different degrees, a concept of law can be more or less coherent, whereas consistency is a

[186] HG Krenzler and HC Schneider, 'Die Gemeinsame Außen—und Sicherheitspolitik der Europäischen Union—Zur Frage der Kohärenz' (1994) 29 *Europarecht* 144–61; 'The Question of Consistency' in Regelsberger, de Schoutheete de Tervarent and Wessels, above n 122, at 133–52.

[187] SJ Nuttall, *European Foreign Policy* (OUP, Oxford, 2000) at 25.

[188] See for example *Effectiveness of the Union's External Action: Conclusions*, General Affairs Council, Luxembourg, 9 October 2000, at http://ue.eu.int/Newsroom.

[189] The French text of the TEU uses the term *cohérence* and the German text the word *Kohärenz*, both terms actually mean coherence and not consistency. The Italian *coerenza*, Spanish *coherencia*, Portuguese *coerência*, Dutch *samenhangend* and Danish *samenhæng* are similar terms.

[190] A Missiroli, 'European Security Policy: The Challenge of Coherence' (2001) 6 *European Foreign Affairs Review* 177, at 182.

[191] Example taken from Missiroli, above, at 179.

static concept: a concept of law is either consistent or not.[192] A measure not meeting the requirements of consistency could be invalid whereas the concept of coherence allows a more balanced assessment. This balanced assessment is necessary because the CFSP is evolving: what was considered sufficiently coherent in 1992 might not be considered sufficiently coherent today. For this reason and because most versions of the TEU use the word 'coherence' rather than 'consistency', the earlier should be used when analysing Second Pillar measures in relation to external action on the basis of other legal bases.[193]

As will be explained below and in further chapters, coherence is a challenge for the non-inclusive CFSP. Vertically, the continued presence and strong position of the individual Member States in foreign policy compared to the EU, and possibly the more intergovernmental nature of the CFSP,[194] have the potential to lead to fragmentation. Competence for external action is not only a matter for the CFSP, but is contained in all three pillars.[195] The special competencies for First and Third Pillar external action override the general Second Pillar competence for foreign policy.[196] This *lex specialis* principle continues the regime governing the EPC according to which the powers retained by the Member States must be exercised in a manner consistent with Community law.[197] Therefore, horizontally, the three-pillar structure leading, amongst other things, to a split of responsibility for external action over several institutions, can undermine coherence as well. Horizontal fragmentation is increased by the fact that defence integration is also taking place in international organisations outside the already fragmented three-Pillar structure of the EU, most notably within NATO. The use of the WEU for the implementation of the CFSP with regards to defence implication under the Maastricht and Amsterdam Treaties is another aspect of horizontal fragmentation. During a joint exercise in June 1998 the WEU and the EU tested the Amsterdam provisions. 25 different procedural steps were needed to manage an international crisis. Up to 45 steps were needed when NATO assets were to be used.[198] These procedural steps

[192] Tietje, above n 176, at 212–13.

[193] Wessel, *Foreign and Security Policy*, above n 75, at 297.

[194] Former President of the Commission Romano Prodi, speech before the European Parliament, Strasbourg, 3 October 2000, at http://www.europa.eu.int/rapid/start. Former Commissioner Chris Patten, speech to the International and Foreign Relations Institute, Paris, 15 June 2001, at http://www.europa.eu.int/comm./external_relations.

[195] First Pillar: economic sanctions, association agreements, trade policy, monetary issues, development co-operation, visa policy, immigration and asylum issues, education, vocational training, culture, public health, trans-European networks, research and technical development, and the environment. Third Pillar: external border issues, international organised crime, trafficking in persons and offences against children, illicit drugs or arms trafficking, corruption and fraud.

[196] Wessel, *Foreign and Security Policy*, above n 75, at 295.

[197] Joined Cases C–6/69 and 11/69, *Commission v France* [1969] ECR 523, at para 17; Case C–57/86, *Greece v Commission* [1988] ECR 2855, at para 9; Case C–129/87, *Commission v Greece* [1988] ECR 3333, at para 7; Case C–221/89, *R v secretary of State for Transport, ex parte Factortame* [1991] ECR I–3905, at para 14. See also the Preamble to the SEA: '[Europe needs] to aim at speaking ever increasingly with one voice to act with consistency and solidarity in order more effectively to protect its common interests' and Article 30(5) SEA: '[the] external policies of the European Community and the policies agreed in the European Political Cooperation (EPC) must be consistent'.

[198] WEU CM (98) 39, Modus Operandi of Article J4.2/Article 17.3 and Flow Chart (13 November 1998).

take time and effort. Moreover, only in an ideal word will they be taken without delay. The crisis situation can change faster than it takes to implement 45 procedural steps and those who caused the crisis will be less than impressed by the pace of the reaction of the EU. Therefore efficiency and effectiveness can seriously be undermined by this lack of horizontal coherence.

The principle of coherence shall be addressed again in the final two chapters on the background of the discussion of the fragmentation of European defence integration discussed in the remainder of the book.

4. THE RECORD OF THE COMMON FOREIGN AND SECURITY POLICY UNDER THE TREATIES OF MAASTRICHT AND AMSTERDAM

The record of the CFSP under the Maastricht and Amsterdam Treaties has to be assessed on the basis of the coherence, independence, and ultimately the success of measures taken in response to a major crisis. The major crises during the lifetime of the Maastricht and Amsterdam Treaties were the conflicts resulting from the dissolution of the SFR Yugoslavia. This included the war between Croatia and Serbia, the civil war in Bosnia and Herzegovina, and the Kosovo conflict. As these conflicts erupted on the European continent they are clearly within the responsibility the EU made the world believe it was determined to shoulder. The dissolution of the Soviet Union and Czechoslovakia also took place during this period. However, the parties involved were quite capable of handling the situations responsibly without help from the EU.

Regarding the initial dissolution of the SFR Yugoslavia starting in summer 1991, the response of the Member States of the then European Community had to be co-ordinated within the EPC framework. The instruments available at the time did not suffice to produce a coherent response that might have prevented the eruption of violence. Slovenia and Macedonia seceded with only limited hostilities between their forces and the Federal Yugoslav Army. For Croatia, however, 1991 marks the start of a long war of independence and also a classical war on borders with the new Federal Republic of Yugoslavia, consisting of Serbia and Montenegro.

The introduction of the CFSP in 1992 brought the 'Common Position' as an instrument to respond to the conflict. However, this required the political will to produce a unified approach. The lack of such unity, due primarily to differences in the assessment of the most appropriate means to deal with the conflict, prevented a decision from being reached which might have prevented an escalation of violence.[199]

Therefore it is a means which is suited to a long-term policy approach, as well as to responding quickly to a sudden political crisis. Yet, it is not surprising that in the initial phase the EU appeared to be concentrating on more restricted actions, such as support for the elections in Russia and South Africa, and providing

[199] Fink-Hooijer, above n 30, at 180.

humanitarian aid to Bosnia and Herzegovina, which build upon earlier initiatives and do not entail the risk of failure or a loss of face.[200]

5. CONCLUSIONS

By the turn of the 21st century European defence integration was firmly back on the agenda. However, the Maastricht and Amsterdam Treaties see the 's' of security only as an extension of the 'f' for foreign policy and a 'd' for defence as an area only to be developed in the future. The TEU set high objectives. According to the Preamble and Article 2 the EU should assert its identity on the international scene, but the three-Pillar structure positioning the CFSP in a separate intergovernmental Pillar prevented in many cases the emergence of a coherent and effective foreign policy. The EU would have to rethink the three-Pillar structure and the strict intergovernmental nature of the CFSP. According to the Preamble the CFSP was to reinforce EU independence, but the implementation of foreign policy decisions having defence implications was impossible without the EU availing itself to the WEU. Moreover, the military capabilities of the Member States did not allow military action without drawing on NATO assets. The EU would have to rethink the integration of the WEU and Member States would have to invest in their military capabilities. According to the Preamble and Article 11, the CFSP was to promote peace, security and progress in Europe and in the world, but the CFSP proved insufficient to react adequately to the lack of peace, security and progress caused by the break-up of the SFR Yugoslavia, a neighbouring region of the Union. The EU would have to start thinking about the development of an autonomous military capability. According to Article 11 the EU was to develop and consolidate democracy, the rule of law, and respect for human rights and fundamental freedoms, but the rule of law and the democracy principle do not apply to the CFSP itself. Judicial scrutiny through the European Court of Justice and parliamentary scrutiny through the European Parliament would have to be introduced or improved in order to establish a credible CFSP.

The lack of an independent EU military capability made it difficult if not impossible to back up a coherent policy with a Petersberg type peacekeeping or peacemaking action. Proposals regarding such a capability marked the beginning of the next chapter of European defence integration.

[200] Above, at 181.

3

Between Saint-Malo and a New Rome: The Current State of European Defence and Security Integration 1998–2005

1. INTRODUCTION

THIS CHAPTER CONTINUES the story told in chapters 1 and 2 up to 2005. Hence it provides a discussion of the current state of European defence and security integration with regards to what currently is the Second Pillar of the Treaty on European Union (hereinafter TEU). The current state can be described as a 'moving target'. This is mainly due to the fact that the European Union (hereinafter EU) is currently in the middle of a process possibly leading to a new Constitutional Treaty. After the envisaged passing of this Constitutional Treaty had failed at the Brussels Summit in December 2003,[1] the now 25 Heads of State and Government finally agreed on a slightly amended Draft during another Brussels Summit on 18th June 2004.[2] The final text was signed on 29th October 2004 in Rome.[3] Its entering into force is not certain since this depends on national referenda in several Member States which are scheduled for 2005 and 2006. The Constitutional Treaty includes significant changes to the existing framework of the TEU in the version agreed in Nice in late 2000, including amendments to the defence and security structure. Most importantly, it aims to overcome the current

[1] See *Declaration of the President*, Conference of the Representatives of the Governments of the Member States, Brussels, 13 December 2003, in A Missiroli, *From Copenhagen to Brussels: European Defence: Core Documents*, Chaillot Paper No 67, (Institute of Security Studies of the European Union, Paris, 2003), at 456 (hereinafter 'Core Documents'). Changes were inserted by the meeting, see: Document CIG 84/04. Changes relevant to the subject matter of this chapter occurred in Articles III-322–329.

[2] 'EU Leaders Reach Deal on Constitution' *Financial Times*, 21 June 2004; 'Public Don't Want any Part of It: Europe's Leaders Reach Agreement, But the Debate Rages On', *Guardian*, 21 June 2004; 'Constitution et Désunion' editorial, *Le Monde*, 20 June 2004; 'EU Gipfel: Europa mit neuer Verfassung–Prodi ohne Nachfolger', *Frankfurter Allgemeine Zeitung*, 19 June 2004.

[3] 'Leaders sign EU Treaty', *Financial Times*, 30 October 2004; 'Krönung des Einigungsprozesses', *Frankfurter Allgemeine Zeitung*, 29 October 2004; 'Le'Europe de 25 a Singé sa Constitution et Cherche sa Nouvelle Commission', *Le Monde*, 29 October 2004.

three-Pillar structure of the Union discussed in chapter 2.[4] As the outcome of the referenda mentioned above is far from certain the Constitutional Treaty belongs to the future rather than the history or present 'state' of European defence and security integration and will therefore be discussed in Part III.

Chapter 3 completes Part I on the evolution of European defence integration. Together the three chapters will facilitate the understanding of Part II, which deals with the contribution of Community law to the process of European defence integration. Part I provides the context for Part II. Furthermore, chapter 3 represents a link to Part III on the Constitutional Treaty consisting of chapters 10, 11, and 12.

This chapter is divided into three main sections. The first section deals with the developments that let to and immediately preceded the legal framework of European defence integration currently in force. This legal framework, the 2000 Nice version of the TEU, will be covered in the second section. The Treaty of Nice is not only important as a crucial chapter in the evolution of European defence and security integration. It will also be its legal foundation until the implementation process of the Constitutional Treaty is completed. Moreover, as it is not entirely unlikely that this implementation process will fail, the Treaty of Nice might be in force for longer than anticipated. The discussion will highlight the differences and innovations compared to the Maastricht and Amsterdam versions discussed in chapter 2. Moreover, the analysis will cover the shortcomings of the Treaty of Nice with regards to security and defence. The third and last section will discuss the developments between the Treaty of Nice and the Constitutional Treaty to provide the link between chapter 3 and Part III of this book.

2. TOWARDS A EUROPEAN SECURITY AND DEFENCE POLICY

The transition from the limited defence component of the Common Foreign and Security Policy (hereinafter CFSP) discussed in chapter 2 to a European Security and Defence Policy (hereinafter ESDP) occurred through a political move of two Member State governments. This move was soon followed by the other governments. The following section will describe this transition thereby explaining the evolutionary step to a distinct ESDP.

2.1. The Saint-Malo Declaration

During the Franco-British summit of 3–4 December 1998 in Saint-Malo the President and Prime Minister of France and the Prime Minister of the United Kingdom agreed on a *Joint Declaration on European Defence*.[5] The declaration

[4] At 57–91.

[5] Franco-British Summit, 'Joint Declaration on European Defence: Saint-Malo', 3–4 December 1998, http://www.weu.int/eng/info/d981204a.htm. See also M Rutten, (ed), *From St-Malo to Nice, European Defence: Core Documents*, Chaillot Paper 47 (Institute of Security Studies of the Western European Union, Paris, 2001) 8.

referred directly to the CFSP and its more intergovernmental basis. In order for the EU "to be in a position to play its full role on the international stage", so Chirac and Blair stated,

> "the Union must have the capacity for *autonomous* action, backed up by credible military forces, the means to decide to use them and a readiness to do so, in order to respond to international crises [emphasis added]".

The declaration suggested nothing less but the establishment of a military force within the framework of the CFSP. Regardless of its size and organisational structure, an autonomous military force had not been on the agenda since the days of the European Defence Community and would represent a major step beyond the *acquis* of the Maastricht Treaty in force at the time. However, it should be pointed out that although an independent military capacity for the EU represents a significant innovation of security and defence policy, such a capability is inadequate if it is introduced without structural change to the basic framework of the CFSP described in chapter 2, ranging from voting procedures in the Council to new military structures. The Declaration also emphasised the importance of NATO. The EU is to act only when NATO as a whole is not involved. But in order to be able to act in such a case the EU:

> "must be given appropriate structures and a capacity for analysis of situations, sources of intelligence and a capability for relevant strategic planning, [and] will also need to have recourse to suitable military means."

This suggests the establishment of a permanent European military organisational structure, including at least temporary control of that structure over military forces. Moreover, the need for "strengthened armed forces that can react rapidly to the new risks", and "a strong and competitive European defence industry and technology" are emphasised. Therefore the Declaration calls for an autonomous and comprehensive security and defence policy within the framework of the EU that complies with NATO obligations.[6]

The summit had been a United Kingdom initiative.[7] The main reason was that the ineffectiveness of the CFSP framework described in chapter 2 was clearly

[6] See on the Declaration: A Deighton, 'The Military Security Pool: Towards a New Security Regime for Europe?' (2000) 35 *The International Spectator* 41–54; J Howorth, 'Britain, France and the European Defence Initiative' (2000) 42 *Survival* 33–55.

[7] The Prime Minister already made first allusions to a United Kingdom policy change at a press conference after an informal EU meeting of the Heads of State and government at Pörtschach (Austria) 24–25 October 1998: '[...] as Kosovo has brought home to us, it is right that Britain and other European countries, as part of Europe, play a key and leading role and that we enhance our capability to make a difference in those situations'. See Rutten, *From Saint Malo to Nice*, above n 5, p 2. The final Declaration of the Franco-German Summit in Potsdam (Germany) on 1 December 1998 had also mooted the idea of European capabilities: 'nous recherchons les voies permettant à l'Union européenne de disposer des capacités opérationelles qui lui font défault en la dotant soit des moyens européens propres', Rutten, *From Saint Malo to Nice*, above, at 4. Hence the idea of European military capabilities had been floated during the year or so before Saint Malo.

demonstrated by the failure of the Union to play a significant role in the long crisis in the Balkans of the 1990s.[8] This ineffectiveness continued to show in the Kosovo crisis.[9] Moreover, a certain frustration with the hesitant Clinton administration in particular in relation to the deployment of ground troops in Bosnia and a general rapprochement with France contributed to this change of mind.[10] However, the fact that the United Kingdom reversed her long-standing position on European defence and security was ultimately triggered by the results of a Ministry of Defence strategic review using only European forces, ordered by the Prime Minister.[11] The review concluded that in an emergency situation the EU Member States could only mobilise a very limited force, heavily dependent on the support of the USA regarding transportation, logistics, and communications. Europe simply lacks the skills and equipment for independent military action. The EU Member States spend about two-thirds of what the USA spends on defence but can only deploy about 10 per cent of what the USA can deploy.[12] Therefore the perceived necessity of the modernisation of the armed forces to equip them for new tasks is an important motive of the initiative. This modernisation will be expensive, too expensive for a purely national effort. The British Prime Minister understood that the relevant modern armed forces of the future, capable and equipped to be deployed world wide without the help of the USA, are too expensive for any single Member State of the EU.[13] The only alternative to national military dependent on the USA is a European force.[14] Another reason for the change in the British attitude was the wish to take the lead in a major European development and the possibility to sell Europe to the population of the United Kingdom.[15] Saint-Malo "triggered" a number of corresponding decisions by the EU.[16]

[8] O Croci, 'A Closer Look at the Changing Transatlantic Relationship' (2003) 8 *European Foreign Affairs Review* 469, 485–86.

[9] Above. See also Rutten, *From Saint Malo to Nice*, above n 5, in her preface at IX.

[10] See N Gnesotto, *et al*, *European Defence: A Proposal for a White Paper*, (Institute of Security Studies of the European Union, Paris, 2004) 46 (hereinafter 'White Paper').

[11] PV Howell, 'Policy Assessment Framework to Evaluate the Operational Capability of the European Union's Rapid Reaction Force (ERRF)' (paper presented at the *8th Biannual Conference of the European Union Studies Association*, Nashville, 2003).

[12] W Sandholtz and AS Sweet, (ed), *European Integration and National Governance* (OUP, New York, 1998) 259.

[13] Rutten, *From Saint Malo to Nice*, above n 5, at IX calls the British policy that followed the review a 'U-turn'.

[14] The initial response of the US administration of the day was positive, provided that the 'three D's' were avoided: (1) decoupling of Europe from the USA, (2) duplication of NATO efforts, and (3) discrimination of NATO member States that are not Member States of the EU, see US Secretary of State Madeleine K Albright, 'The Right Balance Will Secure NATO's Future', *Financial Times*, 7 December 1998. In a speech to the Annual Session of the NATO Parliamentary Assembly, Amsterdam, 15 November 1999, NATO Secretary-General Lord Robertson of Port Allen presented an alternative set of principles, the 'three I's': '[1] improvement in European defence capabilities, [2] inclusiveness and transparency for all allies, and the [3] indivisibility of Trans-Atlantic security based on shared values', (reproduced in Rutten, *From Saint Malo to Nice*, above n 5, 60 at 63).

[15] RA Wessel, 'The EU as Black Widow: Devouring the WEU to Give Birth to a European Security and Defence Policy' in V Kronenberger, (ed), *The European Union and the International Legal Order—Discord or Harmony?* (TMC Asser Press, The Hague, 2001) 405, 423 (hereinafter 'Black Widow'); RA Wessel, 'The State of Affairs in EC Security and Defence Policy: The Breakthrough in the Treaty of Nice' (2003) 8 *Journal of Conflict and Security Law* 265, 273 (hereinafter 'State of Affairs').

[16] Above.

2.2. The Cologne European Council

Six months later the Franco-British proposal of the Saint-Malo Declaration on European Defence was made an EU objective.[17] At the Cologne European Council, on 3–4 June 1999, the fifteen Heads of State or Government and the President of the Commission declared:

> "In pursuit of our Common Foreign and Security Policy, we are convinced that the Council should have the ability to take decisions on the full range of conflict prevention and crisis management tasks defined in the Treaty on European Union, the 'Petersberg Tasks.' To this end, *the Union must have the capacity for autonomous action*, backed up by credible military forces, the means to decide to use them and a readiness to do so, in order to respond to international crises without prejudice to actions by NATO. The EU will thereby increase its ability to contribute to international peace and security in accordance with the principles of the UN Charter [emphasis added]."[18]

The Cologne European Council 'Europeanised' the Franco-British Saint-Malo initiative in two ways. First, what had been the proposal of two Member States became the official policy of all the then 15 Member States. Second, the references to the 'Petersberg Tasks' and the UN Charter bring the proposal in line with the *acquis* of the CFSP. These references also limit the scope of the proposals, although these limitations where already implied in the Declaration of Saint-Malo.

Cologne also developed Saint-Malo by starting a discussion on the guiding principles of such a capacity and the decision making structures. However, it also emphasised that decisions in the Council would still be taken by unanimity:

> "Decisions relating to crisis management tasks, in particular decisions having military or defence implications, will be taken in accordance with Article 23 of the Treaty on European Union. Member States will retain in all circumstances the rights to decide if and when their national forces are deployed."[19]

So decisions were to be taken by unanimity and ultimately the Member States were to decide whether their contribution to a future European force would be deployed or not. This raises the question what Saint-Malo and Cologne mean by an 'autonomous' military capability. The word 'autonomous' implies some form

[17] Before Cologne the 11–12 December 1998 European Council in Vienna had welcomed the Declaration of Saint-Malo, see Presidency Conclusions, at point 76. A German Presidency Paper Informal Reflection at WEU on Europe's Security and Defence, Bonn, 24 February 1999, at point I 2, and a Declaration of the Franco-German Defence and Security Council on 29 May 1999 in Toulouse, had also welcomed Saint Malo, as cited by Rutten, *From Saint Malo to Nice*, above n 5, at 14 and 40 respectively. The Cologne European Council coincided with the last dates of the air campaign of the Kosovo crisis, as pointed out by Gnesotto *et al*, *White Paper*, above n 10, at 44.

[18] Declaration of the European Council on Strengthening the Common European Policy on Security and Defence, European Council Meeting in Cologne, 3–4 June 1999, at point 1 para 2, as cited by Rutten, *From Saint Malo to Nice*, above n 4, at 42–43.

[19] Above, at 44. Article 23(1) sentence 1 TEU reads: 'Decisions under this title shall be taken by the Council acting unanimously.'

of independence. The question is independence from whom or from what? In the context of the EU this can only mean independence from the Member States and this would require the possibility of decisions, including the deployment of troops, taken against the will of Member States. If decisions in the context of an EU military capability are taken by unanimity voting in the Council, the capability is not autonomous or independent from the Member States since they have a right to *veto*. As outlined in chapter 2,[20] decisions in the context of the CFSP are always taken by unanimity. Hence the new military capability is no special case. However, it is submitted that in order to establish an 'autonomous' military capability, decisions concerning this capability including its deployment have to be taken by majority voting. Therefore the implementation of the Saint-Malo and Cologne initiative requires fundamental structural changes to the Second Pillar of the TEU.

2.3. The Helsinki Headline Goal

During the Helsinki European Council of December 1999 it was agreed that Member States would co-operate voluntarily in EU-led operations. In this context Member States made a number of substantial and detailed commitments.[21] Helsinki accepted the proposals of the Anglo-French summit on 25 November 1999 in London as a policy of the EU.[22] However, the London summit did not have the same importance in relation to the Helsinki European Council as the 1998 Saint-Malo summit had on the 1999 Cologne European Council. Since the latter the development of an 'autonomous' military capability was a European policy.

First, the EU was to be able, by 2003, to deploy within 60 days and to sustain for at least one year, military forces of up to 50,000–60,000 persons or up to 15 brigades, capable of the full range of the 'Petersberg tasks'. Co-operation in EU-led operations was to be voluntary. The forces were to be militarily self-sustaining with the necessary command, control and intelligence capabilities, logistics and other combat support services and additionally, as appropriate air and navel elements.[23] The requirement to sustain a deployment for at least a year would require an additional pool of deployable units and supporting elements at lower readiness

[20] At 68–72.

[21] European Council, Presidency Conclusions: European Council Meeting in Helsinki, 10–11 December 1999, http://europa.eu.int/council/off.concl.

[22] (Anglo-French) Joint Declaration on European Defence, London, 25 November 1999, at point 5, reproduced in Rutten, *From Saint Malo to Nice*, above n 5, at 77. The plan for a Rapid Reaction Force had already been launched by the United Kingdom and France during the first ever Council of ministers for foreign affairs and ministers of defence on 15 November 1999. See: Conclusions of the General Council of 15 November 1999, Council Press Release No. 12642/99, para 4. This meeting of defence ministers itself highlights the revolution after Saint-Malo. See Wessel, 'Back Widow', above n 14, 1, at 24. The Paris Declaration of the Franco-German summit on 30 November 1999 in Paris made proposals regarding institutional structures and the transformation of the Eurocorps, at paragraphs 3 and 10, Rutten, *From Saint Malo to Nice*, above, at 80.

[23] Presidency Progress Report to the Helsinki European Council on Strengthening the Common European Policy on Security and Defence, Annex 1 to Annex IV of the Presidency Conclusions.

to provide replacement for the initial forces.[24] Hence the size of the envisaged 'European Rapid Reaction Force' (hereinafter ERRF) would actually exceed the figure of 50,000–60,000. During an informal meeting on 22 September 2000 in Ecouen (France) the defence ministers of the EU estimated that the figure would be nearer to 80,000 men.[25] The French Presidency Report at the European Council in Nice speaks of a "pool of 100,000 persons, [...] 400 combat aircraft and 100 vessels."[26] The 'Helsinki Headline Goal' lacks "detail for the purposes of military planning, raising questions such as where EC-led forces might be expected to operate, with whom, and how often."[27] This lack of detail was addressed later and will be discussed in more detail below.[28] In late 2004 the 2003 target of the Helsinki Headline Goal had not been met.[29] During the informal meeting of defence ministers in Rome in October 2003 the High Representative for the CFSP Javier Solana already implied that the Headline Goal is likely to be met only in 2010.[30] This delay[31] shows that the Helsinki Headline Goal represents a rather ambitious plan not easily put into practice considering the capability shortfalls of the armed forces of the Members States. The plan to set up 13 battle groups of 1,500 men each by 2007 with the capability of dealing with up to two crises a year agreed in November 2004[32] already represents a more modest approach.[33] However, this does not necessarily mean that the Helsinki Headline Goal has been completely replaced by this battle group solution. The latter might just be a step on the way to the earlier.

Second, new political and military bodies and structures would be established within the Council to enable the EU to ensure the necessary political guidance and strategic direction of such operations, while respecting the single institutional framework. These bodies were the standing Political and Security Committee

[24] Above.

[25] Presidency Conclusions, see Rutten, *From Saint Malo to Nice*, above n 5, 143, at 144.

[26] European Council in Nice, 7–9 December 2000, Presidency Conclusions, 4 December 2000, Annex VI Presidency Report on the European Security and Defence Policy, Annex I to Annex VI Military and Capabilities Commitment Declaration, para 4, A. Concerning forces, see Rutten, *From Saint Malo to Nice*, above, 176, at 177.

[27] 'Food for Thought' Paper, Annex Elaboration of the Headline Goal, presented at the Meeting of EU defence ministers in Sintra (Portugal), 28 February 2000, cited by Rutten, *From Saint Malo to Nice*, above n 5, 94, at 103.

[28] On the feasibility of the Helsinki Headline Goal: NATO Parliamentary Assembly Interim Report *Building European Defence: NATO's ESDI and the European Union's ESDP*, Rapporteur Van Eeklen, 5 October 2000; R de Wijk, 'Concergence Criteria: Measuring Input or Output' (2000) 5 *European Foreign Affairs Review* 397–417.

[29] Gnesotto *et al*, *White Paper*, above n 10, at 12.

[30] 'Il nous faudra développer cet horizon ensemble en vue d'un ofjectif de moyen terme pour 2010. Cette dimension temporelle nous offre le plus de possibilités de coopération et de synergie entre less efforts des Etats membres et nous donne le plus de flexiblité budgétaire.' Remarks by Javier Solana, EU informal meeting of defence ministers, Rome, 3–4 October 2003 (official version available in French only) as cited by Gnesotto *et al*, White Paper, above.

[31] Gnesotto *et al*, *White Paper*, above n 10, at 60 already speaks of the 'Headline Goal 2010'.

[32] *Financial Times*, 2 December 2004, at 17.

[33] According to Gnesotto *et al*, *White Paper*, above n 10, at 59, 2–3 such battle groups, which should be deployable within 15 days should be ready by 2005 and another 9–10 by 2007.

(hereinafter PSC) in Brussels, a Military Committee, and the Military Staff.[34] These will be discussed in more detail below in the context of the Nice Treaty.[35]

Third, modalities would be developed for full consultation, co-operation and transparency between the EU and NATO, taking into account the needs of all EU Member States.

Fourth, appropriate arrangements would be defined that would allow, while respecting the Union's decision-making autonomy, non-EU European NATO members and other interested States to contribute to EU military crisis management.

Fifth, a non-military crisis management mechanism would be established to co-ordinate and make more effective the various civilian means and resources, in parallel with the military ones, at the disposal of the Union and the Member States.

The Presidency Conclusions of the Helsinki Summit emphasised that the EU would contribute to international peace and security in accordance with the principles of the UN Charter and recognised the primary responsibility of the United Nations Security Council for the maintenance of international peace and security. The Presidency Conclusions also stated:

> "The European Council underlines its determination to develop an autonomous capacity to take decisions and, where NATO as a whole is not engaged, to launch and conduct EU-led military operations in response to international crises. This process will avoid unnecessary duplication and does not imply the creation of a European army."[36]

The European Councils in Santa Maria de Feira (Portugal) on 19-20 June 2000 and Nice in December 2000 confirmed the results of the Cologne and Helsinki meetings. Moreover, the Heads of State and Government of the Member States agreed to add a 'Feira Headline Goal' of 5,000 police officers for international conflict prevention[37] to the military 'Helsinki Headline Goal'. This added a civilian crisis management component to the evolving ESDP.

While Helsinki and Feira develop and clarify the 'autonomous military capacity' envisaged in Saint-Malo and Cologne as an attempt to create a military force,[38] it also adds some ambiguity by excluding the creation of a European army. More importantly, it does not address the structural changes of the CFSP framework necessary to establish the autonomy of such a force. Helsinki rather reiterates a commitment to unanimity and individual Member State influence that appears to conceptualise the new force as effectively a combined national military capacity

[34] Presidency Progress Report to the Helsinki European Council on Strengthening the Common European Policy on Security and Defence, Annex 1 to Annex IV of the Presidency Conclusions.

[35] At 108–112.

[36] Presidency Conclusions, above n 25.

[37] Presidency Conclusions, European Council, Santa Maria da Feira, 19–20 June 2000, in Rutten, *From Saint Malo to Nice*, above n 4, 120, at 121.

[38] Wessel, 'State of Affairs', above n 15, at 274.

dependent on Member States. The idea seems to be that of an ERRF label only. These issues where to be addressed in the first Treaty revision after Saint-Malo, Cologne, and Helsinki.

3. THE COMMON FOREIGN AND SECURITY POLICY UNDER THE TREATY OF NICE

The political move towards an 'autonomous' European defence capability, which started with the 1998 Saint-Malo Declaration on European Defence, acquired a limited Treaty status in Nice two years later. The Treaty of Nice represents the current version of the basic constitutional document of the EU and builds on the Maastricht and Amsterdam versions discussed in chapter 2. On the one hand, the amendments to the provisions relevant to defence and security in Title V of the TEU were rather limited. On the other hand, these changes are arguably the most significant innovations of the Treaty of Nice as a whole.[39] Moreover, the larger part of the Second Pillar innovations introduced or confirmed by the European Council in Nice were not Treaty-dependent, in other words developments could go ahead without being stipulated in the Treaty.[40] The French Presidency Report and in particular its annexes contained most of these innovations. Therefore they were not dependent on the ratification and entering into force of the Treaty of Nice in 2003 and allowed the ESDP to become operational quickly.

The following section provides an analysis of these innovations and amendments: the deletion of the sections on the WEU in Article 17 TEU, the institutional changes regarding the Political and Security Committee in Article 25 TEU and the introduction of permanent military structures, the extension of qualified majority voting, and the insertion of enhanced co-operation in Articles 27a to 27e TEU.

3.1. The 'Deletion' of the Western European Union[41]

As discussed in chapter 2,[42] the Western European Union (hereinafter WEU) featured prominently in the Maastricht and Amsterdam Treaties. Article 17 (1) subparagraph 2 (ex Article J.7) TEU recognised the WEU as "an integral part of the development of the [European] Union providing the Union with access to an operational capability". It was to assist the EU in "framing the defence aspects" of the CFSP. Close institutional relations with the WEU were envisaged and the possibility of the future integration of the WEU into the EU was expressly stipulated. The WEU was to develop into the defence arm of the EU.[43] Not surprisingly, as

[39] P Craig and G de Búrca, *EU Law*, 3rd edn, (OUP, Oxford, 2003) 45.
[40] S Duke, 'CESDP: Nice's Overtrumped Success?' (2001) 6 *European Foreign Affairs Review* 155.
[41] Duke, (above, p 157), calls this the '*removal* of all but one reference to the WEU [emphasis added]'.
[42] At 80–84.
[43] For further details see ch 2 at 80–84.

most of its member States are also Member States of the EU, the WEU responded positively[44] and has taken over tasks of the EU when asked to do so.[45]

In Article 17 of the Treaty of Nice the provisions referring to the WEU were repealed.[46] Duke called these deletions the "only notable contextual change"[47] and the "most significant treaty change"[48] of the Treaty of Nice in relation to the ESDP. The removal of the WEU from Article 17 TEU is a reflection of the fact that the EU itself will assume direct responsibility for its own operational capability, rather than leaving that to another organisation.[49] The principle of an autonomous EU military capacity, proposed in Saint-Malo and Cologne and further developed in the Helsinki Headline Goal, is not specifically mentioned in the provision. However, the wording of Article 17 of the Treaty of Nice leaves only the EU as a framework to implement the ESDP through an operational capability. Therefore, the deletion of all references to the WEU as the defence arm of the Union clearly implies, as Duke put it, "that it [is] now the job of the EU to do [it]".[50]

The 'deletion' of the WEU from the TEU is also reflected in the ongoing process of transfer of WEU capabilities and institutions[51] and politico-strategic concepts and other documents to the EU.[52] An example is the 'Arrangements for Consultations and Cooperation Between EU and NATO' in the French Presidency Report on the ESDP.[53] In this paper an assessment of the existing procedures governing WEU-NATO relations is suggested with a view of their possible adaptation to an EU-NATO framework. It can be said that the WEU functions are currently

[44] *Declaration on the Role of the WEU*, Maastricht, December 1991, in A Bloed and RA Wessel, *The Changing Functions of the Western European Union: Introduction and Basic Documents* (Kluwer, The Hague, 1994) Document 28.

[45] Wessel, 'Black Widow', above n 15, 1, at 3.

[46] The only reference to the WEU can be found in para 4, which provides: 'The provisions of this Article shall not prevent the development of closer cooperation between two or more Member States on a bilateral level, in the framework of the [WEU] and NATO, provided such cooperation does not run counter to or impede that provided for in this title.'

[47] Above.

[48] S Duke, 'Nice's Overtrumped Success', above n 40, at 159.

[49] Wessel, 'Black Widow', above n 15, at 3 and 17; Craig and de Búrca, above n 39, at 45. This is not the same as having an operational capability, as Duke, above, pointed out.

[50] S Duke, 'Nice's Overtrumped Success', above n 40, at 157.

[51] Porto Declaration, WEU Ministerial Council, Porto, 15–16 May 2000: 'They [the WEU defence ministers] underlined that WEU remains ready to make available to the European Union if it so wishes the WEU Satellite Centre [at Torrejon] and Institute for Security Studies.' Rutten, *From Saint Malo to Nice*, above n 5, 112 at 113. See also the transmission of a draft document on the status of forces to be used in the event of WEU operations to the EU, mentioned in the same Declaration, at 114.

[52] Above. Section V of the Presidency Report on the European Security and Defence Policy, Annex VI to the Presidency Conclusions of the European Council in Nice is entitled 'Inclusion in the EU of the Appropriate Functions of the EU', see Rutten, *From Saint Malo to Nice*, above, 168, at 173.

[53] European Council in Nice, 7–9 December 2000, Presidency Conclusions, 4 December 2000, Annex VI Presidency Report on the European Security and Defence Policy, Annex VII [to Annex VI] Standing Arrangements for Consultation and Cooperation between the EU and NATO, Rutten, *From Saint Malo to Nice*, above n 5, at 202. See also European Council in Santa Maria da Feira, 19–20 June 2000, Presidency Conclusions, Annex I Presidency Report on Strengthening the Common European Security and Defence Policy, Appendix 2 on the Principles for Consultation with NATO on Military Issues and Recommendations on Developing Modalities for EU/NATO Relations, Rutten, *From Saint Malo to Nice*, above, 120, at 131.

in a process of transition to the EU[54] and that this process is already quite advanced. Therefore the purpose and remaining status of the 'rump WEU' itself is now unclear.[55] Whether the organisation will become completely redundant depends on whether the EU will take over all its tasks. Only when the EU incorporates the entirety of the *acquis* of the WEU, can and should the latter be dissolved. The demise of the WEU before having transferred all its functions to the EU would represent a step back in European defence integration. The WEU has three main policies: a security policy within the confines of the Petersberg Tasks, a defence policy through the mutual defence commitment in Article 5 of the Modified Brussels Treaty (hereinafter MBT), and an armaments policy.[56] Moreover, the WEU represents the European pillar of NATO and is therefore a link between the American and European members of the Alliance. A separate European defence and security organisation could have a purpose by providing a solution to problems caused by the asymmetric memberships of the EU and NATO. Austria, Finland, Ireland and Sweden are not member States of NATO[57] but of the EU, whereas Norway and Turkey are not Member States of the EU but of NATO. Denmark has a position comparable to the latter two Member States, as it does not participate in the ESDP. Memberships became even more complex after the enlargement of both organisations as there are new Member States inside and outside NATO.[58] Finally, the functions of the WEU Parliamentary Assembly might have to be transferred to the EU.

3.1.1. The Petersberg Tasks and the European Security Policy

It should be emphasised that, as far as the Nice *acquis* is concerned, the EDSP is limited to the Petersberg Tasks stipulated in Article 17 (2) of the Treaty of Nice.[59] The Saint-Malo move towards an 'autonomous' military capability is directed at the availability of an ERRF for missions related to these security tasks. This excludes mutual defence: the EDSP is not aimed at the defence of the territorial integrity or political independence of the Union or its Member States. However, the EU is assuming the main part of the WEU security policy within the confines of the Petersberg Tasks. Theoretically this leaves little for the WEU. The latter

[54] The WEU itself uses the term 'transition', see the Marseille Declaration, WEU Ministerial Council, Marseille, 13 November 2000, Para 5: 'They [the ministers] also agreed to suspend application of the routine consultation mechanisms in force between the WEU and the EU, without prejudice to the cooperation required within the framework of the transition process.' During the same meeting it was decided that the dialogue and co-operation, which the WEU at 28 and 21 had developed with the associate members, associate partners and observers, would cease. See at Para 4: '[...] these responsibilities would be taken up within the existing framework of political dialogue between the EU and the countries concerned.' Rutten, *From Saint Malo to Nice*, above n 5, 147, at 148.

[55] Craig and de Búrca, above n 39, at 45.

[56] Other activities of the WEU include disarmament and non-proliferation of weapons.

[57] Austria, Sweden, and Finland participate in NATO's 'Partnership for Peace'.

[58] The Czech Republic, Hungary, Poland, the Slovak Republic, Latvia, Estonia, Lithuania, and Slovenia are member States of NATO. Cyprus and Malta are not.

[59] Article 17(2) TEU reads: 'Questions referred to in this Article shall include humanitarian and rescue tasks, peacekeeping tasks and tasks of combat forces in crisis management, including peacemaking.'

seems to assume a residual function in crisis management once the EU security policy is operational.[60] The precise scope of this residual function, however, remains yet to be defined. Moreover, a residual function implies duplication, which is to be avoided. Therefore, it is submitted that once the EU Petersberg capability is operational, the separate WEU Petersberg function is terminated, unless missions already in action at the time still need to be continued and cannot be transferred to the EU. The deletion of the detailed WEU Petersberg provisions from Article 17 TEU and the move towards an autonomous EU capability support this interpretation.

3.1.2. Mutual Defence and the European Defence Policy

Whether the WEU will become completely redundant depends on whether the EU will take over all its tasks. This depends to a large extent on whether the mutual defence commitment in Article 5 MBT will also be transferred to the EU. The WEU is not just about common crisis management in the context of the Petersberg Tasks. In addition to being a security organisation, Article 5 MBT makes the WEU a defence organisation or military alliance that is also about a common defence against an invasion of the territories of its member States. Hence the WEU is about classical territorial defence. According to Article 17 (1) of the Treaty of Nice "The [CFSP] shall include all questions relating to the security of the Union, including the progressive framing of a common defence policy, which might lead to a common defence". Common defence can be interpreted as the EU term for collective defence.[61] However, this part of the provision is vague, uncertain, and set in the future. Therefore the Treaty of Nice does not contain a defence element comparable to Article 5 MBT for the EU. This gives the WEU a clear *raison d'être* in providing its member States with the only European defence guarantee aside from NATO.[62] Moreover, the defence guarantee of Article 5 MBT goes beyond that of Article V of the Washington Treaty establishing NATO.[63] In 2001 the WEU Council listed the "maintenance of the Treaty-based commitments" as one of the residual functions the performance of which the WEU is limited to since the 2000 Marseille Declaration.[64]

Six Member States of the EU, Austria, Finland, Ireland, Cyprus, Malta, and Sweden are neither member States of NATO nor the WEU. These countries do not wish to be part of a defence alliance. As will be explained in more detail in

[60] See the Marseille Declaration, WEU Ministerial Council, Marseille, 13 November 2000, Para 1: 'Ministers requested that the necessary administrative and accommodation measures now be taken, to ensure that the residual WEU structures are in place when the EU becomes operational', see Rutten, *From Saint Malo to Nice*, above n 5, 147.

[61] Wessel, 'The State of Affairs', above n 15, at 287.

[62] Duke, 'Nice's Overtrumped Success', above n 40, at 158.

[63] See the discussion of these provisions in ch 1.

[64] Reply of the WEU Council to a written question of WEU Parliamentary Assembly member Mr Martinez-Casan on the results of the (classified) WEU Council Meeting in Brussels, 28 June 2001, cited by M Rutten, *From Nice to Laeken, European Defence: Core Documents, Volume II*, Chaillot Paper No 51, (Institute of Security Studies of the European Union, Paris, 2002), at 69.

chapter 11,[65] these EU Member States support the security (Petersberg) element but would not support a (mutual) defence element of the ESDP. This leads to another problem crucial to EU-WEU relations: the asymmetric membership of the WEU and EU makes it difficult to claim that the WEU is a proxy defence for the EU.[66] Mutual defence through the WEU cannot be a substitute for the lack of a defence element in what claims to be European Security and Defence Policy. Moreover, it is doubtful that the post-Nice rump-WEU could invoke an effective defence.[67] Nevertheless, it is submitted that for the time being the WEU has an important role in relation to the development of the ESDP through the mutual defence commitment in Article 5 MBT. An EU controversy on the inclusion of a mutual defence commitment could undermine the less controversial development of the (Petersberg) security issues of the ESDP. The existence of a European defence guarantee in addition to NATO could defuse the "potentially divisive and damaging debate within the EU on common defence".[68]

NATO is the dominating military alliance in Europe providing a mutual defence guarantee with Article V of the Washington Treaty. This guarantee is credible due to the substantial conventional and nuclear deterrence provided by the USA as the leading member State of NATO. The WEU and its mutual defence commitment are designed as the European pillar of NATO. Due to the considerable 'capabilities gap' of the armed forces of the Member States, it is highly unlikely for the foreseeable future that the EU can provide a comparable defence guarantee.[69] Moreover, NATO is also developing a security policy covering the Petersberg Tasks, including the establishment of a NATO Rapid Reaction Force. In contrast to the EU, it already has most of the necessary assets and capabilities for the implementation of such a policy. An ESDP that included a mutual defence commitment could lead to an almost complete overlap with NATO, which could lead to duplication. Moreover, it could lead to transatlantic rifts, which would undermine a mutual defence commitment with more credibility than any defence guarantee that the EU could provide at the moment. Therefore the defence element of the WEU cannot be transferred to the EU before the boundaries between NATO and EU mandates are clearly defined and the links between the two organisations are firmly established and operational.

3.1.3. The European Armaments Policy

A third important element of the WEU is its armaments policy. In the European context armaments policy covers the co-ordination of collaborative weapons development and production programmes, procurement, and other policies aimed at strengthening the European defence industrial base. The defence industry has a double nature. First it is a major industry and part of the market. Second it has a

[65] At 332–335.
[66] S Duke, 'Nice's Overtrumped Success', above n 40, at 158.
[67] Duke, above.
[68] Above, at 158.
[69] Above, at 158–59.

strategic nature and is part of the foreign, defence, and security policy of the Member States. For this reason armaments are largely outside the application of European Community law, as will be discussed in detail in chapters 5 and 7. Instruments of both the First and the Second Pillar have to be used to regulate armaments in the EU. To replace the WEU with regards to armaments policy, its armaments structures, the Western European Armaments Group (hereinafter WEAG) and the Western European Armaments Organisation (hereinafter WEAO), would also have to be transferred to the EU. Beyond these WEU structures European defence procurement and industrial reform is discussed in the POLARM forum within the EU, the Conference of National Armaments Directors (CNAD) of NATO, the Organisation of Joint Armaments Co-operation (OCCAR), and the Letter of Intend (LOI) forum.

The Nice European Council failed to agree on the establishment of a true European armaments agency that would allow a transfer of the puzzle of European armaments initiatives in general and relevant WEAG and WEAO structures of the WEU to the EU. Hence its contribution to a European armaments policy gives the WEU another *raison d'être*. "Support for WEAG/WEAO" was listed as one of the residual functions the performance of which the WEU is limited to since the Marseille Declaration.[70] A European Defence Agency is envisaged in the Constitutional Treaty discussed in Part III of this book.[71] However, with Joint Action 2004/551/CFSP of 12 July 2004 the Council established an agency in the field of defence capabilities, development, research, acquisition and armaments. Hence, the Agency was detached from the uncertain fate of the Constitutional Treaty and has become reality before the completion of the latter's implementation process. Nevertheless, as it is not yet fully operational and follows the Agency outlined in the Constitutional Treaty it is part of the future rather than the current state of European defence integration and will be discussed in the context of chapter 11[72] of this book.

3.1.4. The NATO Member States Outside the EU

Again, the purpose and remaining status of the 'rump WEU' itself is now unclear.[73] One purpose could be to include the European member States of NATO which are not Member States of the EU. Currently these are Norway, Turkey, Bulgaria, and Romania,[74] the latter two at least until accession to the EU in 2007 or 2008. However, the EU framework will be open to contributions from non-EU countries and consultations between EU institutions and the institutions of non-EU

[70] Reply of the WEU Council to a written question of WEU Parliamentary Assembly member Mr Martinez-Casan on the results of the (classified) WEU Council Meeting in Brussels, 28 June 2001, cited by Rutten, *From Nice to Laeken*, above n 64, at 69.

[71] At 319–328.

[72] At 319–328.

[73] Craig and de Búrca, above n 39, at 45.

[74] Bulgaria and Romania joined NATO in 2004 together with the Baltic States, Slovenia, and the Slovak Republic.

member States of NATO are prescribed on all levels. As discussed below, non-EU countries participated in all the EU missions conducted so far. These mechanisms of participation are attractive for countries outside Europe, such as Canada and South Africa. However for a European country (yet) outside the EU, being able to participate in EU missions is less attractive than being an EU Member State involved in the decision making process. Hence for countries such as Norway and Turkey the WEU still provides a link between the EU and NATO. Nevertheless, it is debatable whether this function alone suffices to justify the WEU's continued existence.

3.1.5. The Functions of the WEU Parliamentary Assembly

The WEU Council considers the "relations with the WEU Assembly" to be one of the residual functions of the WEU. In other words the parliamentary scrutiny exercised by the WEU Assembly over the activities of the WEU Council is one of the residual functions of the WEU. Residual are the functions not (yet) transferred to the EU.[75] The Assembly of the WEU[76] in Paris has three main functions. First, it represents the parliamentary dimension of the WEU based on its consultative powers vis-à-vis the WEU Council. Article 9 MBT states that "the Council of Western European Union shall make an annual report on its activities [...] to an Assembly composed of representatives of the Brussels Treaty Powers to the Consultative Assembly of the Council of Europe." Second, following the transfer of the operational activities of the WEU to the EU in 2000, it acts as the interim European Security and Defence Assembly, focusing on ESDP. Third, it scrutinises intergovernmental co-operation in the field of armaments and armaments research and development, which is funded and carried out by WEAG and WEAO. The Assembly comprises 370 parliamentarians from the national parliaments of all 28 WEU countries, including all Member States of the EU. Cyprus and Malta send observer delegations to plenary sessions. However, only the 115 representatives from the ten member States have full rights.

According to the WEU Assembly,[77] the European Parliament has the remit necessary to ensure the same level of parliamentary scrutiny of ESDP activities as is provided in the MBT. This includes in particular the fundamental obligation on the part of the WEU Council to provide a written annual report on its activities and to reply to parliamentary recommendations and questions. Therefore, despite all the institutional changes in Europe as a whole, the Assembly of the WEU is still the only European parliamentary institution that allows national parliamentarians to monitor security and defence issues. According to the Treaty of Nice, the ESDP is not subject to any formal scrutiny or approval by the European Parliament. Article 20 TEU states:

[75] Reply of the WEU Council to a written question of WEU Parliamentary Assembly member Mr Martinez-Casan on the results of the (classified) WEU Council Meeting in Brussels, 28 June 2001, cited by Rutten, *From Nice to Laeken*, above n 64, at 69.

[76] This brief description of the WEU Assembly is based on the web-site at http://www.assembly-weu.org/en/presentation/presentation.html.

[77] Above.

> "The Presidency shall consult the European Parliament on the main aspects and the basic choices of the common foreign and security policy and shall ensure that the views of the European Parliament are duly taken into consideration. The European Parliament shall be kept regularly informed by the Presidency and the Commission of the development of the Union's foreign and security policy.
>
> The European Parliament may ask questions of the Council or make recommendations to it. It shall hold an annual debate on progress in implementing the common foreign and security policy."

Since the Treaty of Amsterdam the Council has prepared an annual report on the main aspects and basic choices of the CFSP, including the financial implications. However, the wording of Article 20 TEU does not suggest that there is an obligation to present such annual reports. The European Parliament presents its own annual report in which it regularly criticises Council and Commission. In the 2001 Report, for example, it criticised the substance of a report submitted to it by Council and Commission, the transfer of the WEU Institute for Security Studies to the EU in the form of a Joint Action adopted by the Council without consulting or informing the European Parliament, and the lack of coherence of EU policy in the Western Balkans.[78] It is submitted that due to the obligation to submit an annual report, the extent of parliamentary scrutiny through the WEU Assembly goes beyond that exercised by the European Parliament. The lack of parliamentary scrutiny through the European Parliament has to be seen in addition to the lack of judicial scrutiny caused by the exclusion of the CFSP from the jurisdiction of the European Court of Justice in Article 46 TEU.[79] It is submitted that this lack of judicial and parliamentary scrutiny amounts to a considerable democratic deficit of the ESDP.[80] Foreign policy and in particular defence and security policy are traditionally a domain of the executive branch of government. Apart from historical reasons, this is due to the need for efficiency in a policy field addressing threats to the very existence of the State. The government supported by their military staff have the expertise and means to react to security threats. Parliament and the judiciary can potentially undermine the efficiency of the executive in this field by interfering in their activities. Nevertheless, these arguments of efficiency need to be balanced against arguments of democracy and the rule of law, involving both the legislature and the judiciary in defence and security policy. Moreover, in the constitutional context of the EU, CFSP and EDSP remain intergovernmental, giving the Member States a central position. Therefore the Council is the central

[78] European Parliament Report on the progress achieved in the implementation of the CFSP, Strasbourg, 25 October 2001, in Rutten, *From Nice to Laeken*, above n 64, 86, at 87 and 89.

[79] Article 46 TEU as amended by the Treaty of Nice reads: 'The provisions of the Treaty establishing the European Community, the Treaty establishing the European Coal and Steel Community and the Treaty establishing the European Atomic Energy Community concerning the powers of the Court of Justice of the European Communities and the exercise of those powers shall apply only to the following provisions of this Treaty: [... followed by a list that does not include Title V].'

[80] This is also argued by Wessel, 'State of Affairs', above n 15, at 267 citing W Wessels, *et al*, *The Parliamentary Dimension of CFSP/ESDP: Options for a European Convention*, (Study submitted to the European Parliament, December 2002).

institution of the EDSP. Nevertheless, in an EU based on democracy and the rule of law, no policy can be completely exempt from parliamentary scrutiny. Compared to the EU *acquis* of Article 21 TEU, the WEU *acquis* regarding parliamentary scrutiny in Article 9 MBT is further developed. As long as the parliamentary scrutiny of the EDSP exercised by the European Parliament has not reached the level of that exercised by the WEU Parliamentary Assembly on the basis of Article 9 MBT, the WEU *acquis* on parliamentary scrutiny makes the functions of the WEU Assembly a *raison d'être* for the WEU. These functions, in particular with regards to Article 9 MBT, would have to be transferred to the European Parliament.

3.1.6. 'Reunification' of the Strains of European Defence Integration?

Maastricht, Amsterdam and Nice aim to overcome the separation between defence integration and the mainstream of European integration, which had started in the 1950s.[81] In contrast to the Treaties of Maastricht and Amsterdam which envisaged a progressive integration of the WEU as a 'defence arm' into the EU, Article 17 of the Treaty of Nice envisages an EU that is developing its own military capabilities. However, the developments of the last decade or so show that the borderline between integrating the WEU as a defence arm into the EU and developing an 'independent' EU military capability is somehow blurred. During the 1990s the dormant process of European defence integration was revived both in the EU and the separate WEU frameworks. The WEU developed the Petersberg Tasks and put them into action. Step-by-step institutions, facilities, functions, and concepts of the WEU have been and will be transferred to the EU. To a certain extent this re-unites a substantial part of the European defence integration process with the EU as the mainstream of European integration. After almost 50 years, defence integration is under the same roof, within the same organisation. Nevertheless, for two reasons most of defence integration is still separate. First, the WEU still has several *raisons d'être* because many of its functions, mutual defence and armaments policy in particular, have not been transferred yet. Second, CFSP and ESDP remain more intergovernmental in nature. The functions of the WEU are transferred to the more intergovernmental Second Pillar. In contrast, the mainstream of integration enshrined in the First Pillar is more supranational. Part II of this book will show that this Community Pillar also regulates substantial parts of defence. The process of European defence integration continues in the WEU, in other organisations, the Second Pillar, and the First Pillar of the TEU and is therefore fragmented. This questions the coherence of the approach.

3.2. The Military Structures of the European Security and Defence Policy

The European Council of Helsinki had decided to let the ministers of defence attend the General Affairs Council meetings when issues relating to the ESDP are

[81] See ch 1 at 44–49.

discussed. Moreover it decided to create a number of new ESDP organs: the Political and Security Committee, the European Union Military Committee (hereinafter EUMC), the European Union Military Staff Organisation (hereinafter EUMS). Moreover, it was decided to create a Committee for the Civilian Aspects of Crisis Management.

3.2.1. The Political and Security Committee

According to Article 25 (1) of the Treaty of Amsterdam (Article J.15 Treaty of Maastricht) a Political Committee was to monitor the international situation in the areas covered by the CFSP. It was to contribute to the definition of policies by delivering opinions to the Council at the request of the Council or on its own initiative. It was also to monitor the implementation of agreed policies, without prejudice to the responsibility of the Presidency and the Commission. Apart from referring to the new name 'Political and Security Committee' (hereinafter PSC) this first paragraph remained unaltered in Nice. Hence the basic political role of the PSC was confirmed. Nevertheless, due to the increased role of the Committee stipulated in paragraphs (2) and (3) of Article 25 TEU outlined below, it is accurate to say that the Treaty of Nice replaces the Political Committee with the PSC.[82]

According to the new Article 25 (2) of the Treaty of Nice, the PSC shall exercise, under the responsibility of the Council, political control and strategic direction of crisis management operations. According to the new Article 25 (3) of the Treaty of Nice, the Council may authorise the Committee, for the purpose and for the duration of a crisis management operation, as determined by the Council, to take the relevant decisions concerning the political control and strategic direction of the operation. This possibility is subject to Article 47 TEU, which provides that nothing in the TEU shall affect the EC Treaty or the subsequent treaties and acts modifying or supplementing them. The PSC is the "linchpin" of the ESDP.[83] It will prepare the EU's response to a crisis by keeping track of the international situation, examining the options, recommending them to the Council, drawing opinions for the Council to adopt Joint Actions, supervising the implementation of the recommended measures and assessing their effects.[84] The Committee also has an important role to enhance consultations with NATO and the third states involved. The PSC plays a crucial role in the institutional structure of the ESDP by providing the framework for the EU political-military dialogue and for the support structure.[85] It connects the military structures of the CFSP described below with the political institution of the Union.

The PSC is part of the institution Council and part of the more intergovernmental Second Pillar of the TEU. The prescribed tasks are without prejudice to the decision making and implementation procedures of each Pillar. Within their own

[82] S Duke, 'Nice's Overtrumped Success', above n 40, at 160.

[83] Annex VI to the Presidency Report, Annex III to Annex VI on the PSC, Rutten, *From Saint Malo to Nice*, above n 5, at 191.

[84] Above, at 192.

[85] Duke, 'Nice's Overtrumped Success', above n 40, at 160.

areas of power, only the Council and the Commission have powers to take legally binding decisions.[86] Nevertheless, the role of the PSC is to prepare a response of the EU as a whole within the single institutional framework. This response can be conducted within the Second Pillar, for example by sending peacekeeping troops, or within the First Pillar, for example through sanctions.

Article 25 (2) and (3) of the Treaty of Nice gives Treaty status to the PSC as one of the three defence and security 'institutions' proposed in the 'French Action Plan',[87] which had already been established as interim structures in Helsinki.[88] The other two are the EUMC and the EUMS. The mission, functions, and structure of these institutions are outlined in the Presidency Report on the European Security and Defence Policy to the European Council of Nice.[89] They were established as permanent bodies by Council Decision 2001/78/CFSP for the PSC[90], Council Decision 2001/79/CFSP for the EUMC[91] and Council Decision 2001/80/CFSP for the EUMS on 22 January 2001.[92] Although, as Wessel observes, Article 25 TEU does not mention defence and the PSC is not the Political, Security, and Defence Committee,[93] their tasks include the entire ESDP. After all, the Nice reforms of the PSC were designed to react to the institutional demands of the new policy.[94]

3.2.2. The European Union Military Committee

The EUMC is the highest military body established within the Council and composed of the Chiefs of Defence, normally represented by their military representatives.[95] It provides military advice and makes recommendations to the PSC and provides military direction to the EUMS. In a crisis situation the EUMC

[86] Above.

[87] French action plan: Letter from M Jacques Chirac, President of the French Republic, to the Finnish presidency of the European Union, 22 July 1999, printed in Rutten, *From Saint Malo to Nice*, above n 5, 48, at 51–52. This resulted in the first outline of the institutions in the Presidency Progress Report to the Helsinki European Council on Strengthening the Common European Policy on Security and Defence (Annex 1 to Annex IV Presidency Reports to the Helsinki European Council on 'Strengthening the Common European Policy on Security and Defence' and on 'Non-Military Crisis Management of the European Union'), Rutten, above, 84, at 87. However, it was actually already broadly proposed in Saint-Malo where France and the United Kingdom had said: 'the Union must be given appropriate structures and a capacity for the analysis of situations, sources of intelligence, and a capacity for relevant strategic planing [...]', Rutten, above, at 9–10.

[88] Presidency Progress Report on the Helsinki European Council on Strengthening the Common European Policy on Security and Defence, Rutten, *From Saint Malo to Nice*, above n 5, 84 at 87.

[89] Annex VI to the Presidency Report, Annex III to Annex VI on the PSC, Annex IV to Annex VI on the EUMC, and Annex V to Annex VI on the EUMS, Rutten, *From Saint Malo to Nice*, above n 5, at 191, 193, and 196, respectively.

[90] The PSC became permanent on 22 January 2001, according to the Gothenburg European Council, Presidency Report on the European Security and Defence Policy, cited by Rutten, *From Nice to Laeken*, above n 64, at 35.

[91] The EUMC became permanent on 9 April 2001, above.

[92] The EUMS became permanent on 11 June 2001, Gothenburg Presidency Report on EDSP, Rutten, *From Nice to Laeken* , above n 64, at 35.

[93] Wessel, 'State of Affairs', above n 15, at 276.

[94] Above.

[95] Annex VI to the Presidency Report, Annex IV to Annex VI on the EUMC, Rutten, *From Saint Malo to Nice*, above n 5, at 193–96.

will evaluate the strategic options upon a request of the PSC. It will forward options to the PSC. On the basis of the military option selected by the Council, the EUMC will authorise an Initial Planning Directive for the Operations Commander. Based on the recommendations of the EUMS evaluation the Committee will provide advice to the PSC on the Concept of Operations, the Draft Operation Plan, and the termination option for an operation. During an operation the Committee monitors the proper execution of military operations conducted under the responsibility of the Operations commander. The EUMC has a permanent Chairman who chairs the meetings of the Committee, acts as its spokesperson, conducts the work of the Committee, acts as the primary point of contact for the Operations Commander during military operations.

3.2.3. The European Union Military Staff

The EUMS is to perform 'early warning situation assessment and strategic planning for Petersberg tasks including identification of European national and multinational forces' and to implement policies an decisions directed by the EUMC.[96] It is the source of EU military expertise, assures a link between the latter and the available military resources, and provides an early warning capability. It plans, assesses, and makes recommendations regarding the concept of crisis management and the general military strategy, implements the decisions and guidance of the EUMC, and has numerous other related tasks. The Military Staff is composed of personnel seconded from the Member States acting in an international capacity under the statute to be established by the Council.

EUMC and EUMS provide the necessary structures for situation assessment and the military of EU crisis management operations. Moreover, they provide the links to the national force contributions of the Member States assembled to fulfil the 'Helsinki Headline Goal' and the parallel civil and military NATO structures they need to liase with.[97]

3.2.4. The Committee for Civilian Aspects of Crisis Management

In addition to the three bodies dealing with security and defence in the strict sense, the Council decided on the 22 May 2000 to establish a Committee for Civilian Aspects of Crisis Management (hereinafter CCACM).[98] The CCACM is a working group of the Council and will co-ordinate the civil crisis management of the EU. It reports to the COREPER and supplies the PSC, EUMC, and EUMS with information, recommendations, and opinions. A co-ordination mechanism next to the CCACM was established in the Council Secretariat to co-ordinate a databank on available police capacity, which has led to the creation of the European Security and Intelligence Force (hereinafter ESIF). Similar to the Helsinki Headline Goal, the ESIF will consist of 5,000 well-armed police, 1,000 of

[96] Above, at 196–99.
[97] Duke, 'Nice's Overtrumped Success', above n 40, at 160.
[98] Council-Decision 2000/143/CFSP, 22 May 2000, [2000] OJ L–127.

them deployable within thirty days, able to carry out preventive as well as repressive actions in support of peacekeeping missions under the control of the PSC.

3.3. Qualified Majority Voting

The Treaty of Nice extended decision-making by qualified majority (hereinafter QMV) to the appointment of special representatives in Article 23 TEU. The 'emergency brake provisions'[99] were retained. Article 24 of the Treaty of Nice provides for QMV for the conclusion of international agreements in the context of the CFSP. If the agreement is required for the adoption of a Joint Action or Common Position, the Council may act by QMV but shall act unanimously when the agreement covers an issue for which unanimity is required for the adoption of internal decisions. Similarly, when the adoption of an internal decision requires QMV, the Council shall act by QMV.

3.4. Enhanced Co-operation

The Treaty of Nice also amended the TEU by inserting Articles 27a to 27e on enhanced co-operation. These provisions introduce a new element of flexibility into the CFSP as part of a general concept regulated in Articles 43 to 45 TEU. Enhanced co-operation allows a group of Member States to integrate certain aspects of policy beyond the Nice *acquis* when it is not possible to establish an EU-wide consensus. Such vanguard Member States[100] would use the institutions, procedures, and mechanisms of the Union to deepen integration between them, while inviting all other Member States to join them later. The provisions of the Treaty of Nice develop the previous concept of 'closer co-operation' in the Treaty of Amsterdam. In contrast to the latter, which was discussed in chapter 2,[101] the Treaty of Nice provides reformed procedures and a wider scope for flexible integration. Part of this wider scope is the inclusion of the CFSP through Articles 27a to 27e TEU. The new concept coexists with older Second Pillar mechanisms of

[99] S Duke, 'Nice's Overtrumped Success', above n 40, at 159–60. In particular Article 23(2) subpara 2 TEU provides: 'If a member of the Council declares that, for important and stated reasons of national policy, it intends to oppose the adoption of a decision to be taken by qualified majority, a vote shall not be taken. The Council may, acting by a qualified majority, request that the matter be referred to the European Council for a decision by unanimity.' Hence, although a matter might be subject to QMV, a Member State can pull Article 23(2) subpara 2 TEU as an emergency break and avoid QMV. Subpara 3 provides: The votes of the members of the Council shall be weighted in accordance with Article 205(2) of the Treaty establishing the European Community. For their adoption, decision shall require at least 62 votes in favour, cast by at least 10 members. This para shall not apply to decisions having military or defence implications [?!].'

[100] T Jaeger, 'Enhanced Cooperation in the Treaty of Nice and Flexibility in the Common Foreign and Security Policy' (2002) 7 *European Foreign Affairs Review* 297, at 298.

[101] At 85.

flexibility, such as constructive abstention according to Article 23 (1) TEU[102] and the rule on grave difficulties in implementing a Joint Action in Article 14 (7) TEU.[103]

The advantages in comparison to further integration through a framework outside the EU are efficiency, transparency, and coherence. For the participating Member States it renders the new policy less expensive and more efficient through the use of the already existing EU framework. Moreover, the fact that the policy move carries the EU trademark enhances its credibility. For the non-participating Member State it renders the extent and content of such an effort foreseeable and controllable. The procedural requirements ensure that they are informed about a policy move in which they might be unable or unwilling to participate. Those Member States can control the process leading to enhanced co-operation. Moreover, they ultimately have a "Luxembourg-style"[104] *veto* right through Articles 27c sentence 4[105] and 23 (2) subparagraph 2 TEU. The Treaty of Nice abolished this 'emergency-brake' mechanism in the other Pillars but retains or rather introduces it for the CFSP.[106] This allows Member States to avoid being bound by such a policy move under international law if they consider that necessary.

Such a move of only a group of Member States could undermine the coherence of the CFSP of the EU as a whole. Therefore the relevant Member States have to follow a notification and consultation procedure involving the Council and other EU institutions. The specific CFSP provisions of Articles 27a to 27e TEU have to be read together with the general provisions in Articles 43-45 TEU. In comparison to enhanced co-operation in other policy fields, the roles of Parliament and Commission are reduced with regards to the CFSP, whereas the roles of the Council and the Member are paramount.[107] Commission and Parliament are only

[102] Article 23(1) TEU reads:

> Decisions under this Treaty shall be taken by the Council acting unanimously. Abstentions by members present in person or represented shall not prevent the adoption of such decisions.
>
> When abstaining in a vote, any member of the Council may qualify its abstention by making a formal declaration under the present subparagraph. In that case, it shall not be obliged to apply the decision, but shall accept that the decision commits the Union. In a spirit of mutual solidarity, the Member States concerned shall refrain from any action likely to conflict with or impede Union action based on that decision and the other Member States shall respect its position. If the members of the Council qualifying their abstention in this way represent more than one third of the votes weighted in accordance with Article 250(2) of the Treaty establishing the European Community, the decision shall not be adopted.

The disadvantage of this mechanism is that it introduces a much more visible split in a CFSP move of the EU, see Jaeger, above, at 299.

[103] Article 14(7) TEU reads: 'Should there be any major difficulties in implementing a joint action, a Member State shall refer them to the Council which shall discuss them and seek appropriate solutions. Such solutions shall not run counter to the objectives of the joint action or impair its effectiveness.' This is considered a concealed possibility for differentiated application of Union decisions. See Jaeger, above n 92, at 300, citing K Ehlermann, 'Differentiation, Flexibility, Closer Cooperation', EUI Working Paper, (San Domenico di Fiesole, 1997) at nr. VI5.

[104] Craig and de Búrca, above n 39, at 46.

[105] Article 27c sentence 4 TEU reads: 'Authorisation shall be granted by the Council, acting in accordance with the second and third subparagraphs of Article 23 (2) and in compliance with Articles 43 to 45.'

[106] Jaeger, above n 100, at 303.

[107] Craig and de Búrca, above n 39, at 46.

informed and the Commission has an advisory role regards consistency of the policy in line with other EU policies. The Council decides in accordance with the provisions of Article 23 (2) TEU by qualified majority, with a protective *veto* for a Member State which wishes to refer the matter to the European Council instead for a unanimous decision, as explained above.

There are two important exclusions or limitations. First, according to Article 27b sentence 1 TEU enhanced co-operation "shall relate to [the] implementation of a Joint Action or a Common Position." This excludes a Common Strategy. Therefore enhanced co-operation is limited to measures implementing agreed policies and not for setting new policies in order to square coherence with flexibility in the CFSP context.[108] Second, according to Article 27b sentence 2 TEU "[enhanced co-operation] shall not relate to matters having military or defence implications". This exclusion is left unexplained[109] and is a result of pressure exercised by the United Kingdom government during the Intergovernmental Conference.[110] It means that the concept cannot be used for defence integration. Therefore it is not part of the current state of defence integration and shall not be discussed further in this chapter.[111]

3.5. The Record of the European Security and Defence Policy Under Nice

The record of the ESDP under the Treaty of Nice has to be assessed on the background of the general political situation at the beginning of the 21st century, the military capabilities of the Member States, and the fact that ESDP is still in its infancy. The missions conducted within the evolving ESDP framework are therefore test cases, representing a learning experience for the participating forces and structures. The benchmark has to be comparable missions conducted within the framework of other international organisations, such as the United Nations, NATO, OSCE, or the Economic Organisation of West African States ECOWAS. The crucial point is whether ESDP provides the EU with the necessary coherence and independence to react to a military task.

The general political situation at the beginning of the 21st century is characterised by the war on terrorism triggered by the 11 September 2001 terrorist attacks on the World Trade Centre in New York and the Pentagon in Washington, DC. Although not directly related to these attacks, the 2003 United States-led invasion of Iraq is also a crucial aspect of the global security situation, which forms the background of the evolving ESDP. This situation had two main effects on ESDP. First, the resulting UN and NATO commitments of the Member States of the EU in Afghanistan, Iraq, and the Balkans left fewer military and financial resources for missions within the ESDP framework. The EU Member States cover

[108] Jaeger, above n 100, at 303.
[109] As pointed out by S Peers, 'Common Foreign and Security Policy 1999–2000' (2001) 21 *Yearbook of European Law* 531, 547.
[110] Craig and de Búrca, above n 39, at 46.
[111] Jaeger, above n 100, 297.

more than 40 per cent of the United Nations Department for Peacekeeping.[112] Germany, for example, has armed forces of about 280,000 men and women, but with 8,000 soldiers on UN and NATO missions it has reached its limits. Second, the invasion of Iraq caused an at least momentary transatlantic rift, which might lead those Member States who opposed the invasion to put a stronger emphasis on ESDP as a possible alternative to NATO. This will be discussed in more detail below.

Another important aspect of the background of the ESDP record to date is the military capabilities of the Member States. These are currently characterised by a significant capabilities gap, which the RAND Corporation estimates at between US$ 24 and 26 billion.[113] In other words, since the end of the cold war Europe has not been spending enough on defence with the result that European armed forces lack sufficient cutting edge equipment. Moreover, they lack the specific equipment necessary for out of area missions. Based on the results of the 2001 NATO Capabilities Improvement Conference, the armed forces of the Member States are short of 20–50 types of critical equipment.[114] For example, these missions require airlift capabilities to transport troops to the areas of their engagement. The USA has 250 long-range aircraft, the United Kingdom has 4 and the other EU countries have none.[115] In the current economic climate European governments are reluctant to spend the resources to close this gap.[116] The lack of resources and adequate equipment has an effect on the size and independence of ESDP missions. ESDP missions have to be small with regards to costs, the number of deployed troops and their required equipment. ESDP missions need the support of NATO assets, which means United States assets. The 2002 'Berlin-plus' arrangement gives the EU fairly reliable access to NATO assets, although this still depends on formal NATO decisions which will be taken on a case-by-case basis.[117] As independence is a benchmark for the assessment of ESDP, the dependence on NATO assets has to be logged on the negative side.

In 2003 the three first missions were conducted within the ESDP framework.[118]

The European Union Policy Mission (hereinafter EUPM) in Bosnia-Herzegovina was launched in January 2003, taking over from the United Nations International Police Task Force. 531 police officers and 400 support staff, 80 per cent from EU Member States and 20 per cent from third countries including Canada, will perform monitoring, mentoring, and inspection activities to establish local law enforcement capabilities to contribute to the stability of the region until December 2005. The mission has an annual budget of € 38 million, of which

[112] A Missiroli, 'The European Union: Just a Regional Peacekeeper?' (2003) 8 *European Foreign Affairs Review* 493.

[113] Figures quoted in R Ginsberg, 'European Security and Defence Policy: The State of the Play' (2003) 16 *EUSA Review* 1; see also DS Yost, 'The NATO Capabilities Gap and the European Union' (2000) 42 *Survival* 97.

[114] Howell, above n 11, at 30.

[115] Lord Robertson of Port Ellen, 'Our Grandchildren's NATO' (2003) 8 *European Foreign Affairs Review* 509, at 511.

[116] Croci, above n 8, at 487.

[117] Missiroli, above n 112, at 495.

[118] The following brief descriptions of these missions are based on Missiroli, above, at 498–500.

€ 20 million are financed from the EU budget. EUPM is based on a Council Decision, a UN Security Council endorsement and an agreement with the Bosnian authorities. EUPM, which is not a military mission but nevertheless the first ESDP mission ever, has its own structure headquartered in Sarajevo.

'Concordia' in the Former Yugoslav Republic of Macedonia was launched in March 2003, taking over NATO's Operation Allied Harmony. 357 lightly armed military personnel, 85 per cent from 13 EU Member States[119] and 15 per cent from third countries including Canada, contributed to a stable and secure environment in the country by ensuring the implementation of the 2001 Ohrid Framework Agreement between Macedonian Slavs and Albanians until October 2003. In practice the European troops patrolled the Macedonian Albanian-populated regions to the north and west of the country. This first military mission within the ESDP framework had a budget of € 6.2 million. Concordia was based on a Council decision, a UN Security Council Resolution and was requested by Macedonia. France acted as "framework nation" and the mission drew heavily on NATO assets under the 'Berlin-plus' arrangement. The headquarters were located at the NATO Supreme Headquarter Allied Powers (SHAPE) in Belgium. Hence Concordia was also a test case for the NATO-EU relationship under the 'Berlin-plus' arrangement.

In response to an appeal by the UN Secretary General 'Artemis' was launched in the Ituri region of the Democratic Republic of Congo (DRC) in June 2003. 1,800 soldiers, mostly French were deployed in Bunia to contribute to the stabilisation of security conditions and the improvement of the humanitarian situation until September 2003 when the UNO took over. France again acted as a framework nation and the operational headquarters were located at the *Centre de Planification et de Conduite des Opérations* (CPCO). Apart from France the United Kingdom and Sweden contributed combat forces and Belgium and Germany non-combat forces. Canada, South Africa and Brazil also contributed to the mission, which was based on a Council decision and a UN Security Council Resolution. Artemis was the first military operation within the ESDP framework out of area, in other words out of Europe. Moreover, it is the first ESDP mission that did not rely on NATO assistance.

Police and military operations within the ESDP framework are still in their infancy and the first three missions do not represent a sufficient sample to make fair assessment. Nevertheless, EUPM, Concordia, and Artemis have a number of features in common that are likely to be characteristics of future missions.

First, they are very limited in scope. This is due to the capabilities gap described above, which is enhanced by the fact that the armed forces of the Member States are already stretched through other missions, especially the NATO missions in Kosovo and Afghanistan. However, they are also small because there are also budget problems involved, both in relation to Member State budgets as in relation to the EU budget. Small missions can be covered by current budgets. Moreover, the political-military structures of the ESDP are still in their infancy. This is

[119] Exceptions were Ireland and Canada.

another reason why larger crisis management operations are currently not a realistic option.[120] In the short term ESDP missions will remain small. It seems sensible to learn through smaller missions before tackling large conflicts. However, in the medium and long term the EU has to take on the responsibility for larger operations if it wants to leave its reputation as a military midget behind. The scale of ESDP missions so far confirms this military midget status of the Union.

Second, they concern crisis situations of a low degree of danger. In Bosnia and Herzegovina the worst was over when the European policemen came, hence it could be called a 'second-hand' operation.[121] The same is true of FYROM, if the situation ever was as dangerous as Bosnia. The DRC situation and most African conflicts in general can be contained with rather limited efforts.[122] This fact might make Africa a preferred destination for the next missions. The small scale and the low degree of danger give the ESDP an opportunity of 'learning by doing', of testing abilities, of making experiences. However, it seems sensible to test the ESDP with small, cheap, and limited operations.

Third, the missions depended on the interest, leadership, and commitment of the major EU Member States,[123] in particular on France, which briefly before had intervened autonomously in Ivory Coast. It is not certain that Member States such as France or the United Kingdom will always engage their assets and capabilities within the ESDP framework. Moreover, the ESDP has no independent military capabilities at its disposal yet and depends on the support of all Member States in the Council. The missions were organised on an *ad hoc* basis and the *ad hoc* character of the missions is likely to continue for the time being as the more permanent ERRF envisaged in Helsinki is not operational yet.

Fourth, the military missions Concordia and Artemis were not led by the already existing EU Military Committee and Staff, but through NATO and national French headquarters. It remains to be seen whether the model of France or another Member State acting as a framework nation will be followed in future missions. Developing and using an independent headquarter structure could be an imminent evolutionary step.

Fifth, the Artemis mission does not contradict the presumption that for the foreseeable future any larger and more complex military mission would depend on NATO support.[124] This dependence could only be overcome through long-term investment in military capabilities, including a European defence industrial policy. Nevertheless, it is possible that the EU will be able to cover more demanding missions with developing assets and capabilities.[125]

At the time of completion of this book the EU had just taken over from the NATO Peacekeeping Stabilisation Force (SFOR) in Bosnia and Herzegovina on 2

[120] Duke, 'Nice's Overtrumped Success', above n 40, at 160.
[121] Wessel, 'State of affairs', above n 15, at 283.
[122] See: 'Bundeswehr: Globaler Militärdienstleister' *Der Spiegel* 4/2004, 24, at 25.
[123] Missiroli, above n 112, at 501.
[124] Above.
[125] Wessel, 'State of affairs', above n 15, at 285.

December 2004.[126] The 7,000 strong EU force (EUFOR) has the same size as SFOR and 80 per cent of the troops forming the latter will "change their shoulder and cap badges" and join EUFOR. A crucial task of the new force is to hunt down war criminals. While this is the largest ESDP operation to date, it still shares most of the qualities of the 2003 operations. It is a 'second hand' operation on the low end of security. Nevertheless the size of EUFOR represents a new dimension of the ESDP showing that the Union is prepared and willing to take responsibility for larger missions.

4. TOWARDS THE CONSTITUTIONAL TREATY

Compared to the momentum of the European defence integration between Saint-Malo and Nice, the process slowed down during the last few years. 2001 was characterised by routine and revolution. On the one hand, routine set in. This was necessary to allow the institutional structures to settle in and the EU institutions and the Member States to digest and implement the *acquis* of the Treaty of Nice. The adaptation of the Petersberg Tasks, budgetary and other finance questions, the improvement of capabilities,[127] and the development of a common perception of threats and strategy were on the agenda. On the other hand, the terrorist attacks of 11 September 2001 led to considerable changes in the basic political framework that had existed since the break-up of the Soviet Union. The dream of a civil European power in a civilised world has to face the reality of terrorism and the unilateralism of the USA. The ESDP, however, was continued on the basis of the traditional lines and therefore excluded from the revolution in international relations that started with the attacks in New York and Washington, DC. As Gnesotto put it: "the attacks of 1 September changed everything – except ESDP."[128] Although the Laeken Council on 14–15 December 2001 addressed terrorism,[129] it was impossible to reach a consensus on its inclusion in the ESDP. Laeken also declared the EU capable to conduct crisis management operations and the intention to "take on progressively more demanding operations".[130] The *European Capability Action Plan* in Annex I to the *Presidency Report on European Security and Defence Policy*, however, also acknowledged the considerable shortcomings and deficiencies with regards to military capabilities.[131]

[126] *Financial Times*, 2 December 2004, at 17; BBC online of 23 October 2004, 'EU Troops Prepare for Bosnia Swap', at http://news.bbc.co.uk/1/hi/world/europe/3944191.stm.

[127] See for example the *Statement on Improving European Military Capabilities*, Conference on EU Capability Improvement, Brussels, 19 November 2001, in Rutten, *From Nice to Laeken*, above n 64, at 95.

[128] N Gnesotto, 'Preface, EDSP 2001: routine and revolution', in Rutten, *From Nice to Laeken*, above, at vii.

[129] Presidency Report on European Union Action Following the Attacks in the United States, European Council in Laeken, 14–15 December 2001, Rutten, *From Nice to Laeken*, above n 64, at 186–91. See also: Common Position on Combating Terrorism, Council. Brussels, 27 December 2001, Rutten, *From Nice to Laeken*, above, at 192–98.

[130] Above. Especially the *Declaration on the Operational Capability of the Common European Security and Defence Policy*, at 119.

[131] See Rutten, *From Nice to Laeken*, above n 64, at 131–32.

2002 was to a large extent a continuation of the 'routine and revolution' of 2001 with respect to European defence integration. As explained above, the first missions in Bosnia and Macedonia took shape. Moreover, informal and formal meetings of the EU defence ministers became a regular occurrence, work on the improvement of military capabilities continued, a first crisis management exercise was conducted,[132] EU–NATO relations were formalised,[133] and the Berlin-Plus Agreement provided a framework for the EU drawing on NATO assets.

2003 was characterised by the split between the Member States caused by the US-led invasion of Iraq. Member States such as the United Kingdom and Spain and candidate countries such as Poland supported and participated in the invasion whereas France, Germany, Belgium, and Luxembourg opposed military action without a mandate of the UN Security Council. This even led the latter Member States to consider a separate Defence Community during a 'Four-Power-Conference' in Brussels in April 2003, which ultimately amounted to nothing.

Another important development reached a critical stage at the end of 2003: the Draft Constitutional Treaty. In December 2000, in Nice, the European Council reached an agreement on the revision of the Treaties. The objective was to adapt the institutions of the EU to enlargement, thereby expressing the need to initiate a wider and deeper debate on the future of the Union.[134] In December 2001 the Laeken European Council adopted the Declaration on the Future of the European Union[135] thereby committing the EU to becoming more democratic, more transparent, and more efficient and to preparing the way for a Constitution for the citizens of Europe. For this purpose, it decided to organise a convention bringing together the main stakeholders to examine the vital questions raised by the future development of the Union and to seek different possible responses, which are presented in the Draft Treaty establishing a Constitution for Europe. One of the four central questions to be addressed was how to ensure the cohesion and effectiveness of the external action of the EU.[136] Meeting from February 2002 to July 2003 the Convention formulated a Draft Constitutional Treaty.[137] This draft formed the working basis for the negotiations of the Intergovernmental Conference, composed of the Heads of State and Government of the Member States and the

[132] See the press information in: J-Y Haine, *From Laeken to Copenhagen*, Volume III, Chaillot Paper No 57, (Institute of Security Studies of the European Union, Paris, 2003) 65.

[133] This process started already in 2001, see the First Meeting of EU and NATO Military Committees, Brussels, 12 June 2001, press release, printed in Rutten, *From Nice to Laeken*, above n 64, at 69, see also the Joint Press Statement by the NATO Secretary General and the EU Presidency, after the EU–NATO ministerial meeting in Reykjavik, 14–15 May 2002, printed in Haine, above, at 60; *European Union–NATO Declaration on EDSP*, Haine, above, at 178.

[134] See Declaration 23 on the Future of the Union, Final Act, Treaty of Nice Amending the Treaty on European Union, the Treaties Establishing the European Communities and Certain Related Acts, [2001] OJ C–80/01.

[135] http://europa.eu.int/futurum/documents/offtext/doc151201_en.htm.

[136] The fundamental questions were how to organise the division of responsibilities between the Union and the Member States, how to better define the respective tasks of the European institutions, how to ensure the coherence and effectiveness of the Union's external action, and how to strengthen the Union's legitimacy? See Laeken Declaration, above.

[137] http://european-convention.eu.int/docs/Treaty/cv00850.en03.pdf.

accession countries. The envisaged passing of the Constitutional Treaty on the Brussels Summit in December 2003 failed but succeeded in June 2004. The Treaty was signed on 29th October 2004.

5. CONCLUSIONS

There is a possibility that 2005 is the eve of a new and crucial phase of European defence integration. The Constitutional Treaty might address many of the shortcomings of the ESDP discussed in this chapter. On the positive side the EU has formed military structures to organise and supervise the ESDP in practice, there has been a decisive move towards an independent military capability, and a number of modest first missions could be completed successfully. On the negative side European defence integration remains fragmented. NATO and the WEU continue to play significant roles, certain Member States still conduct military missions outside the EU framework, and the ESDP is part of the more intergovernmental Second Pillar of the TEU, separate from the more supranational First Pillar. The next six chapters of this book will show that the First Pillar is also an instrument of European defence integration. The understanding of this function will facilitate the understanding of the full extent of the fragmentation of European defence integration.

Part II

Community Law as an Instrument of European Defence Integration

4

A Fine Balance: Free Movement and Public Security in the EC Treaty

1. INTRODUCTION

PART I OF this book discussed the evolution of European defence integration from the 1950s until 2005. As described in chapter 1,[1] in the 1950s, after the failure of the European Defence Community, defence integration was enshrined in the Modified Brussels Treaty of the more intergovernmental Western European Union (hereinafter WEU) and thereby separated from the more supranational mainstream of European integration conducted in the framework provided by the European Communities (hereinafter EC). The latter was designed mainly as a commercial enterprise, establishing a common and later an internal market. This included a number of social and other policies but excluded defence. In a Europe dependent on the United States and NATO for its defence, the WEU remained largely dormant. In the early 1990s the Member States of the EC revived the European defence integration process by establishing the Common Foreign and Security Policy (hereinafter CFSP) discussed in chapter 2 as a Second more intergovernmental Pillar separate from the more supranational Community Pillar. As explained in chapter 3,[2] in the late 1990s a distinct European Security and Defence Policy (hereinafter ESDP) including an autonomous military capability was added to the CFSP. Both the WEU and the CFSP/ESDP are designed as frameworks separate from the economic and social framework of the EC. This separation of defence from the other policies assumes and requires defence to be completely separable from other fields of integration.

Defence, however, has commercial and social implications. The regulation of exports, intra-Community transfers, public procurement,[3] State aids, competition,[4] and mergers are substantial parts of the internal market established by the EC Treaty. They affect the defence sector just like any other part of industry. The automatic exemption of that sector for national security reasons would exclude a significant part of industry from the application of the Treaty and might

[1] At 44–49.
[2] At 92–120.
[3] See ch 7 for details on public procurement.
[4] See ch 8 for details on competition law.

be detrimental to the functioning of the common market as a whole. Similarly, the substantial body of social law developed in the framework of the Community, for example with regards to sex equality at the workplace, affects the armed forces just like any other profession. The automatic exclusion of the military for reasons of national security would exclude a significant part of the workforce from the application of the Treaty.[5] Therefore the founders of the EC had to strike a balance between the objectives of the common market and other interests of the Community and the national security interests of the Member States.

The EC Treaty provides a sophisticated mechanism to strike this balance: Articles 296 (ex223), 297 (ex224), 30 (ex36), 39 (3) (ex48), 46 (1) (ex56) and 58 (1) (b) (ex73d) EC, represent exemptions from the Treaty justified by security considerations. Measures normally ruled out are allowed under certain circumstances. The mechanism could be described using the metaphor of scales. The scales strike a balance between the internal market and other interests of the Community on one side and the security interests of the Member States on the other side. In practice this balancing mechanism is applied by the Member States. They have to decide whether exemption is legal in an individual case. However, using the balancing mechanism the Member States may give disproportionate weight to their own national security interests. Such a tendency can be detected in all the cases discussed in this chapter. An affected private party, the Commission, or other Member States may have a different opinion on the legality of exemption. Therefore they may be the second 'users' applying the balancing mechanism. A dispute between the first and the second 'users' of the balancing mechanism can involve a third 'user', the European Court of Justice. The latter will be the last instance regarding the application of the balancing mechanism to an individual case. In such a case the balancing mechanism consists of two aspects: the very exemption provided in the EC Treaty and its application by the European Court of Justice. The Court striking a balance between the internal market interests of the Community and the security interests of the Member States on the basis of the exemptions is also the Court setting the limits between the competencies of the Community and the Member States regarding cases with security implications.

In relation to Articles 30, 39 (3), 46 (1) and 58 (1) (b) EC, the European Court of Justice exercises strict scrutiny over national measures, including a detailed and intense proportionality test. This will be discussed in this chapter. On the basis of recent judgments of the Court it will be explained that the Member States are not the sole judges on whether a measure involving national security is lawful under the national security exceptions in Articles 296 and 297 EC either. This will be discussed in chapters 5 and 6. Moreover, the security exemptions in the Treaty are also present in the relevant instruments of secondary Community legislation where they operate within specific fields of law. Chapters 7 and 8 deal with areas of economic law. Chapter 7 will discuss the public procurement directives and chapter 8 the areas of competition law, State aids, merger control, exports, imports, and intra-community transfers. Chapter 9 discusses the operation

[5] See ch 9 for details on EC sex equality law and the armed forces.

of the Equal Treatment Directive in the armed forces of the Member States as an example of the effect of EC social law on defence. These six chapters forming Part II of this book will show that Community law is an instrument of European defence integration within the limits of the security exemptions and the scrutiny exercised by the European Court of Justice. The EC Treaty and relevant subsidiary Community legislation affect the governments of the Member States, their armed forces, and their defence industries. Hence, in addition to the effect of the WEU and the Second Pillar discussed in Part I of this book there is an effect of Community law on the defence of the Member States.

The degree of scrutiny exercised over the use of the security exemptions by the Court is crucial. A wide margin of discretion left to the Member States and a power for the Court to review their measures is the solution to balance the conflicting interests of security and the Community. The Court will apply the proportionality test to different degrees of intensity. The weaker the commercial link and the stronger the security link of a provision, the lower the degree of intensity. This ranges from a strict test in relation to a low degree of scrutiny in relation to Article 297 EC at the other end of the spectrum. Article 296 (1) (b) EC is situated between these two extremes. The information privilege in Article 296 (1) (a) EC also needs to be subject to scrutiny to avoid its abuse. The following short chapter 4 looks at the exemptions in Articles 30, 39 (3), 46 (1) and 58 (1) (b) EC, which are situated at the other end of the spectrum where scrutiny is very intense. First, the chapter will highlight the common ground and the differences between the security-type exemptions of the Treaty including the basic rules for their interpretation and the rationale for these rules. Second, it will analyse the functioning of the balancing mechanism provided by Articles 30, 39 (3), 46 (1) and 58 (1) (b) EC including the procedures for the judicial review of their use and the standard of review. Unlike Articles 296 and 297 EC, Articles 30, 39 (3), 46 (1) and 58 (1) (b) EC do not mainly operate in areas of defence and national security. However, a discussion of these provisions is required in the context of Part II of this book for two reasons. First, the case law of the European Court of Justice on these exemptions is far more developed than the jurisprudence on Articles 296 and 297 EC and its discussion is therefore to a certain extent necessary for the understanding of the latter provisions. Second, Articles 30, 39 (3), 46 (3) and 58 (1) (b) EC may to a limited extent affect defence and national security. Therefore, an analysis of these provisions is needed to provide a comprehensive discussion of the security exemptions in Community law.

2. THE LIMITED SCOPE OF THE SECURITY EXCLUSIONS IN THE EC TREATY

The leading judgment for the exemptions in Articles 30, 39 (3), 46 (1) and 58 (1) (b) EC and the security exemptions in general is *Marguerite Johnston* v. *Chief Constable of the Royal Ulster Constabulary*.[6] The case concerned a prohibition for

[6] Case C–222/84, *Marguerite Johnston v Chief Constable of the Royal Ulster Constabulary* [1986] ECR 1651, [1986] 3 CMLR 240.

female officers of the Royal Ulster Constabulary, now called the Police Service of Northern Ireland, to wear firearms. This excluded women from a considerable part of police activity and was challenged under the EC Equal Treatment Directive.[7] The Court ruled "the only articles in which the Treaty provides for derogations applicable in situations which may involve public safety are [...] Articles [30, 39, 46, 296 and 297 EC], which deal with exceptional and clearly defined cases. Because of their limited character", said the Court, "those articles do not lend themselves to a wide interpretation and it is not possible to infer from them that there is inherent in the Treaty a general proviso covering all measures taken for reasons of public safety".[8] Article 58 (1) (b) EC (ex73d) was inserted into the Treaty after this judgment and needs to be added to the list of exemptions set out in *Johnston*.[9]

The Court also gave a reason for this basic interpretation of the security exemptions: "If every provision of Community law were held to be subject of a general proviso, regardless of the specific requirements laid down by the provisions of the Treaty, this might impair the binding nature of Community law and its uniform application".[10] There is an underlying principle that security exclusions from the Treaty are exhaustive and have to be interpreted narrowly. This principle applies to all security type exclusions. There are no general and automatic national security exemptions from the Treaty, as this would bring the effectiveness of Community law into question. The internal market is absolute, unless a Member State can invoke one of the exemptions allowing derogation from the Treaty on a case-by-case basis. These are the fundamental principles governing the security type exemptions of the EC Treaty and secondary Community law. Therefore the *Johnston* ruling will feature prominently in all chapters of Part II of this book.

Returning to the 'scales metaphor' outlined above, the very existence of security exemptions represents a heavy weight on the side of the security interests of the

[7] For a detailed discussion of this case see ch 9 at 266–269.

[8] C-222/84, *Johnston*, above n 6, para 26. See also Case C–13/68 *SpA Salgoil v Italian Ministry of Foreign Trade* [1968] ECR 453, 463; [1969] CMLR 181, 192; and Case C–7/68 *Commission v Italy* [1968] ECR 633, 644.

[9] The provision allows measures restricting the free movement of capital similar to Articles 30, 39(3) and 46(1) EC The Court, however, never mentioned Article 58(1)(b) EC when it listed the security exemptions: Case C–285/98, *Kreil v Germany*, [2000] ECR I–69, para 26 (for a detailed discussion of this case see ch 9 at 277–284); Case C–414/97, *Commission v Spain*, [1999] ECR I–5585, [2000] 2 CMLR 4, para 21 (for a detailed discussion of this case see ch 5 at 152–154); Case C–273/97 *Sirdar v The Army Board*, [1999] ECR I–7403, [1999] 3 CMLR 559 para 16 (for details see below and ch 9 and 269–277). In these cases the Court referred to the judgment in *Johnston*, which in 1986 could not take the provision, which was adopted in 1994, into account. The fact that the Court did not add the provision to the list in *Kreil* or *Sirdar* appears to be an oversight. The advisory opinion of Advocate General Cosmas in Case C–423/98, *Alfredo Albore* [2000] ECR I–5965, at para 47, seems to support this finding: 'Nous avons précédement indiqué que les auteurs du traité instituant la Communauté économique européenne utilisent l'expression "sécurité publique" pour traduire une même dimension de l'intérêt public, tant dans le contexte de l'article 73 D [now 58] que dans celui des articles 36, 56 et 66 [now 30, 46 and 55] du traité CE.' The judgment, [1999] ECR I–5965, para 19, explicitly refers to Article 73d EC as one of the public security derogations to which the *Johnston* judgment applies.

[10] Case C–222/84, above n 6, para 26.

Member States. This is counterbalanced in favour of the internal market and other interests of the Community by the exhaustive character of the list of security exemptions and their narrow interpretation provided by the Court in *Johnston*.

The security type exemptions can be divided into two groups on the basis of the level of scrutiny the European Court of Justice can exercise and thus their importance for the constitutional debate. These are Articles 30, 39 (3), 46 (1) and 58 (1) (b) EC on the one hand and Articles 296 and 297 EC on the other hand. In relation to the second group, the Court cannot interpret these provisions without defining the limits of sovereignty over national security. Therefore the Court avoided ruling on these provisions until recently. As explained above, chapter 4 will deal with the first group of exemptions. Chapter 5 will deal with Article 296 EC and chapter 6 with Article 297 EC.

3. PUBLIC SECURITY EXEMPTIONS

The EC Treaty contains a set of free movement regimes aimed at establishing an internal market between the Member States. A first regime concerns the free movement of goods, which are defined as products that can be valued in money and subject to commercial transactions.[11] This regime can be subdivided into two prohibitions. First, Article 25 EC[12] prohibits customs duties, in other words levies on goods simply for the reason that they cross a border between Member States. Measures having equivalent effect to customs duties are also prohibited.[13] The prohibition is absolute. In other words, this part of the free movement of goods regime does not provide for an exemption that could justify customs duties or measures having equivalent effect for reasons of security, health, or other public interest reasons.[14] The abolition of customs duties makes the Community a customs union. It already represents a substantial commitment of the Member States since customs duties used to be a considerable source of income for the national treasuries. Second, Articles 28 and 29 EC Treaty[15] prohibit quantitative

[11] The European Court of Justice provided this definition in *Case C–7/68, Commission v Italy ('Arts Treasures')* [1968] ECR 423.

[12] Article 25 EC reads: 'Customs duties on imports and exports and charges having equivalent effect shall be prohibited between Member States. This prohibition shall not apply to customs duties of a fiscal nature.'

[13] Case C–24/68, *Commission v Italy ('Statistical Levy')* [1969] ECR 193 and Case C–2 and 3/69, *Sociaal Fonds voor de Diamantarbeiders v SA Ch Brachfeld & Sons ('Diamond Workers')* [1969] ECR 211.

[14] However, certain measures can be outside the prohibition of Article 25 EC. This applies in particular: (1) when the charge is merely a payment for a service the Member State has rendered to the importer as argued in Case C–87/75, *Breciani v Amministrazione Italiana delle Finanze dello Stato* [1976] ECR 129; (2) when the charge is made to pay for inspections carried out in fulfilment of legal requirements imposed by EC law as argued in Case C–18/87, *Commission v Germany* [1988] ECR 5427; or (3) when the charge is covered by the regime on discriminatory tax provisions of Articles 90–93 EC.

[15] Article 28 EC Treaty reads: 'Quantitative restrictions on imports and all measures having equivalent effect, shall be prohibited between Member States.' Article 29 EC Treaty reads: 'Quantitative restrictions on exports and all measures having equivalent effect, shall be prohibited between Member States.'

restrictions, that is restraints of trade in goods according to quantity or value,[16] on imports and exports respectively.[17] Measures having equivalent effect on customs duties are also prohibited. Subject to a rule of reason[18] and certain exceptions,[19] all Member State measures that directly or indirectly, actually or potentially restrict trade between Member States[20] are thus prohibited. The prohibition is the crucial component of the free movement of goods regime of the EC Treaty, which is at the heart of the internal market, the core of the European Community. However, in contrast to the prohibition of customs duties and measures having equivalent effect, the prohibition is not absolute. Article 30 EC Treaty[21] allows Member States to justify measures violating these prohibitions *inter alia* for reasons of public security. For example, a dangerous chemical can be stopped at the border when its import would pose a threat to public security. The prohibition of quantitative restrictions and measures having equivalent effect and the additional regimes described below make the Community more than just a customs union, they establish an internal market between the Member States.

A second regime concerns the free movement of workers, in other words of people who for a certain period of time perform services for and under the direction of another person in return for which they receive remuneration.[22] Article 39 EC Treaty[23] prohibits restrictions on the free movement of workers from other

[16] Case C–2/73, *Geddo v Ente Nazionale Risi* [1973] ECR 865, [1974] 1 CMLR 13.

[17] See: P Oliver, *Free Movement of Goods in the EC,* 3rd edn, (Sweet & Maxwell, London, 1996); C Barnard and J Scott (eds), *The Law of the Single European Market* (Hart Publishing, Oxford, 2002); P Craig and G de Búrca, *EU Law: Text, Cases and Materials* (OUP, Oxford, 2003) 613–79 (hereinafter *EU Law*); JHH Weiler, 'From Dassonville to Keck and Beyond: An Evolutionary Reflection on the Text and Context of the Free Movement of Goods' in P Craig and G de Búrca, (eds), *The Evolution of EU Law* (OUP, Oxford, 1999) ch 10 (hereinafter *Evolution*); J Snell, *Goods and Services in EC Law* (OUP, Oxford, 2002).

[18] The concept of 'mandatory requirements' or 'public interest grounds' established by the European Court of Justice in their jurisprudence since Case C–120/78, *Rewe-Zentrale AG v Bundesmonopolverwaltung für Brantwein* [1979] ECR 649. Paragraph 8 of the judgment reads: 'Obstacles to movement within the Community resulting from disparities between the national provisions may be recognised as being necessary in order to satisfy mandatory requirements relating in particular to the effectiveness of fiscal supervision, the protection of public health, the fairness of commercial transactions and the defence of the consumer.' Comparable to measures taken on the basis of Article 30 EC, measures taken within the concept of mandatory requirements have to be proportionate. However, according to the traditional jurisprudence mandatory requirements cannot take discriminatory measures outside the ambit of Article 28 EC.

[19] In particular rules that refer to selling arrangements rather than to the characteristics of the goods are outside the prohibition of Article 28 EC since the jurisprudence after Cases C–267 and 268/91, Criminal Proceedings against *Keck and Mithouard* [1993] ECR I–6097, para 16.

[20] Case C–8/74, *Procureur du Roi v Dassonville* [1974] ECR 837, para 5.

[21] The relevant sections of Article 30 EC Treaty read: 'The provisions of Articles 28 and 29 shall not preclude prohibitions or restrictions of imports, exports or goods in transit justified on grounds of [...] public security [...]'.

[22] Case C–66/85, *Lawrie-Blum v Land Baden-Württemberg* [1986] ECR 2121, para 17; Case C–3/90, *Bernini v Minister van Onderwijs en Weterschapen* [1992] ECR I–1071.

[23] Article 39 paras (1) and (2) EC Treaty reads: '1. Freedom of movement for workers shall be secured within the Community. 2. Such freedom of movement shall entail the abolition of any discrimination based on nationality between workers of the Member States as regards employment, remuneration and other conditions of work and employment.' Paragraph 3 contains a non-exhaustive list of free movement rights.

Member States.[24] However, similar to Article 30 EC Treaty for quantitative restrictions and measures having equivalent effect, Article 39 (3) EC Treaty[25] allows Member States to justify measures restricting the free movement of workers *inter alia* for reasons of public security. For example, a worker from another Member State can be stopped at the border or deported, if he or she is already on the territory of the Member State, if he or she poses a threat to public security. This could apply to a notorious criminal or terrorists.

Moreover, Article 39 (4) EC[26] excludes the public service from the free movement of workers. This exemption has another rationale than the public security exemptions. It accommodates the special relationship between the public servant and his or her Member State and the fact that he or she exercises power over citizens. The European Court of Justice interprets the term 'public service' restrictively[27] to avoid the removal of large parts of the workforce from the ambit of Community law, which would undermine the free movement of workers[28] and eventually lead to barriers to trade. The armed forces are clearly covered by the public service exception.[29] Therefore the EC Treaty allows discrimination on grounds of nationality with regards to the armed forces, which are allowed to exclude the nationals of other Member States. However, this does not mean that they are allowed to discriminate for example on grounds of sex, as will be explained in detail in chapter 9.

A third and fourth regime concerns free movement in relation to self-employed persons, such as lawyers or dentists, and companies. Article 43 EC Treaty[30] prohibits restraints on self-employed persons and companies[31] in relation

[24] See Craig and de Búrca, *EU Law*, above n 17, at 701–64; A Castro-Oliveira, 'Workers and Other Persons: Step-by-Step from Movement to Citizenship' (2002) 39 *Common Market Law Review* 77; F Weiss and F Wooldridge, *Free Movement of Persons within the European Community* (Kluwer, The Hague, 2002).

[25] The relevant sections of Article 39(3) EC Treaty read: 'It shall entail the right, subject to limitations justified on grounds of [...] public security [...]'. However, it needs to be emphasised that the provision can only justify limitations on free movement stipulated in para 3 itself. It cannot justify discrimination of workers from other Member States once they were allowed to immigrate.

[26] Article 39(4) EC Treaty reads: 'The provisions of this Article shall not apply to employment in the public service.'

[27] In his advisory opinion in Case C–307/84, *Commission v France ('French Nurses')* [1986] ECR 1725, at 1727–33 Advocate General Mancini pointed out: 'the duties must involve acts of which affect private individuals by requiring their obedience or, in the event of disobedience, by compelling them to comply. To make a list [...] is practically impossible; but certainly the first examples which come to mind are posts relating to policing, defence of the State, the administration of justice and assessments to tax.' See D O'Keeffe, 'Judicial Interpretation of the Public Service Exception to the Free Movement of Workers' in D Curtin and D O'Keefe, (eds), *Constitutional Adjudication in European Community and National Law* (Butterworths, Dublin, 1992) 89, at 101–3.

[28] Case C–149/79, *Commission v Belgium ('Belgian Local Authorities')* [1980] ECR 3881, para 11.

[29] See advisory opinion of Advocate General Mancini in Case C–307/84, *Commission v France*, above n 27, at 1727–33.

[30] Article 43 EC Treaty reads: 'Within the framework of the provisions set out below, restrictions on the freedom of establishment on the nationals of a Member State in the territory of another Member State shall be prohibited. [...]'.

[31] Article 48(1) EC reads: 'Companies and firms formed in accordance with the law of a Member State and having their registered office, central administration or principal place of business within the Community shall, for the purposes of this Chapter, be treated in the same way as natural persons who are nationals of the Member States.'

to establishment. Establishment involves the permanent integration into the economic framework of another Member State.[32] Similar to Article 30 EC in relation to the free movement of goods and Article 39 (3) EC in relation to the free movement of workers, Article 46 EC Treaty[33] allows Member States to justify measures in violation of that prohibition *inter alia* for reasons of public security. Article 49 EC Treaty[34] provides for the free movement of services.[35] In contrast to establishment this regime prohibits restraints of the temporary economic activities of self-employed persons and companies. According to Article 55 (1) EC[36] the public security exemption in Article 46 EC also applies to the free movement of services.

A fifth and sixth regime concerns capital and payments. Article 56 (1) EC Treaty[37] prohibits restrictions of the free movement of capital.[38] Article 56 (2) EC prohibits restrictions of the free movement of payments.[39] However, Article 58 (1) (b) EC Treaty[40] allows Member States to justify measures in violation of that prohibition for reasons of *inter alia* public security.[41] Hence the Treaty accommodates the public security competence of the Member States by allowing derogation from its core regimes in certain circumstances and if a number of requirements are met. The public security exemptions have two characteristics in common. They all allow derogation for reasons of 'public security' and are subject to strict judicial scrutiny exercised by the European Court of Justice.

[32] See Craig and de Búrca, *EU Law*, above n 17, at 765–99.

[33] Article 46(1) EC Treaty reads: '1. The provisions of this chapter and measures taken in pursuance thereof shall not prejudice the applicability of provisions laid down by law, regulation, or administrative action providing for special treatment for foreign nationals on grounds of public policy, public security or public health'.

[34] The relevant section of Article 49 EC Treaty reads: 'Within the framework of the provisions set out below, restrictions on freedom to provide services within the Community shall be prohibited in respect of nationals of Member States who are established in a State of the Community other than that of the person for whom the services are intended [...].'

[35] See Craig and de Búrca, *EU Law*, above n 17, at 800–23; Snell, above n 17.

[36] Article 55(1) EC reads: 'The provisions of Articles 45 to 48 shall apply to the matters covered by this chapter.'

[37] Article 56 (1) EC Treaty reads: 'Within the framework of the provisions set out in this Chapter, all restrictions on the movement of capital between Member States and between Member States and third countries shall be prohibited.'

[38] Article 56 (2) EC Treaty reads: 'Within the framework of the provisions set out in this Chapter, all restrictions on the movement of payments between Member States and between Member States and third countries shall be prohibited.'

[39] See S Peers, 'Free Movement of Capital: Learning Lessons or Slipping on Split Milk?' in C Barnard and J Scott, (eds), *The Legal Foundations of the Single Market* (Hart Publishing, Oxford, 2000); Craig and de Búrca, *EU Law*, above n 17, at 680–84.

[40] The relevant sections of Article 58(1)(b) EC Treaty read:

1. The provisions of Article 56 shall be without prejudice to the right of Member States: [...] (b) to take all requisite measures to prevent infringements of national law and regulations, in particular in the field of taxation and the prudential supervision of financial institutions, or to lay down procedures for the declaration of capital movements for purposes of administrative or statistical information, or to take measures which are justified on grounds of public policy or public security.

[41] On the fact that Article 58(1)(b) EC was not mentioned in the *Johnston* judgment, n 6 above.

3.1. Public Security

Articles 30, 39 (3), 46 (1) and 58 (1) (b) EC allow restrictions on grounds of 'public security'. Public security is a wide concept covering all aspects of security, internal and external,[42] including the concept of national security. Schwarze defines public security as "the entire field of rules, laid down by the sovereign authorities and incapable of being waived, which have been adopted in the interest of the political and social integrity of society".[43] This would cover all laws, regulations, and individual decisions enacted to protect the integrity of a Member State. A situation causing a Member State to take such a measure is a situation posing a threat to its integrity. In contrast, the exemptions in Articles 296 and 297 EC discussed in chapters 5 and 6 relate to a narrower concept of security.[44] The latter concept could be called 'national security' or 'external military security',[45] although these expressions are not used in the Treaty itself.[46] On the basis of the definition of public security provided by Schwarze, national security could be defined as the entire field of rules which have been adopted to protect the territorial integrity, important strategic interests and political independence of a State. Article 296 and 297 EC are special provisions superseding the wider public security provisions in Articles 30, 39 (3), 46 (1) and 58 (1) (b) EC in most cases involving national security. For example, Article 30 EC only applies to material not covered by Article 296 (1) (b) EC and only to situations not covered by Article 297 EC, as will be explained in more detail in chapters 5 and 6. The exemptions of the first group cover only a small number of situations relating to the notions of national security and therefore defence, which are the main focus of this book.

3.2. Procedures of Judicial Review

The use of Articles 30, 39 (3), 46 (1) and 58 (1) (b) EC is subject to judicial review. According to Article 220 EC the European Court of Justice has the jurisdiction to ensure that in the interpretation and application of the EC Treaty the law is observed. Two procedures are relevant in the context of the use of the public security exemptions by Member States: the preliminary ruling procedure in Article

[42] Case C–367/89, Criminal Proceedings against *Aimé Richardt and Les Accessoires Scientifiques SNC* [1991] ECR I–4621, para 22; Case C–70/94, *Fritz Werner Industrie-Ausrüstungen GmbH v Germany* [1995] ECR I–3989, para 25; Case C–83/94, Criminal Proceedings against *Peter Leifer* [1995] ECR I–3231, para 26.

[43] J Schwarze, *European Administrative Law* (Sweet & Maxwell, London, 1992), at 778, based on Wägbaur, in H von der Groeben, *v* Boeckh, Thiesing, Ehlermann, Kommentar zum EWG Vertrag, 3rd edn, (Nomos, Baden-Baden, 1983) Article 36, margin nos. 18 *et seq.*

[44] Advocate General Sir Gordon Slynn, Case C–72/83, *Campus Oil Limited v Minister for Industry and Energy*, [1984] ECR 2727, at 2764; [1984] 3 CMLR 544, at 558.

[45] Above.

[46] The term 'essential interests of [...] security' is used in Article 296(1)(a) and (b) EC. Security is not mentioned explicitly in Article 297 EC, but the situations described are situations affecting national security.

234 EC and enforcement actions under Articles 226 and 227 EC.[47] Preliminary rulings and enforcement actions on the same matter are possible, as the procedures are not mutually exclusive.[48]

3.2.1. Preliminary Rulings

First, the interpretation of the public security exemptions can be the subject of a preliminary ruling according to Article 234 (1) (a) EC.[49] Under this procedure, when a question concerning the interpretation of Community law is raised before a national court of a Member State, that court may request the European Court of Justice to give a ruling on that question if it considers such an interpretation necessary for its own judgment.[50] The reference is drafted in the form of one or more questions to the Luxembourg court. The principles of supremacy of Community law and direct effect outlined in chapter 1 can make provisions of Community law decisive issues in many proceedings before national courts. The preliminary ruling procedure provides for a dialogue between the national court and Luxembourg. However, the national court will decide on the individual case.[51] Normally an individual or a company will be in conflict with a Member State. Therefore this procedure can indirectly involve individuals who are affected by a Member State measure based on one of the public security exemptions. Most judgments concerning the public security exemptions discussed in this book were made in the context of a preliminary reference.[52]

3.2.2. Enforcement Actions

According to Article 226 (1) EC the Commission can send a reasoned opinion to a Member State if they consider that it has failed to fulfil an obligation under the EC Treaty. There are two stages before the reasoned opinion is delivered. First, a

[47] Case T–26/01, *Fiocchi Munizioni SpA v Commission of the European Communities*, (30 September 2003), is the only case where the judgment was made in the context of a procedure for failure to act under Article 232 EC. However, as the case concerned the national security exemption in Article 296(1)(b) EC it will be discussed in ch 5. Case C–120/94 R, *Commission v Greece (FYROM)* [1996] ECR I–1513 was the only case in the context of the special enforcement procedure of Article 298 EC. However, as the case concerned the national security exemption in Article 297 EC it will be discussed in ch 6.

[48] See Case C–26/62, NV AlgemeneTransport - en Expeditie Oderneming *van Gend en Loos v Nederlandse Administratie der Belastingen* [1963] ECR 1, at 13: 'The fact that these Articles of the Treaty enable the Commission and the Member States to bring before the Court a State which has not fulfilled its obligations does not mean that individuals cannot plead these obligations, should the occasion arise, before a national court.' See also: Case C–28/67, *Molkerei-Zentrale Westfalen v Hauptzollamt Paderborn* [1968] ECR 143, 153.

[49] Article 234(1)(a) EC reads: 'The Court of Justice shall have jurisdiction to give preliminary rulings concerning: (a) the interpretation of this Treaty; [...]'.

[50] Article 234(2) EC.

[51] For details on this procedure see Craig and de Búrca, *EU Law*, above n 17, at 432–81; M Andenas (ed), *Article 177 References to the European Court—Policy and Practice* (Butterworths, London, 1994).

[52] See Case C–13/68, *Salgoil*, above n 8; Case C–15/69, *Südmilch v Ugliola* [1969] ECR 363; Case C–72/83, *Campus Oil*, above n 44; Case C–222/84, *Johnston*, above n 6; Case C–367/89, *Aimé Richardt*, above n 42; Case C–70/94, *Werner*, above n 42; Case C–83/94, *Leifer*, above n 42; Case C–124/95, *The Queen, ex parte Centro-Com Srl v HM Treasury and Bank of England* [1997] ECR I–81; Case C–285/98, *Sirdar*, above n 9; Case C–285/98, *Kreil*, above n 9; Case C–423/98, *Albore*, above n 9.

pre-contentious stage of negotiations gives the Member State the opportunity to explain its legal position and reach an accommodation with the Commission.[53] Second, failing that the Commission will formally notify the Member State of the alleged infringement giving it two months to reply, except in matters of urgency. Failing that the Commission will issue the reasoned opinion as a third stage. The latter sets out the grounds on which the alleged infringement rests and marks the beginning of a time period in which the Member State in question must comply. Failure to comply can lead to the fourth stage. According to Article 226 (2) EC the Commission may refer the matter to the European Court of Justice if the Member State does not comply with the reasoned opinion within the period laid down by the Commission. The Court may rule against the Member State. If a Member State failed to comply with such a judgment in Article 226 EC proceedings, the Commission may request the Court to impose a penalty payment according to Article 228 (2) EC.[54] Hence the procedure has potentially four stages. The procedure has three main functions.[55] First it serves as a diplomatic instrument for removing infringements of Community law without having to resolve to litigation.[56] The procedure is successful here as most infringements are removed before a reasoned opinion has to be delivered. The second function is to allow individuals and companies to complain to the Commission about infringements of Community law by Member States. Finally, the procedure is an instrument of objective law enforcement allowing the Commission to fulfil its function as a watchdog over compliance with Community law. The procedure has also been criticised: "Commission discretion allows and scarce resources dictate, an ordered policy of selective enforcement"[57] and a successful enforcement action does not necessarily lead to compliance.[58] According to Article 227 EC another Member State can also bring proceedings. However, this procedure is not used very often.[59] This is probably due to the fact that such proceedings could disrupt the political relations of two Member States. Moreover, the Commission will take care of most cases anyway.

Only very few judgments concerning the public security exemptions discussed in this book were made in the context of enforcement proceedings.[60] As pointed out above most cases were decided in the context of preliminary references under Article 234 EC, cases initiated by private parties affected by Member State measures based on the public security exemptions. The question is, whether this can be

[53] Craig and de Búrca, *EU Law*, above n 17, at 400.

[54] The first penalty was imposed in Case C–387/97, *Commission v Greece* [2000] ECR I–5047.

[55] R Rawlings, 'Engaged Elites: Citizen Action and Institutional Attitudes in Commission Enforcement' (2000) 6 *European Law Journal* 4.

[56] See the *8th Annual Report* on Commission Monitoring of the Application of Community Law (1990), [1991] OJ C–338/6–7 as cited by Craig and de Búrca, *EU Law*, above n 17, at 397.

[57] Rawlings, above n 55, at 26.

[58] Craig and de Búrca, *EU Law*, above n 17, at 401.

[59] Above, at 429. Exceptions are: Case C–141/78, *France v United Kingdom* [1979] ECR 2923 and Case C–388/95, *Belgium v Spain* [2000] ECR I–3121.

[60] Case C–414/97, *Commission v Spain* [1999] ECR I–5585, [2000] 2 CMLR 4; Case C–62/96, *Commission v Greece* [1997] ECR I–6725.

interpreted as an indication for a certain reluctance by the Commission to initiate enforcement proceedings in cases involving the public security exemptions. In case of an affirmative answer, this might give rise to other questions concerning an extremely wide margin of discretion left to the Member States regarding measures taken to protect public security. However, it is submitted that the small number of judgments concerning public security cannot be interpreted as reluctance of the Commission to bring enforcement proceedings in these cases. First, references for preliminary rulings account for the biggest share of cases brought before the European Court of Justice generally.[61] Therefore it is hardly surprising that most judgments concerning public security were also made in the context of Article 234 EC proceedings. Second, the enforcement procedure in Article 226 EC with its informal and formal pre-judicial stage is designed to avoid court proceedings. In most cases this pre-judicial stage is successful and therefore there are fewer proceedings that end with a judgment. It can be assumed that most cases involving the public security exemptions are also resolved at the pre-judicial stage.

3.3. Standard of Judicial Review: Proportionality

Measures justified by one of the public security exemptions are subject to strict judicial scrutiny. The crucial element of this scrutiny is the application of the proportionality test.[62] Proportionality was developed from German administrative law by the European Court of Justice and is explicitly provided in Article 5 EC since the 2000 Treaty of Nice. In general terms the proportionality test involves a reasonable relationship of the relevant interests involved,[63] which in the context of this chapter can be identified as the internal market interest of the Community on one side and the public security interest of the Member States on the other. The test has three elements.[64] First, the measure in question has to be suitable to promote the objective of public security. Second, the measure has to be adequate. This means that there is "no other measure, less restrictive from the point of view of the free movement of goods, capable of achieving the same objective". The measure must "not restrict intra-Community trade more than is absolutely necessary". Third, the measure needs to be proportionate in the strict sense. The positive effect of the measure on the objective of public security has to be balanced with the negative effect on the internal market. Moreover, the weight of these interests in EC law needs to be determined as a precondition for the subsequent balancing operation.[65] This strict test will be

[61] Craig and de Búrca, *EU Law*, above n 17, at 474.

[62] Other elements of this scrutiny are legitimate expectations, non-discrimination and the emergent principle of transparency.

[63] G de Búrca, 'The Principle of Proportionality and its Application in EC Law' (1993) 13 *Yearbook of European Law* 105.

[64] Formulated by Advocate General van Gerwen in Case C–159/90, *SPUC v Grogan* [1991] ECR I–4685 as cited by de Búrca, above, at 113 including the more controversial third element. Also in favour of the three-part test (based on the same test in German administrative law, see Craig and de Búrca, *EU Law*, above n 17, at 372); Schwarze, above n 43, at 712.

[65] Craig and de Búrca, *EU Law*, above, at 372.

applied to all free movement exclusions. Many measures will already fail to meet the first or the first and second requirements of the test. Thus in many cases it will not be necessary to test all three elements. Moreover, whereas a clear distinction between elements two and three is made in many cases, in others stage three is folded back into stage two.[66] If the test is not satisfied the European Court of Justice will rule against the use of the exemption.

The test is applied to varying degrees of intensity depending on the type of case. In cases involving individual rights, scrutiny will be intense as judicial scrutiny is a necessary element of the recognition of these rights. It is the proper function of courts to adjudicate on whether State interference with individual rights is proportionate.[67] The margin of discretion left to the Member States is relatively narrow. In cases involving policy choices, scrutiny will be less intense as it is the task of the executive and the legislature to make policy choices and the judiciary is not to replace the political judgment of politicians and administrators with that of judges.[68] This is connected to the experience and skills of the executive compared to that of the judiciary which also needs to be taken into account.[69] Hence the intensity of scrutiny will vary depending on the subject matter of the case. However, as pointed out above scrutiny will be intense in cases where individuals challenge Member State action restricting their free movement for reasons of public security.

There is a tendency in the jurisprudence of the Court to apply the proportionality test to an ever-increasing intensity as time moves on. A Member State measure considered proportionate by the Court in the past might not get passed today.[70] Moreover, when the Court feels that public security considerations are simply argued as a pretence to cover protectionist measures the Member State arguments will be subjected to the strictest scrutiny.[71]

Three cases decided by the Court shall briefly be discussed to illustrate and clarify the application and limits of the free movement exemptions.

3.3.1. Campus Oil

Campus Oil Limited v. *Minister for Industry and Energy*[72] concerned an Irish law requiring companies dealing with oil products to buy 35 per cent of their requirements for crude oil from the only national refinery in the Republic. The reason for this requirement was to preserve a national refinery capacity. Article 28 EC Treaty

[66] Above.

[67] Craig and de Búrca, *EU Law*, above n 17, at 373.

[68] Above.

[69] De Búrca, above n 63, at 112.

[70] See for example Case C–41/74, *Van Duyn v Home Office* [1974] ECR 1337 and Cases C–115 and 116, *Adoui and Cornuaille v Belgium* [1982] ECR 1665 concerning the free movement of workers and the public security exemption in Article 39(3) EC.

[71] See for example Case C–40/82, *Commission v United Kingdom ('Poultry Meat')* [1982] ECR 2793 concerning the free movement of goods and disproportionate measures based on the public health exemption in Article 30 EC.

[72] Case C–72/83, above n 44.

(then 30) prohibited this Irish requirement. As a State measure which restricted intra-Community trade, it represented a measure having equivalent effect to a quantitative restriction. Ireland invoked Article 30 EC Treaty (then 36) for reasons of public security. The Court applied the proportionality test in relation to the measure. It considered the Irish purchase requirement to be suitable and necessary because of the strategic importance of a national refining capacity and the connected importance of petroleum products for the functioning of the State. The Court also took the geographic isolation of Ireland and her status of neutrality into account. The judgment is probably the best example of a successful use of Article 30 EC Treaty in a security context. Moreover, *Campus Oil* concerns the narrower national security context, which will be explained in more detail in chapters 5 and 6.

Campus Oil suggests a wide margin of discretion left to the Member States for measures taken in the narrower national security context included in the notion of public security in Article 30 EC. For a number of reasons, however, it is submitted that the ruling cannot be interpreted as a general rule giving Member States a wide margin of discretion. Again, exclusions have to be interpreted narrowly.[73] Thus a unique national industrial or technological capability or the only provider of a particular service has to be in danger of going out of business without the measure in question. Without the respective provider, for example, government and private companies would have to procure the goods or services from abroad. The capability has to be unique to a small country or it has to be the only provider in a certain region of a Member State with a large territory, such as France or Sweden. Therefore the exemption will only apply to a few markets.

Furthermore, the capability has to be relevant to national security. As could be seen in *Campus Oil*, the only national provider for fuel, for example, will meet this requirement, as tanks do not roll without fuel. The only provider for cheese, for example, will not meet this requirement, as soldiers can do without cheese and eat something else instead.[74] Therefore the exemption will only apply to a few goods and services.

Moreover, the acceptance of economic means to implement security objectives by the Court in *Campus Oil* cannot necessarily be applied to other Member States. The Republic of Ireland is geographically isolated and it would be hard to deliver crucial supplies from other parts of the Union during a serious crisis.[75] Furthermore, unlike most other Member States the Republic is neutral and in

[73] Case C–222/84, *Johnston*, above n 6, at para 26. See also Case C–13/68, *Salgoil*, above n 8, at 192.

[74] In Case C–231/83, *Cullert v Centre Leclerc* [1985] ECR I–306, at 313; [1985] 2 CMLR 524, at 535. Advocate General Verloren van Themaat referred to paras 34 and 47 of *Campus Oil* and pointed out: 'reliance upon public security can be justified only in so far as the production capacity in question is necessary for the proper functioning of Irish public institutions and essential public services and even the survival of its inhabitants.'

[75] See Advocate General Slynn in Case C–72/83, *Campus Oil*, above n 44, at 2764, and the arguments of the Irish Government, at 2735.

theory would have no allies in times of war.[76] A Member State in the heart of Europe who is also a member State of NATO might find it harder to justify the implementation of security interests by economic means. Therefore the ruling can only apply to certain Member States.

Finally, any reliance on this exemption will be subject to a strict proportionality test. This proportionality test will take the outlined considerations in relation to markets, products and neutrality into account. A justification based on Article 30 EC will probably not be accepted as necessary when the respective industrial capability is not crucial for defence or when a NATO ally in the vicinity can easily supply the products in question. Thus reliance on this situation is not likely to be accepted easily by the Court.

This interpretation of *Campus Oil* is confirmed by the judgment in *Commission* v. *Greece*.[77] The facts of the case were almost identical with that of *Campus Oil* and the Court pointed out:

> "Admittedly, in its judgment in Case 72/83 Campus Oil Ltd v Minister for Industry and Energy [1984] ECR 2727, paragraph 51, the Court stated that a Member State which is totally or almost totally dependant on imports for its supplies of petroleum products may rely on grounds of public security within the meaning of Article 36 of the Treaty for the purpose of requiring importers to cover a certain proportion of their needs by purchases from a refinery situated in its territory at prices fixed by the competent ministry on the basis of the costs incurred in the operation of that refinery, if the production of the refinery cannot be freely disposed of at competitive prices on the market concerned ."

However, the Court continued:

> "[...] it must be pointed out that Greece has not shown that if the State' s rights with regard to the importation and marketing of petroleum products were not maintained in force, the public-sector refineries would be unable to dispose of their products on the market at competitive prices and thereby ensure their continued operation. Consequently, the argument relied upon in that regard by Greece must be dismissed."

3.3.2. Richardt

Criminal Proceedings against Aimé Richardt and Les Accessoires Scientifiques SNC[78] concerned the transit of strategic goods from France through Luxembourg to the

[76] See the arguments of the Irish National Petroleum Corporation Limited in Case C–72/93, *Campus Oil*, above, at 2738, referring to 'Austria, Barbados, Cyprus, Jamaica, New Zealand and Thailand which are in a geo-political and economic situation similar to that of Ireland' and who 'all consider a domestic refining capacity to be an essential element of national security.' Because of Article 297 the principle of Community solidarity might be compromised in times of crisis or war. This principle requires Member States to help each other and is a foundation of the Union, see Case C–77/77, *BP v Commission* [1978] ECR 1513, [1978] 3 CMLR 174, at para 15.

[77] Case C–347/88, *Commission v Greece* [1990] ECR I–4747.

[78] Case C–367/89, above n 42.

Soviet Union. The question was whether Article 30 (then 36) EC allowed a Member State to require an additional authorisation for the transit of strategic goods and could confiscate the goods in consequence of a failure to comply with such a requirement. The Grand Duchy of Luxembourg considered the goods in question to be of a strategic nature and had made the transit through its territory subject to the grant of a special permission on grounds of external security. The Court ruled that the importation, exportation, and transit of goods capable of being used for strategic purposes might affect the public security of a Member State. Based on its judgment in *Campus Oil* the proportionality of the measure was the crucial issue. As a Member State might consider it necessary for public security reasons to verify the nature of goods described as strategic material, the Court considered making their transit subject to the grant of a special authorisation a proportionate use of the exemption in Article 30 EC.[79] The decision on the proportionality of the confiscation of the goods was referred back to the national Luxembourg court which had made the reference for a preliminary ruling.[80] *Richardt* confirms the basic rules established in *Campus Oil*: measures based on Article 30 EC need to be proportionate but the Member States have a certain margin of deciding which measures are necessary for their public security.

3.3.3. Albore

The intensity of the scrutiny applied by the Court became particularly clear in *Alfredo Albore* v. *Italy*.[81] The case concerned an Italian law requiring non-Italians to acquire the consent of the local administration before buying property in certain areas of the country. These areas were classified as of military interest and included all the small islands of Italy (!). Mr Albore, a notary handling the purchase of land for two German citizens on the island of Ischia, challenged the law as representing discrimination on grounds of nationality. The Italian government justified the law by referring to Articles 58 (1) (b) and 297 EC.

The Court pointed out that "a mere reference to the requirement of defence of the national territory, where the situation of the Member State concerned does not fall within the scope of Article [297 EC] cannot suffice" to justify a measure contrary to the Treaty.[82] "The position would be different only if it were demonstrated", said the Court, that to refrain from that measure contrary to the Treaty,

> "would expose the military interest of the Member State concerned *to real, specific and serious risk* which would not be countered by less restrictive procedures."[83]

Thus a risk for the military interest ("specific") of the Member State has to actually exist ("real"), the risk has to be military-specific and the risk has to reach a

[79] Above, para 23.
[80] Case C–367/89, above n 42, para 25.
[81] Case C–423/98, above n 9.
[82] Case C–423/98, above, para 21.
[83] Case C–423/98, above n 9, para 22.

certain level ("serious"), possibly excluding smaller risks. This represents a detailed three-limb suitability test as part of the proportionality test. Moreover, the measure has to be adequate ("which would not be countered by less restrictive procedures"). Thus in the context of the exemptions of the first group relating to military interests, the Court will apply a strict proportionality test including a specific three-limb suitability test. Furthermore, the Court emphasises the clear differentiation between the first and second group of exemptions, as indicated by the words "where the situation does not [...] fall within the scope of Article [297 EC]".

This degree of scrutiny is appropriate for two reasons. First, in the context of the crucial free movement provisions all restricting measures have to be proportional to ensure the functioning of the internal market. Second, the military interests of the Member States are sufficiently safeguarded by the exemptions of the second group. Thus there is no need to limit scrutiny in the context of the first group.

4. CONCLUSIONS

Defence and security are at the heart of the sovereignty of the Member States. The free movement regimes on goods, workers, establishment, services, capital, and payments are at the heart of the Community. Security considerations can affect the free movement regimes of the EC Treaty. Therefore conflicts between security and the internal market, which in the constitutional framework of the EU are attributed to different levels of governance, are possible. The EC Treaty provides a mechanism to solve these conflicts. Articles 30, 39 (3), 46 (1) and 58 (1) (b) EC allow Member States to derogate from the free movement regimes for reasons of public security. The exemptions need to be specifically invoked and the Member State in question has the burden of proof for the existence of a situation that justifies exemption. The use of these provisions is subject to judicial review by the European Court of Justice under the usual procedures.

Using the metaphor of scales which balance the conflicting interests involved, the Community and Member State interests can be balanced on three levels. The very existence of public security exemptions is a heavy weight on the side of the Member States' interests as they make clear that the free movement regimes are not absolute. However, the exhaustive character and narrow interpretation of these provisions counterbalances this heavy weight in favour of the Community side of the scales. The fact that judicial scrutiny is exercised at all is a weight in the side of the Community interests. The proportionality test allows balancing both sides of the scales. Finally, if necessary, proportionality in the strict sense provides a mechanism to achieve an almost perfect balance.

Article 296 EC, which is the subject matter of the next chapter 5, and Article 297 EC, which is the subject matter of chapter 6, are special provisions superseding the wider public security provisions in Articles 30, 39 (3), 46 (1) and 58 (1) (b) EC in most cases involving national security. For example, Article 30 EC only applies to material not covered by Article 296 (1) (b) EC and only to situations not covered by Article 297 EC. The exemptions of the first group cover only a small number of situations relating to the notion of national security and therefore defence, which is the main focus of this book. However, the exemptions of the first group form part of the borderline between Community and Member State competence for defence that serves to define the limits of the EC Treaty as an instrument of European defence integration. Moreover, due to a lack of case law on the exemptions of the second group, the rich case law helps to clarify the interpretation of Articles 296 and 297 EC and serves as a benchmark for their operation in practice.

5

An Even Finer Balance: Armaments, Secrecy, and Article 296 EC

1. INTRODUCTION

THE PREVIOUS CHAPTER 4 discussed the public security exclusions of the free movement regimes of the EC Treaty in Articles 30, 39 (3), 46 (1) and 58 (1) (b) EC. They constitute a first group of security exemptions which forms part of the borderline between Community and Member State competence for defence. This borderline defines the limits of the EC Treaty as an instrument of European defence integration. The exemptions of the first group are superseded by the national security exemptions of the second group of exclusions, which consists of Articles 296 and 297 EC. Article 30 EC, for example, only applies to material not covered by Article 296 (1) (b) EC and only to situations not covered by Article 297 EC. A common feature of the second group of exclusions is that in cases of "improper use" they can be subject to a special procedure under Article 298 subparagraph 2 EC.[1] Until recently the European Court of Justice has shown a great reluctance to deal with this second group of exemptions. Even in *Marguerite Johnston* v. *Chief Constable of the Royal Ulster Constabulary*, a judgment on all security exemptions, the Luxembourg court considered it unnecessary to answer the specific question on Article 297 EC.[2] In Criminal Proceedings against *Aimé Richardt and Les Accessoires Scientifiques SNC*[3] the Court, referring to *Johnston*, repeated the ruling on the narrow application of the exemptions in relation to Article 30 EC. However, following the advisory opinion of Advocate General Jacobs,[4] it considered it unnecessary to deal with Articles 296 and 297 EC. In *Fritz*

[1] Article 298 EC reads:

[1] If measures taken in the circumstances referred to in Article 296 and 297 have the effect of distorting competition in the common market, the Commission shall, together with the State concerned, examine how these measures can be adjusted to the rules in the Treaty.

[2] By way of derogation from the procedure laid down in Articles 226 and 227, the Commission or any Member State may bring the matter directly before the Court of Justice if it considers that another Member State is making improper use of the powers provided for in Articles 296 and 297. The Court shall give its ruling in camera.

[2] Case C–222/84, *Marguerite Johnston v Chief Constable of the Royal Ulster Constabulary* [1986] ECR 1651; [1986] 3 CMLR 240, para 60.

[3] Case C–367/89, Criminal Proceedings against *Aimé Richardt and Les Accessoires Scientifiques SNC* see:[1991] ECR I–4621. See ch 4 at 137–138 for details.

[4] Case C–367/89, above, at para 30.

Werner Industrie-Ausrüstungen GmbH v. *Germany*[5] and Criminal Proceedings against *Peter Leifer and others,*[6] again, the Court, following the advisory opinion of Advocate General Jacobs,[7] considered it unnecessary to deal with the national security exemptions in the EC Treaty as there was a special provision in Article 11 (Export) Council-Regulation 2603/69/EEC.[8] In *Alfredo Albore* v. *Italy*[9] the Court, following the advisory opinion of Advocate General Cosmas, considered Article 297 EC not to apply to the case. Article 296 (1) (b) EC was the first provision of the second group that the Court dealt with specifically.

This chapter will discuss Article 296 EC followed by chapter 6 on Article 297 EC. Article 296 EC consists of two national security exemptions. The first section of this article will discuss the armaments exemption in Article 296 (1) (b) EC. The second section will cover the secrecy exemption in Article 296 (1) (a) EC. It will be shown that compared to the provisions of Articles 30, 39 (3), 46 (1) and 58 (1) (b) EC discussed in chapter 4, the use of these exemptions is subject to different pre-judicial and judicial review procedures and to a different standard of review. Judicial scrutiny is less intense than that applied in the context of the public security exemptions, leaving a wider margin of discretion to the Member States. The exemptions in Article 296 (1) (b) and 296 (1) (a) EC are part of the sophisticated mechanism provided in the Treaty to balance the internal market and other interests of the Community with the national security interests of the Member States. This balancing mechanism allows its users, the Member States, the Commission, and if necessary the European Court of Justice to determine the borderline between Community and Member State competence in individual cases. This borderline defines the limits of Community law as an instrument of European defence integration.

2. THE ARMAMENTS EXEMPTION OF ARTICLE 296 (1) (B) EC

Article 296 (1) (b) EC allows a Member State "to take such measures as it considers necessary for the protection of the essential interests of its security which are connected with the production or trade in arms, munitions and war material". According to Article 296 (2) EC[10] the Council had to draw a precise list of such "arms, munitions, and war material" to which Article 296 (1) (b) EC applies. The list has to be understood as an integral part of Article 296 (1) (b) EC, detailing and replacing the words "arms, munitions, and war material" in the Treaty provision. Inserting the list in Article 296 (1) (b) EC itself would have made the provision

[5] 'Case C–70/94, *Fritz Werner Industrie-Ausrüstungen GmbH v Germany* [1995] ECR I–3189.

[6] Case C–83/94, Criminal Proceedings against *Peter Leifer* [1995] ECR I–3231.

[7] Cases C–83/94, above, and C–70/94 above n 5, para 51.

[8] Regulation 2603/69/EEC [1969] OJ L–324/25 as amended by Council–Regulation 3918/91/EEC [1991] OJ L–372/3.

[9] Case C–423/98, *Alfredo Albore v Italy* [2000] ECR I–5965. See ch 4 at 138–139 for details.

[10] Article 296 (2) EC reads: 'The Council may, acting unanimously on a proposal from the Commission, make changes to the list, which it drew up on 15 April 1958, of the products to which the provision of para 1 (b) apply.'

very long. Moreover, it might have prolonged the negotiations leading to the Rome Treaties as it might have led to disputes over individual items on the list. Hence it was adequate to move this question of detail to a later Council meeting. The difference between the list stipulated in the Treaty itself on the one hand and the separate list to be decided on by the Council on the other hand is, that in the earlier case amendments to the list could only have been decided by an Intergovernmental Conference. As the latter is the case, amendments are subject to a unanimous decision of the Council. Even in the European Defence Community Treaty discussed in chapter 1,[11] similar lists of armaments are stipulated in Annexes I and II to Article 107 of that Treaty rather than being included in the text of the Treaty itself.

2.1. The List of Armaments According to Article 296 (2) EC

In 1958 the Council drew up the list of products to which Article 296 (1) (b) EC applies.[12] There have been no amendments since then[13] and the list was often assumed outdated.[14] Products on this list are also called warlike or hard defence material, although these expressions are slightly misleading, as will be explained below. The list was never officially published and the governments of the Member States had different attitudes regarding its confidentiality. Some governments and the Commission treated it as a confidential document. Other governments were happy to supply a copy to anybody interested. In the 1980s and 1990s it was produced in academic publications.[15] Hence it has been in the public domain. However, not everybody found it easy to get a copy. The problem with this half-secrecy was, that governments could abuse Article 296 (1) (b) EC by extending it to products which were not on the list. It is obviously difficult to argue against such a policy in practice without knowing the precise contents of the list.

In a written question dated 4 May 2001 a Member of the European Parliament asked the Council: "which products appear on the list of 15 April 1958 to which Article 296(1)(b) refers?"[16] In a reply dated 27 September 2001 the Council provided the following list.

[11] At 41, footnote 135.

[12] Council–Decision 298/58 (15 April 1958).

[13] Commission Answer to a Written Question 573/85 [1985] OJ C–269; Advocate General Jacobs in his advisory opinion in Case C–367/89, *Richardt*, above n 5, at para 30; P Gilsdorf, 'Les reserves de sécurité du Traité CEE, à la lumière du Traité sur L'Union Europénne' (1994) *Revue du marché commun et l'Union europénne* 17, at 20.

[14] RA Wessel, *The Foreign and Security Policy of the European Union: A Legal Institutional Prespective* (Kluwer, The Hague, 1999) 312.

[15] See: A Courades Allebeck, 'The European Community: from the EC to the European Union' in H Wulf, (ed), *Arms Industry Limited* (OUP, Oxford, 1993) 214; M Trybus, *European Defence Procurement Law: International and National Procurement Systems as Models for a Liberalised Defence Procurement Market in Europe* (Kluwer, The Hague, 1999) 14–15 (n 41). It was also published in a publication of the Independent European Programme Group, the predecessor of the Western European Armaments Group of the Western European Union, called *Towards a Stronger Europe* (Brussels, 1987).

[16] Written Question E–1324/01 by Bart Staes (Verts/ALE) to the Council, [2002] OJ C–364 E, 20 December 2001, at 85–86.

"[List according to Article 296 (2) EC]

1. Portable and automatic firearms, such as rifles, carbines, revolvers, pistols, sub-machine guns and machine guns, except for hunting weapons, pistols and other low calibre weapons of the calibre less than 7 mm.
2. Artillery, and smoke, gas and flame throwing weapons such as:
   (a) cannon, howitzers, mortars, artillery, anti-tank guns, rocket launchers, flame throwers, recoilless guns;
   (b) military smoke and gas guns.
3. Ammunition for the weapons at 1 and 2 above.
4. Bombs, torpedoes, rockets and guided missiles:
   (a) bombs, torpedoes, grenades, including smoke grenades, smoke bombs, rockets, mines, guided missiles, underwater grenades, incendiary bombs;
   (b) military apparatus and components specially designed for the handling, assembly, dismantling, firing or detection of the articles at (a) above.
5. Military fire control equipment:
   (a) firing computers and guidance systems in infra-red and other night guidance devices;
   (b) telemeters, position indicators, altimeters;
   (c) electronic tracking components, gyroscopic, optical and acoustic;
   (d) bomb sights and gun sights, periscopes for the equipment specified in this list.
6. Tanks and specialist fighting vehicles:
   (a) tanks;
   (b) military type vehicles, armed or armoured, including amphibious vehicles;
   (c) armoured cars;
   (d) half-tracked military vehicles;
   (e) military vehicles with tank bodies;
   (f) trailers specially designed for the transportation of the ammunition specified at paragraphs 3 and 4.
7. Toxic or radioactive agents:
   (a) toxic, biological or chemical agents and radioactive agents adapted for destructive use in war against persons, animals or crops;
   (b) military apparatus for the propagation, detection and identification of substances at paragraph (a) above;
   (c) counter-measures material related to paragraph (a) above.
8. Powders, explosives and liquid or solid propellants:
   (a) powders and liquid or solid propellants specially designed and constructed for use with the material at paragraphs 3, 4 and 7 above;
   (b) military explosives;
   (c) incendiary and freezing agents for military use.

9. Warships and their specialist equipment:
   (a) warships of all kinds;
   (b) equipment specially designed for laying, detecting and sweeping mines;
   (c) underwater cables.
10. Aircraft and equipment for military use.
11. Military electronic equipment.
12. Cameras specially designed for military use.
13. Other equipment and material.
14. Specialised parts and items of material included in this list insofar as they are of a military nature.
15. Machines, equipment and items exclusively designed for the study, manufacture, testing and control of arms, munitions and apparatus of an exclusively military nature included in this list."

There are a few comments to be made about this Council response.[17] First, the list contained in this response is shorter and less detailed than those previously in the public domain.[18] There are more categories of weapons on the other lists. Moreover, categories such as warships (point 9), tanks (point 6) or firearms (point 1) are stipulated in more detail on these lists. An exception is artillery (category 2), which is more detailed on this list provided by the Council. Therefore the Council response does not contain a complete version of the list. However, it is submitted that these variations do not amount to substantial differences. Most of the additional categories in previously accessible lists refer to spare parts and components of the main categories. Hence the list was not altered in substance. The background to the variations might be a lack of meticulousness of the Council officials or *stagaires* compiling the list for the response in Parliament. An indicator for this theory is that the category "aircraft and their devices for military purposes" in a previously published list 'makes sense' whereas the related category 10 on the list provided in the parliamentary response "aircraft and equipment for military use" does not. The "equipment for military use" is meant to relate to "aircraft", hence the category should be named "aircraft and related equipment for military use". However, a look at the German[19] and French[20] versions of the list reveals that this is a case of an inaccurate English translation rather than a sloppy compilation of the list.[21] Another reason might be the intention not to go into too

[17] Most of the comments in this section were published before in M Trybus, 'On the List According to Article 296 EC Treaty' (2003) 12 *Public Procurement Law Review* NA15–21.

[18] See above n 15.

[19] 'Luftfahrzeuge und *ihre* Ausrüstungen zu militärischen Zwecken'. [emphasis added].

[20] 'Aéronefs et *leurs* équipments à usage militaire.' [emphasis added].

[21] As the list was drafted in 1958 it can be assumed that the German and French versions of this Council response are at least based on the original list. As the mainly English speaking United Kingdom and Republic of Ireland were not yet Member States of the European Communities, it is possible that the English version was specifically translated for the recent Council response. The French version of the list provided in the Council response is: '1. Armes à feu portatives et automatiques, telles que fusils, carabines, revolvers, pistolets, mitraillettes et mitrailleuses, à l'exception des armes de

much detail in the context of a written answer given in Parliament. It cannot be assumed that the Council wanted to provide a tailored list.

Second, *prima facie* category 13 on "other equipment and material" represents an open category where the Council or the Member States could add any type of product they could not think of when first compiling the list in 1958. This would undermine the exhaustive character of the list. This exhaustive character, however, is an essential part of the narrow interpretation of Article 296 EC. As explained in chapter 4, a narrow interpretation has to be applied to all exemptions from the Treaty as a wide interpretation could undermine the functioning of the internal market as a whole.[22] However, this first impression is only caused by the lack of detail of the list provided by the Council. On previously available versions of the list this category was just a heading for all kinds of material that could not be listed under other categories, such as parachutes or devices to cross water.[23] Hence it is submitted that category 13 of the list provided by the Council is not designed to undermine the exhaustive character of the list.

chasse, pistolets et autres armes à petit calibre, d'un calibre inférieur à 7 mm. 2. Matériel d'artillerie et lance-fumées, gaz, flammes, tels que: a) canons, obusiers, mortiers, pièces d'artillerie, armes antichars, lance-roquettes, lance-flammes, canons sans recul; b) matériel militaire pour le lancement des fumées et des gaz. 3. Munitions destinées aux armes reprises aux points 1 et 2 ci-dessus. 4. Bombes, torpilles, roquettes et engins guidés: a) bombes, torpilles, grenades, y compris les grenades fumigènes, pots fumigènes, roquettes, mines, engins guidés, grenades sous-marines, bombes incendiaires; b) appareils et dispositifs à usage militaire, spécialement conçus pour la manutention, l'amorçage, le désamorçage, la détonation ou la détection des articles repris sous a) ci-dessus. 5. Matériel de conduite du tir à usage militaire: a) calculateurs de tir et appareils de pointage en belowrouges et autre matériel de pointage de nuit; b) télémètres, indicateurs de position, altimètres; c) dispositifs d'observation électroniques, gyroscopiques, optiques et acoustiques; d) viseurs de bombardement et hausses de canons, périscopes pour les articles repris dans la présente liste. 6. Chars et véhicules spécialement conçus pour l'usage militaire: a) chars; b) véhicules de type militaire, armés ou blindés, y compris les véhicules amphibies; c) trains blindés; d) véhicules militaires semi-chenillés; e) véhicules militaires de dépannage des chars; f) remorques spécialement conçues pour le transport des munitions énumérées aux points 3 et 4. 7. Agents toxiques ou radioactifs: a) agents toxiques biologiques ou chimiques et agents radioactifs adaptés pour produire en cas de guerre des effets destructifs sur les personnes, les animaux ou les récoltes; b) matériel militaire pour la propagation, la détection et l'identification des substances reprises sous a) ci-dessus; c) matériel de protection contre les substances reprises sous a) ci-dessus. 8. Poudres, explosifs et agents de propulsion liquides ou solides: a) poudres et agents de propulsion liquides ou solides spécialement conçus et fabriqués pour le matériel repris aux points 3, 4 et 7 ci-dessus; b) explosifs militaires; c) compositions incendiaires et gélifiants pour usage militaire. 9. Navires de guerre et leurs équipements spécialisés: a) navires de guerre de toutes espèces; b) équipements spécialement conçus pour le mouillage, la détection et le dragage des mines; c) filets sous-marins. 10. Aéronefs et leurs équipements à usage militaire. 11. Matériel électronique pour l'usage militaire. 12. Appareils de prise de vues spécialement conçus pour l'usage militaire. 13. Autres équipements et matériel. 14. Parties et pièces spécialisées du matériel repris dans la présente liste pour autant qu'elles ont un caractère militaire. 15. Machines, équipement et outillage exclusivement conçus pour l'étude, la fabrication, l'essai et le contrôle des armes, munitions et engins à usage uniquement militaire repris dans la présente liste.'

[22] C–222/84 *Johnston*, above n 2, at para 26.

[23] Parachutes and devices to cross water appear to be out of place on a list of hard defence material. They seem to be dual use material. As this type of dual use material is on the list and all other material is not, this is another argument for the interpretation that only material on the list is covered by Article 296(a)(b) EC. Dual use material, with the exception of these two categories, is outside the ambit of the exception.

Third, the list is remarkably up-to-date for a document compiled in 1958. Most military equipment available to the armed forces of the Member States in 2004 is covered by one of the categories on this list. A stealth bomber, for example, is covered by category 10 "aircraft and equipment for military use". This shows that the categories are reasonably wide to accommodate technical progress in the military sector. The list is not outdated. Major changes were not and will not be necessary to take technological progress into account.

Fourth, with a view of the future liberalisation of the European hard defence equipment market, category 7 "toxic or radioactive agents" needs to be considered. This category concerns highly sensitive material. Whereas liberalisation is feasible with regards to categories like military aircraft or firearms, a liberalisation with regards to nuclear weapons is highly unlikely. Only France and the United Kingdom have nuclear arsenals and consider this military capacity a constituting factor of their status as a major power; a status reflected, for example, in a permanent seat in the Security Council of the United Nations. In its communication *Public Procurement in the European Union*[24] the Commission divided the goods procured by military procurement agencies into the following three categories:

(1) "Products intended for the armed forces but not for military use therefore not covered by Article 223 (1) (b) E. C. [now Article 296 (1) (b) E. C.] nor by Article 2 of the directive 93/36 (markets declared secret, protection of vital interests, national security, etc.). As these products are already subject to the Community public procurement rules, the Commission will specify, where appropriate, in the most suitable form the conditions for the application of these rules;

(2) products intended for the armed forces and for military use, but not constituting highly sensitive defence equipment. The Commission should work out a fairly flexible set of rules, while respecting the principles of transparency and non-discrimination, inspired by the existing public procurement rules;

(3) highly sensitive equipment covered by the scope of Article 223 E. C. [now Article 296 (1) (b) E. C.]. These products could be exempted from the rules referred to above, when safety or the protection of vital interests of the country in question so require. A notification for this mechanism should be foreseen in order to ensure a degree of control and transparency."

Hence the Commission assumes that "highly sensitive equipment" will require special treatment in a future liberalised hard defence equipment market or might never be liberalised at all. The differentiation between hard defence material and "highly sensitive equipment" envisaged by the Commission is currently not set out in any legally binding instrument. Member States might find it easier to invoke Article 296 (1) (b) EC in relation to this kind of equipment than in relation to 'regular' hard defence material. This might lead to a more frequent use of the exemption that could undermine its exceptional character. An option to be

[24] COM (98) 143, 25 May 1999, [1999] OJ C–150, at 64.

considered in this context is the automatic exclusion of "highly sensitive equipment" in separate exclusions from the Treaty. However, it might be difficult to reach an agreement on what constitutes "highly sensitive equipment".[25]

Fifth, the Council response does not amount to an official publication of the list. This means that the list contained in this response is not legally binding. Nevertheless one form of abuse of Article 296 (1) (b) EC might be more difficult now: extending the application of the exclusion to material which is not on the list. However, for the sake of good governance, an official publication of the list in the Official Journal would be preferable to this bizarre erosion of secrecy.

Finally, all items on this list are goods in the sense of Article 23 EC as they are all "products which can be valued in money and which are capable of forming the subject of commercial transactions."[26] This means that the provisions on the free movement of goods in Title I of Part III as the core regime of the EC Treaty apply, subject to the national security exemption in Article 296 (1) (b) EC rather than the public security exemption in Article 30 EC discussed in chapter 4.[27] The latter is superseded by the earlier.

2.2. Dual-use Material and the Exhaustive Character of the List

The list is exhaustive: material not stipulated on the list is not covered by the exemption.[28] Therefore Article 296 (2) EC and the list it refers to are a limitation to Article 296 (1) (b) EC.[29] An argument for this interpretation is that the wording of Article 296 (2) EC clearly limits the application of Article 296 (1) (b) EC to goods on the list. Moreover, the general rule from *Johnston* that exemptions need to be interpreted narrowly to protect the functioning of the internal market as a whole[30] requires the limitation of the provision to products stipulated on the list. The very concept of a list as part of an exemption indicates that it is exhaustive. Finally, Article 296 (2) EC allows the Council to amend the list in case they consider it necessary to add another product. For such a case unanimity would be required[31] as this would effectively amount to an amendment of the Treaty. An amendment of this kind never occurred. Nevertheless, a specific mentioning of an amendment of the list by the Council indicates its exhaustive character. A merely illustrative list does not need a special legal base for its amendment, as a piece of equipment would not have to be on the list in order to be covered.

[25] The European Defence Community Treaty discussed in ch 1 differentiated between two categories of armaments. Annex I to Article 107 EDC Treaty contained a list of armaments (the Treaty applied to these products) whereas Annex II contained more sensitive equipment including nuclear material which was subject to a special regime.

[26] Case C–7/69, *Commission v Italy* (*'Arts Treasures'*) [1968] ECR 42; [1969] CMLR 1.

[27] At 131 and 134–138.

[28] See Case T–26/01, *Fiocchi Munizioni SpA v Commission of the European Communities*, (30 September 2003). For details see below and ch 8 at 249–250.

[29] Wessel, above n 14, at 312.

[30] Case C–222/84, *Johnston*, above n 2, at para 26. See also Case C–13/68, *SpA Salgoil v Italian Ministry of Foreign Trade* [1968] ECR 453, at 463; [1969] CMLR 181, at 192; and Case C–7/68, *Commission v Italy* [1968] ECR 633 at 644.

[31] Wessel, above n 14, at 312.

The crucial effect of the exhaustive character of the list is, that dual-use goods, materials that can be used for both military and civil purposes, are not on the list and therefore are not covered by the exemption in Article 296 (1) (b) EC.[32] Examples for dual use goods are transport aircraft, cross-country vehicles, and tents. It has been argued that the question of central significance was the criteria which determined the primary function of a product as either civil or military. Moreover, it has been argued that the absence of such criteria may result in an interpretative vacuum undermining the application of Community law to the defence industries in practice.[33] However, it is suggested here that such criteria are not needed. The list according to Article 296 (2) EC is exhaustive. The only criterion to differentiate hard defence material, to which Article 296 (1) (b) EC applies, from civil material, to which it does not apply, is the list. Material not on the list is not covered by Article 296 (1) (b) EC. Even the expression 'hard defence material', understood as a legal category, is slightly misleading, although almost all of the material on the list is hard defence material. Due to the exhaustive character of the list, there could be a product that could clearly be classified as hard defence material but not on the list. Such a piece of hard defence material would not be covered by Article 296 (1) (b) EC and could only be exempt through Article 30 EC. Similarly there could be a piece of civil or dual-use material on the list to which Article 296 (1) (b) EC applied, such as "parachutes and devices to cross water" in category 13 of the list. Hence the only decisive factor is whether the product is on the list or not. The existence of the list does not leave room for an interpretative vacuum. A more accurate expression than 'hard defence material' would be 'material stipulated on the list according to Article 296 (1) (b) EC'. However, as this is quite 'a mouth-full' the expression 'hard defence material' shall be used in the remainder of this book.

[32] This was subject to debate. In Case C–70/94, *Werner*, above n 5, the United Kingdom argued 'that the list should not be regarded as exhaustive and that Article 223(1)(b) EC [now Article 296(1)(b) EC] is capable of applying to products which were not included in that list.' In contrast, France and Germany 'considered that those provisions cannot be invoked in respect of products [not on the list compiled in] 1958 pursuant to Article 223(2) EC [now Articles 296(2) EC], see the advisory opinion of Advocate General Jacobs, above, at para 62. On the discussion on the applicability of Article 296(1) (b) EC to dual use goods see: K Eikenberg, 'Article 296 (ex 223) EC and External Trade in Strategic Goods' (2000) 25 *European Law Review* 117, at 125–28, who advocates that the provision does not apply to dual use goods. See also the Commission in *The Challenges Facing the European Defence-Related Industries, A Contribution for Action at European Level*, COM (96) 10 final, 24 November 1996 (hereinafter '*The Challenges Facing the Defence-Related Industries*'), at 14; O Lhoest, 'La production et la commerce des armes, et l'article 223 du traité constituant la Communauté européene' (1993) 26 *Revue belge de droit international* 176, at 184–85; S Arrowsmith, *The Law of Public and Utilities Procurement* (Sweet & Maxwell, London, 1996) 858–59; and JB Wheaton, 'Defence Procurement and the European Community: The Legal Provisions' (1992) 1 *Public Procurement Law Review* 432, at 434; W Hummer, 'Artikel 223' in E Grabitz and M Hilf, (eds), *Kommentar zum EWGV* (CH Beck Verlag, Munich, 1997) loose-leaf, volume II, Art 223, at para 12; Wessel, above; N Emiliou, 'Restrictions on Strategic Exports, Dual-Use Goods and the Common Commercial Policy' (1997) 22 *European Law Review* 68, at 72.

[33] P Koutrakos, *Trade, Foreign Policy and Defence in EU Constitutional Law* (Hart Publishing, Oxford, 2001) 176 referring to JB Wheaton, 'Defence Procurement and the European Community: the Legal Provisions' (1992) 1 *Public Procurement Law Review* 432, 434 and the approaches by various countries to distinguish military from dual-use products discussed by M Bothe and T Marauhn, 'The Arms Trade: Comparative Aspects of Law' (1993) 26 *Revue belge de droit international* 20, at 27 *et seq*.

2.3. Disagreement on the Effect of Article 296 (1) (b) EC

There has been considerable disagreement as to the effect of Article 296 (1) (b) EC.

Voices in favour of a limited interpretation of Article 296 (1) (b) EC argue that the exemption needs to be narrowly construed and is not automatic but must be expressly invoked by Member States who wish to rely on it.[34] The EC Treaty applied to hard defence material unless a Member State can prove a situation justifying derogation.

Most Member States on the other hand have interpreted the provision as a general, categorical, and automatic exemption of hard defence material from the application of the Treaty.[35] According to them they retained *unlimited* jurisdiction regarding these products and their national security concerns automatically overrule the objectives of the internal market.

Due to the lack of an interpretation, the exemption was open to abuse and was successfully used accordingly.[36] Abuse took mainly two forms. One was to extend the exclusion to goods that are not on the 1958 list. The other was to protect the national hard defence markets without justification, thereby leading to separate national markets for warlike products in practice. There are several reasons for this situation.

[34] Most notably the Commission, see *The Challenges Facing the European Defence-Related Industry* COM (96) 10 final, at 14 (following Arrowsmith, above n 32, at 861–63); most recently in *Green Paper Defence Procurement* COM (2004) 608 final, at 5. See also Answer to written Question 1088/89 [1991] OJ C–130/2 as cited by Koutrakos, above, at 176; Lhoest, above n 32, at 183; Eikenberg, above n 32, at 119 and the references referred to in her n 8; N Emiliou, 'Strategic Export Control, National Security and the Common Commercial Policy' (1996) 1 *European Foreign Affairs Review* 55, at 59.

[35] For example France: *La notion de sécurité en droit européen*, ministère de la défense, secretariat général pour l'administration, direction des affaires juridiques (DAJ), études juridiques No 17 September 1999 at 7: 'Cependant, une partie des Etats membres, et notament la France, on jusqu'ici considéré qu'en vertue de cette disposition [Article 296 (1) (b) E. C. (ex 223)] les règels du traité ne sont pas applicables au secteur de l'armement.' This opinion has been put forward by the respective Member States in all cases referred to in this article. See the United Kingdom in *Johnston*, above n 3, at 1671: 'The EEC Treaty itself leaves intact the power of the Member States to take such measures as they may consider necessary or expedient for the above mentioned purposes [safeguarding national security or for protecting public safety or public order] as is shown by the "safeguard clauses" contained in Articles 36, 48, 66, 223 and 224 [now 30, 45, 55, 296 and 297]'. According to Advocate General la Pergola's advisory opinion in Case C–285/98, *Sirdar v The Army Board*, [1999] ECR I–7403, [1999] 3 CMLR 559, at para 10: 'the French and Portuguese Governments submit that the activities of the armed forces are intimately linked to the concept of sovereignty, which the Member States have, in accordance with the Treaty, "shared" only in certain areas other than defence. Defence, therefore, remains within their exclusive competence'. At n 9 the Advocate General reports that 'The French Government, in particular, takes the view that defence should be treated in the same way as the other functions traditionally reserved to States, such as justice, diplomacy, public finances and the police'. In Case C–285/98, *Kreil v Germany*, [2000] ECR I–69, at para 12 it is stated: 'According to it [the German Government], Community law does not in principle govern matters of defence, which form part of the field of common foreign and security policy and which remain within the Member State's sphere of sovereignty' and at paragraph 13 'the Italian and United Kingdom Governments, which presented oral arguments, argue basically that decisions concerning the organisation and combat capacity of the armed forces do not fall within the scope of the Treaty'.

[36] S Mezzadri, *L'ouverture des marchés de la defense: enjoux et modalités*, Occasional Paper No 12, (Institute for Security Studies of the Western European Union, Paris, 2000), at 5.

First, as explained in chapter 1,[37] the EEC Treaty was introduced in 1957 after the unsuccessful attempt to create the EDC in 1954. This initiative had failed because of opposition in some Member States caused by concerns about their sovereignty, especially in France. Therefore the EC Treaty was widely considered to completely exclude any notion of a common regime or policy on defence issues. Article 296 (1) (b) EC was considered a manifestation of this general exclusion.

Second, this historical background is connected to the reluctance of the European Court of Justice to interpret the exception. This reluctance facilitated abuse. Perhaps the Court did not want to jeopardise the acceptance of its judicial activism in other areas by avoiding this politically particularly sensitive provision. However, the provision was not the issue in many cases anyway. Thus there was probably also a reluctance of the Commission to bring an action in cases involving Article 296 (1) (b) EC. This reluctance could have been motivated by the search for a "clear case". The Commission might have wanted a safe chance to win a precedent that provides a narrow interpretation to limit the application of the provision in practice.

Finally, cases involving defence also involve secrecy. Therefore the Commission finds it difficult to detect and prove abuses in practice. Attempts to amend or abolish Article 296 (1) (b) EC have not been successful.[38] The provision remained untouched in Maastricht, Amsterdam and Nice. The 2004 Constitutional Treaty also contains this exclusion,[39] although the European Convention had discussed deletion.[40] This shall be discussed in more detail in chapter 11.[41]

[37] At 47–49.

[38] E Klepsch, *Klepsch-Report: European Armaments Procurement Co-operation* (Luxembourg, 1978); D Greenwood, *Greenwood-Report, European Technological Co-operation and Defence Procurement* (Brussels, 1979); L Tindemanns, *Tindemanns-Report,* in A Drown, *A Single European Arms Industry? European Defence Industries in the 1990s* (London, 1990) at 77–78.

[39] Article III-436 of the Constitutional Treaty (version of 16 December 2004) reads:

1. The Constitution shall not preclude the application of the following rules:

(a) no Member State shall be obliged to supply information the disclosure of which it considers contrary to the essential interests of its security;

(b) any Member State may take such steps as it considers necessary for the protection of the essential interests of its security which are connected with the production of or trade in arms, munitions and war material; such steps shall not adversely affect the conditions of competition in the internal market regarding products which are not intended for specifically military purposes.

2. The Council of Ministers, on a proposal from the Commission, may unanimously adopt a European decision making changes to the list, which it drew up on 15 April 1958, of the products to which the provisions of para 1(b) apply.

[40] See the 'Contribution on "European Defence"' made by L Dini, Brussels, 26 September 2002, in J-Y Haine, *From Laeken to Copenhagen, European Defence: Core Documents*, Chaillot Paper No 57, (Institute of Security Studies of the European Union: Paris, 2003) 203, 205: 'It is also worth asking whether it would not be desirable to revise Article 296 of the European Community Treaty, which excludes armaments from the scope of the single market.' The last half of the sentence reveals an understanding of the provision as an automatic exemption of armaments from the scope of the Treaty. See also: D de Villepin and J Fischer, 'Joint Proposal', Prague, 21 November 2002, in J-Y Haine, above, 214, 217: 'La France et l'Allemagne proposent d'inscrire dans le Traité: les fonctions d'une politique européenne d'armement, dont la création progressive d'un marché européen d'armement, moyennant des procédures spécifiques, notament d'une adaption de l'article 296 du TCE'. However, the ministers did not specify how the provision should be adapted. See ch 10 for further details on the Draft Constitutional Treaty.

[41] At 343–347.

Excluding certain types of material from the application of the Treaty is hard to justify. The example of the USA and her large and competitive defence equipment market shows that the benefits of an internal market, such as economies of scale and synergy effects, are especially prevalent in the defence sector. It is nebulous how the national security of Member States would permanently be compromised in a common market for hard defence material. Most of them are allies in NATO, they co-operate in most major weapons development programmes, and there is no piece of major defence equipment without foreign components. National security appears to be a mere excuse to protect non-competitive industries.

2.4. The Effect of Article 296 (1) (b) EC

In a 1999 judgment the Court defined the application of the exemption in favour of a narrow interpretation. *Commission v. Spain*[42] involved a Spanish law exempting exports and intra-Community transfers of hard defence material from value-added tax (VAT). An EC Directive subjects all exports, imports and intra-Community transfers to VAT. During the eventual Court proceedings Spain submitted that its national legislation complied with Community law, particularly in view of Article 296 (1) (b) EC and that the Spanish law must be understood as having been adopted on the basis of that provision. Exemption from VAT constituted a necessary measure for the purposes of guaranteeing the achievement of the essential objectives of its overall strategic plan and, in particular, to ensure the effectiveness of the Spanish armed forces. The Commission had brought an action under Article 226 EC rather than Article 298 subparagraph 2 EC because Spain had not based her argument on Article 296 (1) (b) EC in the pre-judicial stage. Taking action in this case was possibly also motivated by the fact that the law in question affected the revenue of the Community.

The Court, not being able to avoid the provision, repeated their ruling in *Johnston* and for the first time applied it directly to the exemption in Article 296 (1) (b) EC. Thus they decided in favour of a limited interpretation advocated by the Commission and others. On the basis of this general rule the Court considered that:

> "In the present case, [...] Spain has not demonstrated that the exemptions provided for by the Law [...] are *necessary* for the protection of the essential interests of its security. [...]. It follows that the VAT exemptions are not *necessary* in order to achieve the objective of protecting the essential interests of the security of [...] Spain".[43]

[42] Case C–414/97, *Commission v Spain*, [1999] ECR I–5585; [2000] 2 CMLR 4. See M Trybus, 'On the Application of the EC–Treaty to Armaments' (2000) 25 *European Law Review* 633–38; M Trybus, 'The Recent Judgment in *Commission v Spain* and the Procurement of Hard Defence Material' (2000) 9 *Public Procurement Law Review* NA99–105.

[43] Case C–414/97, above, at para 22, emphasis added.

The judgment in *Commission* v. *Spain* is significant in that in confirms that the Court has the power to review the decision of a Member State to invoke Article 296 (1) (b) EC, including a review of the justification. This is the first time this was done in relation to an exemption of the second group. Carefully respecting the sovereignty of Spain, the Court rejected the use of a provision designed to protect the national security of the Member States. The ruling was possible and unavoidable as Spain provided such a clear and manifest case.

It is submitted that the use of the word 'necessary'[44] in this judgment amounts to scrutiny in the form of a proportionality test in relation to Article 296 (1) (b) EC.[45] This does not necessarily mean that the Court applied the same level of scrutiny as it did in relation to Article 30 EC in *Campus Oil*[46] discussed in chapter 4.[47] It is suggested that in the context of the security type exemptions, the Court apply the proportionality test to different degrees of intensity, leaving differently wide margins of discretion to the Member States. In relation to the exemptions of the first group the test is applied strictly, leaving a relatively narrow margin of discretion to the Member States. This was discussed in chapter 4.[48] Article 297 EC is at the other end of the spectrum leaving a maximum margin of discretion to the Member States. This will be discussed in chapter 6.[49] Article 296 (1) (b) EC is between these two extremes but closer to the latter provision.

As the exemption from VAT in the Spanish law was manifestly unnecessary, the decision does not support the assumption that a very strict scrutiny was applied. This scrutiny leaves a wide margin of political discretion to the governments of the Member States.[50] The question is whether they acted within the ambit of that discretion, whether they acted arbitrarily or in bad faith. The Court will only consider a measure disproportionate when it (1) is clearly unsuitable to promote national security and national security is put forward in bad faith; (2) when the Member State has arbitrarily chosen a measure which is more detrimental to the internal market than necessary; or (3) when the balance between the two interests is manifestly not present.

Due to the subject matter of national security the level of intensity of the Court's scrutiny has to be low. First, because the decision to exempt defence

[44] Case C–414/97, above n 39, at para 22, emphasis added. Advocate General Saggio also used the word in the same sense (at para 12, referred to by the Court at para 23).

[45] Other possible elements of scrutiny are legitimate expectations, non-discrimination and the emergent principle of transparency. Against the application of a proportionality test: A Georgopoulos, 'European Defence Procurement Integration: Evaluating the Teleological Boundaries of Article 296(1b) EC and the Applicability of the New Public Procurement Directive in the Field of Intra-Community Armaments Procurement' forthcoming in the *European Law Review*.

[46] C–72/83, *Campus Oil Limited v Minister for Industry and Energy*, [1984] ECR 2727, at 2764; [1984] 3 CMLR 544.

[47] At 135–137.

[48] At 134–135.

[49] At 188–189.

[50] This was later confirmed by the Court of First Instance in Case T–26/01, *Fiocchi munizioni SpA v Commission of the European Communities*, above n 28, in para 58 where it was stated: 'Article 296(1)(b) EC confers on the Member States a particularly wide discretion in assessing the needs receiving such protection [measures taken for the protection of the essential interests of its security].'

exports from VAT was a policy choice. In cases involving the restriction of individual rights scrutiny will be rigorous, as proportionality is a necessary component of the recognition of such rights.[51] However, as was explained in the context of the discussion of proportionality in chapter 4, policy choices are the reserve of the executive and legislative branches of government (division of powers dimension). Second, because in the field of military security it is the government supported by the military staff, which has the responsibility, training and expertise to take decisions (competence dimension). Their judgement cannot easily be substituted by a court of law. This aspect was already mentioned in the context of the discussion of the principle of proportionality in chapter 4.[52] Third, in the constitutional system of the EU matters of defence and military security are primarily attributed to the Member States and not to the Union[53] (federalism dimension). Thus, if the Court applied a proportionality test, it only considered the Spanish law to be disproportionate because it represented a clearly unsuitable and manifestly inappropriate measure to ensure national security. In the context of Article 296 (1) (b) EC a State measure will only be ruled out in clear and manifest cases where the measure is wholly unreasonable and disproportionate.[54] In less clearly established and manifest cases the Court is likely to be more cautious.

There are arguments for this interpretation. The term 'necessary' implies a balance between the objective of a measure and its negative side effects. The use of this word in certain Treaty provisions led to the very establishment of the proportionality principle in EC law.[55] In *Commission* v. *Spain* the Court refers to the ruling in *Johnston* in which no differentiation between the security type exemptions in the Treaty is made but only the first group of exemptions was discussed.[56] In the recent cases of *Tanja Kreil* v. *Germany* and *Angela Maria Sirdar* v. *the Army Board ex parte Ministry of Defence* the Court applied the proportionality test in relation to the notion of public security, again, without differentiating between the security type exemptions of the Treaty.[57] There are possible arguments against the assumption of the application of a proportionality test, which need to be considered.

2.4.1. The Wording of the Treaty

First, Article 296 (1) (b) EC allows a Member State to take measures "*as it considers* necessary for the essential interests of its security" (emphasis added). Thus,

[51] P Craig and G de Búrca, *EU Law,* 3rd edn, (OUP, Oxford, 2003) 373.

[52] At 135.

[53] G de Búrca, 'The Principle of Proportionality and its Application in EC Law' (1993) 13 *Yearbook of European Law* 105.

[54] Advocate General Jacobs on Article 297 EC in Case C–120/94 R, *Commission v Greece (FYROM)* [1996] ECR I–1513, para 46.

[55] Craig and de Búrca, above n 48, at 371–72.

[56] Case C–222/84, above n 2, at para 26.

[57] Case C–273/97, *Kreil,* above n 35, at para 26; similar in Case C–285/98, *Sirdar,* above n 35, at para 25. However, the Court only said that no general exclusion of security-related matters could be deduced from these exemptions. This does not necessarily mean that there is no differentiation between the two groups of exemptions and that the proportionality test will be applied equally to the second group.

prima facie, the wording supports the 'necessity' of the measure to be determined by the Member States. It could be argued that if the Court were to decide otherwise, it would be against the wording of the Treaty. The words of a Treaty always form the foundation of its interpretation.[58]

The wording in Article XXI (b) of the General Agreement on Tariffs and Trade (GATT)[59] is similar to Article 296 (1) (b) EC. The earlier served as a model for the latter. Moreover, the European Court of Justice considers the GATT "to be relevant for the purpose of interpreting a Community instrument governing international trade."[60] In the famous *Nicaragua* Case,[61] the International Court of Justice compared the wording of Article XXI GATT with that of Article XXI (d) of the 1956 US-Nicaragua Treaty of Friendship, Commerce and Navigation (hereafter 'Friendship Treaty').[62] The Court emphasised that the latter provision speaks simply of "necessary" measures, not of those considered by the parties as such. This different wording means *a contrario*, that the Court could scrutinise the necessity of the measure under the Friendship Treaty.

However, the decision still leaves room for the interpretation of Article XXI GATT as far as the justiciability of 'necessity' is concerned. In *Nicaragua* the World Court did not interpret Article XXI GATT but only the provision in the Friendship Treaty. The wording of the latter in contrast to the earlier supported its interpretation. However, it does not exclude the justiciability of measures taken under Article XXI GATT.[63] Thus the wording of Article XXI GATT, which is very similar to Article 296 (1) (b) EC, does not exclude a court from reviewing 'necessity'. Moreover, in contrast to the GATT, Article 298 subparagraph 2 EC makes clear that there is at least some form of review to be exercised by the European Court of Justice. Finally, the low intensity of the scrutiny suggested here would leave a wide margin of discretion to the Member States thereby respecting the wording of the Treaty. Thus, it is submitted that in *Commission* v. *Spain* the Court did not refer to the word 'necessary' in Article 296 (1) (b) EC.

[58] In relation to the interpretation of the EC Treaty this principle was already established in Case C–26162, *Van Gend en Loos v Nederlandse Administratie der Belastingen*, [1963] ECR 1, at 12; [1963] CMLR 105, at 129. For treaties in general see Articles 31 and 32 on the 1969 Vienna Convention on the Law of Treaties, 1155 UNTS 331.

[59] Article XXI GATT (also Article XIV *bis* General Agreement on Trade in Services GATS and Article 73 Agreement on Trade Related Aspects of Intellectual Property Rights TRIPS): 'Nothing in this Agreement shall be construed [...] (b) to require any contracting party from taking any action which it considers necessary for the protection of its essential security interests [...]'.

[60] Case C–83/94, *Leifer*, above n 6, at para 24.

[61] Military and Paramilitary Activities in and against Nicaragua (*Nicaragua v USA*), Merits, 1986 ICJ-Reports 14, 116 para 222 (June 27).

[62] Article XXI of the Treaty of the Friendship Treaty: '1. The present Treaty shall not preclude the application of measures: [...] (d) necessary to fulfil the obligations of a Party for the maintenance or restoration of international peace and security, or necessary to protect its essential security interest.'

[63] C Schloemann and S Ohloff, '"Constitutionalisation" and Dispute Settlement in the WTO: National Security as an Issue of Competence' (1999) 93 *American Journal of International Law* 424, at 443 (n 104, last paragraph).

2.4.2. Effet Utile *of Articles 296 et seq. EC*

Second, the inclusion of Articles 296 *et seq.* EC in addition to the exemptions of the first group suggests that the creators of the Treaty wanted to include a separate set of derogations.[64] It could be argued that if proportionality applied, these circumstances could be dealt with in the context of the exemptions of the first group; the second group exemptions would be superfluous. They would be deprived of their *effet utile.*

However, the *effet utitle* of the derogations in Article 296 and 297 EC is taken into account by the low intensity of scrutiny suggested above. Moreover, even with the application of scrutiny, Article 296 and 297 EC still form a second and separate set of exclusions as Article 298 subparagraph 2 EC offers the possibility to subject the review of their use to a distinct procedure.

2.4.3. The Special Review Procedures of Article 298 Subparagraph 2 EC

Finally, the special procedure for reviewing abuse of Articles 296 *et seq.* EC in Article 298 subparagraph 2 EC could be interpreted as indicating that the creators of the Treaty wanted these exemptions to be subject to a different kind of scrutiny than those of the first group. The judgments in *Johnston*, *Salgoil*, *Kreil* and *Sirdar* merely say that no exemption excludes security issues completely from the application of the Treaty. None of these cases involved Articles 296 *et seq.* EC directly. Thus they do not rule out a treatment of the second group different from that of the first group of exemptions.

However, it is submitted that the purpose of Article 298 subparagraph 2 EC is not to introduce a different level of scrutiny. In *Commission* v. *Spain* the enforcement procedure in Article 226 EC and not the special enforcement procedure in Article 298 subparagraph 2 EC was used. This was because the Spanish Government invoked Article 296 (1) (b) EC only during the Court hearings and not during the pre-litigation procedure.[65] Thus it was simply too late. It can be assumed that the Commission would have initiated Article 298 subparagraph 2 EC proceedings, had Spain invoked the provision earlier on. However, as argued by Hummer the use of the word "may" in Article 298 subparagraph 2 EC indicates that the use of this procedure, rather than those of Articles 226 and 227 EC, is not obligatory in any case.[66]

The major difference to the enforcement procedure in Article 226 EC is that there is another kind of pre-judicial stage in Article 298 EC proceedings[67] and that the public is excluded. The earlier difference is partly due to the urgency of these situations and their political sensitivity. Thus the bilateral consultations according to Article 298 subparagraph 1 EC are less formalised than Article 226 and 227 EC

[64] Advocate General Cosmas in Case C–423/98, *Alfredo Albore*, above n 9, dealing with Article 297 EC.

[65] Case C–414/97, above n 41, at para 18.

[66] W Hummer, in Eberhardt Grabitz and Meinrad Hilf, (eds), *Kommentar zum EWGV* (CH Beck Verlag, Munich, 1997) loose-leaf, Article 225, at para 8 and before Article 223–25, at para 8. The case of Fiocchi Munizioni, discussed at 158–160 below seems to indicate that the Commission is confined to Article 298 EC proceedings, once a Member State invoked Article 296 EC.

[67] Hummer, in Grabitz and Hilf, above, Article 225, at para 8.

proceedings.[68] There is no formal notification and no reasoned opinion. The procedure has a stronger diplomatic emphasis thereby taking account of the fact that the sovereignty of the Member States over defence and security issues was not transferred to the Community and that the latter does not have the capacity to shoulder this particular responsibility. In contrast to Article 296 EC, in the context of Article 297 EC the Member States also have the opportunity to put forward their arguments during the consultations, as will be discussed in chapter 6.[69] Moreover the public is excluded from Article 298 subparagraph 2 EC proceedings in order to take the national security and secrecy interests of the Member States into account.[70] This suggests that exclusion of the public and the accommodation of the Member State responsibility for security and defence in a different prejudicial stage, rather than the introduction of a different kind of scrutiny, are the purpose of Article 298 subparagraph 2 EC.

The general approach of the Court to subject measures taken under Article 296 (1) (b) EC to scrutiny is welcomed. It reduces the possibility of abuse, as Member States have to justify protective measures thereby possibly facilitating a liberalised market for defence products.[71] Member States, being aware of the possibility of scrutiny, might refrain from using the provision too easily.

2.5. Burden of Proof

According to *Commission* v. *Spain* it is for the respective Member State to prove a situation covered by Article 296 (1) (b) EC:

> "[...] it is for the Member State which seeks to rely on those exemptions to furnish the evidence that the exemptions in question do not go beyond the limits of such cases."[72]

It could be argued that the Court has not taken the division of powers and federalism dimensions of Article 296 (1) (b) EC sufficiently into account when establishing this evidence rule. In the constitutional framework of the EU the governments of the Member States are responsible for defence. They require flexibility to fulfil this responsibility in a sensitive policy field. Part of this flexibility is their wide margin of discretion. Putting the burden of proof for having acted within that margin of discretion on the Member States compromises their flexibility to an extent that might be considered as contradicting the very attribution of this flexibility. It could be argued that there is no reason why the Member State

[68] See ch 4 at 132–134 on Article 226 EC proceedings.

[69] At 178–182.

[70] According to Article 28 of the Statute of the Court of Justice of the European Community as amended by Council-Decision 94/993/EEC OJ [1994] L–379/1 and the Treaty of Amsterdam the Court can decide against Court hearings for serious reasons any way. By derogation from Article 34 of the Statute not all parts of the judgment have to be read in public.

[71] See also the later discussion of Article 296(1)(a) EC below.

[72] Case C–414/97, above n 41, at para 22.

should have to prove the legality of its measures and there is no authority for this requirement in the Treaty. The burden of proof for bad faith or arbitrariness could be put on the Commission or other Member State challenging the legality of the measure. In order to safeguard the necessary flexibility there might be an argument for an evidentiary presumption in favour of the respective government including the benefit of any reasonable doubt.[73] In *Commission* v. *Spain* the Court might have gone too far on this point. This issue will be discussed again below in the context of the information privilege in Article 296 (1) (a) EC.[74]

2.6. Procedural Requirements and Hard Defence Material Intended for Export

All exemptions from the EC Treaty need to be interpreted narrowly.[75] In the recent judgment of *Fiocchi Munizioni SpA* v. *Commission of the European Communities*[76] the Court of First Instance appears to have narrowed the scope of Article 296 (1) (b) EC even further. The case concerned an Italian manufacturer of arms and munitions who had made a formal complaint to the Commission concerning subsidies Spain had granted to a Spanish State-owned undertaking producing arms, munitions, and tanks. The Commission started bilateral communications with Spain on the issue within the context of Article 298 subparagraph 1 EC. Spain argued that the activities of the Spanish undertaking in question were covered by Article 296 (1) EC and recognised in Spanish law as being in the interest of the national defence of Spain and that its production was intended principally to provide for the requirements of the Spanish armed forces. Moreover, these activities were also subject to the Spanish law on State secrets. The Italian manufacturer brought an action for failure to act against the Commission under Article 232 subparagraph 3 EC after the latter had not taken any action for over a year.[77] The Spanish manufacturer had successfully participated in invitations to tender in other Member States including Italy. The perception that this resulted in distortions of competition had motivated the Italian manufacturer to take action.

The Court clarified a few procedural points in relation to Articles 296 (1) (b) and 298 EC. First, where a Member State considers it necessary to invoke the exemption in Article 296 (1) (b) EC it does not have to notify the Commission in advance as the rules on competition do not apply. Moreover, the Commission cannot use the examination procedure laid down in Article 88 EC.[78] Second, the Court emphasised that two specific remedies are prescribed by the Treaty in relation to measures adopted by Member States on the basis of Article 296 (1) (b) EC:

[73] See the approach of the German *Bundesverfassungsgericht* in cases involving defence and foreign policy in TM Franck, *Political Questions/Juridical Answers: Does the Rule of Law Apply to Foreign Affairs?* (Princeton University Press, Princeton, 1992) 107–25.

[74] See below.

[75] Case C–222/84, *Johnston*, above n 2, at para 26.

[76] Case T–26/01, *Fiocchi Munizioni SpA v Commission of the European Communities*, above n 28.

[77] Article 232 subpara 4 EC reads: 'Any natural or legal person may, under the conditions laid down in the preceding paragraphs, complain to the Court of Justice that an institution of the Community has failed to address to that person any act other than a recommendation or an opinion.'

[78] Case T–26/01, above n 28, at para 59.

bilateral examinations according to Article 298 subparagraph 1 EC and court proceedings according to Article 298 subparagraph 2 EC. Within the context of bilateral examination it is within the discretion of the Commission to decide whether the invocation by the Member State concerned is prima *facie* credible. Contrary to the situation in the context of Article 88 EC, the Commission is under no obligation to adopt a decision concerning the measure at issue. Moreover, it has no power to address a final decision or directive to the Member State concerned.[79] In this context the Court also differentiated the facts of *Fiocchi Munizioni* from the facts behind Commission Decision 1999/763/EC of 17 March 1999 on the measures, implemented and proposed, by the Free and Hanse City of Bremen, Germany in favour of 'Lürssen Maritime Beteiligungen GmbH & Co. KG'.[80] In the latter case the Commission had opened the procedure provided in Article 88 (2) EC ending with a decision in the course of which Germany relied in her defence on the application of Article 296 (1) (b) EC. By contrast, in *Fiocchi Munizioni* the Commission had opened bilateral examinations under Article 298 subparagraph 1 EC.

Moreover, the Court made a couple of references to the argument of the applicant that the production of hard defence material intended for export rather than to satisfy domestic needs was outside the protection of essential security interests within the meaning of Article 296 (1) (b) EC.[81] However, the Court did not establish this rule in *Fiocchi Munizioni*. An argument for this interpretation would be that, based on the general rule that exemptions have to be interpreted narrowly, a Member State can only consider the production and trade of hard defence material intended for its own armed forces as necessary for the protection of its essential security interests. The equipment of the armed forces of Germany, for example, cannot be an essential security interest of Spain. However, it is submitted that Article 296 (1) (b) EC covers measures concerning hard defence material intended for export. First, as mentioned above, the Court did not establish a rule excluding hard defence material intended for export from the application of the exemption in *Fiocchi Munizioni*. The impression that the Court considered this argument was partly due to the State aid context of this case. Second, the Court did emphasise that Article 296 (1) (b) EC has a general effect affecting the whole EC Treaty.[82] This means that, if successfully invoked, the provision allows derogation from the entire Treaty, without exception. Excluding measures regarding hard defence material intended for exports from the application of Article 296 (1) (b) EC on a general basis would contradict this general nature of the provision. There is no segment in the wording of the exemption that suggests it being limited to hard defence material intended exclusively to satisfy domestic needs. Third, the Court pointed out that the provision confers on the Member States a particularly wide discretion in assessing the needs of their security.[83] A Member State might

[79] Case T–26/01, above, at para 74.
[80] [1999] OJ L–301/8.
[81] Case T–26/01, above n 28 at para 77 referring back to para 8, see also para 63.
[82] Case T–26/01, above, at para 58.
[83] Above.

consider a national defence industrial capability to be essential for its national security interests. That national defence industrial capability might not be economically viable, if dependent on the requirements of the armed forces of that Member State alone. Exports to other Member States might be necessary to keep that company in business. This general effect of the provision and the wide discretion of the Member States need to be differentiated from the necessity of such a measure and the judicial scrutiny applied to it by the Community courts. The earlier points are strong arguments against a general exclusion of measures regarding hard defence material intended for export from the application of Article 296 (1) (b) EC, not against such an exclusion in an individual case.

Fiocchi Munizioni represents a case decided on procedural grounds rather than an example for judicial scrutiny over Article 296 (1) (b) EC. Whether State aids to the defence industries are necessary to protect national security interests is another question that will be discussed in the context of chapter 8.[84] However, the case emphasised that once a Member State has invoked Article 296 (1) (b) EC the Commission is confined to the special procedure in Article 298 EC and that it has discretion to decide whether the Member State's claim is credible or not.

2.7. Article 296 (1) (b) EC and the Common Foreign and Security Policy

The effect of Article 296 (1) (b) EC not only describes the limits of the EC Treaty as an instrument of European defence integration with regards to armaments. It also raises the question of the relationship of the First and Second Pillars in relation to these materials. As outlined in chapter 2, Article 17 (1) subparagraph 3 TEU explicitly indicates that the progressive framing of a common defence policy will be supported, as Member States consider appropriate, by co-operation between them in the field of armaments. The "production of and trade in arms, munitions, and war material" referred to in Article 296 (1) (b) EC is clearly related to security and defence policy and therefore covered by Title V TEU. There are no mutual references in Article 296 (1) (b) EC and 17 (1) subparagraph 3 TEU that would clarify the relationship of the two provisions.

2.7.1. The Effect of Article 296 (1) (b) EC on the Common Foreign and Security Policy

There is a danger that Article 296 (1) (b) EC could contradict Article 17 (1) subparagraph 3 TEU. European Community law prevails over the law of the Common Foreign and Security Policy (hereinafter CFSP). This 'rule of supremacy' of Community law over the law of the Second and Third Pillars emanates from Article 47 TEU, which provides that "nothing in this Treaty [on European Union] shall affect the Treaties establishing the European Communities or the subsequent Treaties and Acts modifying or supplementing them." The 'protection' of the EC

[84] At 249–252.

Treaty applies to the entire treaty, including the security exemptions. This is a necessary consequence of the nature of the interests accommodated in these exemptions and the attribution of competencies in the constitutional framework of the EU. The wider public security interests and the narrower national security interest accommodated in the exemptions are within the responsibility of the Member States. The EU does not have the capacity to take responsibility for security. As explained in chapter 2,[85] a common defence mentioned in Article 17 (1) subparagraph 1 TEU is vague, uncertain and set in the future. There is no European army and no European police that could provide security. The security exemptions allow derogation from the EC Treaty and the CFSP. Therefore Article 296 (1) (b) EC does not only represent an exemption from the EC Treaty but also from Article 17 (1) subparagraph 3 TEU.

Theoretically Article 296 (1) (b) EC could be invoked in order to ignore an adopted Common Position or Joint Action under the CFSP. The older Article 296 (1) (b) EC is intended to allow the Member States to derogate from their obligation under the EC Treaty in relation to armaments. It potentially takes hard defence material outside the legal order of the Community. It was not changed when the Second Pillar was introduced. Therefore it also potentially takes hard defence material outside the legal order of the Union. The younger Article 17 (1) TEU brings armaments inside the CFSP. However, the narrow interpretation of Article 296 (1) (b) EC needs to be taken into account. The provision only applies to material on the 1958 list according to Article 296 (2) EC, needs to be interpreted narrowly, and is subject to review by the European Court of Justice.

It has been argued that invoking Article 296 (1) (b) EC in order to ignore an adopted Common Position or Joint Action under the CFSP would probably be regarded as an improper use of the provision.[86] However, it is submitted that it would be possible for a Member State to justify derogation from a Common Position or a Joint Action, just as it is possible to derogate from a Directive or Regulation. Moreover, Article 298 subparagraph 2 EC subjecting the use of Article 296 (1) (b) EC to the judicial review of the Court has to be read together with Article 46 TEU that excludes the CFSP from the jurisdiction of the Kirchberg. Therefore there is no judicial review of measures derogating from Second Pillar instruments in Luxembourg. Furthermore, even if there was such a jurisdiction, the margin of discretion left to the Member States concerning measures they consider necessary for the protection of their essential national security interests and taken in the context of Article 296 (1) (b) EC would probably be even wider in relation to Second Pillar instruments than it is in relation to First Pillar instruments. This wider margin of discretion would make a ruling against a Member State measure unlikely and only thinkable in the case of the most blatant abuse. Finally, measures taken in the context of the CFSP rather than the Community are already of a national security nature. If Article 296 (1) (b) EC already justified a measure in relation to armaments derogating from the EC Treaty for national

[85] At 64–66.
[86] Wessel, above n 14, at 313.

security reasons, derogation from the CFSP in relation to the same measure will be equally justifiable in most cases. Considering the interpretation of Article 296 (1) (b) EC after *Commission* v. *Spain* outlined above, it is difficult to think of a measure taken by a Member State in relation to armaments where derogation from the EC Treaty would be proportionate whereas derogation from the CFSP would not.

2.7.2. Armaments and Pillars

This leads to the question by which Pillar of the TEU armaments are actually covered. The easiest and most straightforward solution would be to regulate armaments under only one pillar. The interpretation of Article 296 (1) (b) EC as an automatic exclusion of armaments from the application of the EC Treaty would allow such an easy solution: Article 17 (1) subparagraph 3 TEU would place armaments in the Second Pillar.

The Member States seem to have based the coexistence of Articles 296 (1) (b) EC and 17 (1) subparagraph 3 TEU on their wide interpretation of Article 296 (1) (b) EC as an automatic exemption of hard defence material from the application of the EC Treaty.[87] Article 17 (1) subparagraph 3 (then subparagraph 4) TEU was drafted in the early 1990s. At the time Article 296 (1) (b) EC was understood as a categorical exclusion of all armaments. Secondary legislation drafted during the same period confirms that this was the understanding that prevailed in the Council.[88] Material not covered by the First Pillar can easily be placed under the Second Pillar. This was probably the intention of the Member States: to address armaments, which they perceived to be excluded from the EC Treaty, under the CFSP. It was not before 1999 that the European Court of Justice ruled against the automatic exclusion from the application of the EC Treaty in *Commission* v. *Spain*. Since then it is clear that armaments are not generally outside the application of the EC Treaty, but only when Article 296 (1) (b) EC can successfully be invoked on a case-by-case basis, subject to review of the Court. Thus it is clear that the Member States could not that easily regulate armaments under the Second Pillar because the First Pillar, subject to Article 296 (1) (b) EC, already covered hard defence material. The situation for armaments is comparable but, due to different margins of discretion and standards of review, not equal to that of civil goods, which are covered by the First Pillar, subject to the public security exemption of Article 30 EC.[89] The Member States did not intend to move armaments from the First to the Second Pillar by drafting Article 17 (1) subparagraph 3 TEU.

[87] On evidence for the interpretation of the Member States see above n 35 above.

[88] See Article 3 of the Consolidated Public Supplies Directive, Council Directive 93/36/EC of June 14, 1993 co-ordinating procedures for the award of public supply contracts [1993] OJ L–199/1: '[...] this Directive shall apply to all products [...] including those contracts awarded by contracting authorities in the field of defence except for the products to which Article 223(1)(b)[now 296(1)(b)] applies.' The reference to products implies an understanding of Article 296(1)(b) EC as an automatic exclusion of all armaments from the application of the EC Treaty. The provision will be discussed in more detail in ch 7 at 203–208.

[89] See ch 4 at 127–128 and 135–137 for details.

According to their understanding of Article 296 (1) (b) EC as an automatic exclusion there was nothing to move from the First Pillar. Moreover, such a move would have involved a considerable step back from the *acquis communautaire*. Such a step back had contradicted their intention to make a step forward in Maastricht, in particular with regards to foreign policy and security.

Therefore, in the current situation it depends on the circumstances of each individual case where a Member States invoked Article 296 (1) (b) EC, whether the EC Treaty covers armaments, whether they are not covered by the EC Treaty but by the CFSP, or outside both the EC Treaty and the CFSP. The narrow interpretation of Article 296 (1) (b) EC, judicial review under Article 298 subparagraph 2 EC, and the wide margin of discretion of the Member States leaves armaments in a legal limbo. Ultimately such a situation does not provide a sufficient legal basis for a coherent European armaments policy. The institutions need to know the right legal base for the necessary legislation on public procurement, exports, and mergers in the defence industrial sector. The Member States should make a clear decision on the legal base of the European armaments policy. They could place the policy firmly in the First Pillar. This would require the deletion of Article 17 (1) subparagraph 3 TEU. Alternatively they could place it firmly in the Second Pillar. This would require changing Article 296 (1) (b) EC to an automatic exclusion of armaments from the EC Treaty. Finally the abolition of the three-Pillar structure of the TEU as envisaged in the Constitutional Treaty could overcome the current lack of coherence. This shall be discussed in more detail in chapter 12.[90]

Wessel pointed out in the context of Article 296 (1) (a) EC and Article 16 TEU that the judicial review exercised by the Court under Article 298 subparagraph 2 EC allows correction of the measures of Member States taken under Article 296 EC.[91] Therefore the conflict or contradiction between the two provisions can be avoided in practice and *a posteriori*. To a certain extent the coherence of the Second Pillar of the CFSP with the Community can therefore be ensured by the review of the Court. However, it would be preferable to ensure the *a priori* coherence of Community and CFSP by placing armaments in one of the two Pillars.

3. THE SECRECY EXEMPTION OF ARTICLE 296 (1) (A) EC

According to Article 296 (1) (a) EC "no Member State shall be obliged to supply information the disclosure of which it considers contrary to the essential interests of its security". This rule confers certain procedural privileges on the Member States in relation to national security and secrecy. It represents a derogation from the general obligation of Member States to supply information to the institutions

[90] From 354.
[91] Wessel, above n 14, at 311 discussing Article 296(1)(a) EC, see further below.

of the Union according to Articles 284[92] and 10 EC.[93] The Member States have a political discretion to decide whether their essential security interests are affected.[94] The use of the provision is nevertheless subject to the scrutiny of the Court, especially through Article 298 subparagraph 2 EC. However, such a case has never occurred in practice. Moreover, it is subject to the bilateral communication between the Commission and a Member State provided in Article 298 subparagraph 1 EC if the Commission considers that necessary. The move to a narrow interpretation of Article 296 (1) (b) EC, described above, however, might give a greater practical importance to this privilege in the future.

3.1. Abuse

There is a danger of abuse of Article 296 (1) (a) EC. Member States could, for example, withhold the evidence necessary for the Court to scrutinise a measure taken on grounds of national security. According to *Commission* v. *Spain* it is for the Member States to prove a situation covered by Articles 296 (1) (b) EC.[95] Thus the necessity to disclose the information needed to decide on the application of letter (b) might compromise the use of the privilege in letter (a), when the information in question is the only proof available.

In the context of the GATT, it was argued that the exercise of a legitimate procedural right must not be used against a Member State.[96] Applied to the European Community context this would mean that if a Member State refuses to disclose information under Article 296 (1) (a) EC, the Court will accept the use of Articles 296 (1) (b) or 297 EC in good faith. In such a case a Member State would not be required to prove the situation.

3.2. The Special Review Procedure of Article 298 Subparagraph 2 EC

However, the exercise of the discretion under Article 296 (1) (a) EC can be subjected to the scrutiny of the Court under the *in camera* procedure of Article 298 subparagraph 2 EC. As the public is excluded from these proceedings, Member States are not able to use the privilege in Article 296 (1) (a) EC in the context of these proceedings

[92] Article 284 EC reads: 'The Commission may, within the limits and under the conditions laid down by the Council in accordance with the provisions of this Treaty, collect any information and carry out any checks required for the performance of the tasks entrusted to it.'

[93] Article 10 EC reads:

Member States shall take all appropriate measures, whether general or particular, to ensure fulfilment of the obligations arising out of this Treaty or resulting form action taken by the institutions of the Community. They shall facilitate the achievement of the Community's tasks.

They shall abstain from any measure which could jeopardise the attainment of the objectives of this Treaty.

[94] W Hummer, Article 223, in Grabitz, *et al*, above n 66, at para 4.

[95] Case C–414/97, above n 41, at para 22, discussed above.

[96] In relation to the similar provision of Article XXI (a) GATT see: Schloemann and Ohloff, above n 64, also referring to the statement of United States delegate Evans in the 1949 *Czechoslovakia* dispute, Doc GATT/CP3/38, at 9 (1949).

again to avoid having to supply information to the Court on the previous use of the same provision. If the use of Articles 296 (1) (b) or 297 EC is the subject of these proceedings the respective Member State is not able to use the privilege either.

First, the alternative view could make the review of the Court redundant. The narrow interpretation of Article 296 (1) (b) EC in *Commission* v. *Spain* for example, would be deprived of its practical effect if Member States could use their discretion to withhold information the Court needs to scrutinise a measure taken under that exemption. A Member State who abused letter (b) will not hesitate to abuse letter (a). Moreover, the Court allocated the burden of proof clearly on the Member States.

Second, the secrecy needs of the Member States are sufficiently accommodated in Article 298 subparagraph 2 EC proceedings, as the public is excluded. By derogation from Article 34 of the Statute of the Court, for example, secrecy also has to be taken into account when reading the judgment to the public.[97]

Finally, it is unlikely that a Member State will push it that far and abuse Article 296 (1) (a) EC again in a case where the previous abuse of the same provision is the issue of Court proceedings. This would involve a political confrontation between Member States and institutions that does not occur very often in practice. Member States normally follow judgments of the European Court of Justice and try to co-operate with the institutions of the Union.

For the same reasons discussed in the context of Article 296 (1) (b) above and 297 EC in chapter 6,[98] the Court will apply a low-intensity proportionality test leaving wide discretion to the Member States. It will only consider a measure disproportionate when a measure is outside the ambit of that discretion, when the Member State acted arbitrarily or in bad faith.

To put the burden of proof on the Member States, similar to the position with respect to Article 296 (1) (b) EC,[99] could compromise their wide discretion. Moreover, it might be considered not to take the nature of secrecy into account. On the other hand the Commission would find it difficult to supply the evidence for a disproportionate use of the provision. This would make its role under Article 298 subparagraph 2 EC almost redundant. Furthermore, the evidence rules in relation to Article 296 (1) (b) EC and Article 297 EC discussed above have to be taken into account, assuming a similar evidence rule for all exceptions of the second group. Thus it is submitted that the Member States carry the burden of proof for the use of Article 296 (1) (a) EC.

3.3. Article 296 (1) (a) EC and the Common Foreign and Security Policy

There is a danger that Article 296 (1) (a) EC could contradict Article 16 TEU which provides that under the CFSP the Member States are under the obligation,

> "to inform and consult one another within the Council on any matter of foreign and security policy of general interest."

[97] See also: Hummer, in Grabitz and Hilf, above n 59, commentary on Article 223, para 4.
[98] At 188–189.
[99] See above.

European Community law prevails over the law of the CFSP. Therefore Article 296 (1) (a) EC does not only represent a derogation from the general obligation of Member States to supply information to the institutions of the Union according to Articles 10 and 284 EC but also a derogation from Article 16 TEU. Considering the privileges the older Article 296 (1) (a) EC is intended to bestow on the Member States to protect their national security, the coexistence with the younger Article 16 TEU, which equally deals with sensitive information, is contradictory.[100] Because of the supremacy of Community law over the law of the CFSP this can potentially undermine the coherence of the CFSP. Moreover, it can potentially undermine the coherence of the First and Second Pillars. However, the limited interpretation of Article 296 (1) (a) EC which allows them to invoke the provision only when their essential interests of security are affected limits the use of the exception. Moreover, based on this limited interpretation, the judicial review exercised by the Court under Article 298 subparagraph 2 EC allows correcting the measures of Member States. Therefore the conflict or contradiction between Article 296 (1) (a) EC and Article 16 TEU can be avoided in practice and *a posteriori*. The coherence of the Second Pillar and of the CFSP with the Community can therefore be ensured by the review of the Court. However, it would be preferable to ensure the a *priori* coherence of Community and CFSP though mutual reference in Articles 296 (1) (a) EC and 16 TEU.

4. CONCLUSIONS

In addition to the public security exemptions from the free movement regimes in Articles 30, 39 (3), 46 (2), and 58 (1) (b) EC as a first group of security exemptions, the EC Treaty contains a second group of national security exemptions in Articles 296 and 297 EC. In contrast to the earlier, which only allow exemption from their specific regimes on goods, workers, services, establishment, capital and payments respectively, the latter allows derogation from the Treaty as a whole. Moreover, they are subject to the special review procedure in Article 298 subparagraph 2 EC. However, the armaments exemption in Article 296 (1) (b) EC and the secrecy exemption in Article 296 (1) (a) EC also have to be interpreted narrowly. They do not represent automatic exclusions but need to be justified, invoked, and proven by the Member State that wishes to rely on them. The narrow interpretation is necessary to avoid these exemptions being used as loopholes that could potentially undermine the functioning of the internal market as a whole. In comparison to the first group of exemptions Member States have a wider margin of discretion as regards the measures they consider necessary in relation to armaments and secrecy in the context of Article 296 EC.

The relationships between Articles 296 (1) (b) EC and 17 (1) subparagraph 3 TEU and Articles 296 (1) (a) EC and 16 TEU are not clarified by mutual references in the provisions. The coexistence of Articles 296 (1) (b) EC and 17 (1) subparagraph 3 TEU and the interpretation of the earlier provision put armaments in a legal limbo undermining the coherence and consistency of the armaments policy of the Union.

[100] Wessel, above n 14, at 311 calls this: 'at the very least, surprising'.

6

The Finest Balance: Article 297 EC and Community Law in Times of Crisis and War

1. INTRODUCTION

CHAPTER 4 DISCUSSED the public security exemptions from the free movement regimes of the EC Treaty, namely Articles 30, 39 (3), 46 (1), and 58 (1) (b) EC. The exemptions of this first group only apply to their specific free movement regimes, the use of these provisions is subject to the usual review procedures and the European Court of Justice will apply a strict proportionality test. Chapter 5 discussed the national security exemptions on armaments and secrecy in Article 296 EC. They allow derogation from the Treaty as a whole; the use of these provisions is subject to bi-lateral communications between the Commission and the Member State in question under Article 298 subparagraph 1 EC and to a special review procedure under Article 298 subparagraph 2 EC. The lower level of intensity of the scrutiny exercised by the Court leaves a wider margin of discretion to the Member States.

This chapter will deal with the third security exemption of the second group. Article 297 EC shares most of the characteristics of the other national security exemptions in Article 296 (1) (a) and (1) (b) EC.[1] It will be explained that the highly exceptional character of the situations accommodated in the earlier provision necessitates an even wider margin of discretion for the Member States. This makes the scrutiny that would be exercised by the Court even less intense than in cases where Article 296 EC was invoked. However, this is to a large extent counterbalanced by the highly exceptional character of the provision. This character limits the use of Article 297 EC considerably, thereby almost eliminating its practical relevance. Chapter 6 will complete the discussion on the EC Treaty as an instrument of European defence integration.

[1] An earlier version of this ch was presented at the Hart Workshop *European Union Law for the 21st Century: Defining the New Legal Order*, in June 2003 in London under the title 'At the Borderline between Member State and Community Competence'. It was published as M Trybus, 'At the Borderline between Community and Member State Competence: the Triple-Exceptional Character of Article 297 EC' in T Tridimas and P Nebbia, (eds), *European Union Law for the 21st Century: Defining the New Legal Order* (Hart Publishing, Oxford, 2004) 137.

Article 297 EC provides for a special consultation procedure between Member States taking together the steps needed to prevent the functioning of the common market being affected by measures, which a Member State may be called upon to take in a number of situations involving national security. These situations apply:

> [1] "in the event of serious internal disturbances affecting the maintenance of law and order,
> [2] in the event of war,
> [3] serious international tension constituting a threat of war; or
> [4] in order to carry out obligations it [the Member State] has accepted for the purpose of maintaining peace and international security".

The provision is a typical national security exemption, and it is not unusual in international treaties for this kind of crisis situation to be covered by a special exemption.[2] It is a reflection of the fact that, unlike the European Defence Community of the 1950s discussed in chapter 1, neither the European Economic Community of 1958 nor the European Union of 2005 can shoulder the responsibility for defence and security. Article 297 EC can relieve a Member State of its obligations under the EC Treaty and the Treaty on European Union in extreme crisis situations that threaten its very existence. In these extreme situations the response to a threat takes precedence over the entirety of the law of the EU, with or without a provision such as Article 297 EC.[3] The commercial link of Article 297 EC is weaker than that of Article 296 (1) (b) EC. In contrast to the latter provision, the former does not relate to the free movement of goods, a core regime of the Treaty. Thus the exemption is even closer to the notion of national security as reserved to the sovereignty of the Member States and therefore, together with Article 296 EC, represents the very borderline between Community and Member State competence over defence and security. Article 297 EC is the only security exemption the Court had avoided interpreting so far, although Member States had invoked it in many cases and the Kirchberg once got very close to a ruling.

The analysis in the following chapter will be based on legal principles developed by the Court in the context of the other security exemptions discussed in chapters 4 and 5 and will evaluate the extent to which these principles apply to Article 297 EC. In order to define the provision this chapter will first put it in the context of the other exclusions in the Treaty. Second, the scarce references to the

[2] See provisions in multilateral treaties such as Article XXI(b)(iii) and (c) of the General Agreement on Tariffs and Trade (GATT); Article XIV *bis* of the General Agreement on Trade in Services (GATS); Article 73 of the Agreement on Trade-Related Intellectual Property Rights (TRIPS); Article 15(1) of the European Convention of Human Rights (ECHR); or provisions in bilateral treaties such as Article XX(1)(d) of the Treaty of Amity, Economic Relations and Consular Rights Between the United States of America and Iran 1955; and Article XXI(1)(d) of the United States-Nicaragua Treaty on Friendship, Commerce and Navigation.

[3] In Case C–423/98, *Alfredo Albore v Italy* [2000] ECR I–5965, para 27, Advocate General Cosmas considered Article 297 EC to be forming a dividing line between the situations where national and Community institutions function normally and situations of severe national danger. See below for details.

provision in the case law of the Court will be analysed in order to provide a workable interpretation. Finally, as this is the ultimate chapter on the EC Treaty as opposed to secondary Community legislation as an instrument of European defence integration, the results of chapters 4, 5, and 6 will be summarised to explain the limits of this function of the EC Treaty.

2. THE POSITION OF ARTICLE 297 EC IN THE TREATY

The following section will briefly recapitulate the legal principles developed by the European Court of Justice in relation to the main security exemptions in the Treaty: Articles 30, 39 (3), 46 (1), 58 (1) (b), and 296 EC. This will facilitate the subsequent analysis of Article 297 EC for which no 'direct' case law is available. First, the common principles governing all security exemptions will be discussed. Second, the differences between the provisions will be explained to provide an understanding of the 'borderline position' of Article 297 EC.

2.1. Common Principles

Before locating the position of Article 297 EC in the Treaty, a number of common features of all security exemptions need to be discussed. First, as explained in chapter 4 the Court ruled in *Marguerite Johnston* v. *Chief Constable of the Royal Ulster Constabulary*, that the exemptions, including Article 297 EC, have a "limited character" and that they do not amount to "a general proviso covering all measures taken for reasons of public safety".[4] This "limited character" leads to a narrow interpretation of all exemptions. Moreover, with the exception of Article 58 (1) (b) EC, the list of security exemptions provided in *Johnston* is exhaustive.[5] The reason for this interpretation was also provided in *Johnston*: "If every provision of Community law were held to be subject of a general proviso, regardless of the specific requirements laid down by the provisions of the Treaty, this might impair the binding nature of Community law and its uniform application."[6] This interpretation limits the possibilities of Member States to justify measures for reasons of public and national security as otherwise the functioning of the internal market could be undermined. With regards to defence, the security exemptions provide a mechanism to balance the national security interests as part of the wider public security interests of the Member State on the one side with the internal market

[4] Case C–222/84, *Marguerite Johnston v Chief Constable of the Royal Ulster Constabulary* [1986] ECR 1651; [1986] 3 CMLR 240, para 26. The case concerned the exclusion of women from service in the Royal Ulster Constabulary (RUC), now the Police Service of Northern Ireland (PSNI). The Equal Treatment Directive, Council-Directive 76/207/EEC on the implementation of the principle of equal treatment of men and women as regards access to employment, vocational training and promotion [1976] OJ L–39/40, contains a 'quasi-security' exemption in Article 2(2) when sex is a determining factor for certain activities. See ch 9 for details.

[5] The list consisted of Articles 30, 39(3), 46(3), 296 and 297 EC See ch 4 at 126, n 9 on the reasons why Article 58(1)(b) EC needs to be added to this list.

[6] Case C–222/84, *Johnston*, above n 4.

and other interests of the Community on the other side. Similar to the discussion in chapter 4,[7] this balancing mechanism could also be explained with the metaphor of scales balancing the weight of these two interests. The narrow interpretation represents a heavy weight on the scale of the Community interests. This weight counterbalances the weight on the scale of the Member State interest brought about by the very existence of the exemptions.

Second, all exemptions, including Article 297 EC, are subject to judicial scrutiny exercised by the Court. For Articles 296 and 297 EC this is emphasised by a specific review procedure in Article 298 subparagraph 2 EC. As will be explained below, the intensity of scrutiny differs depending on the exemption.

2.2. Differences

As explained in chapters 4 and 5,[8] the security type exemptions can be divided into two groups.[9] The first group of exclusions discussed in chapter 4, namely Articles 30, 39 (3), 46 (1) and 58 (1) (b) EC, allows restrictions of the free movement of goods, workers, services, capital, payments, or the freedom of establishment for reasons of public security. They allow restrictions on grounds of "public security", a wide concept covering all aspects of security, internal and external, including the concept of national security.[10] In contrast, the exemptions in Articles 296 and 297 EC relate to a narrower concept of national security or military security. The term "essential interests of [...] security" is used in Article 296 (1) (a) and (b) EC and security is not mentioned explicitly in Article 297 EC. However, the situations described are situations affecting national security. The exemptions of the first group are restricted to their respective free movement regimes: goods, workers, services, establishment, payments or capital. In contrast, the national security exclusions of the second group apply to the Treaty as a whole. Measures justified by provisions of the first group are subject to strict scrutiny exercised by the Court. The crucial element of this scrutiny is the application of the proportionality test.[11] In general terms this involves a reasonable relationship of the relevant interests involved,[12] which in the context of this chapter can be identified as the internal market and other interests of the Community on one side and the public security interest of the Member States on the other side. As explained in

[7] At 139.

[8] Chapter 4 at 125 and ch 5 at 141–142.

[9] M Trybus, 'The EC Treaty as an Instrument of European Defence Integration: Judicial Scrutiny of Security and Defence Exclusions' (2002) 39 *Common Market Law Review* 1347, at 1350 (hereinafter 'Instrument').

[10] J Schwarze, *European Administrative Law* (Sweet & Maxwell, London, 1992) 778, based on Wägbaur, in H von der Groeben, *v* Boeckh, Thiesing, Ehlermann, *Kommentar zum EWG Vertrag*, 3rd edn, (Nomos, Baden, 1983) Article 36, margin nos. 18 *et seq.* defines public security as 'the entire field of rules, laid down by the sovereign authorities and incapable of being waived, which have been adopted in the interest of the political and social integrity of society'.

[11] Other elements of this scrutiny are legitimate expectations, non-discrimination and the emergent principle of transparency.

[12] G de Búrca, 'The Principle of Proportionality and its Application in EC Law' (1993) 13 *Yearbook of European Law* 105.

chapter 4, the Member State measure in question has to be suitable to promote public security. Moreover, it needs to be adequate or necessary, meaning that there is no possible measure which is equally effective to promote public security but less detrimental to the internal market. Finally, the measure has to be proportionate in the strict sense, which requires a fine balance between the public security interests of the Member States and the internal market interests of the Community.[13] Generally, scrutiny is very intense which is appropriate for two reasons. First, in the context of the crucial free movement provisions, all restricting measures have to be proportionate to ensure the functioning of the internal market.[14] Exemption has to be the exception. Second, the military interests of the Member States are sufficiently safeguarded by the exemptions of the second group. Thus there is no need to limit scrutiny in the context of the first group. In the context of the first group the Community and Member State interests can be balanced on three levels: through the existence but narrow interpretation of the provisions, through the proportionality test in general, and if necessary, through proportionality in the strict sense.

The second group of exclusions consists of Article 296 and 297 EC. The common feature of these exclusions is that in cases of "improper use" they can be subject to special procedures under Article 298 EC. Moreover, they apply to the Treaty as a whole.

Article 296 (1) (b) EC was described in chapter 5. It allows a Member State "to take such measures as it considers necessary for the protection of the essential interests of its security which are connected with the production or trade in arms, munitions and war material". In *Commission* v. *Spain* the Court held that a measure Spain had tried to justify on the basis of Article 296 (1) (b) EC was "not *necessary* in order to achieve the objective of protecting the essential interests of the security of [...] Spain."[15] It was argued in chapter 5 that in particular the word "necessary" implies that the Court applied a proportionality test. However, as the case represented a clear case of abuse, the ruling does not represent sufficient authority to assume a proportionality test comparable to the intensity applied in the context of, for example, Article 30 EC. Luxembourg takes the Member State discretion over national security issues into account by adapting the standard of review: scrutiny is less intense and will only overrule a measure if there is a clear case of abuse. Articles 296 (1) (b) and 297 EC are parts of the same group of exemptions. Hence the ruling in *Commission* v. *Spain* represents an important

[13] Formulated by Advocate General van Gerwen in Case C–159/90, *SPUC v Grogan* [1991] ECR I–4685 as cited by de Búrca, above, at 113 including the more controversial third element. Also in favour of the three-part test (based on the same test in German administrative law, see P Craig and G de Búrca, *EU Law,* 3rd edn, (OUP, Oxford, 2003) 350); Schwarze, above n 10, at 712.

[14] Case C–222/84, above n 4, at para 26.

[15] Case C–414/97, [1999] ECR I–5585; [2000] 2 CMLR 4. As outlined in chapter 5 the case concerned the exemption of armaments exports form Value Added Tax (VAT). According to an EC Directive all exports had to be subjected to VAT. Spain justified the exemption of armaments on the basis of Article 296(1)(b) EC. See also: M Trybus 'The Recent Judgment in *Commission v Spain* and the Procurement of Hard Defence Material' (2000) 9 *Public Procurement Law Review* NA99; and M Trybus 'On the Application of the EC-Treaty to Armaments' (2000) 25 *European Law Review* 633.

benchmark for the interpretation of Article 297 EC, because there is no ruling on the interpretation of the provision itself.

2.3. Exceptional Character

Another way to describe the position of Article 297 EC in the Treaty appears from the relevant case law and advisory opinions. The provision has an exceptional character within the framework of the Treaty that is connected to a subsidiary character in relation to the other exemptions.

In *SpA Salgoil* v. *Italian Ministry of Foreign Trade* the Court ruled that Article 297 EC has a limited framework and corresponds to a particular, hypothetical and well-defined situation. It is an exceptional provision, calling for a strict interpretation and cannot be invoked to deny the existence of rights created by other provisions of the Treaty.[16]

In his advisory opinion in *Johnston* Advocate General Darmon, and in his advisory opinion in *Fritz Werner Industrie-Ausrüstungen GmbH* v. *Germany* and *Criminal Proceedings against Peter Leifer and others*, Advocate General Jacobs pointed out that Article 297 EC is a safeguard clause of general application that only applies as *ultima ratio* in the absence of special rules.[17]

2.3.1. Double-Exceptional Character

In his advisory opinion in *Alfredo Albore* v. *Italy* Advocate General Cosmas attributed a "double-exceptional character" to Article 297 EC.[18] First, the provision has an exceptional character in the framework of the EC Treaty. Similar to the other security exemptions, it is an established rule that Article 297 EC concerns "exceptional, hypothetical cases, which are well defined and do not lend themselves to any extensive interpretation".[19] This refers to the *Johnston* principle: as these provisions allow derogation from the Treaty, they have to be limited to exceptional cases. Otherwise the functioning of the common market as a whole could be affected. Article 297 EC shares this first aspect of its 'double-exceptional character' with all the other security exemptions discussed in chapters 4 and 5.

[16] Case C–13/69, *SpA Salgoil v Italian Ministry of Foreign Trade* [1968] ECR 453, at 463; [1969] CMLR 181, at 192, 198.

[17] Case C–222/84, above n 4, at para 5; Case C–70/94, *Fritz Werner Industrie-Ausrüstungen GmbH v Germany* [1995] ECR I–3189 (hereinafter '*Werner*'); and Case C–83/94, Criminal Proceedings against *Peter Leifer* [1995] ECR I–3231, at para 63 (hereinafter '*Leifer*'). The *Werner* and *Leifer* cases concerned the export of defence-related goods, see annotations of N Emiliou, 'Restrictions on Strategic Exports, Dual-use Goods and the Common Commercial Policy' (1997) 22 *European Law Review* 68 and P Koutrakos, 'Exports of Dual Use Goods under the Law of the European Union' (1998) 23 *European Law Review* 235.

[18] Advocate General Cosmas in Case C–423/98, above n 3, at para 23. The case concerned an Italian law that required non-Italians purchasing property in certain 'military areas' of Italy including all small islands of Italy, to seek the prior consent of the local administration. See ch 4 for details.

[19] Case C–13/68, *Salgoil*, above n 16; Case C–222/84, *Johnston*, above n 4, at para 26.

Second, the provision has a "wholly exceptional character"[20] in the framework of the Treaty. Unlike the other provisions it allows to derogate from the Treaty as a whole. Thus it can only be used as an "*ultima ratio*" when the other provisions cannot be used.[21] This second aspect is shared with Article 296 EC but not with the public security exemptions of the first group.

2.3.2. Triple-Exceptional Character

It is submitted that, building on the concept of the 'double-exceptional character' developed by Advocate General Cosmas, that Article 297 EC actually has a 'triple-exceptional character'. This is because, in addition to being exceptional within the framework of the Treaty (exceptional) and in relation to the public security exemptions of the first group (double-exceptional), it is also exceptional in comparison to Article 296 EC which also allows derogation from the Treaty as a whole (triple-exceptional). In contrast to the latter, it does not directly relate to the internal market. Moreover, partly because of this missing link to trade, partly because of the highly exceptional character of the crisis situations stipulated therein, the provision was never successfully abused as an automatic exemption the way Article 296 (1) (b) EC was.[22] It was never successfully used in practice at all.[23] This third aspect of its 'triple exceptional character', brought about by the extreme and unlikely crisis situation it seeks to accommodate, could also be called the 'extremely exceptional character' of Article 297 EC.

2.3.3. Subsidiary Character

The subsidiary character of Article 297 EC is linked to this 'triple-exceptional character'. As an exemption the provision does not only have a subsidiary character in relation to the public security exemptions of the free movement regimes. It also has a subsidiary character in relation to Article 296 EC: it can only be invoked when no other exemption can be used. In *Albore* Advocate General Cosmas considered Article 297 EC to have a supplementary character to the other exemptions, forming a dividing line between the situations where national and Community institutions function normally and situations of severe national danger. Article 297 EC implied significant modifications according to the nature, the intensity and the understanding of the connection between the legal order of the Community and that of the Member States.[24]

[20] Case C–222/84, above, at 1684; Case C–273/97, *Angela Maria Sirdar v The Army Board ex parte Ministry of Defence*, [1999] ECR I–7403; [1999] 3 CMLR 559 (hereinafter '*Sirdar*'), at para 19. The case concerned the exclusion of women from the Royal Marines of the United Kingdom armed forces. It was decided on the basis of the Equal Treatment Directive rather than Article 297 EC and will be discussed in detail in ch 9 at 269–277.

[21] Advocate General Cosmas in Case C–423/98, above n 3, at para 24.

[22] On this abuse of Article 296(1)(b) EC see ch 5 at 150.

[23] As far as the case law of the European Court of Justice is concerned. It might have been used successfully in preliminary proceedings or might have had an indirect effect by convincing the Commission not to act on a particular measure.

[24] Case C–423/98, above n 3, at para 27.

On the basis of this 'triple-exceptional' and subsidiary character as an *ultima ratio* the possible application of Article 297 EC in practice is very limited. Situations that would justify the use of the provision have been rare over the last five decades. Article 297 EC possibly only applies to the Falklands War.[25] The exceptional and subsidiary character and resulting limited application of Article 297 EC is possibly the strongest safeguard against its abuse.

3. ARTICLE 297 EC IN THE CASE LAW OF THE COURT

The previous section of this chapter explained the common principles of the security exemptions and the 'triple-exceptional character' of Article 297 EC, which form crucial components of its interpretation. The following section will attempt to refine the definition of the provision on the basis of scarce case law and advisory opinions. As mentioned above, there is no direct judgment of the European Court of Justice on the provision. However, there are references to Article 297 EC in a number of cases. Moreover, several advisory opinions discussed the provisions. These reference and advisory opinions can be added to the discussion of the other exemptions above. Together they provide material forming the foundation of the subsequent interpretation. The basic rule is that the provision has to be interpreted narrowly.[26] Defining means identifying limits. Possible limits of Article 297 EC are judicial scrutiny, procedural requirements, and time limits.

3.1. Jurisdiction

A first question in this context is, whether the Court has jurisdiction to review measures taken by Member States under Article 297 EC at all. Going back to the scales metaphor: if answered in the negative, the provision could be seen either as a decisive weight in favour of the Member States interest in national security, or even as a mechanism to exit or *veto* any balancing operation. In other words, Member States could exclude a measure from review by invoking Article 297 EC. Accommodating the Member State interest further still, the provision could be interpreted as an automatic exemption, without even the necessity to invoke it. The measure would be immune from judicial scrutiny; the rule of law would not apply. This interpretation sees Article 297 EC as a general safeguard clause, a "reserve of sovereignty"[27] for defence matters that goes well beyond its wording.

The Court's jurisdiction has been questioned frequently in the past. Some Member States argued the provision generally "reserved the field of defence

[25] See the second recital in the preamble to Council Regulation No 877/82 of 16 April 1982 suspending imports of all products originating in Argentina [1982] OJ L-102/1, which states that: '[...] following the measures already taken by the United Kingdom, the Member States have consulted one another pursuant to Article 224 of the Treaty [now 297] establishing the [EEC]'.

[26] Case C–222/84, *Johnston*, above n 4, at para 26.

[27] Expression of P Koutrakos, 'Is Article 297 EC a "Reserve of Sovereignty"?' (2000) 37 *Common Market Law Review* 1339 (hereinafter 'Reserve'). However, as indicated by the question and quotation marks, he does not advocate this interpretation.

matters to the exclusive competence of the Member State[s]".[28] The provision made clear that defence matters fall outside the provisions of the Treaty and remain the "exclusive competence" of the Member States. In accordance with the Treaty the Member States have transferred their sovereignty rights only in limited fields other than defence.[29]

In *Commission* v. *Greece ('FYROM')*, a case on trade sanctions imposed by Greece against the Former Yugoslav Republic of Macedonia (FYROM), the Greek government argued that questions regarding the external security of a Member State are not matters open to consideration by the Court.[30] However, in contradiction to this bold statement, it also submitted that Article 225 EC (now298) *restricts* judicial review to cases of "improper use".[31] Exclusion and restriction of jurisdiction, however, are two entirely different concepts: a court with restricted jurisdiction still has jurisdiction. Similarly contradictory the Danish government argued in *Johnston*: "a Member State's discretion in that regard [the use of Article 297 EC] is not subject to judicial review, save in the case of abuse".[32] This line of argument appears to be courtroom tactics: first the Member State argues for the exclusion of jurisdiction. Second, in case the Court assumes jurisdiction, it argues for a restriction of review. Nevertheless, these arguments are significant because they show the opinion of the Member States regarding their competence over defence matters in relation to the EC.

It is clear from the expressly stipulated Article 298 subparagraph 2 EC that the Court has jurisdiction to review measures taken by Member States under Article 297 EC. It has dealt with cases involving this exemption on numerous occasions. In *Salgoil*, *Sirdar*, *Johnston*,[33] and *Tanja Kreil* v. *Germany*[34] the Court considered the scope of the exemption. The advisory opinions of Advocate General Darmon in *Johnston*[35] and of Advocate General Jacobs in *Criminal Proceedings against Aimé*

[28] See the observations of the government of the Federal Republic of Germany in Case C–15/69, *Südmilch v Ugliola* [1969] ECR 363, at 367. The case concerned an Italian worker in Germany who wanted a guarantee that he could return to his post in Germany after his compulsory military service in Italy. German legislation provided for such a guarantee for German conscripts. Mr Ugliola considered that to be discrimination on grounds of nationality. The Court agreed. See also the observations of the United Kingdom, French, and Portuguese governments in Case C–273/97, *Sirdar*, above n 20, as referred to by Advocate General La Pergola, at para 10. According to the Advocate General the French government in particular takes the view that defence should be treated in the same way as the other functions traditionally reserved to States, such as justice, diplomacy, public finance, and police.

[29] Above.

[30] Case C–120/94 R, *Commission v Greece ('FYROM')* [1996] ECR I–1513, at para 56.

[31] Above, at para 59.

[32] See the observations of the representative of the Danish government in Case C–222/84, above n 4, at 1676.

[33] Case C–13/68, above n 16 at 192, 198; Case C–273/97, above n 20, at para 16; Case C–222/84, above n 4, at paras 26, 27 and 60.

[34] Case C–285/98, *Tanja Kreil v Germany* [2000] ECR I–69 (hereinafter '*Kreil*'), at para 16. The case concerned the exclusion of women from service in arms in the German armed forces. See ch 9 at 277–284 for details.

[35] Case C–222/84, above n 4, at 1658.

Richardt and Les Accessoires Scientifiques,[36] *Leifer* and *Werner*[37] discussed Article 297 EC but considered it to be irrelevant for the respective case. In his advisory opinion in *Albore*, Advocate General Cosmas dealt extensively with the provision but considered it not to apply to the case.[38] The Court agreed.[39] Hence it is submitted that the Court clearly has jurisdiction to review measures justified by Article 297 EC. However, by the time of completion of this book in late 2004 there has never been a case where the provision was invoked as the only exemption available and subsequently rejected or approved by the Court.

The jurisdiction of the Court to review measures taken on the basis of Article 297 EC in Article 298 subparagraph 2 EC represents in itself a considerable limitation of sovereignty. By specifically stipulating judicial review of their decisions to derogate from the Treaty during crisis situations involving national security, the Member States have transferred a part of their competence over defence to the Community. They could have avoided that transfer by creating an automatic exemption or by limiting review to political procedures, for example through the Council. Judicial scrutiny by the Court, however restricted, involves Community institutions in defence related decisions. Within the balancing operation, Article 297 EC represents a weight on the scale of the Member States counterbalanced by the judicial review of Article 298 subparagraph 2 EC as a weight on the scale of the Community interests.

Community law prevails over the law of the Second and Third Pillars of the TEU.[40] Therefore Article 297 EC can also be used to derogate from the provisions of the CFSP discussed in chapters 2 and 3.[41] This issue will be discussed in a separate section on Article 297 EC and the CFSP below. The question in the context of this section of the chapter is whether the Court has jurisdiction to review the use of Article 297 EC to derogate from the CFSP. Whereas according to Article 46 TEU[42] the

[36] Case C–367/89, Criminal Proceedings against *Aimé Richardt and Les Accessoires Scientifiques* [1991] ECR I–4621 (hereinafter '*Aimé Richardt*'), at 4643–44. *Aimé Richardt* concerned the export of sensitive material to Eastern Bloc countries and subsequent criminal proceedings. See also: P Eeckhout, 'On Dual Use Goods and Dualist Case Law: the *Aimé Richardt* Judgment on Export Controls' (1992) 29 *Common Market Law Review* 941.

[37] Case C–83/94, above n 17, at para 51; Case C–70/94, above n 17, at para 63.

[38] Case C–423/98, above n 3, at para 35.

[39] Above, at paras 22–24.

[40] RA Wessel, *The European Union's Foreign and Security Policy: A Legal Institutional Perspective* (Kluwer, The Hague, 1999) 311.

[41] Above.

[42] Article 46 TEU reads:

(a) The provisions of the Treaty establishing the European Community, the Treaty establishing the European Coal and Steel community and the Treaty establishing the European Atomic Energy Community concerning the powers of the Court of Justice of the European communities and the exercise of those powers apply only to the following provisions of this Treaty:
(b) provisions amending the Treaty establishing the European Economic Community with a view of establishing the European Community, the Treaty establishing the European Coal and Steel Community and the Treaty establishing the European Atomic energy Community;
(c) provisions of Title VI, under the conditions provided for by Article 35;
(d) provisions of Title VII, under the conditions provided for by Article 11 of the Treaty establishing the European Community and Article 40 of this Treaty;
(e) Article 6 (2) with regard to action of the institutions, insofar as the Court has jurisdiction under the Treaties establishing the European Communities and under this Treaty; [...]

European Court of Justice has no jurisdiction over the CFSP, it has jurisdiction to review the use of Article 297 EC on the basis of Article 298 paragraph 2 EC. There are arguments for and against the assumption that the Court has jurisdiction to review a Member State measure taken on the basis of Article 297 EC to derogate from the CFSP.

On the one hand the wording of Article 298 subparagraph 2 EC refers to "improper use" and therefore does not limit review to the use of Article 297 EC with regards to derogation from the EC Treaty. On the other hand the bilateral examination to be conducted by the Commission and the Member State in question according to Article 298 subparagraph 1 EC is limited to cases where "measures taken in the circumstances referred to in Articles 296 and 297 have the effect of distorting the conditions of competition in the common market". It is submitted that this reference to competition in the common market limits bilateral examination of the use of Article 297 EC according to Article 298 subparagraph 1 EC to effects on the Community Pillar. This excludes effects on the CFSP.

The bilateral examination according to Article 298 subparagraph 1 EC preceding judicial review according to Article 298 subparagraph 2 EC is comparable to the pre-judicial stage in enforcement proceedings of the Commission according to Article 226 (1) or 227 (2) and (3) EC preceding judicial review according to Article 226 (2) or 227 (1) EC. These procedures were discussed in chapter 4.[43] The reference "by derogation from the procedure laid down in Articles 226 and 227" in Article 298 subparagraph 2 EC clarifies that judicial review is conducted under a special procedure that derogates from these general procedures stipulated in Part Five of the EC Treaty and conducted under 'normal' circumstances. The use of the special procedure leads to the proceedings being conducted *in camera* thereby accommodating the national security and secrecy implications of such a case. The pre-judicial stage according to Articles 226 (1) and 227 (2) and (3) EC and judicial review according to Articles 226 (2) and 227 (1) EC are two parts of one enforcement mechanism. The pre-judicial stage is designed to remove infringements of Community law in a non-confrontational and almost diplomatic manner thereby avoiding judicial review.[44] It is widely considered to be successful in achieving this aim making judicial review merely a matter of last resort.[45] Therefore the co-operation of the pre-judicial phase rather than the confrontation of judicial review characterise the removal of infringements of Community law. The co-operation between the Commission and the Member States makes the mechanism more effective than a mechanism based on confrontation would be. It is submitted that the special mechanism in Article 298 EC is based on the same principles. Moreover, the politically sensitive nature of the use of Articles 296 and

[43] At 132–134.

[44] See for example the XVIIIth Annual Report on Monitoring the Application of Community Law (2000), COM (2001) 309.

[45] According to the XXth Annual Report on Monitoring the Application of Community Law (2002), COM (2003) 669, Annex II, in 2002 in 995 cases formal notices were issued, leading to 487 reasoned opinions. In only 180 of these cases the matter had to be referred to the Court. This confirms a general pattern.

297 EC makes avoiding confrontation between Member States or between the Commission and Member States even more important to make the mechanism effective. This means that, just like the pre-judicial stage according to Articles 226 (1) and 227 (2) and (3) EC and judicial review according to Articles 226 (2) and 227 (1) EC are two parts of one enforcement mechanism, the pre-judicial stage of bilateral examination according to Article 298 subparagraph 1 EC and judicial review of Article 298 subparagraph 2 EC are two parts of one 'enforcement' mechanism. The result of understanding paragraphs 1 and 2 of Article 298 EC as one mechanism is that the limitation to "effect[s] of distorting competition in the common market" in Article 298 subparagraph 1 EC extends to Article 298 subparagraph 2 EC. Therefore judicial review under the latter paragraph does not extend to the use of Articles 296 and 297 EC to derogate from the CFSP.

Moreover, Article 46 TEU clearly excludes the CFSP in Title V of the TEU from the jurisdiction of the Court. Review of a measure derogating from the CFSP on the basis of Article 297 EC would necessarily involve a review of the Title V provisions, Common Position, or Joint Action the Member State in question wants to derogate from. In other words it would necessarily involve a review of the CFSP, which is explicitly ruled out in Article 46 TEU. As argued in chapter 2[46] this exclusion leads to a limitation of the rule of law and is therefore lamented. However, it is the clear will of the Member States to exclude the CFSP from judicial review.

Finally, the authority of the Court to define the limits of Community law as defined in recent case law[47] does not by its very nature extend beyond the borderline of Community law into the CFSP. Therefore judicial review exercised by the European Court of Justice under Article 298 (2) EC is limited to measures derogating from Community law.

3.2. Consultation Procedure

The consultation procedure stipulated in the exemption itself is a second issue that has to be discussed. This consultation procedure needs to be differentiated from the bilateral communication according to Article 298 subparagraph 2 EC. Article 297 EC provides that "Member States shall consult each other with a view to taking together the steps needed to prevent the functioning of the common market being affected by measures which a Member State might be called upon to take [...]." Member States invoking the exemption have a duty to engage in consultations with the other Member States. According to Advocate General Jacobs' advisory opinion in *FYROM* they must do so "in order to minimise the effects of the national measures on the functioning of the common market, in accordance with the duty of co-operation and genuine assistance imposed on Member States

[46] At 79–80.

[47] See Case C–84/95, *Bosphorus Hava Yollari Turizim AS v Minister for Transport, Energy and Communications, Ireland and the Attorney General* [1996] ECR I–3953; [1996] 3 CMLR 257; Case C–124/95, *The Queen, ex parte Centro-Com Srl v HM Treasury and Bank of England* [1997] ECR I–81; Case C–177/95, *Ebony Maritime SA and Loten Navigation Co Ltd v Prefetto della Provincia di Brindisi and Ministero dell'Interno* [1997] ECR I–1111; [1997] 2 CMLR 24.

with regard to the Community, the principle enshrined in Article 5 EC [now 10]".[48] The purpose of the consultation is to take the opinion of the other Member States into account and in order to prevent any disruptive effect on the internal market. This might lead to an adapted measure which is less detrimental to the internal market, to a measure of the Union as a whole instead of the planned individual Member State action, or even to the Member State refraining from taking a measure all together. Another purpose is to keep the other Member States informed and to resolve possible disputes which could lead to Article 298 subparagraph 2 EC proceedings.[49] Thus the use of Article 297 EC is subject to procedural requirements and the Court has jurisdiction to determine compliance under Article 298 subparagraph 2 EC.[50] Advocate General Jacobs expressly stated this in his advisory opinion in *FYROM*.[51]

Consultation must be carried out before the measure in question is adopted. Otherwise the purposes to take the opinion of the other Member States into account and to find alternative solutions would be undermined.[52] Moreover, modifications to an adopted measure as a result of consultations after adopting a measure would be politically difficult for a Member State, as this could easily be perceived as a retreat.[53]

Contrary to the interpretation of some Member States,[54] consultation must be carried out irrespective of whether the internal market is affected by the measure in question. Otherwise it would be within the discretion of the Member State in question whether consultations have to be conducted.[55] Moreover, it is not possible to detect an affection of the internal market without actually conducting the

[48] Case C–120/94 R, *FYROM*, above n 30, at para 47.

[49] C Stefanou and H Xanthaki, *A Legal and Political Interpretation of Articles 224 and 225 of the Treaty of Rome: The Former Yugoslav Republic of Macedonia Cases* (Ashgate: Dartmouth, Aldershot, 1997) at 56.

[50] P Koutrakos, *Trade, Foreign Policy and Defence in EU Constitutional Law* (Hart Publishing, Oxford, 2001) 157. Koutrakos, 'Reserve', above n 27, at 1356.

[51] Case C–120/94 R, *FYROM*, above n 30, at para 49.

[52] Koutrakos, 'Reserve', above n 27, at 1358.

[53] Above, at 1358–59.

[54] Arnull cites the United Kingdom government in the context of cases concerning sex equality in the armed forces: '[...] it is quite clear that on an issue [...] which is not related to the common market and such matters, consultation is not appropriate.' See A Arnull, 'EC Law and the Dismissal of Pregnant Servicewomen' (1995) 24 *Industrial Law Journal* 215, 233. See ch 9 on sex equality in the armed forces.

[55] Koutrakos, 'Reserve', above n 27, at 1357 cites two incidents with differing approaches. In the context of the sanctions against Rhodesia in the 1970s the consultation procedure had not been carried out. This omission was due to the fact that there was 'no evidence to suggest that sanctions imposed by Member States have affected the functioning of the common market or that they are being evaded across intra-Community frontiers', Written Question, Patijn, No 527/75, [1976] OJ C–89/8, at 9. During the Iraq Hostage Crisis the Commission was to use the consultation procedure 'for the exchange of information regarding the implementation of the various measures, particularly in order to identify any risk of distorting the conditions of competition in the common market', Bulletin EC 5–1980 at 27–28. Consultations conducted by the Commission, however, go beyond the wording of the provisions. Article 297 EC provides for consultations to be carried out only by the Member States.

procedure.[56] Finally, the wording of Article 297 EC does not qualify the effect on the common market as 'direct',[57] 'important', 'considerable', or 'significant'. This indicates that any effect on the internal market must be prevented.[58]

The requirement of a consultation procedure also implies that Article 297 EC needs to be specifically invoked and does not automatically exclude certain measures from the application of the Treaty.[59] Moreover, the start of the consultation can be interpreted as an implied invocation of Article 297 EC, although there might be cases where a Member State changes its mind and refrains from invoking the exemption. The consultation gives other Member States an opportunity to persuade the Member State in question to refrain from the measure or to modify it in a way that is less detrimental to the internal market.[60] It is submitted that it is one of the purposes of the provision to provide such an opportunity.

The consultation procedure gets the other Member States involved. The procedure is described as "taking together the steps needed to prevent the functioning of the common market being affected". Consultation goes beyond a mere information requirement; it involves discussion, possibly even attempts by other Member States to convince the derogating Member State to refrain from the measure. The Member States are no Community institution. However, they are constitutional players and their involvement in the national security decisions of each other represents another, yet very limited, transfer of sovereignty. Moreover, the consultation's objective of "preventing the common market from being affected" is significant: it introduces the Community interest in the internal market into the national security decision. Hence the Member States have to balance the Member State's national security interest with Community interests during consultations. However, there are two reservations. First, the other Member States have no *veto* power regarding a determined Member State. Within the limits of Article 10 EC,[61] such a Member State can reduce consultation to a mere ritual, leaving her sovereignty 'intact'. Second, the balancing and safeguard mechanism is easily made redundant in practice when the procedure is not followed.

Koutrakos pointed out that in *FYROM* the Greek government failed to follow the procedural requirements of Article 297 EC.[62] Moreover, it was never followed in any of the other relevant cases. This raises three issues. First, the fact that Greece did not follow the procedural requirements could be interpreted as an indication that they did not seriously believe that the use of the provision was feasible or even

56 Koutrakos, 'Reserve', above n 27, at 1357.

57 See Article 94 EC: 'The Council shall, acting unanimously on a proposal from the Commission and after consulting the European Parliament and the Economic and Social Committee, issue directives for the approximation of such laws, regulations or administrative provisions of the Member States as *directly* affect the establishment or functioning of the common market [emphasis added].'

58 Koutrakos, 'Reserve', above n 27, at 1357.

59 Koutrakos, 'Reserve', above, at 1356.

60 Above.

61 Article 10 EC reads: 'Member States shall take all appropriate measures, whether general or particular, to ensure fulfilment of the obligations arising out of this Treaty or resulting from action taken by the institutions of the Community. They shall facilitate the achievement of the Community's tasks.'

62 Koutrakos, 'Reserve', above n 27, at 1356–59 also citing Stefanou and Xanthaki, above n 48.

legally possible. In that case Article 297 EC would only have been used for tactical reasons, as an additional argument. However, the facts of the case seem to indicate that at least in the perception of the Greek government and public opinion in Greece the FYR of Macedonia posed a threat to the national security of Greece. National security was not merely a pretence.

Second, the case raises the question whether the situations described in Article 297 EC, for example war, allow a Member State to follow time-consuming procedures *before* taking measures. In other words, is it appropriate to impose procedural requirements on a Member State in an extreme crisis situation? Surely, the functioning of the internal market is of secondary importance when a Member State's existence is at stake. On the other hand the case shows that there is a danger of abuse. Therefore the availability of *ex post facto* judicial review is imperative. The urgency of a situation should be taken into account when a Member State did not follow the procedural requirements. However, the facts of the *FYROM* case seem to indicate that there would have been time for Article 297 EC consultations.

Third, the case raises the question of the legal effect of non-compliance with the procedural requirements of Article 297 EC. It has been argued that adherence to the procedure is a condition for the legal invocation of the exemption by a Member State.[63] In *FYROM* Advocate General Jacobs did not address the fact that Greece had not followed the procedure. Member States using the provision in their arguments in the Court, for example in the cases of *Johnston*,[64] *Sirdar*,[65] and *Kreil*,[66] had never followed the procedure. However, the Court never addressed the fact. In particular in *FYROM* it would have been easy to reject the use of Article 297 EC simply because the government of Greece had not followed the procedure. Advocate General Jacobs' advisory opinion represents a thorough legal analysis; it contains the most thorough discussion of Article 297 EC written to date. Hence it is unlikely that he overlooked the Greek lack of adherence to the procedure. He deliberately ignored it. This indicates that adherence to the procedure is not a condition for the legal invocation of the exemption. Moreover, the second point made above may be recalled in this context. It is questionable whether it is appropriate to impose procedural requirements on Member States in extreme crisis situations. Therefore it is submitted that non-compliance with the procedural requirement of Article 297 EC does not render a Member State measure illegal as such. Nevertheless, it can be taken into account as an argument in the Court proceedings. Thus the Court has jurisdiction to determine compliance. It is not the purpose of the procedure to serve as a legal condition for the use of Article 297 EC

[63] Koutrakos, *Trade, Foreign Policy and Defence in EU Constitutional Law*, above n 50, at 158 n 101. The argument for this opinion is the wholly exceptional character of the provision as repeatedly emphasised by the Court.

[64] Case C–222/84, above n 4.

[65] Case C–273/97, above n 20.

[66] Case C–285/98, above n 34. The case concerned the exclusion of women from service in arms in the armed forces of Germany. See ch 9 at 277–284 for a detailed discussion.

but to provide for the possibility of consultation on and adaptation of Member State measures before they are actually taken.

A related problem concerns the CFSP. As mentioned above, the use of Article 297 EC is subject to procedural requirements and the Court has jurisdiction to determine compliance. The question is whether it has this jurisdiction when the exemption is used to derogate from the CFSP. On the basis of the clear wording of the provision it is submitted that the objective of the consultation procedure, which is "to prevent the functioning of the common market being affected", limits the jurisdiction of the Court to determine compliance with the procedural requirement of Article 297 EC only when the provision is used to derogate from the EC Treaty.

3.3. Provisory Measures

Third, the question is, whether anticipatory measures are covered by Article 297 EC. Alternatively it is strictly limited to the time the situations actually occur. Examples for anticipatory or permanent measures are the establishment of a military area excluded from the application of Community law, as argued in *Albore*, or the recognition of the military as a profession to which the Treaty does not apply, as argued in *Sirdar*. This would add certain lands and certain people to the material allegedly not covered by the Treaty according to Article 296 (1) (b) EC. There is an important difference between allowing Member States to derogate from the Treaty to react to actual crisis situations and to allow derogation to prepare for these situations, without the requirement that they actually occur. The second interpretation would allow the exclusion of a large percentage of territory, people, or the economy from Community law. This, if abused on a large scale, would undermine the functioning of the internal market. However, based on a narrow interpretation of the provision,[67] it is submitted that Article 297 EC only applies within a certain time limit which does exclude anticipatory measures. This considerably limits the application of the provision in practice and prevents its abuse. However, there has been no ruling on the matter so far.

In his advisory opinion in *Sirdar* Advocate General La Pergola pointed out "that the cases envisaged by Article 297 EC concern temporary and non-permanent situations".[68] He also gave an example in the adoption of unilateral measures under Article 297 EC by the United Kingdom in a temporary situation of serious crisis which arose in 1982 when Argentine troops occupied the British Falkland Islands.[69] Thus in contrast to Article 296 (1) (b) EC, which refers to the

[67] Case C–222/84, *Johnston*, above n 4, at para 26.

[68] Case C–273/97, above n 20, at para 21. The case concerned the exclusion of women from service in the Royal Marines. It was argued by the United Kingdom that Community law did not apply to the armed forces. See ch 9 at 269–277 for a detailed discussion.

[69] See the second recital in the preamble to Council Regulation No 877/82 of 16 April 1982 suspending imports of all products originating in Argentina [1982] OJ L–102/1, which states that: '[...] following the measures already taken by the United Kingdom, the Member States have consulted one another pursuant to Article 224 of the Treaty [now 297] establishing the [EEC]'.

general measures a Member State adopts in 'normal' times for the purpose of safeguarding its security, Article 297 EC refers to the special measures which prove necessary in an actual crisis situation which has already developed.[70] This limitation seems necessary as the measures which Member States can adopt on the basis of Article 297 EC go far beyond those which can be adopted pursuant to Article 30 EC, precisely in view of the exceptional circumstances envisaged by Article 297 EC.[71]

In his advisory opinion in *Albore* Advocate General Cosmas argued that, because of the exceptional character of the situations described, Article 297 EC only applies to provisory and not permanent measures.[72] He therefore considered the requirement under Italian law, for non-nationals to acquire prior consent of the local administration before buying property in so called military zones, to be outside the scope of the exemption.[73]

The Court did not specifically address the problem but ruled that Article 297 EC did not apply to this case. It is submitted that this has to be interpreted as excluding anticipatory measures from the application of the provision.

3.4. Situations

Article 297 EC can only be invoked in one of the situations stipulated therein. It is submitted that, due to the narrow interpretation of exemptions,[74] the list of situations is exhaustive. Hence, as a second stage of judicial scrutiny,[75] the existence of one of the stipulated situations has to be determined. The question is, whether the European Court of Justice is authorised to make that decision.[76] Can they, for example, rule that there is a war or serious internal tension? As the Court never applied the provision, this is still open to debate.

[70] J Verhoeven, in V Constantinesco, R Kovar and D Simon, JP Jacqué, (eds), *Commentaire du Traité instituant la CEE* (Economica, Paris, 1992) entry dealing with Article 224 EC (now 297), at point 2. One commentator even refers to unilateral measures of 'strictly necessary duration' designed to deal with 'exceptional and particularly serious circumstances': see R Quadri, R Monaco, A Trabucchi, *Commentario al Trattato istitutivo della Communità economica europea* (Giuffré, Milan, 1965) vol III, entry dealing with Article 224, at 1633–34 (as cited by Advocate General La Pergola in his advisory opinion in *Sirdar*).

[71] PJG Kapteyn and P Verloren van Themaat, *Introduction to the Law of the European Communities*, 2nd edn, (Kluwer, Deventer, 1990) 406 (as cited by Advocate General La Pergola his advisory opinion in *Sirdar*).

[72] C–423/98, above n 3, at para 32.

[73] C–423/98, above, at para 35. At para 32 he considers anticipatory measures to be covered in exceptional circumstances.

[74] Case C–222/84 *Johnston*, above n 4, at para 26.

[75] After the first stage of deciding on whether the procedural requirements of Article 297 EC have been followed.

[76] F Schloemann and S Ohloff, 'Constitutionalisation and Dispute Settlement in the WTO: National Security as an Issue of Competence' (1999) 93 *American Journal of International Law* 424, 431 call this power the 'justiciability' of measures taken under such exemptions with reference to the GATT. See also the more recent D Akande and S Williams, 'International Adjudication on National Security Issues: What Role for the WTO?' (2003) 43 *Virginia Journal of International Law* 306.

The Commission has been advocating a narrow interpretation of the discretion conferred to Member States. It argues that they must demonstrate by reference to objective circumstances that one of the situations outlined in Article 297 EC actually exists.[77] If the Member States have to refer to objective circumstances, these circumstances would be subject to review. In *FYROM* the Court accepted that this view of the Commission was arguable. However, this was only accepted in so far as it proved a *prima facie* case for the purpose of interim relief.[78]

The Member States on the other hand have been advocating a wider interpretation of Article 297 EC. For example, the United Kingdom government argued in *Johnston* that it is for the Member State alone to determine whether one of the situations set out in that provision exists.[79] The assessment of the situation is considered subject to the subjective judgement of the Member States. The denial of any competence of the Court to assess whether one of the situations outlined in Article 297 EC actually existed is linked to the denial of jurisdiction. However, according to Article 298 subparagraph 2 EC the Court has jurisdiction. If the Court did not have the competence to decide whether an Article 297 EC situation existed, this jurisdiction would be very limited. It had to automatically accept the existence of a situation as alleged by the Member State and decide on the proportionality or abuse of the measure taken because of it. However, a decision on the abuse of the provision requires some form of assessment whether one of the situations actually exists.[80] Otherwise the Member States as parties to the proceedings autonomously determine the factual background of the assessment. Taken to the extreme, the Court would review a measure taken to react to a situation that actually does not exist. The effective judicial review required in Article 298 subparagraph 2 EC would be very difficult or even impossible. Moreover, this approach would be open to abuse.

Article 297 EC was the subject of the 1999 judgment in *Albore*.[81] The case concerned an Italian law that required foreign buyers of property in military areas to seek prior permission of the local government. All the small islands of Italy were classified as military areas! In his very detailed advisory opinion Advocate General Cosmas pointed out that Article 297 EC dealt with very special situations affecting the relationship between the Community and the Member States. Therefore it would be necessary to determine in every individual case whether the conditions for the application of the provision are met.[82] The situations described in Article 297 EC, so said the Advocate General citing the advisory opinion of Advocate General Jacobs in *FYROM*, are directly related to a political, military and geopolitical appreciation in principle reserved to the Member States. The intensity of scrutiny applied by the Court is diminished due to the absence of

[77] Referred to in Case C–222/84 *Johnston*, above n 4, at 1674; Case C–120/94 R, *FYROM*, above n 30, at para 47.

[78] Case C–124/94 R, above, at para 70.

[79] See the observations of the United Kingdom government in Case C–222/84, above n 4, at 1673.

[80] Advocate General Jacobs in Case C–120/94 R, *FYROM*, above n 30, at para 50.

[81] Case C–423/98, above n 3.

[82] Case C–423/98, above, at para 32.

appropriate legal criteria susceptible to application by the Court in relation to categories like 'war'.[83] Therefore the understanding of the judicial control exercised by the Court under Article 298 EC is very limited, not only because of the terminology of that article but also because of the subject matter.[84] In essence he argues against the competence of the judge to determine whether one of the situations exists, as he or she does not have the tools to do it.

This argument is not entirely convincing. The intensity of scrutiny applied by the Court might be diminished but review is not entirely impossible. Moreover, the intensity of scrutiny might vary depending on which of the four situations has been invoked by the Member State. The situations in Article 297 EC should be differentiated.

3.4.1. War

The first situation is 'war'. This is predominantly a category of international law the international judge has to handle. The European judge can do so as well. There are two ways to define war in international law.

The first way is subject to a formal requirement: a formal declaration of war between States.[85] It should be noted, however, that nowadays formal declarations of war are not very common in State practice. Therefore the formal definition of war is largely redundant in international law. The modern definition requires the actual outbreak of hostilities whereas a "threat of war" is tension between States falling short of actual hostilities.[86]

Under both interpretations there is no reason why the European judge could not decide whether a situation constituting "war" in the sense of Article 297 EC actually exists. This interpretation is based on the fact that with a potentially wide situation "serious international tension constituting a *threat* of war", the requirement that hostilities have broken out would be the best way to differentiate these two situations. The drafters of the Treaty had an international law background. This is an additional indication that the word "war" in Article 297 EC refers to the notion of war in international law. Reserving these situations to the subjective judgement of the Member States would not make sense when a visible situation such as the actual outbreak of hostilities is the subject matter of the assessment of the Court.

It is submitted that this situation only covers war situations in which the Member State in question is leading a defensive war or is involved in a Petersberg mission authorised by the Security Council of the United Nations authorised under Chapters VII and VIII of the UN Charter. An aggressive war, for example a war of conquest, started by a Member State would certainly not be covered. Article

[83] Case C–120/94 R, above n 30, at para 50. This line of argument is also followed by others: Lord Wilberforce citing the Court of Appeal in *Buttes Gas v Hammer* [1982] AC 888, at 936.

[84] Case C–120/94 R, above, at para 63.

[85] See in particular Articles 3 of the Resolution on the Definition of Aggression, General Assembly Resolution. 3314 (XXIX). 14 December 1974. GAOR 29th Sess, Supp 31, p 142: (1975) 69 *Amercian Journal of International Law* 480.

[86] Above, Articles 1–3.

2 (4) UN Charter and customary international law[87] prohibit the use of force. The only exceptions to this golden rule of modern international law are self-defence as provided in Article 51 UN Charter and corresponding customary international law[88] or under the authorisation of the Security Council.[89] All Member States of the EU are member States of the United Nations and are therefore and by virtue of customary international law bound by the prohibition to use force. According to Article 103 UN Charter the Charter prevails over all other treaties including the TEU and the EC Treaty. The TEU expressly recognises the principles of the UN Charter in Article 11 (1) hyphen 3 TEU. Therefore 'in the event of war' has to be interpreted in the light of the requirements of the UN Charter as 'in the event of a defensive war'. A war of aggression cannot justify derogation.

3.4.2. Obligations Accepted for the Purpose of Maintaining Peace and International Security

The second situation arising in the context of 'obligations accepted for the purpose of maintaining peace and international security' is a category equally susceptible to judicial scrutiny. It covers measures taken in the context of the United Nations, the WEU[90] or more recently NATO, or the EU,[91] for example peacekeeping operations. The international or European judge is qualified to evaluate this category simply by interpreting the treaties or other sources that establish these international obligations and by assessing whether they require the respective measure. Reserving these situations to the subjective judgment the Member States is not necessary.

3.4.3. Serious Internal Disturbances Affecting the Maintenance of Law and Order

The third situation of 'serious internal disturbances affecting the maintenance of law and order' is also susceptible to review. However, this category requires a wider margin of appreciation for the Member States as it deals with internal affairs. Advocate General Jacobs pointed out in *FYROM* that the "serious internal disturbances affecting the maintenance of law and order" must be construed as a "breakdown of public order on a scale much vaster than the type of civil unrest, which might justify recourse to Article 36 EC [now 30]."[92] Article 30 EC was discussed in chapter 4. For Article 297 EC to apply it has to be a "massive breakdown of public order."[93] The category could include revolutions, *coups d'état*, civil wars, natural and nuclear disasters, epidemics, and organised crime on a large scale.

[87] Following the 1928 Kellogg–Briand Pact, see B Simma, *et al*, *The Charter of the United Nations: A Commentary, Volume I*, 2nd edn, (OUP, Oxford, 2002) entry on Article 2 (4), margin no 10; see also citations in n 13; I Brownlie, *International Law and the Use of Force* (OUP, Oxford, 1963) 110.

[88] Above.

[89] Chapter VII UN Charter.

[90] See ch 2 at 80–84.

[91] See ch 3 at 102–103.

[92] Case C–120/94 R, above n 30, at para 47.

[93] Above, at para 49.

3.4.4. Serious International Tension Constituting a Threat to War

The fourth and final situation of 'serious international tension constituting a threat to war' is potentially very wide as it covers all clear and present dangers to national security falling short of the outbreak of hostilities. However, as Peers pointed out, the comparable Article XXI (b) (iii) GATT speaks of "emergencies". Article 297 EC is based on this provision.[94] Moreover, the European Court of Justice considers the GATT "to be relevant for the purpose of interpreting a Community instrument governing international trade."[95] Hence the use of the words "threat to war" in Article 297 EC can be interpreted as narrowing the GATT clause.[96]

In contrast to war, which is normally a visible situation, a "threat" is a very subjective concept, which is difficult to detect. The subjective evaluation of the Member States as, for the time being, the only guardians of their military security in the EU, is crucial. A wide margin of appreciation has to be left to the political and military decision makers in the Member States. The main limitation to this margin would be a time limit, as explained under 3.3. above. However, as the category is potentially very wide there is also a danger of abuse which necessitates judicial scrutiny. The Court as a supranational institution can determine whether this situation is given, just like the international institution the UN Security Council can determine a "threat to peace" under Article 39 UN Charter.

All the situations in Article 297 EC are to a certain degree subject to international law. Scrutiny of the European Court of Justice is not excluded "due to the absence of appropriate legal criteria susceptible to be applied by the Court".

3.4.5. The Situations in Practice

In practice judicial scrutiny could be very effective. There are only a few cases, most notably *FYROM*, where Member States argued that a situation covered by Article 297 EC existed at the time the measure in question was taken. Normally they simply refer to the provision without arguing the existence of one of the situations. So if the existence of such a situation is not argued, the provision is hard to abuse. The Court can simply note that a Member State does not argue the existence of a situation envisaged by Article 297 EC and reject the use of the provision. In *Albore* the Court considered the national security interests in the context of the concept of public security in Article 58 (1) (b) EC rather than in that of Article 297 EC. They pointed out that "a mere reference to the requirement of defence of the national territory, where the situation of the Member State concerned does not fall within the scope of Article [297 EC,] cannot suffice" to justify a measure contrary to the Treaty.[97] Thus the Court considered Article 297 EC not to apply.

[94] S Peers, 'National Security and European Law' (1996) 15 *Yearbook of European Law* 363, 382.
[95] Case C–83/94, *Leifer*, above n 17, at para 24.
[96] Above.
[97] Case C–423/98, above n 3, at para 21.

3.5. Standard of Review

A crucial question that follows is, whether the Court, after having determined that one of the situations stipulated in Article 297 EC exists, will apply a proportionality test to measures taken by the Member State to respond to it. This very strict standard of review is applied to the public security exemptions of the first group discussed in chapter 4[98] and requires the measure to be suitable, necessary, and proportionate in the strict sense in relation to the aim in view, which is public security. If applied, it would represent a considerable limitation of the Member States to use or abuse the provision and, returning to the scales metaphor, a heavy weight on the scale of the Community interests as part of the balancing operation.

The Commission argues that the means used under Article 297 EC must be proportionate to and necessary for the aim in view.[99] This describes a proportionality test. In *FYROM* the Court accepted that this view of the Commission was arguable in so far as it proved a *prima facie* case for the purpose of interim relief.[100] In his advisory opinion in *Aimé Richardt* Advocate General Jacobs considered measures taken under Article 297 EC without further explanation to be subject to proportionality.[101] The Member States, however, argued against a proportionality test in relation to measures taken under Article 297 EC.[102] As there has been no judgment in which the Court applied Article 297 EC so far, the precise standard of review is still open to debate.

In his advisory opinion in *Albore* Advocate General Cosmas argued that Member States retain a margin of appreciation as large as possible to deal with the exceptional and truly dangerous situations. A full proportionality test is not necessary; the requirement of a measure to be directed at one of the situations described in the exemption and to serve the interest of national security is sufficient. A totally restrictive interpretation of Article 297 EC subjecting it to a scrutiny including proportionality might deprive the provision of its *effet utile*. If a proportionality test is applied to measures taken under Article 297 EC, the existence of this provision is unnecessary as the measure could be justified by the notion of public security in the exemptions of the first group.

As discussed in chapter 5,[103] in *Commission* v. *Spain* the Court considered the measure for which Spain had invoked Article 296 (1) (b) EC to be "not necessary to achieve the objective of protecting the essential interests of the security of Spain".[104] Articles 296 (1) (b) and 297 EC are parts of the same group of exemptions subject to the special review procedure in Article 298 subparagraph 2 EC and *Commission* v. *Spain* is the only ruling on these. It is submitted that in relation to Article 297 EC, the Court will apply a test of "improper use" as stipulated

[98] Articles 30, 39(3), 46, and 58(1)(b) EC.
[99] Referred to in Case C–120/94 R, above n 30, at para 47.
[100] Above, at para 70.
[101] Case C–367/89, above n 36, at para 33.
[102] For example the Hellenic Republic in Case C–120/94 R, *FYROM*, above n 30, at para 56; Case C–70/94 *Werner*, above n 17.
[103] At 152–154.
[104] Case C–414/97, above n 15, at para 22.

in Article 298 subparagraph 2 EC similar to the test applied to measures taken under Article 296 (1) (b) EC. This involves a larger margin of appreciation for Member States than in the context of measures justified under Article 30 EC. The margin of appreciation accommodates their subjective judgement when dealing with the stipulated situations of national security. The Court will only review whether this is wholly unreasonable and disproportionate. This review will look at the suitability and necessity of a measure in a way similar to a proportionality test. The wider margin of appreciation, however, will make it much easier for a Member State to satisfy the test.

This test of 'abuse' or 'low intensity proportionality' does not deprive the provision of its *effet utile* as the standard of scrutiny differs from that applied to exemptions such as Article 30 EC. Moreover, it takes constitutional considerations into account. As far as the national security situations described in Article 297 EC are concerned, it is the executive branch of government supported by its military staff that has the competence, responsibility, training, and expertise to take the decisions. Their subjective *ex ante* judgement, which within the time limits of Article 297 EC has to be made quickly, cannot easily be substituted by an objective *ex post* assessment of a court of law. In the context of the extreme crisis situations of Article 297 EC, this dimension is even more prevalent than in the case of Article 296 (1) (b) EC. Furthermore, in the constitutional system of the EU, the Member States and not the Community are responsible for defence and military security. Hence the Court will only overrule a measure in cases of manifestly disproportionate abuse.

4. ARTICLE 297 EC AND THE COMMON FOREIGN AND SECURITY POLICY

There is a danger that Article 297 EC could contradict Title V TEU on the CFSP.[105] As discussed in a similar context in chapter 5,[106] European Community law prevails over the law of the CFSP. Therefore Article 297 EC does not only represent an exemption from the EC Treaty but also an exemption from the CFSP. Theoretically, Article 297 EC could be invoked in order to ignore an adopted Common Position or Joint Action under the CFSP. The older Article 297 EC is intended to allow the Member States to derogate from their obligation under the EC Treaty in relation to the situations affecting national security described therein. It potentially takes measures that are considered necessary in these extreme crisis situations outside the legal order of the Community. The provision was not changed when the Second Pillar was introduced. Therefore it also potentially takes measures reacting to extreme crisis situations outside the legal order of the TEU. The younger Title V TEU introduces the CFSP. The security and defence components of that CFSP, the latter slowly taking shape only since the late 1990s, appear

[105] Wessel, above n 40, at 313 cites the Commission (1991): '[la] mise an place d'une politiques commune de securité entraîne l'abrogation [del'article] 224, don't le champ d'application est désormais covert part cette politique'.
[106] At 160–163.

to be partly designed to cover the same area as Article 297 EC. Therefore it could be argued that there is a contradiction in the coexistence of Article 297 EC and the CFSP. As discussed in chapter 2,[107] contradictions undermine coherence and consistency. However, it is argued that the *acquis* of the CFSP does not amount to a contradiction to Article 297 EC.[108]

The following last section of this chapter will first discuss the extent of an overlap between Article 297 EC and the CFSP. The section will conclude with an evaluation of the effect of the narrow interpretation of Article 297 EC on possible derogations from the CFSP.

4.1. Overlap Between Article 297 EC and the Common Foreign and Security Policy?

The discussion of a contradiction between Article 297 EC and the CFSP requires the detection of an overlap. The detection of an overlap requires a comparison of the extreme crisis situations accommodated in the safeguard clause with the Second Pillar *acquis*. The extent of the overlap indicates the extent of contradiction and of the inconsistency of the current approach.

4.1.1. In the Event of Serious Internal Disturbances Affecting the Maintenance of Law and Order

The first situation of 'serious internal disturbances affecting the maintenance of law and order' describes a situation wholly internal to one Member State. As outlined above, the category could include revolutions, *coups d'état*, civil wars, natural and nuclear disasters, epidemics, and organised crime on a large scale. Some of the possible cases can have a magnitude that goes beyond a wholly internal dimension; a civil war can quickly involve a neighbouring Member State and nuclear disaster will not stop at a national border. However, such a case would become the internal disturbance of whatever other Member State would be affected and would allow it to use Article 297 EC in its turn. The use of the word 'internal' takes this situation outside any overlap with the CFSP, which by its very nature and history is part of a foreign policy which is an external policy. Therefore there is no contradiction between the CFSP and this situation of Article 297 EC.

4.1.2. In the Event of War

The second situation allows derogation "in the event of war". As outlined above, the modern definition of war requires the actual outbreak of hostilities whereas a "threat of war" is tension between States falling short of actual hostilities.[109] As outlined above a defensive war, in other words a situation where a Member State

[107] At 87–90.

[108] Exceptions are the cases of Article 16 TEU regarding secrecy and Article 17(1) subpara 3 TEU regarding armaments discussed in ch 5.

[109] Articles 1–3 of the Resolution on the Definition of Aggression, General Assembly Resolution 3314 (XXIX), above n 81.

is defending itself against an aggressive military campaign would allow derogation under Article 297 EC.

The CFSP under the Treaty of Nice does not yet cover this situation. Article 17 (1) subparagraph 1 TEU includes "the progressive framing of a common defence policy [...] which might lead to a common defence". However, as discussed in chapter 2,[110] this common defence is vague, uncertain, and set in the future. There clearly is no common defence at this moment in time. The European Security and Defence Policy is yet underdeveloped and has a clear emphasis on security within the context of the Petersberg Tasks rather than defence. The envisaged European Rapid Reaction Force is a Petersberg force and not a defence force. It is not intended and not capable to be even a part substitution for the armed forces of the individual Member States. In the history of European defence integration it was only the failed European Defence Community discussed in chapter [111]1 that envisaged a comprehensive replacement of the defence of the Member States by a Community defence that would have made the accommodation of the defensive war situation in a safeguard clause unnecessary.[112] The Treaty of Nice does not even include a mutual defence commitment comparable to Articles 5 of the Modified Brussels and Washington Treaties. In the history of European defence integration only the failed EDC Treaty,[113] the WEU's Modified Brussels Treaty,[114] and the EU as envisaged by the Constitutional Treaty discussed in Part III contain such a commitment.[115] Therefore with regards to the TEU the situation of a defensive war remains exclusively within the responsibility and competence of the Member States. There is no overlap and hence no contradiction between the situation "in the event of war" as accommodated in Article 297 EC and the CFSP.

4.1.3. Serious International Tension Constituting a Threat of War

The situation of 'serious international tension constituting a threat of war' is potentially very wide as it covers all clear and present dangers to national security falling short of the outbreak of hostilities. However, as outlined above, there is an important time limit: Article 297 EC refers to the special measures which prove

[110] At 61.

[111] At 22–43.

[112] The supranational character of the European Defence Community in Article 1 EDC comprised of common institutions, common armed forces and a common budget. According to Article 20 EDC a supranational Board of Commissioners served as the main executive and even legislative institution. The European Defence Force would have replaced the national armed forces of the individual Member States. No Member State could recruit or maintain national armed forces other than those for which the Treaty had made special provision. See ch 1 at 37–39 for details.

[113] Article 2(3) and (4) EDC provided: '3. Any armed attack against any of the Member States in Europe or against the European defence forces shall be considered an armed attack on all Member States. 4. The Member States and the European Defence Forces shall afford to the State or force so attacked all the military and other aid in their power.' See ch 1 at 25–27 for details.

[114] Article V of the Modified Brussels Treaty. 'If any of the High Contracting Parties should be the object of an armed attack in Europe, the other High Contracting Parties will, in accordance with the provisions of Article 51 of the Charter of the United Nations, afford the Party so attacked all the military and other aid and assistance in their power.' See ch 1 at 16–18 for details.

[115] On the innovations suggested by the 2004 Constitutional Treaty see ch 11 at 328–337.

necessary in an actual crisis situation which has already developed. This limitation brings the situation very close to the situation of war where hostilities actually broke out. The situation complements the war situation. It is submitted that the current CFSP under the Treaty of Nice does not extend to situations where Member States need to act in the interest of their national security to respond to a situation just falling short and possibly leading to the outbreak of hostilities. This is for the same reasons that there is no overlap with the situation 'in the event of war'. Therefore, with regards to the TEU such a situation remains exclusively within the responsibility and competence of the Member States. There is no overlap and hence no contradiction between the situation "serious international tension constituting a threat to war" as accommodated in Article 297 EC and the CFSP.

4.1.4. In Order to Carry out Obligations It has Accepted for the Purpose of Maintaining Peace and International Security

The situation arising in the context of 'obligations accepted for the purpose of maintaining peace and international security' covers measures taken in the context of the United Nations or more recently NATO, for example peacekeeping operations. The wording "obligations it has accepted" indicates that there has to be someone, for example, an international organisation, the Member State has accepted the obligation from. Under international law only the Security Council of the United Nations can legally ask a Member State to carry out such an obligation. Regional security organisations such as the WEU or the Economic Community of West African States (ECOWAS) only act within the limits of the UN Charter. Similarly, NATO would be an organisational structure between the UN and a Member State equally required to act in compliance with UN instruments. A Member State may derogate from the EC Treaty and, through the supremacy of Community law over EU law, the CFSP in order to carry out such obligations. The provision was drafted at a time when the Community did not have a CFSP and the Member States were the only carriers of such obligations. As discussed in chapter 2,[116] according to Article 17 (2) TEU the CFSP includes "humanitarian and rescue tasks, peacekeeping tasks and tasks of combat forces in crisis management, including peacemaking." Therefore with regards to these Petersberg Tasks there is a potential overlap between Article 297 EC and Article 17 (2) TEU.

The potential overlap raises the question of the relationship of coexisting EU and individual Member State Petersberg-type missions. Even with a developing European Security and Defence Policy there have been missions of the latter kind recently, for example of the United Kingdom in Sierra Leone and France in Ivory Coast. *Prima facie* there seems to be potential for inconsistencies and contradictions. However, it is submitted that the coexistence of contradicting EU and individual Member States missions is legally almost impossible. As explained in

[116] At 65.

chapter 2,[117] Article 17 (1) subparagraph 3 part 2 TEU and Article 17 (3) subparagraph 4 TEU require the CFSP to be compatible with NATO obligations. This rules out the possibility of an EU mission incompatible with NATO requirements. According to Articles 11 (1) hyphen 3 TEU and 103 UN Charter the CFSP has to be compatible with UN obligations. This rules out the possibility of an EU mission incompatible with UN requirements. The most probable case would be a mission carried out by an individual Member State because the EU as a whole decided against an EU mission, for example because there is no unanimity in the Council. Two categories of individual Member State missions are thinkable: missions with and without the blessing of the other Member States. In the former case the proportionate use of Article 297 EC would have to be tolerated by the other Member States and would not lead to inconsistency with the CFSP. In the latter case the use of Article 297 EC to derogate from the EC Treaty and the TEU could lead to inconsistency. However, any mission would have to be authorised by the UN Security Council whose decisions are subject to the *veto* of the EU Member States France and the United Kingdom. According to Article 23 (2) subparagraph 4 TEU qualified majority voting does not apply to decisions having military or defence implications. Hence the Council would decide on a Petersberg-type mission by unanimity, including the votes of France and the United Kingdom. Therefore only these two Member States could possibly carry out an individual mission without the blessing of the other Member States as the votes of France and the United Kingdom would already block a UN Security Council decision, which is a condition for the EU to take action. Moreover, France would have to tolerate the United Kingdom mission or *vice versa* or both would have to carry out the mission together. As the recent examples of Sierra Leone and Ivory Coast have shown, such a scenario is not entirely unlikely as France and the United Kingdom have the armed forces and foreign policy interests that might move them to such an individual mission. In contrast, Italy, for example could not carry out an individual mission against the will of France or the United Kingdom as the latter have the power of *veto* in the UN Security Council.

4.2. Impact of the Narrow Interpretation of Article 297 EC

In the context of the EC Treaty, the narrow interpretation and the triple-exceptional character of Article 297 EC limit the possible use of the exemption and make it almost insignificant in practice. In the context of the CFSP the effect is also limited and only potentially significant with regards to the fourth situation on obligations a Member State has accepted for the purpose of maintaining peace and international security. However, even here Article 297 EC is not an automatic exclusion, no reserve of sovereignty. Member States need to invoke the exemption, prove it, and follow the procedural requirements. Most importantly the measure in question has to be proportionate. There is the bilateral procedure

[117] At 84–85.

under Article 298 subparagraph 1 EC and judicial review under Article 298 subparagraph 2 EC. Theoretically the Court could rule against a measure taken in the context of an individual Member State Petersberg-type mission. There have been no such cases in practice. For missions such as the United Kingdom intervention in Sierra Leone no measures leading to a Member State invoking Article 297 EC were reported. A mission would have to be of considerable size to force a Member State to take measures requiring derogation from the CFSP. Even in the context of peacekeeping the significance of Article 297 EC appears to be merely academic. An imaginable situation could be that the EU unanimously decided to employ a Petersberg-type mission to a particular country or region and an individual Member State decided to employ a competing mission with objectives that could undermine the EU mission. For example, one could imagine an EU mission favouring one party in a civil war situation whereas the individual Member State mission favoured the other side. Theoretically the individual Member State could invoke Article 297 EC to justify its mission. However, due to the lack of any real cases the speculative nature of this imagined scenario reveals that such a situation would be highly unlikely. Moreover, the individual Member State in question would contradict its consent to the unanimous Council decision leading to the EU mission. Such extreme cases of estoppel are highly unlikely. Finally, it would be difficult to argue with regards to the other Member States, in the context of Article 298 subparagraph 1 EC the Commission, and in the context of Article 298 subparagraph 2 EC the Court, that such a competing mission was necessary.

Therefore it is submitted that the practical relevance of the overlap between the CFSP and Article 297 EC with regards to situation 4 is insignificant and merely academic. There is almost no overlap and therefore no contradiction that could undermine consistency.

5. CONCLUSIONS

Chapters 4, 5, and 6 of this book advocate that the borderline between Member State and Community competence over defence issues is determined by the security exemptions in the Treaty. These exemptions are not automatic and need to be narrowly construed as otherwise they might develop into major loopholes undermining the functioning of the internal market as a whole. Member States need to specifically invoke the exemptions, they have the burden of proof of a situation justifying derogation from the Treaty for reasons of security exists, the Commission can try to communicate with the Member State with a view to removing disproportionate or improper use of the exemptions, and eventually the European Court of Justice may review these measures.

These exemptions form a spectrum with regards to the standard of review applied by the Court. At one end of the spectrum are the security exemptions of the free movement regimes where scrutiny is very intense. At the other end of the spectrum is Article 297 EC where scrutiny is least intense. Nevertheless, the use of this exemption is limited. Similar to all security exclusions, it has a limited character and has to be interpreted narrowly. First, the jurisdiction of the Court to review measures justified by the provision represents a limitation. Second, the exemption cannot be used when the required consultation procedure was not followed. Third, Article 297 EC is subject to a time limit: it can only justify measures in response to an actual crisis situation that has already developed. Fourth, the provision can only be invoked in one of the situations stipulated therein and the Court can determine whether the situation exists. Fifth, the Court would apply a low-intensity proportionality test to measures taken to respond to these situations. Finally, its exceptional and subsidiary character in the framework of the Treaty limits the provision. Overall it is argued that the scope of application of Article 297 EC is very narrow.

The Treaty covers the economic aspects of defence, unless one of the exemptions discussed in chapters 4, 5, and 6 applies. Within these limits the EC Treaty can be considered an instrument of European defence integration.

7

Heavy Equipment, Food, Fodder, and Stores for the Armies of Europe: Community Law and the Regulation of European Defence Procurement

1. INTRODUCTION[1]

THE PREVIOUS CHAPTERS 4, 5, and 6 of this book discussed the EC Treaty as an instrument of European defence integration. This function is mainly determined by the Member States. First, the Member State included two sets of security exemptions in the EC Treaty, namely the public security exemptions in Articles 30, 39 (3), 46 (1), and 58 (1) (b) EC and the national security exemptions in Articles 296 and 297 EC. Second, this function is determined by how often and in which types of cases the Member States actually invoke these exemptions to derogate from their obligations under the Treaty. Moreover, this function is determined by the scrutiny the European Court of Justice exercises over the use of these clauses. It was submitted that the security exemptions and the judicial scrutiny exercised over their use represent a mechanism to balance the interests of the Community with the interests of the Member States. The national security interests of the Member States can be balanced with the internal market and other interests of the Community.

Similar provisions are contained in secondary Community law. Secondary or subsidiary Community law consists of the Regulations, Directives, and Decisions created by the Community institutions, in particular the Council and the European Parliament, in contrast to the primary law of the EC Treaty created by the Member States. In the following chapters 7, 8, and 9 of this book a discussion of secondary Community law as an instrument of European defence integration will be added to the discussion of primary Community law. Moreover, the discussion of secondary Community law involves the discussion of specific defence related subject areas affected by these rules. This will facilitate the understanding

[1] An earlier version of this chapter was published as M Trybus, 'Procurement for the Armed Forces: Balancing Security and the Internal Market' (2002) 27 *European Law Review* 692–713 and presented as a paper at the conference *Public Procurement: Global Revolution II*, 5–7 September 2001 in Nottingham.

and provide a more comprehensive analysis of the contribution of Community law to European defence integration.

The Member States are sovereign. This means that, leaving their obligations under international and Community law aside, they have unlimited competencies, in other words the power to regulate and decide on everything and everyone within their territorial and personal jurisdiction. Their competence does not require a written authorisation in a constitution. In contrast, the EU is not a sovereign state. According to the classical understanding, the competencies of the Community are governed by the principle of attributed or conferred powers. The Member States voluntarily transferred strictly determined objects to the supranational jurisdiction of the Community.[2] In the words of the European Court of Justice: "the [Member] States have limited their sovereign rights, *albeit in limited fields* [emphasis added]."[3] This means that the Community has competencies but they are limited to those stipulated in the EC Treaty. The principle of attributed or conferred powers[4] requires a legal base for Community action in the Treaty. A legal base is a provision in the EC Treaty that expressly allocates the competence for action on a particular subject matter, for example legislation on sex equality at the workplace, to the Community. It prescribes the legal instrument to be used, the Community institutions involved in the legislative process, and the required majorities for legislation to pass. The importance of this strict requirement of a legal base was recently clarified and emphasised by the European Court of Justice.[5]

There is no legal base for defence in the EC Treaty. The Community is mainly a commercial enterprise, with a substantial social agenda, and other policies, such as the protection of the environment. It does not seem to be concerned with defence at all.[6] However, as pointed out in chapter 4,[7] defence has commercial,

[2] Joined Cases C–7/56 and 3–7/57, *Dinecke Algera v Common Assembly of the European Coal and Steel Community* (1957) 58 ECR 39.

[3] Case C–26/62, *NV Algemene Transport-en Expeditie Onderneming van Gend en Loos v Nederlandse Administratie der Belastigen* [1963] ECR 1. This key judgment also established the principle of direct effect described in ch 1 at 20–21.

[4] However, the strict principle of attributed powers is not the last word on the matter of Community competencies. During the 1970s and 1980s the principle eroded to a point where it left no core of sovereign Member State competencies out of the reach of the Community. See J Weiler, 'The Transformation of Europe' (1991) 100 *Yale Law Journal* 2403, cited from *The Constitution of Europe: 'Do the New Clothes have an Emperor?' and other Essays on European Integration* (CUP, Cambridge, 2002) at 44. Theoretically Community action is possible within any field of activity. A full evaluation of this process would go beyond the aim of this ch. Suffice it to say that the principle of enumerated powers does not provide a comprehensive mechanism to divide Community and Member State competencies.

[5] See the Tobacco Advertising Case: Case C–376/98, *Germany v European Council and Parliament* [2000] ECR I–8419; [2000] 3 CMLR 1175; T Hervey, 'Up in Smoke? Community (Anti) Tobacco Law and Policy' (2001) 26 *European Law Review* 101; S Crosby, 'The New Tobacco Control Directive: An Illiberal and Illegal Disdain for the Law' (2002) 27 *European Law Review* 177; P Syrpis, 'Smoke Without Fire: The Social Policy Agenda and the Internal Market' (2001) 30 *Industrial Law Journal* 271; C Hillion, 'Tobacco Advertising: If You Must, You May' (2001) 60 *Cambridge Law Journal* 486.

[6] As discussed in Part I, since 1992 defence is the subject matter of the Second Pillar of the Treaty on European Union with the Common Foreign and Security Policy and since 1999 also the European Security and Defence Policy. However, Part II of this book is concerned with the First Pillar, the Community pillar.

[7] At 123–124.

social, and other Community-related implications. Defence procurement, competition (anti-trust), merger-control and state aids (subsidies) in the defence industrial sector, trade of strategic goods, and sex equality in the armed forces are examples. There *are* legal bases for these fields in the EC Treaty.[8] The crucial question is whether they extend into the defence sector. For example, does the competence of the Community to regulate public procurement apply to the acquisitions of the ministries of defence, or the power to regulate sex equality in the workplace to the armed forces? It will be argued in the following three chapters that the relevant instruments of secondary Community law contain a set of security exemptions that largely reflect the security exemptions in the EC Treaty described in chapters 4, 5, and 6. The European Court of Justice will scrutinise the use of these exemptions in secondary Community law in a way comparable to the scrutiny exercised over the security exemptions in the EC Treaty. Therefore the answer to the question whether the legal bases and therefore the competence for procurement or sex quality extend into the defence sector is determined by these security exemptions.

The remainder of Part II will discuss mainly secondary Community law as an instrument of European defence integration. Sometimes, relevant policy fields such as competition law can be affected by provisions of both primary and secondary Community law. The discussion will not cover all instruments of legislation relevant to defence. It will be limited to examples considered particularly important influences on the defence law of the Member States. The chapters will discuss legislation affecting the governments of the Member States, the defence industrial sector, and the armed forces directly. Chapter 7 will analyse the current and future EC Public Procurement Directives as the prime example for secondary legislation directly affecting activities of the national governments. Public procurement regulation was also chosen because it is currently subject to reform allowing for the analysis of various versions and proposed versions of the exemptions relevant to defence. Chapter 8 will discuss secondary legislation affecting competition in the defence industrial sector. The discussion will also cover connected policy fields such as State aids, merger control, and trade in arms. Chapter 9 will explore EC sex equality legislation as a prime example for secondary Community legislation affecting the armed forces.

2. EC PUBLIC PROCUREMENT REGULATION

Public procurement represents a significant part of the economy. Government purchasing in the Member States of the European Union, including central governments, regional governments, municipalities, and utilities, is approaching an annual value of €1.5 trillion.[9] This is about 16.3 per cent of the GDP of

[8] See Article 95(1) EC Treaty for public procurement and the free movement of goods as matters relating to the internal market, Article 141(3) EC Treaty for sex equality at the workplace, Article 83 EC Treaty for competition law, Article 89 EC Treaty for state aids.

[9] See information provided by the Commission: http://simap.eu.int/EN/pub/src/welcome.htm.

the EU, with the national percentages of the Member States varying from 11 to 20 per cent.[10] Therefore market access to public procurement contracts is an essential requirement for the functioning of the internal market. The EC Treaty regimes on the free movement of goods and services described in chapter 4[11] apply to this area of government activity. The main objective of EC public procurement law is to open the public procurement markets of the Member States against a traditional tendency of governments to award contracts to their own national suppliers and service providers.[12] However, the broad principles of the EC Treaty are not sufficient to ensure an internal public procurement market. Therefore the Community regulated the details in secondary legislation, the EC Public Procurement Directives.[13] In short, the Directives stipulate their coverage, in other words who has to purchase according to the Directives, procedures including publication requirements, award criteria, remedies, and many other details. The legal basis for these Directives were Article 95 (1) EC Treaty,

[10] Above, see also *A Report on the Functioning of Public Procurement Markets in the EU: Benefits from the Application of EU Directives and Challenges for the Future*, European Commission, Brussels, 3 February 2004, at 2, 4, http://europa.eu.int/comm/internal_market/publicprocurement/docs/public-proc-market-final-report_en.pdf. The Organisation for Economic Cooperation and Development (OECD) provided lower figures in *Government Procurement: A Synthesis Report*, OECD, Paris, 2001: 9.24 % of GDP with and 8.03 without armaments purchases.

[11] At 127–129.

[12] Green Paper Public Procurement in the European Union: Exploring the Way Forward, Chapter 2, I, para 2.3:

> The primary objectives of the Union's public procurement policy, set within this context, have remained unchanged: to create the necessary competitive conditions in which public contracts are awarded without discrimination and value for taxpayers' money is achieved through the choice of the best bid submitted; to give suppliers access to a single market with major sales opportunities; and to ensure that the competitiveness of the European supplier base is strengthened.

Leading works on EC public procurement law: S Arrowsmith, *The Law of Public and Utilities Procurement*, 2nd ed, (Sweet & Maxwell, London, 2005); P Trepte, *Public Procurement in the EC* (CCH, Cheltenham, 1994); JM Fernández-Martín, *The EC Public Procurement Rules* (OUP, Oxford, 1996); H-J Prieß, *Handbuch des europäischen Vergaberechts*, 3rd edn, (Carl Heyermanns Verlag, Heidelberg, 2005).

[13] The procurement laws of most Member States are currently still based on the following directives: Consolidated Public Supplies Directive, Council Directive 93/36/EC of 14 June 1993 co-ordinating procedures for the award of public supply contracts, [1993] OJ L–199/1; Public Services Directive, Council Directive 92/50/EEC of 18 June 1992 relating to the co-ordination of procedures for the award of public services contracts [1992] OJ L–209/1; Consolidated Public Works Directive, Council Directive 93/37/EC of 14 June 1993 concerning the co-ordination of procedures for the award of public works contracts [1993] OJ L–199/54; Council Directive 89/665/EEC of 21 December 1989 on the co-ordination of the laws, regulations and administrative provisions to the application of review procedures to the award of public supply and public works contracts [1989] OJ L–395/33. See also Council Directive 93/38/EEC of 14 June 1993 co-ordinating the procurement procedures of entities operating in the water, energy, transport and telecommunications sectors [1993] OJ L–199/84; Council Directive 92/13/EEC of 25 February 1992 co-ordinating the laws, regulations and administrative provisions relating to the application of Community rules on the procurement procedures of entities operating in the water, energy, transport and telecommunications sector [1992] OJ L–76/14. The new Directives cited in n 17 are already in force. However, they only have to be implemented by 31 January 2006. Therefore the national procurement laws of the Member States, (with the exception of Denmark which has already implemented the new Directives) are still based on the Directives cited in this footnote. The Remedies Directives 89/665/EEC and 92/13/EEC will also be ammended soon.

which gives the Community the competence to pass legislation concerning the internal market,[14] Article 47 (2) EC which gives the Community the competence to pass legislation concerning the taking up and pursuit of activities as self-employed persons,[15] and Article 55 subparagraph 2 EC which gives the Community the competence to pass legislation concerning the free movement of services.[16] Member States had to implement these Directives by amending their existing public procurement laws or by introducing new legislation. The Council and European Parliament recently adopted a new Directive for public purchases.[17] There are no doubts about the competence of the Community to regulate public procurement.[18]

Even in a political environment of decreasing defence budgets after the end of the Cold War, defence procurement represents a substantial part of the purchasing

[14] Article 95 EC Treaty reads:

> 1. By way of derogation from Article 94 and safe where otherwise provided in this Treaty, the following provisions shall apply for the achievement of the objectives set out in Article 14. The Council shall, acting in accordance with the procedure referred to in Article 251 and after consulting the Economic and Social Committee, adopt the measure for the approximation of the provisions laid down by law, regulation or administrative action in Member States which have as their object the establishment and functioning of the internal market.

[15] Article 47(2) EC reads:

> [...] the Council shall, acting in accordance with the procedure referred to in Article 251, issue directives for the co-ordination of provisions laid down by law, regulation or administrative action in Member States concerning the taking-up and pursuit of activities as self-employed persons. The Council, acting unanimously throughout the procedure referred to in Article 251, shall decide on directives the implementation of which involves in at least one Member State amendment of the existing principles laid down by law governing the professions with respect to training and conditions of access for natural persons. In other cases the Council shall act by qualified majority.

[16] Article 55 subpara 2 EC reads: 'The Council, acting unanimously after consulting the European Parliament, shall take a decision with a view to providing for all parts of the areas covered by this Title to be governed by the procedure referred to in Article 251 and adapting the provisions relating to the powers of the Court of Justice.'

[17] Directive 2004/18/EC of the European Parliament and the Council on the coordination of procedures for the award of public works contracts, public supply contracts and public service contracts, [2004] OJ L–134/114. For a general analysis see S Arrowsmith, 'An Assessment of the New Legislative Package on Public Procurement' (2004) 41 *Common Market Law Review* 1277. For an analysis based on a previous version of the 'legislative package': Proposal for a Directive of the European Parliament and the Council, on the coordination of procedures for the award of public supply contracts, public service contracts and public works contracts (presented by the Commission), 10 May 2000, COM (2000) 275 final [2001] OJ C–29E/1, see: S Arrowsmith, 'The European Commission's Proposal for New Directives on Public and Utilities Procurement' (2000) 10 *Public Procurement Law Review* NA 125–38; R Boyle, 'Critique of the Commission's Proposal for a New Directive on the Co-ordination of procedures for Public Contracts COM (2000) 275 final, as Updated by the discussions in the Working Group' (2001) 10 *Public Procurement Law Review* NA 65–74. Council and European Parliament also passed a new Utilities Directive: Directive 2004/17/EC of the European Parliament and of the Council of 31 March 2004 coordinating the procurement procedures of entities operating in the water, energy, transport and postal services sectors, [2004] OJ L–134/1. However, this instrument is not relevant to defence procurement.

[18] There are only doubts about the competence for certain provisions that follow other objectives than market access, such as value for money, efficiency, and probity. See S Arrowsmith, 'The EC Procurement Directives, National Procurement Policies and Better Governance: The Case for a New Approach' (2002) 27 *European Law Review* 3.

activities of the Member States.[19] It has special characteristics that differentiate it from civil purchasing. Defence procurement agencies have to operate in a politically sensitive environment, dominated by national security and secrecy concerns. The government is normally the only client of its national defence industry. Sophisticated and advanced equipment is expensive but can offer decisive advantages in relation to both deterrence and actual warfare.[20] State of the art equipment is just as crucial for success in battle as are trained and motivated servicewomen and men, the right strategy, and an able leadership. Millennia ago the ancient Chinese strategist Sun Tzu remarked about this connection between the armed forces and their supplies: "[...] an army, which lacks heavy equipment, fodder, food and stores, will be lost."[21]

Defence procurement has to be seen in its political context. Chapter 3[22] discussed the importance for the Member States to increase their capabilities. Therefore procurement actually has to increase over the next decade. However, due to budgetary constraints and a lack of political will and public support, it is far from certain that this will actually happen. Even after the introduction of the Common Foreign and Security Policy (hereinafter CFSP) discussed in chapter 2, defence remains mainly within the national competence of the Member States. Thus EC defence procurement regulation requires mechanisms to balance the internal market interests of the Community with the national security interests of the Member States.

[19] 'In particular, military expenditure in Western Europe remained flat in 2002.' E Sönks, *et al*, *SIPRI Yearbook 2003: Armaments Disarmament and International Security* (OUP, Oxford, 2003) ch 10. In a previous edition of the Yearbook the authors noted: 'A decade after the end of the cold war the decline in world military spending is changing into growth', E Sönks, *et al*, *SIPRI Yearbook 2001: Armaments Disarmament and International Security* (OUP, Oxford, 2001) ch 4. In 2000 the Western European NATO States (excluding France) spent US$22,273 million on equipment, the United Kingdom with US$9937 million almost half of that, Germany spent US$4723 million, see NATO, *Financial and Economic Data Relating to NATO Defence: Defence Expenditures of NATO Countries* (1980–2000), Press Release M-DPC-2 (2000) 107, 5 December 2000, URL http://www.nato.int/docu/pr2000/p00–107e.htm. During the same year France spent US$12,386 million on equipment, see French Assemblée Nationale, 'Avis présenté au nom de la commission de la défense nationale et des forces armées sur le projet de loi de finances pour 2001, tomé VIII, Défense: credits d'équipment', Report 2627, tomé VIII, Paris, 11 October 2000, p 11: and French Assemblée Nationale, 'Avis présenté au nom de la commission de la défense nationale et des forces armées sur le projet de loi de finances rectificative pour 2000', Report 2764, Paris, 29 November 2000.

[20] On European defence procurement see: M Trybus, *European Defence Procurement Law: International and National Procurement Systems as Models for a Liberalised Defence Procurement Market in Europe* (Kluwer, The Hague, 1999); M Trybus, 'Procurement for the Armed Forces: Balancing Security and the Internal Market', above n 1; A Cox, 'The Future of European Defence Policy: The Case of a Centralised Procurement Agency' (1994) 3 *Public Procurement Law Review* 65; S Walker and P Gummmet, *Nationalism, Internationalism and the European Defence Market*, Chaillot Paper No 9, (Institute for Security Studies of the Western European Union, Paris, 1993); J Wheaton, JM Buckworth and L Cientanni, *Developing Trends in the EC Defence Sector*, Clifford Chance Paper, (unpublished); P de Vestel, *Defence Markets and Industries in Europe; time for political decisions?*, Chaillot Paper No 21, (Institute of Security Studies of the Western European Union, Paris, 1995) p 26; A Cox and K Hartley, *The Costs of Non-Europe in Defence Procurement—Executive Summary*, (The Commission of the European Communities DG III, 1992).

[21] S Tzu, *The Art of War*, ch 7, verse 9 (6th Century BC).

[22] At 115.

The objective of this chapter is to provide an understanding of these mechanisms in the current and future EC Public Procurement Directives. The exemptions relevant to the supplies, works, and services acquired by military procurement agencies will be analysed.[23] They allow derogation from the Directives in certain circumstances. These exemptions can serve as examples for security exemptions in secondary Community law in general.[24] Most secondary law exemptions correspond to exemptions in the EC Treaty. Based on the dominant interpretation of one of these Treaty exemptions; the current EC Public Procurement Directives were drafted on the assumption that trade in weapons is wholly outside the application of the EC Treaty.[25] Thus the regulation of defence procurement was left to the Member States.[26] However, recent case law of the European Court of Justice discussed in the context of chapter 5,[27] indicates a narrower interpretation of the respective Treaty exemption. In brief, the exemption is not an automatic one but applies only when there is a specific national security justification for derogation from the Treaty. This chapter explains that the new Public Sector Procurement Directive (hereinafter 'the new Directive') appears to have taken this new jurisprudence into account to ensure conformity with the Treaty. This would mean that the new instrument would apply to all purchases made by the military procurement agencies of the Member States, including the acquisition of armaments. It will be argued that this solution does not take the specific characteristics of defence procurement sufficiently into account. These characteristics require a separate 'Defence Procurement Directive'.

The analysis has to start with the exemptions in the Directives in force until 31 January 2006, the date when the period for Member States to implement the new Directive expires.[28] There are currently separate instruments for supplies, works and services.[29] The new Directive consolidates these into a single instrument.

[23] Articles 2–4 Directive 93/36/EEC, Articles 4 (1) and (2) and 5 Directive 92/50/EEC, Articles 4(b) and 5 Directive 93/37/EEC, and Article 10 Directive 93/38/EEC.

[24] Other examples in secondary Community law are: Articles 6 and 9 Council-Directive 64/221/EEC on the co-ordination of special measures concerning the movement and residence of foreign nationals which are justified on grounds of public policy, public security or public health [1963–64] OJ English Sp Ed, 117 (on the free movement of persons), Article 21(3) Council-Regulation 4064/89/EEC on the control of concentrations between undertakings [1989] OJ L–395/1 (on merger control, to be discussed in detail in ch 8), and Article 11 Council-Regulation 2603/69/EEC establishing common rules for exports [1969] OJ L–324/25, [1991] OJ L–372/31 (on exports). There are also security provisions in the EC trade agreements, see S Peers, 'National Security and European Law' (1996) 15 *Yearbook of European Law* 363, 374–78.

[25] On the interpretation of Article 296(1)(b) EC see ch 5 at 142–163.

[26] On the national regimes of France, Germany and the United Kingdom see the respective chapters VI, VII and VIII in: Trybus, *European Defence Procurement Law*, above n 20.

[27] At 152–154.

[28] According to Article 80 (1) of the new Directive 2004/18/EC the Member States shall bring into force the laws, regulations, and administrative provisions necessary to comply with the Directive no later than 31 January 2006. According to the introduction to the new Directive the Conciliation Committee of Council and European Parliament approved the final text of the new Directive on 9 December 2003. It was published 30 April 2004 on the eve of the accession of ten new Member States to the EU.

[29] See n 11 above.

Utilities procurement will continue to be regulated by a separate Directive 2004/18/EC.[30] Moreover, two versions of the initial Draft Proposal, which led to the final version of the new Directive, will be referred to where appropriate. The relevant exemptions can be subdivided into those related to armaments (section 3), those related to security (section 4) and those related to international organisations (section 6).

3. HARD DEFENCE MATERIAL EXCLUSIONS

A first type of exemption relates to hard defence material, a category of goods defined by Article 296 (1) (b) EC. As discussed in chapter 5,[31] this provision allows a Member State "to take such measures as it considers necessary for the protection of the essential interests of its security which are connected with the production or trade in arms, munitions and war material". In 1958 the Council drew up a list of products to which this provision applies according to Article 296 (2) EC which has never been officially published but is part of the public domain. It includes classical military material such as tanks, fighter aircraft and warships. The application of Article 296 (1) (b) is strictly limited to the material on the list, which can also be called warlike or hard defence material.[32]

3.1. The Current Directives

The most important example of a hard defence material exemption can be found in the Supplies Directive which regulates public procurement in relation to goods. Article 3 Supplies Directive reads:

> "Without prejudice to article 2, 4 and 5 (1), this Directive shall apply to all products to which Article 1 (a) relates, including those contracts awarded by contracting authorities in the field of defence except for the *products* to which Article 223 (1) (b) [now 296 (1) (b)] of the EEC Treaty applies [emphasis added]."

Article 4 (1) Services Directive, which regulates public procurement in relation to services, is a similar provision:

> "This Directive shall apply to public service contracts awarded by contracting authorities in the field of defence, except for *contracts* to which the provisions of Article 223 [now 296] of the Treaty apply [emphasis added]."

Due to these direct references, the interpretation of Article 296 (1) (b) EC forms the background for the interpretation of these exclusions in the Directives. As

[30] Directive 2004/17/EC of the European Parliament and the Council of 31 March 2004 co-ordinating procurement procedures of entities operating in the water, energy, transport and postal services sector [2004] OJ L-134/1.

[31] At 142–143.

[32] See ch 5 at 148–149 for details of this discussion.

explained in chapter 5,[33] the Member States have interpreted Article 296 (1) (b) EC as an automatic exclusion of hard defence material from the application of the Treaty whereas the Commission advocated a narrower approach. In *Commission* v. *Spain*[34] the European Court of Justice clarified the interpretation of the provision. According to the previous judgment in *Marguerite Johnston* v. *Chief Constable of the Royal Ulster Constabulary*[35] there is a general rule that all exemptions from the Treaty have to be interpreted narrowly to avoid a detrimental effect on the functioning of the internal market as a whole. This involves the application of a proportionality test. A Member State measure has to be suitable and necessary to serve a public interest, for example security. The interest of security is balanced with the interest of the internal market. On the basis of this ruling, the Court in *Commission* v. *Spain* applied a narrow interpretation of Article 296 (1) (b) EC. Member States have to invoke the exemption and have the burden of proof that its requirements are met. On this general basis the Court ruled that:

> "In the present case, [...] Spain has not demonstrated that the exemptions provided for by the Law [of 1987] are *necessary* for the protection of the essential interests of its security. [...]. It follows that the VAT exemptions are not *necessary* in order to achieve the objective of protecting the essential interests of the security of [...] Spain".[36]

This narrow interpretation ensures the Community interests in the internal market in relation to measures taken for national security reasons connected to armaments. The national security interests of the Member States are also accommodated as they are left a wide margin of appreciation. *Commission* v. *Spain* was a clear case. In other cases the Court is likely to be more careful. The proportionality test allows balancing the internal market interests with the national security interests of the Member States. It is of essential significance for the interpretation of the hard defence exemptions in the Procurement Directives.

The Supplies Directive regulates the procurement of goods. It is submitted that the purpose of Article 3 Supplies Directive[37] is to clarify that the Directive does not cover hard defence material. In contrast to Article 4 (1) Services Directive, which excludes "*contracts* to which the provision of Article 223 [now 296] of the Treaty apply", this provision excludes "*products* to which the provision of Article 223 (1) (b) [now 296 (1) (b)] of the Treaty apply". As the provision in the Supplies

[33] At 150–152.

[34] Case C–414/97, [1999] ECR I–5585; [2000] 2 CMLR 4. See also: M Trybus, 'On the Application of the EC–Treaty to Armaments' (2000) 25 *European Law Review* 633; and M Trybus, 'The Recent Judgment in *Commission v Spain* and the Procurement of Hard Defence Material' (2000) 9 *Public Procurement Law Review* NA99.

[35] Case C–222/84, *Marguerite Johnston v Chief Constable of the Royal Ulster Constabulary* [1986] ECR 1651; [1986] 3 CMLR 240, at para 26. See also Case C–13/68, *SpA Salgoil v Italian Ministry of Foreign Trade* [1968] ECR 453, at 463; [1969] CMLR 181, at 192; and Case C–7/68, *Commission v Italy* [1968] ECR 633, at 644.

[36] Case C–414/97, above n 32, at para 22, emphasis added.

[37] See above.

Directive is based on "products" and not on "contracts" it has to be interpreted as a general exclusion of hard defence material from the application of that Directive.

Alternatively, it could be argued that Article 296 (1) (b) EC has to apply, irrespective of whether to a contract or a product. Following the interpretation of the Treaty exemption following *Commission* v. *Spain* discussed in chapter 5,[38] it only applies when it is successfully invoked by one of the Member States. Hence the notion of "products" in Article 3 Supplies Directive could be interpreted as products in respect of which Article 296 (1) (b) EC was successfully invoked.[39] However, it is submitted that the wording of Article 3 Supplies Directive is sufficiently clear in automatically excluding armaments. Article 296 (1) (b) EC applies to these products irrespective of whether it was invoked or not. This interpretation is supported by the wording of Article 296 (2) EC which speaks of the "list [...] of the products to which the provisions of paragraph 1 (b) apply". Article 296 (1) (b) EC applies to the products on this list irrespective of whether it was invoked or not.

Another detail supporting the interpretation of Article 3 Supplies Directive as an automatic exclusion of armaments is that the provision in the Supplies Directive refers specifically to Article 296 (1) (b) EC which concerns products. The provision in the Services Directive, on the other hand, refers to "the provisions of Article 296", including Article 296 (1) (a) EC.[40] It has always been clear that Article 296 (1) (a) EC has to be specifically invoked by the Member State who wishes to rely on it. This requirement is necessary in relation to this provision. Otherwise secrecy would allow the uncontrolled derogation from the Treaty in relation to civil and dual-use goods. Article 3 Supplies Directive refers only to section (1) letter (b) of Article 296 EC, which at the time was the part of Article 296 EC interpreted as an automatic exclusion from the Treaty. This is a strong indication that Article 3 Supplies Directive constitutes an automatic exclusion of hard defence material. This means that national defence procurement authorities do *not* have to follow the Directive when procuring a piece of hard defence equipment, such as a fighter aircraft, a warship, or a tank.

The provision of the Services Directive, when based on the interpretation of Article 296 (1) (b) EC provided by the Court in *Commission* v. *Spain* outlined above, does not necessarily constitute such a wide exclusion. Service *contracts* involving hard defence material still have to be advertised and procured on the basis of the rules of the Directive, unless a Member State invokes Article 296 (1) (b) EC, via Article 4 (1) Services Directive, for security reasons. This means that normally a national defence procurement authority must follow the Directive when procuring a service related to a piece of hard defence equipment, such as a maintenance contract for a fighter aircraft, a warship, or a tank. However, also created years before the ruling in *Commission* v. *Spain*, the provision was drafted on the understanding that services contracts related to hard defence material were

[38] At 152–154.

[39] Thanks to Peter Trepte, Barrister (London) for bringing this possible interpretation to my attention.

[40] Article 296(1)(a) reads: 'no Member State shall be obliged to supply information the disclosure of which it considers contrary to the essential interests of its security'.

also exempt from the Treaty. Therefore, historically, it could be interpreted as an automatic exemption. Nevertheless, in contrast to Article 3 Supplies Directive, its wording leaves room for an interpretation accommodating *Commission* v. *Spain*. According to the narrow interpretation of Article 296 (1) (b) EC in *Commission* v. *Spain*, Article 4 (1) Services Directive does not necessarily constitute an automatic exclusion of services contracts related to hard defence material from the application of the Treaty. It might be necessary to specifically invoke Article 296 (1) (b) EC and to prove a situation justifying its use. In that case it would also be subject to review by the Court. Article 3 Supplies Directive, however, is an automatic exclusion. Thus the EC Treaty generally applies to hard defence material whereas the Supplies Directive does not. This means that a national defence procurement authority normally has to follow the EC Treaty but not the Supplies Directive when procuring a piece of hard defence equipment, such as a fighter aircraft, a warship, or a tank.

This is a situation comparable to that of contracts below the thresholds of the Directives.[41] The EC Treaty governs the award of public contracts mainly through the prohibition of discrimination on grounds of nationality stipulated in the free movement regimes of Articles 28, 49, and 43 EC.[42] The prohibition imposes a negative obligation to refrain from discrimination irrespective of whether the Directives apply.

As the Treaty applies to armaments unless a Member State can invoke Article 296 (1) (b) EC, the negative obligation applies to hard defence procurement contracts as well. This means, for example, that a contract can not be limited to domestic bidders,[43] can not require the use of only domestic materials[44] or require the use of domestic standards.[45]

[41] The current Directives apply only to contracts above a certain threshold, for example, subject to certain specific cases, to supply contracts above a value of €200,000, services contracts above a value of €200,000, and for works contracts above a value of €5,000,000: [2003] OJ C–309/14, 15 and 16 respectively.

[42] The Court established a set of fundamental principles derived from the Directives that have to be followed. The most important principles are equal treatment, see Case C–243/89, *Commission v Denmark ('the Storebaelt Case')* [1993] ECR I–3353, at para 33, see annotation by JM Fernández-Martín (1993) 2 *Public Procurement Law Review* CS153, and transparency, see Case C–87/94, *Commission v Belgium (the 'Wallonia Buses Case')* [1996] ECR I–2043, at para 82, also confirming the principle of equal-treatment, see annotation by S Arrowsmith, (1994) 3 *Public Procurement Law Review* CS130. The principles of mutual recognition and proportionality apply as well. The European Commission argues that these principles can be derived from the Treaty and apply also to contracts not covered by the Directives, see *Interpretative Communication on Concessions under Community Law* [2000] OJ C–121/2, *Public Procurement in the European Union*, COM (98) 143 final, at para 2.1.2.4. However, in *Storebaelt* and *Wallonia Buses* the Court considers the principles of equal treatment as directly stemming from the Directives and not from the Treaty, see on this in detail P Braun, 'A Matter of Principle(s)—The Treatment of Contracts Falling Outside the Scope of the European Public Procurement Directives' (2002) 9 *Public Procurement Law Review* 39.

[43] In relation to civil procurement: Case C–31/88, *Du Pont de Nemours Italiana SpA v Unità Sanitaria Locale No 2 Di Carrara* [1990] I–ECR 889; [1990] 3 CMLR 239. The authority had reserved 30% of their supply purchases for undertakings established in the *Mezzogiorno*, analysed in S Arrowsmith, *A Guide to the Procurement Cases of the Court of Justice* (Earlsgate Press, Winteringham, 1992) 10.

[44] In relation to civil procurement see the *Storebaelt* Case C–243/89, above n 41.

[45] In relation to civil procurement see Case C–45/87, *Commission v Ireland ('Dundalk')*, [1988] ECR 4929; [1989] 1 CMLR 225, analysed in S Arrowsmith, above n 42, at 7.

Whether the Treaty also imposes positive obligations, in particular in the form of procedural requirements, was subject to debate until recently. According to the Court in *Unitron Scandinavia A/S, 3-S A/S, Danske Svineproducenters serviceselckab* v. *Ministeret for Fødvaer, Landbrug og Fiskeri*[46] the prohibition of discrimination "implies, in particular, an obligation of transparency in order to enable the contracting authority to satisfy itself that the principle has been complied with". Hence the prohibition of discrimination implies an obligation of transparency. Transparency facilitates the negative obligation to refrain from discrimination. On the basis of this principle the Court ruled in *Telaustria Verlags GmbH und Telefonadress GmbH* v. *Telekom Austria AG*[47] that:

> "That obligation of transparency which is imposed on the contracting authority consists in ensuring, for the benefit of any potential tenderer, a degree of *advertising* sufficient to enable the services *market to be opened up* to *competition* and the *impartiality of procurement procedures* to be *reviewed* [emphasis added]".[48]

Hence the Treaty also imposes positive obligations, for example requirements in relation to award procedures. This probably implies some form of advertising, some form of competitive procedure, objective award criteria, and a review mechanism. The easiest way to comply with the Treaty requirements and the positive obligation is to follow the Directives. Nevertheless, following the detailed rules of the Directive will be considerably more onerous than following the Treaty. On the other hand, following the Treaty without following the Directives can be difficult in practice. The Directives represent a detailed 'Guide to Procurement in Conformity with Community Law', the Treaty does not.

Whether the requirements of the Treaty are followed in practice in relation to hard defence material is another question. This will depend on the acceptance of the Member States,[49] the attitude of the Commission to enforcement, the readiness of the Court to review these cases, and the intensity of scrutiny applied. Until recently Article 296 (1) (b) EC was widely understood as an automatic exclusion. Both the interpretation in *Commission* v. *Spain* and the principles of *Unitron Scandinavia* are relatively recent developments.

Another purpose of Articles 3 Supplies Directive and 4 (1) Services Directive is to clarify that, apart from hard defence material, the Directives cover all other

[46] Case C–275/98, *Unitron Scandinavia A/S, 3-S A/S, Danske Svineproducenters serviceselckab v Ministeret for Fødvaer, Landbrug og Fiskeri* [1999] ECR I–8291, para 31.

[47] Case C–324/98, *Telaustria Verlags GmbH und Telefonadress GmbH v Telekom Austria AG* [2000] ECR I–10704. The contract was not covered by the Directive because: 'such a contract is excluded, [...] by reason of the fact, in particular, that the consideration provided by the first undertaking to the second consists in the second obtaining the right to exploit for payment its own service.' See annotations by M Dischendorfer, 'Service Concessions under the EC Procurement Directives: A Note on the Telaustria Case ' (2001) 10 *Public Procurement Law Review* NA57.

[48] Above, at para 62.

[49] According to the Commission in *Green Paper Defence Procurement*, COM (2004) 608 final, at 6: 'the low number of publications in the Official Journal of the European Union appears to imply that some Member States believe they can apply the derogation automatically.'

purchasing activities of defence procurement authorities. This is confirmed by the fact that the defence procurement authorities of the Member States are listed in the Annexes to the Directives. There is no exclusion based on the type of the contracting authority but exclusion based on the type of material to be procured. Thus the Directives cover civil goods and dual use material and related services procured by national defence procurement authorities unless one of the other exemptions applies. The undisputed application of the EC Treaty and the Directives to the procurement of civil goods, services, and works represents a considerable transfer of sovereignty over defence from the Member States to the Community. The purchase of civil and dual-use goods for the armed forces has national security implications. It would have been possible to exclude all purchasing activities for the armed forces and their civil administration from the application of Community law. Civil and dual-use goods, works, and services amount for a considerable percentage of the purchases of the ministries of defence. Many procurement laws exclude the ministries of defence as a whole, irrespective of whether this refers to civil, dual-use, or hard defence materials.[50] Defence procurement can be understood as all procurement for the armed forces. As only hard defence material is currently excluded from secondary Community law, the remaining field of application of the EC Treaty and the Directives leaves an important body of EC defence procurement law.

3.2. The New Directive

Similar to Article 3 Supplies Directive and Article 4 (1) Services Directive, Article 10 of the new Directive deals explicitly with hard defence procurement. It reads:

> "This Directive shall apply to public contracts awarded by contracting authorities in the field of defence, subject to Article 296 of the Treaty."

There are two main observations to be made on this provision. First, it clarifies that the procurement activities of the "contracting authorities in the field of defence" are in principle covered by the new Directive. Moreover, Annex I of the new Directive lists the ministries of defence and defence procurement agencies of the Member States amongst the contracting authorities covered by the new Directive. In this regard the new Directive follows the tradition of the old Supplies and Services Directives.

Second, the wording suggests that, in contrast to the old Article 3 Supplies Directive, the provision does not constitute an automatic exclusion of hard

[50] See Article 1(2)(a) of the UNCITRAL (United Nations Commission for International Trade Law) Model Law on the Procurement of Goods, Construction and Services, which provides for the option to exclude all defence procurement from its application: '[...] this Law does not apply to: (a) *Procurement involving national defence or national security*, [...]' [emphasis added]. This law is designed as a model for countries desiring to introduce domestic procurement laws.

defence material and related services from the application of the new Directive. The Explanatory Memorandum attached to the initial 2000 Draft Proposal for the new Directive[51] said that the then Article 7 (now Article 10) "*corresponds* to the provisions of the current Article 4 (1) of [the Services Directive] and [...] the current Article 3 of [the Supplies Directive] [and] is *unchanged in substance* [emphasis added]." This referred to the wording of Article 7 in the initial Draft Proposal, which had read:

> "This Directive shall apply to public contracts awarded by contracting authorities in the field of defence, except for public supply and service *contracts* to which the provisions of Article 296 of the Treaty apply [emphasis added]."

As outlined above, the use of the word "*contracts*" rather than "*products* to which the provisions of Article 296 [(1) (b)] of the Treaty apply" infers, on the basis of the interpretation in *Commission* v. *Spain*, that Article 296 EC has to be specifically invoked. The requirements have to be proven and the use of the provision is subject to review by the European Court of Justice. Thus it appears that Article 7 of the initial Draft Proposal corresponds to Article 4 (1) Services Directive but not to Article 3 Supplies Directive. It follows that the wording of the Explanatory Memorandum is inaccurate.

The wording of Article 7 of the initial Draft Proposal which eventually led to the wording of Article 10 of the new Directive could be explained in two ways. One explanation is that the Commission explicitly took the new interpretation of Article 296 (1) (b) EC into account when drafting the provision. It adapted the exemption in the Draft Proposal to that in the Treaty. The wording of Article 7 of the initial Draft Proposal, which differs from that of the automatic exemption in Article 3 Supplies Directive, is the strongest argument for this explanation.

An alternative explanation is that the Commission overlooked the difference between the current Article 4 (1) Services Directive and Article 3 Supplies Directive. An indication for this "oversight theory" is the Explanatory Memorandum, which says that the provision in the Draft Proposal "corresponds" to the current provisions and "is unchanged in substance". In the Memorandum the Commission does not seem to assume a difference between the two current provisions. However, the difference is quite substantial.[52] As explained above, the current Article 3 Supplies Directive has to be interpreted as an automatic exclusion of hard defence material from the application of the Directive, which goes beyond the narrow interpretation of Article 296 (1) (b) EC in *Commission* v. *Spain*. Article 4 (1) Services Directive can be reconciled with that interpretation. The wording of Article 7 of the initial Draft Proposal follows the wording of Article 4 (1) Services Directive but not that of Article 3 Supplies Directive.

[51] COM (2000) 275 final, above n 15.

[52] Assuming, on the basis of the alternative interpretation of Article 3 Supplies Directive outlined above, according to which the provision does not represent an automatic exemption either, it would of course make sense for the Commission not to see a difference between the two exclusions in the Explanatory Memorandum.

An argument against this explanation is that the word "contracts" might have been used to refer to both services and supplies. However, in order to include an unequivocal exclusion of hard defence material and related services, the provision would have to refer to "*products* to which Article 296 (1) (b) of the EEC Treaty applies including services in relation to these products". The wording or the initial Draft Proposal does not support the assumption of an express exclusion.

Moreover, should the Commission have intended to draft an express exclusion, this would not be in conformity with the interpretation of Article 296 (1) (b) EC provided in *Commission* v. *Spain*, as long as there is no separate instrument regulating the procurement of hard defence material. When the Treaty provision setting the basic rule has to be interpreted narrowly, the secondary law instrument setting the details has to conform to this basic rule. The EC Treaty introduces the free movement of hard defence material, subject to a derogation for security reasons that has to be specifically invoked and is subject to review by the Court. A Procurement Directive including an express exclusion of hard defence material from its application would contradict this basic rule in the Treaty. Such an exemption would represent a barrier to trade and the legislator would work against the objectives of the EC Treaty. On the basis of the wording, Article 7 of the initial Draft Proposal corresponds to Article 4 (1) Services Directive.

The wording of Article 7 of the initial Draft Proposal contains another detail indicating that it was drafted on the basis of the old provision in the Services Directive and not on the basis of the provision in the Supplies Directive. It refers to "the provisions of Article 296 of the Treaty" rather than "Article 223 (1) (b) of the EEC Treaty [now Article 296 (1) (b) EC]". As explained above, this includes Article 296 (1) (a) which needs to be specifically invoked. This is another indication for assuming that Article 7 of the initial Draft Proposal refers to cases where Article 296 EC has to be invoked, proven and is subject to review by the Court.

This assumption is confirmed by the wording of Article 7 in an amended version of the Draft Proposal put forward in April 2001, which is very close to Article 10 of the new Directive of March 2004:

> "This Directive shall apply to public contracts awarded by contracting authorities in the field of defence, *subject to the provisions of Article 296 of the Treaty* [emphasis added]."

In the final version of the new Directive only the words "the provisions of" are omitted from this April 2001 version of the Draft Proposal. This does not amount to a change of substance but the April 2001 version is clearer about the fact that both exemptions, Article 296 (1) (b) and 296 (1) (a) EC, are covered. Nevertheless, the wording of the final version also includes both Treaty exemptions. The deletion of "the provisions of" is merely the result of an editing process omitting unnecessary phrases in order to provide a more concise draft of the Directive. It is submitted that the narrow *Commission* v. *Spain* interpretation is accommodated in Article 10 of the new Directive. Thus hard defence material seems to be in principle covered by the new Directive unless a Member State can justify derogation for national security reasons within the context of Article 296 (1) (b) EC.[53]

Even when assuming that the above interpretation of the provision is accurate, it is not certain that Article 10 of the new Directive will lead to an internal market for hard defence material in practice. This will depend on how often the Member States invoke Article 296 (1) (b) EC, on the attitude of the Commission to enforcement in this context, and on the approach of the European Court of Justice in scrutinising measures justified by the exemption. It might well be that the Member States will invoke the provision frequently, that the Commission will accept the use of the provision, and that in the context of the few cases it initiates the enforcement procedures, the Court will be very cautious to consider a measure unnecessary. *Plus ça change*? On the other hand, Article 10 might also lead to the application of the new Directive to most hard defence procurement in practice. Assuming the application of the Directive to hard defence material in practice two questions need to be briefly addressed.

First, the question is whether the EC should regulate hard defence procurement at all. The Community lacks the competence for the regulation of defence. There is clearly no legal basis for a common defence policy in the EC Treaty and it was introduced after an unsuccessful attempt to establish a European Defence Community, as discussed in chapter 1.[54] As will be explained in section 6 below, other organisations are preparing proposals for European defence procurement regulation. It could be argued that the Community institutions lack the necessary experience and expertise for the defence sector. In other words it is arguable that the Community institutions are not suitable to deal with defence procurement regulation in both absolute terms and in relative terms when compared with other organisational frameworks. Discussions of the author with defence procurement officials from various Member States and international organisations indicate a strong opposition against any Community involvement. However, the EC institutions have decades of expertise on multinational public procurement, an advantage not shared by the 'competing' organisations. Moreover, outside the First Pillar the CFSP discussed in chapters 2 and 3 indicates that the Member States are "moving to an ever closer union" in defence matters. Defence procurement regulation through the Community could be part of that move. Finally and most importantly, civil and dual-use purchases[55] are regulated by the EC Public Procurement Directives. Europe should avoid a dual-use market managed by the Community and a hard defence market managed by some other organisation. Splitting efforts and jurisdiction will weaken the whole approach towards a competitive European

[53] This is also the interpretation of the *Commission in Green Paper Defence Procurement* COM (2004) 608 final, at 5. For an alternative interpretation see A Georgopoulos, 'European Defence Procurement Integration: Evaluating the Teleological Boundaries of Article 296(1b) EC and the Applicability of the New Public Procurement Directive in the Field of Intra-Community Armaments Procurement' forthcoming in *European Law Review*.

[54] At 47–49.

[55] Material that can be used for both military and civil purposes not on the list according to Article 296(2) EC.

defence equipment market. It is very unlikely that the power to regulate civil and dual-use purchases made by military authorities will be taken from the Community and moved to the Second Pillar. Therefore the only solution towards the integration of the European defence equipment market is to make the Community the legislator for European defence procurement.[56]

Second, it has to be asked whether the extension of the civil regime to hard defence procurement in the new Directive is appropriate.[57] There is not even a special section for hard defence procurement. The civil rules could be considered as too inflexible thereby not accommodating the special characteristics of the military sector sufficiently. These special features include the high-technology nature of the products concerned, the high level of costs, the long duration of many projects, the complexity of the defence procurement cycle, the need for secrecy, national security concerns in particular requirement of security of supply, the sensitive political nature of most procurement decisions, and monopsony.[58] These characteristics require, for example, the more flexible use of less competitive procedures allowing to award contracts to bidders who have been selected beforehand and registered on a contractors list on the basis of objective criteria. They might also require another set of award criteria taking into account considerations such as security of supply,[59] a different set of remedies, a safeguard clause for national security or other principles of contract awards. A detailed analysis of the new Directive as an instrument of defence procurement, however, is beyond the aim of this chapter.[60]

It is submitted that it would be preferable to produce a separate piece of legislation on defence procurement: a "Defence Procurement Directive". The special characteristics of the utilities sector led to the creation of a special and more flexible piece of legislation rather than the extension of the public sector rules to utilities.[61] This is also necessary for the defence sector.[62] Alternatively there should at least be a hard defence section in the new Directive.

[56] See M Trybus, 'The Changes Facing the European Defence-Related Industry—Commission Communication COM (96) 08' (1996) 5 *Public Procurement Law Review* CS98, at CS101–2.

[57] The Commission also recently asked this question in *Green Paper Defence Procurement*, COM (2004) 608 final, at 9.

[58] The fact that the government is the only buyer on a national defence market, see A Cox and K Hartley, above n 20, at 3. These characteristics where also identified by the Commission as special features of defence markets in the recent *Green Paper Defence Procurement*, COM (2004) 608 final, at 4–5. For an overview of the special characteristics of the defence sector see Trybus, *European Defence Procurement Law*, above n 20, at 24–26.

[59] Following the judgment in Case C–448/01, *EVN v Austria*, (4 December 2003), see [2004] OJ C–21/5 a criterion such as security of supply might legally be taken into account. See M Dischendorfer, 'The Rules on Award Criteria Under the EC Procurement Directives and the Effect of Using Unlawful Criteria: The *EVN* Case' (2004) 13 *Public Procurement Law Review* NA74.

[60] See Trybus, *European Defence Procurement Law*, above n 20, ch 2.

[61] This point was made by the Commission in *Green Paper Defence Procurement*, COM (2004) 608 final, at 9.

[62] On detailed proposals see M Trybus, *European Defence Procurement Law*, above n 20, chs 9–12; M Trybus, 'Developing a Model for the Regulation of European Defence Procurement' (1999) 11 *European Review of Public Law* 115; M Trybus, 'National Models for the Regulation of the Acquisition of Armaments: Towards a European Defence Procurement Code?' in S Arrowsmith and A Davies, (eds), *Public Procurement: Global Revolution* (Kluwer, London, 1998) 71.

The fact that the special characteristics of the defence sector are not taken into account might also lead to a more frequent use of Article 296 (1) (b) EC. Defence procurement authorities not seeing their security or secrecy needs accommodated in the Directive could invoke Article 10 of the new Directive as their last resort. This would prevent an internal market for hard defence material in practice.

Finally, it is unlikely that the extension of the civil regime to hard defence procurement can simply 'creep in' without an express commitment of all the Member States or even against their will. Article 10 of the new Directive has not been the subject of much discussion so far. This might be an indication that neither the Commission nor the Member States have fully appreciated the possible consequences of the provision. The Member States could, however, use the exemption frequently thereby preventing an internal defence equipment market. Alternatively, the Commission knows what they are doing, and is hoping to use the provision to establish a European defence equipment market in practice.

4. SECRECY AND SECURITY EXCLUSIONS

A second category of defence related exemptions also concerns security. A good example for these security type exclusions is Article 2 Supplies Directive:

> "The Directive shall not apply to [...] b) supply contracts which are declared secret or the execution of which must be accompanied by special security measures in accordance with the laws, regulations or administrative provisions in force in the Member States concerned or when the protection of the basic interests of the member State's security so requires."

Article 4 (b) Works Directive,[63] Article 4 (2) Services Directive[64] and Article 10 Utilities Directive[65] contain similar exclusions. Article 14 of the new Public Procurement Directive has the same wording as the provisions in these Directives.[66] According to the Explanatory Memorandum, the then Article 16 (now Article 14) of the initial Draft Proposal leading to the new Public Procurement Directive corresponds to the provisions of the current Directives

[63] Article 4(b) Works Directive reads: 'The Directive shall not apply to [...] b) works contracts which are declared secret or the execution of which must be accompanied by special security measures in accordance with the laws, regulations or administrative provisions in force in the Member States concerned or when the protection of the basic interests of the member State's security so requires.'

[64] Article 4(2) Services Directive reads: 'The Directive shall not apply to services which are declared secret or the execution of which must be accompanied by special security measures in accordance with the laws, regulations or administrative provisions in force in the Member States concerned or when the protection of the basic interests of the member State's security so requires.'

[65] Article 10 Utilities Directive reads: 'The Directive shall not apply to contracts when they are declared to be secret by Member States, when their execution must be accompanied by special security measures in accordance with the laws, regulations or administrative provisions in force in the Member States concerned or when the protection of the basic interests of the security of that State so requires.'

[66] Article 14 of the new Directive reads: 'This Directive shall not apply to public contracts when they are declared to be secret, when their execution must be accompanied by special security measures in accordance with the laws, regulations or administrative provisions in force in the member State concerned, or when the protection of the basic security interests of that State so requires.'

and "is unchanged". Thus the following interpretation is based on Article 14 of the new Directive, which contains a set of three exclusions from the application of the Directive. It applies to contracts involving civil and dual use goods, services, and works. Contracts involving hard defence material and related services are already covered by the specific exclusion of Article 10 of the new Directive.

4.1. Security Exclusion No. 1 "Contracts Declared Secret"

The first exclusion applies to contracts declared secret, when the publication of the contract would betray sensitive military information. Here the secrecy is so sensitive that it does not even allow publication of the contract. The very existence of the plan for the contract is a secret.

An example might be the Second Gulf War of 1991. A publication of a contract for the acquisition of heat resistant tents, for example, might have given Iraqi intelligence an indication on how many soldiers the British forces wanted to send to the Gulf region.[67] Another example could be a secret mission that requires special supplies. Advertising these supplies could be equal to advertising the secret mission.

It has been put forward that this need for secrecy does not necessarily have to be narrowly interpreted as only referring to the publication of the contract.[68] It may also include any aspect or requirement of the Directive that would adversely affect secrecy. Examples of such aspects could be the requirement to supply equal information to competitors for a particular contract or requirements to send reports to the Commission when using non-competitive procedures.

As discussed in chapter 5,[69] Article 296 (1) (a) EC deals with information to be kept secret for national security reasons. As explained above, Article 10 of the new Directive refers to the whole of Article 296 EC, which includes paragraph (1) letter (a) of the provision. Thus the security exclusion No. 1 "contracts declared secret" covers aspects outside the ambit of Article 296 (1) (a) EC, such as aspects covered by the public security aspect of exemptions like Article 30 EC, which were discussed in chapter 4. Exceptions in Community law have to be interpreted narrowly.[70] Moreover, public security exemptions such as Article 30 EC are subject to a strict scrutiny in the form of a proportionality test.[71]

[67] Arrowsmith, above n 10, at 152.

[68] Arrowsmith, above.

[69] At 163–166.

[70] Case C–222/84 *Johnston*, above n 33, at para 26. See also Case C–13/68 *Salgoil*, above n 33, at 192.

[71] Case C–72/83, *Campus Oil Limited v Minister for Industry and Energy*, [1984] ECR 2727, at 2764; [1984] 3 CMLR 544 at 558 (see discussion in ch 4 at 135–137). The test has three elements. First, the measure in question has to be suitable to promote the objective of public security. Second, the measure has to be adequate in that there is 'no other measure, less restrictive from the point of view of the free movement of goods, capable of achieving the same objective'. Third, the positive effect of the measure on the objective of public security needs to be balanced with the negative effect on the internal market. Formulated by Advocate General van Gerven in Case C–159/90, *SPUC v Grogan* [1991] ECR I–4685 as cited by G de Búrca, 'The Principle of Proportionality and its Application in EC Law' (1993) 13 *Yearbook of European Law* 105, 113 including the more controversial third element. Also in favour of the three-part test (based on the same test in German administrative law), see P Craig and G de Búrca, *EU Law*, 3rd edn, (OUP, Oxford, 2003) 350; and J Schwarze, *European Administrative Law* (Sweet & Maxwell, London, 1992) 712. Other elements of the Court's scrutiny are legitimate expectations, non-discrimination and the emergent principle of transparency.

On the basis of the narrow interpretation and the requirement of proportionality it is submitted, that the first security type exclusion "contracts declared secret" would be difficult to invoke and justify in practice. It is most likely to be accepted in exceptional situations of crisis or close to wars. This does not mean that the exemption can never apply outside such situations. Moreover, the concept of crisis can also include serious situations in times of peace, in particular terrorist attacks such as the hijacking incidents of the 1970s in Entebbe and Mogadishu. However, it is unlikely to be accepted as proportionate when such a situation does not exist. There are two main arguments for this assumption.

First, there is a danger of abuse. This type of exclusion does not apply to hard defence supplies and related services as a more specific type of exclusion already covers those. Thus the "contracts declared secret" exemption applies to civil and dual-use goods[72] and related works and services. Theoretically, almost any procurement activity of a defence purchasing authority in relation to these contracts could come under this secrecy exclusion. Thus a wide interpretation would be contrary to the inclusion of the procurement of civil and dual use goods, works, and services through defence procurement agencies. Clear manifestations of this inclusion are Article 5 (1) (a) Supplies Directive[73] and the fact that the defence procurement authorities of the Member States are listed as contracting authorities in the Annexes to the Directives, for example in Annex IV to the new Directive. Moreover, Article 10 explicitly subjects the purchasing activities of military procurement agencies to the regime of the new Directive. Limiting the exclusion to crisis situations is necessary to avoid this exemption to develop into a major loophole for defence procurement agencies to avoid the application of the Directive to civil and dual use goods, works, and services.

Second, a wide interpretation would delete the differentiation between civil and dual use goods on the one side and hard defence material on the other side directed by Article 296 (1) (b) EC. Again, the secrecy exclusion applies to civil and dual use contracts as hard defence material is already covered by Article 10 of the new Directive. However, hard defence contracts are the contracts that will normally require a certain degree of secrecy. Other contracts normally do not. If the legislator had intended a general exclusion of all procurement activities of defence procurement authorities from the application of the Directives they would have formulated a clear and unequivocal exemption to that end.[74] The fact that the

[72] Material that can be used for both military and civil purposes not on the list according to Article 296(2) EC.

[73] 'Titles II, III and IV and Articles 6 and 7 shall apply to public supply contracts: —awarded by the contracting authorities [...], including contracting authorities listed in Annex I in the field of defence [...]'.

[74] See for example Article XXI of the General Agreement on Tariffs and Trade GATT (also Article XIV *bis* of the General Agreement in Trade in Services GATS and Article 73 of the Agreement on Trade Related Aspects of Intellectual Property Rights TRIPS):

> 'Nothing in this Agreement shall be construed [...] to prevent any contracting party from taking any action which it considers necessary for the protection of its essenital security interests [...] (ii) relating to the traffic in arms, ammunition and implements of war *and to such traffic in other goods and materials as is carried out directly or indirectly for the purpose of supplying a military establishment*; [...].' [emphasis added].

legislator did not insert such an exemption, in either the old Directives, the new Directive, or the 2000 Draft Proposal, shows clearly that it wants the Directives to apply to civil and dual use goods, works, and services procured by defence procurement authorities. Alternatively, the legislator could have inserted this as a general exemption without inserting a special hard defence material exemption. In that case a wider interpretation of this exemption in Article 14 of the new Directive could be assumed, as it would be the main way to justify exemption in relation to hard defence material. However, according to information received from the Commission and the representatives of several national defence ministries, the exemption is not used very often in practice. The purpose of this exclusion is only to accommodate exceptional war and crisis situations.

4.2. Security Exclusion No. 2 "Special Security Measures"

The second exclusion applies where the execution of the contract in question must be accompanied by special security measures in accordance with the laws, regulations or administrative provisions in force in the Member State concerned. The exclusion covers defence but is not confined to it. This could refer to the delivery of sensitive supplies, such as equipment for combating crime or terrorism, which could be diverted to improper purposes.[75] For the reasons discussed above, the exemption applies to civil and dual use contracts only.

Again, according to the jurisprudence of the European Court of Justice, exclusions have to be interpreted narrowly[76] and are subject to a proportionality test. This means that exemption of an individual contract has to be suitable and necessary to achieve the security objectives. The latter requirement requires that there is no other measure less detrimental to the internal market than exemption.

In *R. v. Secretary of State for the Home Department ex parte Evans Medical*[77] the European Court of Justice indicated that this exclusion does not cover a contract for the delivery of drugs. The Court suggested that the objective of preventing the improper diversion of sensitive material could be achieved in an open or restricted procurement procedure[78] by taking account of a firm's ability to provide adequate security as an award criterion. Alternatively, contracting authorities could simply write stringent security standards into the minimum specifications of a

See also Article 1(2)(a) of the UNCITRAL (United Nations Commission for International Trade Law) Model Law on the Procurement of Goods, Construction and Services which provides for the option to exclude all defence procurement from its application: '[...] this Law does not apply to: (a) *Procurement involving national defence or national security*, [...]' [emphasis added]. This law is designed as a model for countries desiring to introduce domestic procurement laws.

[75] Example suggested by Arrowsmith, above n 11, at 153.

[76] Case C–222/84, *Johnston*, above n 33, at para 26. See also Case C–13/68, *Salgoil*, above n 33, at 192.

[77] Case C–324/93, *R v Secretary of State for the Home Department ex parte Evans Medical ('Evans Medical')* [1995] ECR I–563.

[78] All directives provide the open, restricted and negotiated procurement procedures. The new Directive introduces a new procedure called 'competitive dialogue', see Chapter V 'Procedures', in particular Article 28 of the new Directive.

contract. The same argument applies for other sensitive equipment. Therefore this exemption can only be invoked when exclusion of the contract is the only way to achieve the objective of preventing the improper diversion of sensitive material. The Member State invoking it has to prove that the objective cannot be achieved by other means, such as those indicated by the Court. Exclusion is a drastic measure not likely to pass the strict proportionality test very easily.

In the recent judgment of *Commission* v. *Belgium*[79] the European Court of Justice accepted the use of security exemption No. 2 for the first time. The case concerned a service contract for the surveillance of the Belgian coast awarded by the Belgian Waterways and Maritime Affairs Authority to a Belgian contractor by negotiated procedure without competition. The Authority required the possession of a military security certificate from contractors. The Court considered this requirement to be a special security measure in the sense of Article 4 (2) Services Directive thereby allowing exemption. As Belgium, so the Court, is responsible for protecting the security of its national installations and those of international organisations within its territory, such as NATO, it is for the Belgian authorities to lay down the security measures necessary for the protection of such installations.[80] Contractors have access to data, sites, or equipment classified by Belgium or NATO. They can obtain the military security certificate after undergoing certain security checks, which allows them to work directly on the results of their photography and, before publishing or distributing them, conceal classified objects on the base of a list of such items which they receive from the Belgian authorities.[81] The procedure for obtaining the military security certificate is strictly applied and involves a thorough vetting of the contractor concerned. The past record, circle of contacts, trips abroad and membership of organisations of every member of staff who has access to the photographs, as well as of shareholders and managers of that contractor, is looked at in detail.[82] In order to guarantee the protection of classified information in its possession, the undertaking in question must fulfil conditions as to security commensurate with the level of confidentiality of the information held. Special procedures for accessing the recorded material are necessary and the equipment for storing and using uncensored results of photography must meet certain security requirements, such as that photographs and related documents must be kept in a bombproof building with a metal clad main door protected by a double alarm system permanently linked to a security firm.[83] Therefore obtaining a military security certificate does not constitute merely an administrative formality but requires that the certified contractor meet certain operational conditions. Contractors not in possession of a military security certificate must, before processing the data, transmit the results of their photography to the general intelligence services, which will

[79] Case C–252/01, *Commission v Belgium ('re coastal photography')*, [2003] ECR I - 11859.
[80] Case C–252/01, above, at para 30.
[81] Case C–252/01, above n 79, at para 26.
[82] Case C–252/01, above n 79, at para 32.
[83] Case C–252/01, above n 79, at para 33.

conceal classified objects if necessary. Classified material is of strategic importance. The dissemination of geographical information concerning such objects entails serious risks of terrorism, sabotage, or espionage.

In *Commission* v. *Belgium* the European Court of Justice appears to deviate from the sophisticated criteria of its jurisprudence with regards to exemptions in favour of a wide margin of discretion for the Member States in questions affecting their security. According to *Commission* v. *Belgium* derogation under Article 4 (2) No. 2 Services Directive is justified when in the opinion of the Member State in question the execution of the services under the contract in issue must be accompanied by special security measures.[84] This deviates from the *Johnston* principle that all exemptions have to be interpreted narrowly and that their use is subject to the principle of proportionality.[85] Moreover, it is in sharp contrast to *Commission* v. *Spain* where the principle of proportionality was even applied to the hard defence material exemption in Article 296 (1) (b) EC.[86] The findings of the Court in *Commission* v. *Belgium* do not even mention these principles. Moreover, the ruling deviates from the principles set out in *Evans Medical* according to which the use of the exemption is only justified when the security concerns cannot be addressed in other ways, for example by the use of a less competitive procedure or by including stringent security standards in the contract specifications.[87] The findings of the Court do not even mention this principle. Finally, this deviates from the principles set out in *Telaustria* according to which the procurement contracts not covered by the Directives still have to comply with the principles of non-discrimination and transparency deriving from the EC Treaty.[88] Exemption from the Directive and exemption from the Treaty need to be differentiated. The Court neither argued for an exemption from the Treaty nor scrutinised the procurement with regards to transparency and non-discrimination.

The Court had to accept the Belgian argument that the contract had to be accompanied by special security measures, although this is not necessarily convincing.[89] However, the deviation from all relevant previous jurisprudence is not welcome as it leads to an incoherent jurisprudence. Moreover, the reason for this deviation is not clear. It was suggested that the changes in international politics

[84] Case C–252/01, above n 79, at para 36.

[85] Case C–222/84, *Johnston*, above n 33, at para 26. See also Case C–13/68, *Salgoil*, above n 33, at 192.

[86] Case 414/97, *Commission v Spain*, above n 32.

[87] Case C–324/93, *R v Secretary of State for the Home Department ex parte Evans Medical*, above n 76. In a decision of the procurement chamber of the *Oberlandesgericht* (High Court) Düsseldorf of 30 April 2003, Verg 61/02, published with annotations by F-J Hölzl in (2004) *Vergabrecht* 3/6, concerning a services contract on air transport to Afghanistan awarded by the German Ministry of Defence, the use of the implemented Article 4(2) No 2 Services Directive (§100 II lit d Variation 3 GWB) was rejected because the existing security interests could be accommodated during the qualification and award stages of the procurement procedure.

[88] Case C–324/98, *Telaustria Verlags GmbH und Telefonadress GmbH v Telekom Austria AG*, above n 47.

[89] A Brown, annotation in (2004) 12 *Public Procurement Law Review* NA 33: 'Indeed, those familiar with the highly populated and accessible Belgian coastline may be surprised to know that the view of its features from the air raises such intense security concerns.'

after 11 September 2001 might be part of the reason and that the Court would have decided differently before that date.[90] This suggests that the European Court of Justice threw its sophisticated standards to deal with security out of the window in favour of a wide margin of discretion for the Member States, just because of '9/11'. A similar change of jurisprudence, from a sophisticated mechanism based on a narrow interpretation and proportionality, occurred recently in the context of sex equality and the armed forces and will be discussed in chapter 9. However, this would ignore the concerns that led to the 'old' sophisticated jurisprudence. A wider interpretation of the security exemptions could undermine the functioning of the internal market as a whole.[91] In the context of public procurement contracts, exemption from the Directives considerably reduces the protection of bidders with negative implications for the functioning of the internal market in this sector.[92] If these sensible considerations weigh less after '9/11' the European Court of Justice should clearly say so. Nevertheless, the considerations concerning the internal market and the protection of bidders still have some weight. Therefore, as before *Commission* v. *Belgium*, they should be balanced with the security interests of the Member States on the basis of the principle of proportionality. This balance was struck convincingly in *Evans Medical*. The wide discretion rule in *Commission* v. *Belgium* lacks clarity and is not a useful substitute for a mechanism that balances the interests involved. 9/11 might represent an argument to give more weight to the security interests of the Member States, however, this additional weight has to be taken into account as part of a balancing operation to be conducted on the basis of the exemptions and a previous jurisprudence based on proportionality.

Commission v. *Belgium* was a recent judgment and judgments on security issues are relatively rare. Therefore it might take some time before it can be assessed whether it represents an isolated decision or a coherent deviation from the previous jurisprudence.

4.3. Security Exclusion No. 3 "Basic Interests of Security"

The third exclusion applies when the protection of the basic interests of a Member State's security so requires. This reason can be relied upon when the authority wishes to procure from a national firm in order to preserve a certain 'industrial capability' for strategic reasons. The exemption applies to civil and dual use contracts only.

The exclusion is to be interpreted as covering the same circumstances as the security derogation from the free movement of goods provision in Articles 30 EC discussed in chapter 4, which includes national security as a part of the wider concept of public security as a reason to derogate from the Treaty.[93] In *Campus Oil*

[90] F-J Hölzl, 'Circumstances Alter Cases' (2004) *Neue Zeitschrift für Bau-und Vergaberecht* 256.

[91] C-222/84, *Johnston*, above n 33, at para 26. See also Case C–13/68, *Salgoil*, above n 33; and Case C–7/68, *Commission v Italy*, above n 33.

[92] Hölzl, above n 90.

[93] See ch 4 at 131 for details.

Limited v. *Minister for Industry and Energy*,[94] a case discussed in detail in the context of chapter 4, the Court decided in relation to the Republic of Ireland that these security interests could be implemented by economic means. The case involved a rule for importers of crude oil to buy 35 per cent of their requirements from the only Irish refinery. However, the ruling has a limited application.

Again, exclusions have to be interpreted narrowly.[95] Thus a national industrial or technological capability with regards to civil or dual use goods or services has to be in danger to go out of business without orders from the national defence procurement authority. Without the respective provider, for example, the authority would have to procure the good in question from abroad. The capability has to be unique to a small country or it has to be the only provider in a certain region of a Member State with a large territory, such as France or Sweden. Most hard defence material will meet this requirement.[96] This exemption, however, applies to civil and dual use goods and services where there is more than just a single provider for most products. Therefore the exemption will only apply to a few markets.

Furthermore, the capability has to be relevant to national security. The only national provider for fuel, for example, will meet this requirement, as tanks do not roll without fuel. The only provider for cheese, for example, will not meet this requirement, as soldiers can do without cheese and eat something else instead.[97] Therefore the exemption will only apply to a few products.

Moreover, the acceptance of economic means to implement security objectives by the Court in *Campus Oil* cannot necessarily be applied to other Member States. The Republic of Ireland is geographically isolated and it would be hard to deliver crucial supplies from other parts of the Union during a serious crisis.[98] Furthermore, unlike most other Member States the Republic is neutral and in theory would have no allies in times of war.[99] A Member State in the heart of Europe who is also a member State of NATO might find it harder to justify the implementation of security interests by economic means. Therefore the ruling can only

[94] Case C–72/83, above n 70.

[95] Case C–222/84, *Johnston*, above n 33, at para 26. See also Case C–13/68, *Salgoil*, above n 35, at 192.

[96] See the country chapters of France, Germany and the United Kingdom and chapter I in M Trybus, *European Defence Procurement Law*, above n 20.

[97] In Case C–231/83, *Cullert v Centre Leclerc* [1985] ECR I–306, at 313; [1985] 2 CMLR 524, at 535 Advocate General Verloren van Themaat referred to paras 34 and 47 of *Campus Oil* and pointed out: 'reliance upon public security can be justified only in so far as the production capacity in question is necessary for the proper functioning of Irish public institutions and essential public services and even the survival of its inhabitants.'

[98] See Advocate General Slyn in Case C–72/83, *Campus Oil*, above n 69, at 2764, and the arguments of the Irish Government, at 2735.

[99] See the arguments of the Irish National Petroleum Corporation Limited in *Campus Oil*, above, at 2738, referring to 'Austria, Barbados, Cyprus, Jamaica, New Zealand and Thailand which are in a geopolitical and economic situation similar to that of Ireland' and who 'all consider a domestic refining capacity to be an essential element of national security.' Because of Article 297 EC the principle of Community solidarity might be compromised in times of crisis or war. This principle requires Member States to help each other and is a foundation of the Union, see Case C–77/77, *BP v Commission* [1978] ECR 1513; [1978] 3 CMLR 174, at para 15.

apply to a few Member States, namely Ireland, Sweden, Malta, Cyprus, and Finland.

Finally, any reliance on this exemption will be subject to a strict proportionality test. This proportionality test will take the outlined considerations in relation to markets, products and neutrality into account. The exclusion of the Directives will probably not be accepted as necessary when the respective industrial capability is not crucial for defence or when the supplies can easily be supplied by a near-by NATO ally. Thus reliance on this situation is not likely to be accepted easily by the Court. Briefly afterwards this narrow interpretation of *Campus Oil* was confirmed in a judgment of the European Court of Justice in *Commission* v. *Greece.*[100] This security type exemption could also be interpreted as covering the situations stipulated in Article 297 EC. An argument for this interpretation is that otherwise these situations are not dealt with in the Directives and that hence even in times of war defence procurement agencies would have to procure civil and dual use goods on the basis of the Directives. However, there are two arguments against this interpretation. First, the legislator could have included an exemption expressly referring to Article 297 EC as they did with Article 296 EC. They did not do so in the current Directives nor in the new Directive or the Draft Proposal. Second the situations in Article 297 EC are already sufficiently accommodated in the security type exemptions. In these situations derogation will easily be accepted as proportionate.

5. EXCLUSIONS IN THE TREATY AND IN THE DIRECTIVES

These exemptions from the Directives are not exemptions from the EC Treaty. This is the substantial difference between the exemptions in Article 2 (1) (b) Supplies Directive and Article 14 of the new Directive on one side and Article 4 (1) Services Directive and Article 10 of the new Directive on the other side.

The latter are exclusions which have an equivalent in the Treaty: Article 296 EC. Thus the possibility to invoke an exemption in relation to the procurement of hard defence material and related services if national security concerns so require applies to both the Directives and the Treaty.

In contrast the exemptions in Article 2 (1) (b) Supplies Directive, Article 4 (b) Works Directive, Article 4 (2) Services Directive, Article 10 Utilities Directive and Article 14 of the new Directive have no direct equivalent in the Treaty. An example where this difference might become important could be that the need to keep a contract secret may justify the non-advertisement of the contract in the Official Journal thereby invoking the first exemption in Article 14 of the new Directive. The same need for secrecy, however, may not be sufficient to invoke Articles 30 EC, to impose a condition that only domestic providers will be considered. It may be possible to ensure secrecy, even when the contract is awarded to providers in other Member States, by including secrecy clauses in the contract. As the Treaty still has

[100] Case C–347/88, *Commission v Greece* [1990] ECR I–4747.

to be followed even when a security type exemption in the Directive applies, the effect of the latter is limited.

6. CONTRACTS OF INTERNATIONAL ORGANISATIONS IN THE FIELD OF DEFENCE

The most important example for an international organisation exemption is Article 4 (c) Supplies Directive:

> "This Directive shall not apply to public supply contracts governed by different procedural rules and awarded: [...] (c) pursuant to the particular procedure of an international organisation."

Articles 5 (c) Works Directive and Article 5 (c) Services Directive are similar provisions. Article 15 (c) of the new Directive has the same wording as the provisions in the previous Directives.[101] According to the Explanatory Memorandum, Article 17 of the initial Draft Proposal, which has the same wording, corresponds to the current provisions "and adapts these provisions without modifying their scope". Thus it is submitted that the following interpretation of the current Directives equally applies to the new Directive.

6.1. The Background

With the emergence of new European international organisations in the area of defence procurement, such as the Organisation for Joint Armaments Procurement (hereinafter OCCAR)[102] and the Western European Armaments Group (hereinafter WEAG),[103] this type of exclusion could gain importance.

6.1.1. Western European Armaments Group and Organisation

The WEAG is a caucus within the Western European Union (hereinafter WEU) aiming at the formation of a European Armaments Agency (hereinafter EA) operating on the basis of mandatory rules.[104] Within the WEAG the participating nations and not the WEAG as an international organisation will purchase

[101] 'This Directive shall not apply to public contracts governed by different procedural rules and awarded: [...] (c) pursuant to the particular procedure of an international organisation'.

[102] Abbreviation from the French name 'Organisme conjoint de coopération en matière d'armement'. The founding structure is based in Bonn. The four participating nations are France, Germany, United Kingdom and Italy. Spain and Sweden joined for the '1998 Letter of Intent'. Belgium and the Netherlands have applied to participate. See Prieß, above n 11, at 322–23; Trybus, *European Defence Procurement Law*, above n 20, at 20. On 10 September 1998 the defence ministers of the participating nations signed the OCCAR Treaty in Farnborough, see: http://defence-data.com/f98/pfa46.htm.

[103] Prieß, above, at 321–22; Trybus, *European Defence Procurement Law*, above, at 18–20 and 31–44.

[104] Full members of the WEAG are Austria, Belgium, the Czech Republic, Denmark, Finland, France, Germany, Greece, Hungary, Italy, Luxembourg, the Netherlands, Norway, Poland, Portugal, Spain, Sweden, Turkey, United Kingdom, see: http://www.weu.int/weag/index.html.

material.[105] Therefore the exemption in Article 15 of the new Directive does not apply to the WEAG anyway.

In the early 1990s the WEAG[106] established an Ad Hoc Study Group to review the possibilities of creating a European Armaments Agency (hereinafter WEU-EAA). Due to a lack of the necessary political, legal, and economic conditions, the Study Group did not recommend the implementation of a fully-fledged WEU-EAA at the time.[107] However, the Ad Hoc Study Group continued its work and prepared an organisational framework for such an agency. On this basis, on 19 November 1996, a week after OCCAR was created, in Ostend the WEAG ministers of defence established the Western European Armaments Organisation (hereinafter WEAO) by signing the WEAO Charter[108] and the European Understanding of Research Organisation, Programmes and Activities (EUROPA). It was intended as a formal subsidiary body of the WEU. According to Article 1 of the WEAO Charter, the aim of the organisation is to assist in promoting and enhancing European armaments co-operation, strengthening the European defence technology base and creating a European defence equipment market, in accordance with the policies agreed by the WEAG. The executive body of the WEAO, the Research Cell (abbreviated WRC) is co-located with the WEU Secretariat and the Armaments Secretariat of the WEAG in Brussels. The WRC is considered a possible precursor for the proposed agency, since Article 7 of the 1997 WEAO Charter provides for a broad range of possible activities. These are defence research and technology activities, procurement of defence equipment, studies, management of assets and facilities, and other functions to carry out the aim of the Organisation.

The WEAO is an integral part of the WEU and will share her fate.[109] The latter features prominently in the Maastricht and Amsterdam versions of the TEU but is deleted from Article 17 of the Nice version. As explained in chapter 2 and 3,[110] it can be said that the WEU functions are currently in a process of transition to the EU and that this process is already quite advanced. This is also reflected in the ongoing process of transfer of WEU capabilities, institutions, and politico-strategic concepts and other documents to the EU. Therefore the purpose and remaining status of the 'rump WEU' itself is now unclear.[111] Whether the organisation will become completely redundant depends on whether the EU will take over all her tasks. "Support for WEAG/WEAO" was listed as one of the residual functions

[105] On the WEAG see: M Trybus, *European Defence Procurement Law*, above n 20, Part II 'The Western European Armaments Group and the European Defence Equipment Market as a Model for Regulating Defence Procurement', at 31–45.

[106] Austria, Belgium, the Czech Republic, Denmark, Finland, France, Germany, Greece, Hungary, Italy, Luxembourg, the Netherlands, Norway, Poland, Portugal, Spain, Sweden, Turkey and the United Kingdom are full members of the WEAG. See: http://www.weu.int/weao/site/frameset.htm.

[107] B Schmitt, 'Introduction to WEAO Charter' in *European Armaments Cooperation: Core Documents*, Chaillot Paper No 59, (Institute for Security Studies of the European Union, Paris, 2003) 11.

[108] Reproduced in Schmitt, above, at 11–22.

[109] Article 8(a) WEAO Charter.

[110] Ch 1 at 44–47 and ch 2 at 80–84.

[111] P Craig and G de Búrca, *EU Law*, 3rd edn, (OUP, Oxford, 2003) 45.

the WEU still has after Nice.[112] As will be discussed in detail in chapter 11,[113] the European Defence Agency (hereinafter EDA) which was established in July 2004 has a fairly comprehensive mandate. After the eventual entering into force of the Constitutional Treaty and the establishment of an EDA, the continued co-existence of WEAO and WEAG could lead to a wasteful duplication of efforts. Therefore it seems likely that the functions of WEAG and WEAO will be transferred to the EDA once the latter is operational.

6.1.2. Organisation for Joint Armaments Procurement

On 12 November 1996 France, Germany, Italy and the United Kingdom created OCCAR. The organisation developed from the earlier Franco-German armaments co-operation structure as a result of the French-German dissatisfaction with the lack of progress to establish a European Armaments Agency within the WEU.[114] The purpose is that of a management organisation for joint programmes involving two or more member nations. The ability of OCCAR to centrally administer contracts was curtailed until it obtained legal status.[115] The OCCAR Convention[116] (hereinafter OCCAR) was signed on 9 September 1998. The ratification process was completed in December 2000 and OCCAR attained legal status on 28 January 2001. According to Article 8 OCCAR the organisation can cover a large range of activities and may become a fully-fledged armaments agency. OCCAR is situated in Bonn and manages several programmes.[117]

Such organisations[118] could use the kind of exemption contained in Article 15 of the new Directive to exclude all their acquisitions, hard defence, soft defence and civil, from the application of the Directives. Thus the effect of the new interpretation of Article 296 (1) (b) EC discussed in chapter 5[119] and above might be compromised in practice. These organisations might not only draft competing rules for the hard defence sector but also develop into a peril for the *acquis communautaire* in the dual use and even civil sectors. Acquisitions of national defence authorities now covered by the Directives might be excluded if transferred to the responsibility of new international organisations.

[112] Reply of the WEU Council to a written question of WEU Parliamentary Assembly member Mr Martinez-Casan on the results of the (classified) WEU Council Meeting in Brussels, 28 June 2001, cited by M Rutten, *From Nice to Laeken, European defence: core documents*, Volume II, Chaillot Paper No 51, (Institute of Security Studies of the European Union, Paris, 2002) 69.

[113] At 319–328.

[114] *Defence Trade: European Initiatives to Integrate the Defence Market*, United States General Accounting Office, Report to the Secretary of Defence, Washington DC, October 1997, at 7.

[115] Above, at 9.

[116] Convention on the Establishment of the Organisation for Joint Armaments Co-operation OCCAR, printed in Schmitt, above n 107, at 45–59.

[117] The Franco–German 'Tiger' attack helicopter, the Franco–Italian Future Surface-to-Air Missile Family, the Belgian–British–French–German–Spanish–Turkish A400M transport aircraft. The latter involves non-OCCAR members.

[118] Worth mentioning in this context is also the LoI (Letter of Intent) initiative of France, Germany, Italy, Spain, Sweden, and the United Kingdom which is aimed at facilitating industrial restructuring in the defence sector.

[119] At 152–154.

6.2. Interpretation

It is submitted that the notion of an international organisation in the sense of Article 15 (c) of the new Directive has to be interpreted as an organisation of which only States or other international organisations are members. This covers contracts awarded according to the rules of the United Nations or the organisations of the World Bank Group, in other words contracts awarded by contracting authorities of the Member States but financed by one of these international organisations. Contracts awarded by these organisations themselves are not covered in any case, as they are not contracting authorities within the definitions of the Public Procurement Directives.

The notion of an international organisation has to be narrowly interpreted as an organisation with a membership including States that are not Member States of the EU (third countries). Thus an organisation with a membership consisting only of Member States of the EU is not an international organisation in the sense of Article 15 (c) of the new Directive.

Moreover, an organ of an organisation formed by two or more Member States of the European Union is to be considered a contracting authority under the Directives. This is due to the fact that such an organ or organisation would only represent a substitute for a contracting authority now covered by the Directives and expressly listed in the Annexes.

It is not the objective of provisions like Article 15 (c) of the new Directive to provide Member States with an extremely flexible way to avoid the application of the Directives. Otherwise they could simply found new international organisations to avoid the application of the Directives to large parts of their procurement activities. A Franco-German Road Agency, for example, would be able to award large works contracts now covered by the Directives without applying the Directives.

The objective of provisions like Article 15 (c) of the new Directive is to provide for the case of conflict between the EC Directives and regulations of another international organisation, for example Eurocontrol or the European Space Agency. These provisions only clarify that the Union does not want to interfere with the procurement activities of other international organisations.

This interpretation corresponds with Article 307 EC which provides that the rights and obligations arising from agreements concluded before the entry into force of the Treaty between one or more Member States on the one hand, and one or more third countries on the other, shall not be affected by the provisions of the EC Treaty. This applies to agreements entered into after the entry into force of the Treaty. Only agreements with third countries remain unaffected. All existing agreements between Member States not compatible with the Treaty must be adapted, as is stated in the second paragraph of Article 307 EC. This means that any agreement between Member States without the participation of a third country concluded after the entry into force of the Treaty that is not compatible with it, is superseded by the Treaty. Therefore an organisation like OCCAR-EA would have to follow the Directives while conducting its procurement activities unless it could use one of the other exclusions.

The intergovernmental EDA mentioned in chapter 3[120] and discussed in more detail in chapter 11[121] is similar to OCCAR-EA and the WEAO and an organisational structure established by the Member States with the exception of Denmark. The only difference is that the EDA is part of the CFSP. The Commission does not appear to be sure about the application of the Directives to the EDA.[122] Following the requirements for Article 15 (c) of the new Directive discussed above, the exemption does not apply to the EDA. However, the exemption could apply to *ad hoc* projects involving third countries. The application of the Directive to EDA projects involving only Member States of the European Union is determined by Article 10 and the other relevant exemptions of the Directive, not by its Article 15 (c).

7. OTHER EXCLUSIONS

The other exclusions in the Directives are of less relevance to defence procurement. These exemptions include those on contracts pursuant to international agreements involving other States, on contracts pursuant to international agreements on the stationing of troops, on contracts for the acquisition of land, on provision by another contracting authority pursuant to exclusive rights[123] and on public housing scheme works contracts.

The exclusions with regards to contracts pursuant to international agreements on the stationing of troops in Article 4 (b) Supplies Directive, Article 5 (b) Works Directive and Article 5 (b) Services Directive, and Article 15 (b) of the new Directive *prima facie* seem to have a certain relevance to purchases made by defence procurement authorities. However, the exclusions seem to be of little practical relevance and have never been the subject of a judgment or academic analysis.[124] It can be assumed that they were specifically designed for the American, British, French and other forces stationed in Germany. Based on the wording, they also apply to the German troops stationed in the Netherlands. Article 17 (b) of the new Directive contains a provision that, according to the Explanatory Memorandum, "adapts these provisions without modifying their scope". Thus this type of exclusion is also part of the Draft Proposal. It is understandable that American troops stationed in a Member State should be excluded from the application of the Directives. These troops are not part of a public entity of a Member State. The rationale for the exclusion of troops of one Member State stationed in another Member State, however, is unclear. The Directives, subject to the other exclusions, should therefore cover acquisitions for these troops. The new Directive should have made that clear.

[120] At 105.
[121] At 319–328.
[122] *Green Paper Defence Procurement*, COM (2004) 608 final, at 10: 'Application of the directive to other bodies, such as the new Defence Agency, would have to be determined by the appropriate fora.'
[123] Article 2(2) Supplies Directive.
[124] See the brief coverage in Arrowsmith, above n 11, at 155.

8. CONCLUSIONS

The current EC Public Procurement Directives and the new Directive contain exemptions relating to national security and defence. The legislator had to include these exemptions to balance the European interests of the internal market with the national security interests of the Member States with respect to the regulation of the procurement activities of the Member States for their armed forces.

Article 296 (1) (b) EC forms the background to the hard defence material exclusions in the Directives. As discussed in chapter 5[125] the Court clarified in *Commission* v. *Spain* that Article 296 (1) (b) EC has to be interpreted narrowly. The provision is not an automatic exclusion of hard defence material from the application of the Treaty but needs to be specifically invoked by the relevant Member State, who has the burden of proof and needs to justify its use. The current Supplies Directive contains an automatic exclusion of hard defence material not required by the Treaty. The wording of Article 10 of the new Directive seems to have taken the new and narrow interpretation into account. Thus the new Directive might be intended to apply in principle to hard defence material unless a Member State can invoke the exemption for national security reasons subject to scrutiny by the Court. This is a significant change. It is not clear whether the Commission and the Member States are fully aware of the consequences: the application of the Directive to hard defence material without adaptations taking the specific characteristics of the defence sector into account. These specific characteristics require the introduction of a special 'Defence Procurement Directive'.

Furthermore, the Directives contain certain exclusions with regards to national security and secrecy that allow Member States to derogate from the Directives in exceptional circumstances. These circumstances have to be narrowly construed and apply only to civil and dual use goods, works and services. In order to invoke the exemption the Member State has to justify and prove the circumstances on a case-by-case basis.

On the basis of the treatment of international agreements in the EC Treaty, the exceptions with regards to international organisations in the Directives have to be interpreted as being limited to organisations with third country participation. The activities of new international organisational structures formed by Member States of the Union would have to be conducted on the basis of the EC Public Procurement Directives unless one of the other exceptions applies. The exemption in relation to agreement on the stationing of troops should only apply to troops of third countries stationed in a Member State and not to troops of a Member State stationed in another Member State.

The legislator recently passed the new Directive. This Directive will not be implemented into the national laws of the Member States before 2006. Implementation problems are likely. Time will show whether the legislator produced an appropriate legal framework for the survival of the European defence industrial base or whether Europe needs a 'Defence Procurement Directive'.

[125] At 152–154.

The discussion of European defence procurement in this chapter has shown how secondary Community law affects an important aspect of the national defence law of the Member States. Civil and dual use goods, related services, and works are normally covered by the EC Procurement Directives, unless one of the security-type exemptions is successfully invoked. This subjects a large part of the acquisitions of the ministries of defence of the Member States to secondary Community law. Hard defence material is not covered by the old Supplies Directive. However, the new Directive normally covers hard defence material, unless the hard defence material exemption in Article 10 is invoked, justified, and proven. The only difference to the security–type exemptions is, that the margin of discretion left to the Member States is wider and the scrutiny exercised by the European Court of Justice is less intense. The exemption of hard defence material and related services is therefore a matter to be decided on a case-by-case basis. This makes the coverage of this type of material and services uncertain. The clear exemption from Community law would open the way for regulation under the Second Pillar. The clear inclusion in Community law would help to establish a competitive European defence equipment market but represent a transfer of sovereignty. A possible solution for the medium term could be an agreement between Member States to limit the use of Article 10 of the new Directive. This would allow the development of an integrated defence equipment market without entailing a final transfer of sovereignty.

8

Policing an Armed Market: The Regulation of the European Defence Industries[1]

1. INTRODUCTION

THE PREVIOUS CHAPTER discussed the effect of the EC Public Procurement Directives on the procurement activities of the ministries of defence of the Member States. These Directives are addressed to the defence procurement agencies as part of the wider military apparatus of the Member State governments. Their aim is to open the public procurement markets to contractors from other Member States, including to a certain extent the procurement of armaments. However, the regulation of the purchasing activities of the national procurement authorities is not sufficient to establish a competitive internal defence equipment market. It needs to be complemented with regimes directed at the mainly private defence industries. Regimes on competition law[2] and merger control are required to prevent private undertakings from undermining competition and thereby the internal market by concerted practices, abuses of dominant positions, and by merging to form dominant companies or even monopolies. The regulation of State aids[3] is connected to the regimes on competition law and merger control since subsidies can distort competition. Similar to the public procurement regime, it is directed at the Member States and not the private companies, which benefit from State aids directly. Nevertheless, similar to the regimes on competition law and merger control it is designed to ensure competition by limiting subsidies. Therefore, these regimes should be discussed together in one chapter.

Competition law, merger control and the regime on State aids are needed to ensure competition and the functioning of internal market with regards to the defence industries. Moreover, they are particularly important in the defence sector. In an environment of decreasing defence budgets after the end of the Cold War many companies left the armaments market. Defence equipment is getting

[1] An earlier version of this chapter was published as M Trybus, 'European Defence Procurement: Towards a Comprehensive Approach' (1998) 4 *European Public Law* 111–33.

[2] Also know as 'anti-trust law'.

[3] Also called 'subsidies'.

increasingly expensive and involves considerable investments in research and development. There are more and more types of equipment, for example fighter aircraft and warships, which can only be produced by a few companies or consortia in Europe. Finally, some Member States might consider it necessary to ensure the survival of a defence industrial capability by granting State aids.

Together with the defence administration and the armed forces, the still mainly national producers of armaments are part of the defence effort of those Member States large enough to support national defence industries.[4] Therefore, competition law, merger control, and the State aids regime in relation to the defence sector are affected by national security considerations. A Member State might consider the preservation of a national defence industrial capability as necessary for its national security.[5] With respect to competition policy this could allow concerted practices between national defence undertakings that would be unacceptable in the civil industries where these national security considerations do not exist. With respect to merger control national security considerations could prevent the merger of a national defence company with a defence company from another Member State that would normally be allowed. Finally, with respect to subsidies, national security considerations could necessitate State aids to an undertaking producing armaments that would otherwise go out of business. Nevertheless, this special treatment may lead to all the negative effects competition law aims to prevent: complacency, high prices, and the low quality of goods and services. Moreover, for an increasing number of crucial products and services not even a maximum of 'immunity' will be sufficient to preserve national defence industrial capabilities, not even in the largest Member States. Finally, as it is getting increasingly difficult to separate defence industrial capabilities from civil capabilities, which are often produced by a different part of the same company, there is a danger that the exclusion of competition law from armaments production has a negative effect on competition in civil sectors. Therefore, a mechanism is needed to balance the Community interests in competition and the internal market with the national security interests of the Member States in their defence industrial capabilities.

Chapter 8 complements the discussion of the effect of Community economic law on the defence of the Member States explored in chapters 4 to 7. It discusses the application of the Community regimes on competition law (section 2), merger control (section 3) and State aids (section 4) to the defence industrial sectors of the Member States. It will be shown that EC competition law represents an

[4] France, Germany, Italy, United Kingdom and Sweden. The Netherlands, Poland, Hungary, and the Czech Republic have limited capabilities. Greece, Portugal, and Spain have developing defence industries.

[5] See for example France, in M Trybus, *European Defence Procurement Law: International and National Procurement Systems as Models for a Liberalised Defence Procurement Market in Europe* (Kluwer, The Hague, 1999) ch 5 at 100–101 and 'Defence Procurement and the EC Treaty', at 79–96 (hereinafter '*European Defence Procurement Law*').

instrument of European defence integration within the limits of the security exemptions of the EC Treaty and secondary legislation.[6]

2. COMPETITION LAW: ARTICLES 81 AND 82 EC

EC competition law[7] is regulated in primary and secondary Community law. Articles 81 to 86 EC deal with the rules on competition. Council-Regulation 1/2003/EC[8] is the secondary instrument dealing with the enforcement of Articles 81 and 82 EC. Article 81 (1) EC prohibits agreements between undertakings, decisions by associations of undertakings and concerted practices which prevent, restrict or distort competition and which may affect trade between Member States.[9]

Competition law is extremely relevant to the defence industries. Many defence companies are large in size and turnover. Looking at each Member State separately there are many products which only a few firms can produce, and some for which there is only one single manufacturer.[10] For example, in France there is only one company producing fighter aircrafts.[11] Moreover, as explained below, mergers are taking place on a national and increasingly on a European level, thereby leading to even fewer and even bigger companies. Where firms are large in size and few in number, there is a danger they may become involved in practices covered by

[6] The 2004 Constitutional Treaty adopted the Community regimes on competition law, merger control, and State aids. Therefore the discussion in this chapter remains relevant, irrespective of whether the Constitutional Treaty enters into force or not. For details see Part III of this book.

[7] As opposed to competition law in the wider sense, including competition law, merger control, and State aids. Leading works on EC competition law: C Bellamy and G Child, PM Roth, (ed), *European Community Law of Competition,* 5th edn, (Sweet & Maxwell, London, 2001); D Goyder, *EC Competition Law,* 4th edn, (OUP, Oxford, 2003); V Korah, *EC Competition Law,* 7th edn, (Hart Publishing, Oxford, 2000); R Wish, *Competition Law,* 5th edn, (Butterworths, London, 2004).

[8] Council Regulation 1/2003/EC of 16 December 2002 on the implementation of the rules on competition laid down in articles 81 and 82 of the Treaty [2003] OJ L–68/1.

[9] Article 81(1) EC reads:

> 1. The following shall be prohibited as incompatible with the common market: all agreements between undertakings, decisions by associations of undertakings and concerted practices which may affect trade between Member States and which have as their object or effect the prevention, restriction or distortion of competition within the common market, and in particular those which:
> (a) directly or indirectly fix purchase or selling prices or any other trading conditions;
> (b) limit or control production, markets, technical development, or investment;
> (c) share markets or sources of supply;
> (d) apply dissimilar conditions to equivalent transactions with other trading parties, thereby placing them at a competitive disadvantage;
> (e) make the conclusion of contracts subject to acceptance by the other parties of supplementary obligations which, by their nature or according to commercial usage, have no connection with the subject of such contracts.

The 2003 Convention on the Future of Europe adopted Article 81 EC in Article III–161 Constitutional Treaty (December 2004 version). On the Constitutional Treaty see Part III of this book.

[10] See the overview of the French (ch 6), German (ch 7) and United Kingdom (ch 8) defence industries in Trybus, *European Defence Procurement Law,* above n 5, at 102–4, 140–41, and 174–75 respectively.

[11] For example, for large combat aircraft, there are only three producers in the entire European Union: the British–German–Italian–Spanish 'Eurofighter/Typhoon', the French 'Rafale' and the Swedish–British 'Grippen'.

Article 81 EC, which is not to imply that the provision applies only to monopolies and oligopolies.

Various violations of Article 81 EC by defence firms can be contemplated in a liberalised market as the case of *GEC-Siemens* v. *Plessey* has shown, which is discussed further below.[12] Infringements may occur where undertakings decide to divide the market according to products (Firm A for missiles, Firm B for tanks, etc.) or according to territory (Firm A for Southern Europe, Firm B for Northern Europe, etc.).[13] In a nutshell, all kinds of anti-competitive practices happening in the civil sector are equally possible in the defence sector. Moreover, an internal market is likely to indirectly promote anti-competitive practices, as these practices would be made easier on a European-wide level. Thus, the application of Article 81 EC is clearly needed to deal with these kinds of problems, if there is to be a truly competitive defence market ensuring value for money in Europe and market opportunities in third countries.

Article 82 EC prohibits the abuse of a dominant position.[14] It is designed to control the activities of undertakings enjoying an economic strength that makes them immune from the influence of the normal constraints of a competitive market. As with Article 81 EC, the application of Article 82 EC is obviously increasingly needed to ensure the ultimate success of a liberalised defence market in achieving its ultimate objectives of value for money and market opportunities in third countries through competition. These could be negatively affected by the abuse of a dominant market position, in particular of the larger defence firms. As explained below, mergers are already taking place, to some extent in response to market pressures, and mergers in the future may increase the prospect of undertakings obtaining a dominant position in the European market which they then might abuse. In many segments of the defence market, for example of fighter air-

[12] See under the next heading below.

[13] See P de Vestel, *Defence Markets and Industries in Europe: Time for Political Decisions?*, Chaillot Paper No 21, (Institute of Security Studies of the Western European Union, Paris, 1995) 84 and S Walker and P Gummet, *Nationalism, Internationalism and the European Defence Market*, Chaillot Paper No 9, (Institute for Security Studies of the Western European Union, Paris, 1993) 65 on the scenario where the Member States share the markets for their national champions.

[14] Article 82 EC reads:

Any abuse by one or more undertakings of a dominant position within the common market or in a substantial part of it shall be prohibited as incompatible with the common market insofar as it may affect trade between Member States.

Such abuse may, in particular, consist in:

(a) directly or indirectly imposing unfair purchase or selling prices or other unfair trading conditions;
(b) limiting production, markets or technical development to the prejudice of consumers;
(c) applying dissimilar conditions to equivalent transactions with other trading parties, thereby placing them at a competitive disadvantage;
(d) making the conclusion of contracts subject to acceptance by the other parties of supplementary obligations which, by their nature or according to commercial usage, have no connection with the subject of such contracts.

The 2003 Convention on the Future of Europe adopted Article 82 EC in Article III–162 Constitutional Treaty (December 2004 version). On the Constitutional Treaty see Part III of this book.

craft, missiles, or warships, some national producers have a dominant position even without mergers with companies from other Member States. A liberalised defence procurement regime will further promote such mergers as they are a condition for achieving the policy objectives such as avoiding duplication, minimising defence budgets, and building up competitiveness with countries outside the Union.[15]

The armaments exemption of Article 296 (1) (b) EC discussed in chapter 5 is crucial for the application of Articles 81 and 82 EC in the defence sector. It is not entirely clear whether Article 296 (1) (b) EC can only be invoked by Member States or also by private persons, for example companies active in the defence industrial sector. If only Member States can invoke the armaments exemption, companies would be subject to Articles 81 and 82 EC in the usual way, and would only be exempt if Member States authorised such an exemption. In other words, a defence company would need the protection of a Member State to benefit from the exemption.

These questions were considered in *GEC-Siemens* v. *Plessey*.[16] To defend itself against a take over bid from GEC-Siemens, Plessey complained to the Commission alleging breaches of Article 81 and 82 EC (then Articles 85 and 86 EC). The practice involved was the right of a licensee to grant sub licences in respect of applications of a patented invention to military equipment. The Commission argued that Article 296 (1) (b) EC can only be invoked by Member States and not by undertakings. Application of the competition rules was precluded only where an undertaking is required or encouraged to take action by a Member State within the terms of Article 296 (1) (b) EC.[17] According to a notice of the Commission, Article 296 EC does not have the effect of posing any restrictions on the application of competition law within the meaning of Article 81 (1) EC as far as products destined for defence purposes are concerned.[18] This rule applied at least when the practices in question are not authorised or encouraged by Member States. In *GEC-Siemens/Plessey*, however, the Commission found, *inter alia*, that even if Article 81 EC applied, an exemption would be justified, and that there was no infringement of Article 82 EC.

Two questions addressed in *GEC-Siemens* v. *Plessey* have to be discussed separately. The first question is whether Article 296 (1) (b) EC can be invoked by private defence companies, in particular against the Commission. The Commission themselves argued that Article 296 (1) (b) EC can only be invoked by Member States and not by undertakings. It is submitted that this limitation to Member States is the correct interpretation of the provision. First, the wording of the exemption, "any *Member State* may take such measures as *it* considers necessary [emphasis added]", clearly limits the use of the exemption to Member States. Thus,

[15] On defence procurement see ch 7 for details.

[16] Notice relating to a proceeding under Articles 85 and 86 of the EEC–Treaty (IV/33.018 *GEC–Siemens/Plessey*), [1990] OJ C–239/2.

[17] Answer given by Sir Leon Brittan, on behalf of the Commission (16 May 1990) to a question of Mr James Ford (S) in the European Parliament (19 December 1989) in [1991] OJ C–130/2.

[18] *GEC–Siemens/Plessey*, above n 16.

allowing private companies to invoke Article 296 (1) (b) EC would be against its wording. Second, only the Member States can take the relevant measures, which, according to the narrow interpretation of Article 296 (1) (b) EC advocated in chapter 5[19] following the judgment in *Commission* v. *Spain*,[20] require the Member States to specifically invoke the exemption. This requirement includes that a Member State and only a Member State has to specifically invoke Article 296 (1) (b) EC in order to justify exemption of a measure regarding armaments. A Member State cannot be substituted or represented by a private company. Third, as Article 296 (1) (b) EC is not an automatic or categorical exemption, invoking it requires a rather complex assessment of the national security considerations involved. It requires making a judgement which only a Member State government with its expertise and trained staff is competent to make and which is necessarily at least partly subjective. A private defence industrial company cannot make this judgement and assessment. Fourth, an extension of the right to invoke the exemption to private companies would imply a widening of its interpretation. However, the security exemptions have to be interpreted narrowly.[21] Finally, the Member States conferred parts of their sovereignty to the Community. The security exemptions represent a limitation of this transfer. The Member States have reservations regarding the transfer of sovereignty over defence and security issues to the Community and to international organisations in general. Moreover, the governments of most Member States have problems to even involve their national parliaments or courts of law in decisions regarding questions of national security.[22] Considering this jealousy of Member State governments over questions of national security, it appears highly unlikely that they intended to allow private companies to decide whether their national security is affected or not. Therefore the right to invoke Article 296 (1) (b) EC is an exclusive privilege of the Member States.

The second question is whether Article 296 (1) (b) EC prevents the application of Articles 81 and 82 EC as far as armaments are concerned. Not even the Commission is entirely sure about this question. In the 2003 *Communication European Defence – Industrial and Market Issues: Towards an EU Defence Equipment Policy* they declared to "intend to continue [their] reflection on the application of competition rules in the defence sector".[23] The same Communication announced

[19] At 152–154.

[20] Case C–414/97, *Commission v Spain*, [1999] ECR I–5585; [2000] 2 CMLR 4. See M Trybus, 'On the Application of the EC–Treaty to Armaments', (2000) 25 *European Law Review* 633–38; M Trybus, 'The Recent Judgment in *Commission v Spain* and the Procurement of Hard Defence Material' (2000) 9 *Public Procurement Law Review* NA99–105.

[21] Case C–222/84, *Marguerite Johnston v Chief Constable of the Royal Ulster Constabulary* [1986] ECR 1651; [1986] 3 CMLR 240, at para 60. See also Case C–13/68, *SpA Salgoil v Italian Ministry of Foreign Trade* [1968] ECR 453, at 463; [1969] CMLR 181, at 192; and Case C–7/68, *Commission v Italy* [1968] ECR 633 at 644.

[22] See on this issue: TM Franck, *Political Questions/Juridical Answers: Does the Rule of Law Apply to Foreign Affairs?* (Princeton University Press, Princeton, 1992).

[23] European Commission Communication COM (2003) 113 final, Brussels, 11 March 2003, in B Schmitt, *European Armaments Cooperation: Core Documents*, Chaillot Paper No 59, (Institute of Security Studies of the European Union, Paris, 2003) 162, at 163, 174, and 179 (hereinafter '*Towards an EU Defence Equipment Policy*').

an Interpretative Communication on "several important Court judgements in recent years that are relevant [...] especially in helping to define the scope of Article 296" was anticipated for late 2003.[24] However, at the time of writing this book the Commission had not yet issued such an Interpretative Communication. There is no judgment of the Court on the application of Articles 81 and 82 EC in the defence sector as such. It could be argued that the European Court of Justice could only clarify the situation if a case occured where the Commission prohibits a practice and a company defends itself and takes the Commission to the Court.[25] However, following the judgment in *Commission* v. *Spain*, it is clear that the EC Treaty including Articles 81 and 82 EC applies to armaments unless Article 296 (1) (b) EC is successfully invoked. The Member State in question needs to argue and justify invoking the exemption and prove that a situation affecting its national security actually exists, subject to the review of the Court.[26] Thus, Articles 81 and 82 EC apply to the defence sector unless a Member State successfully invokes Article 296 EC.

There are many cases where Member States do encourage the creation of monopolies and this may lead to distortions of competition or an abuse of a dominant position. France and Germany, for example, actually encouraged the creation of the Eurocopter S.A., which now has a monopoly for combat helicopters in both countries and they encouraged the creation of the national monopolies of Aérospatiale and MBB that existed before that merger. Encouraging monopolies, however, is not the same as encouraging infringements of competition law. This means that anti-competitive practices of undertakings who have monopolies encouraged by Member States may be subject to Articles 81 and 82 EC, unless the actual anti-competitive practices themselves are encouraged by Member States.[27]

3. MERGER CONTROL

The Merger Regulation 139/2004/EC[28] (hereinafter 'Merger Regulation') deals with mergers, acquisitions and certain joint ventures between companies of a certain worldwide turnover, to control the potential distortive impact of these transactions on the competition and the free movement of goods and services in the European Union. The disappearance of competitors through mergers and takeovers is obviously detrimental to competition. The Commission can allow or

[24] Above, Case C–414/97, *Commission v Spain* was not mentioned. Nevertheless it is submitted that the Commission was referring mainly to this judgment.

[25] So the author in 'European Defence Procurement: Towards a Comprehensive Approach', above n 1, 118, published a year (1998) before the decisive judgment in *Commission v Spain* (1999).

[26] See also: Bellamy and Child, above n 7, at 24, 1–040.

[27] Even then there is no 'unlimited unilateral derogation' from the Treaty as Article 298 EC allows for judicial review over the exercise of the derogation in Article 296 EC, [1991] OJ C–130/2.

[28] Council Regulation of 20 January 2004 on the control of concentrations between undertakings, [2004] OJ L–24/1. According to its Article 25(1) Merger Regulation 139/2004 repeals Council Regulation 4064/89/EEC [1989] OJ L–395/1. Leading works on EC merger control: J Cook and C Kerse, *EC Merger Control*, 3rd edn, (Sweet & Maxwell, London, 2000); MP Broberg, *The European Commission's Jurisdiction to Scrutinise Mergers* (Kluwer, The Hague, 1998).

prohibit mergers according to Article 8 Merger Regulation. Article 2 (1) Merger Regulation provides for a list of factors to be taken into account, including market structure, the company's economic power, sources of supply and entry barriers. In deciding the admissibility of mergers the Commission can take account of actual or potential competition from businesses outside the European Union, as will be explained further below.

The Merger Regulation is especially relevant to the defence industries, as mergers, take-overs, and particularly joint ventures are increasingly common in this field. Whereas the combined Western European defence budgets amount to only 60 per cent of that of the United States, there are between two to three times more suppliers.[29] For example, six Member States have at least one supplier of military combat aircraft,[30] while the United States have only two. European companies are too small to be competitive and a certain consolidation through mergers is considered necessary to preserve the European defence industrial base. Such a consolidation is also necessary to meet the capability objectives of the EU described in chapter 3[31] with European products. Consolidation is happening slowly with Article 296 (1) (b) EC in existence, and a more liberalised defence market is likely to increase merger activity, especially mergers involving undertakings from different Member States. However, as the Commission pointed out, this rationalisation is happening mainly in the aerospace sector, not with respect to land-based systems and naval shipyards.[32] Moreover, it is very limited in the ten new Member States which joined the Union in May 2004.[33]

It should be noted, however, that so far there have not been many full mergers between companies from different Member States as such. Instead Europe's defence companies have established project specific joint ventures in particular business areas.[34] Examples are the 'Eurofighter/Typhoon' fighter aircraft project of the German 'Daimler-Benz Aerospace', the Italian 'Alenia', 'British Aerospace', and the Spanish 'CASA' or the 'Horizon' frigate international joint venture of the 'French Direction des Constructions Navales', the Italian 'Fincatieri' and the British 'GEC-Marconi Naval Systems'.[35] Industrial co-operation of this kind offers

[29] B Wiener, *British Aerospace*, Merrill Lynch, Pierce, Fenner and Smith Limited, March 1997 as cited by *Defence Trade: European Initiatives to Integrate the Defence Market*, United States General Accounting Office, Report to the Secretary of Defence, Washington DC, October 1997, at 9 (hereinafter 'US–GAO'). The figure of two thirds of the United States market advocated by former EU External Relations Commissioner Chris Patten is subject to disagreement. The Centre for European Reform argues that the combined annual defence budgets of the EU Member States is about half that of the USA. The latter spends about US$290 billion annually. The defence budgets of the EU Member States have declined by 22% in real terms 1992–2001. See: S Duke, 'CESDP: Nice's Overtrumped Success?' (2001) 6 *European Foreign Affairs Review* 155, at 164.

[30] France, Germany, Italy, Spain, Sweden, and United Kingdom.

[31] At 97–100.

[32] *Towards an EU Defence Equipment Policy*, COM (2003) 113 final, Schmitt, above n 23, at 169.

[33] Above.

[34] See: Global Defence Industry Survey, *The Economist*, 14 June 1997, at 13. An important exception, which can be seen as a first example for future developments, was the full merger of Eurocopter France (Aérospatiale) and Eurocopter Deutschland (MBB) to form Eurocopter in June 1997.

[35] For further examples see: US–GAO, above n 29, table 2 at 11.

advantages, such as economies of scale and learning effects in manufacturing. Moreover, wasteful duplication can be avoided. However, the components of the joint ventures are still run separately. Trans-border mergers involving a change of ownership appear to be problematic.[36] This is mainly due to traditional attitudes in both the governments of the Member States and the defence companies themselves. As the defence industries have a strategic significance and are part of the national defence effort, it is still widely assumed that they cannot be owned or controlled by 'foreigners'. Nevertheless, these co-operation activities create dominant positions or even monopolies and it is very likely that full mergers will be established in the near future. Some European companies already acquired others or established joint ventures or cross share holdings not tied to a particular programme. For example, the French 'Matra' and 'British Aerospace' merged their missiles business to form 'Matra BA Dynamics'.[37] Furthermore, there are numerous full mergers between companies from the same Member State. For example in the United Kingdom 'GEC' bought the military vehicle and shipbuilder 'VSEL' and in Italy 'Finmeccanica' gained control of about 75 per cent of the Italian defence industry through take-overs. Nevertheless, the European defence companies are consolidating at a much slower pace than their competitors from the United States.[38] Moreover, the EC merger control regime is stricter than that in the United States.

The application of the Merger Regulation to concentrations in the defence sector was made clear in the *Eurocopter*-decision.[39] The Commission decided that the Regulation applies, but that the particular merger was compatible with the internal market. The Commission reported in Spring 2003 that several mergers in the military sector were notified to them under the old Merger Regulation, but that so far they have not objected to any of these operations.[40] Nevertheless, they anticipate that they might have to object to individual mergers in the defence sector in the future since recently more cross-border mergers occurred.[41]

3.1. Recital 19

Similar to the Public Procurement Directives discussed in chapter 7, the Merger Regulation is subject to defence and security exemptions. First it is subject to the armaments and secrecy exemptions in Article 296 EC discussed in chapter 5. Recital 19 of the Merger Regulation reads:

> "[...] the exclusive application of this Regulation to concentrations with a Community dimension is without prejudice to Article 296 of the Treaty, and does

[36] *Towards an EU Defence Equipment Policy*, COM (2003) 113 final, Schmitt, above n 23, at 177.

[37] For further examples see: US–GAO, above n 29, figure at 13.

[38] US–GAO, above, at 9.

[39] Case 0.17, *Aérospatiale/MBB* [1992] 4 CMLR M70; see also Case M086, *Thompson/Pilkington*, (23 October 1991).

[40] *Towards an EU Defence Equipment Policy*, COM (2003) 113 final, Schmitt, above n 23, at 173.

[41] Above. 'Recently, however, complex cross-border mergers have occurred, which call for a thorough assessment of their overall impact on competition, notably with respect to dual-use or civil products.'

> not prevent the Member States from taking appropriate measures to protect legitimate interests other than those pursued by this Regulation, provided that such measures are compatible with the general principles and other provisions of Community law."

This recital represents an armaments- and secrecy exemption comparable to Article 10 of the new Public Procurement Directive discussed in chapter 7.[42] It clarifies that the application of the Merger Regulation is subject to the provisions of Article 296 EC. In contrast to Article 10 Public Procurement Directive, Recital 19 of the Merger Regulation is not an 'independent' exemption. This difference could be explained by the different nature of a Directive and a Regulation. A Directive is not final: it depends on the implementation by the Member States it is addressed to. Its provisions have to be as clear as possible and rules and exceptions need to be spelt out to facilitate implementation. A Regulation is final: it does not depend on further implementation. Moreover, in the case of the Merger Regulation it is largely addressed to the Commission who have to apply it in practice. Therefore a clear armaments- and secrecy exemption is less essential and the recognition of Article 296 EC in a recital is sufficient. However, the effect is the same as both provisions make a direct reference to Article 296 EC. Therefore the effect of Recital 19 depends on the interpretation of Article 296 EC discussed in chapter 5[43] and above in the context of Articles 81 and 82 EC. A merger in the hard defence sector, which is imposed or encouraged by a Member State, may escape the application of the Merger Regulation if the Member State or the Member States in question can successfully invoke Article 296 (1) (b) EC. Following the principles developed in *Commission* v. *Spain*,[44] the Member States have to specifically invoke the exemption and prove that a situation justifying its use actually exists, subject to review by the Court. Ten years before the ruling, the Council creating the 1989 Merger Regulation may have interpreted Article 296 (1) (b) EC as an automatic exclusion of hard defence material. However, *Commission* v. *Spain* made clear that the provision has to be interpreted narrowly. Similar to Article 3 Supplies Directive discussed in chapter 7,[45] a Recital 19 automatically excluding all hard defence material from the Merger Regulation would have been against the Treaty. An amendment to overcome this defect, however, was never necessary since the wording of Recital 19 accommodates the ruling in *Commission* v. *Spain*. This is also a possible reason for the fact that the wording of Recital 19 adopted that of Recital 28 of the 1989 Merger Regulation almost *verbatim*, only changing the reference to the provision in the EC Treaty which changed through the Treaty of Amsterdam. Recital 19 has to be interpreted in the light of the case law of the Court.

It is submitted, that Article 296 (1) (b) EC might allow a Member State to authorise a merger in the hard defence sector, even when the Commission has

[42] At 208–213.
[43] At 142–163.
[44] Case C–414/97, *Commission v Spain*, above n 20.
[45] At 203–208.

prohibited that merger. However, this is not clear, as a conflict between a Member State and the Commission about the prohibition of a merger in the hard defence sector has been avoided so far. According to Bellamy & Child, the attitude of Member States with regards to their jurisdiction over defence sector concentrations *vis-à-vis* the Commission differs.[46] While the United Kingdom[47] and France[48] guard their control over mergers in the armaments industries, Germany is less concerned about the matter.

3.2. The Legitimate Interests Exception

Recital 19 also provides that legitimate interests can justify derogation from the Regulation, provided such Member State measures are "appropriate" and "compatible with the general principles and other provisions of Community law". The concept of legitimate interests allowing derogation is spelt out in detail in Article 21 Merger Regulation. According to Article 21 (3) Merger Regulation no Member State may apply its national competition legislation to any concentration with a Community dimension. However, according to Article 21 (4) Merger Regulation Member States may take appropriate measures to protect legitimate interests "other than those taken into consideration by this Regulation and compatible with the general principles and other provisions of Community law". Public security is one of these legitimate interests. Article 21 (4) of the 2004 Merger Regulation adopts the wording of Article 21 (3) of the 1989 Merger Regulation almost *verbatim*.

There is no judgment of the European Court of Justice or the Court of First Instance to clarify the interpretation of the legitimate interest exemption. In *IBM/CGI*[49] the French authorities invoked the then Article 21 (3) Merger Regulation, now Article 21 (4), taking measures to protect public security. Moreover, in *Thomson-CSF/Racal*[50] the Commission cleared the transaction but the United Kingdom authorities announced their intention to consider the public security aspects of the transaction under the United Kingdom Fair Trading Act 1973. However, there has never been a judgment of the European Court of Justice or the Court of First Instance concerning a merger where the legitimate interests exception was invoked for reasons of public security.

[46] Above n 7, at 6–265.

[47] See Case M529, *GEC/VSEL* (27 January 1999); Case M724 *GEC/Thomson CSF (II)* (15 May 1996); Case M820, *British Aerospace/Lagadère* (press release IP (96) 851 of 25 September 1996); Case M1258, *GEC Marconi/Alenia* (press release IP/98/782 of 31 August 1998); Case M1438, *British Aerospace/GEC Marconi* (25 June 1999 and press release IP/99/426 of 28 June 1999); Case M1858, *Thompson/Racal (II)* (15 June 2000 and press release IP/00/628 of 16 June 2000) as cited by Bellamy and Child, above.

[48] According to Bellamy and Child, above n 7, at n 25, p 469, the French attitude might be changing. In M1745, *EADS* (11 May 2000) the French government raised no objection to the Commission's assessment of the merger as far as it affected the markets for military satellites, guided weapons, drones, defence vehicles, and defence electronics under the Merger Regulation.

[49] Case M336, *IBM/CGI*, (19 May 1993), XXII Report on Competition Policy (1993), at point 321.

[50] Case M1858, *Thomson-CSP/Racal (II)*, (15 June 2000, Press Release 18/00/628 of 16 June 2000).

One issue in the context of the interpretation of the exception concerns the competencies with regards to the authorisation or prohibition of mergers. When the Merger Regulation was adopted Council and Commission issued some policy and interpretative statements on individual articles in the Council Minutes. According to these statements the legitimate interests exception does not enable Member States to authorise a concentration that the Commission has prohibited. It seems clear that, as far as soft defence material is concerned, when the Commission prohibits a merger under the Regulation no Member State can permit it but a Member State may prohibit it even if the Commission has permitted it.

Another issue in this context concerns the standard of review that could be applied by the European Court of Justice in case the Commission or another Member State challenged the use of the exemption by a Member State. It is submitted that the Court will subject the use of Article 21 (4) Merger Regulation to a strict level of scrutiny, comparable to that of the first group of exemptions in the EC Treaty discussed in chapter 4. In other words the intensive scrutiny applied to exemptions such as Article 30 EC including the proportionality test is applied to the legitimate interests exemption. First, Article 21 (4) refers to "public security" as a legitimate interest justifying derogation. This is the term used in the public security exemptions in the EC Treaty. Second, as pointed out above, Recital 19 stipulates that legitimate interests can justify derogation from the Regulation, provided such Member State measures are "appropriate" and "compatible with the general principles and other provisions of Community law". The word "appropriate" is a direct reference to the proportionality test and the notion of "general principles and other provisions of Community law" is certainly wide enough to include the test.[51]

Recital 19 introduces two different exemptions. On the one hand there is the national security exemption of hard defence material through the reference to Article 296 (1) (b) EC. On the other hand there is the public security exemption as part of the legitimate interests exemption. This means that the security exemptions in the Merger Regulation reflect the system of security exemption in the EC Treaty discussed in chapters 4–6. The secondary legal instrument adopted the system of primary Community law. This is not surprising since secondary Community law has to comply with the EC Treaty. Thus, comparable to the situation under the EC Treaty, the public security exemption in Article 21 (4) Merger Regulation only applies to material not covered by Article 296 (1) (b) EC. It only applies to civil and dual use material not on the 1958 List according to Article 296 (2) EC.[52]

[51] Proportionality is a general principle of European Community law, see for example: Case C–181/84, *R v Intervention Board, ex parte ED & F Man (Sugar) Ltd* [1985] ECR 2889; P Craig and G de Búrca, *EU Law*, 3rd edn, (OUP, Oxford, 2003) 371–79.

[52] See ch 5 at 143–148 for details.

3.3. Mergers and the Defence Industrial Base

It is a common view that future mergers will be necessary as part of a consolidation process to preserve the defence industrial base.[53] Examples of recent mergers were stipulated above. This trend is likely to continue[54] and is increasingly encouraged by governments.[55] The consolidation process through mergers involves a conflict between the Community interest of competition manifested in the Merger Regulation on the one hand and the survival of the defence industrial base and its strategic implications on the other hand.[56] The Commission argues that this conflict would be eliminated as a result of the establishment of the common market for defence equipment.[57] From a legal point of view there are several possible solutions to this conflict.

3.3.1. Exclusion

One solution could be the general exclusion of the defence industry from the rules on mergers. Four arguments can be put forward in favour of this approach.

First, there would be neither a loss nor a gain in competition after the emergence of large inter-State defence companies. The situation would be very similar to that of today, only on the European rather than the national level, as the 'Eurocopter'-example has shown.

The survival of the European defence industry is a second argument. As mergers are necessary to preserve competitiveness of the defence industrial base with competition outside the EU such as the United States, it would be suicidal to prohibit these mergers and take-overs in order to preserve competition within the Union. There is no room for a competition policy when the industries it seeks to

[53] *Implementing European Union Strategy on Defence-Related Industries*, COM (97) 583 final, 12 November 1997, at 24; W Walker and S Willet, 'Restructuring the European Defence Industrial Base' (1993) *Journal of Defence Economics* 141, 147 and 152; K Hartley, 'Public Procurement and Competitiveness' (1989) 3 *Journal of Common Market Studies* 237, 241; and K Hartley, 'Competition in Defence Contracting in the United Kingdom' (1992) 1 *Public Procurement Law Review* 440, 441; J Lovering, 'Military Expenditure and the Restructuring of Capitalism; the Military Industry in Britain' (1990) 14 *Cambridge Journal of Economics* 453, 458 and 460; S Arrowsmith, *The Law of Public and Utilities Procurement* (Sweet & Maxwell, London, 1996) 849–50; 'Towards a Euro-Mix', *The Economist*, 11 March 1995, at 30; US–GAO, above n 29, at 9–12; implied in *Towards an EU Defence Equipment Policy*, COM (2003) 113 final, above n 22; for an alternative view see Vredeling Report, *Towards a Stronger Europe*, at point 32: 'In our view however, mergers are not the answer for the short term. They will do nothing to counteract the effects of the real barriers to free trading and co-operation which exist between European nations [...]'.

[54] Arrowsmith, above, at 851.

[55] Former Chief of Defence Procurement, Roger Freeman, in a speech on 7 December 1994: see *The Times*, 7 December 1994, 'Freeman to Call for more European Defence Deals'; or 'Conze [former director of the French defence procurement authority Délégation Générale pour l'Armement-DGA] calls for European Mergers, *Jane's Defence Weekly*, 21 January 1996, at 29.

[56] *Implementing European Union Strategy on Defence-Related Industries*, COM (97) 583 final, 12 November 1997, at 24.

[57] Above. '[a]s far as geographic markets remain, further concentration may aggravate monopolistic inefficiencies that can extend into civilian areas of business. On the other hand, if progress towards a common market for defence equipment is achieved, and provided that conditions of competition are preserved, business consolidation may contribute favourably to European competitiveness on a global market.'

keep competitive do not exist any more because their structure makes defence companies too small to compete with the United States. The protection of the indigenous defence industries would certainly be another way to keep them from going out of business; however, this would involve all the negative side effects of protectionism, such as complacency, high prices, and ultimately inferior products.

Competition from outside the EU is another argument to justify the exclusion of the defence industry from the Community rules on competition and mergers. Because of this there is a sufficiently high level of competition and the defence industries are competitive enough to be a part of it.

A last argument is that these mergers are possibly the only way to avoid duplication and to minimise the costs of defence purchases.

The disadvantages would be the restricted influence of the Commission on the defence industries and thereby on a considerable part of the industry as a whole.

3.3.2. Balance System

A solution less restrictive on the influence of the Commission and Community law is the adoption of a balance system. As explained before, the Merger Regulation itself takes only limited account of wider questions of industrial policy and the Commission can only take actual or potential competition from outside the Union into consideration. This will be hardly sufficient to reconcile the interests of competition and of the preservation of the defence industrial base.

Before the adoption of the previous Merger Regulation some of the Member States and the Commission had argued that the regulation should also be used as an instrument of industrial policy. These Member States argued that the Commission should be able to approve concentrations between businesses with strong positions in Europe if they would be better placed to withstand competition from third countries. The European Parliament took a similar stance. Following the decision of the Commission in *Aérospatiale-Alenia/deHaviland*[58] the European Parliament passed a resolution concluding that the Merger Regulation should be revised to require decisions to take account of the concentrations likely impact on European industrial strength and of its social, regional and environmental consequences.[59] However, apart from these considerations account should also be taken of aspects of European or national security issues.

There are a number of ways in which a balance system could be implemented. It is submitted, that a balance system comparable to the balance system for competition law as manifested in exemptions as in Article 81 (3) EC and a rule of reason should be introduced to the Merger Regulation. This system should take into account the preservation of the defence industrial base as a matter of industrial policy. This model is submitted here for the defence sector although it might be viable beyond that.[60] The competition regime of the EU is long established and it

[58] Case M053, [1991] OJ L–334/42 [1992] 4 CMLR M2.
[59] European Parliament Resolution, [1991] OJ C–280/140.
[60] Already proposed by the author in 'European Defence Procurement: Towards a Comprehensive Approach', above n 1, at 1122–23.

provides the experience and case law to be the base for a model to solve the conflicts between the liberalised defence procurement regime and the laws on merger control.

The competition and merger control regimes of the Community are concerned with anti-competitive practices on a Community level. Therefore, only the preservation of the European defence industrial base, rather than the preservation of the national defence industrial bases of the individual Member States, can be a basis for the application of the balance system of the EC-Treaty in the long run. However, political reality in the early 21st Century still makes security a matter of national concern and there is no equivalent Community security interest replacing the national security interests so far—not even with the Second Pillar of the TEU. As discussed in chapters 2 and 3, Article 11 (1) TEU speaks of the "independence and integrity of the Union" and even the "security of the Union" as objectives of the Common Foreign and Security Policy (hereinafter CFSP). The Constitutional Treaty discussed in chapters 10 and 11 also includes "the Union's security" in its Article I-16. Moreover, for the Commission the emergence of a European Security and Defence Policy (hereinafter ESDP) as part of the Common Foreign and Security Policy (hereinafter CFSP) is one of two reasons[61] to present its *Towards an EU Defence Equipment Policy* Communication in 2003,[62] so shortly after its Communications on the same matter in 1996 and 1997.[63] However, CFSP and EDSP remain intergovernmental frameworks outside the more supranational Community Pillar, which includes the competition law regime and the Merger Regulation. The purpose of the exemptions in Recital 19 and Article 21 (4) Merger Regulation is to accommodate the fact that only the Member States can guarantee their national security. The exemptions separate the more supranational Community Pillar from the intergovernmental CFSP Pillar of the TEU. The EU is in no position to take responsibility for national security. Before the Member States have agreed on a common defence, which is also mentioned in Articles 17 TEU and I-16 Constitutional Treaty, there is no such Community or Union security interest that could replace the national security interests of the Member States.[64]

Therefore national security interests must be taken into account when dealing with competition in the defence industries. For the period until the introduction of a common defence this national security interest in a national defence industrial

[61] The other reason being the transformation in the defence industrial sector.

[62] COM (2003) 113 final, Schmitt, above n 23.

[63] *The Challenges Facing the European Defence-Related Industries, A Contribution for Action at European Level*, COM (96) 10 final, 24 November 1996 (hereinafter '*The Challenges Facing the Defence-Related Industries*'); and *Implementing European Union Strategy on Defence-Related Industries*, COM (97) 583 final, 12 November 1997. On the earlier see: M Trybus, 'The Challenges Facing the European Defence-Related Industry-Communication COM (96) 08 of the Commission' (1996) 5 *Public Procurement Law Review* CS 98–103.

[64] Nevertheless the European defence industrial base is an emerging concept. OCCAR and ESA use the term quite frequently as well as the European Defence Industries Group (EDIG), see for example: The European Defence Industry, An Agenda for the 1996 Intergovernmental Conference—Memorandum of EDIG, Brussels, 30 May 1995.

base has to be a part of the balancing of the objectives of competition and national security. The Commission and European Court of Justice should therefore, for the time being, recognise the preservation of the national defence industrial bases, as opposed to the European defence industrial base, as a balance factor. Depending on the individual case, the European institutions should allow mergers in the defence industries if they are justified by the interest in national security to preserve a national defence industrial base. This could be explicitly stipulated in the Merger Regulation as a specific Recital or even exemption – although this is not absolutely necessary.

However, it needs to be pointed out that a balancing system taking account of national defence industrial bases is only a solution for the short term. The importance given to national security as opposed to Union security in Community law does not reflect the economic and technological reality of the European defence industries at the beginning of the 21st Century. Only very few Member States, notably France and Sweden, still had the defence industrial base to produce the 'high end' of the current generation of defence technology, for example large combat aircraft. No Member State will have the base to produce the next generation on a national basis. Member States have to buy most of their equipment from abroad, including the United States and the Russian Federation. Moreover, most large defence equipment has components purchased abroad, there is no purely British or German tank or submarine. The large Member States already reacted to this situation by collaborative projects, such as the British-German-Italian-Spanish 'Eurofighter/Typhoon' mentioned above or the 'Lockheed Martin'-led 'Joint Strike Fighter F-35'.[65] Moreover, they established organisational structures, such as the Western European Armaments Group and Organisation (WEAG/WEAO) and Organisation for Joint Armaments Procurement (OCCAR) described in chapter 7[66] to facilitate these projects. Generally, a national defence industrial base as part of the national defence effort, which is both independent and comprehensive, is technologically, financially, and politically not feasible for any Member State. Therefore the importance of national security should be supplemented with a concept of Union security with respect to the defence industries. In other words, the balancing system should successively move away from taking account of the preservation of national defence industrial bases and move towards taking account of the European defence industrial base. Due to the narrow interpretation of Article 296 (1) (b) EC in *Commission* v. *Spain*, this does not require a repeal of the armaments exemption. The move towards taking account of the European defence industrial base could be conducted within the current legal framework.[67] The provision accommodates national security as opposed to

[65] According to the Commission in *Towards an EU Defence Equipment Policy*, COM (2003) 113 final, Schmitt, above n 23, at 169, the biggest defence programme in history, involving US$200 billion over the next 30 years. The United States and four Member States are co-operating. The order numbers illustrate the purchasing power of the partners. The United States Department of Defence ordered 2900 aircraft and the largest European order is 150 aircraft.

[66] At 222–224.

[67] The Constitutional Treaty discussed in chs 10, 11, and 12 adopted this legal framework.

Union security. However, the emerging concept of Union security could significantly reduce the importance of the armaments exemption in practice. Member States would no longer invoke the exemption to derogate from Community law.

3.3.3. Exemptions Similar to Article 81 (3) EC

This model of a balance system could be introduced in a way similar to an exemption under Article 81 (3) EC.[68] Applied to the Merger Regulation this would not be concerned with restricted practices but with balancing the restrictive effects of the merger itself with other interests such as national security and defence industrial policy considerations. Non-essential restrictions or restrictions that might interfere with the functioning of the internal market are left to be decided under this provision. Article 81 (3) EC envisages a balance between the costs and benefits of the restrictive practice.[69] This balance should be the aim of a provision for mergers in the defence industries as well. To achieve this balance the same requirements as for an exemption under Article 81 (3) EC should be fulfilled.

As a first requirement for invoking this exemption, the practice must contribute to improving the production or distribution of goods or to promoting technical or economic progress. Mergers in the defence sector would lead to economies of scale, learning effects in manufacturing, synergies, and could help to avoid wasteful duplication in research and development.[70] However, real competition is impossible without some duplication – in other words, without having at least two products of the same kind. This duplication is something Europe may wish to avoid because of the high costs this involves, costs ultimately born by the taxpayer in times of tight budgets. Nevertheless, there might be some industries that can support two or more companies in the same segment, for example armoured vehicles or small guns. The question is how to avoid duplication when there is no room for two or more firms, and to secure or even increase competition at the same time. For most equipment at the 'high end' of military technology there is only room for one producer in Europe. The European remaining

[68] Article 81(3) EC reads:

(a) The provisions of para 1 may, however, be declared inapplicable in the case of:
(b) any agreement or category of agreement between undertakings;
(c) any decision or category of decision by associations of undertakings;
(d) any concerted practices or category of concerted practices
(e) which contributes to improving the production or distribution of goods or to promoting technical or economic progress, while allowing consumers a fair share of the resulting benefit, and which does not:
(f) impose on the undertakings concerned restrictions which are not indispensable to the attainment of these objectives;
(g) afford such undertakings the possibility of eliminating competition in respect of a substantial part of the products in question.

[69] S Weatherill and P Beaumont, *EU Law*, 3rd edn, (Penguin, London, 1999) 827.

[70] *Towards an EU Defence Equipment Policy*, COM (2003) 113 final, Schmitt, above n 23, at 174; *The Challenges Facing the Defence-Related Industries*, COM (96) 10 final, at 8; de Vestel, above n 13, at 57; A Cox and K Hartley, *The Costs of Europe in Defence Procurement—Executive Summary*, The Commission of the European Communities DG III, July 1992 (released December 1994) at 22.

companies active in the production of combat aircraft, submarines, or large warships will merge or exit the market.

A possible solution for keeping more than one supplier in business is to make the procurement decisions discussed in chapter 7 at an early stage of equipment developments, after the perception but before the production of the product. This provides competition without duplication, at least of production. Disadvantages, however, are that defects in the production phase can only be detected after the award of the contract and other potential competitors may go out of business so competition may not exist for the next contract. The United States Department of Defence tries to maintain at least two competitors in each sector of arms in order to benefit from competition. The Department of Defence even keeps companies artificially alive by financing all of their research and development to produce different prototypes for each tender. For this reason the unsuccessful company has still gained in technical capability and can survive until the next tender.[71] However, it is doubtful that even all Member States taken together could afford such a practice.

It should also be noted, that the defence industries of the United States represent considerable competition.[72] A certain amount of competition would therefore be secured anyway if the Union were prepared to accept global competition. Problems here may again be national security considerations and the ability to obtain reciprocal agreements with the United States.[73]

Furthermore, technical progress would be promoted by the liberalisation of the market, as the preservation of a defence technological base would keep Europe in the run of technical progress.[74] Without liberalisation and industrial restructuring through mergers the defence industrial base would be in danger, as defence companies would exit the market or be bought by their American competitors. The Member States could eventually be cut off from technical progress in defence.[75] More generally, the preservation of the defence industrial base would at the same time promote economic progress, so this requirement may be fulfilled. Everything will, of course, depend on the facts of the individual case.

The second requirement for invoking an exemption under Article 81 (3) EC is that the agreement or practice allows consumers a fair share in the resulting benefit. Consumers could benefit from a liberalised market and a restructured industry in three ways. First, they would benefit as workers because the preservation of the defence industrial base preserves employment. Second, they would benefit as tax payers, because liberalisation and the avoidance of duplication are the only way to cut defence budgets. Finally, they could benefit as customers, indirectly, as

[71] De Vestel, above n 13, at 45.

[72] See the British 'Policy of Contestable Markets'—where monopolies exist, the United Kingdom Ministry of Defence has threatened to open up the markets to foreign competition.

[73] De Vestel, above n 13, at 95; *EDIG Study Paper on Main US Discriminating Measures and Practices in the Defence Field*, Reference EPP/93/04, EDIG, Brussels 29 September 1993 on the relations on civil procurement see A Halford, 'An Overview of EC - United States Trade Relations in the Area of Public Procurement' (1995) 4 *Public Procurement Law Review* 35.

[74] *The Challenges Facing the Defence-Related Industries*, COM (96) 10 final, at 10.

[75] Above.

the only customer is the State they belong to, because the practices may lead to more competitive products.

The next requirement is, that the agreement must not impose on the undertaking concerned restrictions that are not indispensable. Whether this requirement is fulfilled depends on the individual case.

The last requirement is that the agreement must not afford such undertakings the possibility of eliminating competition in respect of a substantial part of the products in question. There are a lot of competitors outside the Union such as the United States, Brazil, or the Russian Federation. This competition from outside the EU guarantees a sufficient level of competition for undertakings which have merged or adopted practices actually in the scope of Article 81 EC. So this last requirement is often fulfilled as well. The fact that this may well depend on a government's willingness to buy foreign products and that it may be reluctant to do so for security or economic reasons or because of difficulties in achieving reciprocal agreements with third countries has to be noted as a reservation to this result.

This part of the balance system has the advantage, that the law is very clear and therefore easy to handle (uniformity of interpretation).[76] The Commission noted that producers need a transparent framework in which restructuring can take place and that both industry and governments would appreciate clarity.[77] Article 81 (3) EC gives the power to grant exemptions exclusively to the Commission. Article 81 (3) EC therefore gives the Commission the maximum supervision and control.

There are disadvantages too. The Commission has just a limited capacity as far as staff and resources are concerned. This leads to a heavy workload and therefore to long delays. These delays lead to legal uncertainty amongst business people.[78] However, this problem is now addressed to a large extent by the fact that since the new Council-Regulation 1/2003/EC,[79] Article 81 (3) EC is directly effective. Previously national courts could not deal with the question as to whether an exemption could be granted or not.[80] The European Court of Justice could only deal with the case when there was a decision of the Commission beforehand. The increased involvement of the Court of First Instance in competition cases did already help to ease the burden of the Court of Justice. However, the involvement of national courts through the direct effect of Article 81 (3) EC and the increased involvement of national competition authorities as parts of a general decentralisation of EC competition policy introduced by the new Competition Regulation 1/2003/EC will ensure a more efficient competition regime and more legal certainty. Hence this disadvantage does not apply as much as it did before the new Regulation.

[76] J Steiner and N Wood, *Textbook on EC Law*, 8th edn, (OUP, Oxford, 2003) 424.

[77] *Towards an EU Defence Equipment Policy*, COM (2003) 113 final, Schmitt, above n 23, at 173.

[78] Steiner and Wood, above n 76, at 425.

[79] Council Regulation 1/2003/EC of 16 December 2002 on the implementation of the rules on competition laid down in articles 81 and 82 of the Treaty [2003] OJ L–1/1 as amended by Council-Regulation 411/2004/EC [2004] L–68/1.

[80] Weatherill and Beaumont, above n 68, at 825.

A similar provision to Article 81 (3) EC in the Merger Regulation would allow the Commission or another authority to strike a balance between the objectives of the Regulation and the preservation of the defence industrial base and national security issues. A merger could be allowed, for example, if it preserves a particular national or European production capability, if it facilitates collaboration or if it enables indigenous research and development.

In summary, there are two major solutions for the conflict between the interests of competition and the preservation of the defence industrial base submitted here. First, the exclusion of the defence industries from the law of mergers. Second, the adoption of a balance system comparable to the balance system provided by the competition regime of the EC Treaty. The latter solution would allow the competent institution to strike a balance between the objectives involved: competition and merger control on the one side and the preservation of the defence industrial base and national security on the other side.

4. STATE AIDS

Another area of concern is State aids[81] as defined in Articles 87 to 89 EC.[82] Public support constituting State aid may be in breach of Article 87 EC[83] if the measure

[81] Leading works on the law of State aids: A Evans, *EC Law of State Aids* (OUP, Oxford, 1997); I Harden, (ed), *State Aid: Community Law and Policy* (Bundesanzeiger Verlag, Bonn, 1993).

[82] *The Challenges Facing the Defence-Related Industries*, COM (96) 10 final, at 22–24.

[83] Article 87 EC reads:

1. Save as otherwise provided in this Treaty, any aid granted by a Member State or through State resources in any form whatsoever which distorts or threatens to distort competition by favouring certain undertakings or the production of certain goods shall, in so far as it affects trade between Member States, be incompatible with the common market.
2. The following shall be compatible with the common market:
   aid having a social character, granted to individual consumers, provided that such aid is granted without discrimination related to the origin of the products concerned;
   aid to make good the damage caused by natural disasters or exceptional occurrences;
   aid granted to the economy of certain areas of the Federal Republic of Germany affected by the division of Germany, insofar as such aid is required in order to compensate for the economic disadvantages caused by that division.
3. The following shall be considered to be compatible with the common market:
   aid to promote the economic development of areas where the standard of living is abnormally low or where there is serious underemployment;
   aid to promote the execution of an important project of common interest or to remedy a serious disturbance in the economy of a Member State;
   aid to facilitate the development of certain economic activities or of certain economic areas, where such aid does not adversely affect trading conditions to an extent contrary to the common interest;
   aid to promote culture and heritage conservation where such aid does not affect trading conditions and competition in the Community to an extent that is contrary to the common interest;
   such other categories of aid as may be specified by decision of the Council acting by a qualified majority on a proposal from the Commission.

The 2003 Convention on the Future of Europe adopted Article 87 EC in Article III-167 Constitutional Treaty (December 2004 version). On the Constitutional Treaty see Part III of this book.

distorts or threatens competition and is capable of affecting trade between Member States.[84] The Commission is of the opinion that these rules offer an appropriate framework for a European market for defence goods.[85]

European Governments support their defence industries with various benefits,[86] thereby distorting competition and affecting trade between Member States.[87] According to the Commission this is due to the special characteristics of the defence sector and in particular to the close relationship with public authorities.[88] The arms trade between Member States is affected because the beneficiaries of these aids are competing with enterprises in other Member States even if they do not export armaments to these States. Competition is affected because companies who benefited from State aid are competing with companies who have to operate without such public support.

4.1. Application of Article 296 (1) (b) EC

Companies producing hard defence material on the list according to Article 296 (2) EC could be exempt from the State aids regime of the EC Treaty by virtue of Article 296 (1) (b) EC. The armaments exemption applies within the limits of its narrow interpretation after *Commission* v. *Spain* discussed in chapter 5 and above. According to the Commission, Article 296 (1) (b) EC had not yet been applied to State aids in the defence industrial sector until March 2003.[89]

In September 2003 the Court of First Instance decided the case of *Fiocchi Munizioni SpA* v. *Commission of the European Communities* discussed in chapter 5,[90] where they mainly clarified procedural points in relation to Articles 296 to 298 EC. First, in contrast to the normal procedure, a Member State which considers it necessary to invoke the exemption in Article 296 (1) (b) EC from the beginning does not have to notify the Commission in advance. In such a case the rules on competition do not apply. Moreover, the Commission cannot use the examination procedure for State aids laid down in Article 88 EC.[91] Second, the Court emphasised that the two specific remedies of Article 298 EC are prescribed by the Treaty in relation to measures adopted by Member States on the basis of Article 296 (1) (b) EC. Within the context of bilateral examinations according to Article 298 subparagraph 1 EC it is within the discretion of the Commission to decide whether the invocation by the Member State concerned is *prima facie* credible. Contrary to the situation in the context of Article 88 EC, the Commission is under

[84] Case C–730/79, *Philip Morris Holland v Commission* [1980] ECR 2671, at 2688; [1981] CMLR 321.
[85] *The Challenges Facing the Defence-Related Industries*, COM (96) 10 final, at 22–24.
[86] See for example on the 'cash injections' of the French government to major national suppliers: JAC Lewis, 'Keeping French Industry Afloat', *Jane's Defence Weekly*, 16 November 1994, at 26.
[87] *The Challenges Facing the Defence-Related Industries*, COM (96) 10 final, at 22.
[88] *Towards an EU Defence Equipment Policy*, COM (2003) 113 final, Schmitt, above n 23, at 173.
[89] Above.
[90] See Case T–26/01, *Fiocchi Munizioni SpA v Commission of the European Communities*, (30 September 2003), for details see ch 5 at 158–160.
[91] Case T–26/01, above, at para 59.

no obligation to adopt a decision concerning the measure at issue. Moreover, it has no power to address a final Decision or Directive to the Member State concerned.[92] In this context the Court also differentiated the facts of *Fiocchi Munizioni* from the facts of Commission Decision 1999/763/EC of 17 March 1999 on the measures, implemented and proposed, by the Free and Hanse City of Bremen, Germany in favour of 'Lürssen Maritime Beteiligungen GmbH & Co. KG'.[93] In the latter case the Commission had opened the procedure provided in Article 88 (2) EC ending with a decision in the course of which Germany relied in her defence on the application of Article 296 (1) (b) EC. By contrast, in *Fiocchi Munizioni* the Commission had opened bilateral examinations under Article 298 subparagraph 1 EC. However, based on *Commission* v. *Spain*, *Fiocchi Munizioni*, and Commission Decision 1999/763/EC it can be said that the EC Treaty including the State aid regime applies to the hard defence material producing industries unless a Member State specifically invokes Article 296 EC. Moreover, invoking the exemption is subject to bilateral examinations and judicial review under Article 298 EC. Due to their wide margin of discretion over national security issues Member States will normally be successful in practice. However, the exemption is not automatic.

4.2. Other Exceptions

There are a number of exceptions under Article 87 (2) EC[94] which apply automatically and some under Article 87 (3) EC[95] which may be granted at the discretion of the Commission. The most important exceptions potentially relevant to defence are Article 87 (3) (b) and (c) EC.

Article 87 (3) (c) EC provides for aids for the economic development of certain areas and aids in the interest of the development of certain branches of industry. In relation to these sectorial aids the Commission is of the opinion that these can be permitted in relation to the so called "sunset" industries,[96] which have run into difficulties for external reasons or are struggling and "sunrise" industries, which are mainly new technological sectors with good future prospects. The former are to be supported by defined restructuring programmes like modernisation, the latter by any aid to facilitate their development,[97] but marketing aids as well as aids for the expansion of capacity are in principle seen as inadmissible. On the other hand aids may be regularly permitted, subject to strict conditions, in case of serious difficulties making temporary restructuring aid necessary. Greece, Spain, and Portugal are in the process of establishing a national defence industry. Therefore they are called Defence Developing Industries (DDI) countries. Their

92 Case T–26/01, above n 90, at para 74.
93 [1999] OJ L–301/8.
94 See above n 83.
95 Above.
96 PJG Kapteyn and P VerLoren van Themaat, LW Gormley, (ed), *Introduction to the law of the European Communities: from Maastricht to Amsterdam*, 3rd edn, (Kluwer, The Hague, 1998) 935–36.
97 Eighth Report on Competition Policy (Brussels, Luxembourg) 122–23 points 172 ff.

defence industries could be considered "sunrise" industries. New Member States such as the Czech Republic, Poland or the Slovak Republic are for the most part loss making[98] and outdated and their defence industries could be considered "sunset industries".

The defence industries are in a major restructuring process after the end of the Cold War and have to face immense difficulties. These difficulties may make the defence sector eligible for a variety of State aids within the limits described. With regards to the defence industries in a possible EU market for defence goods the Commission is of the opinion that the then possible:

> " [...] rigorous control of State aids will make it possible to distinguish between aid necessary for restructuring, since it accelerates change, encourages research, development and innovation and reduces the social consequences of reorganisation [on the one hand], and aid used for defence reasons that certain Member States might be inclined to use to avoid necessary structural changes and transfer the production and employment adjustment cost onto other Member States [on the other hand]."[99]

Member States under any liberalised regime will probably try to make their national champions more competitive by providing State aids but the current degree of subsidies would not be tolerable under this heading.

Another aspect of this exception is the support of research and technological development for which the Commission has adopted policy guidelines.[100] This is more likely to provide a potential justification for State aids in the defence sector. This support is one of the special features of the defence sector that have to be taken into account:

> "As far as the financing of military R&D [research and development] by member States is required, the Commission takes account of the particularities of the defence related activities, namely a high technology base of production, high costs and a very long development cycle, which, to a large degree, require public financing."[101]

Article 87 (3) (b) EC provides for aid to promote the execution of a project of common European interest. The Commission came close to complaining about the fact that until March 2003 there had been no notification based on this provision.[102] This strongly suggests that notifications would be available regarding State aid granted to major defence equipment projects such as the British-German-Italian-Spanish 'Eurofighter/Typhoon' combat aircraft. The notion "*common* European interest [emphasis added]", however, requires the participation of defence companies from at least two Member States. It is submitted that such a notification would not even require the project to contribute to the survival of the

[98] *Towards an EU Defence Equipment Policy*, COM (2003) 113 final, Schmitt, above n 23, at 169.
[99] *The Challenges Facing the Defence-Related Industries*, COM (96) 10 final, at 22.
[100] [1986] OJ C–83/2.
[101] *The Challenges Facing the Defence-Related Industries*, COM (96) 10 final, at 24.
[102] *Towards an EU Defence Equipment Policy*, COM (2003) 113 final, Schmitt, above n 23, at 174.

European defence industrial base or to be specifically designed to support the European Security and Defence Policy or the European Capabilities Programme described in chapter 3.[103]

Another exception under Article 87 EC is State aid to combat a general economic crisis.[104] These aids are becoming increasingly an instrument of economic policy to counteract structural problems and alterations in the world economy. A good example is aid in the shipbuilding industry.[105]

The State aids regime of the EC Treaty provides for a rule of reason that accommodates and allows aids in cases that are relevant to the defence industries. This enables Member States to support their defence industries even without invoking Article 296 (1) (b) EC. There are, however, still problems here. One is the effect on the civil sector by aid awarded to the military sector. Many firms produce both military and civil materials, and aid to the military arm of a company may affect the civil sector, distorting competition also in the civil sector.[106] This interaction of civil and military sectors represents a major difficulty for the Commission to detect and prove violations of Article 87 EC in companies producing both civil and military goods.

Another problem is the case of dual-use goods, to be used both for military and civil purposes. It seems that indirect distortions of competition in the civil sector are not, however, exempt from the State aid rules, by the national security exemption of Article 296 (1) (b) EC. The armaments exemption clearly says: "such measures shall not, however, adversely affect the conditions of competition in the common market regarding products which are not intended for specifically military purposes."

These State aids might lead to a number of distortions of competition. The co-ordination of national State aids and the integration of that co-ordination into the Union's own policy in the field concerned, such as economic policy, regional policy, etc., is possibly the best way to avoid these distortions.[107] If the European States agreed on a centralised approach, a procurement agency or Directorate General could administer this co-ordination with a new Union fund like the European Regional Development Fund (the "European Defence Industry and Technology Fund").[108]

5. TRADE IN ARMAMENTS

Another important issue to be mentioned in the context of the defence industries is the regulation of trade in armaments.[109] The small size of the national markets

[103] At 104–105.
[104] Gormley, (ed), above n 96. See also COM (85) 310 final, at 39–40.
[105] See Sixth Directive on Aids to Shipbuilding Directive 87/167/EEC in [1987] OJ L–69/55.
[106] *The Challenges Facing the Defence-Related Industries*, COM (96) 10 final, at 22; *Towards an EU Defence Equipment Policy*, COM (2003) 113 final, Schmitt, above n 23, at 174.
[107] Gormley, (ed), above n 96, at 938.
[108] Name suggested by the author.
[109] *The Challenges Facing the Defence-Related Industries*, COM (96) 10 final, at 24.

makes intra-Community transfers and exports of arms and dual-use goods particularly relevant for the performance of the defence industrial base. In 1989, for example, exports in the Community amounted to 9.9 billion ECU or 18 per cent of European armaments sales.[110] The then 12 Member States had a 20 per cent share in global armaments sales, 90 per cent of that coming from the major producers in Germany, France and the United Kingdom.[111] The regulation of trade in armaments has a direct impact on competition in the defence industries.[112] A liberal regime is likely to increase sales thereby leading *inter alia* to economies of scale and competitive prices. A restrictive regime will do the opposite. Therefore, the regulation of trade has an effect on the competitiveness of the defence industries comparable to the regimes on competition law, merger control, and State aids and has to be discussed in the context of this chapter.

5.1. Intra-Community Transfers

The problem of trade in armaments has to be divided into two separate but interrelated aspects. The first aspect covers the trade situation between the Member States. As explained in chapters 4 and 5[113] and above, the free movement of goods regime of the EC Treaty covers these intra-Community transfers, within the limits of Article 296 (1) (b) EC. Intra-Community transfers are subject to numerous time-consuming national procedures. These procedures are normally the same that apply to exports to third countries and take the form of individual licences for firms, import and export licences, checks on delivery and in some cases end user certificates.[114] An important reason for this burdensome 'red tape' is the desire of Member States to control the final destination of defence equipment, especially when this eventually involves third countries.[115] Nevertheless, these procedures represent a considerable barrier to trade and contribute to the fragmentation of the European armaments market.[116]

It is submitted that the Member States can invoke the armaments exemption in Article 296 (1) (b) EC for most of these procedures, since for obvious national security reasons trade in arms requires some form of control. Moreover, licence requirements will normally be proportionate since they are the form of formal control the least detrimental to the internal market. However, it appears that most of these procedural requirements were introduced or continued under the assumption that Article 296 (1) (b) EC is an automatic or categorical exemption

[110] Fouquet, Kohnstamm and Noelke, *Dual Use Industries in Europe*, Eurostrategies, European Commission DG III (Brussels, 1991).
[111] Above.
[112] *Towards an EU Defence Equipment Policy*, COM (2003) 113 final, Schmitt, above n 23, at 175.
[113] Ch 4 at 127–128 and ch 5 at 152–154.
[114] *Towards an EU Defence Equipment Policy*, COM (2003) 113 final, Schmitt, above n 23, at 173.
[115] Above.
[116] *The Challenges Facing the Defence-Related Industries*, COM (96) 10 final, at 19. The intra-Community trade in arms is only 3–4% of the overall armaments trade according to COM (96) 10 final, at 8.

of hard defence material from the application of the Treaty. There are no reports on Member States invoking the exemption to justify their licensing requirements. Following the narrow interpretation of the armaments exemption clarified in *Commission* v. *Spain*, it needs to be specifically invoked for every single national procedural requirement. It is submitted that this clear legal situation after the judgment requires a review and reform of these national procedures. Moreover, the best solution would be the harmonisation of national rules on intra-Community transfers, ideally combined with their simplification.

The Commission and Member States are working towards the simplification of intra-Community transfers, for example by aligning national licensing systems through the adoption of the 'principle of global authorisation' that would apply to intergovernmental programmes and industrial co-operation programmes.[117] Moreover, a common regime on exports to third countries would facilitate the simplification of intra-Community transfers since this would accommodate the main motivation for the licensing requirements: the control of the final destination of defence equipment. The narrow interpretation of Article 296 (1) (b) EC clarifies that the Commission has the competence to work towards this simplification. However, the fact that Member States can invoke the exemption necessitates co-operation between them and the Commission. By the end of 2004 the Commission intends to make an impact analysis to establish the added value of a Community-level legislative initiative towards the harmonisation of national licensing requirements.[118] A proposal for a Regulation or Directive cannot be expected before late 2005 or even 2006.

Moreover, Member States even impose customs duties on intra-Community transfers of armaments.[119] It is submitted that this practice cannot be reconciled with the narrow interpretation of Article 296 (1) (b) EC after *Commission* v. *Spain*, especially when considering the facts behind the judgment outlined in chapter 5.[120] A charge on armaments because they are crossing a border is not a proportionate measure in the interest of national security but a clear case of abuse of Article 296 (1) (b) EC to protect the national defence industries. In other words, it can not be argued that customs duties could be necessary for the national security interest of a Member State. Similarly the Court rules against an exemption of armaments exports from VAT in *Commission* v. *Spain*.[121] The Court is likely to rule against customs duties on intra-Community transfers of armaments.[122]

[117] *Towards an EU Defence Equipment Policy*, COM (2003) 113 final, Schmitt, above n 23, at 173.

[118] Above.

[119] *The Challenges Facing the Defence-Related Industries*, COM (96) 10 final: '[...] it is in the interest of the European Union and the Community that certain imports of arms and equipment for the European armed forces should benefit from exemption from customs duties and a list of equipment suitable for exemption from such duties is therefore needed.'

[120] At 152.

[121] Case C–414/97, above n 20.

[122] The fact that customs duties are not mentioned in *Towards an EU Defence Equipment Policy*, COM (2003) 113 final, Schmitt, above n 23, could be interpreted as an indication that customs duties no longer occur.

5.2. Defence Exports

The second aspect concerns the regulation of exports from the Member States of the EU to third countries. In addition to their economic importance outlined above, armaments exports are a highly political issue in Europe. They are regarded as an important instrument of foreign and economic policy. Governments encourage and control arms exports in order to exert influence in other regions of the world, generate external revenues, sustain internal capacity, maintain employment[123] and keep production lines open to maintain capability for integrating weapons systems. There has been an overall decrease of arms exports during the early 1990s, a trend that seems to have been arrested in the mid-1990s.[124] In 2003 there has been a decrease in arms exports.[125]

Differences in policy and practice have emerged between the governments of the Member States that may affect competition in the defence industries. Due to the fact that the major European arms producers have failed to realise the full potential of developing trade relations with other Member States, protectionism makes Europe no market for Europe, and United States protectionism and the lack of competitive products closes the American market for European producers.[126] The Third World and especially the Middle East have thus become the major export markets for Europe with all the problems this involves.

These problems have led to an intensive arms control debate with Germany and the Netherlands on one side promoting a higher level of control and France and Britain on the other side supporting flexibility. The disparities between arms export regulations in European countries could become a significant impediment to integration. Countries resisting more restrictive arms export policies will be loath to co-operate with their advocates and *vice-versa*. These disparities may also provide a rationale for greater defence industrial co-operation at a company level, as companies attempt to get around strict national export regulations and look for partners in countries with less restrictive policies. These disparities also distort competition as producers in countries with a less strict regulation have a competitive advantage over countries with stricter rules. This situation is inconsistent with the objective of the EC Treaty as it puts arms exports policy outside the common economic foreign policy of the Union.[127]

In December 1991 the Intergovernmental Conference proposed an EC-wide user regime and the establishment of an agency to co-ordinate, maintain and support national efforts on export control on the way to a common export policy. This would have the advantage of reducing the number of decision-making centres thereby making international agreements easier to negotiate. Moreover, it

[123] Walker and Willett, above n 53, at 154: Lovering, above n 53, at 462.

[124] Stockholm International Peace Research Institute (SIPRI), *Armament, Disarmament and International Security, Yearbook 1996* (OUP, Oxford, 1996) 462.

[125] Scientific Service of US Congress in August 2004, as cited in *Der Spiegel*, 6 September 2004.

[126] The rather complex arms export problems with the United States and the resulting export deficit shall not be dealt with in this chapter, see *The Challenges Facing the Defence-Related Industries*, COM (96) 10 final, at 7.

[127] Above, at 27.

would allow the EU and its Member States to exert political and economic leverage over other suppliers of military goods, particularly those from States who receive economic assistance or have applied to join the Union.[128] In the long run the EU should aim for a common export policy in this area, as one of the preconditions of a fair and competitive market. However, with the different approaches in the several Member States this is difficult to achieve. The agency proposed in 1991 had not became reality by the end of 2004.

Member States participate in most international defence-related export control regimes. These include the Australia Group, the Missile Technology Control Regime, the Nuclear Suppliers' Group, the Wassenaar Arrangement,[129] or formerly the Co-ordinating Committee on Multilateral Export Controls (COCOM).[130] These regimes are designed to prevent the transfer of strategic goods and technology to a region or country where the situation could become a cause of serious political, strategic, or economic concern to the participating states. The regimes are not legally binding and contain common criteria for assessing destabilising weapons accumulations and notification procedures for all relevant exports. In the context of the EU the regulation of strategic goods has to be subdivided into the regimes on dual use goods on the one hand and that on armaments on the other hand.

5.2.1. Exports of Dual-Use Goods

Dual-use goods are goods, software and technologies likely to have both civilian and military uses.[131] The export of these goods is regulated in the Dual-Use Regulation 1334/2000/EC,[132] which was based on Article 133 EC and provides for legally binding common principles and rules for the national implementation and enforcement of dual-use export controls by the Member States. Regulation 1334/2000/EC comprises a common list of items subject to control, which is directly derived from the consensus decisions taken in the international regimes mentioned above.[133] The Dual-Use Regulation abolished the previous regime on

[128] *The Challenges Facing the Defence-Related Industries*, COM (96) 10 final, at 25 and 26.

[129] *Towards an EU Defence Equipment Policy*, COM (2003) 113 final, in Schmitt, above n 23, at p 180 (n 18):

> The Australia Group controls exports and transhipments that could result in proliferation of chemical and biological weapons. The Missile Technology Control Regime aims at preventing proliferation of unmanned delivery systems for weapons of mass destruction by controlling exports of missiles and related technologies. The Nuclear Suppliers' Group controls transfers of nuclear-related dual-use equipment, material and technology in order to prevent civilian nuclear trade from contributing to nuclear weapons acquisition. The Wassenaar Arrangement controls transfers of conventional weapons and sensitive dual-use goods and technologies, primarily electronic products defined widely.

[130] Intended to regulate exports to the Soviet bloc and therefore in contrast to the other regimes an instrument for the Cold War, see P d'Argent, 'Les Enseignements du COCOM' (1993) 26 *Revue Belge de droit international* 500.

[131] *Towards an EU Defence Equipment Policy*, COM (2003) 113 final, in Schmitt, above n 22, at 175 citing Regulation 1334/2000/EC, cited in n 132 below. Article 2(a) Regulation 3381/94/EC [1994] OJ L–367/1 denies dual-use products as 'goods which can be used for both civil and military purposes.' See ch 5 for more details.

[132] [2000] OJ L–159/1.

[133] As pointed out by the Commission in *Towards an EU Defence Equipment Policy*, COM (2003) 113 final, in Schmitt, above n 23, at 175.

the same matter. This was based on an inter-pillar approach whereby the regime was regulated in the Community Pillar Regulation 3381/94/EC[134] and the Second Pillar Decision 94/942/CFSP.[135] The latter incorporated the material scope and procedures of the earlier. The inter-pillar approach[136] had been criticised because it relied on an obsolete distinction between trade and foreign policy and rendered the Community measure's *modus operandi* ineffective by excluding it from the legal framework of the Community.[137] Moreover, it was considered contrary to the relevant case law of the European Court of Justice discussed in the previous chapters. In *Criminal Proceedings against Aimé Richardt and Les Accessoires Scientifiques SNC*,[138] *Fritz Werner Industrie-Ausrüstungen GmbH* v. *Germany*,[139] and *Criminal Proceedings against Peter Leifer and others*[140] the Court suggested that the competence of the Member States for foreign policy be protected within the Community legal system of external relations, which may also ensure the effectiveness of the Common Commercial Policy.[141] Chapter 5[142] discussed the narrow interpretation of Article 296 (1) (b) EC, especially after *Commission* v. *Spain*, placing dual-use goods clearly outside the ambit of the armaments exemption and therefore inside the field of application of the EC Treaty.[143] As the EC Treaty covers this material the export of dual-use goods can only be regulated under the Community Pillar.

[134] [1994] OJ L–367/1.

[135] [1994] OJ L–367/8. Decision 2000/402/CFSP [2000] OJ L–159/218 repealed Decision 94/942/CFSP.

[136] Economic sanctions are also imposed on the basis of an inter-pillar approach. Under Articles 60 and 301 EC introduced by the Treaty of Maastricht, sanctions on third countries are to be imposed by means of a Council Regulation adopted by qualified majority and pursuant to a Common Position or Joint Action already adopted under Title V TEU. This formalised the combination of Community and non-Community measures under the European Political Co-operation before 1992. See: P Koutrakos, *Trade, Foreign Policy and Defence in EU Constitutional Law: The Legal Regulation of Sanctions Exports of Dual Use Goods and Armaments* (Hart Publishing, Oxford, 2001) in ch 4 (hereinafter '*Trade, Foreign Policy and Defence*'). See also P Koutrakos, 'Inter-Pillar Approaches to the European Security and Defence Policy—the Economic Aspects of Security' in V Kronenberger, (ed), *The European Union and the International Legal Order: Discord or Harmony?* (TMC Asser Press, The Hague, 2001) 435. Economic sanctions are an instrument of foreign policy with security implications. They do not form part of 'defence' as defined in the introduction to this book and therefore are not subjected to a closer analysis.

[137] Above, in ch 5.

[138] Case C–367/89, [1991] ECR I–4645.

[139] Case C–70/94, [1995] ECR I–3989.

[140] Case C–83/94, [1995] ECR I–3231.

[141] Koutrakos, *Trade, Foreign Policy and Defence*, above n 136, in ch 6, in particular at 122.

[142] At 152–154.

[143] See also the Commission in *The Challenges Facing the European Defence-Related Industries*, COM (96) 10 final, at 14; K Eikenberg, 'Article 296(ex 223) EC and External Trade in Strategic Goods' (2000) 25 *European Law Review* 117, 125–28; O Lhoest, 'La Production et la Commerce des Armes, et l'Article 223 du Traité Constituant la Communauté Européene' (1993) 26 *Revue Belge de Droit International* 176, 184–85; S Arrowsmith, *The Law of Public and Utilities Procurement* (Sweet & Maxwell, London, 1996) 858–59; and JB Wheaton, 'Defence Procurement and the European Community: The Legal Provisions' (1992) 1 *Public Procurement Law Review* 432, 434; W Hummer, 'Artikel 223' in E Grabitz and M Hilf, (eds), *Kommentar zum EWGV* (CH Beck Verlag, Munich, 1997) loose-leaf, vol II, Art 223, at para 12; N Emiliou, 'Restrictions on Strategic Exports, Dual-Use Goods and the Common Commercial Policy' (1997) 22 *European Law Review* 68, 72.

Therefore Regulation 1334/2000/EC is to be welcomed as an instrument of secondary Community law complying with both the EC Treaty and the case law of the Court. Moreover, it shows the acceptance of the Member States.

5.2.2. Exports of Armaments

The significance of Regulation 1334/2000/EC is emphasised when compared to the legal nature of the export control regime for armaments. In June 1998, after long negotiations,[144] the Council adopted the EU Code of Conduct as a Council Decision in the framework of the CFSP.[145] It sets minimum standards for the control of conventional arms exports of Member States to third countries and establishes an exchange and consultation mechanism. Annual Reports monitor the operative provisions of the Code.[146] Its objective is to achieve greater transparency in arms transactions and to lead to a growing convergence of national export policies. The material scope it not expressly laid down and it does not contain a list of products it applies to.[147] Eight criteria[148] are to guide national export officials in the authorisation of armaments exports. A refusal to authorise an export is to be notified and justified through diplomatic channels.[149] The 'no undercutting' rule covers the case where a Member State receives an application for an export licence for a product and country where this has been refused by another Member State. The Member State who received such an application has to consult with the other Member State. The earlier has to inform the latter about the granting of a licence in such a case and justify this decision.[150] The Code of Conduct is not legally binding. Generally, there is more common ground with the international agreements mentioned above than with Regulation 1334/2000/EC. Koutrakos criticised the approach of adopting such a Code in the form of a non-binding Declaration

[144] Koutrakos, *Trade, Foreign Policy and Defence*, above n 136, at 201.

[145] *European Union Code of Conduct on Arms Exports*, European Council Decision 8675/2/98, DG E–PESC IV, Brussels, 5 June 1998, in Schmitt, above n 23, at 23–28. The EU including the new Member States, Turkey, Canada, and South Africa have subscribed to the principles of this Code.

[146] See for example the *Fourth Annual Report according to operative provision 8 of the European Union Code of Conduct on Arms Exports*, Council of the European Union, 13779/02, PESC 446, COARM 14, Brussels, 11 November 2002, in Schmitt, above n 23, at 29–44.

[147] Koutrakos, *Trade, Foreign Policy and Defence*, above n 136, at 202.

[148] Criterion One: respect for the international commitments of Member States, in particular the sanctions decreed by the UN Security Council and those decreed by the Community, agreements on non-proliferation and other subjects, as well as other international obligations; Criterion Two: the respect for human rights in the country of final destination; Criterion Three: the internal situation in the country of final destination, as a function of the existence of tension or armed conflicts; Criterion Four: preservation of regional peace, security and stability; Criterion Five: the national security of the Member States and of territories whose external relations are the responsibility of a Member State, as well as that of friendly and allied countries; Criterion Six: the behaviour of the buyer country with regard to the international community, as regards in particular its attitude to terrorism, the nature of its alliances and respect for international law; Criterion Seven: the existence of a risk that the equipment will be diverted within the buyer country or re-exported under undesirable conditions; Criterion Eight: the compatibility of the arms exports with the technical and economic capacity of the recipient country, taking into account the desirability that states should achieve their legitimate needs of security and defence with the least diversion for armaments of human and economic resources.

[149] Point 3 of the Operative Provisions of the Code.

[150] Above.

of the Council.[151] First, the lack of a legal obligation undermined the effectiveness of the Code. Second, the decision not to have recourse to the formal instruments of the CFSP, such as Joint Action and Common Position, was inconsistent with the rationale underpinning the Code. To ignore the legal machinery of the CFSP questioned the actual significance of the initiative, undermined the role of Common Positions and Joint Actions[152] and was inconsistent with the past practice under the CFSP where embargoes on arms against third countries have been imposed by means of a Common Position.[153] Moreover, it had an undermining effect on the CFSP as a whole: "[f]or the European Union to attempt to regulate this issue by ignoring the most important instruments provided for under Title V is tantamount to denying the CFSP the opportunity to carry out in a meaningful way a policy lying at its very heart."[154] A consideration to be added to this criticism is that the legal form of the Code of Conduct adds to the fragmentation of European defence integration. The form of a Declaration creates a framework separate from the CFSP.[155] The latter is already separate from the Community, which as explained in this and the previous chapters, is also an instrument of European defence integration. The state of fragmentation is complemented by the fact that organisations outside the Union, WEU, NATO or OCCAR, are concerned with defence.

However, according to the *Fourth Annual Report according to operative provision 8 of the European Union Code of Conduct on Arms Exports* "a substantive increase in the number of notified denials and consultations has produced a sizeable body of information which testifies to the growing confidence in the instrument."[156] Hence, it could be argued that a non-legally binding instrument, even when undermining the CFSP and adding to the fragmentation of defence integration, is better than nothing. It serves its purpose in promoting the harmonisation of the arms exports of the Member States through common standards, procedures, mutual information, and the no-undercutting rule. Its application beyond the Member States of the Union can only enhance its effectiveness as an instrument of security policy. If the Code is adhered to in practice the fact that it is not legally binding is of little significance. This can help to overcome the negative effects of the differences in arms export regulations on competition in the defence industries and contribute to the creation of a liberalised defence equipment market.

However, even a Code of Conduct using the machinery of the CFSP had to be criticised as it assumes and requires an automatic exclusion of armaments from the EC Treaty. The narrow interpretation of Article 296 (1) (b) EC, especially after *Commission* v. *Spain*, places armaments inside the field of application of the

[151] Koutrakos, *Trade, Foreign Policy and Defence*, above n 136, at 205–7.
[152] See ch 2 at 69–71 for details.
[153] Koutrakos, *Trade, Foreign Policy and Defence*, above n 136, at 206, for examples see his n 37.
[154] Above, at 207.
[155] It could even be advocated that it had a different 'membership' since Turkey, South Africa, and Canada also participate.
[156] Schmitt, above n 23, at 30.

Community Pillar of the TEU, unless a Member State can derogate from the EC Treaty on a case-by-case basis. Therefore an abstract Code can only be part of the Community framework as the regulation of armaments exports is covered by the EC Treaty unless Article 296 (1) (b) EC is successfully invoked. The foreign policy implications of arms exports might lead to frequently successful invocations of the armaments exemption. Thus even with an 'EC Armaments Exports Regulation' the CFSP would still have a role to play. The solution could be partly based on the inter-pillar approach of the former dual-use export regime. Armaments exports would be covered by a Community Regulation, which would provide a national security exemption based on Article 296 (1) (b) EC. After the successful invocation of this exemption the individual arms export case would be 'transferred' to the CFSP. The Second Pillar would have to provide a Code of Conduct using the CFSP machinery as a catch-up framework for these cases. Moreover, an additional international treaty based on this CFSP framework would allow third states to participate in the framework of such a Code. In extreme cases a Member State should be allowed to derogate from both frameworks and move to the existing Code of Conduct as a second catch-up framework. To summarise, the narrow interpretation of Article 296 (1) (b) EC requires an 'EC Arms Export Regulation' supplemented by a 'CFSP Arms Export Joint Action of Common Position' for cases where the armaments exemption of the EC Treaty can be successfully invoked. This approach reflects the fragmentation of defence integration into two Pillars which could potentially undermine its effectiveness. However, it is submitted that it would contribute to a more coherent arms export policy since fewer 'solo attempts' of individual Member States would get through such a 'filter system'. Moreover, this would almost provide a single export regime of the Union, save for those cases where national security is invoked.

6. CONCLUSIONS

In addition to the set of procurement rules discussed in chapter 7, an internal market for defence equipment also needs common rules on competition, merger control, exports and State aids. Achieving this through the legal instruments already provided in Community law is one possible option, which has a number of advantages. The EC rules are already well established, a competent institution, the European Commission, with the necessary experience and expertise supervises these legal instruments and they have been proven to work, in some areas over decades. Other organisations such as the WEU, a Second Pillar authority, or OCCAR would need time to establish new legal frameworks in these areas. However, the application of the current Community legal instruments to the defence sector has to be clarified further. Moreover, the rules have to be adapted to the special features of the defence sector such as secrecy, national security and the necessity to preserve a European defence industrial base.

First, the application of the competition rules of Articles 81 and 82 EC must be clarified. Second, for the law on mergers the adoption of a balance system comparable to the system provided for competition law, is advocated. This would allow the Commission to strike a balance between the objectives involved. Moreover, the Member States need to harmonise their export rules with regard to third countries as the current disparities distort competition and the abolition restriction on intra-Community transfers of hard defence material is also an essential element of the liberalisation of defence procurement within Europe. Finally, national subsidies to the defence industries can affect competition. These aids must be integrated into the co-ordination policies of the Union regarding State aids.

European Community law has a significant impact on the economic aspects of defence. This impact is often underestimated because the armaments exemption in Article 296 (1) (b) EC is misunderstood as an automatic exclusion of hard defence material from the application of the EC Treaty. The impact of Community law can be increased by the abolition of the provision or by reducing its use in practice. European Community law is not designed as an instrument of European defence integration. However, the discussion in chapters 7 and 8 has shown that it is already well equipped to address the problems of the regulation of defence procurement and the defence industries. It can make a contribution to important aspects of defence integration. The fact that other aspects of defence integration are regulated in a separate Second Pillar of the TEU which does not share the more supranational features of the Community amounts to an EU internal dimension of fragmentation. This internal dimension is added to the external dimension of fragmentation caused by the fact that certain aspects of European defence integration are addressed in organisational structures outside the Union. Measures taken by the Council outside both the framework of the Community and the CFSP, such as the Code of Conduct for Armaments Exports or previously the inter-pillar approach for dual use exports discussed in this chapter lead to additional fragmentation. This situation undermines the coherence of European defence integration.

9

European Bands of Brothers and Sisters: The Regulation of Sex Equality in the Armed Forces of the Member States

1. INTRODUCTION[1]

THE PREVIOUS CHAPTERS 7 and 8 discussed the impact of Community law on the economic aspects of defence, namely defence procurement and the regulation of the European defence industries. It was shown that the EC Public Procurement Directives and other instruments of secondary Community law contain sets of exemptions relevant to defence that largely reflect or resemble the security exemptions in the EC Treaty. The Member States have to specifically invoke these exemptions, justify their use, and prove that a situation justifying exemption actually exists. Also similar to the exemptions in the Treaty discussed in chapters 4, 5, and 6 of this book, the European Court of Justice exercises scrutiny over the use of these exemptions to varying degrees of intensity. The exemptions allow striking a balance between the internal market interests of the Community and the national security interests of the Member States. Within the limits of the exemptions and the scrutiny exercised by the Court over their use the EC Public Procurement Directives, the Merger Regulation, and other instruments apply to the defence procurement agencies and defence industries of the Member States. These instruments concern areas of economic law, which have been at the heart of the EC Treaty from its very beginning.[2]

The European Community is not merely a commercial enterprise. Within the limits of the EC Treaty, the Community is also concerned with issues such as culture, education, the protection of the environment, or health. Most notably the Community has a substantial social agenda, as will be discussed in more detail below.

[1] Earlier versions of this paper were published as 'Sisters in Arms: European Community Law and Sex Equality in the Armed Forces' (2003) 9 *European Law Journal* 631–58 and presented at the Annual Conference of the (United Kingdom) Socio-Legal Studies Association (SLSA) in Aberystwyth (Wales), 5 April 2002 and the Biannual Conference of the European Union Studies Association (EUSA) in Nashville, Tennessee (USA), 29 March 2003. The present version was the subject of a presentation to the Gender and Law Group at the University of Utrecht (The Netherlands), 9 September 2004.

[2] See ch 1 at 47–49 on these beginnings in the 1950s.

This is important for the subject matter of this book since the defence of the Member States is not merely based on the equipment of the armed forces but also on the men and women forming these armies. Social issues such as recruitment, vocational training, promotion, or pensions, affect soldiers just like any other employee.

Recent case law of the European Court of Justice sheds a new light on the limits of Community competence in areas concerned with sex equality in the armed forces. *Sirdar* and *Kreil*[3] deal with access of women to employment in the forces. *Dory* deals with conscription for men. The following chapter 9 discusses this new case law with regards to the effect of Community law on sex equality in the armed forces of the Member States. The cases illustrate that Community law has an impact on an important aspect of defence: the composition of the armed forces of the Member States with regards to sex.[4] The chapter adds an area of social law regulated by secondary Community law to the discussion of areas of economic law regulated by secondary Community law discussed in chapters 7 and 8. It also represents an example for areas of life regulated by EC law that go beyond the economic core areas of the Community. Thereby chapter 9 contributes to a more complete perspective of the effect of secondary Community law on the defence law of the Member States. Sex equality law was also selected for Part II of this book because the secondary Community law exemption relevant to defence is not a reflection of a security exemption in the Treaty. Therefore a new type of security exemption in Community law is introduced and discussed thereby complementing the understanding of the limits of Community law as an instrument of European defence integration facilitated in chapters 4 to 8.

Thousands of women enlist in the armed forces of the Member States every year.[5] For decades they have been working in uniform: as nurses, musicians, and cooks. Female tank drivers, bomber pilots, and submarine commanders, however, are a more recent phenomenon. Generally there is a Community-wide tendency to open more and more military occupations to females. This tendency in the military is part of a wider tendency towards the emancipation of women in society. However, the armed forces are still the strongest bastions of male dominance. Women remain excluded from several areas of frontline activity. Moreover, they are not subject to conscription. The degree of exclusion varies considerably from Member State to Member State.[6] Choices on access of women to the defence sector affect the composition of the armed forces and are therefore perceived as

[3] Case C–273/97, *Angela Maria Sirdar v The Army Board, ex parte Secretary of State for Defence* [1999] ECR I–7403; Case C–285/98, *Tanja Kreil v Germany* [2000] ECR I–69.

[4] On the constitutional dimensions of the *Kreil* case see T Wobbe, 'From Protecting to Promoting: Evolving EU Sex Equality Norms in an Organisational Field' (2003) 9 *European Law Journal* 88.

[5] According to 2001 figures 3190 women (7.7%) serve in the Belgian armed forces, 862 (5%) in the Danish armed forces, 6300 (3.4%) in the German armed forces, 6155 (3.75%) in the Greek armed forces, 438 (0.1%!) in the Italian armed forces, 22 in the Luxembourg armed forces (overall strength 770), 4170 (8%) in the Dutch armed forces, 2875 (6.6%) in the Portuguese armed forces and 9983 (8.2%) in the Spanish armed forces. 8.55% of the French armed forces are women. These figures fall short of the United States where 200,000 (14%) serve in the armed forces and 90% of career fields are open to them. Source: web site of the Committee on Women in NATO Forces: http://www.nato.int/ims/2001/win/.

[6] The percentage can be as high as 8.55% as in France and as low as 0.1% as in neighbouring Italy, above.

an important aspect of national defence. Member States try to justify the total or partial exclusion of women with the argument that choices of defence policy were outside Community competence. More sophisticated arguments say that their presence in the forces compromised combat effectiveness. Safeguarding combat effectiveness was necessary to ensure national security and justified derogation from the EC Treaty and secondary Community law.

This chapter will start by briefly providing an introduction to the sex equality law of the Community (section 2). Second, the case law on sex equality in relation to the armed forces will be discussed (section 3). Third, a general theory on the application of Community social law to the armed forces of the Member States will be provided (section 4). Finally, the conclusions will summarise the findings on Community law as an instrument of European defence integration in Part II of this book.

2. SEX EQUALITY IN COMMUNITY LAW

The list of Community objectives in Article 2 EC[7] implies a commercial emphasis. However, the objectives include a high level of employment and of social protection and equality between men and women. It could be argued that, because of the commercial emphasis, sex equality has to be seen in an economic context. Sex equality at the workplace has economic effects on production and service provision and national differences in regulation can be barriers to trade. If sex equality as an objective of the Community is limited to those areas where it has economic effects, it could be further argued that equality between men and women in the armed forces has no economic effects and is therefore not covered by the Treaty objective. There are three arguments against this interpretation. First, the wording of Article 2 EC does not limit the objective of sex equality and there are strong indications that equality between men and women has a constitutional dimension that exceeds commercial limits.[8] Second, economic

[7] Article 2 EC reads:

> The Community shall have as its task, by establishing a common market and an economic and monetary union and by implementing common policies or activities referred to in Articles 3 and 4, to promote throughout the Community a harmonious, balanced and sustainable development of economic activities, a high level of employment and of social protection, equality between men and women, sustainable and non-inflationary growth, a high degree of competitiveness and convergence of economic performance, a high level of protection and improvement of the quality of the environment, the raising of the standard of living and quality of life, and economic and social cohesion and solidarity among Member States.

[8] In Case C–43/75, *Defrenne v SABENA (No 2)* [1976] ECR 455 the Court described the then Article 119 EC as one of the 'foundations of the Community' to achieve a 'double objective', economic and social. Nevertheless EC sex discrimination law is confined strictly within the economic context, see for example: Case C–184/83, *Hoffmann v Barmer Ersatzkasse* [1984] ECR 3042. J Langer, annotations in (2000) 37 *Common Market Law Review* 1433, 1443 says that the 'principle gradually has been constitutionalised' and that it has 'some autonomous value' in Community law. See also G More, 'The Principle of Equal Treatment: from Market Unifier to Fundamental Right?' in P Craig and G de Búrca, (eds), *The Evolution of EU Law* (OUP: Oxford, 1999) 517, 544 and 548; H Fenwick and T Hervey, 'Sex Equality in the Single Market: New Directions for the European Court of Justice' (1995) 32 *Common Market Law Review* 443; P Craig and G de Búrca, *EU Law*, 3rd edn, (OUP, Oxford, 2003) 885.

integration is at the core of the Community but as outlined above the EC Treaty has objectives in the social, environmental, and other fields that go beyond its commercial emphasis. Third, sex equality in the armed forces has at least indirect economic effects. If, for example, women are generally excluded from the armed forces, these women will seek employment in other parts of the economy or will need the support of the social security system.

Following these considerations this chapter is based on the understanding that sex equality is an objective of the EC Treaty and that the Community has the competence to legislate this area.[9] The question addressed is to what extent the competence of the Member States to regulate their armed forces is limited by the Community competence to legislate on sex equality.

Community law on sex discrimination comprises of Article 141 EC on the general principle of equal pay for equal work for men and women, the Equal Pay Directive,[10] the Equal Social Security Directive,[11] the Equal Occupational Schemes Directive,[12] the Equal Self-Employment Directive[13] and the Equal Treatment Directive (hereinafter 'ETD').[14] Most provisions have at least vertical direct effect.[15] As a provision of the EC Treaty, Article 141 EC has also horizontal direct effect.[16] The employer of soldiers is the national ministry of defence as an organ of the respective Member State. They will therefore always be able to bring cases against their employer on the basis of vertically directly effective provisions of the Sex Equality Directives.[17] The cases discussed in this paper are all concerned with the ETD. However, the principles developed in this case law apply equally to most of the other provisions of Community social law. Article 2 (1) ETD provides:

[9] Article 141 EC is now the legal basis for secondary legislation on the equal treatment of men and women.

[10] Council-Directive 75/117/EEC of 10 February 1975 on the approximation of the laws of the Member States relating to the application of the principles of equal pay for men and women [1975] OJ L–45/19.

[11] Council-Directive 79/7/EEC of 19 December 1979 on the progressive implementation of the principle of equal treatment for men and women in matters of social security [1979] OJ L–6/24.

[12] Council-Directive 86/378/EEC of 24 July 1986 on the implementation of the principle of equal treatment for men and women in occupational social security schemes [1986] OJ L–225/40.

[13] Council-Directive 86/613/EEC of 11 December 1986 on the application of the principle of equal treatment between men and woman engaged in an activity, including agriculture, in a self-employed capacity, and on the protection of self-employed women during pregnancy and motherhood [1986] OJ L–359/56.

[14] Directive 76/207/EEC on the implementation of the principle of equal treatment of men and women regards access to employment, vocational training and promotion, and working conditions [1976] OJ L–39/40.

[15] Case C–91/92, *Faccini Dori* [1994] ECR I–3325; Case C–152/84, *Marshall v Southampton and South-West Hampshire Area Health Authority* [1986] ECR 723, at para 48; Case C–106/89, *Marleasing SA v La Comercial Internacional de Alimentacion SA* [1990] ECR I–4135; Case C–443/98, *Unilever Italia SpA v Central Food SpA* [2000] ECR I–7535. See ch 1 at 20–21 of this book for details on the principle of direct effect of Community law.

[16] Case C–43/75, above n 15; Case C–143/83 *Commission v Denmark* [1985] ECR 427.

[17] Case C–152/84, *Marshall v Southampton and South West Hampshire Area Health Authority (Teaching)* [1986] ECR 723.

> For the purposes of the following provisions, the principle of equal treatment shall mean that there shall be no discrimination whatsoever on grounds of sex, either directly or indirectly by reference in particular to marital or family status.

This wide prohibition is not absolute but subject to several exemptions. These will be discussed below.

3. THE STORY OF SEX EQUALITY IN THE ARMED FORCES

The ETD applies to employment in the public service[18] including the armed forces.[19] It does not contain a security or defence specific exemption or an exemption for the armed forces. It is part of the social provisions of Community law and not part of the free movement of workers regime of the Treaty to which the public service exemption in Article 39 (4) EC discussed in chapter 4 applies.[20] However, the ETD contains an exemption that could potentially be interpreted as justifying discrimination of women in relation to certain dangerous professions, although not on a literal interpretation. Member States have argued that the entirety or parts of their armed forces were one of these dangerous professions[21]. Article 2 (2) ETD reads:

> This Directive shall be without prejudice to the right of Member States to exclude from its field of application those occupational activities and, when appropriate, the training leading thereto, for which by reason of their nature or the context in which they are carried out, the sex of the worker constitutes a determining factor.

This is not an exemption intended to safeguard Member State sovereignty over defence; there is no such safeguard in the ETD. The exclusion is intended to take differences between the sexes into account[22] as will be discussed in more detail below.

3.1. Royal Ulster Constabulary Women Wearing Firearms

The 'mother' of all cases on the armed forces and the exemption in Article 2 (2) ETD is *Marguerite Johnston v Chief Constable of the Royal Ulster Constabluary*,[23] although this original ruling is not itself an armed forces case.

[18] Case C–248/83, *Commission v Germany* [1985] ECR 1459, at para 16; Case C–1/95, *Gerster v Freistaat Bayern* [1997] ECR I–5253, at para 18 (hereinafter '*Gerster*').

[19] Case C–273/97, *Sirdar*, above n 3; Case C–285/98, *Kreil*, above.

[20] See for example: Case C–307/84, *Commission v France* [1986] ECR 1725, 1733. See ch 4 at 129 for details.

[21] Above.

[22] H Fenwick, 'Special Protections for Women in European Union Law' in T Hervey and D O'Keeffe, (eds), *Sex Equality Law in the European Union* (Wiley, London, 1996) 63–80.

[23] Case C–222/84, *Marguerite Johnston v Chief Constable of the Royal Ulster Constabluary* [1986] ECR 1651 (hereinafter '*Johnston*'). See E Ellis, 'Can Public Safety Provide an Excuse for Sex Discrimination?' (1986) 102 *Law Quarterly Review* 496; V Shrubsall, 'Protection Practices and the Equal Treatment Directive' (1987) 19 *Industrial Law Journal* 118; PE Morris, 'Sex Discrimination, Public Order and the European Court' (1987) 32 *Public Law* 334; A Arnull, 'The Beat Goes On' (1987) 12 *European Law Review* 56; R Wallace, 'Free Movement for Workers and Social Security: Remedies for Foul Play' (1988) 13 *European Law Review* 267.

A female officer of the Royal Ulster Constabulary (hereinafter RUC), now called the Police Service of Northern Ireland (hereinafter PSNI), brought an action against a decision of her employer refusing to renew her contract of employment. As women were neither trained in the use of firearms nor permitted to use them, the RUC had decided a new policy not to employ women as full-time members of their reserve. The RUC argued by analogy with Article 39 (3) EC (then 48 (3) EC) that because of the political situation in the province, derogation was justified on public safety or public security grounds. Moreover they considered it justified under Article 2 (2) ETD.[24] Allowing women to carry and use firearms increased their risk of becoming the target for assassinations. The Member States had the discretion to decide whether, "owing to the requirement of national security and public safety or public order, the context in which the occupational activity is carried out prevents that activity from being carried out by a policewoman".[25]

The Court clarified two important points. First, they held that there is no general public safety exemption to the equal treatment principle available under the EC Treaty, thereby rejecting the RUC's argument based on the analogy with Article 39 (3) EC.

Second, they held that derogation could only be examined in the light of the ETD. The Directive provides an exemption in Article 2 (2) that, "being a derogation from an individual right" has to be interpreted strictly.[26] In relation to Article 2 (2) ETD the Court provided the following test.

The derogation can only be applied to specific duties, not to activities in general. Nevertheless it is permissible to take the context in which the activity takes place into account.[27] The context in which the activity is carried out can be a reason for the sex of the person carrying out the activity being a determining factor in the sense of Article 2 (2) ETD. The environment in which the activity is carried out determines this context. In *Johnston* an environment of serious internal disturbances that characterised the situation in Northern Ireland determined the context in which police activities were carried out. In other words, public security considerations determined this context. In the situation of Northern Ireland, said the Court, the carrying of firearms by women can be contrary to public security requirements due to an additional risk of being assassinated.[28] Because of this

[24] The RUC also sought to justify its action under Article 2(3) Directive, as 'concerning the protection of women, particularly as regards pregnancy and maternity'. The Court held that the risks to policewomen arising from the situation in the province were not within the scope of the derogation. Article 3(3) Directive is intended to protect women's biological condition.

[25] Case C–222/84, *Johnston*, above n 23, at para 31.

[26] Above, at para 36.

[27] In Case C–318/86, *Commission v France* [1988] ECR 3559, a case on prison wardens, the Court made clear that derogation is possible only in relation to specific activities, and these exceptions must be sufficiently transparent to permit effective scrutiny. The fact that women cannot perform certain police functions does not justify discriminatory treatment in admission to the police force in general. The application of the derogation requires a specific assessment of the specific duties to be performed in individual cases.

[28] The Court, building on an argument of the United Kingdom, assumes that there is an additional risk for women wearing firearms to be assassinated.

additional risk compromising public security, the sex of a police officer can constitute a determining factor.[29] In such a situation, a restriction of particular tasks to men can be justified on the basis of Article 2 (2) ETD. Thus Article 2 (2) ETD functions as a public security exemption if the deployment of women causes an additional risk.

The questions are: whether the deployment really does cause additional risks, who determines whether it does, and whether the Court has the authority to scrutinise this evaluation made by the Member States. In *Johnston* the Court assumed such an additional risk. The United Kingdom had argued an additional risk caused by "the difference in physical strength between the sexes, the probable reaction of the public to the appearance of armed policewomen and the risk of their being assassinated".[30] They had also argued that the decision about this additional risk was within the discretion of the Member States. The Court did not specifically rule on the discretion of Member States in this context but they assumed that such an additional risk might exist. The term "the possibility cannot be excluded" could be interpreted as indicating that the Court itself made that evaluation and did not assume the discretion argued by the United Kingdom.

However, it seems more appropriate to leave maximum discretion on whether there is an additional risk to the discretion of the Member States. Only when there clearly is no additional risk or the Member State does not argue such a situation in good faith the Court should rule against it. This is because, as argued in the other chapters of Part II of this book, the Member States are the only guardians of security and the Court lacks the expertise to evaluate whether such an additional risk exists. It is the Member States who have the staff and the police forces that have the expertise to evaluate this additional risk. Their judgement, which is necessarily partly subjective, cannot easily be substituted by the judgement of the Court.

It is submitted, however, that *Johnston* represents a case where an additional risk was clearly not given, as the reasons put forward by the United Kingdom are not convincing. The "difference in physical strength between the sexes" is not an important factor when a woman wears a firearm, and the wearing of firearms was the issue in this case. Most women will have the physical strength to pull a trigger. It is not clear what kind of "probable reaction of the public to the appearance of armed policewomen" was anticipated. Did the United Kingdom expect riots in reaction to armed women? The "additional risk of their being assassinated" is also not persuasive. Why are armed women more likely to be attacked than armed men? The government of the United Kingdom did not provide any arguments for this allegation.

Another question related to this 'additional risk test' is the definition of the concept of public security that determines the context that can make sex a determining factor in the sense of Article 2 (2) ETD. It is not taken from Article 39 (3) EC discussed in chapter 4 or Article 297 EC discussed in chapter 6. The Court

[29] Case C–222/84, *Johnston*, above n 23, at para 37.
[30] See reference of the Court in Case C–222/84, *Johnston*, above, at para 30.

made clear that the earlier exemption applies only to the free movement of workers regime of which the ETD is not a part. Moreover it considers Article 297 EC to concern "a wholly exceptional situation" and the subject matter of another question put to the Court.[31]

However, public security in the context of Article 2 (2) ETD is not related to the concepts of security in the exemptions of the Treaty. In the Treaty security is like a national privilege, as such giving Member States the right to derogate from it. In the Directive security is one of several factors, biological differences being one of the others, which can determine a context in which sex is a determining factor to carry out a certain activity. Security does not justify derogation as such. Therefore the concept of security that can apply in the context of Article 2 (2) ETD is distinct from the concepts of security in the Treaty. It is an autonomous concept.

Moreover, derogation is subject to the principle of proportionality. Hence derogation has to be suitable and necessary to accommodate the fact that sex is a determining factor for a specific duty.[32] The derogation was later successfully used to justify limitations in relation to prison wardens and head prison wardens.[33] However, in *Johnston* the Court referred the case back to the national court to decide on proportionality.[34]

Where derogation is justified, the situation must be reviewed periodically to ensure that the justification still exists.[35] Soon after *Johnston* the RUC/PSNI changed its policy and allowed women into activities involving the carrying of arms.[36]

Johnston is important because it shows the impact of security on the application of the ETD and made clear that all security exemptions from the Treaty have to be interpreted narrowly. The foundations for a detailed, intense and balanced scrutiny of Article 2 (2) ETD were laid but not applied. The Court did not go as far as to rule against the discriminatory measure of the Member State but laid the foundation for the application of EC social law to the 'security sector'. This facilitated the access of women to more and more occupations thereby allowing the ETD to achieve its objectives.

3.2. Who is Cooking for the Royal Marines?

It was already clear from *Johnston* that the blanket exclusion of women from the armed forces as a whole would be difficult to justify on the basis of Article 2 (2) ETD. The derogation can only be applied to specific duties, not to activities in general. Moreover, it was clear that the fact that exercising a specific military duty

[31] Case C–222/84, *Johnston*, above n 23, at para 27.
[32] Above, at para 38.
[33] Case C–318/86, *Commission v France*, above n 27.
[34] Case C–222/84, *Johnston*, above n 23, at para 39.
[35] Above.
[36] According to Inspector Ken Cameron of the Emergency Planning Unit of the PSNI, today the PSNI does not have restrictions on female officers in any activity, e-mail dated 20 February 2003.

involved the use of firearms would not suffice to justify the exclusion of women on the basis of this derogation either. However, it took another 15 years before the European Court of Justice finally decided on the application of the exemption specifically in the context of the armed forces.

Angela Maria Sirdar v. *The Army Board ex parte Secretary of State for Defence*[37] continued the line of judgments which had started with *Johnston*.[38] It concerned a female soldier who had been a chef in the British Army since 1983. Before she was made redundant for economic reasons, she received an offer from the Royal Marines who had a shortage of chefs. When the responsible authorities became aware of the fact that she was a woman, they informed her that she was ineligible because there was a general policy to exclude women from that regiment. This policy was adopted on the ground that their presence was considered incompatible with the requirement of 'interoperability'. Every Royal Marine has to be capable of fighting in a commando unit.[39] Compromising interoperability means compromising combat effectiveness. Mrs Sirdar brought the matter before an industrial tribunal who made a reference for a preliminary ruling.

Based on Article 2 (2) ETD and the *Johnston*[40] principles the European Court of Justice ruled:

> [the] application of the equal treatment of men and women is not subject to any general reservation as regards measures for the organisation of the armed forces taken on the grounds of the protection of public security [...].[41]

Therefore decisions taken to ensure the combat effectiveness of the armed forces "do not fall altogether outside the application of Community law". Moreover they ruled that within the context of Article 2 (2) ETD:

> That principle [of proportionality] requires that derogation remain within the limits of what is appropriate and necessary in order to achieve the aim in view and requires the principle of equal treatment to be reconciled as far as possible with the requirements of public security which determine the context in which the activities in question are to be performed.[42]

[37] Case C–273/97, *Sirdar*, above n 3. See reactions: Langer, above n 8; P Koutrakos, 'Community Law and Equal Treatment in the Armed Forces' (hereinafter 'Equal treatment') (2000) 25 *European Law Review* 433; JM Kämmerer, 'Gleichberechtigung am Gewehr' (2000) 35 *Europarecht* 102, 116; J Rideau, 'Overservation sur Sirdar' (2000) No 19 *Receuil Le Dalloz Sommaires Commentés* 191; and J-L Clergerie in No 22, *Commentaire Jursiprudence* at 487–89.

[38] Expression of Koutrakos, 'Equal Treatment', above, 436.

[39] Paragraph 2(b) of the Revised Employment Policy for Women in the Army—Effect on the Royal Marines states: 'In a small corps, in times of crisis and manpower shortage, all Royal Marines must be capable at any time of serving at their rank and skill level in a commando unit [...] Employment of women in the Royal Marines will not allow for interoperability'. Cited by the Court in Case 273/97, *Sirdar*, above n 3, at para 7.

[40] Case C–273/97, *Sirdar*, above, at paras 23–26.

[41] Above, at para 19.

[42] Case C–273/97, *Sirdar*, above n 3, at para 26.

Referring to the judgment in *Criminal proceedings against Werner Leifer and others*,[43] a case on the export of strategic products, the Court said that Member States have a certain margin of discretion when "adopting measures which they consider to be necessary in order to guarantee public security in a Member State". The Court held:

> The question is therefore whether, in the circumstances of the present case, the measures taken by the national authorities, in the exercise of the discretion, which they are recognised to enjoy, do in fact have the purpose of guaranteeing public safety and whether they are appropriate and necessary to achieve that aim.[44]

Hence the Member States have a margin of discretion but the Court will scrutinise the proportionality of the measure and whether it serves the purpose of the narrowly construed exception invoked to justify it.

The Court went on to test whether the total exclusion of women from a particular unit could be justified by the objective of interoperability. It took into account that the organisation of the Royal Marines differs considerably from that of any other unit of the British armed forces, as they are the "point of the arrow head", and that they are a small force intended to be the first line of attack. All members including chefs have to serve as front-line commandos, are trained for the purpose, and there are no exceptions at time of recruitment.[45] On the basis of these considerations the Court ruled that:

> the competent authorities are entitled [...] to come to the view that the specific rules for deployment of the assault units of which the Royal Marines are composed, and in particular the rule on interoperability to which they are subject, justified their composition remaining exclusively male.[46]

Thus, according to the Court, the interoperability of a small combat unit on the first line of attack can justify the total exclusion of women. It is within the discretion of the Member State to consider the principles of interoperability and combat effectiveness being affected by the presence of women. The measure of total exclusion goes very far but it is justifiable in relation to a very particular kind of unit.

Sirdar is important because it clarifies that the ETD in particular and the social provisions of the Treaty and related secondary law in general, apply to the armed forces. This means that to a certain extent Community social law regulates the armed forces of the Member States.[47] This principle was later confirmed in *Kreil* and *Dory*, as will be explained in detail below. In order to evaluate the

[43] Case C–83/94, *Leifer* [1995] ECR I–3231, at para 35.
[44] Case C–273/97, *Sirdar*, above n 3, at para 28.
[45] Above, at para 29.
[46] Case C–273/97, *Sirdar*, above n 3, at para 30.
[47] That is also the interpretation of: Langer, above n 8, 1433; Kämmerer, above n 36, 102; Koutrakos, 'Equal Treatment', above n 36, at 432 and 441.

contribution of *Sirdar*, the following comments first address the more general issue of standard of review and Member State discretion in the context of the armed forces. Second, the more specific problem of the effect of women on combat effectiveness is discussed. The latter issue is at the core of the former.

First, *Sirdar* does not clarify the precise standard of review. This facilitates abuse of Article 2 (2) ETD in the context of the armed forces.[48] The Court left open whether the intensity of scrutiny is that of the public security exemptions of the free movement regimes or whether another standard of review applies.

When functioning as a security exemption in the context of the armed forces, Article 2 (2) ETD has to balance the social interest of the Community to ensure equal treatment with the national security interest of the Member States. The basic tools to achieve this balance are judicial scrutiny to safeguard the Community interest on the one hand and a margin of discretion to safeguard the Member State interest on the other hand. The fact that the composition of the armed forces is a question of defence, which generally is within the competence of the Member States, widens their margin of discretion compared to a case concerning a civil profession. In the constitutional order of the EU it is the Member States and not the Community who have the competence, expertise, and capabilities to safeguard defence. Moreover, national security issues are the responsibility of the executive arm of government and not of the judiciary. It is the government supported by their military staff who have the expertise to take decisions on defence. The Community judge cannot easily substitute the judgement of the executive with his or her own. The military implications limit the intensity of control exercised by the Court.[49]

At the same time the fact that sex equality is a rights issue, intensifies the standard of review because effective judicial review is a necessary component of the recognition of rights.[50] In contrast, the award of an armaments contract discussed in chapter 7, for example, is a policy issue without direct rights implications. Moreover, the baseline for judicial scrutiny is the general rule that exemptions have to be narrowly construed.[51]

The main instrument of judicial scrutiny is the proportionality test, which requires a measure to be both suitable and necessary to promote a public interest.[52] The test was discussed in more detail in chapter 4. Within the proportionality test the suitability of a measure to promote national security is mainly

48 Kämmerer, above, at 115–16.
49 Koutrakos, 'Equal Treatment', above n 36, 438.
50 Craig and de Búrca, *EU Law*, above n 8, p 373.
51 Case C–222/84 *Johnston*, above n 23, at para 39.
52 The test has actually three elements as formulated by Advocate General van Gerwen in Case C–159/90, *SPUC v Grogan* [1991] ECR I–4685 as cited by G de Búrca, 'The Principle of Proportionality and its Application in EC Law' (1993) 13 *Yearbook of European Law* 105, 113 including the more controversial third element. Also in favour of the three-part test (based on the same test in German administrative law, see Craig and de Búrca, *EU Law*, above n 8, at 350); J Schwarze, *European Administrative Law* (Sweet & Maxwell, London, 1992) 712. The third element, proportionality in the strict sense, requires that the positive effect of the measure on, for example, the objective of security has to be balanced with the negative effect, for example, equal treatment.

determined by the additional risk test established in *Johnston*. As will be explained in more detail below, the presence of women in a particular unit or activity may pose an additional risk for security which makes (the male) sex a determining factor in the sense of Article 2 (2) ETD. *Sirdar* established that a negative effect on interoperability and therefore on combat effectiveness can constitute an additional risk. However, this was not clearly spelt out. The ruling is not entirely clear on whether it considers the British rules to be proportionate or just within the margin of discretion of the United Kingdom. However, it is widely interpreted as a ruling on the proportionality of the exclusion of women from certain units.[53] Moreover, for reasons discussed below this is not considered to be convincing. Therefore *Sirdar* makes no contribution to clarity and coherence in the context of the crucial question of the standard of review.

It is submitted that the level of scrutiny possibly applied to Article 297 EC and discussed in chapter 6 would not have been appropriate. Rules on the composition of the armed forces are permanent measures outside the narrowly defined emergency situations envisaged by Article 297 EC.[54] The provision represents a "wholly exceptional clause"[55] and in *Sirdar* the Court considered it not to apply to the case,[56] a view shared by Advocate General La Pergola in his advisory opinion.[57] Hence the Court did not answer the questions put to it by the industrial tribunal regarding the interpretation of Article 297 EC.[58]

It is submitted that only when interoperability is clearly not affected or the measure to ensure it is manifestly disproportionate should the Court intervene. Luxembourg attempted to strike a balance in *Sirdar*: a wide margin of appreciation for the national security interests of the Member States[59] balanced with a narrow interpretation and the principle of proportionality for the Community interest in equal treatment.[60] However, the balance cannot be achieved when the principle of

[53] Kämmerer, above n 36, 115.

[54] In Case C–273/97, *Sirdar*, above n 3, Advocate General La Pergola pointed out 'that the cases envisaged by Article 297 EC concern temporary and non-permanent situations' (para 21). He gave an example in the adoption of unilateral measures under Article 297 EC by the United Kingdom in a temporary situation of serious crisis which arose in 1982 when Argentine troops occupied the British Falkland Islands. Thus, so the Advocate General in contrast to Article 296(1)(b) EC, which refers to the general measures a Member State adopts in times of peace for the purpose of safeguarding its security, Article 297 EC refers to the special measures which prove necessary in an actual crisis situation which has already developed. In Case C–423/98, *Alfredo Albore v Italy* [2000] ECR I–5965, at para 32 Advocate General Cosmas argued that, because of the exceptional character of the situations described, Article 297 EC only applies to provisional and not permanent measures. See chs 4 and 6 for details.

[55] Case C–222/84, *Johnston*, above n 23, at para 27.

[56] Case C–273/97, *Sirdar*, above n 3, at para 19, citing para 27 of Case C–222/84, *Johnston*, above.

[57] Advocate General La Pergola in Case C–273/97, *Sirdar*, above n 3, at paras 19–29.

[58] Case C–273/97 *Sirdar*, above, at para 33. Koutrakos, above n 36, at 437–39 rightly laments the fact that the Court failed to clarify 'the uncertainty that seems to surround the interpretation of Article 297'. This adds to a line of judgments where the Court avoided the provision, see M Trybus, 'The EC Treaty as an Instrument of European Defence Integration: Judicial Scrutiny of Defence and Security Exemptions' (2000) 39 *Common Market Law Review* 1347, and ch 6, above.

[59] See Langer, above n 8, 1441.

[60] Kämmerer, above n 36, 116.

proportionality is not properly applied. As will be explained below, *Sirdar* represented a manifestly disproportionate case where interoperability was clearly not affected. The fact that the Court still considered the disproportionate United Kingdom measure to be proportionate shows that this margin of appreciation is relatively wide.

Second, within the wider issue of standard of review and margin of discretion the precise mechanism to balance the interests involved needs to be discussed. *Prima facie* the Court does not apply the 'additional risk' test established in *Johnston*. However, it is submitted that the notions of 'interoperability' and 'combat effectiveness' point essentially in the same direction. Negative effects on interoperability and combat effectiveness cause additional risks for national security. Hence the Court does not deviate from the additional risk requirement: they only established a variation of it.

The recent *Women in the Armed Forces* report of the United Kingdom Ministry of Defence[61] supports this interpretation. The report refers to *Sirdar* and spells out the 2002 United Kingdom position on exclusion. It indicates that the additional risk notion was the determining factor for the decision of the Secretary of Defence to continue to exclude women from certain units such as the Royal Marines.[62] It concludes that the final decision on lifting the exclusions has to be "based on military judgement":

> The military viewpoint was that under the conditions of a high intensity close-quarter battle, group cohesion becomes of much greater significance to team performance and, in such an environment consequences of failure can have far reaching and grave consequences. To admit women would, therefore, involve a *risk with no gains in terms of combat effectiveness to offset it.* [emphasis added][63]

In this context "military judgment" is another way of saying 'Member State discretion'. A "risk with no gains [...] to offset it" is another way of saying 'additional risk'. This indicates that sex is considered a determining factor when the presence of women poses an additional risk.

However, in *Sirdar* the European Court of Justice fails to explain how the presence of women in small combat units affects interoperability thereby posing an additional risk.[64] This needs explanation to justify exclusion on the basis of Article

[61] *Women in the Armed Forces*, Ministry of Defence, May 2002, for the summary report see: http://www.mod.uk/linked_files/women_af_summary.pdf, at para 11: 'Differences between women and men in their capacity to develop muscle strength and aerobic fitness are such that only approximately 1% of women can equal the performance of the average man.' It should be pointed out, however, that this does not exclude that there are a substantial number of women capable to fulfil the requirements with regards to physical fitness.

[62] Royal Marines, General Service (RMGS), Household Cavalry and Royal Armoured Corps (Hcav/RAC). Infantry, and Royal Air Force Regiment, *Women in the Armed Forces*, above, at para 1.

[63] *Women in the Armed Forces*, above n 61, at para 17.

[64] Koutrakos, 'Equal Treatment', above n 36, 436, considers the answer to this question to be a part of the discretion enjoyed by the Member States. However, the answer to this question is crucial for determining whether the measure in question is aimed at ensuring the combat effectiveness and interoperability of the Royal Marines. This determination necessitates the consideration of possible alternative motives and a discussion of the effect of the presence of women on combat effectiveness and interoperability.

2 (2) ETD: without the presence of one sex posing an additional risk, the other sex cannot be a determining factor. The advisory opinion of Advocate General La Pergola cites material provided by the United Kingdom arguing that Royal Marines have to "maintain a high level of physical fitness". This seems to argue that the principle of interoperability is negatively affected by the presence of women because they do not have the required level of physical fitness. This appears to be connected to the cohesion argument discussed below: women physically unable to 'pull their weight' disrupt the interoperability of small units.

Soldiers not meeting certain requirements of physical fitness can obviously degrade or compromise combat effectiveness. Most women might not have the necessary level of physical fitness to be Royal Marines. However, some women do. Moreover, most men are not fit enough to be Royal Marines. Surely it is necessary to look at the individual applicant to decide on his or her physical fitness. If a female applicant has the required level of physical fitness, her level of fitness cannot compromise the principle of interoperability as far as physical fitness is concerned.[65] Hence the total exclusion of a group of society because of their sex is manifestly unsuitable to achieve interoperability. Moreover, the exclusion of women from the Royal Marine Corps is not appropriate when there is a measure less restrictive on the equal treatment of women but equally effective to achieve interoperability. The definition of objective access requirements would be such a less restrictive measure.[66] Moreover, in contrast to the total exclusion of women it would be a measure suitable to ensure interoperability with regards to physical fitness.

Physical ability was also put forward as a reason for the exclusion of women from certain units in *Women in the Armed Forces*.[67] The report also argues the possibility that the cohesion of small units, such as fire teams or individual tank crews, is achieved more easily in single sex teams. Hence the presence of women in these small teams might have a negative effect on the cohesion of such a unit and therefore on interoperability.[68] This negative effect, says the report, is caused by "the attitudes of group members, particularly positive and negative attitudes to

[65] *Women in the Armed Forces*, above n 61, accepts this at para 16:

> The Secretary of State is satisfied that as some women will certainly be able to meet the standard required of personnel performing in close combat roles, the evidence of women's lower physical capacity could not, in itself be a reason to maintain restrictions. Nor are the identified psychological differences between men and women, or the gap in the capacity for aggression, compelling evidence that women would perform less well in close combat.

[66] Kämmerer, above n 36, 116. A related question that cannot fully be explored in the context of this chapter is whether requirements of physical fitness should be formulated on the basis of male performance alone. 'Objective' requirements cannot be based on the performance of one sex. This might require the introduction of lower requirements. However in the context of this chapter it is assumed that the physical requirements for frontline combat units such as the Royal Marines remain at the current level.

[67] *Women in the Armed Forces*, above n 61, at para 16.

[68] *Women in the Armed Forces*, above, at para 13: 'There is some evidence from the literature survey that the inclusion of small numbers of women adds to the difficulty of creating the necessary degree of cohesion.' For the full report: http://www.mod.uk/linked_files/ewaf_full_report.pdf. It should be pointed out that a single sex team could also be a team exclusively made up of female soldiers.

gender and gender stereotypes [that] could affect group dynamics and ultimately group effectiveness".[69] Hence there is an assumed chain reaction connected by a causal link: bad attitudes – bad group dynamics – bad group cohesion – bad interoperability and combat effectiveness.

The same doubts with regards to proportionality presented in the context of physical fitness above apply to this cohesion argument. It assumes that the average Royal Marine, for example, is a rather conservative character, finding it difficult to work with women, particularly in a combat situation. He would be too sexist to fight side by side with a female comrade, let alone to accept orders from a female superior.[70] This traditionalist male opposition would compromise interoperability. Moreover, the average Royal Marine is a gentleman. Rather than fighting side by side with a female Marine, he might feel the urge to protect her in a combat situation.[71]

From a legal point of view, this argument cannot easily be accepted. The question is, whether governments or courts should accept male chauvinism or protective instincts as an argument for the lawful exclusion of women from a particular activity.[72] Community law and the law of all Member States clearly prohibit the discrimination of women.[73]

Moreover, the question arises whether differences and attitudes in relation to religion, race and sexual orientation can lead to a similar chain reaction affecting the interoperability of small units. Especially race is similar to sex, as in contrast to religion and sexual orientation it cannot be hidden or ignored.[74] This would mean that in order to ensure combat effectiveness, small units have to be composed exclusively of white, protestant, and heterosexual males. At least they all have to be males of the same race. This cannot be right: it would turn the armed forces into a uniform ghetto within a society based on equality. The armed forces,

[69] Above.

[70] See A Utley, 'Army Struggles to Integrate Women', *The Times Higher Education Supplement*, 7 February 2003, 5: 'Masculine culture still dominates the British army, whose top brass echoed tabloid stereotypes of female soldiers as gutsy types who would never be good enough to be real soldiers.' The article reflects on research done by Newcastle and Sunderland universities. Also see Wobbe, above n 4, 100–2 on 'The Military, Gender, and Equality'.

[71] Male soldiers tend to protect each other in combat situations to a certain extent. This comradeship rather than 'the love for King and country' keep most soldiers in the ranks during combat.

[72] These phenomena are very present in many other professions traditionally reserved to men. Examples include the fire and police services, the legal professions and even academia.

[73] Austria: Article 7(1) of the Constitution; Belgium: Article 10(2) of the Constitution; Denmark: Section 83 of the Constitution; Finland: Section 6(1)(2) of the Constitution of 2000; France: Article 1 Declaration de Droi*t de* l' Hommes et de Citoyens; Germany: Article 3(2) Basic Law; Greece: Article 4(1)(2) of the Constitution; Italy: Article 3(1) of the Constitution; Luxembourg: Article 11(2) of the Constitution; The Netherlands: Article 1 of the Constitution; Portugal: Article 13 of the Constitution; Spain: Article 14 of the Constitution; Sweden: Article 16, Chapter 2 of the Constitution; United Kingdom: Article 14 of the Human Rights Act 1998 (the United Kingdom is the only Member State of the European Union without a written constitution). *Women in the Armed Forces,* above n 61, at paras 17 and 18.

[74] These potential reasons for discrimination also have to be differentiated. Race and sex are characteristics that are difficult or impossible to hide and ignore. Religion and sexual orientation, however, can be hidden and ignored. In relation to sexual orientation, for example, many armed forces apply a 'don't ask, don't tell' policy, effectively ignoring the homosexuality of individual soldiers and asking them to hide it.

just like any other employer, have to work against negative stereotypes regarding sex, race, religion, and sexual orientation. For many obvious reasons the British armed forces cannot, for example, compose single-race units. They cannot guarantee that an individual soldier is not homosexual or, for example, Catholic or Buddhist, as these characteristics can be hidden and are often ignored. Allowing negative attitudes and stereotypes in the forces might even have in itself negative effects on combat effectiveness. Individual members who hate each other for whatever reason obviously compromise cohesion in small combat units.

Furthermore, assuming the validity of the cohesion argument, keeping a number of commando units or the Royal Marines as a whole exclusively female could also ensure interoperability of small combat units. Hence the cohesion of small units cannot be a justification for the exclusion of women from the Royal Marines as a whole.

The *Women in the Armed Forces* report could not find any conclusive evidence for the cohesion argument. Neither the field experiments nor the literature survey backed the assumption that the presence of women in small combat units has a negative effect on interoperability.[75] However, it was because of interoperability that the Court considered the British exclusion policy proportionate. The results of the surveys carried out as part of the report do not even suggest that many male Marines have negative attitudes regarding the presence of women. Due to this lack of evidence the Defence Secretary had to base his decision to keep the exclusions on "military judgement", by which he seems to assume a margin of discretion safe from any court's scrutiny. According to *Sirdar*, however, such a margin does not exist in this context.

Finally, the presence of women in the US Marine Corps shows that the British attitudes are not shared everywhere.

Hence it is submitted that, due to the lack of an additional risk in the form of a negative effect on interoperability, the total exclusion of women from small combat units is neither suitable nor necessary and therefore not proportionate.

3.3. Tank Girls for the Bundeswehr

Sirdar added to *Johnston* by clarifying that the Court itself would scrutinise a measure taken for public security reasons in the context of Article 2 (2) ETD. As the Court considered the measure lawful, the ruling fell short of a 'scrutiny with teeth' which requires a negative judgment on the legality of a Member State measure. However, this 'scrutiny with teeth' manifested itself a few months after *Sirdar* in *Tanja Kreil* v. *Germany*.[76]

Miss Tanja Kreil is a German woman trained in electronics who applied for voluntary service involving weapon electronic maintenance in the *Bundeswehr*, the German armed forces. Her application was rejected on the basis that according to German law women were barred from serving in military positions involving the use of arms. Miss Kreil brought an action in a German court that asked for a

[75] *Women in the Armed Forces,* above n 61, at paras 14 and 17.
[76] Case C–285/98, [2000] ECR I–69.

preliminary ruling. The question concerned the interpretation of Article 2 (2) ETD in the light of Article 1 (1) of the Law of Soldiers[77] and Article 3 (a) of the Regulation on Soldier's Careers.[78] According to these national provisions, women may enlist only as volunteers and only in the medical and military music service. The German provisions are based on Article 12 a (4) Basic Law, the Federal German constitution, which at the time provided:

> If, while a state of defence exists, civilian service requirements in the civilian public health and medical system or in the stationary military hospital organisation cannot be met on a voluntary basis, women between eighteen and fifty-five years of age may be assigned to such services by or pursuant to a law. *They may on no account render services involving the use of arms.* [emphasis added]

The reference question did not include Article 12 a (4) 2 Basic Law itself but only the corresponding Law and the Regulation mentioned above. The motive behind this limitation of the reference was probably to avoid an unnecessary ruling on the constitutional provision. This might have been perceived as potentially raising constitutional questions the solution of which would have been of no help to their case but might have caused delays through long considerations or even rejection and resubmission. Another motive might have been to 'protect' the constitution from the European Court of Justice.[79]

3.3.1. The German Situation Before Kreil

Article 12 a (4) 2 Basic Law had been subject to controversy since it was introduced as part of the 'emergency constitution'[80] in 1968. The political and academic

[77] Article 1(2) of the Law of Soldiers (German: *Soldatengesetz*) provided:

> Any person who voluntarily undertakes to perform military service for life may be appointed to serve as a professional soldier. Any person who voluntarily undertakes to perform military service for a limited period may be appointed to serve as a soldier for a fixed term. Women may also be appointed to serve in the armed forces, in accordance with the first and second sentences above, in posts in the medical and military-music services.

As cited by the Court in *Kreil*, German original:

> In das Dienstverhältnis eines Berufssoldaten kann berufen werden, wer sich freiwillig verpflichtet, auf Lebenszeit Wehrdienst zu leisten. In das Dienstverhältnis eines Soldaten auf Zeit kann berufen werden, wer sich verpflichtet, für begrenzte Zeit Wehrdienst zu leisten. In ein Wehrdienstverhältnis nach Satz 1 und 2 können auch Frauen für Verwendungen im Sanitäts- und Militärmusikdienst berufen werden.

[78] Article 3a of the Regulation of Soldiers´ Careers (*Soldatenlaufbahnverordnung)* provided: 'Women may enlist only as volunteers and only in the medical and military-music services', as cited by the Court in *Kreil*, German original: 'Frauen können nur aufgrund freiwilliger Verpflichtung und nur in Laufbahnen des Sanitäts- und des Militärmusikdienstes eingestellt werden.'

[79] There is extensive case law concerning German courts protecting parts of the constitution, especially the fundamental rights section: *Internationale Handelsgesellschaft mbH v Einfuhr und Vorratsstelle für Futtermittel* [1972] CMLR 177; *Bundesverfassungsgericht in 'Solange I'* [1974] CMLR 540; *'Solange II'* [1987] 3 CMLR 225; *Brunner v The European Union Treaty* [1994] 1 CMLR 57.

[80] Translation of the author, German: *Notstandsverfassung*, inserted into the Basic Law through the 17 *Gesetz zur Ergänzung des Grundgesetzes vom* 24 May 1968, BGBl I S709. This major constitutional reform adapted the Basic Law to the requirements of a national emergency, for example a war situation. The reform was very controversial and one of the reasons for the student protests of the late 1960s.

discussion concerned both the interpretation and, based on a wide interpretation, the utility of the resulting State practice to completely exclude women from service in arms in the *Bundeswehr.*

The Federal Constitutional Court,[81] the Federal Administrative Court[82] and the majority of academic writers[83] interpreted the provision as an outright ban for women to render services involving the use of arms. This ban was understood as an exemption from the freedom of profession in Article 12 Basic Law,[84] the

[81] BVerfGE 48, 127, at 165; BVerfG, 2nd Senate, 1st Chamber, decision of 30 April 1996, 2 BvR 471/96 and decision of 5 September 1997, BvL 8/97, on the reference of the *Truppendienstgericht Nord* (Military Tribunal North), Decision of the 20 June 1997, N 7 Bla 1/97 published in (1997) 50 *Neue Juristische Wochenschrift* 2834–35. BVerfG is the official abbreviation for *Bundesverfassungsgericht*, the Federal Constitutional Court, which is the highest federal court. BVerfGE contains the official publication of the judgements of the Court.

[82] BVerwGE 72, 241, at 246; BVerwGE 103, 301, (1996) 49 *Neue Juristische Wochenschrift* 2173, at 2174; (1996) 38 *Neue Zeitschrift für Wehrrecht* 122. BVerwG is the official abbreviation for *Bundesverwaltungsgericht,* the Federal Administrative Court. BVerwGE contains the official publication of the judgments of the Court.

[83] R Scholz, 'Artikel 12 a' in T Maunz, *et al*, (eds), *Grundgesetz–Kommentar, Band II*—Art *12 a–37 GG* (CH Beck–Verlag, Munich, 1989) Rdnr 198, pp 67–68; M Gubelt, 'Artikel 12 a Wehrdienst und andere Dienstverpflichtungen' in I v Münch and P Kunig, (eds), *Grundgesetz-Kommentar, Band I (Präambel bis* Art *20 GG),* 4th edn, (CH Beck–Verlag, Munich, 1992) Rdnr 20, p 785; W Heun and H Dreier, *Grundgestz-Kommentar, Band I, Artikel 1–19 GG* (Mohr Siebeck, Tübingen, 1996) 'Artikel 12 a', Rdnr 33, pp 802–3; B Schmidt-Bleibtreu, 'Artikel 12 a' in B Schmidt-Bleibtreu and F Klein, (eds), *Kommentar zum Grundgesetz,* 9th edn, (Luchterhand: Neuwied, 1999) Rdnr 10, p 354; G Gornig, 'Artikel 12 a Abs IV' in C Starck, (ed), *v Mangolt/Klein, Das Bonner Grundgesetz, Band 1, Präambel bis* Art *19 GG,* 4th edn, (Verlag Franz Vahlen, Munich, 1999) Rdnr 158, p 1540; C Grimm, 'Freiwilliger Waffendienst für Frauen?' (1987) *Zeitschrift für Rechtspolitik* 394, 394–95; HD Jarras, 'Artikel 12a' in HD Jarras, B Pieroth, (eds), *Grundgesetz für die Bundesrepublik Deutschland—Kommentar,* 3rd edn, (CH Beck–Verlag, Munich, 1995) Rdnr 13, p 308 (more critical at Rdnr 3, p 305); K Dau, 'Ernstfall für die Gleichberechtigung?' (1990) 32 *Neue Zeitschrift für Wehrrecht* 45; E-D Maar, 'Frauen im Bundesgrenzschutz' (1989) 42 *Der Öffentliche Dienst* 249; E Barth, '10 Jahre Wehrverfassung im Grundgesetz' (1966) 19 *Die Öffentliche Verwaltung* 153, 156 (although he asks whether 'the Basic Law went to far in its ambition to protect women'); B Walter, 'Frauen im BGS—Präzedenzfall für die Bundeswehr?' (1992) 34 *Neue Zeitschrift für Wehrrecht* 89; C Lutze, 'Kein Verfassungsverbot für eine Verteidigungsministerin' (1996) 38 *Neue Zeitschrift für Wehrrecht* 196; A Steinkamm, 'Der "Ernstfall für die Gleichberechtigung" ist in Sicht' (1994) 36 *Neue Zeitschrift für Wehrrecht* 133 (although he appreciates the arguments of the minority view, see below in n 111, at 136 and argues against a majority view on the prohibition of the voluntary service of women, at 138).

[84] Article 12 Basic Law reads:

> (1) All Germans have the right freely to choose their trade or profession their place of work and their place of training. The practice of trades and professions may be regulated by law. (2) No one may be compelled to perform a particular work except within the framework of a traditional compulsory public service which applies generally and equally to all. (3) Forced labour may be imposed only in the event that a person is deprived of his freedom by the sentence of a court.

German original:

> (1) Alle Deutschen haben das Recht, Beruf, Arbeitsplatz und Ausbildungsstätte frei zu wählen. Die Berufsausübung kann durch Gesetz oder auf Grund eines Gesetzes geregelt werden. (2) Niemand darf zu einer bestimmten Arbeit gezwungen werden, außer im Rahmen einer herkömmlichen allgemeinen, für alle gleichen öffentlichen Dienstleistungspflicht. (3) Zwangsarbeit ist nur bei einer gerichtlich angeordneten Freiheitsentziehung zulässig.

equality rights in Article 3 (2) and (3) Basic Law,[85] and the free access of all Germans to public offices in Article 33 (2) Basic Law.[86] The actual State practice in Germany was based on this wide interpretation: women were not allowed to serve in arms. Female applicants were rejected. The wording, "on no account"[87] and the history of the provision seem to support this interpretation.[88] The reasons for the ban were less clear. The Federal Administrative Court said that the ban aimed to prevent women from participating in hostilities.[89] However, this is the effect of the provision rather than a reason for it. The Court also said that the ban aims at preventing that women as combatants are subject to the effects of enemy weapons, again without explaining why the constitution seeks to provide this protection and whether this protection would be effective.[90]

A minority of academic writers[91] offered a narrow interpretation. According to this minority view, the ban in sentence 2 was limited to the emergency situations

[85] Article 3(2) Basic Law reads: 'Men and women are equal. The State supports the effective realisation of equality of women and men and works towards abolishing present disadvantages.' German original: 'Männer und Frauen sind gleichberechtigt. Der Staat fördert die tatsächliche Durchsetzung der Gleichberechtigung von Frauen und Männern und wirkt auf die Beseitigung bestehender Nachteile hin.' Article 3(3) Basic Law reads: 'No one may be disadvantaged or favoured because of his sex, parentage, race, language, homeland and origin, his faith, or his religious or political opinions. No one may be disadvantaged because of his handicap.' German original: 'Niemand darf wegen seines Geschlechtes, seiner Abstammung, seiner Rasse, seiner Sprache, seiner Heimat und Herkunft, seines Glaubens, seiner religiösen oder politischen Anschauungen benachteiligt oder bevorzugt werden. Niemand darf wegen seiner Behinderung benachteiligt werden.'

[86] Article 33(2) Basic Law reads: 'Any German is equally eligible for any public office, according to his aptitude, qualifications and professional achievements.' German original: 'Jeder Deutsche hat nach seiner Eignung, Befähigung und fachlichen Leistung gleichen Zugang zu jedem öffentlichen Amte.'

[87] Gornig, above n 83, at 1543 (Rdnr 164).

[88] See the MP Dr Schwarzhaupt, 132. Session of the Deutscher Bundestag of 6 March 1956, Stenographischer Bericht, Bd 28 at 6819; Bundestags-DrucksacheV/2873, p 7; Protokoll Nr 106 des 16. Ausschusses, Deutscher Bundestag, 2. Wahlperiode, 1953, as cited by Gornig, above, 1542, n 29; Bundestag-Drucksache 2/2150, 6858–59, as cited by M Zuleeg, 'Frauen in die Bundeswehr' (1997) 50 *Die Öffentliche Verwaltung* 1017, at 1018 n 11; Grimm, above n 83.

[89] BVerwG, above n 82.

[90] Above.

[91] Very comprehensively on the basis of a PhD thesis at the University of Trier: I Seidner, *Der freiwillige Dienst von Frauen in der Bundeswehr mit der Waffe als Gleichheitsproblem. Zum verfassungsrechtlichen Kontext von* Art 12a IV S 2 GG (Shaker Verlag,Tübingen, 1997) at 80–110 and 114–18; Zuleeg, above n 88, 1018; R Jahn, 'Frauen zu den Waffen?' (1988) 30 *Neue Zeitschrift für Wehrrecht* 177; V Slupik, 'Bewaffneter Dienst von Frauen in der Bundeswehr' (1990) 31 *Zeitschrift für Rechtspolitik* 305; J Kokott, 'Artikel 12 a' in J Kokott and M Sachs, (eds), *Kommentar zum Grundgesetz* (C. H. Beck, Munich, 1996) Rndnr 4; H D Jarras and B Pieroth, *Kommentar zum Grundgesetz*, 5th edn (C H Beck, Munich, 2000), 'Article 12 a', RdNr. 3; HG Edelmann, 'Freiwilliger Waffendienst für Frauen?' (1988) 29 *Zeitschrift für Rechtspolitik* 144; L Broker, 'Frauen als Kombattanten' (1996) 37 *Zeitschrift für Rechtspolitik* 127; A Poretschkin, 'Frauen in der Bundeswehr' (1990) 31 *Zeitschrift für Rechtspolitik* 482; A Poretschkin, 'Innere Führung, Recht und Frauen. Zufall oder Ironie?', (1990) 32 *Neue Zeitschrift für Wehrrecht* 195; very cautiously for the narrow (minority) interpretation: H-J Berg, 'Zum grundgesetzlichen Verbot eines uneingeschränkten Dienstes von Frauen in den Streikräften' (1979) 21 *Neue Zeitschrift für Wehrrecht* 81, also cautious: U Repkewitz, 'Verbietet Art 12 a Abs 4 Satz 2 GG Frauen den freiwilligen Dienst mit der Waffe?' (1990) 32 *Neue Zeitschrift für Wehrrecht* 177. I v Münch, an advocate of the majority view, above n 83, argued in a report for the German liberal party FDP: 'more reasons can be put forward for the constitutional legality of a voluntary service of women than against it', *Gutachten zur Verfassungsmäßigkeit des Dienstes von Frauen in der Bundeswehr*, printed in Beschluss des 38. Ordentlichen Bundesparteitages der FDP in Kiel, 5 and 6 September 1987, *Frauen in der*

described in sentence 1 of Article 12 a (4) Basic Law: women could be forced to serve in the health system but not to serve in arms. This interpretation could be reconciled with the sex equality provisions in Article 3 (2) and (3) Basic Law and the free access to public office and employment in Article 33 (2) Basic Law.[92] Moreover, as will be explained in more detail below, this interpretation could be reconciled with the requirements of Community law.[93]

As Zuleeg[94] pointed out, the fathers and mothers of the German Constitution were free to introduce a special provision as an exemption to sex equality. However, when two different interpretations of a provision are possible, the government, the legislature and the courts are required to choose the interpretation that can be reconciled with other relevant provisions of the Constitution and with the requirements of Community law.

The question whether the total ban suggested by the Courts and the majority of academic writers can be reconciled with other provisions of the German Constitution depends on whether the ban can be justified by reasonable considerations. This depends on the purpose of the ban. Possible purposes of the ban were gallantry,[95] to protect women as 'reproductive elements of society',[96] to ensure security, as women are considered physically and psychologically incapable to serve in arms,[97] to accommodate traditional role models and division of work,[98] and to protect women from participation in armed conflicts.[99]

These purposes, however, are not convincing and reasonable considerations to justify discrimination. Discrimination is not gallant;[100] it is rather offensive to women and contradicts their basic rights in Articles 3, 12 and 33 Basic Law.[101] Women cannot be protected in war situations anyway, as modern warfare does

Bundeswehr. Many authors advocating the minority view published their thoughts in the *Neue Zeitschrift für Wehrrecht* (English: New Journal for Defence Law), a specialist law journal not available in most university law libraries in times of tight budgets. The author found the journal only in the State library of Westphalia in Münster, not, for example, in the otherwise well equipped law library of the Ruhr University in Bochum. In contrast the authors advocating the wide (majority) view published their views in commentaries of the Basic Law, a form of legal literature widely available in university, government, court and even private law libraries. However, many authors advocating the minority view published in the *Zeitschrift für Rechtspolitik* (English: Journal for Legal Policy), a 'free supplement' to the *Neue Juristische Wochenschrift*, the legal journal with the widest circulation in Germany. Every German lawyer (over 120,000 attorneys) recieves a weekly copy.

92 Zuleeg, above n 88.

93 An exhaustive record of the arguments for this interpretation would go beyond the aims of this chapter.

94 Zuleeg, above n 88, at 1019. In this excellent article the former judge at the European Court of Justice anticipates the results and reasoning of the *Kreil* judgment, see 1021–25. He also wrote a report on the question for the Law Committee of the *Bundestag*, the Lower House of the German Federal parliament, before Article 12a(4) sentence 2 Basic Law was amended in October 2000.

95 Above, at 1019.

96 Zugleeg, above n 88, at 1019.

97 Above.

98 Zugleeg, above n 88, at 1019–20.

99 Above, at 1020.

100 Assuming that gallantry as such is a good thing, it can also be seen as an expression of the fact that women are not seen as equal or as a compensation for inequality. Hence, gallantry is controversial.

101 Zugleeg, above n 88, at 1019; Edelmann, above n 91, at 144.

not spare any part of the population.[102] Moreover, an armed female soldier can protect herself better than an unarmed woman. The successful service of women in many other armies of the world,[103] in the Federal German Police,[104] and the police forces of the German states, has shown that many women are physically and psychologically capable of serving in arms. On the other hand many men are not capable of being useful soldiers. The fostering of traditional role models is no legitimate purpose for an exemption in the Constitution, and in fact the amended Article 3 (3) Basic Law explicitly prohibits this.[105] Finally protection against their will comes close to denying women their right to self-determination: the free will of women overrides rules for their protection.[106] The Federal Constitutional Court ruled in the *Night Work Judgment*[107] that women can decide themselves about advantages and disadvantages of their work. The motives of the majority view seem patronising and based on atavistic notions of masculinity and femininity and male and female roles.

Hence, as the total ban cannot be justified by a legitimate purpose, only the narrow interpretation of Article 12 a (4) 2 Basic Law can be reconciled with the other provisions of the Constitution. Nevertheless, it was the wide interpretation, understanding Article 12 a (4) 2 Basic Law as a total ban for women to serve in arms, that was applied in practice.

3.3.2. The Judgment

Building on the established case law in *Johnston,*[108] *Criminal proceedings against Richardt and 'Les Accessoires Scientifiques',*[109] *Leifer,*[110] *Commission* v. *Germany,*[111] *Gerster,*[112] *Commission* v. *France,*[113] and *Sirdar,*[114] the Court focussed on the fact that the German law in question represented an outright ban from military posts involving the use of arms. The ban applied to almost the entirety of military posts in the *Bundeswehr*. Thus the provisions could not be justified by the specific nature of the post in question as in *Sirdar* or by the particular context in which the activities in question are carried out as in *Johnston*. Article 2 (2) ETD did not

[102] Zugleeg, above; Dau, above n 83, 45; Poretschkin, above n 91, 198; Steinkamm, above n 91, at 140 also referring to the consideration of Parliament when discussing female soldiers: Protokoll der 106. Sitzung des Ausschusses tür Rechtswesen und Verfassungsrecht v 6.2.1956, Deutscher Bundestag, 2. Wahlperiode 1953, BT–Drs 2154, v 1.3.1956.

[103] Dau, above n 91, at 45.

[104] M Hellenthal, *Frauen im Bundesgrenzschutz* (Schrifen zum Öffentlichen Recht (No. 537), Berlin, 1988); Maar, above n 83, at 249–52; Walter, above n 83, at 93–94.

[105] Zuleeg, above n 88, 1020 citing BVerfGE 87, 234, 258 (judgment of 1992).

[106] HD Jarras and B Pieroth, *Grundgesetz für die Bundesrepublik Deutschland, Kommentar,* 3rd edn, (CH Beck Verlag, Munich, 1996) 'Art 3', Rdnr 58, as cited by Zugleeg, above, at 1020.

[107] BVerfGE 85, 191, at 209–10 as cited by Zugleeg, above n 88, at 1020 (n 39).

[108] Case C–222/84, *Johnston*, above n 23.

[109] Case C–367/89, *Richardt and 'Les Accessoires Scientifiques'* [1991] ECR I–4621. See ch 4 at 137–138 for details.

[110] Case C–83/94 *Leifer*, above n 43.

[111] Case C–248/83, *Commission v Germany* [1985] ECR 1459.

[112] Case C-1/95, *Gerster v Freistaat Bayern*, above n 18.

[113] Case 318/86, *Commission v France*, above n 27.

[114] Case C–273/97, *Sirdar*, above n 3.

apply. The nature of a post in the armed forces as at least potentially involving the use of arms cannot in itself justify the exclusion of women. Even for the posts that are accessible to women in the *Bundeswehr*, basic training in the use of arms for self-defence and assistance purposes is provided. On this basis the Court ruled:

> In those circumstances, even taking account of the discretion which they have as regards the possibility of maintaining the exclusion in question, the national authorities could not, without contravening the principle of proportionality, adopt the general position that the *Bundeswehr* had to remain exclusively male.[115]

Moreover, the Court ruled that the ban was not justified by Article 2 (3) ETD[116] out of concern to protect women. The Court concluded that:

> the [Equal Treatment] Directive precludes the application of national provisions, such as those of German law, which impose a general exclusion of women from military posts involving the use of arms and which allow them access only to the medical and military music services.[117]

The judgment is important for several reasons. First, it is constitutionally important. It confirms *Sirdar*: Community law applies to the armed forces. Measures taken on the basis of Article 2 (2) ETD need to be proportionate. Second, it develops the tests developed in *Johnston* and *Sirdar* further into a 'scrutiny with teeth'. For the first time the European Court of Justice declares incompatible with the ETD a rule relating to the armed forces. Politically that goes a step further than confirming a national rule, as the Court did in *Sirdar*. This means that the Court is prepared to rule against national provisions regulating the organisation of the armed forces. The sovereignty of the Member States over their defence is not absolute. Community social law has an impact on defence. Third, this ruling on the incompatibility of the Law of Soldiers and the Regulation of Soldiers' Careers with the Directive implies a ruling on the incompatibility of Article 12 a (4) 2 Basic Law, a provision of the Constitution.

3.3.3. The German Situation After Kreil

Reactions to the judgment in Germany were divided.[118] Negative reactions considered the judgment to be *ultra vires*: the Court failed to respect the reserved defence domain of the Member States by expanding Community competence.[119]

[115] Above, at para 29.

[116] Article 3(3) reads: 'This Directive shall be without prejudice to provisions concerning the protection of women, particularly as regards pregnancy and maternity.'

[117] Case C–273/97, *Sirdar*, above n 3, at para 32.

[118] See the annotation by Langer, above n 8, 1433, citing mainly negative reactions in n 2. Kämmerer, above n 36 speaks of mainly positive reactions.

[119] See TM Spranger, 'Die Entscheidungen "Sidar" und "Kreil" des EuGH–Diskriminierung oder Gleichberechtigung de luxe?' (2000) 42 *Neue Zeitschrift für Wehrrecht* 117, also citations in n 4; K Eichen, 'Erosion der deutschen Wehrverfassung durch sekundäres Gemeinschaftsrecht?' (2000) 42 *Neue Zeitschrift für Wehrrecht* 45.

In October 2000 the German parliament decided to amend Article 12 a (4) 2 Basic Law.[120] The amended version reads: "They [women] may on no account be forced to render services involving the use of arms."

Before the *Kreil* judgment a proposal of the parliamentary group of the liberal party FDP had suggested to delete the provision.[121] However, as the protocol of the debate preceding the vote reveals,[122] the amendment was a direct reaction to *Kreil*. The incompatibility of the provision with Community law was the strongest argument for the amendment releasing a decades old deadlock in the legislature.

3.4. Who Wants to be a Legionnaire?

The legislative reaction to *Kreil* made *Alexander Dory* v. *Germany*[123] inevitable. The amended Article 12 a (4) 2 Basic Law stipulates that women can serve in arms and according to Article 12 a (1) Basic Law, men are subject to conscription.[124]

[120] *Gesetz zur Änderung des Grundgesetzes (Artikel 12a) vom* 19 December 2000, BGBl I–2000, 1755 [decision of the *Bundestag*, the Federal Diet (lower house, directly elected representatives) in October of the *Bundesrat*, the Federal Council (upper house, members sent by the state governments) in November.

[121] Deutscher Bundestag, 14. Wahlperiode, Drucksache 14/1728 (neu), at 2. The FDP was, however, aware of the reference pending before the Court (see motives of the proposal, at 3). The motives for the proposal were also to take the change of the reality of society of the Federal Republic of Germany after five decades into account. The motives cited the Annual Report of the Young Officers of the *Bundeswehr* 1997 according to which female young people are increasingly interested to serve in the armed forces and considered the old interpretation and State practice an 'extreme violation of equal treatment', a 'violation of the law' or even 'misogynist'.

[122] See the speeches of the MPs Anni Brandt-Elsweiler (social democrat SPD), Professor Rupert Scholz (Christian democrat CDU/CSU but also majority view commentator, above n 103, *spiritus rector* of the 'constitutional revision' after the reunification of Germany, and former Federal Defence Secretary under Helmut Kohl), Volker Beck (green BÜNDNIS 90/DIE GRÜNEN), Jörg van Essen (liberal FDP) Petra Bläss (socialist or post-communist PDS), Margot von Renesse (SPD) and Christina Schenk (PDS). Deutscher Bundestag, 14. Wahlperiode, Bundestagsprotokolle, 128. Sitzung, Berlin, Freitag, den 27. Oktober 2000, at 12338–12348. All refer to the judgment in their speeches.

[123] Case C–186/01, *Alexander Dory v Germany* [2003] ECR I–2479 (hereinafter '*Dory*'). First reactions in Germany: 'Wehrpflicht für Männer Rechtens', *Frankfurter Allgemeine Zeitung*, 12 March 2003; 'Nun muss Alexander Dory doch "seine Zeit vergeuden" EuGH: Wehrpflicht nur für Männer ist rechtens', *Westdeutsche Allgmeine Zeitung*, 12 March 2003; 'EuGH zur Wehrpflicht für Männer' (2003) 56 *Neue Juristische Wochenschrift*, VI. Reactions outside Germany: M Trybus, annotations in (2003) 40 *Common Market Law Review* 1269; F Dorssemont, 'Militaire dienstplicht en gelijke toegang tot de arbeidsmarkt' (2003) 7/8 *Sociaal Recht* 231; P Koutrakos, 'How Far is Far Enough? EC Law and the Organisation of the Armed Forces after Dory' (2003) 66 *Modern Law Review* 759.

[124] Article 12a(1) of the Basic Law provides: 'Men who have attained the age of eighteen years may be required to serve in the Armed Forces, in the Federal Border Guard, or in a Civil Defence organisation.' German original; 'Männer können vom vollendeten achtzehnten Lebensjahr an zum Dienst in den Streitkräften, im Bundesgrenzschutz oder in einem Zivilschutzverband verpflichtet werden.' The Netherlands and Belgium abolished conscription in the 1990s, France in 2001, Spain in 2002, Portugal in 2003. Italy aims for having professional armed forces by 2006 and there is discussion on phasing out conscription in Austria and Greece. The United Kingdom abolished conscription in the 1950s. Ireland and Luxembourg have professional armed forces. Germany (since July 2003—6 months), Denmark (4–11 months), Finland (6, 9 or 12 months) and Sweden (7–11 months) plan to continue the practice of conscription. Source: BBC, http://news.bbc.co.uk/1/hi/world/europe/1414033.stm and the European Council of Conscripts Organisations (ECCO) in Stockholm, Sweden, http://www.xs4all.nl/~ecco/servicetimes.html. Only men are subject to compulsory military service in the armed forces of the Member States. The European Defence Community Treaty had also envisaged conscription only for men, see ch 1 for details.

This means that, subject to the possibility of conscientious objection in Article 12 a (2) Basic Law, men can be forced to serve in arms. Having to serve in arms (in Germany conscripts had to serve for nine months)[125] represents a considerable loss of time and earnings and is thoroughly unpleasant for those not cut out to be soldiers.[126] *Prima facie* this situation, armed service as a right for women but an obligation for men, represents discrimination against men on grounds of sex. This 'other side of the same coin' is at issue in the final case considered in this chapter.

The German national Alexander Dory was called up. He unsuccessfully applied for exemption from conscription to his local drafting authority arguing that the Law on Conscription[127] violated Community law. Section 1 (1) of that Law reflects Article 12 a (4) 2 Basic Law and reads: "From the age of 18 all men who are Germans within the meaning of the Basic Law are subject to conscription".[128] He took his case to a German court where he argued that after *Kreil* there were no reasonable reasons to justify the exemption of women from conscription on grounds of sex. Conscription only for men represented an unlawful discrimination of men: women now had a right but no duty to serve in arms. The matter fell within the material scope of the ETD, as conscription has the effect of delaying the access of men to civil work. They have access only after their service. The German court referred the following question to Luxembourg: "Having regard in particular to the interpretation of Article 2 [...] Directive [...], is the fact that in Germany military service is compulsory only for men contrary to Community law?" Mr Dory applied to both the German court and Luxembourg for an injunction. Both applications were rejected[129] for procedural reasons. According to Advocate General Stix-Hackl[130] the Law on Conscription is not directed at a delayed access of men to civil work. Delayed access was only an effect of the Law, which was exclusively directed at safeguarding the external security of Germany.[131] Community law did not cover the safeguarding of the external security of a Member State.

[125] Conscription was reduced to six months from July 2003.

[126] K Meyer, 'Der Rechtsschutz der Grundrechte im Wehrdienst' (1954) 8 *Die Öffentliche Verwaltung* 66, at 66 speaks of 'particularly intrusive duties' and names 'interruption of his professional career, separation from his family, limitation with regards to his residence, subordination under the special duty of obedience of the soldier'. Conscription can interfere with the fundamental right in Articles 1(1): human dignity; 2: personal freedom; 3: equality; and 4(3): conscientious objection, of the Basic Law. Moreover the right to strike and the freedom to organise trade unions in Article 9 Basic Law 'cannot be reconciled with the nature of the armed forces' (at 68, translated by the author). This article was published before German rearmament in 1955.

[127] *Wehrpflichtgesetz*, English: Federal Law on Military Service (translation of the Court), better: 'Law on Conscription', in the version of 15 December 1995, applicable from 1 January 1996, BGBl. 1995 I, at 1756.

[128] Translation of the author, original German: 'Wehrpflichtig sind alle Männer vom vollendeten achtzehnten Lebensjahr an, die Deutsche im Sinne des Grundgesetzes sind'. Translation of the Court in Case C–186/01 *Dory*, above n 123, at para 12: 'All men who have attained the age of 18 years and are Germans within the Grundgesetz are obliged to perform military service [...]'.

[129] See on the decision of the European Court of Justice: C–186/01 R, *Dory* [2001] ECR I–7823.

[130] Advocate General Stix-Hackl in Case C–186/01, *Dory*, delivered on 28 November 2002, not yet reported, available in French and German.

[131] Above. at para 78. She based her findings on a narrow application of the Directive based on Cases C–63/91 and C–64/91, *Sonia Jackson and Patricia Cresswell v Chief Adjudication Officer* [1992] ECR I–4737; Case C–116/94, *Meyers* [1995] ECR I–2131; Case C–79/99, *Julia Schnorbus v Hesse* [2000] ECR I–10997.

The application of Community law to conscription (for men) is the crucial issue in this ruling. First, the Court confirms the pre-existing case law on defence[132] culminating in the application of Community law and the ETD to the armed forces in *Sirdar* and *Kreil*. Application is subject to narrowly defined public security derogations, the use of which is scrutinised by the Court.[133] Second, however, the Court emphasises Member State competence over defence.[134] Third, the Court establishes the rule that:

> Choices of military organisation for the defence of the territory or of the essential interests [of the Member States] take precedence over policies aimed at the work prospects of young people.[135]

Conscription is an "expression of such a choice of military organisation to which Community law is consequently not applicable."[136] The Court then recognises that conscription for men delays the career of the men concerned. But this delay:

> is an inevitable consequence of the choice made by the Member States regarding military organisation and does not mean that that choice comes within the scope of Community law.[137]

Hence conscription is both expression and inevitable consequence of choices of military organisation that take precedence over social policy. The Court ruled:

> The existence of adverse consequences for access to employment cannot, without encroaching on the competencies of the Member States, have the effect of compelling [them] either to extend the obligation of military service to women, thus imposing on them the same disadvantages with regard to access to employment, or to abolish compulsory military service.[138]

Here the European court of Justice evaluates Germany's options in case of a 'negative' ruling on conscription for men. The Court finishes: "Community law does not preclude compulsory military service being reserved to men."[139]

Rather than building on the previous case law that balances discrimination and security within the context of the ETD, the Court establishes a new precedence rule. This rule neutralises EC social law by making it secondary to the choices of

[132] Case C–222/85, *Johnston*, above n 23; Case C–273/97, *Sirdar*, above n 3; Case C–285/98, *Kreil*, above n 3; Case C–367/89, *Richardt*, above n 109; cited by the Court in C–186/01, *Dory*, above n 123, at paras 31 and 32. In para 33 the Court cites Case C–248/83, *Commission v Germany*, above n 111, at para 16 and Case C–1/95, *Gerster*, above n 18, on the application of the Directive to employment in the public service together with *Sirdar* and *Kreil*.

[133] Case C–186/01, *Dory*, above n 123, at paras 30–34.

[134] Above, at para 36.

[135] Case C–186/01, *Dory*, above n 123, at para 38.

[136] Above, at para 39.

[137] Case C–186/01, *Dory*, above n 123, at para 41.

[138] Above.

[139] Case C–186/01, *Dory*, above n 123, after the last paragraph.

military organisation of the Member States. At the same time the rule implies a precedence of these Member State choices over Community law as a whole. The legal reasoning leading to these implications is not convincing.[140]

First, the Court does not address the issue of sex discrimination. The German court wanted to know whether, conscription "*only for men*" was contrary to Community law. Luxembourg ruled that Community law does not apply to conscription. But there is a difference between the choice to have conscription and the choice to have conscription only for one sex. The answer in paragraph 42 is hardly connected to the rest of the findings.

This leads to a second point. *Dory* established a precedence of choices of military organisation over Community social law.[141] In itself the decision that the choice of conscription in general is outside the application of Community law is consistent with previous case law. However, a decision leading to the differential treatment of men and women with regards to access to employment is definitely within the application of Community law. Before *Dory* the fact that the different treatment was motivated by defence or national security did not compromise the application of Community law, unless of course one of the exemptions applied. *Sirdar* and *Kreil* clarified that Community law applies to access to employment in the armed forces and that sex is not a determining factor for serving in arms. Applying the precedence rule in *Dory* to *Kreil* would lead to a completely different outcome. It would be entirely consistent with *Dory* if excluding women from service in arms were considered a choice of military organisation just like conscription only for men. Excluding women would be "an expression of such a choice" and the resulting discrimination an "inevitable consequence" of that choice. From this viewpoint the *Dory* precedent makes the "line of judgments" on sex discrimination in the armed forces incoherent and messy.

Third, the Court does perhaps not correctly assess the two options left to Germany in case of a negative ruling on conscription only for men.[142] The first option would indeed be the abolition of compulsory military service. This is a choice of military organisation that the European Court of Justice cannot make because it would encroach on the competence of Member States. The second option, the extension of compulsory military service to women, would encroach on the competence of the Member States no more than the obligation to provide

[140] Another question is whether German conscription is directed at defence at all. Germany is not very concerned about her defence, with 1.5% of the GDP it has the lowest defence budget of all major NATO States, for an overview see: E Sönks, *et al*, *SIPRI Yearbook 2001: Armaments, Disarmament and International Security* (OUP, Oxford, 2001) ch 4. It is more likely that the reason to keep conscription in Germany is the financial viability of the social security system. Many young Germans subject to conscription are conscientious objectors. According to BBC News Online http://news.bbc.co.uk/1/hi/wordl.europe/1414033.stm 124,000 young Germans or 30% of those subject to conscription do social work in hospitals and old peoples homes every year. According to the *Westdeutsche Allgemeine Zeitung*, 15 April 2003, the figure in 2002 was 190,000 and will be even higher in 2003. These young men receive little more than pocket money and without them the social services would have to pay proper wages.

[141] Case C–186/01, *Dory*, above n 123, at para 38.

[142] Case C–186/01, *Dory*, above, at para 41.

access for women to service in arms in *Kreil*. No one denies that conscription for women is politically very sensitive and a negative judgment would probably have had the abolition of conscription as a consequence. Nevertheless, the option to extend conscription to women leaves the choice of military organisation of the Member States intact and opens the way for a negative ruling without encroaching on the competence of Germany. From a constitutional point of view *Dory* is a step back from *Kreil*.

Fourth, the admissibility of conscription only for men may be assessed in the light of the ETD, Article 1 (1) of which stipulates that there shall be no discrimination on grounds of sex. Ever since Aristotle discrimination involves treating equal issues unequally or unequal issues equally. There might be an argument that, at this moment in time, service in the armed forces is substantially different for men and women. The current working environment in most armed forces is male dominated and there is an increased danger for women of being sexually abused. Women joining any force face fierce male opposition.[143] Male opposition and dominance as well as the danger of being sexually abused affect male recruits considerably less or not at all. It is these additional negative aspects that constitute a difference between the male and female military experience and could be put forward as arguments for the legality of compulsory military service for men in conjunction with only voluntary service for women under the ETD.[144] However, this situation should periodically be assessed in a way similar to that envisaged by Article 9 (2) ETD.[145] The female military experience might gradually change over the next few years, especially with the military leadership making an effort to improve it and more women joining the forces. A full discussion of this point goes beyond the aims of this chapter. Suffice to say that the absence of any reasoning from the Court in this respect is a missed opportunity. Reasoning along these lines would have allowed Luxembourg to revisit the issue in a new case in a few years time, provided conscription will still be an issue.[146] Possibly they wanted to avoid this happening.

[143] See Utley, 'Army Struggles to Integrate Women', above n 70.

[144] However, at least the first point on fierce male opposition applies whenever women enter a male-dominated workforce. Thanks to Thérèse Murphy of the University of Nottingham for bringing this point to my attention. It could be argued that women have to face and overcome this opposition in order to ensure sustainable access of women to this particular profession or workforce.

[145] Article 9(2) ETD reads: 'Member States shall periodically assess the occupational activities referred to in Article 2(2) in order to decide, in the light of social developments, whether there is justification for maintaining the exclusions concerned. They shall notify the Commission of the results of this assessment.' The *Women in the Armed Forces* report of the United Kingdom Ministry of Defence, above n 61, is an example of such an assessment.

[146] German conscription is 'on the way out'. A Commission on the future of the German armed forces chaired by the former Head of State Richard von Weizsäcker suggested in 2000 to cut the manpower of the forces from 340,000 to 240,000 and the number of conscripts from 130,000 to 30,000 (!). Then Defence Secretary Rudolf Scharping wanted to retain 70,000 conscripts and cut 100,000 personnel over five years. Compare the figure of 70,000 or 30,000 with the number of conscientious objectors of 124,000 given in the previous footnote. Source: BBC News Online http://news.bbc.co.uk/1/hi/wordl. europe/760330.stm. In 2001 conscription was reduced from 10 to 9 months. In April 2003 the Federal

4. THE APPLICATION OF EC SOCIAL LAW TO THE ARMED FORCES OF THE MEMBER STATES

According to *Sirdar* and *Kreil*, EC legislation on the equal treatment of men and women applies to the armed forces of the Member States. Compliance with the Treaty and the ETD depends on whether a Member State can successfully invoke one of the security exemptions. The European Court of Justice scrutinises the use of these exemptions. In particular the proportionality test is applied in varying degrees of intensity. *Dory* seems to deviate from this sophisticated mechanism to balance Community and Member State competence, in favour of a crude precedence rule of choices of national military organisation over EC (social) law. Luxembourg should return to the old mechanism.

Most women are not interested in serving in the armed forces. First, this is for the same reasons most men are not interested. The work is hard, repetitive, dangerous, badly paid, and carries little prestige in most European countries. Second, they can do without the fierce opposition, abuse and chauvinism from some male soldiers. Third, they might fear the increased danger of being sexually abused. Finally, many women know that they do not have the necessary level of physical fitness or that they are not cut out for being soldiers for other reasons. However, some or all of these reasons will prevent most but not all women from applying for the service in the armed forces. There are a considerable number of women that have the physical strength and the ability and who are interested in the services. It is a task of the ETD to make sure that these women get their chance and that the 'band of brothers' includes sisters: sisters in arms.

5. CONCLUSIONS

The analysis in chapters 7 and 8 has shown that secondary Community law, for example on public procurement, applies to the purchasing activities of the defence procurement agencies of the Member States. Similarly, EC legislation on anti-trust, merger control, State aids and trade affects the European defence industries. The Public Procurement Directives and other secondary instruments contain a number of exemptions relevant to defence procurement which largely reflect the security exemptions in the EC Treaty discussed in chapters 4, 5, and 6. The European Court of Justice will exercise scrutiny over the use of these exemptions with varying degrees of intensity. The existence of these exemptions and the judicial scrutiny exercised over their use represent a mechanism that allows to strike a balance between the internal market and other interests of the Community and the national security interests of the Member States.

Ministry of Defence announced that from 1 July 2003 married men, men above the age of 23 (formerly 25), graduates of universities of applied science with an employment contract, and those not reaching top physical requirements ('Tauglichkeitsstufen eins und zwei') would no longer be called up. Moreover conscription is reduced to six months. According to Jürgen Meinberg of the military trade union *Bundeswehrverband* (representing conscripts and professional soldiers) these measures put the sense of conscription into question. The overall strength of the *Bundeswehr* in 2003 was 283,000 with 83,000 conscripts. Source: *Westdeutsche Allgmeine Zeitung*, 15 April 2003.

Chapter 9 discussed the extent to which secondary Community law on sex equality applies to the armed forces of the Member States. The ETD contains an exemption that, although not specifically intended to accommodate security considerations, allows Member States to derogate from their obligations under the Directive in situations involving national security. The European Court of Justice can use this exemption as a basis for a balancing mechanism similar to that used in the context of the security exemptions in the EC Treaty and instruments of secondary Community law, for example the Public Procurement Directives. While until recently the Court provided a coherent jurisprudence applying these balancing mechanisms, the recent judgments in *Commission* v. *Belgium*[147] with regards to public procurement law discussed in chapter 7,[148] *Fiocchi Munizioni*[149] with regards to the law on State aids discussed in chapter 8,[150] and *Dory* with regards to sex equality law seem to deviate from these sophisticated mechanisms in favour of a crude exclusive Member State competence rule regarding defence. These three judgments in three different areas affected by defence could be interpreted as the start of a new jurisprudence. However, it is clearly too early to interpret these judgments as a general move away from the balancing mechanisms described in Part II of this book.

What emerges from Part II is that within the limits of the security exemptions in the EC Treaty and relevant instruments of secondary Community law, European Community law is an instrument of European defence integration. The limits of this function are not clearly determined. They are 'unstable' as they depend on how often the exemptions are used in practice, whether Member States and the Commission will challenge the use of the exemptions, and on the intensity of scrutiny the European Court of Justice will exercise.

Beyond the limits of (1) the more supranational European Community law as an instrument of European defence integration lie (2) the areas of law within the exclusive competence of the Member States, (3) areas regulated by the more intergovernmental CFSP and ESDP, and (4) the areas governed by international obligations, in particular in the context of the WEU, NATO, or the armaments organisations described in chapter 7.[151] Hence it could be said that in 2005 European defence integration is fragmented since it is divided into different frameworks. This fragmentation could lead to inconsistencies and therefore incoherence undermining the efficiency of European defence integration, just as the incoherence of a small combat unit undermines its effectiveness.

[147] Case C–252/01, *Commission v Belgium ('re coastal photography')*, [2003] ECR I-11859.
[148] At 217–219.
[149] See Case T–26/01, *Fiocchi Munizioni SpA v Commission of the European Communities*, (30 September 2003).
[150] At 249–250.
[151] Organisation for Joint Armaments Co-operation (OCCAR), the Western European Armaments Organisation (WEAO), and the Letter of Intent, see ch 7 at 222–224 for details.

Part III

European Defence Integration Under the Constitutional Treaty

10

Joining Pillars, Joining Forces: the Objectives and Principles of the Common Security and Defence Policy

1. INTRODUCTION

THE PREVIOUS PART II of this book presented European Community law as an instrument of defence integration. Integration through the First Pillar is distinct from that in the Second Pillar of the Treaty on European Union (hereinafter TEU). Moreover, it is distinct from organisational structures outside the EU (hereinafter EU), such as the Western European Union (hereinafter WEU), NATO, the Organisation for Security and Cooperation in Europe (hereinafter OSCE), or the Organisation for Joint-Armaments Cooperation (hereinafter OCCAR). Therefore European defence integration is fragmented. With regards to the EU, this fragmentation has an internal dimension through the regulation of defence integration in two different pillars of the TEU. Moreover, it has an external dimension through the defence and security organisations outside the EU. The external dimension was addressed in the Treaties of Amsterdam and Nice, mainly with the transfer of the functions of the WEU to the EU, as described in chapter 3.[1] The internal dimension of fragmentation was addressed by the Convention for the Future of Europe, who in 2003 presented a *Draft Treaty Establishing a Constitution for Europe*. Under this new Treaty the EU will have legal personality and replaces the European Communities.[2] The Constitutional Treaty envisages the abolition of the three-Pillar structure of the TEU by establishing a single legal framework of the Union. Therefore the Constitutional Treaty has to be discussed in a separate and final Part III of this book. The discussion continues and completes the story told in Part I. However, it also continues and completes

[1] At 100–108.

[2] Article IV–438(1) Constitutional Treaty (December 2004 version, see below) 'Succession and legal continuity' reads: 'The European Union established by this Treaty shall be the successor to the European Union established by the Treaty on European Union and to the European Community.' Article IV–437(1) Constitutional Treaty reads: 'Repeal of earlier Treaties. This Treaty establishing a Constitution for Europe shall repeal the Treaty establishing the European Community, the Treaty on European Union and, [...] the acts and treaties which have supplemented or amended them, [...].'

the analysis in Part II since the Convention adopted the defence *acquis communautaire* for the new legal order of the EU.[3]

The following Part III will discuss the Constitutional Treaty as an instrument of European defence integration. The crucial question addressed in the Part of the book is whether the Constitutional Treaty provides a coherent legal framework for defence, in other words whether it overcomes the fragmentation of European defence integration. A critical analysis in this chapter will cover the objectives of the Union's Common Security and Defence Policy (hereinafter CSDP) under the Constitutional Treaty before discussing its scope in chapter 11 and the institutions and legal instruments in chapter 12. Chapter 11 will also cover the organisational and institutional security and defence structures outside the legal order of the Constitutional Treaty, such as the United Nations or NATO, and their connection to the 'new EU'. This discussion will show that the CSDP is built and dependent on the United Nations and NATO.

At the time of completion of this book at the end of 2004 the entering into force of the Constitutional Treaty is uncertain. In many of the now 25 Member States this will depend on a national referendum. Therefore chapters 10, 11, and 12 will also address alternative options for European defence integration beyond the *acquis* of the Treaty of Nice in general and in particular with regards to defence integration. As the book is also written for an audience reading it after the possible entering into force of the Constitutional Treaty the present tense is used. The discussion is based on the 13 October 2004 version of the Constitutional Treaty signed in Rome on 29 October 2004,[4] unless indicated otherwise.

2. TOWARDS THE CONSTITUTIONAL TREATY 2000–2004

The Common Foreign and Security Policy (hereinafter CFSP) and the European Security and Defence Policy (hereinafter ESDP) outlined in chapters 2 and 3 are currently parts of a wider process towards a new European Constitutional Treaty. This process is part of a future that has already begun. In December 2000, in Nice, the European Council reached an agreement on the revision of the Treaties. The objective was to adapt the institutions of the EU to enlargement, thereby expressing the need to initiate a wider and deeper debate on the future of the Union.[5] In December

[3] See Article IV–438(3) Constitutional Treaty (December 2004 version) reads: 'The acts of the institutions, bodies, offices and agencies adopted on the basis of the treaties and act repealed by Article IV–437 shall remain in force. Their legal effects shall be preserved [...]. The other components of the acquis of the Community and the Union existing at the time of the entry into force of this Treaty [...] shall also be preserved [...].'

[4] Treaty establishing a Constitution for Europe, Conference of the Representatives of the Governments of the Member States, Brussels, 13 October 2004 (ORfr.) CIG 87/1/04 REV 1. This version included a number of considerable changes in comparison to the Draft Treaty and the June version of the Constitutional Treaty. The version published on 16 December 2004 [2004] 03 C–31011 contained only minor changes to the October 2004 version. Chapters 10–12 will refer to the published December 2004 verison of the Constitutional Treaty unless indicated otherwise.

[5] See Declaration 23 on the Future of the Union, Final Act, Treaty of Nice Amending the Treaty on European Union, the Treaties Establishing the European Communities and Certain Related Acts, [2001] OJ C–80/01.

2001 the Laeken European Council adopted the *Declaration on the Future of the European Union*[6] thereby committing the EU to becoming more democratic, more transparent, and more efficient and to preparing the way for a Constitution for the citizens of Europe. For this purpose, it decided to organise a Convention bringing together the main stakeholders to examine the vital questions raised by the future development of the Union and to seek different possible responses, which were presented in the *Draft Treaty establishing a Constitution for Europe*. One of the four central questions to be addressed was how to ensure the cohesion and effectiveness of the external action of the EU.[7] Meeting from February 2002 to July 2003 the Convention formulated a *Draft Constitutional Treaty*.[8] This Draft formed the working basis for the negotiations of the Intergovernmental Conference, composed of the Heads of State and Government of the Member States and the accession countries. After the envisaged passing of the Constitutional Treaty had failed on the Brussels Summit in December 2003,[9] the now 25 Heads of State and Government finally agreed on the Draft during another Brussels Summit on 18th June 2004.[10] The discrepancies between the December 2003 and the June 2004 versions of the Draft are only limited. The final text of the Constitutional Treaty was signed on 29 October 2004 in Rome. This final text differs, in parts considerably, from the previous December 2003 and June 2004 versions of the Draft. As mentioned above, the entering into force of the Constitution is not certain since this depends on national referenda in at least nine Member States. These referenda are scheduled for 2005 and 2006.

One of the most important innovations of the Constitutional Treaty is the intention to remove the differentiation between the three Pillars of the TEU. The more supranational First Community Pillar and the two more intergovernmental Second and Third Pillars, on CFSP and Police and Judicial Co-operation in Criminal Matters respectively, are merged into one 'Pillarless' framework. *Prima facie* this would overcome the internal fragmentation of European defence integration. However, it is submitted and explained in detail in chapters 10, 11, and 12 that this 'merger' has no effect on the more intergovernmental nature of the CFSP and what under the Constitutional Treaty is called the 'Common Security and

[6] http://europa.eu.int/futurum/documents/offtext/doc151201_en.htm.

[7] The fundamental questions were how to organise the division of responsibilities between the Union and the Member States, how to better define the respective tasks of the European institutions, how to ensure the coherence and effectiveness of the Union's external action, and how to strengthen the Union's legitimacy? See Laeken Declaration, above.

[8] Draft of the Constitutional Treaty presented by the European Convention in July 2003 and published in [2003] OJ C–169/1 and http://european-convention.eu.int/docs/Treaty/cv00850.en03.pdf.

[9] See *Declaration of the President*, Conference of the Representatives of the Governments of the Member States, Brussels, 13 December 2003, in Antonio Missiroli, *From Copenhagen to Brussels: European Defence: Core Documents*, Chaillot Paper No 67, (Institute of Security Studies of the European Union, Paris, 2003) 456 (hereinafter '*From Copenhagen to Brussels*'). Changes were inserted by the meeting, see: Document CIG 84/04. Changes relevant to the subject matter of this chapter occurred in what was then Articles III-322–III-329. The final version of the Constitutional Treaty signed on 29 October 2004, above n 3, contained more substantial changes.

[10] 'EU Leaders reach Deal on Constitution', *Financial Times*, 21 June 2004; 'Public Don't Want Any Part of it: Europe's Leaders reach Agreement, but the Debate Rages On', *Guardian*, 21 June 2004; 'Constitution et désunion', editorial, *Le Monde*, 20 June 2004; 'EU Gipfel: Europa mit neuer Verfassung–Prodi ohne Nachfolger', *Frankfurter Allgemeine Zeitung*, 19 June 2004.

Defence Policy' (hereinafter CSDP). The term CSDP replaces the term ESDP used in the Treaty of Nice. This will be discussed in more detail below.

The Constitutional Treaty consists of the Treaty itself, divided into four parts, preceded by a preamble, and 36 Protocols and 2 Annexes.[11] Part I covers, in 60 articles (I-1 to I-60) divided into nine titles, the objectives, principles, competencies, legal instruments, finances, membership and institutions of the Union. Part II consists of the Charter of Fundamental Rights of the Union, consisting of a separate preamble and 54 articles (II-61 to II-114) divided into seven titles. Part III consists of 322 articles (III-115 to III-436) divided into seven titles containing the detailed provisions on the *acquis communautaire* and the *acquis*' of the Second and the Third Pillars. Finally Part IV contains twelve general and final articles (IV-437 to IV-448). A reference to the relevant part needs to be included when indicating individual articles of the Constitutional Treaty, for example Article I-40 or III-210 Constitutional Treaty. Parts I and III regulate Community policies and the CFSP and CSDP. The following discussion will cover the objectives and principles of the CFSP and CSDP before examining their scope in chapter 11.

3. THE OBJECTIVES OF THE COMMON SECURITY AND DEFENCE POLICY

The objectives of the CFSP and CSDP are stipulated in various parts and provision of the Constitutional Treaty. These include the preamble, Articles I-3, I-40, I-41, III-292, and III-195 Constitutional Treaty.

3.1. Strive for Peace

The short preamble to the Constitutional Treaty[12] already contains an indirect reference to the CSDP, as "to strive for peace" is stipulated as one of the objectives

[11] Article IV–442 Constitutional Treaty reads: 'The Protocols and Annexes to this Treaty shall form an integral part thereof.'

[12] The preamble to the Constitutional Treaty reads:

> Drawing inspiration from the cultural, religious and humanist inheritance of Europe, from which have developed the universal values of the inviolable and inalienable rights of the human person, freedom, democracy, equality and the rule of law,
>
> Believing that Europe, reunited after bitter experiences, intends to continue along the path of civilisation, progress and prosperity, for the good of all its inhabitants, including the weakest and most deprived; that it wishes to remain a continent open to culture, learning and social progress; and that it wishes to deepen the democratic and transparent nature of its public life, and to strive for peace, justice and solidarity throughout the world,
>
> Convinced that, while remaining proud of their own national identities and history, the peoples of Europe are determined to transcend their ancient divisions and, united ever more closely, to forge a common destiny,
>
> Convinced that, thus 'united in diversity', Europe offers them the best chance of pursuing, with due regard for the rights of each individual and in awareness of their responsibilities towards future generations and the Earth, the great venture which makes of it a special area of human hope,

and basic values of the EU. The promotion of peace is also stipulated as one of the Union's objectives in Article I-3 (1) Constitutional Treaty.[13] However, these references do not only relate to the promotion of peace in relation to third countries, in other words to peace as an aspect of foreign and security policy. It also refers to internal peace between the Member States, which is promoted and secured through European integration. The 'peace objective' is both inward and outward looking.[14] This fundamental objective of European integration, first expressed in the Schuhman Declaration of 1950, and later continuously contained in the preambles of the European treaties, most notably the European Defence Community Treaty,[15] the EC Treaty[16] and the TEU,[17] has found a prominent place in the Constitutional Treaty.[18] The legal significance of this peace objective of the Union is not clear. It is submitted that it would exclude the use of the CSDP for an act of armed aggression. Moreover, the different aspects of the CSDP discussed below have to be interpreted on the background of this objective. In practical terms the peace objective has been successful in the past 50 years. It enjoys public and political support and for these reasons deserves its prominent place in the Constitutional Treaty.

3.2. The Relations with the Wider World: The Union's Values and Interests

Article I-3 Constitutional Treaty contains a list of the values and interests of the Union. These are crucial since any security and defence policy embodies values and interests and their combination creates the identity of an international actor.[19] In other words the values and interests explain why the Union wants and needs a

> Determined to continue the work accomplished within the framework of the Treaties establishing the European Communities and the Treaty on European Union, by ensuring the continuity of the Community acquis,
>
> Grateful to the members of the European Convention for having prepared this Constitution on behalf of the citizens and States of Europe, [...].

[13] Article I–3(1) Constitutional Treaty reads: 'The Union's aim is to promote peace, its values and the well being of its peoples.'

[14] The notions of inward looking and outward looking objectives was taken from RA Wessel, *The European Union's Foreign and Security Policy: A Legal Institutional Perspective* (Kluwer, The Hague, 1999) 68.

[15] Paragraph 2 of the Preamble to the EDC Treaty: 'to contribute to the maintenance of peace'. See ch 1 at 22–44 for details.

[16] Paragraph 9 of the Preamble to the EC Treaty: 'Resolved by thus pooling their resources to preserve and strengthen peace and liberty, and calling upon the other peoples of Europe who share their ideal to join in their efforts.'

[17] Paragraph 11 of the Preamble to the TEU: 'Resolved to implement a common foreign and security policy including the progressive framing of a common defence policy, which might lead to a common defence [...] thereby reinforcing European identity and its independence in order to promote peace, security and progress in Europe and in the world.' See chs 2 and 3.

[18] Schuman Declaration of 9 May 1950, 13 (1980) *Bulletin of the European Communities*, 14, 15; available at: http://www.cec.org.uk/whatsnew/schuman.htm. See ch 1 at 19–21 for details.

[19] N Gnesotto, *et al*, *European Defence: A Proposal for a White Paper*, (Institute of Security Studies of the European Union, Paris, 2004) at 25 (hereinafter 'White Paper').

security and defence policy. Thus it also sets the basic framework for the scope of this policy discussed in chapter 12. Article I-3 (1) Constitutional Treaty repeats the part of the Preamble outlined above and stipulates that the Union's aim is *inter alia*, the promotion of peace. Article I-3 (4) Constitutional Treaty provides:

> In its relations with the wider world, the Union shall uphold and promote its values and interests. It shall contribute to peace, security, the sustainable development of the Earth, solidarity and mutual respect among peoples, free and fair trade, eradication of poverty and protection of human rights, in particular the rights of the child, as well as to strict observance and the development of international law, including respect for the principles of the [UN] Charter.

First, by contrast to the preamble and Article I-3 (1) Constitutional Treaty outlined above, the reference "[I]t shall contribute to peace, security [...]", in Article I-3 (4) Constitutional Treaty only refers to peace as an objective of foreign, in other words external policy. This interpretation can be made on the basis of the context of the other objectives stipulated in paragraph 4 of the provision. These are all foreign policy objectives.[20] Moreover, the paragraph begins with the words: "in its relations with the wider world", which clarifies that it concerns the foreign policy objectives of the EU.

Second, whereas the Union's "interests" are not defined, it's "values" are clearly stipulated in the second sentence of paragraph 4. However, the difference between values and interests is not always clear. Free trade and security are clearly interests as well as values. It is submitted that the references to peace, the "strict observance" of international law, and the UN Charter, limit the use of force by the EU and therefore the CSDP as a whole. The deployment of EU troops in whatever form would only be possible when this would be legal under international law. Therefore the use of force outside the limits of Article 51 UN Charter or without authorisation by a resolution of the UN Security Council can be excluded. This is confirmed by other provisions of the Constitutional Treaty which shall be discussed in the context of the scope of the CSDP in chapter 12. Following the tradition of all preceding treaties described in chapters 1, 2, and 3,[21] the reference to the UN Charter also builds the EU and her CSDP on the foundations of the United Nations.[22]

In contrast to the Treaties of Maastricht, Amsterdam and Nice discussed in chapters 2 and 3, the external relations and action objectives of the Union are stipulated in detail and take a more prominent place in the Constitutional Treaty.[23] This is partly due to the fact that all Union policies are now regulated in one Treaty which, at least in theory, overcomes the three-Pillar system of the TEU.

[20] Above.

[21] See ch 1 at 14,15 and 25, ch 2 at 63, and ch 3 at 84.

[22] See Gnesotto, *et al*, 'White Paper', above n 19, at 35.

[23] Article 2 indent 2 TEU (ex Article B) listed '[...] to assert its identity on the international scene, in particular through the implementation of a [CFSP] including the progressive framing of a common defence policy, which might lead to a common defence, in accordance with the provisions of Article 17; [...]' as one of the objectives of the EU More details on the objectives of the CFSP are provided in Article 11 TEU (ex J1), which includes all objectives stipulated in Article I–3(4) Constitutional Treaty.

Article I-3 (4) Constitutional Treaty therefore addresses both aspects of EU external action. It stipulates the objectives of the Second Pillar CFSP, for example security, and of the First Pillar EC external relations, for example free and fair trade.

Part III of the Constitutional Treaty contains Article III-292 as a provision having general application and introducing Title V on the Union's external action, which includes the CFSP and CSDP. Article III-292 (2) Constitutional Treaty contains a list of objectives of EU external action, including EC external relations, CFSP, and CSDP. These objectives repeat and expand the ones stipulated in Article I-3 (4) Constitutional Treaty:

> The Union shall define and pursue common policies and actions, and shall work for a high degree of cooperation in all fields of international relations, in order to:
>
> (a) safeguard its values, fundamental interests, security, independence and integrity;
>
> (b) consolidate and support democracy, the rule of law, human rights and international law;
>
> (c) preserve peace, prevent conflicts and strengthen international security, in conformity with the principles of the United Nations Charter, with the principles of the Helsinki Final Act and with the aims of the Charter of Paris, including those relating to external borders;
>
> (d) foster the sustainable economic, social and environmental development of developing countries, with the primary aim of eradicating poverty;
>
> (e) encourage the integration of all countries into the world economy, including through the progressive abolition of restrictions on international trade;
>
> (f) help develop international measures to preserve and improve the quality of the environment and the sustainable management of global natural resources, in order to ensure sustainable development;
>
> (g) assist populations, countries and regions confronting natural or man-made disasters;
>
> (h) promote an international system based on stronger multilateral cooperation and good global governance.

Similar to Article I-3 (4) Constitutional Treaty this list combines CFSP and EC external relations objectives. Letters (a)–(c) and (h) contain the CFSP objectives also stipulated in Article 11 hyphens 1–5 TEU.[24] The differences are minimal. Only

[24] Article 11(1) TEU (ex Article J1.) reads:

- The Union shall define and implement a [CFSP] covering all areas of foreign and security policy, the objectives of which shall be:
- to safeguard the common values, fundamental interests, independence and integrity of the Union in conformity with the principles of the United Nations Charter;
- to strengthen security of the Union in all ways;
- to assert its identity on the international scene, in particular through the implementation of a common foreign and security policy, including the progressive framing of a common defence policy, which might lead to a common defence, in accordance with the provisions of Article 17;
- to promote international cooperation;
- to develop and to consolidate democracy and the rule of law, and respect for human rights and fundamental freedoms.

the promotion of good governance was added.[25] The separate objective of "to strengthen the security of the Union in all ways" was deleted and the security objective inserted instead in Article III-292 (2) letter (a) Constitutional Treaty. Letter (d) is similar to the EC objective in Article 3 (1) letter (r) EC,[26] letter (e) is similar to the EC external relations objective in Article 131 EC,[27] and letter (f) is similar to the EC objective in Article 3 (1) letter (l) EC.[28] However, in contrast to the EC Treaty, the objectives relating to environmental protection and development are phrased in a way emphasising the foreign policy aspect. Generally, however, the Constitutional Treaty adds little to the *status quo* of the Treaty of Nice with regards to the objectives of external action.

3.3. The EU Operational Capacity

According to Article I-41 (1) Constitutional Treaty the "common security and defence policy shall be an integral part of the [CFSP]". First, this suggests a name other than European Security and Defence Policy for the defence component of the EU. Therefore, hereinafter the abbreviation of this term 'CSDP' shall be used. This will also make it easier to distinguish the different versions of the defence component of the CFSP. Whether this name change also entails an innovation in relation to substance is a different matter, which shall be discussed in more detail in chapter 11. Second, the nature of the CSDP as an integral part of the CFSP entails that the provisions on the institutional structure discussed in chapter 12 and other basic features of the latter equally apply to the earlier. The CSDP shares most of the CFSP structures.

Article I-41 (1) Constitutional Treaty provides that the CSDP shall provide the EU with an operational capacity drawing on civil and military assets. This establishes an independent EU military capacity as an objective of the EU. However, the EU may use this independent military capacity only on missions outside the Union for peacekeeping, conflict prevention and strengthening international security in accordance with the principles of the UN Charter. Therefore the objective is limited to the framework of the European Rapid Reaction Force (hereinafter ERRF) already envisaged before.[29] Moreover, "the performance of these tasks shall be undertaken using capabilities provided by the Member States." This clarifies that the independent military capability should not amount to a permanent European Army. This can be concluded from the final act of the Helsinki Summit discussed in chapter 3[30] in which this was spelt out. The Constitutional

[25] References to the Helsinki Final Act and the Paris Charter and one reference to the UN Charter did not appear in the December 2003 and June 2004 versions of the Treaty, but reappeared in the October 2004 and December 2004 versions.

[26] Article 3(1) letter (r) EC reads: 'a policy in the sphere of development cooperation, [...]'.

[27] Article 131(1) EC reads: 'By establishing a customs union between themselves Member States aim to contribute, in the common interest, to the harmonious development of world trade, the progressive abolition of restrictions on international trade and the lowering of customs barriers.'

[28] Article 3(1) letter (l) EC reads: 'a policy in the sphere of the environment, [...]'.

[29] See ch 3 at 93–98 for details.

[30] Above.

Treaty would contain a specific reference to a European Army if the objective were to establish such a body. However, the difference between an ERRF and a European Army is not entirely clear, as the latter is not further defined. A European Army would probably require a certain independence of its component units from the Member State governments who sent them and a certain element of permanence. It does not necessarily require all the attributes of the European Defence Forces of the European Defence Community envisaged in the 1950s and described in chapter 1,[31] for example a common uniform, common procurement, and common ranks. The final act of the Helsinki Summit also provides that the ERRF would be "sustained for at least one year." It could be argued that during a longer period in which the ERRF were deployed and sustained it would be a *de facto* European Army. Such an ERRF would be composed of national units but integrated into European military structures and outside the control of their individual Member States for a longer period. It is submitted that this would be an EU Army in everything but name. The ERRF shall be discussed in more detail in the context of crisis management in chapter 11.[32]

4. THE PRINCIPLES OF THE COMMON SECURITY AND DEFENCE POLICY

The principles of the CFSP and CSDP are stipulated in various parts and provisions of the Constitutional Treaty. These include the preamble, Articles I-16, III-292, and III-294 Constitutional Treaty.

4.1. The Principles of External Action

Article III-292 (1) subparagraph 1 Constitutional Treaty contains the principles of the external action of the EU. It provides:

> "The Union's action on the international scene shall be guided by the *principles* which have inspired its own creation, development and enlargement, and which it seeks to advance in the wider world: democracy, the rule of law, the universality and indivisibility of human rights and fundamental freedoms, respect for human dignity, the principles of equality and solidarity, and respect for the principles of the United Nations Charter and international law. [emphasis added]"

This contains a number of principles which shall be advanced by EU external action on the one hand and shall guide EU external action on the other hand. In other words, it is both outward and inward looking. The references to human rights, international law, and in particular the UN Charter repeat the values of the Union stipulated in Article I-3 (4) Constitutional Treaty and discussed above. These are 'I-3 (4)-values' as well as 'III-292 (1) 1-principles' of the Union. Democracy and the rule of law are mentioned for the first time in Article III-292

[31] At 37–39.
[32] At 309–319.

(1) Constitutional Treaty. The notion of a principle "having general application" to the Union's external action implies that the specific rules on external action as well as the practical implementation of external action have to comply with these principles. The wording "shall be guided by" supports this impression. Article 11 TEU does mention the development and consolidation of democracy, the rule of law, and respect for human rights and fundamental freedoms as objectives of the CFSP. However, this was meant as an objective of the CFSP which should be advanced by this policy in relation to third countries. The notion of a 'foreign policy objective' implies an outward looking character. In contrast, Article III-292 (1) Constitutional Treaty also provides an inward looking principle guiding external action including the CFSP and CSDP. The rules on the CFSP and CSDP therefore have to comply with the principle of democracy and the rule of law. It will be shown in the context of the discussion of the European Parliament and the European Court of Justice as parts of the institutional framework of the CFSP and CSDP in chapter 12[33] that the relevant rules do not comply with these principles. The CFSP and CSDP suffer from both a democratic deficit and a deficit regarding the rule of law.

4.2. The CFSP and the Member States: Mutual Solidarity, Loyalty, and Convergence

A number of provisions deal with the internal relationship between the CFSP and the Member States. Article I-16 (2) Constitutional Treaty on the CFSP provides:

> Member States shall actively and unreservedly support the Union's [CFSP] in a spirit of loyalty and mutual solidarity and shall comply with the acts adopted by the Union in this area. They shall refrain from action contrary to the Union's interests or likely to impair its effectiveness.

This is repeated in Article III-294 (2) Constitutional Treaty.[34] Moreover, Article III-294 (2) subparagraph 2 Constitutional Treaty makes the Council and the newly created Union Minister for Foreign Affairs responsible for safeguarding this principle. These provisions leave the rule in Article 11 (2) TEU discussed in chapter 2[35] almost unchanged, with the exception of the role of the Union Minister for Foreign Affairs. Article I-40 Constitutional Treaty on "specific provisions for implementing common foreign and security policy" provides in paragraph 1:

[33] At 382–392.

[34] Article III–294(2) Constitutional Treaty reads:

> The Member States shall support the [CFSP] actively and unreservedly in a spirit of loyalty and mutual solidarity. The Member States shall work together to enhance and develop their mutual political solidarity. They shall refrain from any action which is contrary to the interests of the Union or likely to impair its effectiveness as a cohesive force in international relations.
> The Council and the Union Minister for Foreign Affairs shall ensure that these principles are complied with.

[35] Ch 2 at 61–64.

> The European Union shall conduct a [CFSP], based on the development of mutual political solidarity among Member States, the identification of questions of general interest and the achievement of an ever-increasing degree of convergence of Member States' actions.

These provisions introduce the principles of mutual political solidarity, loyalty, and convergence as objectives of the CFSP. Solidarity and convergence are the internal or inward-looking objectives of the CFSP: they refer to the behaviour of Member States towards each other as a precondition for the (external) effectiveness of the CFSP. There is no enforcement mechanism as such, the Council and the Union Minister for Foreign Affairs can merely impose political pressure on Member States violating these principles.

4.3. Consistency

Another inward looking principle is provided in Article III-292 (3) subparagraph 2 sentence 1 Constitutional Treaty:

> The Union shall ensure consistency between the different areas of its external action and between these and its other policies.

Consistency is the lack of contradictions which undermine coherence. In the context of this provision the principle applies to the consistency between the different areas of external action, in particular the CFSP and trade, and to the consistency between external action and the other EU policies. According to subparagraph 2 of the provision the Council and the Commission, assisted by the Union Minister for Foreign Affairs, shall ensure consistency and co-operate to that effect. This indicates that consistency is a guiding principle for the institutions in the conduct of external action. They shall avoid contradictions. The consistency that is stipulated in Article III-292 (3) Constitutional Treaty is not required of the external action framework of the Constitutional Treaty. However, inconsistencies in this framework would make it difficult for the institutions to fulfil their obligation under Article III-292 (3) Constitutional Treaty. It will be argued in chapters 11 and 12 that the continued fragmentation of the various aspects of European defence integration will make it very difficult to adhere to the principle of consistency.[36]

5. CONCLUSIONS

The Constitutional Treaty aims to overcome the three-Pillar structure of the Treaties of Maastricht, Amsterdam, and Nice. Theoretically, this unites the previously separate CFSP and ESDP/CSDP with the Community Pillar of the Union. Therefore, *prima facie* one important aspect of fragmentation of European defence integration will be addressed in the Constitutional Treaty. Whether this

[36] Ch 11 at 353 and ch 12 at 392–394.

really decreases the degree of fragmentation depends partly on whether the new Treaty does not introduce new dimensions of fragmentation. This shall be discussed in the context of the scope of the CSDP in chapter 11. Moreover, whether the three-Pillar structure of the TEU is really removed thereby addressing the problem of fragmentation depends on whether the separation between a more supranational Community and a more intergovernmental CFSP is removed. This shall be discussed in the context of the institutional structure of the CSDP in chapter 12.

11

Crisis Management, Armaments, and Collective Defence: the Scope of Defence Integration Under the Constitutional Treaty

1. INTRODUCTION

AS DISCUSSED IN the previous chapter, the Constitutional Treaty aims to overcome the separation between the more intergovernmental Second Pillar on the Common Foreign and Security Policy (hereinafter CFSP) and the more supranational First Community Pillar of the Treaties of Maastricht, Amsterdam and Nice discussed in chapters 2 and 3. The European Security and Defence Policy (hereinafter ESDP) of these Treaties, renamed Common Security and Defence Policy (hereinafter CSDP) is part of the CFSP. Hence *prima facie* defence integration through the CSDP is united with European defence integration through Community law as described in chapters 4 to 9 of this book.

The Constitutional Treaty develops the ESDP by adding to its scope. The different areas of activities of the envisaged CSDP shall be discussed first. Second, the Constitutional Treaty also adopts the *acquis communautaire* including the defence *acquis* of the Community which shall be discussed next. A developed CSDP and the Community defence *acquis* in a 'Pillarless' legal order may lead to overlaps and inconsistencies. Finally, following the tradition of the TEU, the Constitutional Treaty links its aspects of defence integration to other international organisations in the field of security and defence, most notably to the United Nations and NATO.

2. THE SCOPE OF THE COMMON SECURITY AND DEFENCE POLICY

The scope of the CSDP is described in Article I-41 and Articles III-309 to 312 Constitutional Treaty. These provisions use the terms CFSP, CSDP, 'common Union defence policy', and 'common defence'.

The relationship of CFSP and CSDP is clarified in Article I-41 (1) Constitutional Treaty:

> The [CSDP] shall be an integral part of the [CFSP]. It shall provide the Union with an operational capacity drawing on civil and military assets. The Union may use

> them on missions outside the Union for peace-keeping, conflict prevention and strengthening international security in accordance with the principles of the [UN] Charter. The performance of these tasks shall be undertaken using capabilities provided by the Member States.

According to this paragraph crisis management on the basis of an operational capability is one of the aspects of the CSDP. This aspect shall be discussed in detail below. The introduction of this aspect and the rule on the relationship between CSDP and CFSP in the same paragraph is no coincidence. As explained below, crisis management is the CSDP aspect closest to foreign policy, it is an aspect of security policy as a form of foreign policy. Moreover, as outlined in chapters 2 and 3,[1] crisis management is also the most established and least disputed aspect of EU security and defence policy. A common security policy, which started in 1992, was an offspring of an older foreign policy, which had started with European Political Cooperation.[2] Similarly with the Constitutional Treaty, a common defence policy as a policy going beyond crisis management, will be the offspring of the common security policy. The 'F' in CFSP gave birth to the 'S', which in turn gave birth to the 'D' in CSDP.[3] However, Article I-41 (1) Constitutional Treaty cannot be read in isolation, the CSDP is more than crisis management. This will be discussed in detail below.

With regards to a 'common defence', the Convention adopted the approach of Article 17 (1) TEU described in chapter 2.[4] According to Article I-41 (2) the Constitutional Treaty does not envisage a common defence. The provision reads:

> The [CSDP] shall include the progressive framing of a common Union defence policy. This will lead to a common defence, when the European Council, acting unanimously, so decides. It shall in that case recommend to the Member States the adoption of such a decision in accordance with their respective constitutional requirements.

This keeps intact the *status quo* of the Treaty of Nice regarding a common defence described in chapter 3. A common defence remains uncertain and set in the future. However, Article I-41 (2) Constitutional Treaty is useful for the definition of the scope of the CSDP since it clearly spells out that it does *not* amount to the establishment of a common defence.

Article I-41 (2) also introduces the notion of a 'common Union defence policy' as a fourth aspect. As outlined in the introduction to this book, security can be understood as a wide concept which includes defence. Alternatively, it can be understood as a narrow concept which refers to crisis management as an aspect of foreign policy only. The Constitutional Treaty follows the latter approach.

[1] Ch 2 at 65–66 and ch 3 at 102–103 and 114–118.

[2] See ch 2 at 52–57 for details.

[3] A Missiroli, 'European Security Policy: The Challenges of Coherence' (2001) 6 *European Foreign Affairs Review* 177, at 184.

[4] Ch 2 at 64–65.

Defence, is considered an aspect of the CSDP which is different and additional to security. This is already implied in the use of the word "and" in "Common Security *and* Defence Policy". The word "defence" refers to the aspects of the CSDP which are additional to crisis management, in particular mutual defence and defence procurement. These will be discussed below. The express mentioning of a 'common Union defence policy' clarifies that the CSDP goes beyond crisis management. Article I-41 (2) Constitutional Treaty stipulates the "progressive framing" of such a defence policy. This describes the common Union defence policy as a process set in the future but starting with the entering into force of the Constitutional Treaty. Moreover, the words "progressive framing" imply a process of defence integration growing in substance and coherence over time, of an ever closer defence policy. It is submitted that this refers to the flexible character of all three main aspects of the CSDP, in particular those going beyond crisis management. This shall be explained in the context of these aspects below. Moreover, it might refer to the possible inclusion of additional aspects at a later stage. Additional aspects could include permanent European armed forces, a Union Minister for Defence and Security, or a European defence budget. The possibility of the addition of aspects at a later stage is implied in the notion of a 'common defence' as the 'final destination' of the "progressive framing of a common Union defence policy".

The flexible character of the three aspects of the CSDP is not due to the applicability of enhanced co-operation in the field. Up to October 2004 all three aspects had their own flexible framework. Under the Constitutional Treaty enhanced co-operation is possible in the context of the CFSP. Article III-419 (2) provides:

> The request of the Member States which wish to establish enhanced cooperation between themselves within the framework of the [CFSP] shall be addressed to the Council. It shall be forwarded to the Union Minister for Foreign Affairs, who shall give an opinion on whether the enhanced cooperation is consistent with the Union's common foreign and security policy, and to the Commission, which shall give its opinion in particular on whether the enhanced cooperation proposed is consistent with other Union policies. It shall also be forwarded to the European Parliament for information.
>
> Authorisation to proceed with enhanced cooperation shall be granted by a European decision of the Council acting unanimously.

Article III-420 (2) provides:

> Any Member State which wishes to participate in enhanced cooperation in progress in the framework of the [CFSP] shall notify its intention to the Council, the Union Minister for Foreign Affairs and the Commission.
>
> The Council shall confirm the participation of the Member State concerned, after consulting the Union Minister for Foreign Affairs. It shall note where necessary that

> any conditions of participation have been fulfilled. The Council, on a proposal from the Union Minister for Foreign Affairs, may also adopt any transitional measures deemed necessary with regard to the application of the acts already adopted within the framework of enhanced cooperation. However, if the Council considers that any conditions of participation have not been fulfilled, it shall indicate the arrangements to be adopted to fulfil those conditions and shall set a deadline for re-examining the request for participation.
>
> For the purposes of this paragraph, the Council of Ministers shall act unanimously and in accordance with Article I-44 (3).

The words "acting unanimously" in Articles III-419 (2) and III-420 (2) Constitutional Treaty were not part of the Draft presented by the Convention in July 2003 but inserted by the Brussels European Council on 18 June 2004 and carried on to the final version signed in October 2004 and published in December 2004. The requirement of unanimity is absolute since the possibility to move to qualified majority voting through Articles III-422 (1) and (2)[5] Constitutional Treaty was also blocked by the Brussels European Council of June 2004 which inserted paragraph 3 to Article III-433 (then Article III-328) Constitutional Treaty: "Paragraphs 1 and 2 shall not apply to decisions having military or defence implications."

As explained in chapter 3,[6] under the Treaty of Nice enhanced co-operation is available in the context of the CFSP. However, it is not easily applied and it is subject to derogations. In regard to CFSP, enhanced co-operation is possible with respect to the implementation of Joint Actions only. Not only does the Treaty of Nice require the acquiescence of all the Member States, there is a "right to delay" by asking for a referral to the European Council in accordance with Article 23 (2) subparagraph 2 TEU. As a result, enhanced co-operation is difficult to obtain.

Military and defence aspects are currently explicitly excluded from the Nice procedures for enhanced cooperation. A derogation clause was inserted in the Treaty of Nice at the request of the United Kingdom[7] for reasons still not explained.[8] Article 27b TEU simply provides that: "Enhanced cooperation pursuant to this title [Title V on CFSP] shall relate to implementation of a Joint Action

[5] Article III-422(1) and (2) Constitutional Treaty read:

1. Where a provision of the Constitution which may be applied in the context of enhanced cooperation stipulates that the Council shall act unanimously, the Council, acting unanimously in accordance with the arrangements laid down in Article I-43(3), may, adopt a European decision stipulating that it will act by a qualified majority.
2. Where a provision of the Constitution which may be applied in the context of enhanced cooperation stipulates that the Council of Ministers shall adopt European laws or framework laws under a special legislative procedure, the Council, acting unanimously in accordance with the arrangements laid down in Article I-43(3), may, adopt a European decision stipulating that it will act under the ordinary legislative procedure. The Council shall act after consulting the European Parliament.

[6] At 112–114.

[7] P Craig and G de Búrca, *EU Law*, 3rd edn, (OUP, Oxford, 2003) 46.

[8] As pointed out by S Peers, 'Common Foreign and Security Policy 1999–2000' (2001) 21 *Yearbook of European Law* 531, 547.

or a Common Position. It shall not relate to matters having military or defence implications."[9] The concept of defence is not defined, nor that of "having military implications". In a broad conception, the fight against terrorism, peacekeeping actions, weapons exports and exports of dual use goods could come under this term. As a result of such a wide definition, enhanced co-operation would be excluded and the way to progress barred in these fields other than by having recourse to action by the twenty-four,[10] or by a core group of Member States acting outside the EU.

In comparison to the Treaty of Nice, the right to delay and the limitation to Joint Actions described above no longer apply. Nevertheless, because of the requirement of unanimity, enhanced co-operation in the CSDP is still difficult to obtain. However, a closer look at the provisions on the individual aspects of the CSDP shows that they contain their own flexibility regimes. Therefore, the field of application for enhanced co-operation is limited anyway.

The future CSDP, enshrined in the Constitutional Treaty, consists of the three main aspects of European defence integration mentioned above: crisis management, defence procurement, and collective defence. Articles I-41 and III-309 to III-312 Constitutional Treaty deal with these defence issues.

2.1. Crisis Management

As a first aspect of the CSDP, crisis management is addressed in Articles I-41 (1) and III-309 (1) Constitutional Treaty. These provisions roughly cover the Petersberg Tasks initially developed by the WEU. Article I-41 (1) Constitutional Treaty defines crisis management as "peacekeeping, conflict prevention and strengthening international security in accordance with the [UN] Charter". This short definition is described in more detail in Article III-309 (1) Constitutional Treaty:

> The tasks referred to in Article I-41 (1), in the course of which the Union may use civilian and military means, shall include, joint disarmament operations, humanitarian and rescue tasks, military advice and assistance tasks, conflict prevention and peace-keeping tasks, tasks of combat forces in crisis management, including peacemaking and post-conflict stabilisation. All these tasks may contribute to the fight against terrorism, including by supporting third countries in combating terrorism in their territories.

This represents a comprehensive list of military and police operations outside the Union territory which are compatible with international law. This list is more

[9] The delay according to Article 2(2) subpara 2 TEU is not available in the context of defence either: 'This para shall not apply to decisions having military or defence implications.'

[10] According to Article 6 of the 5th Protocol to the Treaty of Amsterdam, 'Denmark does not participate in the elaboration and implementation of decisions and actions of the Union which have defence implications, but will not prevent the development of closer cooperation between Member States in this area. Therefore Denmark will not participate in their adoption.' For the Constitutional Treaty see Protocol on the position of Denmark, in particular Article 5.

extensive in comparison to the Petersberg Tasks stipulated in the Nice version of Article 17 (2) TEU[11] discussed in chapter 3.[12] Joint disarmament operations, military advice and assistance tasks, conflict prevention, post-conflict stabilisation, and the fight against terrorism were added to the list in the Treaty of Nice. This 'modernisation' of the Petersberg Tasks clarifies the range of activities relevant to the CSDP[13] and broadens them considerably.[14] It represents the first amendment or modernisation since the WEU Petersberg Declaration of 1992[15] first introduced them. As outlined in chapters 2 and 3,[16] the tasks were adopted by the Treaty of Maastricht and remained unchanged in Amsterdam and Nice. The new set of tasks represents a more holistic approach[17] and an adequate reaction to international developments, in particular the fight against terrorism after the attacks of 11th September 2001 in New York and Washington DC.

An important question is whether this list is strictly exhaustive or whether the notion of "strengthening international security in accordance with the [UN] Charter" in Article I-41 (1) Constitutional Treaty would include missions beyond that expressly stipulated in Article III-309 (1) Constitutional Treaty. This could include the armed intervention in a country authorised by a UN Security Council resolution under Chapter VII of the UN Charter, such the UN interventions in Somalia or Bosnia-Herzegovina. It is submitted that such a mission would be included.[18] First, this is indicated by the reference to the UN Charter. Second, the notion of "strengthening international security" is sufficiently wide to allow this interpretation. Third, the exclusion of such a mission would run counter to the obligations of the Member States as members of the UN. There is no hint in the Constitutional Treaty or any version of the TEU that would indicate that the Member States want to keep these missions within their exclusive national competence. On the contrary, the CSDP is also intended as an instrument to be made available to the UN.

2.1.1. Ad hoc Flexibility

As mentioned above, the crisis management regime of the Constitutional Treaty contains elements of flexibility. One element concerns the implementation of

[11] Article 17(2) TEU reads: 'Questions referred to in this Article shall include humanitarian and rescue tasks, peacekeeping tasks and tasks of combat forces in crisis management, including peacemaking.'

[12] At 102–103.

[13] See the British non-paper 'Food for Thought', presented at the informal meeting of EU defence ministers, Rome, 29 August 2003, in A Missiroli, *From Copenhagen to Brussels: European Defence: Core Documents*, Chaillot Paper No 67, (Institute of Security Studies of the European Union, Paris, 2003) 204, at 206 (hereinafter '*From Copenhagen to Brussels*').

[14] A Missiroli, 'The European Union: Just a Regional Peacekeeper?' (2003) 8 *European Foreign Affairs Review* 493 (hereinafter 'Regional Peacekeeper'), at 495.

[15] A Bloed and RA Wessel, (eds), *The Changing Functions of the Western European Union (WEU): Introduction and Basic Documents* (Martinus Nijhoff Publishers, Dordrecht, 1994) 142.

[16] Ch 2 at 65 and ch 3 at 102–103.

[17] 'Food for Thought', above n 14, at 206.

[18] A Missiroli, *CFSP, Defence and Flexibility*, Chaillot Paper No 38, (Institute of Security Studies of the Western European Union, Paris, 2000) (hereinafter '*Defence and Flexibility*'), at 14.

European Decisions regarding crisis management.[19] Article III-310 (1) Constitutional Treaty provides:

> Within the framework of the European decisions adopted in accordance with Article III-309, the Council may entrust the implementation of a task to a group of Member States which are willing and have the necessary capability for such a task. Those Member States, in association with the Union Minister for Foreign Affairs, shall agree between themselves on the management of the task.

This suggests that crisis management can be subject to partial participation, and that there is room for a degree of flexibility. First of all, as will be explained in chapter 12,[20] there will be a unanimous European Decision of the Council, for example, on a peacekeeping or peacemaking mission.[21] At this stage there would be no element of flexibility.[22] However, the European Decision will be followed by an *ad hoc* decision of each individual Member State on whether to contribute troops or other forms of support to the implementation of the European Decision. At this stage there may be an element of informal or *ad hoc* flexibility, as possibly only some of the Member States which would have passed the European Decision would decide to contribute to its implementation. Theoretically a Member State could decide never to participate in a crisis management mission. This is the principle of voluntarism and the normal practice in the UN for crisis management missions.[23] The Member States have shown a clear preference for such "one-off

[19] In the context of the CFSP and the CSDP the institutions generally act by taking 'European Decisions', which are defined as non-legislative acts, binding in their entirety: Article I-33(1) subpara 5 Constitutional Treaty. European Laws and European Framework Laws are explicitly excluded: Article I-40(6) sentence 3 Constitutional Treaty. Definitions are provided in Article I-33(1): 'A European law shall be a legislative act of general application. It shall be binding in its entirety and directly applicable in all Member States. A European framework law shall be a legislative act binding, as to the result to be achieved, on the Member States to which it is addressed, but leave to the national authorities the choice of form and methods.' The European Decision, European Laws and European Framework Laws replace the Decision, Regulations, and Directive defined in Article 249 EC respectively.

[20] At 360–362.

[21] Article III-309(2) sentence 1 Constitutional Treaty reads: 'The Council shall adopt European decisions relating to the tasks referred to in para 1 [the "Petersberg Tasks"], defining the objectives and scope and the general conditions for their implementation.' Unanimity is always required in the context of military action. Article III-297(1) sentence 1 reads: 'Where the international situation requires operational action by the Union, the Council shall adopt the necessary European decisions.' Article I-40(6) sentence 1 reads: 'European decisions relating to the [CFSP] shall be adopted by the European Council and the Council unanimously, except in cases referred to in Part III'. The possibility to move to qualified majority voting in Article III-300(2) and (3) is blocked by para 4 of that provision which provides: 'Paragraphs 2 and 3 shall not apply to decisions having military or defence implications.'

[22] Although, as mentioned above, Denmark does not participate in the CFSP with regards to measures having defence implications under the TEU, Denmark would continue this practice under the Constitutional Treaty.

[23] See Articles 43 and 44 of the Charter of the United Nations. Contributions are voluntary. Nevertheless, the experience of the United Nations also shows that the practice has disadvantages. These concern the uncertainty of contributions, funding, and the coherence of a corps made up of many different national contingents.

ad hoc operational coalitions rather than more structured [formal] multilateral frameworks" in the context of the WEU.[24] These "one off *ad hoc* operational coalitions" are an appropriate practice since Member States differ enormously with regards to their financial and military capabilities. Cyprus or Malta, for example, will not always be in a position to contribute troops to the implementation of European Decisions on crisis management. *Ad hoc* flexibility of this kind is already available under the Treaty of Nice and it has been practised during the first crisis management operations of the EU in Bosnia-Herzegovina, the Former Yugoslav Republic of Macedonia, the Democratic Republic of the Congo in 2003 and late 2004.[25] Such flexible arrangements will only lead to problems when there are no Member States willing to contribute and there is a clear need for action. For example, in 2004 the United Nations had problems getting contributions to a mission in Iraq.

A more efficient alternative to this *ad hoc* arrangement could be a permanent 'Rapid Reaction Force' with long-term contributions from the Member States. This would take the element of uncertainty mentioned above out of the equation. Member States would commit their contributions for longer periods rather than making contributions to a specific mission. The force would be available for the implementation of European Decisions before the Decision is even taken. Some element of flexibility can also be maintained by leaving it to the Member States to decide whether they want to make long-term contributions to such a force or to supplement the contribution of troops on a voluntary basis, for example by (only) providing logistic or financial support. This being said, the autonomous military capacity discussed in chapter 3, proposed by the French President Jacques Chirac and the British Prime Minister Tony Blair in Saint-Malo in 1998,[26] adopted by the Cologne European Council in 1999, and developed into a plan for a European Rapid Reaction Force (hereinafter ERRF) of 60,000 in the Helsinki Headline Goal by the EU,[27] is an example of co-operation developed under the Nice provisions.

[24] Missiroli, *Defence and Flexibility*, above n 13, at vii. See also the Franco-British Declaration: 'Strengthening European Cooperation in Security and Defence', London, 24 November 2003, in Missiroli, *From Copenhagen to Brussels*, above n 9, 280, at 281: 'noting that forces are offered to both the EU and NATO on a voluntary basis'.

[25] See the lists of contributions to these missions ('EUPM' in Bosnia and Herzegovina and 'Concordia' in FYR Macedonia) in Missiroli, 'Peacekeeper', above n 14, at 497 and 499. Notable are the contributions of countries outside the EU, Canada in particular. The 'Artemis' mission in the DR Congo was conducted by 1800 mainly French soldiers. See also ch 3 at 116 for details.

[26] '[In order for the EU] to be in a position to play its full role on the international stage the Union must have the capacity for autonomous action, backed up by credible military forces, the means to decide to use them and a readiness to do so, in order to respond to international crises [emphasis added]'. Franco–British Summit, 'Joint Declaration on European Defence: Saint-Malo', 3–4 December 1998, http://www.weu.int/eng/info/d981204a.htm. See also Maartje Rutten, *From St-Malo to Nice, European Defence: Core Documents*, Chaillot Paper No 47, (Institute of Security Studies of the Western European Union, Paris, 2001) at 8.

[27] European Council, Presidency Conclusions: European Council Meeting in Helsinki, 10–11 December 1999, http://europa.eu.int/council/off.concl.

However, it is not expressly mentioned in the Constitutional Treaty.[28] Moreover, in late 2004 the ERRF was still not fully operational in the form envisaged in Saint-Malo, Cologne, and Helsinki.

2.1.2. Permanent Structured Co-operation

The other important aspect to be mentioned in the context of flexibility and the implementation of crisis management decisions is the possibility for 'permanent structured co-operation' provided in Article I-41 (6) Constitutional Treaty:

> Those Member States whose military capabilities fulfil higher criteria and which have made more binding commitments to one another in this area with a view to the most demanding missions shall establish permanent structured cooperation within the Union framework. Such cooperation shall be governed by the provisions of Article III-312. It shall not affect the provisions of Article III-309.

Sentence 3 of this paragraph clarifies that decisions on Petersberg tasks to be conducted in the framework of the EU are separate from decisions on their implementation through permanent structured co-operation. The earlier are taken by the Council under Article III-309 Constitutional Treaty. The latter are taken by the members of the Council representing the Member States participating in permanent structured co-operation, which will be explained in more detail below. Permanent structured co-operation is intended as a framework for the implementation of Petersberg related decisions of the Council in addition to the *ad hoc* implementation outlined above. According to Article III-312 (1) and (2):

> 1. Those Member States which wish to participate in the permanent structured cooperation referred to in Article I-41 (6), which fulfil the criteria and have made the commitments on military capabilities set out in the Protocol on Permanent Structured Cooperation shall notify their intention to the Council and to the Union Minister for Foreign Affairs.
>
> 2. Within three months following the notification referred to in paragraph 1 the Council shall adopt a European decision establishing permanent structured cooperation and determining the list of participating Member States. The Council shall act by a qualified majority after consulting the Union Minister for Foreign Affairs.

The October 2004 version of these provisions signed by the Member States differs considerably from the June 2004 version of the Constitutional Treaty. First, the predecessor of Article 312 (1) and (2) Constitutional Treaty envisaged that

[28] Article I 41(1) Constitutional Treaty mentions the autonomous military capacity: '[The CFSP] shall provide the Union with an operational capacity drawing on civil and military assets', but not the more tangible Helsinki Headline Goal and the plan for the ERRF.

"structured cooperation" would already be established by the Constitutional Treaty itself.[29]

Second, according to Article III-213 (4) of the June 2004 version "The Council of Ministers may ask the Member States participating in such cooperation to carry out at Union level such tasks as referred to in Article III-210."[30] The reference to Article III-210 in this paragraph and the notion of "the most demanding missions" in Article I-40 (6) of the June 2004 version clarified that structured co-operation was only envisaged for the aspect of crisis management.[31] The latter reference to what is now Article I-41 (6) is still provided in Article III-312 (1) of the October version of the Constitutional Treaty. Hence even without the additional reference to the Petersberg tasks comparable to Article III-210 in the June 2004 version, it is clear that permanent structured co-operation is not designed for the other aspects of the CSDP, namely defence procurement and collective defence discussed below. In comparison to the Treaty of Nice under which enhanced co-operation is not available for matters having military or defence implications, the possibility using structured co-operation with regards to crisis management is a major innovation of the Constitutional Treaty.

Third, while the June 2004 version used the term "structured cooperation", the October 2004 version uses the term "permanent structured cooperation". The notion of "permanent" added by the October 2004 version emphasises the difference to the "one-off *ad hoc*" flexibility regarding the implementation of Article III-309 decisions outlined above. Moreover, it might be interpreted as an argument supporting the thesis that permanent structured co-operation envisages some form of permanent 'ERRF' discussed below.

It should be noted that the concept of 'permanent structured cooperation' is only used in Articles I-41 (6) and III-312 Constitutional Treaty. Other parts of the Constitutional Treaty, in particular Article I-44 and III-416-423, speak of 'enhanced cooperation'. Article III-213 (5) of the June 2004 version of the Constitutional Treaty provided that "[n]otwithstanding the previous paragraphs

[29] The June 2004 version of Article I–213(1) Constitutional Treaty (now I–312) read:

> The Member States listed in the Protocol [title], which fulfil higher military capability criteria and wish to enter into more binding commitments in this matter with a view to the most demanding tasks, hereby establish structured cooperation between themselves within the meaning of Article I–40(6). The military capability criteria and commitments which those Member States have defined are set out in that Protocol. [...].

[30] 'Joint disarmament operations, humanitarian and rescue tasks, military advice and assistance tasks, conflict prevention and peace-keeping tasks, tasks of combat forces in crisis management, including peace-making and post-conflict stabilisation. All these tasks may contribute to the fight against terrorism including by supporting third countries in combating terrorism in their territories.'

[31] This interpretation is confirmed by another provision. Article I–41(5) provides: 'The Council of Ministers may entrust the execution of a task, within the Union framework, to a group of Member States in order to protect the Union's values and serve its interests. The execution of such a task shall be governed by Article III–310.' Article III–310(1) provides: 'Within the framework of the European decisions adopted in accordance with Article III–309, the Council of Ministers may entrust the implementation of a task to a group of Member States which are willing and have the capability for such a task.' Article III–309 is the provision dealing with crisis management tasks.

the appropriate provisions relating to enhanced co-operation shall apply to the structured co-operation governed by this Article". This paragraph was deleted in Article III-312 of the October 2004 version. Thus permanent structured co-operation and enhanced co-operation are completely separate forms of formal flexibility now. Even in the June 2004 version there was a difference between these two forms of differentiation. Most importantly, as expressed in the reference to a list of Member States (to be) provided in a Protocol and the use of the words "hereby establish", the then Article III-213 (1) already established 'structured co-operation' in a specific policy field with regards to the Member States which were to be listed in the Protocol. It was therefore a case of pre-defined flexibility.[32] According to the October 2004 version of the Constitutional Treaty, enhanced co-operation according to Articles I-44 and III-416-423 is the general mechanism provided for non-specified policy fields in the future. The permanent structured co-operation in Article III-312 is not subject to the legal criteria or procedural uncertainty accompanying the procedures set out for enhanced co-operation in Articles III-416-423.

Further differences between structured and enhanced co-operation relate to the participation of Member States at a later stage. In a case of 'ordinary' enhanced co-operation the Commission decides on 'accession' to the respective policy field according to Article III-418 (1) Constitutional Treaty,[33] except for cases in the context of the CFSP where the Council acting on a proposal from the Union Minister for Foreign Affairs takes this decision according to Article III-420 (2) Constitutional Treaty.[34] Enhanced co-operation is open to as many Member States as possible and they can join at any time, provided they comply with the conditions of participation laid down by the authorising European Decision: Article III-418 (1) Constitutional Treaty. This comes close to an automatic right for Member States wishing to do so to participate in enhanced cooperation. Moreover, EU

[32] See Missiroli, '*Defence and Flexibility*', above n 17, at 10.

[33] Article III 418(1) reads:

> When enhanced cooperation is being established, it shall be open to all Member States, subject to compliance with any conditions of participation laid down by the European authorising decision. It shall also be open to them at any other time, subject to compliance with the acts already adopted within that framework, in addition to any such conditions.
>
> The Commission and the Member States participating in enhanced cooperation shall ensure that they promote participation by as many Member States as possible.

[34] Article III 420(2) reads:

> Any Member State which wishes to participate in enhanced cooperation in the framework of the common foreign and security policy shall notify its intention to the Council of Ministers, the Union Minister for Foreign Affairs and the Commission.
>
> The Council shall confirm the participation of the Member State concerned, after consulting the Union Minister for Foreign Affairs. It shall note where necessary that any conditions of participation have been fulfilled. The Council, on a proposal from the Union Minister for Foreign Affairs, may also adopt any transitional measures deemed necessary with regard to the application of the acts already adopted within the framework of enhanced cooperation. However, if the Council of Ministers considers that any conditions of participation have not been fulfilled, it shall indicate the arrangements to be adopted to fulfil those conditions and shall set a deadline for re-examining the request for participation.
>
> For the purposes of this paragraph, the Council of Ministers shall act unanimously and in accordance with Article I–44(3).

institutions, in which all Member States are represented, will take the relevant decisions on 'accession'. In contrast, Article III-312 (3) Constitutional Treaty provides that if a Member State wishes to participate in the structured co-operation at a later stage, "[o]nly the members of the Council that represent the Member States taking part in structured co-operation shall participate in the vote". Moreover, according to Article III-312 (1) structured co-operation is designed for Member States "which fulfil higher military capability criteria". Therefore, structured co-operation is not as open to Member States wishing to join at a later stage as enhanced co-operation is. There is no 'right' for Member States to participate at a later stage. Moreover, a 'Council within the Council' representing only the Member States already participating in structured co-operation will decide on the 'application of the prospective newcomer'. The reasons for this special category of structured co-operation shall be discussed below, after considering what kind of co-operation this special category of formal flexibility is designed for.

It is submitted that the regulations on permanent structured co-operation are mainly designed to accommodate the ERRF envisaged in the Helsinki Headline Goal mentioned above. Such a force would overcome the *ad hoc* nature of the implementation stage of crisis management missions and represent a binding commitment of the participating Member States. Henceforth, after a European Decision (taken by the Council) to deploy troops on a peacekeeping mission, for example, there would be no uncertainty regarding the contribution of troops to implement the European Decision. The Council could deploy the ERRF, a force made up of Member State contributions on the basis of long-term or medium-term commitments. In other words, the forces for the implementation of a European decision would be ready before the European Decision is taken. Such a force would eliminate the element of flexibility formed by the *ad hoc* character of the forces implementing European Decisions hitherto. However, as the force would be formed on the basis of permanent structured co-operation, in other words on the basis of voluntary commitments, another element of differentiation would be introduced instead. Therefore, an ERRF would take an element of uncertainty out of an important aspect of European defence without eliminating the advantages of flexibility.

This connection between permanent structured co-operation on the basis of Articles I-41 (6) and III-312 Constitutional Treaty with the ERRF explains the differences to enhanced co-operation in the Constitutional Treaty. Only Member States making a contribution in practice, by contributing troops, equipment and funds to the ERRF, will be 'allowed' to participate at a later stage. For various reasons, the contribution proposed by such a Member State might not be considered sufficient in exchange for getting a say in the organisation and deployment of the ERRF under Article III-312 (6) Constitutional Treaty, which provides:

> The European decisions and recommendations of the Council within the framework of permanent structured cooperation, other than those provided for in paragraphs 2 to 5, shall be adopted by unanimity. For the purposes of this paragraph, unanimity shall be constituted by the votes of the representatives of the participating Member States only.

Article III-312 (3) Constitutional Treaty regulates the procedure to be followed in case a Member State wishes to participate in permanent structured co-operation at a later stage. First, the Member State in question has to fulfil the criteria and make the commitments on military capabilities set out in the Protocol on Permanent Structured Co-operation. Second, the Council members representing the Member States already participating in permanent structured co-operation will vote on the notification submitted by the 'newcomer' by a qualfied majority of at least 55 per cent of these members of the Council, comprising at least 65 per cent of the population of these Member States. A minority of more than 35 per cent of the Council members representing the already participating Member States plus one member can block this decision on the 'accession' of a Member State at a later stage. This discretion enjoyed by the Member States already participating in the ERRF gives them a strong bargaining position regarding the contribution of newcomers. This will enable them to restrict 'free riding'. This function is enhanced by the fact that the participation of a participating Member State which no longer fulfils the criteria or is no longer able to meet the commitments of permanent structured co-operation can be suspended by a similar qualified majority of the participating Member States under Article III-312 (4) Constitutional Treaty. Moreover, the power to decide over 'accession' also gives them a larger margin of discretion regarding the timing of such an 'accession' to the ERRF. For military or political reasons it might not be considered appropriate to let other Member States join the ERRF at a particular moment in time. Generally, the 'founding' Member States of the ERRF, when exercising their discretion regarding the participation of other Member States at a later stage, are able to take all the necessary political and military considerations into account. This might be interpreted as creating a separate security policy within the CSDP, the institutional dimension of which is the emergence of a 'Council within the Council'. Depending on the number and identity of the Member States participating in the ERRF, this could lead to inconsistencies. On the other hand, it is hardly politically feasible to give Member States not contributing to the ERRF a say in its organisation.

The Finnish Foreign Secretary Erkki Tuomioja criticised this regime of structured co-operation in crisis management under the June 2004 version of the Constitutional Treaty as "in the Union without being of it."[35] He urged efforts to involve the EU as a whole rather than to allow "a self-selecting inner group of countries" to "use the EC 'trademark' without a mandate from the Union."[36] Ultimately he considered the arrangements to be damaging for the EU and suggested to Member States wanting to go ahead to use frameworks outside the Union, such as the WEU. This criticism is, however, closely connected to the criticism on the mutual defence clause, which will be discussed in detail below. Thus it is not mainly directed at (permanent) structured co-operation in crisis

[35] 'Europe Needs to Work as a Whole on Defence', *Financial Times*, 28 October 2003. See also the related publications of the Foreign Secretary with colleagues from the other non-aligned Member States of the EU discussed in the context of the aspect of mutual defence below.

[36] Above.

management. Moreover, there is far reaching agreement on the crisis management component of the CSDP. Therefore it is still possible that all Member States will participate in permanent structured co-operation, in other words the ERRF, from the moment it is established.

If the Constitutional Treaty does not enter into force, crisis management will have to be conducted on the basis of the current framework of the Treaty of Nice. This would have consequences for the establishment of an ERRF. First, it could not be established on the basis of permanent structured co-operation. As explained in chapter 3,[37] because of the military and defence exception in Article 27b TEU an ERRF could not be established on the basis of enhanced co-operation either. It can be conducted only by all Member States acting in unison within the EU or by a number of Member States acting outside the Union. Whether such a force would find the support of all the Member States is uncertain if not unlikely. The force is still not operational in late 2004, although it was to be established by 2003.[38] Whether the establishment of such a force outside the EU is compatible with the obligations under the Treaty of Nice is also unclear. However, it would clearly undermine the CFSP and ESDP when such visible aspects of security and defence policy were conducted outside the EU. This is the main reason why Belgium, France, Germany, and Luxembourg never realised their April 2003 plans for military alliance outside the Union.[39] Assuming the continuation of the *status quo* on the basis of the Treaty of Nice, the forces necessary for the implementation of crisis management decisions would have to be formed on an *ad hoc* basis, with the implication of uncertainty described above.

As mentioned in chapter 3,[40] in 2003 the EU conducted the first three missions within the current framework of the Treaty of Nice in Bosnia and Herzegovina, the Former Yugoslav Republic of Macedonia, and the Democratic Republic of the Congo.[41] However, so far these missions have been small. Moreover, they have been at the "low end" of security, involving police work or

[37] At 112–114.

[38] According to the Presidency Conclusions at the European Council meeting in Thessaloniki, 19–20 June 2003, 'The EU now has operational capability across the full range of the Petersberg Tasks, limited and constrained by recognised shortfalls, which can be attained by the further development of the EU's military capabilities', in Missiroli, *From Copenhagen to Brussels*, above n 13, at point 56, p 144. See also General Affairs and External Relations Council, Brussels, 19–20 June 2003. This appears to fall short of the ERRF envisaged in the Helsinki Headline Goal.

[39] 'French Call for Military Co-operation Divides EU', *The Independent*, 28 April 2003; 'Gang of Four', *Financial Times*, 28 April 2003; 'France and Germany in EU Defence Breakaway', *The Times*, 30 April 2003; 'European Leaders Unveil Plan for Central Military HQ', *Financial Times*, 30 April 2003.

[40] At 115–118.

[41] On brief descriptions of these missions see Missiroli, 'Peacekeeper', above n 14, at 498–500.

military missions in areas that were relatively safe for the troops involved. Finally, the military missions were very limited in terms of time. The EU missions continued the tradition of WEU crisis management, which was equally limited.[42] The EUFOR mission in Bosnia and Herzegovina which started in December 2004 is larger in size but still at the "low end" and "second hand".

Generally it is unlikely that the EU, in contrast to NATO, will be able to react quickly and with a sizeable force to a humanitarian crisis or a substantial security challenge.[43] Without that ability the EU will not develop into 'a power to be reckoned with' on the international scene. With respect to external relations it will stay a civilian power, occasionally conducting limited crisis management operations. The EU has raised expectations it cannot fulfil and therefore its crisis management policy needs the innovations envisaged in the Constitutional Treaty if crisis management is to contribute to the Union asserting its role on the international scene.

2.2. The European Capabilities and Armaments Policy and the European Defence Agency

The second aspect of the CSDP is the European Capabilities and Armaments Policy[44] conducted by the European Defence Agency (hereinafter EDA), called the European Armaments, Research and Military Capabilities Agency by the Convention and the June 2004 version of the Constitutional Treaty.[45] The activities of the Agency include the research and development of new armaments, the preservation of the European defence industrial base, and the European armaments market. Hence the EDA will operate in an area concerned with the economic aspects of defence close to and potentially overlapping with subject matters regulated by Community law.[46] The Agency is

[42] Missiroli, '*Defence and Felxibility*', above n 18, at 16. Missions included co-ordinating mine-clearance operations in Gulf waters: 'Operation Cleansweep'. WEU also contributed to the humanitarian actions for Kurdish refugees in Northern Iraq, WEU/NATO Operation Sharp Guard in the Adriatic, the WEU Danube operation, and the police contingent in Mostar. There was a (police) mission in Albania, a WEU de-mining assistance mission in Croatia, and a general security surveillance mission in Kosovo.

[43] Missiroli, '*Defence and Felxibility*', above, at 14, argues that there is agreement amongst all EU Member States regarding peacekeeping in the sense of Chapter VI of the UN Charter but not (yet) with regards to peacemaking involving the use of force in the sense of Chapter VII of the UN Charter. However, it is likely to become increasingly difficult to exclude the necessity to use force in a peacekeeping mission.

[44] The European Capabilities and Armaments Policy is not abbreviated for the purposes of this chapter to avoid confusion because 'ECAP' is the official abbreviation of the European Capabilities Action Plan.

[45] See Article III–212 of the June 2004 version of the Constitutional Treaty.

[46] The limits of Community law in relation to armaments were addressed in ch 5 and the issue of defence procurement was addressed in detail in ch 7.

covered in Articles I-41 (3) subparagraph 2[47] and III-311[48] Constitutional Treaty.

The Agency was already established by Council Joint Action 2004/551/CFSP on 12 July 2004[49] (hereinafter EDA Joint Action) within the framework of the Treaty of Nice, independent from the entering into force of the Constitutional Treaty.[50] At the end of 2004 it is in the process of being set up. This 'moving ahead'[51] will be discussed in more detail below. However, the EDA provisions of the Constitutional Treaty have to be discussed together with those of the EDA Joint Action since by the time the earlier enters into force the Agency will already be operational on the basis of the more detailed regulatory framework set by the latter.

According to the first sentence of Article I-41 (3) subparagraph 2 Constitutional Treaty "the Member States shall undertake progressively to improve their military capabilities." The second sentence of this subparagraph mentions the creation of

[47] Article I–41(3) subpara 2 Constitutional Treaty reads:

Member States shall undertake progressively to improve their military capabilities. An Agency in the field of defence capabilities development, research, acquisition and armaments (European Defence Agency) shall be established to identify operational requirements, to promote measures to satisfy those requirements, to contribute to identifying and, where appropriate, implementing any measure needed to strengthen the industrial and technological base of the defence sector, to participate in defining a European capabilities and armaments policy, and to assist the Council in evaluating the improvement of military capabilities.

[48] Article III–311(1) Constitutional Treaty reads:

The Agency in the field of defence capabilities development, research, acquisition and armaments (European Defence Agency) established by Article I-43(3) and subject to the authority of the Council shall have as its task to:

a) contribute to identifying the Member States' military capability objectives and evaluating observance of the capability commitments given by the Member States;
b) promote harmonisation of operational needs and adoption of effective, compatible procurement methods;
c) propose multilateral projects to fulfil the objectives in terms of military capabilities, ensure coordination of the programmes implemented by the Member States and management of specific cooperation programmes;
d) support defence technology research, and coordinate and plan joint research activities and the study of technical solutions meeting future operational needs;
e) contribute to identifying and, if necessary, implementing any useful measure for strengthening the industrial and technological base of the defence sector and for improving the effectiveness of military expenditure.

[49] Council Joint Action 2004/551/CFSP of 12 July 2004 on the establishment of the European Defence Agency [2004] OJ L–245/17. Article 1(1) of the Joint Action reads: 'An Agency in the field of defence capabilities development, research, acquisition and armaments (the European Defence Agency), hereinafter referred to as "the Agency", is hereby established.' See A Georgopoulos, 'The New European Defence Agency: Major Development or a Fig Leaf?' (2005)14 *Public Procurement Law Review* 103–112.

[50] This had been indicated before. See 'First major step in setting up the Ad hoc Preparation Group to prepare the creation of an intergovernmental agency in the field of defence capabilities', COREPER, Brussels, 4 September 2003, in Missiroli, *From Copenhagen to Brussels*, above n 13, at 208; and the Presidency Conclusions of the European Council in Brussels, 12 December 2003, in Missiroli, above, at 303, mentioning an Agency Establishment Team (AET) to be set up in January 2004.

[51] Georgopoulos, above n 49 puts it as follows: '[...] its establishment was dissociated with the adoption of the European Constitutional Treaty.'

the EDA. Furthermore it stipulates its tasks in broad terms. Thus the Agency is designed as an instrument to address the recognised military capabilities shortfalls of the Member States.[52] The Agency is to participate in defining a European Capabilities and Armaments Policy and to assist the Council in evaluating the improvement of military capabilities. The European Capabilities and Armaments Policy covers common approaches to the improvement of military capabilities of the Member States in general, not only in relation to their contribution to EU crisis management.[53] The shortfalls affect the implementation of the EU crisis management policy as well as the obligations of many Member States to NATO.

2.2.1. The Tasks of the European Defence Agency

The envisaged EDA is not supposed to replace but rather to complement the defence procurement agencies of the Member States.[54] The principle of attributed or conferred powers applies. Hence the activities are limited to those stipulated in the Constitutional Treaty. They can be divided into three broad groups.

First, the Agency is to be involved in the development of policies. Article I-41 (1) subparagraph 2 gives the EDA a broad mandate. It is "to participate in defining a "European capabilities and armaments policy". Articles I-41 (3) subparagraph 2 and III-311 (1) Constitutional Treaty have to be read together. The provisions give a list of detailed polices in the definition of which the Agency is to participate. These polices include capability objectives,[55] defence industrial and technological policy,[56] procurement policy,[57] and even policy in relation to operational needs.[58] This indicates a comprehensive European Capabilities and Armaments Policy, covering all relevant aspects including a European defence industrial policy. When Articles I-41 (3) subparagraph 2 and III-311 (1) (e) Constitutional Treaty speak of the "industrial and technological base of the defence sector" they refer to the defence sector of the EU as a whole. As far as their participation in the definition of a European Capabilities and Armaments Policy is concerned, there will be a stronger role for the Council than in the rather technical field of multilateral projects and joint defence research discussed below. The Agency will prepare the decisions of the Council. The tasks of the Agency are

[52] The Centre for European Reform argues that the combined annual defence budgets of the EU Member States is about half that of the USA. The latter spends about US$290 billion annually. The defence budgets of the EU Member States have declined by 22% in real terms 1992–2001. See: S Duke, 'CESDP: Nice's Overtrumped Success?' (2001) 6 *European Foreign Affairs Review* 155, at 164. See also for example the findings of the Conference on EU Capability Improvement, Brussels, 19 November 2001, in Rutten, *From Nice to Laeken, European Defence: Core Documents*, above n 26, at 95–101.

[53] The 2003 Franco–British Summit in Le Touquet called the improvement of rapid reaction capabilities a 'European priority', see: Missiroli, *From Copenhagen to Brussels*, above n 13, 36, at 37.

[54] In contrast to the Agency envisaged by the 1952 EDC Treaty, which was to replace national defence procurement, see ch 1 at 39–42.

[55] Article III–311(1)(a) Constitutional Treaty.

[56] Article III–311(1)(e) Constitutional Treaty.

[57] Article III–311(1)(b) Constitutional Treaty.

[58] Article III–311(1)(b) and (d) Constitutional Treaty.

stipulated in more detail in the Preamble and Article 5 of the EDA Joint Action.[59] However, these detailed tasks do not go beyond those stipulated in the Constitutional Treaty.

The EDA is designed as a more intergovernmental instrument.[60] The European Capabilities and Armaments Policy is also more intergovernmental. According to Article III-311 Constitutional Treaty all activities are carried out "subject to the

[59] Article 5 EDA Joint Action reads:

Functions and tasks

1. In fulfilling its functions and tasks, the Agency shall respect the competences of the European Community and those of the EU institutions.
2. The Agency's fulfilment of its functions and tasks shall be without prejudice to the competences of Member States in defence matters.
3. The Agency shall work in the following principal fields:

3.1. Development of defence capabilities in the field of crisis management, in particular by:

3.1.1. identifying, in association with the competent Council bodies, and utilising the Capability Development Mechanism (CDM), the EU's future defence capability requirements in quantitative and qualitative terms (encompassing both forces and equipment);

3.1.2. coordinating the implementation of the European Capabilities Action Plan (ECAP) and any successor plan;

3.1.3. scrutinising, assessing and evaluating against criteria to be agreed by the Member States the capability commitments given by the Member States through the ECAP process, and utilising the CDM;

3.1.4. promoting and coordinating harmonisation of military requirements;

3.1.5. identifying and proposing collaborative activities in the operational domain;

3.1.6. providing appraisals on financial priorities for capabilities development and acquisition.

3.2. Promotion and enhancement of European armaments cooperation, in particular by:

3.2.1. promoting and proposing new multilateral cooperative projects to meet ESDP capabilities requirements as they stand now and develop in the future;

3.2.2. working for coordination of existing programmes implemented by Member States;

3.2.3. assuming, at the request of Member States, responsibility for managing specific programmes (through OCCAR or other programme management arrangements as appropriate);

3.2.4. promoting cost-effective and efficient procurement by identifying and disseminating best practices.

3.3. Working to strengthen the DTIB and for the creation of an internationally competitive European Defence Equipment Market in particular by:

3.3.1. developing relevant policies and strategies, in consultation with the Commission and industry as appropriate;

3.3.2. pursuing EU-wide development and harmonisation of relevant rules and regulations (particularly by an EU-wide application of relevant rules of the LoI Framework Agreement).

3.4. Enhancement of the effectiveness of European Defence Research and Technology (R & T), in particular by:

3.4.1. promoting, in liaison with the Community's research activities where appropriate, research aimed at fulfilling future defence and security capability requirements and thereby strengthening Europe's industrial and technological potential in this domain;

3.4.2. promoting more effectively targeted joint defence R & T, drawing on the experience of relevant elements of the WEAG and the WEAO;

3.4.3. coordinating and planning joint research activities;

3.4.4. catalysing defence R & T through studies and projects;

3.4.5. managing defence R & T contracts;

3.4.6. working in liaison with the Commission to maximise complementarity and synergy between defence and civil or security related research programmes.

[60] The more intergovernmental character of the Agency has been emphasised repeatedly, see European Council Meeting at 20–21 March 2003 in Brussels, Missiroli, *From Copenhagen to Brussels*, above n 13, at 70 (seen as the starting point of the EEA) and the Presidency Report on ESDP, European Council Meeting, Thessaloniki, 20 June 2003, Missiroli, above, 153, at 159.

authority of the Council". This is also stipulated in the Preamble and Articles 1 (2) and 4 of the EDA Joint Action. Moreover, Article I-41 (3) subparagraph 2 Constitutional Treaty and Article 2 (2) EDA Joint Action emphasise that the Agency is "to support the Council". This means that the EDA will be supervised by the main more intergovernmental institution of the EU. According to Article III-311 (2) Constitutional Treaty, the EDA shall liaise with the Commission where necessary. Article 24 of the EDA Joint Action clarifies that the Commission shall be a member without voting rights in the EDA Steering Board and participate in the programmes and projects of the Agency. Moreover, the EDA shall establish the necessary arrangements with the Commission "in particular with a view of exchanging expertise and advice in those areas where the activities of the Community have a bearing on the Agency's missions and where the activities of the Agency are relevant to those of the Community." These arrangements indicate an only limited involvement of the more supranational institution and only when absolutely necessary. The European Parliament, which is not mentioned at all with regards to the EDA, neither in the Constitutional Treaty nor the EDA Joint Action, demands to be involved in the Agency's practical organisation not least regards decisions on financing[61] and warns that the creation of shadow budgets totally outside parliamentary control should be avoided.[62] According to Article III-376 subparagraph 1 Constitutional Treaty the jurisdiction of the European Court of Justice is excluded. Consequently, the Court is neither mentioned in the EDA provisions of the Constitutional Treaty nor the EDA Joint Action. To summarise, the role of the more supranational institutions, Parliament and Court, concerning the EDA and the European Capabilities and Armaments Policy is non-existent and that of the Commission is very limited. However, this is the arrangement for all three aspects of the CSDP. The institutional structure of the CSDP will be discussed in detail in chapter 12.

It should be noted that so far the Commission has been a major player with regards to European defence industrial and technological policy and general procurement policy. The Constitutional Treaty leaves the *acquis communautaire* and all competencies of the Commission and the other supranational institutions intact. This is also emphasised in a reference to Article 47 TEU in the Preamble[63] and Article 1 (2) of the EDA Joint Action.[64] Hence the new arrangements might

[61] *European Parliament Resolution on the Annual Report from the Council to the European Parliament on the Main Aspects and Basic Choices of CFSP, including Financial Implications for the General Budget of the EU*, Strasbourg, 23 October 2003 (hereinafter '2003 Parliament Resolution'), in Missiroli, *From Copenhagen to Brussels*, above n 9, 229, at 240 (point 17).

[62] Above, at 243 (point 41).

[63] Point 19 of the Preamble reads: 'The Agency should fulfil its mission in accordance with Article 3 TEU and in full respect of Article 47 TEU'.

[64] Article 1(2) EDA Joint Action reads: 'The Agency shall act under the Council's authority, in support of the CFSP and the ESDP, within the single institutional framework of the European Union, and without prejudice to the responsibilities of the EU institutions and the Council bodies. The Agency's mission shall be without prejudice to the competences of the European Community, in full respect of Article 47 TEU'.

cause an overlap between the Community competencies for industrial policy and public procurement on one side and the Council and the EDA competencies for defence industrial policy and procurement on the other side. However, as was explained in Part II of this book, the limits of Community competence are determined by the limits of Community law as an instrument of defence integration. These limits depend on the interpretation and practical use of the security exemptions in the Treaty. The existence of an EDA will make a clear interpretation even more important. For example, according to Article III-311 (1) (b) Constitutional Treaty the EDA will be involved in the harmonisation of procurement procedures with the objective of making the laws compatible. The regulation of defence procurement was addressed in chapter 7. Suffice it to point out and repeat at this point, that the procurement of weapons is not automatically or categorically excluded from the application of the EC Treaty and all the EC Public Procurement Directives. The same applies to the Constitutional Treaty and the new Public Sector Procurement Directive. As will be explained below, the Constitutional Treaty adopted the relevant rules of the EC Treaty. By addressing defence procurement rules in the context of the more intergovernmental CSDP, the Convention and the Member States seem to assume that the procurement of armaments is automatically excluded from *the acquis communautaire*. It is submitted that liaising with the Commission will be necessary in most cases involving defence industrial policy and public procurement as these areas are not categorically excluded from Community law. As explained below, the Commission may bring proceedings to the European Court of Justice under Article III-132 Constitutional Treaty if they think that the Member States are making improper use of *inter alia* Article III-436 (1) (b) Constitutional Treaty (what is now Article 296 (1) (b) EC).

Second, according to Article III-311 (1) (a) Constitutional Treaty and Article 5 (3.1.3.) EDA Joint Action the Agency will evaluate observance of the capability commitments given by the Member States. This seems to indicate the role of an oversight authority for capability commitments. The precise limits of this function are not clearly spelt out.

Third, according to Article III-311 (1) (c) and (d) Constitutional Treaty and Article 5 (3.4.) EDA Joint Action the Agency will be in charge of joint research programmes and multilateral projects (practical project management function). This refers to projects where a group of Member States decides to approach the development of a certain piece of equipment on a common basis. Such a project may also concern research only. In such a case the common programme would normally replace individual Member State programmes. However, there is no rule preventing a Member State from continuing or starting a similar project on a national basis. Nevertheless, in times of tight defence budgets this is very unlikely. The EDA will have the role of a practical co-ordinator and manager for joint projects. Multinational collaborative programmes such as the British-German-Italian-Spanish 'Eurofighter/Typhoon' would be conducted by the EDA. This task is not mentioned in Article I-41 (3) subparagraph 2 Constitutional Treaty and it is submitted that this indicates that this rather technical matter was not considered controversial. It is mentioned in Article 5 (3) EDA Joint Action. Moreover, the Member States decide on their participation in an individual research programme or joint project on an *ad hoc* basis anyway. No Member State is forced to participate, as will be explained in more detail below.

2.2.2. Partial Participation and the European Defence Agency

Similar to the crisis management aspect of the CSDP discussed above, the armaments aspect also provides for some form of flexibility. Article III-311 (2) Constitutional Treaty provides:

> The Agency shall be open to all Member States wishing to be part of it. [...] That decision should take account of the level of effective participation in the Agency's activities. Specific groups shall be set up within the Agency bringing together Member States engaged in joint projects. [...].

This provision suggests that, somewhat comparable to the framework for crisis management discussed above, the EDA be construed as a flexible framework. No Member State is obliged to participate. Two levels of flexibility need to be differentiated. First, there is flexibility regarding participation in the Agency. This is also expressed in the definition of 'participating Member States' as Member States of the EU who participate in the Agency in Article 3 EDA Joint Action. When there are participating Member States there have to be non-participating Member States at least in theory.[65] Thus neither the Constitutional Treaty nor the EDA Joint Action envisage all Member States participating in the Agency. This is also confirmed by Article 1 (3) and (4) EDA Joint Action which differentiate between Member States who wish to participate immediately on the one hand and those who wish to participate after its adoption or withdraw from it.[66] Thus the basic institutional framework of the EDA is designed as a flexible framework. Second, there is flexibility regarding participation in the individual programme and projects conducted within this basic institutional framework. This is also expressed in the definition of 'contributing Member States' as Member States of the EU contributing to a particular project or

[65] Apart from Denmark which does not participate in the EDA, see section 21 of the Preamble to the EDA Joint Action.

[66] Article 1(3) EDA Joint Action reads: 'The Agency shall be open to participation by all Member States bound by this Joint Action [not Denmark, see above]. Member States who wish to participate immediately in the Agency shall notify their intention to do so to the Council and inform the [Secretary General/High Representative for the CFSP] at the time of the adoption of this Joint Action.'

Paragraph (4) reads: 'Any Member State wishing to participate in the Agency after the adoption of this Joint Action or wishing to withdraw from the Agency shall notify its intention to the Council and inform the SG/HR. Any necessary technical and financial arrangements for such participation or withdrawal shall be determined by the Steering Board.'

programme in Article 3 EDA Joint Action. The groups of Member States co-operating in a particular project, for example a new fighter aircraft or tank, are always formed on a one-off and *ad hoc* basis. This follows the tradition of European collaborative projects conducted within the organisational structures described in chapter 7[67] or outside any permanent structure, which under the Constitutional Treaty are to be conducted in the framework of the EU. Theoretically, a Member State could decide never to participate in a procurement project. Nevertheless, Member States participating in individual projects will have to make long-term commitments regarding such a project. Given the one-off and *ad hoc* character of procurement projects, however, it could be said that this area is covered by informal flexibility as well as a form of more permanent co-operation. This finding is confirmed *inter alia* by the Preamble[68] and Chapter IV[69] of the EDC Joint Action.

The incorporation of the EDA in the Constitutional Treaty will help to overcome the external fragmentation of European defence integration with regards to armaments. As explained above, organisational structures outside the EU, such as the Western European Armaments Group and Organisation (hereinafter WEAG/WEAO)[70] and the Organisation for Joint Armaments Co-operation (hereinafter OCCAR),[71] are currently promoting European co-operation in defence procurement. It will no longer be necessary for those Member States wishing to establish a more coherent defence procurement regime to do so in organisations outside the Union. To avoid wasteful duplication, in particular the British–French–German–Italian OCCAR can be dissolved or incorporated after the EEA has become operational. In other words, similar to the functions of the WEU, the establishment of the EDC could lead to the import of the external *acquis* of the WEAG/WEAO and OCCAR into the EU.[72] The Agency is intended to replace OCCAR and WEAG/WEAO, the latter

[67] At 222–224.

[68] Section 17 of the Preamble to the EDA Joint Action reads: 'The Agency, while being open to participation by all Member States, should also provide for the possibility of specific groups of Member States establishing ad hoc projects or programmes.'

[69] On 'ad hoc projects or programmes and associated budgets'.

[70] Austria, Belgium, the Czech Republic, Denmark, Finland, France, Germany, Greece, Hungary, Italy, Luxembourg, the Netherlands, Norway, Poland, Portugal, Spain, Sweden, Turkey and the United Kingdom are full members of the WEAG, which forms the background for the WEAO See: http://www.weu.int/weao/site/frameset.htm.

[71] See: Convention on the Establishment of the Organisation for Joint Armaments Co-operation OCCAR, printed in Burkardt Schmitt, *European Armaments Cooperation: Core Documents*, Chaillot Paper No 59, (Institute for Security Studies of the European Union, Paris, 2003) 45–59. OCCAR is based in Bonn and manages several programmes: the Franco-German 'Tiger' attack helicopter, the Franco–Italian Future Surface-to-Air Missile Family, the Belgian–British–French–German–Spanish–Turkish A400M transport aircraft. The latter involves non-OCCAR members.

[72] Missiroli, *Defence and Flexibility*, above n 18, at 37; P de Vestel, 'The Future of Armament Cooperation in NATO and the WEU' in KE Eliassen, (ed), *Foreign and Security Policy in the European Union* (Sage, London, 1998) 197–215.

are to be transferred to the earlier.[73] These organisational structures outside the Union are addressed in the Preamble,[74] Article 5 (3.2.3.),[75] and Article 25 (2) EDA Joint Action[76] which imply their eventual assimilation into the new EDA structure.

2.2.3. The European Defence Agency and the Constitutional Treaty

As mentioned above, the EDA was first established by Council Joint Action 2004/551/CFSP on 12 July 2004 within the framework of the Treaty of Nice, independent from the entering into force of the Constitutional Treaty.[77] First, this shows that this aspect of the CSDP is not controversial. Second, moving ahead of the Constitutional Treaty shows that Member States rightly consider the matter to be important and urgent. They are not prepared to leave this crucial aspect of the common defence policy to the uncertainty of the implementation process of the Constitutional Treaty. Without the EDA, collaborative projects would continue to be conducted on the basis of the current patchwork of national, EU, WEU, and other initiatives. This would take the larger part of these projects outside the framework of the EU thereby making the establishment of a liberalised European defence equipment market more difficult to achieve. Without such a market, the European defence industries are deprived of economies of scale making it difficult

[73] This was clearly spelled out in the Conclusions of the General Affairs and External Relations Council in Brussels on 17 November 2003, in Missiroli, *From Copenhagen to Brussels*, above n 13, 256, at 263 with respect to OCCAR and at 264. At 266 it says: 'The Agency should establish close working relations with existing arrangements/groupings/organisations, such as Lo I, OCCAR, WEAG/WEAO, including the R&T mechanism of EUROPA MoU, with a view to incorporate them or assimilate their principles and practices in due course, as appropriate.' The United Kingdom–Italy Summit on 21 February in Rome, Missiroli, above, at 42 concluded: '[...] agency which would incorporate, at the appropriate time, existing bodies such as WEAG/WEAO, OCCAR, and LOI'. The progressive enlargement of OCCAR suggested on the Franco-German Summit on the occasion of the 40th Anniversary of the Elysée Treaty on 22 January 2003 in Paris, Missiroli, above, at 23 and the Franco–British Summit at 4 February 2003 in Le Touquet, Missiroli, above, at 39 are aiming in the same direction.

[74] Section 8 of the Preamble to the EDA Joint Action reads:

> The Agency should develop close working relations with existing arrangements, groupings and organisations such as Letter of Intent (LoI), Organisation de coopération conjointe en matière d'armement (OCCAR) and Western European Armaments Group (WEAG)/Western European Armaments Organisation (WEAO), with a view to assimilation or incorporation of relevant principles and practices as appropriate.

[75] Article 5(3.2.3.) EDA Joint Action on the tasks of the Agency reads 'assuming, at the request of Member States, responsibility for managing specific programmes (through OCCAR or other programme management arrangements as appropriate) [...].' Section 3.4.2. reads: 'promoting more effectively targeted joint defence R & T, drawing on the experience of relevant elements of the WEAG and the WEAO; [...].'

[76] Article 25(2) EDA Joint Action reads: 'The Agency shall develop close working relations with the relevant elements of OCCAR, the LoI Framework Agreement, and WEAG/WEAO with a view to incorporate those elements or assimilate their principles and practices in due course, as appropriate and by mutual agreement.'

[77] This had been indicated before. See 'First major step in setting up the Ad hoc Preparation Group to prepare the creation of an intergovernmental agency in the field of defence capabilities', COREPER, Brussels, 4 September 2003, in Missiroli, *From Copenhagen to Brussels*, above n 13, at 208 and the Presidency Conclusions of the European Council in Brussels, 12 December 2003, in Missiroli, above, at 303, mentioning an Agency Establishment Team (AET) to be set up in January 2004.

to survive in a world dominated by the highly competitive US arms industries. Finally, the armed forces of the Member States suffer from a substantial 'expectations-capabilities' gap. Their defence procurement activity and consequently their equipment are considered widely as insufficient to fulfil their NATO obligations, let alone new obligations under the CSDP. Without the EDA the Member States of the EU would lose a major instrument to improve their capabilities in a coherent and cost-effective manner. Therefore the EDA was singled out for 'accelerated integration' ahead of the Constitutional Treaty.

The establishment of an agency has been on and off the agenda for a long time.[78] As discussed in chapter 1,[79] the EDC Treaty had envisaged the supranational Board of Commissioners as the armaments agency of the European Defence Community.[80] As discussed in chapter 3[81] the TEU, much more modestly, included co-operation between Member States in the field of armaments without making a special reference to an agency.[82] Since the late 1980s the WEAG, since the 1990s the WEAO of the WEU, and since the 1990s the British–French–German–Italian OCCAR-EA have similar tasks.[83] Provided European defence integration continues on the basis of the current wording of the Constitutional Treaty and the EDA Joint Action, the creation of the EDA is to be welcomed to avoid duplication and to preserve the consistency of the CSDP. However, it can be doubted that the arrangements of the Constitutional Treaty will be sufficient to create a liberalised European defence equipment market and to preserve the greater part of the European defence industrial and technological base. The latter needs a liberalised European defence equipment market to survive and the Constitutional Treaty leaves the *status quo* intact, as will be explained below. A more supranational and central defence procurement agency could take advantage of economies of scale and European technological transfer. It appears the Convention did not equip the EDA with the necessary powers to achieve its objectives. However, the supranational agency which was envisaged by the 1952 EDC Treaty is not politically feasible at this time.

2.3. Collective Defence

The third and last aspect of the CSDP is an innovation of the Constitutional Treaty. In the Draft Constitutional Treaty proposed by the Convention and the

[78] See for example in the context of the EU: A Cox, 'The Future of European Defence Policy: The Case of a Centralised Procurement Agency' (1994) 3 *Public Procurement Law Review* 65; A Cox and K Hartley, *The Costs of Non-Europe in Defence Procurement—Executive Summary*, The Commission of the European Communities DG III, July 1992.

[79] At 39–42.

[80] Article 101–11 EDC Treaty.

[81] Ch 3 at 104–105.

[82] Article 17(1) last subpara TEU (ex Article J6).

[83] For an overview see ch 1 in Martin Trybus, *European Defence Procurement Law: International and National Procurement Systems as Models for a Liberalised Defence Procurement Market in Europe* (Kluwer, The Hague, 1999).

June 2004 version of the Constitutional Treaty collective defence was covered in Article I-40 (2) and (7). Most notably this included a mutual defence commitment in Article I-40 (7). The first sentence of this paragraph provided:

> Until such time as the European Council has acted in accordance with paragraph 2 of this Article, closer co-operation shall be established, in the Union framework, as regards mutual defence.

The paragraph would have established the concept of closer EU co-operation in mutual defence. This would have been an important innovation because, as was explained in chapters 2 and 3, the establishment of a fully-fledged "common defence" is uncertain and envisaged for a distant future. Article I-40 (7) of the June 2004 version of the Constitutional Treaty would have regulated the period between the entering into force of the Constitutional Treaty and the establishment of a common defence by a decision of the European Council according to Article I-40 (2). Therefore this provisory or intermediate arrangement might well have governed the CSDP for a long time. The Treaties of Maastricht, Amsterdam, and Nice do not contain a comparable provision or concept of collective defence.[84] 'Common defence' is not defined in any version of the Constitutional Treaty or the TEU. However, the fact that it is also mentioned in the June 2004 version of the Constitutional Treaty indicates that a common defence would go beyond the CSDP. It could include a supranational defence policy controlled by a supranational institution, a European Army in addition to or replacing the national armies of the Member States, and a European defence budget as envisaged in the EDC Treaty. The following discussion shall explain the concepts of collective defence and closer co-operation before addressing the problems of the neutral Member States with this envisaged innovation of the June 2004 version, and their impact of the October 2004 version of the Constitutional Treaty.

2.3.1. The Mutual Defence Clause in the December 2003 and June 2004 Version of the Constitutional Treaty

The contents of closer co-operation in collective defence was defined in sentence 2 of Article I-40 (7) of the June 2004 version:

> Under this cooperation, if one of the Member States participating in such cooperation is the victim of armed aggression on its territory, the other participating States shall give it aid and assistance *by all the means in their power*, military or other, in accordance with Article 51 of the United Nations Charter [emphasis added].

[84] As explained in ch 2 at 64–66 and ch 3 at 103, Article 17(1) TEU (ex Article J7) did envisage a common defence in an uncertain future. However, mutual defence was not mentioned in the provision.

This is a mutual assistance clause comparable to Article 5 of the Modified Brussels Treaty 1954,[85] the founding document of the WEU, or Article V of the Washington Treaty 1949,[86] the founding document of NATO. However, the notion "by all the means in their power" implies a stronger commitment than that in the Washington Treaty, following the tradition of the Modified Brussels Treaty. In contrast to the earlier, the WEU founding document leaves no discretion to the Member States with regards to their assistance in case of an armed attack. They have to consider the armed attack on another Member State an attack on themselves. Member States have to act as if they were defending themselves with all the means at their disposal. Article 2 EDC included a similar 'automatic action commitment', speaking of "all the military and other aid in their power".[87] Therefore the wording of Article I-40 (7) of the December 2003 and June 2004 versions of the Constitutional Treaty was based on a European tradition of mutual defence clauses.

Prima facie, the mutual assistance clause in the December 2003 and June 2004 versions would have made the EU a military alliance comparable to the WEU. Moreover, as mentioned above, according to Article I-40 (2), this military alliance would have represented a provisory or intermediate arrangement for the period before the eventual creation of a common defence. Therefore the EU might even develop into a military alliance going beyond the WEU or NATO. The mutual assistance clause would have united most of the *acquis* of the WEU with the *acquis* of the EU in defence and security, thereby reuniting the separate defence integration 'stream', so far conducted within the framework of the WEU, with the 'mainstream of European integration'. While the October 2004 version of the collective

[85] Article V of the modified Brussels Treaty reads: 'If any of the High Contracting Parties should be the object of an armed attack in Europe, the other High Contracting Parties will, in accordance with the provisions of Article 51 of the Charter of the United Nations, afford the Party so attacked all the military and other aid and assistance in their power.' Protocol (with Exchange of Letters) Modifying and completing the Brussels Treaty, signed 23 October 1954, 211 UNTS 342.

[86] Article 5 Washington Treaty, 34 UNTS 243, reads:

> The Parties agree that an armed attack against one or more of them in Europe or North America shall be considered an attack against them all and consequently they agree that, if such an armed attack occurs, each of them, in exercise of the right of individual or collective self-defence recognised by Article 51 of the Charter of the United Nations, will assist the Party or Parties so attacked by taking forthwith, individually and in concert with the other Parties, such action as it deems necessary, including the use of armed force, to restore and maintain the security of the North Atlantic area.
> Any such armed attack and all measures taken as a result thereof shall immediately be reported to the Security Council. Such measures shall be terminated when the Security Council has taken the measures necessary to restore and maintain international peace and security.

JS Ignarski, entry on 'NATO' in R Bernardt, *Encyclopedia of Public International Law* (North Holland, Amsterdam, 1983) 264, at 269, considers this a qualified provision which 'compares unfavourably with the equivalent Article V of the Modified Brussels Treaty'. See also T Marauhn, *Building a European Security and Defence Identity, Bochumer Schriften zur Friedenssicherung und zum Humaniären Völkerrecht 30* (Universitätsverlag Dr N Brockmeyer, Bochum, 1996) 7. Article 5 was invoked only once. The USA invoked it after the attacks on New York and Washington on 11 September 2001.

[87] See ch 1 at 25–27 for details.

defence clause contained many changes which shall be discussed below, this 'reunification' of the different streams of integration would still be achieved through what is now Article I-41 (7) of the Constitutional Treaty.

2.3.2. Closer Co-operation

The concept of closer co-operation in Article I-40 (7) sentence 1 of the December 2003 and June 2004 versions of the Constitutional Treaty and the wording "Member States participating in such co-operation" and "the other participating Member States" in Article I-40 (7) sentence 2 suggest there could have been partial participation and flexibility in the context of mutual defence under the Constitutional Treaty. This is confirmed by the wording of the related Article III-214 (1) of the June 2004 version, which provides that "The closer co-operation on mutual defence provided for in Article I-40 (7) shall be open to all Member States of the Union". Although it is similar to (permanent) structured co-operation which only applies to crisis management in the context of what was then Articles I-40 (6) and III-213 (Articles I-41 (6) and III-312 in the December 2004 version), closer co-operation only applied to collective defence in the context of what was then Articles I-40 (7) and III-214 (Articles I-40 (7) and III-313 in the December 2004 version). Therefore it represented a special kind of formal flexibility, separate from the general concept of enhanced co-operation. Closer co-operation can also be distinguished from the formal flexibility of the same name under the Treaty of Amsterdam.[88]

Closer co-operation would have been a special form of flexibility in mutual defence which does not share the *ad hoc* character of informal flexibility in crisis management and the EDA discussed above. Member States wishing to participate in closer co-operation in collective defence would have had to commit themselves for a foreseeable future. Such a longer-term commitment is in the very nature of collective defence. In the context of the WEU it has been in existence for over 50 years since 1954[89] and in the context of NATO even for over 55 years since 1949. An *ad hoc* mutual defence commitment, where the participating Member States could decide on a case-by-case basis whether they will come to the rescue of one of the other participating Member States, is almost worthless. The purpose of an automatic action commitment is deterrence, a message to the outside world that possible attackers would face the combined defence effort of many Member States in case of an armed attack on one of them. In order for deterrence to work, it has to be clear that in case of an attack on Greece or Estonia, for example, the armed forces of all the other participating Member States will come to their rescue. Otherwise, the EU risks not being taken seriously as a military alliance. If this

[88] Title VII (Articles 43–45) of the Treaty of Amsterdam.

[89] 56 years when the preceding *Brussels Treaty for Collaboration in Economic, Social and Cultural Matters and for Collective Self-Defence* signed by the United Kingdom, France, the Netherlands, Belgium, and Luxembourg on 17 March 1948, 19 UNTS 51, is taken into account. The Brussels Treaty built on the *Treaty of Dunkirk* between the United Kingdom and France of 4 May 1947, 9 UNTS 187. See ch 1 at 16–18 for details.

combined reaction is not certain but will be decided on a case-by-case basis, the deterrent effect is significantly reduced.

With regards to collective defence, the coherence of the EU and therefore the effectiveness of the Union as a military alliance would have depended largely on the number and identity of Member States participating. It is submitted that if all the large Member States, France, Germany, Italy, Poland, Spain, the United Kingdom and the majority of medium sized and small Member States had participated in closer co-operation in mutual defence by making the necessary commitment to help each other in case of an armed attack, the EU would have represented a veritable military alliance. This would have been possible, since these Member States all participate in the WEU, which has a very similar commitment in Article 5 of the Modified Brussels Treaty. The fact that Austria, Cyprus, Finland, Ireland, Malta, and Sweden might not be able or willing to participate due to their neutral status would not have undermined the emergence of a sufficiently coherent military alliance.[90] Closer co-operation might even be one of very few solutions to address the issue of neutrality in this context. This shall be discussed in more detail below. However, if some of the large Member States, such as the United Kingdom, Italy, or Poland would have stayed outside closer co-operation in mutual defence the EU would not that easily have developed into a coherent military block providing its Member States with deterrence and a combined political weight on the international scene.

2.3.3. The Neutral Member States and Mutual Defence

The 'automatic action commitment' in Article I-40 (7) 2 of the December 2003 and June 2004 versions of the Constitutional Treaty caused problems with the neutrality of some Member States of the EU. They would have participated in a military alliance. Neutrality means not to participate in such an arrangement. The neutral Member States Austria, Finland, Ireland, and Sweden made their reservations clear before the December 2003 Brussels Summit.[91] "Formal binding security guarantees would be inconsistent with our security policy or constitutional requirements," the four Member States said. They argued against the automatic nature of the clause, which was however defended by various other Member States

[90] See also the argument of Missiroli, *Defence and Flexibility*, above n 18, at 14, first paragraph.

[91] See in particular the letter, dated 4 December 2003, written by the Finnish Foreign Secretary Erkki Tuomioja and his colleagues Brian Cowen from Ireland, Benita Ferrero-Waldner from Austria, and Leaila Freivalds from Sweden, Missiroli, *From Copenhagen to Brussels*, above n 9, at 437 (hereinafter 'Letter of 4 December 2003'), the article by E Toumioja, 'Europe Needs to Act as a Whole on Defence', *Financial Times*, 28 October 2003, and the article he published together with his colleague Laila Freivalds from Sweden, in *Dagens Nyhetter*, 11 November 2003, a translation into English was provided by Sweden's Permanent Representation to the EU in Missiroli, above, at 430. See also: 'Four EC States Fight to Guard Neutrality', *The Guardian*, 9 December 2003; 'Neutral States Baulk and EU Defence Provisions', *The Age*, 10 December 2003; 'Selbst entscheiden wie wir helfen', *Kurier* (Austria), 11 December 2003; 'Tuomioja Welcomes Italian Compromise on Security Guarantees' *Helsingin Sanomat* (Finland), 10 December 2003.

and EU institutions.[92] The Italian Presidency proposed to change the wording to "may request that the other Member States give it aid" by all possible means.

The example of Article V of the Washington Treaty shows that the mutual assistance commitment can be worded in a way that leaves more discretion to the participating nations without compromising the effectiveness of NATO as a military alliance. However, NATO is not necessarily a comparable alliance. It can be argued that NATO is only effective because the USA with the overwhelming military means of the only remaining superpower drives it. NATO does not need the military support of all Member States acting in concert to be effective. It is sufficient for the USA to act alone.

The neutral Member States are also opposed to the flexible character of closer co-operation in mutual defence. This would allow a self-selecting inner group of Member States to develop its security and defence policy without trying or even wanting to involve the Union as a whole. This would split the Union and allow a group of Member States to use the "EU trademark" without the full EU taking responsibility.[93] Instead the Constitutional Treaty should include a solidarity clause acceptable to all. This is spelt out in an article written by the Finish Foreign Secretary Erkki Tuomioja and his Swedish counterpart Laila Freivalds published in November 2003:

> We therefore support the idea of a new solidarity clause that builds on the voluntary principle while expressing the political solidarity that already exists between EU-members. This clause will make it possible to mobilise and coordinate all instruments available to the Union, including military resources, to prevent terrorist attacks or other disasters in any EU country and to be able to mange the effects should any such event ever occur.[94]

Similarly in the Letter of 4th December 2003 the foreign secretaries of the then four non-aligned Member States in the EU were "prepared to underline the principle of EU solidarity more widely in the field of security, including situations referred to in Article 51 [UN Charter]."[95] They proposed the following text for the then Article I-40 (7) Constitutional Treaty:

> If a Member State is victim of an armed aggression, it may request that the other Member States give it aid and assistance by all the means in their power, military or other, in accordance with Article 51 of the UN Charter.[96]

[92] 'Security Guarantee Initiative of Non-Aligned EU Countries meets Resistance in Brussels', *Helsingin Sanomat*, 9 December 2003.
[93] Tuomioja, *Financial Times*, 28 October 2003, above n 91.
[94] Tuomioja and Freivalds, *Dagens Nyhetter*, 11 November 2003, above n 91.
[95] Tuomioja, Cowen, Ferrero-Waldner, and Freivalds, above n 91.
[96] Above.

Moreover, those Member States wanting to go further should do so outside the Union.[97] Due to its voluntary basis, the proposal of a revised solidarity clause does not provide a substitute for the mutual solidarity envisaged in Article I-40 (7) of the December 2003 and June 2004 versions of the Constitutional Treaty. Similarly, the proposed text of Article I-40 (7) weakens the obligation of Member States to help each other in case of an armed aggression considerably. It is submitted that this would not be sufficient to develop the EU into a military alliance, as the commitment must be unconditional and unlimited. Even under the Treaty of Nice Member States "may request" assistance from each other in a case of military aggression. The proposals therefore suggest the creation of a military alliance outside the Union.

It could be argued, however, that the wording and conception of Articles I-40 (7) and III-214 provides sufficient flexibility to accommodate the neutral Member States. As discussed above, mutual defence is subject to closer co-operation. Therefore no Member State commits itself to an automatic action commitment just yet, simply by passing and implementing the Constitutional Treaty. A decision to participate in closer co-operation in mutual defence would not have to be made until later and on the basis of the Constitutional Treaty. Neutral Member States are still free not to participate in such closer co-operation.

It is submitted that the EU has to be based on some kind of automatic action commitment for two reasons. First, all Member States are small or medium sized military powers. Even all the 25 Member States together would be a military power considerably smaller than the USA. In order to establish a deterrent effect, which was the objective of the then Article I-40 (7), the commitment needs to be automatic to send the clear message that any possible aggressor will face the combined military response of as many of the 25 Member States as possible. It has to be certain that in case of an attack on Greece or Estonia the armed forces of all the other Member States come to their rescue. Otherwise, the EU risks not being taken seriously as a military alliance. Ultimately, the lack of an automatic action commitment would not only undermine the "security of the Union" but also the establishment of the EU as an actor on the international stage. A possible aggressor would have good reason to believe that the EU will show her usual lack of unity in an international crisis situation.

Second, the EU military alliance of Article I-40 (7) of the December 2003 and June 2004 versions is only designed as a transition to a common defence. The common defence envisaged by Article I-40 (2) Constitutional Treaty (Article 41 (2) of the October 2004 version), but also by Article J.7 (1) of the Treaty of Maastricht and Article 17 (1) of the Treaties of Amsterdam and Nice, goes well beyond a military alliance. Ireland did not object to the prospect of a common defence in any of these provisions. Ireland, Austria, Finland, and Sweden did not object to the same concept in the Treaties of Amsterdam and Nice. Therefore there is a contradiction in the position of the neutral Member States. This is probably to a large

[97] Tuomioja, *Financial Times*, 28 October 2003, above n 91.

extent due to the vague and uncertain character of the concept, which made it easy to agree with it. However, since the Treaty of Amsterdam the common defence has been a future destination, a prospect, and an objective of the EU. It is hard to see how the agreement with a concept going far beyond a military alliance can be reconciled with a fundamental objection to an automatic action commitment. A military alliance is a necessary step on the way to a common defence of the Union. If there is not even agreement on an automatic action commitment, a common defence becomes less likely. The Member States opposing it are not even prepared to accept the *acquis* of the WEU. Therefore the removal of the automatic action commitment would also require the removal of the concept of a common defence from the Constitutional Treaty to ensure its consistency.

2.3.4. Collective Defence in the October 2004 Version of the Constitutional Treaty

The mutual defence clause of the October 2004 version of the Constitutional Treaty published on 16 December 2004 provides in what is now Article I-41 (7):

> If a Member State is the victim of an armed aggression on its territory, the other Member States shall have towards it an obligation of aid and assistance by all the means in their power, in accordance with Article 51 [UN] Charter. This shall not prejudice the specific character of the security and defence policy of certain Member States.
>
> Commitments and cooperation in this area shall be consistent with commitments under the [NATO], which, for those States which are members of it, remains the foundation of their collective defence and the forum for its implementation.

In comparison to the mutual defence clause in the December 2003 and June 2004 versions discussed above, this provision introduces considerable changes. First, the concept of closer co-operation is removed from the provision. This accommodates part of the reservations of the neutral Member States since this removal of flexibility from the mutual defence clause prevents a vanguard of Member States from using the "label of the EU" in collective defence without really representing the entire EU.

Second, the notion "military or other" was deleted after the notion of "all the means in their power". However, this does not exclude military means, since the notion of "all the means in their power" is sufficiently wide to include military means. Moreover, the provision still deals with the response to an "armed aggression". Therefore it is submitted that Article I-41 (7) would have to expressly stipulate the exclusion of military means to exclude them.

Third, the reference to a close co-operation with NATO was omitted. However, subparagraph 2 introduces an even clearer requirement of consistency with NATO. Moreover, it even introduces a hierarchy of norms and organisations. Subparagraph 2 could be interpreted as reducing the mutual defence commitment of subparagraph 1 to a commitment subsidiary to NATO. In other words, the collective defence clause in subparagraph 1 can only be invoked after the mutual defence commitment in Article V of the NATO (Washington) Treaty was unsuccessfully invoked. This corresponds to the general arrangements between the two organisations and shall be addressed again in the context of the discussion of the relationship of the EU of the Constitutional Treaty with other international organisations.

Fourth, the reference to detailed arrangements in what was then Article III-214 and Article III-214 itself were deleted. Taken together the deletion of "military or other", the deletion of the reference to NATO, and the deletion of Article III-214, which included references to the EU Political and Security Committee, the EU Military Committee, NATO and the UN Security Council could be interpreted as a 'demilitarisation' of the defence clause. In other words, these deletions could be interpreted as a transformation of the mutual defence clause into a mere solidarity clause excluding military means. However, all versions of the Constitutional Treaty, including that of October 2004, include a separate solidarity clause in Article I-42, now Article I-43, covering terrorist threats as well as natural or man-made disasters. Hence, Article I-41 (7) is not meant to be a mere solidarity clause as such a clause already exists in Article I-43.

Fifth, the sentence "[t]his shall not prejudice the specific character of the security and defence policy of certain Member States" was added. This accommodates the reservations of the neutral Member States with regards to Article I-40 (7) in the June 2004 version outlined above. Article I-41 of the October 2004 version of the Constitutional Treaty does not oblige the neutral Member States to aid and assistance of the other Member States in case of an armed aggression. This sentence could also be interpreted as an argument against the "demilitarisation" of the clause, since it could be argued that such a reservation would not be necessary for a mere solidarity clause. It could also be argued that even a solidarity clause would have to exclude military aid to accommodate the neutral Member States.

Sixth, on a literal interpretation Article I-40 (7) subparagraph 1 sentence 1 of the October 2004 version of the Constitutional Treaty does not exclude the neutral Member States, who under Article I-40 (7) subparagraph 1 sentence 2 are under no obligation to aid and assist the other Member States in case of an armed aggression, from being entitled to such aid and assistance. In other words, a Member State such as Sweden, for example, is entitled to aid and assistance in case of an armed aggression, without being obliged to give it. Hence the October 2004 version of the Constitutional Treaty legalises 'free riding' in collective defence. *Prima facie* this appears unfair and excessively favourable to the interests of the neutral Member States. However, due to the fact that an armed aggression against any of the Member States seems very unlikely, the collective defence commitment is mainly of a political and diplomatic rather than a military and strategic nature. Therefore this arrangement has clear advantages since it accommodates the reservations of the neutral Member States while at the same time including them in collective defence.[98] Moreover, since this arrangement addresses a serious concern of

[98] The notion of 'mutual defence' is not accurate here, since the arrangement is one-sided and the notion of 'mutual' requires some form of 'give and take'.

the neutral Member States, it is to be welcomed. Having regards to the strategic situation in Europe today, collective defence is simply not important enough to risk the entire Constitutional Treaty over it.

An important feature of the collective defence clause in the December 2003 and June 2004 versions of the Constitutional Treaty remained unchanged in the October 2004 version. Compared to the mutual defence clause in Article 5 of the Washington Treaty, Article I-41 (7) Constitutional Treaty provides a commitment that goes further since it obliges Member States to provide all the aid and assistance in their power, rather than just the assistance they consider necessary. It is submitted that this transfers the WEU collective defence element in Article 5 Modified Brussels Treaty to the EU.

Without the Constitutional Treaty entering into force the EU will not develop into a military alliance. Moreover, as the military alliance is an important step on the way to a common defence, the latter will be delayed. However, Member States aiming at a defence alliance and possibly a common defence, such as Belgium, France, Greece, Hungary, Luxembourg, Spain, and Germany, will not necessarily wait for the next Treaty revision. Therefore a military alliance of EU Member States outside the EU becomes a possibility. Apart from numerous legal problems, which would go beyond the aim of this chapter, such an alliance outside the EU could undermine the coherence and consistency of the CFSP and *vice versa*.

3. THE DEFENCE *ACQUIS* OF THE EUROPEAN COMMUNITY

The defence *acquis* of the European Community discussed in Part II of this book was adopted by the Convention in the Constitutional Treaty. This comprises of the entire *acquis communautaire* of the First Pillar, including the EC Treaty, all secondary legislation,[99] and the case law of the European Court of Justice and the Court of First Instance.[100] This includes the *acquis* on public procurement discussed in chapter 7, that on the regulation of the European defence industries covered in chapter 8, and that on sex equality discussed in chapter 9. The defence *acquis* of the Community was discussed in Part II of this book and is not a part of the CSDP. However, it forms an important part of the legal order of security and defence under the Constitutional Treaty. Under the Treaties of Maastricht, Amsterdam, and Nice, the European Community formed the more supranational First Pillar of the TEU whereas the Common Security and Defence Policy formed part of the more intergovernmental Second Pillar. However, as outlined

[99] Article IV–438(3) Constitutional Treaty reads: 'The acts of the institutions, bodies, office, and agencies adopted on the basis of the treaties and acts repealed by Article IV–437 [inter alia EC Treaty and TEU] shall remain in force. Their legal effects shall be preserved until those acts are repealed, annulled or amended in implementation of this Treaty. [...]'

[100] Article IV–438(4) Constitutional Treaty reads: 'The case law of the European Court of Justice of the European Communities and the Court of First Instance on the interpretation and application of the Treaties and acts repealed in Article III–437, as well as the acts and conventions adopted for their application, shall remain, mutatis mutandis, the source of interpretation of Union law and in particular of the comparable provisions of the Constitution.'

above, the Constitutional Treaty aims to abolish the old three-pillar structure of the TEU. Therefore it is appropriate to discuss the defence *acquis* of the European Community in the Constitutional Treaty within this context. The defence *acquis* of the European Community is defined by the security exemptions in the EC Treaty and secondary legislation discussed in chapters 4 to 9, which determine the limits of Community law as an instrument of European defence integration. It will be shown that the Constitutional Treaty contains exactly the same set of security exemptions as the EC Treaty. Hence the Constitutional Treaty adopted the entire defence *acquis* of the European Community.

Under the Treaty of Nice the security exemptions of the EC Treaty formed the borderline between Community and Member State competence for defence on the one hand and between the Community and CFSP Pillars of the TEU on the other hand. Under the Constitutional Treaty, which does not differentiate between Pillars, the second function of the security exemptions of forming the borderline between the First and Second Pillars is *prima facie* no longer needed. However, the loss of this function depends on whether the differentiation between a more supranational Community and a more intergovernmental CFSP and CSDP is actually deleted. Since there is neither the intention nor a legal possibility to 'intergovermentalise' the *acquis communautaire*, this would require the 'communitarisation' of the CFSP. The more intergovernmental character of the CFSP is mainly reflected in the institutional provisions regarding the CFSP in the Constitutional Treaty and shall be discussed in the context of chapter 12.

Assuming for the moment that the Constitutional Treaty did overcome the differentiation between the First and Second Pillars of the TEU, a borderline between these Pillars would no longer be needed. Therefore, the security exemptions would only be a borderline between Union and Member State competence for defence. Under the Treaty of Nice matters exempt from Community law through the security exemptions, for example regarding armaments, could still be regulated in the context of the CFSP. Under the Constitutional Treaty such matters are exempt from the law of the Union as a whole, including from what formerly was the Second Pillar. In other words, under the Constitutional Treaty the security exemptions go further than under the TEU. This could be interpreted as a step back from the Union *acquis* under the Treaty of Nice and will be discussed in more detail in the context of the individual security exemptions below.

The discussion will cover the relevant exemptions in the EC Treaty: the public security exemptions of the free movement provisions discussed in chapter 4, the armaments and secrecy exemptions discussed in chapter 5, and the extreme crisis exemption discussed in chapter 6. These exemptions were also inserted into the Constitutional Treaty. The *acquis communautaire* of secondary legislation remains untouched by the Constitutional Treaty. Therefore the security exemptions discussed in chapters 7, 8 and 9 of this book would still apply after the entering into force of the Constitutional Treaty.

3.1. Free Movement and Public Security

The Constitutional Treaty adopted the free movement regimes of the EC Treaty including their respective public security exemptions. Similar to Article 30 EC, Article III-154 Constitutional Treaty allows limitation of the free movement of goods on grounds of *inter alia* public security.[101] Similarly, Article III-133 (3) Constitutional Treaty adopts Article 39 (3) EC and allows limitations of the free movement of workers justified on grounds of public security.[102] In addition, Article III-133 (4) Constitutional Treaty follows the tradition of Article 39 (4) EC and excludes the public service from the regime.[103] Article III-140 (1) Constitutional Treaty allows limitation of the freedom of establishment and the free movement of services.[104] The provision continues the situation under Article 46 EC. Finally, Article III-158 (1) (b) Constitutional Treaty[105] contains a public security exemption regarding the free movement of capital and payments. The relevant case law is part of the *acquis communautaire* and also applies in the context of the Constitutional Treaty. Corresponding to the discussion in chapter 4,[106] these exemptions need to be interpreted narrowly[107] and the European Court of Justice will exercise strict scrutiny over the use of the exemptions by the Member States and apply a proportionality test.[108]

As explained in chapter 4,[109] the relevance of the public security exemptions for defence is limited. Moreover, under the Treaty of Nice they are mainly part of the

[101] Article III–154 Constitutional Treaty reads:

> Article III–153 shall not preclude prohibitions or restrictions on imports, exports or goods in transit justified on grounds of public morality, public policy or public security; the protection of health and life of humans, animals or plants; the protection of national treasures possessing artistic, historic or archaeological value; or the protection of industrial and commercial property. Such prohibitions or restrictions shall not, however, constitute a means of arbitrary discrimination or a disguised restriction on trade between Member States.

[102] Article III–133(3) Constitutional Treaty provides 'Workers shall have the right, subject to limitations justified on grounds of public policy, public security or public health: [...]'

[103] Article III–133(4) Constitutional Treaty reads: 'This Article shall not apply to employment in the public service.'

[104] Article III–140 Constitutional Treaty reads: 'This Subsection and measures adopted in pursuance thereof shall not prejudice the applicability of provisions laid down by law, regulation or administrative action in Member States providing for special treatment for foreign nationals on grounds of public policy, public security or public health.'

[105] Article III–158(1)(b) Constitutional Treaty reads:

> Article III–156 shall be without prejudice to the right of Member States: [...] (b) to take all requisite steps to prevent infringements of national provisions laid down by law or regulation, in particular in the field of taxation and the prudential supervision of financial institutions, or to lay down procedures for the declaration of capital movements for purposes of administrative or statistical information, or to take steps which are justified on grounds of public policy or public security.

[106] At 125–127.

[107] Case C–222/84, *Marguerite Johnston v Chief Constable of the Royal Ulster Constabulary* [1986] ECR 1651; [1986] 3 CMLR 240. See also Case C–13/68, *SpA Salgoil v Italian Ministry of Foreign Trade* [1968] ECR 453, at 463; [1969] CMLR 181, at 192; and Case C–7/68, *Commission v Italy* [1968] ECR 633, at 644.

[108] Case C–72/83, *Campus Oil Limited v Minister for Industry and Energy*, [1984] ECR 2727, at 2764; [1984] 3 CMLR 544, at 558.

[109] At 139–140.

borderline between Community and Member State competence. Measures justified by a public security exemption from the EC Treaty will not lead to common approaches within the CFSP Pillar. Therefore the Constitutional Treaty does not introduce any changes to these regimes and their exemptions. Public security exemptions in secondary legislation, for example the Public Procurement Directives discussed in chapter 7, continue to have their foundation and equivalent in the Constitutional Treaty, for example Article III-154 in relation to Article 2 variation 3 of the old Supplies Directive.

3.2. The National Security Exemptions

The Constitutional Treaty also adopted the national security exemptions in Articles 296 and 297 EC, which were discussed in chapters 5 and 6 respectively. A text comparison reveals that the exemptions were adopted almost *verbatim*. Article III-436 (1) (a) Constitutional Treaty[110] contains the secrecy exemption formerly provided in Article 296 (1) (a) EC and Article III-436 (1) (b) Constitutional Treaty[111] contains the armaments exemption contained in Article 296 (1) (b) EC. The latter is clarified by the 1958 List of Armaments according to Article III-436 (2) Constitutional Treaty.[112] The only changes are that "[t]he provisions in this Treaty" was replaced by "[t]he Constitution" and that changes to the list in Article III-436 (2) now have to be in the form of a European Decision.[113] Following the tradition of the EC Treaty, the secrecy and armaments exemptions are still combined in one article. Furthermore, the position of the exemptions in Title VII "Common Provisions" at the very end of Part III of the Constitutional Treaty is comparable to that of Article 296 (1) (b) EC at the very end of the EC Treaty. The exemption to accommodate extreme crisis situations in Article 297 EC discussed in chapter 6 and the communication and review procedures for Article 296 and 297 EC in Article 298 EC are no longer regulated together in the same section. The Convention separated the 'sister provisions' of Article 296 EC from its 'siblings'. Article 297 EC became Article

[110] Article III–436(1)(a) Constitutional Treaty reads: 'The Constitution shall not preclude the application of the following rules: (a) no Member State shall be obliged to supply information the disclosure of which it considers contrary to the essential interests of its security; [...]'

[111] Article III–436(1)(b) Constitutional Treaty reads:

> The Constitution shall not preclude the application of the following rules: [...] (b) any Member State may take such steps as it considers necessary for the protection of the essential interests of its security which are connected with the production of or trade in arms, munitions and war material; such steps shall not adversely affect the conditions of competition in the internal market regarding products which are not intended for specifically military purposes.

[112] Article III–436(2) Constitutional Treaty reads: 'The Council of Ministers, on a proposal from the Commission, may unanimously adopt a European decision making changes to the list, which it drew up on 15 April 1958, of the products to which the provisions of para 1(b) apply.'

[113] See ch 9 at 311 n 19 for details on the new forms of secondary legislation.

III-131[114] Constitutional Treaty and Article 298 EC became III-132 Constitutional Treaty.[115] The only change is that in the latter the word "Treaty" was replaced by the word "Constitution". Nevertheless, the communication and review procedures in Article III-132 still apply to the exemptions in Article III-436 Constitutional Treaty. The treatment of the national security exemptions in the Constitutional Treaty gives rise to several interrelated problems.

3.2.1. The Position of Articles III-131 and III-132 in the Constitution

For almost fifty years the national security provisions were regulated in one section of the EC Treaty. Articles 296 to 298 EC were positioned at the end of the Community's founding document. This was appropriate since the provisions contain exemptions that apply to the Treaty as a whole. In contrast, the public security exemptions are combined with the respective free movement regime to which they apply. Moreover, Article 298 EC deviates from the normal review procedures of the Treaty. An alternative position could have been at the very beginning of the EC Treaty. However, the Treaty is a political as well as a legal document and it would have been against the spirit of the founders to start with a set of exceptions before establishing the rules. Moreover, the position at the end of the EC Treaty could also be interpreted as an indication that the authors assumed an extremely exceptional character of the national security exemptions. Articles 296 to 298 EC are not very well known provisions of the Treaty. Most textbooks hardly mention them and there is little academic literature concerning the interpretation of these exemptions.[116]

In the Constitutional Treaty the secrecy and armaments exemptions retain a position comparable to that in the EC Treaty. In contrast, the extreme crisis exemption and the communication and review procedures now form part of Title III "Internal Policies and Action", Chapter I "Internal market", Section 1

[114] Article III–131 Constitutional Treaty reads:

> Member States shall consult each other with a view to taking together the steps needed to prevent the functioning of the internal market being affected by steps which a Member State may be called upon to take in the event of serious internal disturbances affecting the maintenance of law and order, in the event of war, serious international tension constituting a threat of war, or in order to carry out obligations it has accepted for the purpose of maintaining peace and international security.

[115] Article III–132 Constitutional Treaty reads:

> If steps taken in the circumstances referred to in Articles III–131 and III–436 have the effect of distorting the conditions of competition in the internal market, the Commission shall, together with the State concerned, examine how these steps can be adjusted to the rules laid down in the Constitution. By way of derogation from the procedure laid down in Articles III–360 and III–361, the Commission or any Member State may bring the matter directly before the Court of Justice if it considers that another Member State is making improper use of the powers provided for in Articles III–131 and III–436. The Court of Justice shall give its ruling in camera.

[116] See the literature cited in ch 5 at 149 fn 32 & 33 and ch 6 at 179 fn 49 & 50 of this book. For example in the popular textbook Craig and de Búrca, *EU Law*, above n 6, mentions only Article 296 EC and only once in n 9 on p 827: 'Note that Art 296 (ex Art 223) EC provides for a further exception to the rules of the Treaty (and not only to the free movement rules) where a Member State considers that the essential interests of its security are at stake.'

"Establishment of the Internal Market". In other words, in contrast to the secrecy and armaments exemptions these national security provisions moved to a significantly more prominent position in the Constitutional Treaty. Now the exception comes before the rule. This indicates a gain in importance for the extreme crisis exemption. Moreover, it indicates that the European Convention and the Member States assume a long-term or even permanent inclusion of Articles III-131 and III-132 in the Constitutional Treaty. The position at the beginning of the internal market chapter gives the provisions a certain prominence. The academics, politicians, and lawyers working with the Constitutional Treaty will be unable to overlook them. They might be covered more extensively in the literature. This is slightly surprising since, as discussed in detail in chapter 6, the predecessor of Article III-131 Constitutional Treaty, Article 297 EC, has such a limited field of application through its triple-exceptional character. The prominent position of Articles III-131 and III-132 is an indication of their long-term or permanent inclusion in the Constitution because their deletion at a later stage would leave a noticeable gap in the Constitution. Alternatively, deletion would lead to a significant renumbering of articles, affecting all provisions after the gap left by Articles III-132 and III-132.[117] In contrast, the deletion at a later stage of a provision at a less prominent position of the Constitution, in particular at the end, would be easier. It would just make the Constitutional Treaty one article shorter and would hardly be noticed, even by the informed public. In the case of the crisis exemption and the review procedure the Convention could have left them at their much less prominent position at the end of the Treaty.

It is submitted that the prominent position of Articles III-131 and III-132 in the Constitutional Treaty is appropriate. First, a deletion of Article III-131 would require the EU to be in a position to take over the full responsibility for the extreme crisis situations accommodated in the provision. As outlined above, the Constitutional Treaty does not establish a common defence. It merely establishes a CSDP, which represents a combination of flexible frameworks, including a security policy, a defence alliance, and an armaments policy. This CSDP cannot take over from Member States the responsibility for the extreme crisis situation accommodated in Article III-131. *Prima facie* common defence would be the minimum prerequisite for the deletion of the exemption. However, even the 1952 EDC Treaty, discussed in chapter 1 as the only project for a common defence to date, accommodated extreme crisis situations. Articles 12, 13, and 14 EDC laid down the conditions under which a Member State would have been able, with the authority of the Board of Commissioners, to temporarily withdraw parts of its EDC force contribution to meet national contingencies. The situations envisaged were those of disorder or threatened disorder in the Member State's own territory, in the event of a major crisis affecting a non-European territory for which it has

[117] Another alternative would be to replace Articles III–131 and III–132 with a completely different provision. However, this would be very difficult systematically since the new provisions would have to fit in. Therefore provisions of the EC Treaty were never replaced in this way.

assumed responsibility, or to fulfil an international mission entrusted to it outside the EDC area. These situations are similar to those accommodated in Article III-131 Constitutional Treaty. A deletion of Article III-131 would require a common defence involving a total transfer of responsibility for defence and security from the Member States to the Union, including the responsibility for internal disorder and overseas territories. This is highly unlikely for the foreseeable future. Moreover, the narrow interpretation of the extreme crisis situation discussed in chapter 6 has to be taken into account. The triple-exceptional character of Article 297 EC limited its practical relevance considerably. The narrow field of application prevents the provision from undermining the internal market. Therefore, due to the limits of both the CSDP and a possible common defence and the narrow interpretation of the exemption, the inclusion and position of Article III-131 in the Constitutional Treaty is considered appropriate.

The position of Article III-131 in the 'introduction' to the internal market Chapter I of Title III on "Internal Policies and Action" also indicates a limitation of application in comparison to its predecessor Article 297 EC. The latter was positioned in the final provisions and applied to the EC Treaty as a whole. On the one hand the fact that Article III-131 adopts Article 297 EC *verbatim* could be interpreted as an adoption of the general application of the exemption as well, at least in relation to Part III of the Constitutional Treaty. On the other hand Article III-131 is part of Title III of Part III of the Constitutional Treaty. A systematic interpretation leads to the assumption that Article III-131 only applies to Title III and not to the Constitutional Treaty as a whole. This interpretation is supported by the fact that Article III-131 is not part of Title I "Provisions of General Application". This does not alter the *status quo* with regards to Parts I and II of the Constitutional Treaty. However, Article III-131 does not apply to Titles I , II, and IV to VII of Part III . Therefore it is submitted that the new position of the extreme crisis exemption in the Constitutional Treaty indicates an even narrower application of Article III-131 compared to Article 297 EC.

3.2.2. The Survival of the Armaments Exemption

The Constitutional Treaty adopted the armaments exemption in Articles 296 (1) (b) EC discussed in chapter 5 almost *verbatim* in Article III-436 (1) (b). The provision allows Member States to derogate from their obligations under the Constitution with respect to armaments in cases where they consider this necessary in the interests of their national security. The exemption is clarified by the 1958 List of Armaments according to Article III-436 (2) Constitutional Treaty. The wording of the latter paragraph corresponds almost word for word to that of Article 296 (2) EC. Therefore the Constitution also adopted the 1958 List of hard defence material reproduced and discussed in chapter 5.[118] Following the tradition of the EC Treaty, the secrecy and armaments exemptions are still combined in one article. Furthermore, the position of the exemptions in Title VII "Common

[118] At 143–148.

Provisions" at the very end of Part III of the Constitutional Treaty is comparable to that of Article 296 (1) (b) EC in "Part Six: General and Final Provisions" at the very end of the EC Treaty. This position on the background of the move of the crisis exemption and the review procedures for both exemptions to a more prominent position at the beginning of Part III of the Constitution could be interpreted as the 'beginning of the end' of the armaments exemption. The Convention discussed the deletion of the provision,[119] which had been on the European agenda for decades.[120] The 'abolitionists' were not successful but singled the exemption out for deletion at a later stage. The 'conservatives' were successful but failed to enshrine the provision at the prominent place together with the sister provisions at the beginning of Part III. Hence, the current position of the armaments exemption could be interpreted as a compromise between these two camps. The time is not yet ripe for a deletion of the armaments exemption.

The adoption of the armaments exemption in the Constitutional Treaty adopts the *acquis communautaire* in relation to armaments within its current limits. As explained in chapters 5 and 8 the armaments exemption allows a special treatment of the defence industries in relation to competition law, merger control, and State aids. Moreover, it allows a special treatment of imports, exports, and intra-Community transfers of hard defence material. As explained in chapter 7[121] the exception also allows a special treatment of procurement contracts regarding hard defence material as there is a direct reference to the predecessor of Article III-436 Constitutional Treaty in the EC Public Procurement Directives. Generally that predecessor, Article 296 (1) (b) EC, prevented the establishment of a liberalised European defence equipment market in the context of the Community. This effect was mainly caused by the interpretation of the armaments exemption in Article 296 (1) (b) EC as an automatic or categorical exclusion of all armaments on the 1958 List from the application of the EC Treaty. This categorical interpretation of the armaments exemption, advocated mainly by the Member States, could also be applied to Article III-436 (1) (b) Constitutional Treaty which follows the wording of Article 296 (1) (b) EC.

[119] See the 'Contribution on "European Defence"' made by Lamberto Dini, Brussels, 26 September 2002, in J-Y Haine, *From Laeken to Copenhagen, European Defence: Core Documents*, Chaillot Paper No 57, (Institute of Security Studies of the European Union: Paris, 2003) 203, at 205: 'It is also worth asking whether it would not be desirable to revise Article 296 of the European Community Treaty, which excludes armaments from the scope of the single market.' The last half of the sentence reveals an understanding of the provision as an automatic exemption of armaments from the scope of the Treaty. See also: D de Villepin and J Fischer, 'Joint Proposal', Prague, 21 November 2002, J-Y Haine, above, 214, at 217: 'La France et l'Allemagne proposent d'inscrire dans le Traité: les fonctions d'une politique européenne d'armement, dont la création progressive d'un marché européen d'armement, moyennant des procédures spécifiques, notament d'une adaption de l'article 296 du TCE'. However, the ministers did not specify how the provision should be adapted.

[120] E Klepsch, *Klepsch–Report: European Armaments Procurement Co-operation* (Luxembourg, 1978); D Greenwood, *Greenwood–Report: European Technological Co-operation and Defence Procurement* (Brussels, 1979); L Tindemanns, *Tindemanns–Report*, in A Drown, *A Single European Arms Industry? European Defence Industries in the 1990s* (London, 1990) 77–78.

[121] At 203–213.

In contrast to the wide interpretation of Article 296 (1) (b) EC as an automatic exclusion of hard defence material from the application of the EC Treaty, the narrow interpretation, based on the judgment of the European Court of Justice in *Commission* v. *Spain*,[122] requires Member States to specifically invoke the exemption. Moreover, they have to prove that a situation justifying exemption actually exists. The European Court of Justice can scrutinise the use of the exemption and apply a proportionality test. In contrast to the interpretation as an automatic exemption of armaments which makes exemption the rule, the limited interpretation makes exemption the exception. As explained in chapter 7,[123] it is yet too early to assess whether this new interpretation will prevail and lead to a liberalised defence equipment market in practice. This depends on the frequency with which the Member States invoke the exemption, the vigorousness with which the Commission polices its use and bring cases before the European Court of Justice, and the readiness of the Court to scrutinise measures taken on the basis of the provision. Assuming an only limited and proportionate use, a vigorous Commission, and a strict Court, the new interpretation might well make the use of the exemption an exception thereby providing the EU with a competitive defence equipment market. Thus the deletion of the exemption would not be required. Nevertheless the continued presence of the armaments exemption in the founding document makes the borderline between the Union and Member State competence for armaments uncertain or unstable. The borderline is like a river that can change its bed. It depends on the behaviour of the Member States and the institutions, which can change, for example due to changes in the general political landscape. It lacks certainty and clarity. The deletion of the provision would represent a substantial commitment and send a clear message to the defence industries, defence procurement agencies, and ministries of defence.

3.2.3. The Coexistence of Article III-436 (1) (b) and the European Defence Agency in the Constitutional Treaty

The adoption of the armaments exemption cannot be seen in isolation. As discussed above, the Constitutional Treaty also introduces an EDA dealing with armaments. An automatic exemption of armaments from the application of the Constitutional Treaty would lead to a contradiction with Articles I-41 (3) subparagraph 2 and III-311 which provide a framework for an armaments policy within the field of application of the Constitutional Treaty. The question arises, whether there can be a regime on goods in the Constitutional Treaty which at the same time are categorically excluded from it. Under the Treaty of Nice an automatic exclusion of armaments from the First Pillar can coexist with a Second Pillar EDA. However, in the 'Single Pillar' order of the Constitutional Treaty an automatic exemption of armaments and an EDA are mutually exclusive. The Constitution would require a

[122] Case C–414/97, *Commission v Spain*, [1999] ECR I–5585, [2000] 2 CMLR 4. See ch 5 at 152–154 for details and further references on this judgment.
[123] At 211.

provision that brings the armaments pushed out of the Union's legal order by an automatic armaments exemption back into the field of application of the Constitution to allow the EDA to operate a policy on armaments. Such a provision could be added to Article III-436:

> Paragraph (1) letter (b) shall not compromise the right of Member States to develop a European armaments policy and co-operate in individual armaments projects as envisaged by Articles I-40 (3) subparagraph 2 and III-212.

Alternatively, Articles I-41 (3) subparagraph 2 and III-311 could include a 'derogation from the derogation' in Article III-436. There are various explanations for the fact that such a provision was not included in the Constitutional Treaty. First, the issue of the armaments exemption could have been so controversial that the Convention preferred not to touch it or did not reach an agreement on any adaptations.[124] The almost verbatim adoption of the EC Treaty provision is a strong indication for this explanation. Second, the Convention did not see the contradiction. Third, the Convention followed the narrow interpretation of Article 296 (1) (b) EC advocated in chapter 5[125] and therefore saw no necessity to adapt the provision before adopting it.

It is submitted that the limited interpretation allows the coexistence of the armaments exemption with the flexible framework of the EDA. Member States would co-operate in the context of the EDA but retain Article III-436 (1) (b) as an 'emergency break'. Nevertheless, this emergency break makes the borderline between Union and Member State competence for armaments uncertain even for Member States participating in individual armaments projects. As mentioned above, the borderline is like a river that can change its bed, it lacks legal certainty. A way to address this problem could be that the Member States participating in individual armaments projects could give this river a fixed bed by forfeiting their right to invoke Article III-436 (1) (b) with respect to the project by contract or treaty.

The limited interpretation of the armaments exemption needs to be compared to its deletion. A number of Member States and members of the European Convention advocated this solution. With respect to the EDA, an abolition of the armaments exemption would represent a clear commitment of the Member States to the Agency and its role in the establishment of a European defence equipment market within the Union's legal framework. However, it is submitted that due to the limited interpretation of Article III-436 (1) (b), a deletion of the provision is no longer required.

[124] There clearly was discussion on the adaptation of the provision. See above n 104.
[125] At 152–154.

3.2.4. The Secrecy Exemption in Article III-342 (1) (a) Constitutional Treaty

In Article III-436 the secrecy and armaments exemptions have a position in the Constitutional Treaty comparable to Article 296 in the EC Treaty. As discussed above, the crisis exemption was moved to a more prominent position indicating its long term or even permanent inclusion in the Constitutional Treaty. The secrecy exemption in Article III-436 (1) (a) allows Member States to derogate from their obligations to supply information under the Constitutional Treaty when they consider that to be against the interests of their national security. It is submitted that such a secrecy exemption is necessary unless the EU has taken over the responsibility for security from the Member States. Only when 'national security' has become 'Union security' because a common defence is in place and operational, the Member States can be asked to supply information without considering their national security. Therefore, the security exemption in the current Article 296 (1) (a) EC is closer to Article 297 EC than to Article 296 (1) (b) EC and should have been separated from the latter and moved to the more prominent position at the beginning of Part III of the Constitutional Treaty. A possible explanation for not doing this could be an oversight, the Convention did not properly differentiate between the three national security exemptions and treated Article 296 EC as a unit. However, with a possible deletion of the armaments exemption at a later stage, the armaments exemption in Article III-436 (1) (b) would have to be moved to Article III-131 or continue as the remainder of Article III-436.

4. LINKS WITH RELATED INTERNATIONAL SECURITY ORGANISATIONS

Following the tradition of European defence integration since the times of the European Defence Community the Constitutional Treaty builds the CSDP on the foundations of the existing European defence architecture. First, the commitment to international law expressed in the values, objectives, and principles discussed in chapter 10, includes an adherence to the legal requirements of the UN Charter. Second, it recognises the paramount importance of NATO for the security and defence of Europe. Most Member States of the EU are member States of NATO and as explained in chapter 3[126] the Union needs NATO assets for most of her operations. Third, the Western European Union (WEU) is not mentioned in the Constitutional Treaty. This completes the process of transfer of the functions of the WEU, which started with the Treaty of Amsterdam described in chapters 2 and 3.[127]

4.1. United Nations

The Constitutional Treaty recognises the United Nations as the foundation of their CFSP and CSDP. According to Articles I-3 (4) and III-292 (1) subparagraph 1

[126] At 114–118.
[127] Ch 2 at 80–84 and ch 3 at 100–108.

"respect for the principles of the United Nations Charter and international law" shall be one of the principles of the CFSP. These principles were discussed in chapter 10. Article III-292 (1) subparagraph 2 Constitutional Treaty gives a preference to the "framework of the United Nations" when the Union seeks to develop relations and build partnerships with third countries, international, regional or global organisations. According to Article III-292 (2) letter (c) Constitutional Treaty the EU is to "preserve peace, prevent conflicts, and strengthen international security, in conformity with the principles of the United Nations Charter." The October 2004 version added "with the principles of the Helsinki Final Act and the aims of the Charter of Paris, including those relating to external borders;" to letter (c) of the provision. Articles III-305 (2) subparagraphs 2 and 3 Constitutional Treaty gives special importance to the UN Security Council thereby recognising this UN institution as the ultimate arbiter on security issues.

Article III-214 (3) of the December 2003 and June 2004 version of the Constitutional Treaty provided:

> The [UN] Security Council shall be informed immediately of any armed aggression and the measures taken as a result.

This involved the UN Security Council in the collective defence of the EU. However, as outlined above with the 'reform' of collective defence in the October 2004 version of the Constitutional Treaty this sentence and the entire Article III-214 were deleted. Nevertheless, it is submitted that the references to the UN Charter in the October 2004 version still require the EU and the Member States to inform the UN Security Council immediately of any armed aggression and the measures taken as a result as prescribed in the deleted Article III-214 (3). According to Article 103 UN Charter[128] the Constitutional Treaty has to comply with the UN Charter. This means that the Constitutional Treaty also has to comply with Article 51 UN Charter which stipulates: "Measures taken by members in the exercise of this right to self-defence shall be immediately reported to the Security Council [...]." Article III-214 (3) could have been inserted in Article I-41 (7) of the October 2004 version of the Constitutional Treaty.

The references to the UN introduce a requirement of compatibility with both the UN Charter and the security policy of the UN. This recognises the supremacy of the UN Charter over any other treaty stipulated in Article 103 UN Charter. The requirement will make it necessary for the EU institutions involved in the CSDP to work in close contact with the UN institutions. Crisis management missions can only be conducted with a respective mandate from the UN Security Council. The details regarding co-operation in crisis management were agreed in 2003 in the

[128] Article 103 UN Charter reads: 'In the event of a conflict between the obligations of the Members of the United Nations under the present Charter and their obligations under any other international agreement, their obligation under the present Charter shall prevail.'

Joint Declaration of the UN and the EU.[129] A citation from this Joint Declaration clarifies the requirement of UN compatibility with regards to crisis management:

> The [UN] and the [EU] are united by the premise that the primary responsibility for the maintenance of international peace and security rests with the [UN] Security Council in accordance with the [UN] Charter. Within this framework, the EU reasserts its commitment to contribute to the objectives of the [UN] in crisis management.[130]

Moreover, measures taken in the context of collective defence have to stay within the limits of Article 51 UN Charter. As outlined above, there is an obligation to keep the UN Security Council informed and measures taken in the context of collective defence "shall not in any way affect the authority and responsibility of the [UN] Security Council under the [UN] Charter to take at any time such action as it deems necessary in order to maintain or restore international peace and security."

The Treaties of Maastricht, Amsterdam, and Nice discussed in chapters 2 and 3 also include a requirement of UN compatibility in Article 11 (1) TEU (ex Article J.1) comparable to Article III-292 (2) letter (c) Constitutional Treaty. The reference also expresses the defensive character of the EU as a military alliance. The CSDP respects the prohibition of the use of force in Article 2 number (4) UN Charter and the limits of the right to self-defence in Article 51 UN Charter. As explained in chapter 1, Article 2 (1) EDC Treaty expressly provided for the defensive character of the Community as a whole.[131] Such a provision would also be possible in the context of the Constitutional Treaty. The CSDP includes a regime on crisis management and therefore it could be argued that it is not exclusively defensive. However, the EDC would also have co-operated with the UN in crisis management and this was not considered contrary to its exclusively defensive character. Moreover, Article 2 (1) EDC Treaty has to be seen in its historic context as a provision drafted a few years after the end of World War II and also as a message to the Soviet Union. As the CSDP has another historic context and a message to the Soviet Union or her successors is no longer necessary, the Constitutional Treaty does not need a provision stipulating the exclusively defence character of the EU. The references to the UN are sufficient to express the defensive character of the Union.

The repeated references to the UN are an innovation of the Convention, in particular the reference in Article I-3 (4) making "respect for the principles of the [UN] Charter" a principle of the CFSP. This principle is also an element of European identity, which differentiates all Member States from other parts of the world with less respect for the prohibition of the use of force.

The requirement of UN compatibility does not undermine the coherence, consistency and effectiveness of the CFSP or CSDP. The membership of all

[129] *Joint Declaration of the United Nations and the European Union on Cooperation in Crisis Management*, New York, 24 September 2003, in Missiroli, *From Copenhagen to Brussels*, above n 13, at 217.

[130] Above.

[131] Article 2(1) EDC, Cmd 9127 (HMSO, London, 1954), provided: 'The objectives of the Community are exclusively defensive.' See ch 1 at 25–27.

Member States in the UN alone would make it, due to Article 103 UN Charter, legally impossible and politically unfeasible not to build the CSDP on the foundations of the UN Charter.

4.2. NATO

The connection of the CSDP to NATO is diverse and complex. According to Article I-41 (2) subparagraph 2 Constitutional Treaty the policy of the EU in accordance with Article I-41 shall not prejudice the specific character of the security and defence policy of certain Member States. The provision covers the crisis management,[132] the collective defence,[133] and the capabilities and armaments[134] components of the CSDP. The CSDP shall respect the obligations of certain Member States, which see their common defence realised in NATO and under the 1949 Washington Treaty. The CSDP shall be compatible with the common security and defence policy established within the NATO framework. This compatibility requirement does not only cover the CSDP as envisaged by the Constitutional Treaty but also the uncertain but possible common defence which could be the next step towards defence integration. Consequently, Article I-41 (7) subparagraph 2 Constitutional Treaty extends the requirement of NATO compatibility to the execution of collective defence discussed above:

> Commitments and cooperation in this area shall be consistent with commitments under [NATO], which, for those States which are members of it, remains the foundation of their collective defence and the forum of its implementation.

While this wording accommodates the neutral Member States, this subparagraph introduces a requirement of NATO compatibility also for measures taken for collective defence taken to defend a neutral Member State.

The NATO compatibility requirement covers the entire CSDP as envisaged by the Constitutional Treaty, possible enhanced co-operation between a number of Member States, and the possible but yet uncertain common defence. However, there is no precise definition of NATO compatibility in Article I-41 Constitutional Treaty.

Article I-41 (2) subparagraph 2 Constitutional Treaty refers to "certain Member States" rather than all the Member States. This is due to the fact that four of the 15 Member States before the 2004 accessions, namely Austria, Finland, Ireland, and Sweden are not Member States of NATO. Two of the new Member States, namely Cyprus and Malta, are neutral. The Czech Republic, Hungary and Poland have

[132] Article I–41(1) Constitutional Treaty.
[133] Article I–41(7) Constitutional Treaty.
[134] Article I–41(3) Constitutional Treaty.

been Member States of NATO since 1999 and Estonia, Latvia, Lithuania, the Slovak Republic, and Slovenia joined in 2004. Of the countries currently negotiating accession to the EU, Turkey is a founding member State of NATO and Bulgaria and Romania joined recently. This makes the EU of 25 or 28 an organisation with 19 or 22 Member States inside and six Member States outside NATO. However, the NATO compatibility requirement applies to the EU as a whole.

The requirement of NATO compatibility is a reflection of the fact that Europe and the CSDP are dependent on the Atlantic Alliance. First, neither the WEU nor the EU is in a position to take over the responsibility for the 'homeland' defence of Europe. Second, the capability shortfalls of the Member States mentioned in the context of the discussion of the EDA above are so substantial that crisis management operations on a larger scale can not be conducted without access to NATO assets. Therefore the Berlin-Plus Agreement between NATO and the EU allows the latter to make use of the Alliance's planning and logistic facilities for operations where NATO is not itself engaged.[135] The capability shortfalls and the resulting dependence on NATO assets are a major obstacle to the development of a CSDP that includes an autonomous military capacity. A military capacity, which depends on assets outside the EU is not autonomous but dependent. It is yet too early to say whether the "assured access" of the Berlin-Plus Agreement will give the CSDP the independence it needs to provide the EU with credibility and visibility on the international scene. Duke pointed out, that the NATO Washington Summit decisions, or *Washington Communiqué*, in its Paragraph 10 provides for "assured access" and not for 'guaranteed permanent access'.[136] The EU missions in Bosnia and Herzegovina, the Former Yugoslav Republic of Macedonia, and the Democratic Republic of the Congo do not provide a sufficient set of precedents to prove the reliable and viable access to NATO assets. 'EUPM' was merely a police mission, 'Artemis' was conducted without having recourse to NATO assets, and the 'Althea' mission in Bosnia-Herzegovina only started on 2 December 2004.[137] Moreover, the Berlin-Plus Agreement appears to be the only viable solution. It would be very expensive to improve European military capabilities and many Member States are cutting their defence budgets despite the lip service they pay to

[135] Washington Communiqué, NATO Washington Summit, NAC 5(99) 64, 24 April 1999. See the *European Union-NATO Declaration on ESDP*, Brussels, 16 December 2003, in Haine, *From Laeken to Copenhagen*, above n 117, 178, at 179: 'NATO is supporting ESDP in accordance with the relevant Washington Summit decisions, and is giving the European Union, inter alia and in particular, assured access to NATO's planning capabilities, as set out in the NAC decisions on 13 December 2002.'

[136] Duke, above n 52, at 164.

[137] 'Changing of the Guard: the EU Seeks to Show the US it is Serious about Defence', *Financial Times*, 2 December 2004, at 17.

the importance of improving their capabilities.[138] Even existing commitments are threatened.[139] An EU wide effort to invest in defence procurement is unlikely. Therefore the CSDP will remain dependent on NATO for a long time. However, the dependence on NATO assets reinforces and guarantees the observance of the NATO compatibility requirement in practice. A CSDP that depends on NATO assets is not in a position to be incompatible with NATO.

The requirement of NATO compatibility is a necessary component of the CSDP as long as the Alliance itself is a credible force on the international scene. Although there are signs that NATO is weakening, it will be the dominant military alliance for the foreseeable future. The CSDP has to grow in the shadow and under the shield of NATO. The future will show whether the Union can provide the structures, political resolve, and financial backing to develop an increasingly independent military profile. However, even a well structured- and funded CSDP will have to be compatible with NATO to avoid political and strategic loss through friction. The difference that sufficient funding and political will could make is that between a CSDP where the limits are ultimately determined by NATO and a situation where both organisations need to harmonise their efforts. Only the latter scenario will serve the purpose of the CSDP: to add a credible security and defence component to a strong political actor on the international scene.

4.3. WEU

The Constitutional Treaty completes the process of transfer or transition of WEU functions to the EU, which started with the Treaty of Amsterdam. This was described in chapter 2[140] and in particular in chapter 3.[141] The organisation of the Modified Brussels Treaty is not even mentioned once in the new primary legal document. With the reservations made in the context of chapters 2 and 3 in particular with regards to the WEU Assembly, the WEU is completely integrated in the flexible frameworks of the CSDP and can be dissolved. This overcomes an important aspect of external fragmentation.[142] However, depending on the number and identity of the Member States participating in these frameworks, the fragmentation might be internalised. Moreover, the WEU might be revitalised in case

[138] Duke, above n 52, at 163 points out the German and Swedish cuts in 2000:

> During 2000, Hans Eichel, German Finance Minister, announced plans to save about ECU 9.7 billion ($10.4 billion) over four years [until 2004] while Sweden announced plans to save about SEK 4 billion ($500 million) per annum from its defence budget, mainly through cutting jobs. In Germany's case the cuts were made in spite of Rudolf Scharping's [then Defence Minister] call for an increase in the defence budget of some $16 to $22 billion over the next ten years.

For a more general overview see: A Missiroli, 'Ploughshares into Swords? Euros for European Defence' (2003) 8 *European Foreign Affairs Review* 5–33.

[139] For example the construction of 620 Eurofighter/Typhoon fighter aircraft for the German, Italian, Spanish and United Kingdom air forces, see *Financial Times*, 22 October 1999.

[140] At 80–84.

[141] At 100–108.

[142] Missiroli, 'Challenges of Coherence', above n 3, at 191.

the Constitutional Treaty does not enter into force and the EU has to continue defence integration on the basis of the Treaty of Nice.

5. CONCLUSIONS

The CSDP envisaged in the Constitutional Treaty represents the next chapter in the story of European defence integration. It develops aspects of security and defence policy already addressed in the Treaties of Maastricht, Amsterdam, and Nice. First, the Petersberg Tasks are reformed and put in the flexible framework of structured co-operation in crisis management to facilitate the establishment of a more permanent and deployable ERRF. Second, a European Defence Agency was established to conduct a European Capabilities and Armaments Policy, even before and therefore independent of the entering into force of the Constitutional Treaty. Third, as a major and controversial innovation, the new basic treaty includes a collective defence clause. Fourth, the Constitutional Treaty adopts the defence *acquis communautaire*, allowing the relevant Community policies to impact on the economic and social aspects of the defence laws of the Member States within the limits of the security exemptions. Fifth, following the tradition of the previous treaties, the CSDP is connected to and dependent on other security organisations, in particular on NATO. The objective of these new arrangements is to provide the Union with a coherent and effective CSDP and CFSP in order to speak with one voice on the international scene. On the one hand the fragmentation of European defence integration is addressed in the Constitutional Treaty. Continuing the principles of the Treaty of Nice the new Constitution provides a framework that allows the EU to implement its own crisis management policy, rather than "avail" itself to the WEU. The establishment of the EDA will allow the transfer of armaments structures outside the Union, such as OCCAR, WEAG/WEAO, and LOI, to the new Agency. The introduction of a collective defence commitment allows the transfer of the most important remaining function of the WEU to the EU. Article III-292 (3) subparagraph 2 sentence 2 Constitutional Treaty requires the consistency of the CFSP and CSDP with the other policies of the Union, in other words the *acquis communautaire*. The external dimension of fragmentation of European defence integration is addressed by these measures. However, the flexible frameworks of closer co-operation for crisis management and the armaments policy respectively provide a potential for internalised fragmentation. The next chapter 12 on the institutional structure of the CSDP will show that the separation of a more intergovernmental CFSP and CSDP from the more supranational *acquis communautaire* adds another dimension of internal fragmentation to the discussion.

12

The Old Players and a New Minister: The Institutional Structure of the Common Security and Defence Policy Under the Constitutional Treaty

1. INTRODUCTION

CHAPTER 11 DISCUSSED the scope of the Common Security and Defence Policy (hereinafter CSDP) as part of the Common Foreign and Security Policy (hereinafter CFSP) under the Constitutional Treaty.[1] Moreover, it covered the connection to other security organisations such as the United Nations, NATO or the Organisation for Security and Co-operation in Europe (hereinafter OSCE). The following chapter 12 will discuss the institutional structure, in other words the composition and powers of the institutions involved in decision making in the CSDP. Chapter 12 will complement the discussion in chapters 10 and 11 and complete Part III on the possible next phase of European defence integration. The analysis will include the competencies of the relevant institutions regarding the defence *acquis communautaire*.

The institutions involved in the CSDP are the European Council, the President of the European Council, the Council of Ministers, the Political and Security Committee, the Union Minister for Foreign Affairs, the Commission, and the European Parliament. Moreover, similar to the Treaty of Nice, the Member States, as separate from the Council(s) are to have an important role. The military structures of the Union discussed in chapter 3,[2] such as the European Union Military Committee or the European Union Military Staff, are not mentioned in the Constitutional Treaty. Following the tradition of the Treaty on European Union (hereinafter TEU), the jurisdiction of the European Court of Justice is excluded.

[1] Treaty establishing a Constitution for Europe, Conference of the Representatives of the Governments of the Member States, Brussels, 13 October 2004 (ORfr) CIG 87/1/04 REV 1. This version included a number of considerable changes in comparison to the Draft Treaty and the June version of the Constitutional Treaty. The version published on 16 December 2004 [2004] 0J C-310/1 contained only minor changes to the October 2004 version. Chapters 10–12 refer to the published December 2004 version of the Constitutional Treaty unless indicated otherwise.

[2] At 108–112.

The following discussion will differentiate between the more intergovernmental institutions and their relevant sections on the one hand and the more supranational institutions Commission, European Parliament, and European Court of Justice on the other hand. As outlined in the introduction to this book, the concept 'more intergovernmental (EU) institution' is understood as an institution dependent on the governments of the Member States. Intergovernmentalism is also characterised and reinforced by unanimous decisions or national *veto* and an exclusion of judicial scrutiny. In contrast, the members of a 'more supranational (EU) institution' are independent from the governments of the Member States. Supranationality is characterised and reinforced by (qualified) majority voting and judicial scrutiny. The analysis will show that, following the tradition of the Treaties of Maastricht, Amsterdam, and Nice, the CFSP and CSDP of the Constitutional Treaty are still dominated by the more intergovernmental institutions. Moreover, it will be shown that the exclusion of effective parliamentary and judicial scrutiny amounts to a considerable democratic deficit of the CFSP and CSDP. Finally, it will be argued that CFSP and CSDP continue to form a more intergovernmental 'Pillar' separate from the more supranational policies of the Union, although as outlined in chapter 10[3] the Constitutional Treaty aims to overcome the three-Pillar structure of the TEU.

2. THE MORE INTERGOVERNMENTAL INSTITUTIONS

The more intergovernmental institutions of the Constitutional Treaty are the European Council and the President of the European Council, the Council and its consecutive sections, and the Union Minister for Foreign Affairs. The latter, however, has certain supranational features, as will be explained below. Since these institutions are all connected to the Council these more intergovernmental institutions could also be called 'Council institutions'.

2.1. The European Council

The Constitutional Treaty leaves intact the prominent role of the European Council under the Treaty of Nice. The newly created office of 'President of the European Council' joins the heads of State or government and the President of the Commission. Furthermore, the Union Minister for Foreign Affairs shall take part in its work.[4] The CSDP is an integral part of the CFSP.[5] Therefore the competencies and decision-making procedures of the latter form the basis for action in the context of the CSDP. As far as the crisis management aspect discussed in chapter 11[6] is concerned, the latter is a policy for implementation of the military and defence implications of the CFSP. This shall be discussed in more detail below.

[3] At 293–296.
[4] Article I–21(2) sentence 2 Constitutional Treaty.
[5] Article I–40(1) sentence 1 Constitutional Treaty.
[6] At 309–319.

Unless the Constitutional Treaty provides otherwise, decisions of the European Council shall be taken by consensus.[7] The term 'consensus' rather than 'unanimity' is used as the European Council also includes the Presidents of the Commission and of the European Council. Unanimity describes the consensus of the Member States, although it should be mentioned that abstentions are possible.[8] According to Article I-40 (6) European Decisions relating to the CFSP shall be adopted by the European Council and the Council, acting unanimously, except in the cases referred to in Part III. Hence, in the context of the CFSP, unanimity rather than consensus apply. The European Council shall act on a proposal from a Member State, from the Union Minister for Foreign Affairs or from that Minister with the Commission's support. According to Article I-40 (7) the European Council may unanimously decide that the Council should act by qualified majority in cases other than those referred to in Part III. However, as under the Treaty of Nice unanimity is the rule and qualified majority voting is the exception.

In the context of the CFSP and the CSDP the relevant institutions generally act by taking 'European Decisions', which are defined as non-legislative acts, binding in their entirety.[9] European Laws and European Framework Laws are explicitly excluded.[10] This is not surprising since these are defined as "legislative acts",[11] which in the understanding of the Constitutional Treaty are acts involving the European Parliament. The latter does not take part in the creation of acts in the context of the CFSP and CSDP. This shall be discussed in more detail below. The explicit exclusion of European Laws and European Framework Laws leaves the 'European Regulation' as a non-legislative act which theoretically could be used by the Council institutions for action in the context of the CFSP and CSDP. However, the Constitutional Treaty does not provide for action by European Regulation in the context of these policies.

According to Articles I-40 (2) and III-293 (1) the European Council shall identify the strategic interests of the EU and determine the objectives of its CFSP and together with the Council shall adopt the necessary European Decisions.[12] They shall do so on the basis of the principles and objectives referred to in Article

[7] Article I–21(4) Constitutional Treaty.

[8] See below for details.

[9] Article I–33(1) subpara 5 sentence 1 Constitutional Treaty.

[10] Article I–40(6) Constitutional Treaty. Definitions are provided in Article I–33(1): 'A European law shall be a legislative act of general application. It shall be binding in its entirety and directly applicable in all Member States. A European framework law shall be a legislative act binding, as to the result to be achieved, on the Member States to which it is addressed, but shall leave to the national authorities the choice of form and methods.'

[11] Above.

[12] Article I–40(3) Constitutional Treaty.

III-292 Constitutional Treaty.[13] European Decisions on these strategic interests and objectives shall relate to the CFSP and to other areas of the external action of the EU and may concern the relations of the EU with a specific country or region or may be thematic in their approach. They shall define their duration, and the means to be made available by the EU and the Member States. The European Council shall act unanimously on a recommendation from the Council, adopted by the latter under the arrangements laid down for each area. European Decisions of the European Council shall be implemented in accordance with the procedures provided for by the Constitutional Treaty. According to Article III-295 (1) Constitutional Treaty the European Council shall define the general guidelines for the CFSP, including for matters with defence implications. Hence, following the tradition of the Treaties of Maastricht, Amsterdam, and Nice, the European Council set the basic CFSP and CSDP framework within which the other institutions have to operate. In short, the European Council defines the parameters of the CFSP and CSDP, whereas the details and the day-to-day business are run by other institutions, in particular the Council and the Union Minister of Foreign Affairs. Moreover, the Council have a strong position since in contrast to other decisions of the European Council, they have the exclusive right to initiative regarding these parameters of the CFSP and CSDP decided by the European Council. The practice under the Treaties of Maastricht, Amsterdam, and Nice has shown that the heads

[13] Article III–292(1)-(2) Constitutional Treaty reads:

1. The Union's action on the international scene shall be guided by, and designed to advance in the wider world, the principles which have inspired its own creation, development and enlargement: democracy, the rule of law, the universality and indivisibility of human rights and fundamental freedoms, respect for human dignity, equality and solidarity, and respect for the principles of the United Nations Charter and international law.

   The Union shall seek to develop relations and build partnerships with third countries, and international, regional or global organisations, which share these values. It shall promote multilateral solutions to common problems, in particular in the framework of the United Nations.
2. The Union shall define and pursue common policies and actions, and shall work for a high degree of cooperation in all fields of international relations, in order to:
   a) safeguard its values, fundamental interests, security, independence and integrity;
   b) consolidate and support democracy, the rule of law, human rights and international law;
   c) preserve peace, prevent conflicts and strengthen international security, in accordance with the purposes and principles of the United Nations Charter, with the principles of the Helsinki Final Act and with the aims of the Charter of Paris, including those relating to external borders;
   d) foster the sustainable economic, social and environmental development of developing countries, with the primary aim of eradicating poverty;
   e) encourage the integration of all countries into the world economy, including through the progressive abolition of restrictions on international trade;
   f) help develop international measures to preserve and improve the quality of the environment and the sustainable management of global natural resources, in order to ensure sustainable development;
   g) assist populations, countries and regions confronting natural or man-made disasters;
   h) promote an international system based on stronger multilateral cooperation and good global governance.

of State and government assembled in the European Council will not restrict themselves to a general role of setting guidelines. They will get actively involved in the CFSP and CSDP, *inter alia* by regularly assessing the threats facing the EU and its Member States to take effective action under Article III-329 (3) Constitutional Treaty and by making the final decision in cases of *veto* in the Council in cases where voting by qualified majority is possible under Article III-300 (2) subparagraph 2 sentence 3 Constitutional Treaty.[14]

The Constitutional Treaty does not add to or otherwise change the role of the European Council under the Treaties of Maastricht, Amsterdam, and Nice described in chapters 2 and 3. Its "very prominent and powerful position in the institutional landscape of the Union"[15] remains a crucial element of the more intergovernmental character of the CFSP and the CSDP. As outlined in chapter 2[16] with reference to the Treaties of Maastricht and Amsterdam, the European Council has no supranational features.[17] An organ composed of the highest representatives of the Member State governments takes unanimous decisions. It does not get more intergovernmental than that. The strong position of this intergovernmental institution in the CFSP is a first indication for the more intergovernmental character of the CFSP and CSDP under the Constitutional Treaty. However, the membership of the elected President of the more supranational Commission in the European Council inserts a supranational voice and element. Moreover, the participation of the Union Minister for Foreign Affairs adds another partly supranational element, as will be explained in more detail below. The membership of the President of the European Parliament could add to this voice and element and would increase the democratic legitimacy of the CFSP.

After the Treaties of Maastricht, Amsterdam, and Nice, the Constitutional Treaty is the fourth treaty providing for a strong position for the intergovernmental European Council. In the history of European defence integration, only the European Defence Community (hereinafter EDC) discussed in chapter 1[18] had envisaged an organisation without a comparable organ, dominated by more supranational institutions, most notably the Board of Commissioners. The EDC failed. A strong role for the assembled heads of State or government has been a feature of the emerging European foreign, security, and defence policy[19] since its beginnings. Not only does this organ give the governments a strong position. The European Council is also the instrument to protect the strong position of the

[14] W Wessels, 'A "Saut Constitutionnel" Out of an Intergovernmetnal Trap? The provisions of the Constitutional Treaty for the Common Foreign, Security and Defence Policy' in JHH Weiler and CL Eisgruber, (eds), *Altneuland: The EU Constitution in a Contextual Perspective*, (Jean Monnet Working Paper 5/04, New York University School of Law and Woodrow Wilson School of Public and International Affairs at Princeton University 2004) 18. Article III–329(3) Constitutional Treaty concerns the implementation of the solidarity clause.

[15] D Curtin, 'The Constitutional Structure of the Union: A Europe of Bits and Pieces' (1993) 30 *Common Market Law Review* 17, at 26: 'the intergovernmental organ par excellence'.

[16] At 67–68.

[17] Above.

[18] At 28–34.

[19] Term used by Wessels, above n 14.

heads of State and government in foreign, security and defence policy. The prerogatives of the very top of the executive for these fields of policy have a long tradition. In the history of many Member States these were the last competencies the kings, queens, or grand dukes handed over to parliamentary control and the control of the elected government. They could be called royal prerogatives now held by the elected presidents, prime ministers, or chancellors. Therefore it is not surprising that the European Council still has such a strong position in the CFSP and CSDP. This simply repeats or mirrors the constitutional history of most Member States. These would be the last policy fields which would be fully transferred to the control of supranational institutions. It is likely that any alternative solution to the Constitutional Treaty would also include a comparable institution.

The Constitutional Treaty introduces the new office of President of the European Council. According to Article I-22 (1) Constitutional Treaty the European Council shall elect its President, by qualified majority, for a term of two and a half years, renewable once. The duration of this term may harmonise with the five-year terms of the Commission. The President may not hold a national mandate.[20] Therefore, he or she is not elected out of the midst of the European Council. Under the Treaty of Nice a head of State or government holds the Presidency for half a year. The Presidency covers the work of both the European Council and of the Council. While holding the presidency under the TEU, a head of government would often not be able to devote sufficient time to govern his or her Member State. A President not carrying this double-burden will be able to concentrate on this office and conduct it with a higher degree of independence than under Nice. He or she shall chair and drive forward the work of the European Council, ensure its proper preparation and continuity in co-operation with the President of the Commission, and endeavour to facilitate cohesion and consensus within the European Council. Moreover, he or she shall present a report to the European Parliament after each of its meetings.

The President of the European Council shall ensure the external representation of the Union on issues concerning the CFSP on his or her level, without prejudice to the responsibilities of the Union Minister for Foreign Affairs.[21] According to Wessels, the words "without prejudice to" acknowledge functional overlaps with the Union Minister of Foreign Affairs which are not addressed in the text of the Treaty but left to custom developing from the every day practice once the Constitutional Treaty is operational.[22] Hence much will depend on the individual officeholder. Should he or she successfully link all tasks the office might develop into a CFSP actor in its own right, leaving only the everyday diplomacy and crisis management to the Minster. If not, the office might become merely representative and symbolic. According to Article I-22 (3) Constitutional Treaty the President of

[20] Article I–22(3) Constitutional Treaty.
[21] Article I–22(2) last sentence Constitutional Treaty.
[22] Wessels, above n 14, at 27.

the Council shall hold no national office. This offers the possibility for mutual empowerment by electing the President of the Commission to the office.[23]

Specific competencies of this office in the context of the CFSP and CSDP are rather limited. According to Article III-295 (1) subparagraph 2 Constitutional Treaty if international developments so require, the President of the European Council shall convene an extraordinary meeting of the European Council in order to define the strategic lines of EU policy in the face of such developments. The office is not mentioned once in the section on the CSDP. It will be explained below that the Union Minister for Foreign Affairs has a strong position in relation to the CFSP and the CSDP. This suggests that in relation to the CSDP the power struggle between the two offices anticipated by Wessels[24] might not happen, since the Minister is clearly envisaged as 'Mr or Mrs CSDP' in the Constitutional Treaty.

2.2. The Council

Similar to the European Council, the Constitutional Treaty leaves intact the CFSP and CSDP roles of the Council already envisaged by the Treaties of Maastricht, Amsterdam, and Nice. Moreover, the Convention added certain competencies to the already strong arsenal of the Council. Apart from the basic framework, which as outlined above is decided by the European Council on a recommendation of the Council, the latter takes all decisions. CFSP and CSDP are Council policies. Again, the CSDP is an integral part of the CFSP.[25] Therefore the competencies and decision-making procedures of the latter form the basis for action in the context of the CSDP.

2.2.1. Common Foreign and Security Policy

With respect to the CFSP the strong role of the Council of Ministers is clearly spelt out in Article I-40 (2) sentence 2 Constitutional Treaty. It provides that they shall frame the CFSP within the framework of the strategic guidelines established by the European Council and in accordance with the arrangements in Part III of the Constitutional Treaty. This is repeated in Article III-295 (2) Constitutional Treaty, which provides that the Council shall adopt the European Decisions necessary for defining and implementing the CFSP on the basis of the general guidelines and strategic lines defined by the European Council. According to Article I-40 (3) Constitutional Treaty the European Council and the Council shall adopt the necessary European Decisions. However, the European Decisions to be adopted by the European Council are limited to those concerning the basic framework outlined above. Within this framework the Council takes all decisions.

According to Article III-297 (1) Constitutional Treaty where the international situation requires operational action by the EU, the Council shall adopt the

[23] Above, at 27 and 28.
[24] Wessels, above n 14, at 28.
[25] Article I–41(1) Constitutional Treaty.

necessary European Decisions. 'Operational action' is to be understood as foreign policy action including crisis management missions involving the military. Article III-309 in the section on the CSDP regulates decision making in the area of crisis management with regards to implementation. Decisions under Article III-297 shall lay down the objectives, the scope, the means to be made available to the EU, if necessary the duration, and the conditions for implementation of the action. If there is a change in circumstances having a substantial effect on a question subject to such a European Decision, the Council shall review the principles and objectives of the action and adopt the necessary European Decisions. As long as the Council has not acted, the European Decision on action by the EU shall stand. According to Article III-297 (2) Constitutional Treaty such European Decisions shall commit the Member States in the positions they adopt and in the conduct of their activity. According to Article III-297 (3) Constitutional Treaty whenever there is any plan to adopt a national position or take national action pursuant to a European Decision as referred to in paragraph 1, information shall be provided in time to allow, if necessary, for prior consultations within the Council. The obligation to provide prior information shall not apply to arrangements, which are merely a national transposition of European Decisions. According to Article III-297 (4) Constitutional Treaty in cases of imperative need arising from changes in the situation and failing a new European Decision, Member States may make the necessary arrangements as a matter of urgency, having regard to the general objectives of the European Decision referred to in paragraph 1. The Member State concerned shall inform the Council immediately of any such arrangements. Hence national action pursuant to a European Decision is possible but made dependent on certain procedural requirements. These requirements are designed to limit the potentially damaging effect of national action contradicting EU action. Moreover, Article III-297 (2) to (4) Constitutional Treaty envisages such national action as an exception. Otherwise it may undermine the credibility and consistency of the CFSP as a whole. Similarly, according to Article III-297 (5) should there be any major difficulties in implementing a European Decision, a Member State shall refer them to the Council which shall discuss them and seek appropriate solutions. Such solutions shall not run counter to the objectives of the action or impair its effectiveness. Again, deviations from the action and its implementation envisaged in the European Decision shall be limited and controlled by the Council. The Council not only takes the decisions, it also has the power to control Member State action deviating from it.

According to Article III-299 (1) Constitutional Treaty any Member State, the Union Minister for Foreign Affairs, or that Minister with the support of the Commission may refer to the Council any question relating to the CFSP and may submit initiatives or proposals to it. According to paragraph 2 in cases requiring a rapid decision, the Union Minister for Foreign Affairs, of the Minister's own motion or at the request of a Member State, shall convene an extraordinary meeting of the Council within forty-eight hours or, in an emergency, within a shorter period.

According to Article III-298 Constitutional Treaty the Council shall adopt European Decisions which shall define the approach of the Union to a particular matter of a geographical or thematic nature. Member States shall ensure that their national policies conform to the positions of the Union.

2.2.2. Common Security and Defence Policy

The Council has a particularly strong position regarding the implementation of the CSDP. In the context of crisis management, according to Article I-41 (4) sentence 1 Constitutional Treaty European Decisions on the implementation of the CSDP, including those initiating a crisis management mission shall be adopted by the Council acting unanimously. Decisions are taken on a proposal from the Union Minister for Foreign Affairs or from a Member State. According to Article III-309 (2) Constitutional Treaty the Council also decides the objectives, scope, and general conditions of implementation in this context. Article III-309 gives the Council the competence to take decisions regarding the implementation of decisions on crisis management taken by the same Council on the basis of Article III-297. An Article III-297 Council decision is therefore the precondition for an Article III-309 Council decision. The adoption of a national position or the taking of national action pursuant to a European Decision on operational action of the Union under Article III-297 (3) or the urgency clause in Article III-297 (4) can also apply in the context of crisis management. Within the limits of Article III-297 Constitutional Treaty a Member State may even send a national peacekeeping mission to a particular region after the EU has sent a similar mission. In other parts of Chapter II on the CFSP, decisions having military or defence implications are specifically excluded, for example in Article III-300 (14). Article III-297 does not contain such exclusions.

As explained in chapter 2,[26] under the Treaty of Maastricht the Council would take decisions regarding the CFSP on the basis of Articles J.3, J.4, and J.5 TEU. However, the security aspect was not yet developed enough to include an implementation level for crisis management missions. At the time it was the WEU that developed a crisis management policy. Under the Treaty of Amsterdam the Council of the EU would take the decisions on the basis of Articles 13-15 TEU first before the Union would avail itself to the WEU to elaborate and implement decisions with defence implications. As explained in chapter 3,[27] under the Treaty of Nice the EU itself assumed the implementation role of the WEU following the move towards an autonomous military capability proposed in Saint-Malo, Cologne, and Helsinki. Therefore the separation of a CFSP Council decision on operational action in Article III-297 and a CSDP Council decision on the implementation of the CFSP decision in the Constitutional Treaty has to be seen on the background of this development from Maastricht 1991 to Rome 2004.

[26] At 68–72.
[27] At 100–103.

Alternatively, decision making and implementation could be regulated in one article in the CSDP section of the Constitutional Treaty.

According to Article I-41 (5) Constitutional Treaty the Council may entrust the execution of a task, within the Union framework, to a group of Member States in order to protect the Union's values and serve its interests. The execution of such a task shall be governed by Article III-310 Constitutional Treaty. This informal *ad hoc* flexibility was discussed in chapter 11.[28] In the context of this chapter it is important to note that the Council takes the decisions regarding implementation and has the right to be informed by the participating Member States. On an initiative of the latter the Council can also make amending decisions regarding such implementation. Hence the Council has rights of control regarding the implementation of their decisions by a group of Member States.

In the context of armaments policy, the European Defence Agency (hereinafter EDA) is subject to the authority of the Council according to Articles I-41 (3) subpara 2 and III-311 (1) Constitutional Treaty. According to Article III-311 (2) sentence 2 they also define the Agency's statute, seat, and operational rules. Therefore the EDA has to act under the supervision of the Council. Again, the Council has substantial rights of control.

In the context of permanent structured co-operation, the members of the Council already participating in such permanent structured co-operation decide on the accession of Member States at a later stage according to Article III-312 (2) and (3) Constitutional Treaty. The Council may also entrust the implementation of crisis management missions to a group of Member States having the necessary capability and desire to undertake the mission according to Article III-310 (1) Constitutional Treaty. The participating Member States have to keep the Council regularly informed. The Council controls permanent structured co-operation: the Council as a whole when the initial decision on structured co-operation is taken and as the 'Council within the Council' described in chapter 11[29] when the accession of additional members at a later stage is decided.

2.2.3. Voting on CFSP and CSDP

Generally decisions on the CFSP have to be taken by unanimity. According to Article I-40 (6) Constitutional Treaty European Decisions relating to the CFSP shall be adopted by the acting Council unanimously, except in the cases referred to in Part III. As the last part of the sentence indicates, the principle of unanimity is not absolute.

First, according to Article III-300 (1) Constitutional Treaty European Decisions referred to in Chapter II on the CFSP shall be adopted by the Council acting unanimously. However, abstentions by members present in person or represented shall not prevent the adoption of such decisions. When abstaining in a vote, any member of the Council may qualify its abstention by making a formal declaration.

[28] At 310–313.
[29] At 317.

In that case, it shall not be obliged to apply the European Decision, but shall accept that the latter commits the EU. In a spirit of mutual solidarity, the Member State concerned shall refrain from any action likely to conflict with or impede Union action based on that decision and the other Member States shall respect its position. If the members of the Council qualifying their abstention in this way represent at least one third of the Member States representing at least one third of the population of the EU, the decision shall not be adopted. It is submitted that this procedure represents a derogation from the principle of unanimity which in practice will help to take decisions. It accommodates 'constructive' abstention as a compromise between voting for and voting against a decision. The Council can take a decision without the support of one or two of its members. The EU as represented by the members of the Council voting for the decision is still a sufficiently credible and cohesive force to ensure the efficiency of the action taken. The arrangement could even be seen as a form of differentiation for individual decisions comparable to the other forms of flexibility discussed in chapter 11.[30] A similar arrangement allows the UN Security Council to take decisions and action. Moreover, it is submitted that this arrangement could be well suited for a transitional period before the CFSP and CSDP is operational and the Member States have developed the political will to introduce qualified majority voting in the Council.

Second, Article III-300 Constitutional Treaty provides for cases where the Council may derogate from the principle of unanimity and adopt a decision by qualified majority. According to Article III-300 (2) by derogation from paragraph 1, the Council shall act by qualified majority:

a) when adopting European decisions on Union actions and positions on the basis of a European decision of the European Council relating to the Union's strategic interests and objectives, as referred to in Article III-293(1);

b) when adopting a decision on a Union action or position, on a proposal which the Minister has put to it following a specific request to him or her from the European Council made on its own initiative or that of the Minister;

c) when adopting any European decision implementing a Union action or position;

d) when adopting a European decision concerning the appointment of a special representative in accordance with Article III-302.

This provision is a continuation of the move towards more qualified majority voting since the Treaty of Nice outlined in chapter 3.[31] As explained in chapter 2,[32] under the Treaties of Maastricht and Amsterdam all decisions in the context of the Second Pillar had to be taken by unanimity.

Qualified majority voting in the fields outlined above, however, is potentially limited by Article III-300 (2) sentence 2. A member of the Council may declare

[30] In the context of crisis management at 313–319 and armaments policy at 325–327.
[31] At 112.
[32] At 71–72.

that, for vital and stated reasons of national policy, he or she intends to oppose the adoption of a European Decision to be adopted by qualified majority. In such a case a vote shall not be taken. The wording "a member of the Council" seems to imply that the President of the Commission can also use the provision. However, it is submitted that it only applies to the Member States since only a State can have "vital and stated reasons of *State* policy". An express reference to Union interests would have been added had the Member States wanted to include the President of the Commission. The notion of "vital and stated reasons of national policy" is not defined. Moreover, as there is no judicial review and no other legal remedy to challenge a Member State invoking this *veto* to qualified majority voting, only political pressure can be applied. The Union Minister for Foreign Affairs will, in close consultation with the Member State involved, search for a solution acceptable to it. If he or she does not succeed, the Council may, acting by a qualified majority, request that the matter be referred to the European Council for decision by unanimity. Thus a determined Member State can *veto* decisions in the context of the CFSP by vetoing the decision on qualified majority voting first and by vetoing the decision in the European Council afterwards. However, this *veto* is procedurally very difficult and might be politically damaging to the Member State in question. Hence it might not be used very often in practice.

According to Article III-300 (3) Constitutional Treaty the European Council may decide unanimously that the Council shall act by a qualified majority in cases other than those referred to in paragraph 2. However, according to Article III-300 (4), paragraphs 2 and 3 shall not apply to decisions having military or defence implications. Therefore, in the context of the CSDP the Council always takes decisions by unanimity. This requirement covers the CFSP decision for operational action on the basis of Article III-297 Constitutional Treaty and the CSDP decision for the implementation of the CFSP decision. In contrast to the CFSP where qualified majority voting is at least possible, the CSDP is always subject to unanimity. However, it should be pointed out that the abstention rule in Article III-300 (1) Constitutional Treaty outlined above applies to decisions having military or defence implications. Article III-300 (4) Constitutional Treaty only refers to paragraphs 2 and 3 of the provision.

According to Article III-309 (2) sentence 1 Constitutional Treaty the Council acting unanimously, shall adopt European Decisions relating to the tasks referred to in Article I-41 (1), in the course of which the Union may use civilian and military means.[33] The Council shall define the objectives and scope of these European Decisions and the general conditions for their implementation. On this level of implementation the Council will always decide by unanimity.

[33] According to Article III–309(1) Constitutional Treaty these tasks shall include joint disarmament operations, humanitarian and rescue tasks, military advice and assistance tasks, conflict prevention and peace-keeping tasks, tasks of combat forces in crisis management, including peacemaking and post-conflict stabilisation. All these tasks may contribute to the fight against terrorism, including by supporting third countries in combating terrorism in their territories.

As outlined above decisions on the CSDP are subject to unanimity in the Council without exceptions. The requirement of unanimity is an important element of the more intergovernmental character of the CSDP since every single Member State government has a right of *veto* and needs to agree with every individual decision. France and Germany had proposed to "make decisions in the field of CFSP generally by qualified majority",[34] a proposal which met the opposition of the United Kingdom, relieving other governments to express theirs.[35] The split in the Union caused by the war on Iraq made it difficult for some Member States to accept qualified majority voting and then being outvoted.[36] There are arguments for qualified majority voting in the context of the CFSP. First, Member States will not be prepared to send their armed forces to implement a decision they had not supported.[37] However, the flexible character of the crisis management aspect of the CSDP discussed in chapter 11[38] would allow to accommodate such a situation. Second, as pointed out in the Working Group VII on external action, qualified majority voting could "heighten third country awareness of internal disagreement, thus rendering the CFSP less effective".[39] However, where necessary decisions are not taken because of the requirement of unanimity, third country awareness of internal disagreement is even higher rendering the CFSP even less effective. In a situation where a decision is necessary, a unanimous decision is the best possible solution but a decision taken by qualified majority voting is better than no decision at all.

In a recent resolution the European Parliament criticised the dominance of unanimity voting with regards to the CFSP:

> [Parliament c]riticises the intended retention of the principle of unanimity voting in votes on foreign and security matters, which it regards as a serious obstacle to the capacity for action which the Union needs, at least in relation to decisions on proposals by the Union Minister for Foreign Affairs, for majority voting, involving, where appropriate, a reinforced qualified majority.[40]

[34] Contribution by Joschka Fischer and Dominique de Villepin to the Convention, CONV 489/03, http://register.consilium.eu.int/pdf/de/o3cv00/cv00489deo3.pdf (German version); or CONV422/02, http://register.consilium.eu.int/pdf/fr/o2/cv00/0422f2.pdf (French version) as translated and cited by Wessels, above n 14, at 13.

[35] M Jopp and E Regelsberger, 'GASP und EVSP im Verfassungsvertrag—eine neue Angebotsvielfalt mit Chancen und Mängeln' *Integration* 4/2003, Europa Union, Bonn, 550, at 556; D Thym, 'Reforming Europe's Common Foreign and Security Policy' (2004) 10 *European Law Journal* 5, at 11 as cited by Wessels, above.

[36] Wessels, above n 14, at 13; A Arnull, Editorial: 'War-torn' (2003) 28 *European Law Review* 301–302.

[37] See the Final Report of working Group VII, CONV 459/02, Part B, para 45 and also the 'Contribution franco-allemande à la Convention europénne sur l'architecture de l'Union', CONV 489 as cited by Arnull, above.

[38] At 310–313.

[39] CONV 459/02, Part B, para 45.

[40] *European Parliament Resolution on the Annual Report from the Council to the European Parliament on the Main Aspects and Basic Choices of CFSP, including Financial Implications for the General Budget of the EU*, Strasbourg, 23 October 2003 (hereinafter '2003 Parliament Resolution'), in A Missiroli, *From Copenhagen to Brussels: European Defence: Core Documents*, Volume IV, Chaillot Paper No 67, (Institute of Security Studies of the European Union, Paris, 2003) 243.

This hints at a considerable disadvantage of the requirement of unanimity in the context of the CSDP. The principle can develop into an obstacle to action, in particular in situations where swift action is needed, for example in a crisis situation. Theoretically, a single Member State could block all action by using its *veto*. The European Parliament already hints at possibilities to introduce more qualified majority voting to the CFSP and CSDP. First, it could be limited to proposals by the Union Minister for Foreign Affairs, assuming that the proposals are already sufficiently balanced in comparison to the proposals of the Member States which might be motivated by individual State interests. Second, there could be reinforced qualified majority voting, requiring a bigger majority of, for example, 20 Member States representing 80 per cent of the population. This is particularly important in a Union of 25 or more Member States where unanimity could be increasingly difficult to obtain.[41] These are constructive suggestions and it is likely that the representatives of the European Parliament made these views clear in the Convention but did not succeed. However, the Constitutional Treaty is not the end of the European integration process. The suggestions of the Parliament could be steps on the way towards more qualified majority voting in future revisions of the Constitutional Treaty.

The requirement of unanimity in the context of the CSDP also hints at a considerable contradiction. As outlined above and in the context of the supranational institutions below, the intergovernmental Council takes all the decisions. As explained further below, the European Parliament is not involved, for example, in the decision on crisis management missions and the European Court of Justice has no jurisdiction to review these decisions. A possible explanation for this strong position of the Council is that time consuming consultation of the Parliament or even a co-decision procedure with Strasbourg could prevent swift action in response to security challenges. Moreover, Parliament could vote against the decision. Similarly, judicial review through the European Court of Justice would be time-consuming and might end with a judgment against taking action. In other words, the democratic deficit could be considered 'justified' by national or common security considerations requiring swift action, which can only be ensured when decisions are taken exclusively by the Council.[42] However, this line of

[41] See N Gnesotto, *et al*, *European Defence: A proposal for a White Paper*, (Institute of Security Studies of the European Union, Paris, 2004) 10.

[42] In the United Nations Organisation decisions on crisis management missions are taken by the UN Security Council and not by the UN General Assembly. However, these institutions are not comparable with the institutions of the EU. The UN General Assembly is not an elected parliament but composed of the representatives of the governments of the member States: Article 9 UN Charter. However, there are similarities between the UN Security Council and the Council of Ministers. Both are composed of the representatives of the Member States. The UN Security Council, however, is composed of only a limited number of member State representatives, five permanent members and ten on the basis of rotation: Article 23 UN Charter. The reason for the transfer of responsibility for the protection of World peace from the UN member States to the UN Security Council is to allow swift and effective action: Article 24(1) UN Charter. The requirement of swift and effective action is a reason to allocate the competence and responsibilities for crisis management to a smaller institution, which because of its small size can take quick decisions.

argument is not fully convincing. First, negotiations in the Council to reach a unanimous decision are also time-consuming. Hence it is contradictory that there is time for these negotiations but no time for parliamentary and judicial scrutiny. Second, national procedures regarding parliamentary and judicial scrutiny of foreign and security policy show that the requirement of swift action may well be taken into account. There can at least be parliamentary and judicial scrutiny after action was taken. The coexistence of the requirement of unanimity with the exclusion of parliamentary and judicial scrutiny regarding decisions taken in the context of the CFSP casts suspicion on the latter's justifications. After all the reason might be that the Member States' governments excluded parliamentary and judicial scrutiny to ensure absolute executive power over matters having military or defence implications. The democratic and rule of law deficits of the CSDP might not be due to sensible national security considerations but due to the will of politicians and their civil services to defend and increase executive power. This used to be a general problem of European Community law before the Treaty of Maastricht and it can be argued that it continues to be a general problem under the Treaty of Nice and the Constitutional Treaty. However, the introduction of the co-decision procedure involving the European Parliament in the legislative process and the gradual increase of majority voting in the Council addressed the democratic deficit. The CSDP of the Constitutional Treaty suffers from a democratic deficit comparable to that of the pre-Maastricht EC, made worse by the lack of judicial scrutiny.

The dominance of decision making by unanimity in the Council with regards to the CFSP, subject to only a few complex derogations which are difficult to invoke with regards to the general CFSP, almost absolute with regards to the CSDP, gives the CFSP and CSDP a more intergovernmental character. This character keeps the CSDP separate from the more supranational defence *acquis communautaire* discussed in Part II of this book. The failure of proposals to introduce more qualified majority voting with the Constitutional Treaty and before shows a lack of consensus.

2.2.4. The Council and the Defence Acquis Communautaire

Comparable to the Treaties of Maastricht, Amsterdam, and Nice, the Council is the co-legislator with the supranational European Parliament in the context of the Community policies under the Constitutional Treaty. Moreover, the European Court of Justice has jurisdiction to review Union acts in the Community context. Therefore the Council has a strong but not exclusive role in the legislative process regarding secondary legislation regulating areas covered by Community policies. This includes, for example, the regulation of defence procurement discussed in chapter 7 and the regulation of sex equality in the armed forces discussed in chapter 9. Therefore in these areas of defence law the role of the Council differs substantially from that in the context of the CSDP described above.

First, the Community policies are subject to qualified majority voting in the Council. The defence *acquis communautaire* is characterised by this voting method indicating a balance of intergovernmentalism with supranationality. CFSP and CSDP are determined by Council decisions taken by unanimity indicating an intergovernmental character.

Second, the Community policies are regulated by what the Constitutional Treaty calls European Laws and European Framework Laws, called Regulations and Directives in the EC Treaty. In other words, these areas are regulated by legislative acts with a substantial involvement of the supranational and democratically elected European Parliament. This will be discussed in more detail below. The CSDP is regulated by European decisions without an involvement of the European Parliament.

Third, the European Court of Justice can review legislation in the areas of defence law affected by Community policies. However, with regards to the CFSP and CSDP the jurisdiction of the Court is excluded. This will also be discussed in more detail below.

Article I-24 Constitutional Treaty also differentiates between the Council in its general affairs and legislative functions on the one hand and the Foreign Affairs Council on the other hand. The Member State representatives shall hold the Presidency of the former on the basis of equal rotation.[43] This continues the basic practice of Article 204 (2) EC. The Union Minister of Foreign Affairs, as will be explained in more detail below, heads the Foreign Affairs Council. The latter therefore has a different institutional structure.[44]

The strong role of the Council institutions and the reduced role of the supranational institutions in comparison to the Community policies make the CFSP and CSDP a separate legal order, as distinct from the earlier as the current Second Pillar is from the First. This continues the separate Pillar regime of the Treaty of Nice.

2.2.5. The Political and Security Committee

According to Article III-307 Constitutional Treaty the Political and Security Committee (hereinafter PSC) shall monitor the international situation in the areas covered by the CFSP and contribute to the definition of policies by delivering opinions to the Council. It may do so at the request of the latter, or of the Union Minister for Foreign Affairs, or on its own initiative.[45] It shall also monitor the implementation of agreed policies, without prejudice to the responsibility of the Union Minister for Foreign Affairs. Within the scope of this Chapter II of the Constitutional Treaty, this Committee shall exercise, under the responsibility of the Council and of the Union Minister for Foreign Affairs, political control and strategic direction of crisis management operations, as defined in Article III-309.[46] The Council may authorise the PSC, for the purpose and for the duration of a

[43] Article I–24(7) sentence 1 Constitutional Treaty.
[44] Wessels, above n 14, at 18.
[45] Article III–307 Constitutional Treaty.
[46] See ch 11 at 309–310 for details.

crisis management operation, as determined by the Council, to take the relevant measures concerning the political control and strategic direction of the operation. Article III-307 Constitutional Treaty is almost identical to Article 25 TEU described in chapter 3.[47] The substantial differences refer to the references to the Union Minister for Foreign Affairs who is an innovation of the Convention. Therefore the Constitutional Treaty adds nothing to the role of the PSC described in chapter 3. The PSC is an instrument of the Council for the day-to-day management of crisis management operations. It gives an element of permanence to the CSDP. Moreover, in contrast to the military institutions of the EU described in chapter 3 it is explicitly mentioned in the Constitutional Treaty thereby giving it an added status.

The military institutions of the EU, namely the European Union Military Committee, European Union Military Staff, and the Committee for Civilian Aspects of Crisis Management, are not mentioned in the Constitutional Treaty. However, it is not necessarily the custom to mention structures of this level in a constitutional document or treaty.

2.3. The Union Minister for Foreign Affairs

The Constitutional Treaty introduces the new office of 'Union Minister for Foreign Affairs' (hereinafter also referred to as 'Minister'). It replaces and develops the office of the Secretary-General of the Council and High Representative for the CFSP under the Treaties of Amsterdam and Nice discussed in chapters 2 and 3.[48] The office of the minister has been called the "central innovation"[49] of the institutional framework envisaged by the Constitutional Treaty or a "major innovation".[50]

According to Article I-28 (2) Constitutional Treaty he or she shall conduct the EU's CFSP, which according to Article I-40 (4) he or she and the Member States shall put it into effect, using national and Union resources. The Minister shall contribute by his proposals to the development of the CFSP and CSDP, which he shall carry out as mandated by the Council. Again, the CSDP is an integral part of the CFSP.[51] Therefore the Union Minister for Foreign Affairs is also in all but name the Union Minister for Security and Defence. However, as will be explained below, his or her role in the context of the CSDP is more limited when compared to that in the context of the CFSP proper.

Moreover, the Minister is one of the Vice-Presidents of the Commission and responsible for external relations and for co-ordinating other aspects of the

[47] At 72.

[48] Ch 2 at 73–74.

[49] Wessels, above n 14, at 20.

[50] *A Constitution for the Union*, Opinion of the Commission pursuant to Article 48 of the Treaty on European Union, on the conference of representatives of the Member States' governments convened to revise the Treaties, COM (2003) 584 final.

[51] Article I–41(1) Constitutional Treaty.

Union's external action. In exercising these responsibilities within the Commission, and only for these responsibilities, the Minister shall be bound by Commission procedures.[52] In other words, the Minister is responsible for the portfolios of both the former High Representative for the CFSP and of the Commissioner for External Relations. He or she has both the 'jobs of Solana[53] and Patten'.[54]

2.3.1. The Predecessor Under the Treaty of Nice

As outlined in chapter 2,[55] the Treaties of Maastricht, Amsterdam, and Nice provide that the General Secretariat of the Council led by the Secretary-General is to assist the Presidency.[56] According to Article 18 (3) TEU (ex Article J.8) the Secretary of the Council is to exercise the function of High Representative for the Common Foreign and Security Policy. He or she assists the Presidency and according to Article 26 TEU (ex Article J.16) the Council in matters within the scope of the CFSP. The High Representative can contribute to the formulation, preparation and implementation of policy decisions. This function inevitably has implications for decision-making. Moreover, when appropriate and acting on behalf of the Council at the request of the Presidency, he or she can conduct political dialogue with third parties. The Amsterdam Treaty introduced the office of the High Representative in an attempt to increase the visibility of the CFSP and to remedy certain shortcomings of the CFSP.[57] The personal union with the office of Secretary-General of the Council was a compromise between those who favoured the *status quo ante* and those who wanted a separate new organ.[58] It will be explained below that in contrast to The Secretary-General of the Council and High Representative for the CFSP who is clearly a part of the intergovernmental Council, the new office combines intergovernmental and supranational competencies. He or she will be wearing a 'double hat'.[59]

[52] Article I–27(3) Constitutional Treaty.

[53] Javier Solana, first and only High Representative for the CFSP.

[54] Chris Patten, Commissioner for External Relations of the 2000–5 European Commission.

[55] Ch 2 at 73–74.

[56] Article 207(2) EC, which according to Article 28(1) TEU (ex Article J18) applies to the CFSP.

[57] According to a Report of the Secretary-General, *Setting the CFSP policy planning and early warning unit*, Brussels, 6 November, at para 8 these shortcomings were the external invisibility of the CFSP, its inadequate ability to react quickly to current political events, the difficulty of laying down guidelines which transcend national interests, the insufficient use of the instruments available to the Union, and the lack of forward planning.

[58] RA Wessel, *The European Union's Foreign and Security Policy: A Legal Institutional Perspective* (Kluwer, The Hague, 1999) 87.

[59] The term double hat was probably invented by the German delegate Peter Glotz, quoted in A Maurer, 'Jour Fixe Verfassungskonvent', http://www.swp-berlin.org/produkte/brennpunkte/jour-eu-konvent3druck.htm, 1 October 2002 and Caspar Einem for the Convention on the Future of Europe, CONV202/02, 1–3, here 1 and the final report of the Convention Working Group WG VII—'external action'—WD 21 and Comments, WD 22–54 of 5 November 2002, as cited by Wessels, above n 14, at 21.

2.3.2. The Appointment and Removal of the Minister

In contrast to the Secretary-General of the Council and High Representative for the CFSP of the Treaty of Nice, the Union Minister for Foreign Affairs of the Constitutional Treaty is a member of the Commission.[60] However, he or she has a special and partly independent position within that more supranational institution. The Minister is appointed and dismissed by the European Council acting by a qualified majority with the agreement of the President of the Commission.[61] Hence the heads of State or government of the Member States ultimately appoint him or her. This is similar but not equal to the appointment of Commissioners. First, under the October 2004 version of the Constitutional Treaty Commissioners are selected by the Council "in common accord with the President-elect" of the Commission and then subject as a body to a vote of consent by the European Parliament.[62] Hence the Minister is appointed by the higher authority of the European Council. However, unlike the President of the Commission he or she is not elected into this office by the European Parliament. This already puts the Minister into a position between the President of the Commission and the other Commissioners, a fact also illustrated by his or her competencies outlined below. Moreover, the appointment by the higher authority of the European Council is also an illustration of the intergovernmental competencies of the Minister. Second, the appointment of the Minister is not dependent on the system of equal rotation between the Member States envisaged for the appointment of Commissioners by Articles I-26 (6) and I-27 (2) Constitutional Treaty. Theoretically there could be a succession of Ministers of, for example Italian or Estonian nationality.

The Union Minister for Foreign Affairs is submitted to a vote of approval by the European Parliament together with the voting (European Commissioner) and non-voting (Commissioner) members of the Commission. According to Article III-340 subparagraph 2 Constitutional Treaty the Minister shall resign from the Commission if a motion of censure against the Commission is carried in the European Parliament. Wessels predicts that if the two largest groups of Social Democrats and European Peoples Party continue their 'grand coalition' in the European Parliament they will try to distribute the offices of President and Minister between themselves along party lines.[63] However, it is submitted that this will be more difficult with regards to the Minister since unlike the President who

[60] Article I–26(6) Constitutional Treaty: '[...] the Commission shall consist of a number of members, including its President, the Union Minister of Foreign Affairs [...].'

[61] Article I–28(1) Constitutional Treaty.

[62] Article I–27(2) Constitutional Treaty (October 2004 version). According to Article I–26(3) of the Draft version of the Constitutional Treaty presented by the Convention the President-elect was to choose from a list of three. On this list both genders had to be represented. This was yet another consequence of the continued importance of sex equality in the constitutional framework of the EU discussed in ch 9. However, in the October 2004 version these references to the list of three and gender were omitted.

[63] Wessels, above n 14, at 21.

is elected, he or she is only submitted to a vote of approval as part of the entire Commission.

2.3.3. *The Competencies of the Minister*

In contrast to the tasks of the High Representative for the CFSP under the Treaty of Nice, who according to Articles 18 (3) and 26 TEU is merely the assistant and top-diplomat of the Council, the Union Minister for Foreign Affairs has a considerably more extensive role. Whereas the former is mentioned once or twice in the TEU, the latter plays a role in 17 provisions of the Constitutional Treaty. The competencies of the Minister can be subdivided into CFSP, CSDP, and Community external relations competencies.

2.3.3.1. Common Foreign and Security Policy Competencies The Union Minister for Foreign Affairs shall conduct the CFSP and contribute by his or her proposals to its development, which he or she shall carry out as mandated by the Council.[64] The Minister together with the Member States shall put the CFSP into effect, using national and Union resources.[65] According to Article I-40 (6) Constitutional Treaty European Decisions relating to the CFSP shall be adopted by the European Council and the Council on a proposal from a Member State, or from the Union Minister with or without the Commission's support.

According to Article I-293 (2) Constitutional Treaty the Minister may submit joint proposals to the Council for the field of the CFSP. This gives him or her a right of initiative. Under the Treaty of Nice it was the Member States, the Presidency, and within the limits of Article 14 (4) TEU the Commission who could submit proposals. For other fields of external action it is the Commission which has this right of initiative.[66] This right of initiative reinforces the general right to initiative for EC legislation in Article I-26 (2) Constitutional Treaty and clarifies the protection of the *acquis communautaire* with regards to the competencies of the Commission for external relations, most importantly for trade. It also shows that the Minister has two hats: that of a CFSP organ on the one hand and that as a Commissioner for External Relations on the other hand. This shall be discussed in more detail below.

According to Article III-296 (1) Constitutional Treaty the Minister shall chair the Council for Foreign Affairs. Wessels identifies this as a third major role in addition to the enhanced role of the High Representative and the Commissioner for Foreign Relations and predicts a more efficient and effective external action of the EU than under the previous regime of biannual rotation between the foreign secretaries of the Member States.[67] Moreover, he argues that a significant improvement of the continuity of the external representation of the EU thereby enhancing its role in international relations through this "upgraded" 'face' and

[64] Article I–28(2) Constitutional Treaty.
[65] Article I–40(4) Constitutional Treaty.
[66] Also Article III–293(2) Constitutional Treaty.
[67] Wessels, above n 14, at 23.

'voice'.[68] The Minister shall contribute through his or her proposals towards the preparation of the CFSP and shall ensure implementation of the European Decisions adopted by the European Council and the Council of Ministers. According to Article III-296 (2) Constitutional Treaty, for matters relating to the CFSP, he or she shall represent the EU. The Minister shall conduct political dialogue on the Union's behalf and shall express her position in international organisations and at international conferences. According to paragraph 3 in fulfilling his or her mandate, a European External Action Service shall assist the Minister.[69] This service shall work in co-operation with the diplomatic services of the Member States. A Declaration on the creation of a European External Action Service regulates the details on this last point. Building of the *acquis* of the Treaty of Nice discussed in chapter 3 and to a large extent codifying existing practice under that and the preceding Treaties in the tradition described in chapter 2,[70] Article III-296 develops a more credible representative of the EU. The Minister will have more competencies and the resources to fulfil his or her role.

According to Article III-299 (1) Constitutional Treaty any Member State or the Minister with or without the Commission's support may refer to the Council any question relating to the CFSP and may submit proposals to it. In cases requiring a rapid decision, by the Minister's own motion or at the request of a Member State, he or she shall convene an extraordinary meeting of the Council within forty-eight hours or, in an emergency, within a shorter period.

The Council shall act by qualified majority when adopting a decision on an EU action or position, on a proposal which the Minister has put to it following a specific request to him or her from the European Council made on its own initiative or that of the Minister.[71] If a Council member declares that, for vital and stated reasons of national policy, it intends to oppose the adoption of a European Decision to be adopted by qualified majority, a vote shall not be taken. The Minister will, in close consultation with the Member State involved, search for a solution acceptable to it. If he or she does not succeed, the Council may, acting by a qualified majority, request that the matter be referred to the European Council for decision by unanimity.[72]

When the Union has defined a common approach within the meaning of Article I-40 (5) Constitutional Treaty, the Union Minister and the national Ministers for Foreign Affairs shall co-ordinate their activities within the Council.[73] Moreover, the Council shall, whenever it deems it necessary, appoint, on the initiative of the Minister, a special representative with a mandate in relation to particular policy issues. The special representative shall carry out his or her mandate

[68] Above.
[69] According to Wessels, above n 14, at 23 to reinforce the 'hand' of the EU in addition to its 'face' and 'voice'.
[70] At 73–74.
[71] Article III–300(2)(b) Constitutional Treaty.
[72] Above.
[73] Article III–301(1) Constitutional Treaty.

under the authority of the Minister.[74] The Minister shall consult the European Parliament on the main aspects and the basic choices of the CFSP and shall ensure that the views of the European Parliament are duly taken into consideration. Parliament shall be kept regularly informed by the Minister of the development of the CFSP. Special representatives may be involved in briefing Parliament.[75] Parliament may ask questions of the Council and of the Minister or make recommendations to them. Twice a year it shall hold a debate on progress in implementing the CFSP.[76] The role of the Parliament shall be discussed in more detail below. The Minister shall organise the co-ordination of Member State action in international organisations and at international conferences. Member States represented in international organisations or international conferences where not all the Member States participate shall keep the latter, as well as the Minister, informed of any matter of common interest. Member States, which are also members of the United Nations Security Council shall consult and keep the other Member States and the Minister fully informed. When the Union has defined a position on a subject which is on the UN Security Council agenda, those Member States which sit on the Security Council shall request that the Minister be asked to present the Union's position.[77]

The PSC shall monitor the international situation in the areas covered by the CFSP and contribute to the definition of policies by delivering opinions to the Council at the request of the latter, or of the Minister, or on its own initiative. It shall also monitor the implementation of agreed policies, without prejudice to the responsibility of the Minister. Within the scope of Chapter II, the PSC shall exercise, under the responsibility of the Council and of the Minister, political control and strategic direction of crisis management operations, as defined in Article III-309 Constitutional Treaty.[78]

2.3.3.2. Common Security and Defence Policy Competencies In the context of the CSDP the Minister has a general right of initiative, a right to attend deliberations, and duties regarding co-ordination and information. The Minister shall contribute by his or her proposals to the development of the CSDP, which he or she shall carry out as mandated by the Council.[79] European Decisions on the implementation of the CSDP, including those initiating a crisis management mission, shall be adopted by the Council on a proposal from the Minister or from a Member State.[80] He or she may propose the use of both national resources and Union instruments, together with the Commission where appropriate.[81]

According to Article III-309 (2) sentence 2 Constitutional Treaty the Minister acting under the authority of the Council and in close and constant contact with

[74] Above.
[75] Article III–304(1) sentence 3 Constitutional Treaty.
[76] Article III–304(2) sentence 2 Constitutional Treaty.
[77] Article III–305(2) subparagraph 2 Constitutional Treaty.
[78] Article III–307(2) Constitutional Treaty.
[79] Article I–28(2) sentence 2 Constitutional Treaty.
[80] Article I–41(4) sentence 1 Constitutional Treaty.
[81] Article I–41(4) sentence 2 Constitutional Treaty.

the PSC, shall ensure co-ordination of the civilian and military aspects of crisis management tasks. As outlined in chapter 11,[82] the Council may entrust the implementation of a crisis management task to a group of Member States having the necessary capability and the desire to undertake the task. The Minister shall be associated with those Member States when they agree between themselves on the management of the task.[83] Under the December 2003 version of the Constitutional Treaty. The Minister was to attend the deliberations of the members of the Council that represent the Member States taking part in permanent structured co-operation and was to duly and regularly inform the representatives of the other Member States.[84]

The role of the Minister is most developed with respect to crisis management. This is not surprising since this is the aspect of the CSDP, which is closely linked to foreign policy. Moreover, as explained in chapter 2,[85] the 'S' for security in CFSP was the 'junior policy' of the common foreign policy but also the starting point of the ESDP and CSDP, complemented by a 'D' for defence. Mutual defence and the armaments policy are aspects where a role of the Minister is not expressly stipulated in the Constitutional Treaty. However, his or her right to make proposals includes these fields. Moreover, as explained in chapter 11,[86] the European Defence Agency (hereinafter EDA) of Article III-311 was already established by Council Joint Action 2004/551/CFSP on 12 July 2004[87] within the framework of the Treaty of Nice, independent from the entering into force of the Constitutional Treaty. According to Article 7 of this Joint Action the Secretary General/High Representative shall be the Head of the EDA. I can be assumed that after the entering into force of the Constitutional Treaty the Minister would also take over this function from the current office of the High Representative. As Head of the EDA he will be responsible for its overall organisation and functioning and shall ensure that the guidelines issued by the Council and its Steering Board are implemented by its Chief Executive. Moreover the Head shall be in charge of the negotiations of administrative arrangements with third countries and other organisations, groupings or entities.[88] This gives the predecessor of the new office responsibility for the overall coherence of the evolving European Armaments Policy ahead of the entering into force of the Constitutional Treaty. This adds to the point made in chapter 11 that this policy is currently not considered controversial but urgent.

2.3.3.3. Community Competencies The Minister shall also be responsible in the Commission for handling external relations and for co-ordinating other aspects of

[82] At 313–317.
[83] Article III–310(1) sentence 2 Constitutional Treaty.
[84] Old Article III–210(3) Constitutional Treaty.
[85] At 51–91.
[86] At 320.
[87] Council Joint Action 2004/551/CFSP of 12 July 2004 on the establishment of the European Defence Agency [2004] OJ L–245/17. Article 1(1) of the Joint Action reads: 'An Agency in the field of defence capabilities development, research, acquisition and armaments (the European Defence Agency), hereinafter referred to as "the Agency", is hereby established.'
[88] Above, Article 7(4).

the Union's external action.[89] Therefore the office of the Minister also includes what under the 2000–2005 Commission was the Commissioner for External Relations. This describes the Community part of external action. In exercising these responsibilities within the Commission, the Minister is bound by Commission procedures.

The Union Minister for Foreign Affairs does not have a role in the context of the defence *acquis communautaire* discussed in chapters 4 to 9. Defence procurement, competition in the defence sector, and sex equality in the armed forces will be within the portfolios of other members of the Commission. Hence not all issues affecting defence are within the responsibilities of the Minister. While the Community and the CFSP dimensions of external action are somehow united in the office of the Minister, the Community and CSDP dimensions of defence are not.

2.3.3.4. A Stranger Among Equals The office of Union Minister for Foreign Affairs can be understood as a more intergovernmental part of a more supranational institution or a more intergovernmental attachment to a more supranational institution. On the one hand his or her appointment shares similarities to the appointment of a Commissioner, he or she is part of the Commission, one of their Vice-Presidents, and bound by the procedures of the Commission when exercising responsibilities regarding external relations in the Commission. On the other hand he or she is only bound by these procedural rules when exercising these responsibilities, in other words with regards to what under the Treaty of Nice are the Community competencies for external relations. Hence the Minister has two heads: an intergovernmental CFSP and CSDP hat which separates him or her from the more supranational Commission and a supranational external relations hat which makes him or her part of that supranational Commission. However, there is one crucial element of the position of the Minister which makes his or her office a more intergovernmental one. According to Article I-26 (7) Constitutional Treaty the Commissioners are "completely independent. [They] shall neither seek nor take instructions from any government or other institution, body, office or entity". This rule of independence is "[w]ithout prejudice to Article I-28 (2)". Under that Article I-28 (2) and by contrast to the independence of Commissioners under Article I-26 (7), the Minister "shall carry out the [CFSP and CSDP] as mandated by the Council." In other words, he or she is dependent on and takes instructions from the Council. The Council is composed of representatives of the governments of the Member States. Moreover, in the context of the CFSP and CSDP decisions are mostly adopted by unanimity ultimately giving every single Member State government a right of *veto*. Therefore taking instructions from the Council means taking instructions from the governments of the Member States. Ever since the High Authority of the ECSC and the Board of Commissioners of the EDC discussed in chapter 1,[90] independence from the government of the Member States has been considered the crucial characteristic of a supranational institution.

[89] Article I–28(4) sentence 2 Constitutional Treaty.
[90] At 28–30.

As the Minister does not share the crucial characteristic of independence with his 'colleagues' in the Commission, he or she is an 'intergovernmental outsider' there. Hence the Minister had to be discussed in the context of the intergovernmental rather than the supranational institutions of the EU under the Constitutional Treaty. However, changing the perspective, the Council when meeting as the Foreign Affairs Council could also view the Minister as a 'supranational outsider',[91] or as Wessels put it as an "agent of the Commission and indirectly the [European Parliament]."[92] Due to his or her limited powers vis-à-vis the Member States the use and extension of Community instruments might be the only option to achieve tangible results.[93] The objective of such a spill-over would be a more integrated foreign- and therefore also security and defence policy with stronger supranational features than currently envisaged by the letter of the Constitutional Treaty. Such a spill-over might also be formalised through amendments to the Constitutional Treaty. A possible area of the CSDP to be 'supranationalised' would be the European Armaments Policy and the EDA described in chapter 11.[94] The extent of such a spill-over would depend on the living Constitutional Treaty after its entering into force. The living Constitution will also depend on the personality and attitude of the first Minister or the first few Ministers. In his or her "position of strong inter- and intra-institutional role conflicts"[95] or 'outsider position' he will be influenced by national foreign secretaries in the Council, diplomats in the PSC, his or her colleagues in the Commission, by the latter's Presidents, and by the President of the European Council. However, a strong Minister will also influence them. According to Wessels, the Minister will probably have to adopt a "low profile", in particular in crisis situations when national policies might differ considerably. Here, the "perennial risk when sitting between two or even three institutional chairs, or to bridge two coexisting [a more supranational and a more intergovernmental] pillar, is to fall right through them."[96] However, the 'double hat' could also make the office of the Union Minister for Foreign Affairs a bridge between the more intergovernmental and the more supranational aspects of European defence integration thereby at least partly overcoming the incoherence caused by their separation. Using the chairs metaphor, the Minister firmly sitting on two chairs at the same time might turn these chairs into one piece of furniture. The integration of the outsider in the Commission and the Council through procedures or more practically through regular participation in meetings might give the more supranational Commission considerable influence on the Minister and therefore on the CFSP and CSDP and indirectly the Foreign Affairs Council. The President of the Commission can facilitate this influence by using the requirement of his agreement in Article I-28 (1) Constitutional Treaty to influence the choice

[91] Thym, above n 35, calls this a 'Trojan Horse'.
[92] Wessels, above n 14, at 26.
[93] Above.
[94] At 319–328.
[95] Wessels, above n 14, at 25.
[96] Above.

of the candidate for the office. Generally, the introduction of the office is to be welcomed.

2.3.3.5. A Union Minister for Security and Defence? In the national context of the Member States security and defence are covered by a cabinet minister and ministry separate from the minister and ministry for foreign affairs. This has many reasons. The Member States have permanent armed forces, military administrations, procurement programmes, assets, and security policies, a workload which normally requires a separate department and minister. For diplomatic reasons it might be considered inappropriate when the top diplomat of the country is also its commander in chief.[97] Finally, tradition has always seen defence as connected but separate from foreign affairs. Finally, having a minister for defence is an expression of sovereignty.[98]

This raises the question whether the Constitutional Treaty should provide for the office of Union Minister for Security and Defence similar to but separate from the office of the Union Minister for Foreign Affairs. There are arguments against the introduction of such a Minister. First, as explained in the introduction to this book, there is a move from 'defence' to 'security'. The present and future focus of military action is security, the deployment of troops in the context of the 'Petersberg Task' rather than the defence of the homeland. This makes the deployment of troops an aspect of foreign policy, which justifies its integration into the responsibility of the Union Minister for Foreign Affairs. Moreover, as explained above, the CSDP is an integral part of the CFSP. Second, the CSDP described in chapter 11 could still be considered too limited to justify the introduction of a separate office. The introduction of the office of Union Minister for Security and Defence could raise false expectations.

It is submitted that an evolving CSDP might soon necessitate the introduction of a separate office of Union Minister for Security and Defence. The introduction of an ERRF based on permanent or long-term contributions and the execution of more crisis management missions involving more personnel, funds, being deployed over longer periods, and with an increased degree of danger for the troops involved will give the CSDP an increasingly distinctive profile. The 'defence workload' will increase. Moreover, the possible procurement of most major weapons systems through a successful EDA and the improvement of national defence capabilities in this European framework would add to this development. Finally, the establishment of European Military Headquarters, the creation of a European Security Strategy, and generally an evolving European security culture will give additional impetus to the CSDP. A 'Mr or Mrs CSDP' would be required,

[97] The Minister or Secretary for Defence is not always the commander in chief. Very often the head of State (for example Spain) fills this role. In other Member States the head of State (for example France) or Government (for example Germany) takes over this position from the Defence Secretary in times of war. However, the Minister will normally be responsible for the day-to-day running of the military in times of peace.

[98] Even the smallest Member States Luxembourg and Malta have Ministers for Defence. In France, the Minister of the Interior or Home Secretary is also the Minister for Defence.

similar to the Union Minister for Foreign Affairs with his own civil service, appointed for a longer period, and integrated into the Commission. Such a Minister could also help to overcome the separation of the CSDP from the other policies by taking over the Commission responsibilities for defence issues from the Directorate General for External Relations,[99] Industry, and Internal Market.[100] A Union Minister for Security would obviously add considerably to the visibility of the CSDP on the international scene.

The appointment of a Special Representative under Article III-302 Constitutional Treaty, responsible for the CSDP, could be a solution in the medium term. The supervision through the Union Minister for Foreign Affairs would ensure the consistency of CFSP and CSDP.

3. THE SUPRANATIONAL INSTITUTIONS

The Commission, European Parliament, and European Court of Justice are the more supranational institutions of the European Union. Their members are independent from the governments of the Member States and their decisions are binding. Moreover they take decisions by majority. The governments of the Member States do not even have any influence in the 'nomination' and 'appointment' of the members of the directly elected European Parliament. A strong constitutional position of these supranational institutions is a crucial indicator of the more supranational character of an organisation or a policy as a whole. The supranational Board of Commissioners of the EDC discussed in chapter 1,[101] for example, was almost completely independent from the governments of the Member States and the main decision-maker. The same applied to the supranational High Authority of the European Coal and Steel Community (hereinafter ECSC). The supranational Board and their powers were the crucial component of the supranational character of the EDC. Under both the Treaty of Nice and the Constitutional Treaty the *supranational* institutions have such a strong position regarding the Community policies, although this is balanced with a relatively strong position of the Council. Most notably, the Commission makes proposals for new legislation, the European Parliament is involved in the decision making process through the co-decision procedure, and the European Court of Justice has jurisdiction *inter alia* to review Community legislation. The following discussion of the more supranational institutions will show that they have a considerably weaker position in the context of the CFSP and CSDP.

[99] He or she would have to take over these responsibilities from the Union Minister for Foreign Affairs.

[100] These responsibilities are not to be transferred to the Union Minister for Foreign Affairs. The respective Directorates General will continue their work on these issues. This could contribute to the fragmentation of defence integration.

[101] At 28–30.

3.1. The Commission

The role of the Commission with regards to both CFSP and CSDP is very limited. According to Article I-40 (6) Constitutional Treaty the Commission can support the Union Minister for Foreign Affairs when he makes a proposal to the European Council or the Council for action in the context of the CFSP. However, the Minister may also make a proposal without the support of the Commission. Moreover, Member States can also make proposals. Similarly, the Commission supporting the Minister may refer any question relating to the CFSP and may submit proposals to it according to Article III-299 (1). However, the Minister may also make proposals and refer questions without the support of the Commission. Whether this will happen in practice remains to be seen, but it is not unlikely that both sides will try to avoid that. Moreover, Member States may also refer questions and proposals. In the context of the CSDP the Commission does not even have that possibility of supporting a proposal according to Article I-41 (4) Constitutional Treaty. The only role is limited to the EDA. Article III-311 (2) sentence 4 Constitutional Treaty provides: "The Agency shall carry out its tasks in liaison with the Commission where necessary." The wording "where necessary" indicates a wide margin of discretion for the EDA, a Council body, or the Council itself on whether any involvement of the Commission is necessary. However, it is likely that the EDA will involve the Commission in questions of procurement regulations, industrial policy and, competition policy, in other words in areas where the Agency's role overlaps with 'Community' competencies. This will be crucial to ensure the coherence of this aspect of the CSDP, although it might not be sufficient.

The role of the Commission under the Constitutional Treaty is the absolute minimum.

First, due to the transfer of external relations competencies to the Minister the Commission *prima facie* loses importance in comparison to the regime under the Treaty of Nice. Wessels suggests that they have been removed from the institutional architecture of the CFSP.[102] However, as outlined above, the Minister wears a 'double hat' and one half of that is that of Vice President of the Commission. He or she will partly be a Commissioner in all but name, bound by Commission procedure and Community law with regard to his more supranational competencies. Again, much will depend on constitutional practice and the person of the Minister. He might get fully integrated into the Commission, indentify with their 'supranational ethos' and develop into a Commissioner for Foreign Affairs in all but name, for example, always taking initiatives with the support of the Commission. To the outsider it might become difficult to differentiate the Minister from the Commissioner. In this case the role of the Commission might be enhanced by gaining influence over the CFSP and the CSDP.

Second, the external action role under the Constitutional Treaty is not comparable to its role as the initiator of new legislation under the EC Treaty.

[102] Wessels, above n 14, at 18.

Under the EDC Treaty the Board of Commissioners and under the ECSC Treaty the High Authority described in chapter 1[103] had even stronger roles, as they were also the main legislators.

Most notably through its right of initiative for new legislative acts the Commission has a strong role in the legislative process regarding secondary instruments regulating areas covered by the Community policies. Article I-26 (2) Constitutional Treaty[104] continues the tradition of the EC Treaty. This includes, for example, the regulation of defence procurement discussed in chapter 7 and the regulation of sex equality in the armed forces discussed in chapter 9.

3.2. The European Parliament

The European Parliament has been the most democratic institution of the Union since the citizens of Europe directly elect its members. Moreover, it is a supranational institution since its members are independent from any influence of the Member State governments and take decisions by majority, at least in theory irrespective of any national consideration. Under the Constitutional Treaty the role of the European Parliament with regards to both the CFSP and the CSDP is very limited. Their participatory powers with regards to the CFSP and CSDP have not been increased and it has been argued that they have been sidelined.[105] According to Article I-40 (8) Constitutional Treaty the "European Parliament shall be regularly consulted on the main aspects and basic choices of the [CFSP] and shall be kept informed of how it evolves." Similarly, according to Article I-41 (8) Constitutional Treaty the "European Parliament shall be regularly consulted on the main aspects and basic choices of the [CSDP] and shall be kept informed of how it evolves."

According to Article III-304 (1) Constitutional Treaty the Union Minister for Foreign Affairs shall consult and inform the European Parliament on the main aspects and the basic choices of the CFSP, including the CSDP, and shall ensure that the views of the European Parliament are duly taken into consideration. Special representatives may be involved in briefing the European Parliament. According to Article III-304 (2) the European Parliament may ask questions of the Council and of the Union Minister for Foreign Affairs or make recommendations to them. Twice a year it shall hold a debate on progress in implementing the CFSP, including the CSDP. Generally, the Constitutional Treaty does not add anything substantial to the role of the European Parliament in the CFSP and ESDP under

[103] At 20–21 and 28–30.

[104] Article I–26(2) Constitutional Treaty reads:

> Union legislative acts may be adopted only on the basis of a Commission proposal, except where the Constitution provides otherwise. Other acts shall be adopted on the basis of a Commission proposal where the Constitution so provides.

[105] Wessels, above n 14, at 18.

the TEU discussed in chapter 2.[106] The only difference is that they will hold two debates instead of one annual debate on the CFSP and CSDP.

In October 2003 the European Parliament expressed concerns *inter alia* about its role under the Constitutional Treaty.[107] The criticism concerned its rights to be consulted and kept informed and the budgetary provisions. Generally it considered:

> the status quo wording in respect of Parliament's rights to be consulted and kept informed [is] a retrograde step by comparison with the changes relating to the executive.

This puts the lack of any extension of the rights of the European Parliament with respect to CFSP and CSDP into perspective. While the rights of Parliament stagnated, the role of the Council institutions was substantially increased. Due to the boost of the role of the executive the stagnation of the role of Parliament is effectively a step back. As Parliament is democratically elected, the Constitutional Treaty decreases the level of democratic legitimacy of CFSP and CSDP in comparison to the situation under the Treaty of Nice.

In order to better deliver its political opinion based on firm information and thus to fulfil its duty of scrutiny Parliament considers it necessary to be informed and involved during the early recognition and planing stages of crisis operation in the context of the EDSP.[108] Moreover, Parliament wants to be consulted in advance of decisions on ESDP missions, be they of a civilian or military nature, without prejudice to the need for the EU to act swiftly in crisis situations. Only a well-informed Parliament was in a position to take the requisite personnel and budgetary decisions swiftly and efficiently and such decisions may be rejected unless Parliament is so informed.[109] These demands of the European Parliament to be informed early and in advance about crisis management missions are limited and modest. They do not ask, for example, to take the decision instead or to get a right to *veto* Council decisions in this context. This is not surprising since Parliament was represented in the Convention and had the opportunity to make proposals and to communicate their position. The result was necessarily a compromise and Parliament has no intention to jeopardise the entering into force of the Constitutional Treaty by more substantial criticism.

In chapter 3[110] it was submitted that due to the obligation to submit an annual report, the extent of parliamentary scrutiny through the Western European Union (hereinafter WEU) Assembly goes beyond that exercised by the European Parliament. Compared to the EU *acquis* of Article 21 TEU and Article III-304 (2) Constitutional Treaty, the WEU *acquis* regarding parliamentary scrutiny in Article 9 Modified Brussels Treaty (hereinafter MBT) is further developed. As long as the parliamentary scrutiny of the CSDP exercised by the European Parliament has not

[106] At 76–78.
[107] 2003 Parliament Resolution, above n 40, at 229.
[108] Above, at 243.
[109] 2003 Parliament Resolution, above n 40, at 243.
[110] At 106–108.

reached the level of that exercised by the WEU Parliamentary Assembly, the WEU *acquis* on parliamentary scrutiny makes the functions of the WEU Assembly a *raison d'être* for the WEU. These functions, in particular with regards to Article 9 MBT, would have to be transferred to the European Parliament. The question raised by the comparison with Article 9 MBT is why the Convention did not include a requirement for the Council to present an Annual Report to the European Parliament. Such a requirement could have counterbalanced the increase in executive powers through the Constitutional Treaty. Moreover, the fact that such a requirement is feasible in the context of the WEU is an indication for it being also feasible in the context of the EU. National security considerations can be taken into account in a way similar to the Annual Reports to the WEU Assembly or to national parliaments.

According to the European Parliament the costs of CSDP operations, including those of a civilian or military nature must be financed through the Community budget. Moreover, they ultimately call for a Community defence budget.[111] In the national context the defence budget is normally an aspect of defence policy where Parliament has the strongest influence. Under the Treaty of Nice and the Constitutional Treaty the operational part of the budget for a mission is financed by the participating Member States and third States on the basis of voluntary contributions. Only the smaller part of the costs is financed through the Community budget. However, these budgetary arrangements prevent the European Parliament from any influence in an aspect of defence policy where in most Member States they play the central role.

Generally, the Constitutional Treaty adds nothing to the role of the European Parliament in the context of the CFSP and security and defence policy under the TEU discussed in chapters 2 and 3. Therefore CFSP and CSDP suffer from a democratic deficit. The national parliaments of the Member States are involved in security and defence policy. The German *Bundestag*, for example, takes the decisions on the contribution to crisis management missions. This indicates that it is not general national security considerations that prevent a stronger involvement of the European Parliament. The democratic deficit of the CSDP appears to be just another variation of the democratic deficit as a general congenital defect of the European Community and Union. This defect will have to be overcome step-by-step. Nevertheless, the Constitutional Treaty is a missed opportunity in this respect. A CSDP without proper parliamentary control will place a powerful instrument in the hands of the Member States' governments through the Council. Fortunately the national parliaments will still exercise control over their national contributions.[112] An ERRF made up of permanent contributions based on general national

[111] Above, at 244.

[112] See Article 10 in title II of the Protocol of the Role of national parliaments in the European Union which provides that 'the Conference of European Affairs Committees [COSAC] may [...] organise inter-parliamentary conferences on [...] matters of common foreign and security policy, including common security and defence policy.' However, as Wessels, above n 14, at 20 points out, COSAC has been a body of marginal importance.

parliamentary approval without reference to individual missions would place a powerful instrument in the hands of the Member States' governments through the Council. Such a force would require a stronger role of the European Parliament since otherwise a 'European Army' without parliamentary control would lead to an even more substantial democratic deficit.

Wessels makes two points that might explain this treatment of the Parliament in the Constitutional Treaty. One point was already discussed in the context of the comparison with the WEU Assembly in chapter 3,[113] that defence is a unique policy field that needs "fast, discrete, and discretionary decision making", the DDS syndrome.[114] However, at least the need for speed is more severely undermined by the requirement of unanimity on the CSDP in the Council and the need for secrecy can be accommodated otherwise. National parliaments accommodate the need for secrecy. Another point is that the European Parliament is not seen as a legitimating factor for the CSDP: "national governments and diplomats are perceived to be the only legitimated actors, as they derive their general mandate from domestic sources".[115] In other words the intergovernmental nature of the CSDP is also a justification for its democratic deficit. However, this line of argument has been the background for the parliamentary dimension of the democratic deficit in the context of the Community as well.

Under the Constitutional Treaty the European Parliament retains its influence through the co-decision procedure for secondary legislation on those areas of defence law which are now regulated by the EC Treaty. The public procurement directives discussed in chapter 7 and the sex equality legislation discussed in chapter 9 need a majority in Parliament. Here the democratic deficit is considerably reduced.

The minimal role of the European Parliament in the CFSP and CSDP compared to the central role of the Council institutions and the important role of Parliament in the Community policies is a strong indication for the continuous existence of a separate Second Pillar in the Constitutional Treaty. The justifications for sidelining the European Parliament are not convincing. A stronger role would be desirable.

3.3. The European Court of Justice

Under the Constitutional Treaty the judicial scrutiny exercised by the European Court of Justice with regards to matters having security and defence implications remains almost completely within the limits of the Treaty of Nice. With two exceptions the CFSP and CSDP are excluded from the jurisdiction of the Court. However, the Court has jurisdiction regarding the national security exemptions discussed in Part III of this book.

[113] At 107.
[114] Wessels, above, at 20.
[115] Wessels, above n 14, at 20.

3.3.1. Exclusion of Jurisdiction

According to Article III-376 subparagraph 1 Constitutional Treaty and similar to the Treaty of Nice, the jurisdiction of the European Court of Justice does not include the provisions on the CFSP and CSDP:

> The Court of Justice shall not have jurisdiction with respect to Articles I-40[116] and I-41[117] and the provisions of Chapter II of Title V concerning the [CFSP] and Article III-293 insofar as it concerns the [CFSP].

Exemptions from this exclusion are stipulated in Article III-376 subparagraph 2 Constitutional Treaty. In contrast to Article 46 of the Treaty of Nice, which provided a list of provisions within the jurisdiction of the Court not including Title V of the TEU on the CFSP, Article III-376 Constitutional Treaty represents an express exclusion of the CFSP and CSDP, subject to two exceptions. These exemptions apply only (1) to review compliance with Article III-308[118] and (2) to review the legality of restrictive measures against natural or legal persons adopted by the Council on the basis of Chapter II of Title V[119] and brought in accordance with the conditions laid down in Article III-365 (4).[120] Both exemptions from the exclusion were introduced by the October 2004 version of the Constitutional Treaty.

The first exemption regards the borderline between the Community and the CFSP. According to Article III-308 subparagraph 1, the implementation of the CFSP shall not affect the exclusive competencies listed in Article I-13, nor the areas of shared competence in Article I-14, or the competence for the co-ordination of economic and employment policies in I-15, or the competencies for areas of supporting, co-ordinating, or complementary action in Article I-17. Likewise, the implementation of the policies listed in those articles shall not affect the competence referred to in Article I-16 on the CFSP. Article III-308 Constitutional Treaty is comparable to Article 47 TEU,[121] although the new provision is more explicit. The article represents a protective clause for the Community competencies and

[116] Specific provisions for implementing the common foreign and security policy.

[117] See above n 116.

[118] Article III–308 Constitutional Treaty reads:

> The implementation of the [CFSP] shall not affect the application of the procedures and the extent of the powers of the institutions laid down by the Constitution for the exercise of the Union competences referred to in Articles I–13 to I–15 and I–17 [the Community competencies].
>
> Similarly, the implementation of the policies listed in those Articles shall not affect the application of the procedures and the extent of the powers of the institutions laid down by the Constitution for the exercise of the Union competences under this chapter.

[119] On the CFSP.

[120] Individual action against legislative acts of the EU, formerly Article 230(4) EC Article III–365(4) Constitutional Treaty reads: 'Any natural or legal person may, under the conditions laid down in paragraphs 1 and 2, institute proceedings against an act addressed to that person or which is of direct and individual concern to him or her and does not entail implementing measures.'

[121] Article 47 TEU reads: '[...] nothing in this Treaty [on European Union] shall affect the Treaties establishing the European Communities or the subsequent Treaties and Act modifying or supplementing them.'

the *acquis communautaire* contained in the Constitutional Treaty. This includes the defence *acquis* discussed in Part II of this book, for example with regards to defence procurement discussed in chapter 7 or sex equality in the armed forces discussed in chapter 9. The jurisdiction of the Court to monitor compliance under Article III-376 subparagraph 2 Constitutional Treaty is a jurisdiction to enforce this protection of the *acquis communautaire*. This allows the Court to rule on measures implementing the CFSP if they affect the *acquis*.

This a codification of jurisprudence of the European Court of Justice under the TEU discussed in chapter 2.[122] As Wessel put it, the Court is the "ultimate arbiter to decide where the line of demarcation between the Union's issue-areas lies".[123] This became clear through judgments concerning sanctions,[124] the withdrawal of privileges from Yugoslavia (Serbia and Montenegro),[125] and access to information.[126] The Court would annul a CFSP decision according to Articles 230 and 231 EC if a Community legal base should have been used.[127] This authority of the Court derives from Article 46 TEU, which provides that "[...] nothing in [the TEU] shall affect the Treaties establishing the European Communities [...]". Article 47 TEU is covered by Article 46 TEU and safeguards the Community *acquis*.[128] The Court could, for example, annul parts of a CFSP decision that could harm the *acquis communautaire*.[129] The Constitutional Treaty contains this general rule in Article IV-438 but specifically for the CFSP in Article III-308. The Court is a guardian of the *acquis communautaire* 'from' the CFSP and CSDP. This reinforces the borderline between the Pillars under the Constitutional Treaty.

The second exemption from the exclusion of jurisdiction regarding the review of the legality of restrictive measures against natural or legal persons adopted by the Council on the basis of Chapter II of Title V and brought in accordance with the conditions laid down in Article III-365 (4) is an innovation of the October 2004 version. The December 2003 and June 2004 versions had included an exemption regarding the review of the legality of restrictive measures against natural or legal persons in the context of sanctions as long as the applicants could prove to be directly and individually concerned. It is submitted that the review of this type of action is not excluded from the jurisdiction of the Court under Article III-376 subparagraph 1 Constitutional Treaty, as sanctions are covered and also the main and possibly only case of the second exemption introduced by the October 2004

[122] At 79–80.
[123] Wessel, *Foreign and Security Policy*, above n 58, at 225.
[124] Case C–84/95, *Bosphorus Hava Turizim ve Ticaret AS* v *Minister for Transport, Energy and Communications Ireland and Attorney General* [1996] ECR I–3953; [1996] CMLR 257; Case C–124/95, *The Queen* v *HM Treasury and Bank of England, ex parte Centro-Com Srl* [1997] ECR I–81; Case C–177/95, *Ebony Maritime SA and Loten Navigation Ltd.* v *Prefetto della Provinzia die Brindisi and Ministero dell'Interno* [1997] ECR I–1111; [1997] 2 CMLR 24.
[125] Case 162/96, *A Racke GmbH* v *Hauptzollamt Mainz* [1998] ECR I–3655.
[126] Case T–174/95, *Svenska Jornalistförbundet* v *Council* [1998] ECR II–2289; Case T–194/94, *John Carvel and The Guardian Newspaper Ltd* v *European Council* [1995] ECR II–2765.
[127] Case C–170/96, *Commission* v *Council (the 'Airport Transit Visa Case')* [1998] ECR I–2763.
[128] Wessel, *Foreign and Security Policy*, above n 58, at 224.
[129] S Peers, 'National Security and European Law' (1996) 15 *Yearbook of European Law* 363, at 398–99.

version. The wording also leaves room to interpret it as a general right to review Council measures taken in the context of the CFSP and CSDP when they restrict natural or legal persons. In other words, the Court has jurisdiction to review an action brought by a non-privileged applicant against a CFSP and CSDP measure under what under the Nice version of the Treaty is Article 230 (4) EC. This partly addresses the rule of law deficit discussed in chapter 2[130] regarding the exclusion of jurisdiction under the Treaties of Maastricht, Amsterdam, and Nice in relation to individuals and legal persons. However, sanctions are the main and possibly only CFSP measures that can affect natural and legal persons in a way that could be covered by the second exemption in Article II-376 subparagraph 2 Constitutional Treaty. The second exemption is probably a reaction to cases such as that of *Abdirisak Aden and Others* v. *Council and Commission*[131] where Swedish citizens of Somali origin and an organisation listed in Sweden were listed by the Council to comply with their obligation, through their listing by the Taliban Sanctions Committee of the UN Security Council, brought an action before the Court of First Instance claiming a violation of their right to a fair hearing before any sanctions were imposed on them. The case was partially resolved diplomatically.[132] Nevertheless it shows the necessity to introduce the second exemptions when natural or legal persons are affected by CFSP and CSDP measures. The authors of the Constitutional Treaty have reacted to this necessity. The wording of this exemption from the exclusion of jurisdiction is wider than the one of sanctions in the June 2004 version of the Constitutional Treaty. Hence natural legal persons might bring an action against other types of CFSP and CSDP measures. The living Constitution, if it is ever brought to life, might show in the case law of the European Court of Justice what other types of measures can be reviewed. Possible measures could include a review of the legality of the confiscation, occupation, or destruction of property during a conflict situation. This might be a condition for a claim for damages under Article III-431 subparagraph 2 for which the European Court of Justice has jurisdiction under Article III-380 Constitutional Treaty.

However, as under the EC Treaty it will be difficult for natural and legal persons to prove legal standing under Article III-365 (4) Constitutional Treaty and this requires them to be directly and individually concerned.[133] This will prevent the CFSP and CSDP from being disrupted by frivolous claims.

Excluded is the review of an action brought by a privileged applicant, the Commission, the European Parliament, or a Member State, against a CFSP and CSDP measure under what under the Nice version of the Treaty is Article 230 (2) EC. Hence, administrative actions brought by individuals against the CFSP are

[130] Ch 2 at 78–80.

[131] Case T–306/01, *Abdirisak Aden* v *Council of the European Union and Commission of the European Communities* [2002] OJ C–44/47.

[132] R Cryer and ND White, 'The Security Council and the International Criminal Court: Who's feeling Threatened?' in H Langholtz, B Kondoch and A Wells, (eds), (2002) *8 International Peacekeeping: The Yearbook of International Peace Operations* 143, at 167.

[133] See P Craig and G de Búrca, *EU Law*, (3rd edn, OUP, Oxford, 2003) 486–523.

within the jurisdiction of the Court whereas constitutional actions are excluded. With regards to the CSDP where decision making by unanimity prevails, an action of a Member State would not be likely as no Member State can be outvoted. Actions of the Council would also be unlikely as they are the only decision-maker. Therefore, Article III-376 subparagraph 1 Constitutional Treaty is mainly designed to prevent actions brought by the Commission and European Parliament. The more supranational institutions cannot bring an action, for example against the Council institutions for failing to involve them in the CFSP or CSDP. The fact that their limited rights under the CFSP described above are not enforceable makes them even weaker.

Under the Treaty of Nice the development and consolidation of the rule of law is one of the objectives of the CFSP according to Article 1 TEU. As pointed out in chapter 2,[134] this amounts to a considerable contradiction: one of the three basic values of the EU, the rule of law, is to be promoted by the CFSP without applying to it.[135] As pointed out in chapter 10,[136] under the Constitutional Treaty the development and consolidation of the rule of law is not listed as an objective of the Union in Article I-3. Moreover, the CFSP does not have specific objectives according to Article I-16 Constitutional Treaty or a provision in Chapter II of Title V of Part III. *Prima facie* the contradiction in the Treaty of Nice was addressed by removing the development and consolidation of the rule of law as an objective of the CFSP. However, the rule of law is expressly referred to as a value of the Union according to Article I-2 Constitutional Treaty. Moreover, the rule of law is listed in Article III-292 (1) sentence 1 Constitutional Treaty[137] as one of the principles that shall guide the Union's external action, including the CFSP and CSDP. Therefore it is submitted that the contradiction is still contained in the Constitutional Treaty, although this is less obvious than under the Treaty of Nice. However, as could be seen in the context of exemptions from the principle of sex equality in the German constitution discussed in chapter 9, the authors of a constitution are not necessarily prevented from inserting contradictions into its text. Nevertheless, such contradictions undermine the consistency and coherence of a constitution. Moreover, contradictions might be noted by the citizens of those Member States voting on the Constitutional Treaty in a national referendum and by the members of the national parliaments of those Member States where such a popular vote is not taken.

There are good arguments for the exclusion of the jurisdiction of the European Court of Justice, which resemble those for the exclusion or limitation of jurisdiction with regards to the national security exemptions discussed in chapter 5 and 6.

[134] At 91.

[135] Apart from the limited two exceptions discussed above.

[136] At 301–302.

[137] Article III–292(1) Constitutional Treaty reads:

> The Union's action on the international scene shall be guided by the principles which have inspired its own creation, development and enlargement, and which it seeks to advance in the wider world: democracy, the rule of law, the universality and indivisibility of human rights and fundamental freedoms, respect for human dignity, the principles of equality and solidarity, and respect for the principles of the United Nations Charter and international law.

First, decisions on foreign policy and defence are policy choices. In cases involving the restriction of individual rights scrutiny will be rigorous in order to ensure the proportionality of the measure is a necessary component of the recognition of such rights. The exemption from the exclusion of jurisdiction in Article III-376 subparagraph 2 with regards to natural and legal persons takes this human rights dimension into account. Policy choices, however, are the reserve of the executive and legislative branches of government (division of powers dimension). Second, in the field of military security it is the government supported by the military staff, which has the responsibility, training and expertise to take decisions (competence dimension). Its judgement cannot easily be substituted by a court of law. Third, in the constitutional system of the EU matters of defence and military security are primarily attributed to the Member States and not to the Union[138] (federalism dimension). In the context of the CFSP and CSDP, matters of defence and military security are primarily attributed to the Member States represented in the more intergovernmental institutions of the EU. The Court, however, is a more supranational institution independent from the governments of the Member States. Fourth, the specific nature of measures in the CFSP and CSDP fields makes judicial review very difficult and there is a danger that it could impede the necessary freedom to act on a security challenge. Interim measures against a peacekeeping mission, for example, could delay the start of such a mission thereby undermining its effect. In a defence situation judicial review becomes almost entirely unfeasible. Finally, even in national jurisdictions, such as the United Kingdom or the United States, many of the considerations outlined above limit or exclude judicial scrutiny in the context of foreign policy and defence. However, these countries have strict parliamentary scrutiny of these policies. Moreover, there are also national jurisdictions, such as Germany, where judicial scrutiny over foreign and security policy is limited but not excluded.[139]

However, there are also arguments for a jurisdiction of the Court. First, similar to the jurisdiction under the old Article 298 subparagraph 2 EC discussed in chapters 5 and 6, now Article III-132 subparagraph 2 Constitutional Treaty, judicial review could be conducted in a way that takes the division of powers, competence, and federalism dimensions of judicial review into account. A particularly wide margin of discretion or appreciation could be left to the Member States represented in the Council institutions, similar to that left to the Member States in the context of Article III-132. The standard of review could be based on cases of abuse. Certain actions, for example the action for failure to act under Article III-367 or interim measures under Article III-379 (2) Constitutional Treaty could be excluded rather than excluding jurisdiction completely. Moreover, the burden of proof could be placed on the applicant seeking judicial review of a CFSP or CSDP

[138] G de Búrca, 'The Principle of Proportionality and its Application in EC Law' (1993) 13 *Yearbook of European Law* 105.

[139] See the approach of the German *Bundesverfassungsgericht* in cases involving defence and foreign policy in TM Franck, *Political Questions/Juridical Answers: Does the Rule of Law Apply to Foreign Affairs?* (Princeton University Press, Princeton, 1992) 107–25.

measure. This would make it very difficult for an applicant to succeed. Finally, the exclusion of jurisdiction of the Court has to be read in conjunction with the limited parliamentary scrutiny exercised by the European Parliament. As outlined in chapter 3[140] this scrutiny falls short also of the rights of the WEU Assembly. Therefore there is only very limited scrutiny of the measures taken by the intergovernmental institutions of the EU with regards to CFSP and CSDP. There are no checks and balances between the institutions, there is no division of powers, no involvement of anybody who was directly elected. The most important checks are provided in the national systems of the Member States. National parliaments and courts can be involved in the decision whether a Member State makes a contribution to the implementation of a decision in the context of the CSDP.

In the failed European Defence Community, which was based on a Treaty only on defence policy, the Court had jurisdiction. As outlined in chapter 1,[141] Articles 51 to 67 EDC regulated the Court of the EDC, which according to Article 52 EDC was to be the ECSC Court of Justice. The Court had the function of a constitutional court in the framework of the EDC. However, in contrast to the intergovernmental CFSP and CSDP under the Constitutional Treaty, the defence policy of the EDC was supranational. The founders of the EDC provided for judicial scrutiny of the supranational Board of Commissioners. They probably saw the role of the Court as an important check on the Board. However, according to Article 57 EDC the Court also had jurisdiction to review proceedings of the Council and set aside its decisions. The example of the EDC proves two important points. First, it proves that a foreign and security policy does not, due to its special nature, have to exclude judicial scrutiny. Second, judicial scrutiny is an important characteristic of a supranational organisation and policy. The exclusion of jurisdiction of the European Court of Justice under Article III-376 is an important element of the intergovernmental character of the CFSP and CSDP.

3.3.2. Jurisdiction for the Use of the National Security Exemptions

Finally, the Court has jurisdiction to review measures taken on the basis of Articles III-131 and III-436 on the basis of Article III-132 subparagraph 2 Constitutional Treaty. As explained in chapter 11,[142] the limits applying to Articles 296 to 298 EC discussed in chapters 5 and 6 apply equally to these provisions of the Constitutional Treaty. Both exemptions need to be specifically invoked, justified, and proven and the Court will review their use and apply a proportionality test to the measures in question. Article III-436 applies only to material on the 1958 List of armaments. Article III-131a has triple-exceptional character and can not justify permanent measures. However, in contrast to the situation under the Treaty of Nice, the national security exemptions are no longer a borderline between the Pillars. They are merely a borderline between Union and Member State competencies.

[140] At 106–108.
[141] At 34–36.
[142] At 340–347.

Moreover, the Court has jurisdiction to review measures taken on the basis of the security exemptions in secondary legislation as discussed in chapters 7, 8, and 9. Finally, it has jurisdiction to review measures derogating from the free movement regimes for reasons of public security as discussed in chapter 4.

3.3.4. Jurisdiction for Defence Matters

The Constitutional Treaty does not significantly change the *status quo* of the Treaty of Nice with regards to the jurisdiction of the Court over defence matters. Most of the explanations provided in chapters 2 to 9 are still valid under the Constitutional Treaty. Jurisdiction over CFSP and CSDP is excluded. However, the Court has jurisdiction to protect the *acquis communautaire* from measures implementing the CFSP and the CSDP. Moreover, they have jurisdiction to review the legality of CFSP and CSDP measures when the action is brought by a natural or legal person who is directly and individually concerned by the measure. Finally, the Court has jurisdiction over the review measures taken by Member States on the basis of the national security and public security exemptions in the Constitutional Treaty and secondary legislation.

4. CONCLUSIONS

The institutional framework of the CFSP and CSDP provided in the Constitutional Treaty adds little to the *acquis* of the Treaty of Nice discussed in chapter 3. As before, the intergovernmental institutions adopt all decisions relevant to the CSDP by unanimity, whereas the supranational institutions are almost irrelevant. By contrast, the decisions concerning the defence *acquis communautaire* continue to involve the Commission through its right to initiative, the European Parliament through the co-decision procedure, and the European Court of Justice through jurisdiction. Although the Constitutional Treaty aims to overcome the three-Pillar structure of the TEU, it continues to regulate the defence and security policy in an intergovernmental CFSP and CSDP Pillar. This continued separation of CFSP and the security and defence policy from the rest of the Union policies undermines the coherence and effectiveness of EU external action. Moreover, the exclusion of parliamentary and judicial scrutiny amounts to a substantial democratic deficit undermining the legitimacy of the CFSP and CSDP.

As discussed throughout this book, foreign and security policy, national security, and defence are normally within the competencies of governments. In the national context, the executive has the power to take decisions in these areas. The rights of the legislature and the courts are limited in comparison to other fields. The reasons for this special treatment of foreign and defence policy is, that it is the government supported by its military staff that has the expertise and the means to take decisions in these areas. Moreover, there is also a corresponding constitutional tradition. The urgency of situations involving national security could also be used as an argument against the involvement of parliaments and courts. Similarly, in the EU context, the Council institutions have the power to take decisions on

CFSP and CSDP. The rights of the European Parliament and the European Court of Justice are limited in comparison to other fields. Considerations of national sovereignty and the general constitutional order of the Union reinforce the considerations leading to a strong role of the executive in the national context. Member States consider defence to be at the heart of national sovereignty. The transfer of even parts of this sovereignty is harder than in other areas. The transfer to intergovernmental institutions, where the individual Member State government keeps control through the requirement of unanimity in decision making, is easier than the transfer to a supranational organisation. The transfer to the intergovernmental EU Council is politically feasible. The transfer to a supranational EDC Board of Commissioners is no more acceptable in 2005 than it was fifty years earlier.

The Constitutional Treaty provides a CFSP and CSDP on the background of these considerations. The European Council and the Council take decisions on the basis of the principle of unanimity. The legislative role of the European Parliament is reduced to a right to be regularly informed. The jurisdiction of the European Court of Justice is largely excluded. The intergovernmental institutions are the CFSP and CSDP institutions of the EU, without substantial parliamentary and judicial control. This stands in stark contrast to the rights of some national parliaments in foreign policy and defence and to the rights of the European Parliament in the legislative process regarding Community policies, including those with defence implications. This also stands in stark contrast to the rights of some national courts to review foreign and defence policy and the rights of the European Court of Justice to review Member State and Community measures in the Community context, including those with defence implications.

The Constitutional Treaty adds little to the institutional framework of the CFSP under the Treaty of Nice. The attribution of powers to the intergovernmental institutions, in contrast to a more balanced attribution of powers to both the intergovernmental and supranational institutions in the Community context, keeps the separation of the Second Pillar from the First Pillar of the TEU intact. The Constitutional Treaty does not overcome this separation of the Pillars with regards to the CFSP and CSDP. Innovations introduced by the convention are moderate. The office of the Union Minister for Foreign Affairs will promote the coherence of the different aspects of external action and the permanent Chair of the European Council will provide continuity. With his or her responsibilities for both the CFSP/CSDP and Community external relations the Minister is a potential bridge between the Community and CFSP Pillars of the Constitutional Treaty.

The requirement of unanimity for decisions on the CSDP taken in the Council without exception needs to be reconsidered. It often takes long negotiations to meet this requirement and in the end it might not be possible to get the agreement of all Member States. This could undermine the required quick response to a security challenge. The abstention rule in Article III-300 (1) Constitutional Treaty will be the only possibility of reaching a decision in a case where a number of Member States do not want to support EU action. However, this might not be sufficient.

The possibility to move to qualified majority voting in Article III-300 (2) and (3) should be extended to decisions having military or defence implications by deleting Article III-300 (4) Constitutional Treaty. The issue of qualified majority voting will be back on the agenda as soon as the current arrangement proved too big an obstacle to the emergence of a credible CSDP.

The limited role of the European Parliament in the context of the CSDP is the strongest aspect of its democratic deficit. In the medium term the Union Minister for Foreign Affairs or the Council should be obliged to present an annual Report. In the longer term the rights of the European Parliament in the context of the CFSP and CSDP should be adjusted to its rights in the context of the other Union policies, taking the specific character of foreign, defence, and security policy into account. The role of the national parliaments of the Member States in these policies can serve as an example. The role of the European Parliament will become particularly important when an ERRF, based on permanent and long-term contributions of the participating Member States, should be introduced and the deployment of such a force would not depend on the approval of national parliaments.

The jurisdiction of the European Court of Justice should be extended to the CFSP and CSDP. Judicial review should take the specific characteristics of foreign policy and defence into account by allowing the Member States a wide margin of discretion. Moreover, following the regime of the national security exclusions in the Treaty, scrutiny should not be intense and only set aside a decision when they are clearly disproportionate or not taken in good faith. Finally, the applicant should have the burden of proof.

In order to overcome the three-Pillar structure of the TEU the provisions on the decision-making procedures, the institutions involved in these procedures, and the systems of checks and balances in the CFSP and CSDP should be adjusted to the provisions on the other Union policies. Nevertheless the specific character of security and defence should be taken into account. The national laws of the Member States and European Community law provide examples on how this can be done. After all, consistency promotes security.

By the end of the completion of this book at the end of 2004 the entering into force of the Constitutional Treaty is uncertain due to the unpredictable outcome of the required referenda in many Member States. However, the example of the EDA has shown, that the content of the Constitutional Treaty is not necessarily dependent on the fate of project. Many of the policies, institutions, and procedures might be the subject of Treaty amendments in the event of a failure of the Constitutional Treaty. This possibility includes the CSDP.

Conclusions

THE MEMBER STATES of the European Union enjoy a period of peace and security unprecedented in the history of the continent. The major military threat disappeared with the end of the Cold War and defence seemed less important than ever before. However, the threats posed by international terrorism, crisis and war ridden regions such as the Balkans and the Caucasus, and the vicinity of the Middle East require a security and defence policy.

The United States is withdrawing large parts of its troops from Europe, the transatlantic rifts caused over the war on Iraq show considerable differences regarding foreign and security policy, and NATO is an organisation with an uncertain future. The wars in Bosnia and Kosovo revealed that major military operations in Europe depend on the participation of the United States. However, the latter is not always in agreement with its European allies about how such missions should be conducted. Substantial capability shortfalls of the armed forces have to be addressed against the background of tight budgets, inefficient defence industries, and increasing unit prices for defence equipment. Hence there is a dilemma caused by an increased need for an independent European security and defence policy to address the modern security challenges on the one hand and limited means on the other hand. No Member State has either the financial means, public support, or political will to address this dilemma on a purely national basis. Therefore, a common foreign, security, and defence policy of the European Union provides the only feasible solution. A 'European Security and Defence Union' comprised *inter alia* of common military structures, a European Rapid Reaction Force, a mutual defence guarantee, a European Defence Agency, and a set of rules to harmonise the defence laws of the Member States, could provide the Union with an instrument to face the security and defence challenges of the 21st Century.

This book has shown that the European defence and security architecture is fragmented. European defence integration is an ongoing process towards the uncertain ultimate goal of a common defence which started in the 1940s. This process is conducted within legal frameworks based on treaties, which *inter alia* involve political, military, and financial commitments and establish institutions, including defence-specific institutions. These institutions take the decisions regarding the details of their legal frameworks. Dependent on the degree of independence of decision-making from the governments of the participating Member States, these legal frameworks are either more intergovernmental or more supranational in nature. Since the failure of the European Defence Community Treaty in 1954 the relevant legal frameworks, and, therefore European defence integration are characterised by fragmentation.

First, as explained in Part I of this book, a considerable part of European defence integration was separated from the mainstream or main path of European integration conducted in the framework of the more supranational Communities through the establishment of the more intergovernmental Western European Union in 1954. The Western European Union remained a largely dormant European club within NATO. Nevertheless, it developed crisis management capabilities and structures concerning armaments policy from the early 1990s. In contrast to the European Communities, both WEU and NATO provide mutual defence guarantees. Hence crisis management and collective defence were regulated in legal frameworks separate from the European Communities.

Second, the Communities represent a legal framework of European defence integration. This was discussed extensively in Part II of this book. As defence has, *inter alia*, commercial and social implications, the Community, intended as an instrument of economic and later social integration excluding defence, had to address defence and security. Thus a number of security exemptions were included in the legal instruments of the Community. Exemptions accommodating public security, armaments, secrecy, and crisis situations allow Member States to derogate from their obligations under the Treaty in circumstances involving public and national security. These exemptions have to be specifically invoked on a case-by-case basis and are subject to the judicial scrutiny exercised by the European Court of Justice. The intensity of scrutiny applied to the use of the security exemptions differs depending on the exemption. The public security exemptions in Articles 30, 39 (3), 46 (1), and 58 (1) (b) of the EC Treaty are subjected to a relatively intensive review in the form of a rigorous proportionality test analysed in chapter 4. In the context of the national security exemptions in Articles 296 and 297 of the EC Treaty discussed in chapters 5 and 6 respectively, the Court leaves a wider margin of discretion to the Member States. However, all security exemptions have to be narrowly construed. They do not represent automatic or categorical exclusions. Therefore, the EC Treaty applies to many economic, social, and other aspects of defence, such as defence procurement or sex equality in the armed forces, unless a security exemption is successfully invoked. In other words, Community law is an instrument of European defence integration within the limits of the security exemptions. These exemptions and the judicial scrutiny exercised over their use provide a sophisticated mechanism to balance the internal market and other interests of the Community with the security interests of the Member States. The security exemptions of the EC Treaty are reflected in secondary Community legislation. As explained in chapter 7, this is particularly important in the area of defence procurement. Moreover, chapter 8 covered the impact of Community law on the regulation of the defence industrial sector including competition law, merger control, State aids, as well as intra-Community transfers and exports of armaments and dual-use goods. Finally, chapter 9 explained how even the organisation of the armed forces of the Member States is affected by Community social law. These legal instruments amount to a considerable body of Community defence law affecting the ministries of defence, defence industries, and armed forces of the Member States.

Third, in 1992 a Second Pillar on a Common Foreign and Security Policy was added to the First Community Pillar in the Treaty on European Union. This was covered mainly in chapters 2 and 3. However, in contrast to the more supranational Community Pillar characterised by the principles of supremacy and direct effect, by qualified majority voting in the Council, co-decision of Council and European Parliament, legislative initiative of the Commission, and judicial review of the Court, the Common Foreign and Security Policy remained an intergovernmental framework. Member States retained their right of *veto* in a dominant Council which takes all decisions, the involvement of the Commission and the Parliament is very limited, and the jurisdiction of the Court is largely excluded. Nevertheless, the security element of the Second Pillar was developed to a European Security and Defence Policy. This policy includes the establishment of EU military institutions, such as the Political and Security Committee, the European Union Military Committee, the European Union Military Staff, the European Defence Agency, and eventually an autonomous military capacity in the form of a European Rapid Reaction Force. Moreover, a High Representative for the Common Foreign and Security Policy also gives a face to the European Security and Defence Policy.

Fourth, international organisations such as the Organisation for Security and Co-operation in Europe with regards to crisis management and organisational structures such as the Organisation for Joint Armaments Co-operation or the Western European Armaments Group and Organisation for defence procurement also deal with certain aspects of European defence integration. Moreover, NATO is still the dominant defence and security organisation in Europe covering collective defence, an armaments policy, peacekeeping and peace enforcement including an evolving NATO Rapid Reaction Force. The European Security and Defence Policy is dependent on NATO assets. Hence, from a European Union perspective the fragmentation of European defence integration has two dimensions: an internal dimension caused by the regulation of aspects of defence within a supranational Community Pillar and a separate Second Pillar of the Union, and an external dimension caused by the regulation of defence in various international organisations and frameworks. Fragmentation is increased, when, as described in chapter 8 with regards to exports, the Member States address defence issues outside the Pillars.

Unity is paramount for efficiency in defence. The coherence of a small combat unit of four soldiers is decisive for their efficiency. The coherence of the national armed forces as a whole is also crucial in order for them to reach their objectives. The coherence of a military alliance is equally important. Without unity there will be neither successful deterrence nor consistent responses to security challenges. No aggressor will take a disunited army or alliance seriously. Therefore unity and coherence are of considerable strategic importance.

Since the Treaty of Amsterdam the European Union has been trying to address the external dimension of fragmentation, in particular by slowly integrating the functions of the Western European Union into the Common Foreign and Security

Policy. The Constitutional Treaty discussed in Part III of this book aims to address both the internal and the external dimension of fragmentation. The Convention aimed to overcome the internal dimension of fragmentation by abolishing the current three-Pillar structure. However, as explained in chapter 12 decision-making with regards to the new Common Security and Defence Policy remains intergovernmental whereas it remains more supranational with regards to the Community policies. As under the Treaty of Nice, the security and defence policy of the Union is still dominated by a Council acting by unanimity, the roles of the Commission and the European Parliament remain marginal, and the jurisdiction of the Court is still largely excluded. Therefore the Constitutional Treaty fails to overcome the separation between the supranational and intergovernmental Pillars.

The internal dimension of fragmentation of European defence integration is partly addressed by the introduction of the office of the Union Minister for Foreign Affairs, who in all but name is also the 'Union Minister for Security and Defence'. The Minister is to be responsible for both the Community and the Second Pillar aspects of external action. Hence this office unites competencies from two Pillars. Whether this office will contribute to overcoming the fragmentation of European defence integration will depend on the constitutional practice and to a certain extent the personality of the Minister. However, he does not have responsibility for the areas of procurement, competition, and sex equality discussed in Part II. Moreover, the Constitutional Treaty puts him or her in a difficult position 'between the chairs' of the supranational Commission and the intergovernmental Council.

The external fragmentation is mainly caused by a lack of agreement between the Member States regarding the different aspects of defence integration. Therefore, the Convention aimed to address this dimension by providing a set of flexible frameworks for the different aspects of defence integration, such as crisis management, collective defence, and armaments policy. However, these flexible frameworks might lead to an additional dimension of fragmentation undermining the coherence of European defence integration.

A number of recommendations concerning the legal framework of European defence integration were made to address the problem of fragmentation. First, the armaments exemption in Article 296 (1) (b) EC and Article III-436 (1) (b) Constitutional Treaty should be amended. An amendment could take the form of a redrafting of the Council List of 1958. Such a new list could be limited to the most sensitive weapons thereby subjecting most conventional armaments to the more supranational Community regime of the Treaties. This could lead to a liberalised defence equipment market as a condition for the survival of the European defence industrial base and to address the capabilities gap in an efficient and affordable manner. Second, following the example of the 'Union Minister for Foreign Affairs' proposed in the Constitutional Treaty a 'Union Minister for Defence Affairs' should be in charge of both the Community aspects of defence and the Common Security and Defence Policy.

Third, a permanent European Rapid Reaction Force based on long-term contributions of the participating Member States should be established to provide the Union with an ensured core force to carry out Petersberg missions.

Fourth, the exclusion of the jurisdiction of the European Court of Justice in Article 46 TEU and Article III-376 Constitutional Treaty should be abolished or amended. An amendment could allow judicial scrutiny of the Common Security and Defence Policy in a manner similar to Articles 298 subparagraph 2 EC and Article I-132 subparagraph 2 Constitutional Treaty. This would allow the Court to balance the interests of the Union with the interests of the Member States, leaving a wider margin of discretion to the latter. Fifth, effective parliamentary control of the Common Security and Defence Policy through the European Parliament should be introduced. Moreover, the deployment of the European Rapid Reaction Force should be subject to the assent of the European Parliament to increase the democratic legitimacy of the Policy. Finally, the budgetary control of Strasbourg should be brought in line with that exercised by most national legislatures. Sixth, qualified majority voting should be introduced in the Council for questions relating to the Common Security and Defence Policy. This would allow swift action to be taken by the Union in this policy field.

Seventh, organisations and structures outside the European Union framework, such as the Western European Union, the Western European Armaments Organisation and the Organisation for Joint Armaments Co-operation should be disbanded after their activities have been integrated into the framework of the Union. The Constitutional Treaty will introduce flexible frameworks for collective defence, armaments policy, and crisis management that allow the integration of these external structures but accommodate Member States who do not wish to participate. While this would not necessarily overcome fragmentation as such it would internalise an aspect of fragmentation thereby increasing the coherence of European defence integration as fewer organisations were active in the field.

The European defence integration process through legal frameworks will continue. The next planned step is the Constitutional Treaty which might be rejected in one or more of the national referenda required for its implementation. Nevertheless, many of the innovations of the Common Security and Defence Policy are likely to be introduced either, through the Constitutional Treaty or other Treaty amendments. Theoretically, the ultimate future destination of European defence integration is a "common defence", which is unclear and uncertain. However, while European defence integration is still fragmented it is submitted that the developments of recent years have increased coherence. If the Member States are willing to 'Communitarise' crucial parts of the Common Security and Defence Policy, make the necessary investments in their military capabilities, and find the right relationship with NATO, the European Union might become the dominant European security and defence organisation.

Bibliography

D AKANDE and S WILLIAMS, 'International Adjudication on National Security issues: What Role for the WTO?' (2003) 43 *Virginia Journal of International Law* 306.

A COURADES ALLEBECK, 'The European Community: from the EC to the European Union' in H Wulf, (ed), *Arms Industry Limited* (OUP, Oxford, 1993).

M ANDENAS, (ed), *Article 177 References to the European Court—Policy and Practice* (Butterworths, London, 1994).

A ARNULL, 'The Beat Goes On' (1987) 12 *European Law Review* 56.

——, 'EC Law and the Dismissal of Pregnant Servicewomen' (1995) 24 *Industrial Law Journal* 215.

——, Editorial: 'War-Torn' (2003) 28 *European Law Review.*

R ARON, 'Historical Sketch of the Great Debate' in D Lerner and R Aron, *France Defeats EDC* (Praeger, NewYork, 1957) 2.

S ARROWSMITH, *A Guide to the Procurement Cases of the Court of Justice* (Earlsgate Press, 1992).

——, 'The Award of Interim Measures in Procurement Cases: Implications of the Recent Order in the Wallonia Buses Case' (1994) 3 *Public Procurement Law Review* CS130.

——, *The Law of Public and Utilities Procurement* (Sweet & Maxwell, London, 1996).

——, 'The European Commission's Proposal for New Directives on Public and Utilities Procurement' (2000) 10 *Public Procurement Law Review* NA 125.

——, 'An Assessment of the New Legislative Package on Public Procurement' (2004) 41 *Common Market Law Review* 1277.

D ARTER, *The Politics of European Integration in the Twentieth Century* (Ashgate, Dartmouth,1993).

C BARNARD and J SCOTT, (eds), *The Law of the Single European Market* (Hart Publishing, Oxford, 2002).

E BARTH, '10 Jahre Wehrverfassung im "Grundgesetz"' (1966) 19 *Die Öffentliche Verwaltung* 153.

H-J BERG, 'Zum grundgesetzlichen Verbot eines uneingeschränkten Dienstes von Frauen in den "Streikräften"' (1979) 21 *Neue Zeitschrift für Wehrrecht* 81.

A BLOED and RA WESSEL, (eds), *The Changing Functions of the Western European Union (WEU): Introduction and Basic Documents* (Martinus Nijhoff, Dordrecht, 1994).

M BOTHE and T MARAUHN, 'The Arms Trade: Comparative Aspects of Law' (1993) 26 *Revue belge de droit international* 20.

R BOYLE, 'Critique of the Commission's Proposal for a New Directive on the Co-ordination of procedures for Public Contracts COM (2000) 275 final, as Updated by the discussions in the Working Group' (2001) 10 *Public Procurement Law Review* NA 65.
P BRAUN, 'A Matter of Principle(s)—The Treatment of Contracts Falling Outside the Scope of the European Public Procurement Directives' (2002) 9 *Public Procurement Law Review* 39.
HW BRIGGS, 'The Proposed European Political Community' (1954) 48 *American Journal of International Law* 110–122.
MP BROBERG, *The European Commission's Jurisdiction to Scrutinise Mergers* (Kluwer, The Hague, 1998).
L BROKER, 'Frauen als "Kombattanten"' (1996) 37 *Zeitschrift für Rechtspolitik* 127.
I BROWNLIE, *International Law and the Use of Force* (OUP, Oxford, 1963).
F CAPOTORI, 'Above National Organisations' in R Bernardt, *Encyclopedia of Public International Law*, (North Holland, Amsterdam, 1983) Volume 5.
A CASSESE, (ed), *Parliamentary Control over Foreign Policy: Legal Essays* (Sijthoff & Noordhoff: Alphen aan den Rijn, 1980).
A CASTRO-OLIVEIRA, 'Workers and Other Persons: Step-by-Step from Movement to Citizenship' (2002) 39 *Common Market Law Review* 77.
J-L CLERGERIE, (2000) No 22 *Receuil Le Dalloz* Commentaire Jursiprudence.
J COOK and C KERSE, *EC Merger Control*, 3rd edn, (Sweet & Maxwell, London, 2000).
A COX, 'The Future of European Defence Policy: the Case of a Centralised Procurement Agency' (1994) 3 *Public Procurement Law Review* 65.
A COX and K HARTLEY, *The Costs of Non-Europe in Defence Procurement—Executive Summary*, The Commission of the European Communities DG III, July 1992 (released December 1994).
P CRAIG, 'Constitutions, Constitutionalism and the European Union' (2001) 7 *European Law Journal* 125.
P CRAIG and G DE BÚRCA, *EU Law*, 3rd edn, (OUP, Oxford, 2003).
——, (eds), *The Evolution of EU Law* (OUP, Oxford, 1998).
M CREMONA, 'The European Union as an International Actor: The Issues of Flexibility and Linkage' (1998) 3 *European Foreign Affairs Review* 67.
O CROCI, 'A Closer Look at the Changing Transatlantic Relationship' (2003) 8 *European Foreign Affairs Review* 469.
S CROSBY, 'The New Tobacco Control Directive: An Illiberal and Illegal Disdain for the Law' (2002) 27 *European Law Review* 177.
R CRYER and ND WHITE, 'The Security Council and the International Criminal Court: Who's Feeling Threatened?' in H Langholtz, B Kondoch and A Wells, (eds), (2002) 8 *International Peacekeeping: The Yearbook of International Peace Operations* 143.
DM CURTIN, 'The Constitutional Structure of the Union: A Europe of Bits and Pieces' (1993) 30 *Common Market Law Review* 17.
DM CURTIN and IF DEKKER, 'The European Union as a "Layered" International Organisation: Institutional Unity in Disguise' in P Craig and G de Búrca, (eds), *The Evolution of EU Law* (OUP, Oxford, 1999) 83.

DM CURTIN and RH VAN OOIK, 'Denmark and the Edinburgh Summit: Maastricht without Tears' in D O'Keefe and P Twomey, (eds), *Legal Issues of the Maastricht Treaty* (Wiley Chancery Law, London, 1994) 349.

P D'ARGENT, 'Les enseignements du COCOM' (1993) 26 *Revue Belge de droit international* 500.

P DANKERT, 'The EC—Past, Present, Future' in L Tsoukalis, *The EC—Past, Present Future* (Basil Blackwell, London, 1983).

A DASHWOOD, 'The Role of the Council of the European Communities' in D Curtin and T Heukels, *Institutional Dynamics of European Integration, Essays in Honour of Henry G Schermers* (Martinus Nijhoff Publishers, Dordrecht, 1994) vol II 117.

——, 'The Council of the European Union in the Era of the Amsterdam Treaty' in T Heukels, N Blokker and M Brus, (eds), *The European Union after Amsterdam: A Legal Analysis* (Kluwer, The Hague, 1998) 117.

K DAU, 'Ernstfall für die "Gleichberechtigung ?"' (1990) 32 *Neue Zeitschrift für Wehrrecht* 45.

G DE BÚRCA, 'The Principle of Proportionality and its Application in EC Law' (1993) 13 *Yearbook of European Law* 105.

P DE VESTEL, *Defence Markets and Industries in Europe: Time for Political Decisions?*, Chaillot Paper No 21, (Institute of Security Studies of the Western European Union, Paris, 1995).

——, 'The Future of Armament Cooperation in NATO and the WEU' in KE Eliassen, (ed), *Foreign and Security Policy in the European Union* (Sage, London, 1998).

R DE WIJK, 'Convergence Criteria: Measuring Input or Output' (2000) 5 *European Foreign Affairs Review* 397.

B DE WITTE, 'The Pillar Structure and the Nature of the European Union: Greek Temple or French Gothic Cathedral?' in T Heukels, N Blokker and M Brus, (eds), *The European Union after Amsterdam: A Legal Analysis* (Kluwer, The Hague, 1997).

A DEIGHTON, 'The Military Security Pool: Towards a New Security Regime for Europe?' (2000) 35 *The International Spectator* 41.

M DISCHENDORFER, 'Service Concessions under the EC Procurement Directives: A Note on the *Telaustria* Case' (2001) 10 *Public Procurement Law Review* NA57.

O DÖRR, 'Zur Rechtsnatur der Europäischen Union' (1995) 30 *Europarecht* 334.

F DORSSEMONT, 'Militaire dienstplicht en gelijke toegang tot de arbeidsmarkt' (2003) 7/8 *Sociaal Recht* 231.

S DUKE, 'CESDP: Nice's Overtrumped Success?' (2001) 6 *European Foreign Affairs Review* 155.

MR EATON, 'Common Foreign and Security Policy' in D O'Keefe and P Twomey, (eds), *Legal Issues of the Maastricht Treaty* (Chancery Law Wiley, London, 1994) 215.

HG EDELMANN, 'Freiwilliger Waffendienst für "Frauen?"' (1988) 29 *Zeitschrift für Rechtspolitik* 144.

P EECKHOUT, 'On Dual Use Goods and Dualist Case Law: the *Aimé Richardt* Judgment on Export Controls' (1992) 29 *Common Market Law Review* 941.

K D EHLERMANN, 'Differentiation, Flexibility, Closer Cooperation', (EUI Working Paper, San Domenico di Fiesole, 1997).

K EICHEN, 'Erosion der deutschen Wehrverfassung durch sekundäres Gemeinschaftsrecht?' (2000) 42 *Neue Zeitschrift für Wehrrecht* 45.

K EIKENBERG, 'Article 296 (ex 223) EC and External Trade in Strategic Goods' (2000) 25 *European Law Review* 117.

E ELLIS, 'Can Public Safety Provide an Excuse for Sex Discrimination?' (1986) 102 *Law Quarterly Review* 496.

N EMILIOU, 'Strategic Export Control, National Security and the Common Commercial Policy' (1996) 1 *European Foreign Affairs Review* 55.

——, 'Restrictions on Strategic Exports, Dual-Use Goods and the Common Commercial Policy' (1997) 22 *European Law Review* 68.

A EVANS, *EC Law of State Aids* (OUP, Oxford, 1997).

U EVERLING, 'Reflections on the Structure of the European Union' (1992) 28 *Common Market Law Review* 1053.

——, 'L'avenir de l'organisation jurisdictionelle de l'Union européenne' in G Versanden, (ed), *La Réforme du Système Jurisdictionel Communautaire* (Éditons de l Université de Bruxelles, Brussels, 1994), 1.

J FAUVET, 'Birth and Death of a Treaty' in D Lerner and R Aron, (eds), *France Defeats EDC* (Praeger, NewYork, 1957) 128.

H FENWICK and T HERVEY, 'Sex Equality in the Single Market: New Directions for the European Court of Justice' (1995) 32 *Common Market Law Review* 43.

H FENWICK, 'Special Protections for Women in European Union Law' in T Hervey and D O'Keeffe, (eds), *Sex Equality Law in the European Union* (Wiley, London, 1996).

J M FERNÁNDEZ-MARTÍN, 'Case C-243/89, *Commission v Denmark* (*The Storebaelt Case*), Judgment of June 22, 1993'(1993) 2 *Public Procurement Law Review* CS153.

——, *The EC Public Procurement Rules* (OUP, Oxford, 1996).

F FINK-HOOIJER, 'The Common Foreign and Security Policy of the European Union' (1994) 3 *European Journal of International Law* 173.

TM FRANCK, *Political Questions/Juridical Answers: Does the Rule of Law Apply to Foreign Affairs?* (Princeton University Press, Princeton, 1992).

D FREESTONE and S DAVIDSON, 'Community Competence and Part III of the Single European Act' (1986) 23 *Common Market Law Review* 793.

JA FROWEIN, entry on 'European Political Cooperation' in R Bernardt, *Encyclopedia of Public International Law* (North Holland, Amsterdam, 1983) Volume 6.

——, 'Die Europäische Union mit WEU als Sicherheitssystem' in O Due, *et al*, (eds), *Festschrift fur Ulrich Everling* (Nomos Verlagsgesellschaft, Baden Baden, 1995) 313.

E FURSDON, *The European Defence Community: A History* (Macmillan, London, 1980).

D GALLOWAY, 'Common Foreign and Security Policy: Intergovernmentalism Donning the Mantle of the Community Method' in M Westlake, *The Council of the European Union* (Cartermill, London, 1995).

A GEORGOPOULOS, 'The New European Defence Agency: Major Development or a Fig Leaf?' (2005)14 *Public Procurement Law Review* 103.

——, 'European Defence Procurement Integration: Evaluating the Teleological Boundaries of Article 296 (1b) EC and the Applicability of the New Public Procurement Directive in the Field of Intra-Community Armaments Procurement' forthcoming in *European Law Review*.

P GILSDORF, 'Les reserves de sécurité du Traité CEE, à la lumière du Traité sur L'Union Europénne' (1994) *Revue du marché commun et l'Union europénne* 17.

R GINSBERG, 'European Security and Defence Policy: The State of the Play' (2003) 16 *EUSA Review* 1.

N GNESOTTO, 'Preface, EDSP 2001: Routine and Revolution' in M Rutten, (ed), Chaillot Paper No 51, *From Nice to Laeken, European defence: core documents Volume II*, (Institute of Security Studies of the European Union, Paris, 2002).

L GORMLEY, (ed), Kapteyn & Verloren van Themaat, *Introduction to the Law of the European Communities*, 3rd edn, (Kluwer, Deventer, 1998).

G GORNIG, 'Artikel 12 a Abs IV' in C Starck, (ed), v Mangolt/Klein, *Das Bonner Grundgesetz, Band 1, Präambel bis* Art *19 GG*, 4th edn, (Verlag Franz Vahlen: Munich, 1999) Rdnr 158.

D GOYDER, *EC Competition Law*, 4th edn, (OUP, Oxford, 2002).

E GRABITZ and M HILF, (eds), *Kommentar zum EWGV* (CH Beck Verlag, Munich, 1997) loose-leaf, volume II, Art 223.

SB GRIFFITH (ed), Sun Tzu, *The Art of War* (OUP, Oxford, 1963).

C GRIMM, 'Freiwilliger Waffendienst für "Frauen ?"' (1987) 28 *Zeitschrift für Rechtspolitik* 394.

A GROSSER, 'Germany and France: A Confrontation' in D Lerner and R Aron, (eds), *France Defeats EDC* (Praeger, NewYork, 1957) 54.

T GRUNERT, 'The Association of the European Parliament: No Longer the Underdog in EPC?' in E Regelsberger, P de Schoutheete de Tervarent, W Wessels, *Foreign Policy of the European Union: From EPC to CFSP and Beyond* (Lynne Rienner, Boulder, 1997) 109.

M GUBELT, 'Artikel 12 a Wehrdienst und andere Dienstverpflichtungen' in I v Münch and P Kunig, (eds), *Grundgesetz-Kommentar, Band I (Präambel bis* Art *20 GG)*, 4th edn, (CH Beck-Verlag: Munich, 1992) Rdnr 20.

J-Y HAINE, *From Laeken to Copenhagen*, Volume III, Chaillot Paper No 57, (Institute of Security Studies of the European Union, Paris, 2003).

A HALFORD, 'An Overview of EC—United States Trade Relations in the Area of Public Procurement' (1995) 4 *Public Procurement Law Review* 35.

I HARDEN, (ed), *State Aid: Community Law and Policy* (Bundesanzeiger Verlag, Bonn, 1993).

K Hartley, 'Public Procurement and Competitiveness' (1989) 3 *Journal of Common Market Studies* 237.

——, 'Competition in Defence Contracting in the United Kingdom' (1992) 1 *Public Procurement Law Review* 440.

T Hartley, 'The European Court, Judicial Objectivity and the Constitution of the European Union' (1996) 112 *Legal Quarterly Review* 95.

W Heinzmann, 'Die europäische Verteidigungsindustrie im Wandel', *Deutsch-Französische Rüstungskooperation*, 1996.

M Hellenthal, *Frauen im Bundesgrenzschutz* (Schriften zum Öffentlichen Recht 537, Berlin,1988).

T Hervey, 'Up in Smoke? Community (Anti) Tobacco Law and Policy' (2001) 26 *European Law Review* 101.

W Heun and H Dreier, (eds), *Grundgestz-Kommentar, Band I, Artikel 1–19 GG* (Mohr Siebeck, Tübingen, 1996), 'Artikel 12 a', Rdnr 33.

MJ Hillenbrand, 'American Perceptions of NATO and the European Community' in C Coker, (ed), *Shifting into Neutral? Burden Sharing in the Western Alliance in the 1990s* (Brassey's, London, 1990), 103.

C Hillion, 'Tobacco Advertising: If You Must, You May' (2001) 60 *Cambridge Law Journal* 486.

S Hoffmann, 'The Postmortems' in D Lerner and R Aron, (eds), *France Defeats EDC* (Praeger, NewYork, 1957) 164.

F-J Hölzl in 6 (2004) *Vergaberecht* 376–379.

——, 'Circumstances Alter Cases' [2004] *Neue Zeitschrift für Bau-und Vergaberecht* 256.

D Howarth, 'The Compromise on Denmark and the Treaty on European Union: A Legal and Political Analysis' (1994) 31 *Common Market Law Review* 765.

PV Howell, 'Policy Assessment Framework to Evaluate the Operational Capability of the European Union's Rapid Reaction Force (ERRF)', paper presented at the *8th Biannual Conference of the European Union Studies Association* (Nashville, 2003).

J Howorth, 'Britain, France and the European Defence Initiative' (2000) 42 *Survival* 33.

W Hummer, 'Artikel 223' in E Grabitz and M Hilf, (eds), *Kommentar zum EWGV* (CH Beck Verlag, Munich, 1997) loose-leaf, volume II, Art 223.

——, 'Artikel 225' in E Grabitz and M Hilf, (eds), *Kommentar zum EWGV* (CH Beck Verlag, Munich, 1997) loose-leaf, Art 225.

D Hurd, 'Political Cooperation' (1981) 57 *International Affairs* 383.

JS Ignarski, entry on 'NATO' in R Bernardt, *Encyclopedia of Public International Law* (North Holland, Amsterdam, 1983) 264.

F Jacobs, 'Is the Court of Justice of the European Communities a Constitutional Court?' in D Curtin and D O'Keefe, (eds), *Constitutional Adjudication in European Community and National Law* (Butterworths, Dublin, 1992).

T JAEGER, 'Enhanced Cooperation in the Treaty of Nice and Flexibility in the Common Foreign and Security Policy' (2002) 7 *European Foreign Affairs Review* 297.

R JAHN, 'Frauen zu den "Waffen?"' (1988) 30 *Neue Zeitschrift für Wehrrecht* 177.

HD JARRAS, 'Artikel 12a' in HD Jarras, B Pieroth, (eds), *Grundgesetz für die Bundesrepublik Deutschland–Kommentar*, 3rd edn, (CH Beck-Verlag, Munich, 1995) Rdnr 13.

HD JARRAS and B PIEROTH, *Grundgesetz für die Bundesrepublik Deutschland, Kommentar*, 3rd edn, (CH Beck Verlag, Munich, 1996) 'Art 3', Rdnr 58.

——, *Kommentar zum Grundgesetz*, 5th edn, (C H Beck, Munich, 2000), 'Article 12 a', Rdnr 3.

M JOPP and E REGELSBERGER, 'GASP und EVSP im Verfassungsvertrag–eine neue Angebotsvielfalt mit Chancen und Mängeln' *Integration* 4/2003, Europa Union, Bonn, 550.

T JÜRGENS, *Die Gemeinsame Außen—und Sicherheitspolitik* (Carl Heyermanns Verlag, Cologne, 1994).

JM KÄMMERER, 'Gleichberechtigung am Gewehr' (2000) 35 *Europarecht* 102.

P J G KAPTEYN and P VERLOREN van Themaat, *Introduction to the Law of the European Communities*, 2nd edn, (Kluwer, Deventer, 1990).

S KEUKELEIRE, *Het Buitenlandse beleid van de Europese Unie* (Kluwer, Deventer, 1998).

J KLABBERS, 'Presumptive Personality: The European Union in International Law' in M Koskenniemi, (ed), *International Law Aspects of the European Union* (Kluwer, The Hague, 1998) 231.

J KOKOTT, 'Artikel 12 a' in J Kokott and M Sachs, (eds), *Kommentar zum Grundgesetz* (C H Beck, Munich, 1996) Rndnr 4.

V KORAH, *EC Competition Law*, 7th edn, (Hart Publishing, Oxford, 2000).

P KOUTRAKOS, 'Exports of Dual Use Goods under the Law of the European Union' (1998) 23 *European Law Review* 235.

——, 'Community Law and Equal Treatment in the Armed Forces' (2000) 25 *European Law Review* 433.

——, 'Is Article 297 EC a "Reserve of Sovereignty"?' (2000) 37 *Common Market Law Review* 1339.

——, *Trade, Foreign Policy and Defence in EU Constitutional Law: The Legal Regulation of Sanctions, Exports of Dual Use Goods and Armaments* (Hart Publishing, Oxford, 2001).

——, 'How Far is Far Enough? EC Law and the Organisation of the Armed Forces after Dory' (2003) 66 *Modern Law Review* 759.

HG KRENZLER and HC SCHNEIDER, 'Die Gemeinsame Außen—und Sicherheitspolitik der Europäischen Union–Zur Frage der Kohärenz' (1994) 29 *Europarecht* 144.

——, 'The Question of Consistency' in E Regelsberger, P de Schoutheete de Tervarent, W Wessels, (eds), *Foreign Policy of the European Union: From EPC to CFSP and Beyond* (Lynne Rienner, Boulder, 1997).

EDJ KRUIJTBOSCH, entry on 'Benelux Economic Union' in R Bernardt, *Encyclopedia of Public International Law* (North Holland, Amsterdam, 1983) Volume 6.

RC LANE, entry on 'Federalism in the International Community' in R Bernardt, *Encyclopedia of Public International Law* (North Holland, Amsterdam, 1983) Volume 5.

J LANGER, annotations in (2000) 37 *Common Market Law Review* 1433.

FS LAURSEN and S VANHOONACKER, (eds), *The Intergovernmental Conference on Political Union: Institutional Reforms, New Policies and International Identity of the European Community* (EIPA, Maastricht, 1992).

H LECHELER, 'Der Rechtscharakter der Europäischen Union' in J Ipsen, *et al*, (eds), *Verfassungsrecht im Wandel* (Carl Heyermanns Verlag, Cologne, 1995) 383.

O LHOEST, 'La production et la commerce des armes, et l'article 223 du traité constituant la Communauté europèene' (1993) 26 *Revue belge de droit international* 176.

J LOVERING, 'Military Expenditure and the Restructuring of Capitalism: the Military Industry in Britain' (1990) 14 *Cambridge Journal of Economics* 453.

C LUTZE, 'Kein Verfassungsverbot für eine "Verteidigungsministerin"' (1996) 38 *Neue Zeitschrift für Wehrrecht* 196.

E-D MAAR, 'Frauen im "Bundesgrenzschutz"' (1989) 42 *Der Öffentliche Dienst* 249.

P MACALISTER-SMITH, entry on 'Western European Union' in R Bernardt *Encyclopedia of Public International Law* (North Holland, Amsterdam, 1983).

T MARAUHN, *Building a European Security and Defence Identity, Bochumer Schriften zur Friedenssicherung und zum Humaniären Völkerrecht 30* (Universitätsverlag Dr N Brockmeyer, Bochum, 1996).

JJ MARCHAND, 'A Tableau of the French Press' in D Lerner and R Aron, (eds), *France Defeats EDC* (Praeger, New York, 1957) 102.

A MAURER, 'Jour Fixe Verfassungskonvent', http://www.swp-berlin.org/produkte/brennpunkte/jour-eu-konvent3druck.htm.

K MEYER, 'Der Rechtsschutz der Grundrechte im Wehrdienst' (1954) 8 *Die Öffentliche Verwaltung* 66.

S MEZZADRI, *L'ouverture des marchés de la defense: enjoux et modalités*, Occasional Paper No 12, (Institute for Security Studies of the Western European Union, Paris, 2000).

A MISSIROLI, *CFSP, Defence and Flexibility*, Chaillot Paper 38, (Institute of Security Studies of the Western European Union, Paris, 2000).

——, 'European Security Policy: The Challenges of Coherence' (2001) 6 *European Foreign Affairs Review* 177.

——, *From Copenhagen to Brussels: European Defence: Core Documents*, Chaillot Paper No 67 (Institute of Security Studies of the European Union, Paris, 2003).

——, 'Ploughshares into Swords? Euros for European Defence' (2003) 8 *European Foreign Affairs Review* 5.

——, 'The European Union: Just a Regional Peacekeeper?' (2003) 8 *European Foreign Affairs Review* 493.

J MONAR, 'The European Union's Foreign Affairs System after the Treaty of Amsterdam: A Strengthened Capacity for External Action' (1997) 2 *European Foreign Affairs Review* 413.

G MORE, 'The Principle of Equal Treatment: from Market Unifier to Fundamental Right?' in P Craig and G de Búrca, (eds), *The Evolution of EU Law* (OUP, Oxford, 1999) 517.

PE MORRIS, 'Sex Discrimination, Public Order and the European Court' (1987) 32 *Public Law* 334.

L MÜNCH, 'Die Gemeinsame Außen—und Sicherheitspolitik (GASP): ein Schaf im Wolfspelz?' (1997) 57 *Zeitschrift für Ausländisches Öffentliches Recht und Völkerrecht* 389.

N NEUWAHL, 'Foreign and Security Policy and the Implementation of the Requirement of "Consistency" under the Treaty on European Union' in D O'Keefe and P Twomey, (eds), *Legal Issues of the Maastricht Treaty* (Chancery Law Wiley, London, 1994).

——, 'A Partner with a Troubled Personality: EU Treaty-Making in Matters of CFSP' (1998) 3 *European Foreign Affairs Review* 177.

SJ NUTTALL, *European Foreign Policy* (OUP, Oxford, 2000).

A NUTTING, *Europe will Not Wait: a Warning and a Way Out* (Hollis & Carter, London, 1960).

D O'KEEFFE, 'Judicial Interpretation of the Public Service Exception to the Free Movement of Workers' in D Curtin and D O'Keefe, (eds), *Constitutional Adjudication in European Community and National Law* (Butterworths, Dublin, 1992).

P OLIVER, *Free Movement of Goods in the EC*, 3rd edn, (Sweet & Maxwell, London, 1996).

S PEERS, 'National Security and European Law' (1996) 15 *Yearbook of European Law* 363.

——, 'Free Movement of Capital: Learning Lessons or Slipping on Split Milk?' in C Barnard and J Scott, (eds), *The Legal Foundations of the Single Market* (Hart Publishing, Oxford, 2000).

——, 'Common Foreign and Security Policy 1999–2000' (2001) 21 *Yearbook of European Law* 531.

A PHILIP, 'The Interplay of Interests and Passions' in D Lerner and R Aron, (eds), *France Defeats EDC* (Praeger, NewYork, 1957) 24.

A PORETSCHKIN, 'Frauen in der "Bundeswehr"' (1990) 31 *Zeitschrift für Rechtspolitik* 482.

——, 'Innere Führung, Recht und Frauen. Zufall oder "Ironie?"' (1990) 32 *Neue Zeitschrift für Wehrrecht* 195.

H-J PRIEß, *Handbuch des europäischen Vergaberechts*, 2nd edn, (Carl Heyermanns Verlag, Heidelberg, 2001).

R QUADRI, R Monaco, A Trabucchi, *Commentario al Trattato istitutivo della Communità economica europea*, (Giuffré, Milan, 1965) vol III.

R RAWLINGS, 'Engaged Elites: Citizen Action and Institutional Attitudes in Commission Enforcement' (2000) 6 *European Law Journal* 4.

J RAZ, 'On the Authority and Interpretation of Constitutions: Some Preliminaries' in Alexander, (ed), *Constitutionalism* (CUP, Cambridge, 1998).

G REES, entry on 'European Political Community' in R Bernardt *Encyclopedia of Public International Law* (North Holland, Amsterdam, 1983) Volume 6.

E REMACLE, 'La politique étrangère et de sécurité commun de l'Union européenne après Maastricht' in M Thelò, (ed), *Vers une nouvelle Europe?* (Edites Européennes, Brussels, 1992) 239.

U REPKEWITZ, 'Verbietet Art 12 a Abs 4 Satz 2 GG Frauen den freiwilligen Dienst mit der "Waffe?"' (1990) 32 *Neue Zeitschrift für Wehrrecht* 177.

G RESS, 'Die Europäische Union und die neue Qualität der Beziehungen zu den Europäischen Gemeinschaften' (1992) *Juristische Schulung* 112.

J RIDEAU, 'Overservation sur Sirdar' (2000) No 19 *Receuil Le Dalloz Sommaires Commentés* 191.

AH ROBERTSON, 'The European Political Community' (1952) 29 *British Yearbook of International Law* 383.

ROBERTSON LORD, of Port Ellen, 'Our Grandchildren's NATO' (2003) 8 *European Foreign Affairs Review* 509.

PM Roth, (ed), C BELLAMY and G CHILD, *European Community Law of Competition,* 5th edn, (Sweet & Maxwell, London, 2001).

M RUTTEN, Chaillot Paper No 47, *From St-Malo to Nice, European Defence: core documents,* (Institute of Security Studies of the Western European Union, Paris, 2001).

——, Chaillot Paper No 51, *From Nice to Laeken, European defence: core documents Volume II* , (Institute of Security Studies of the European Union, Paris, 2002).

W SANDHOLTZ and A S SWEET, (eds), *European Integration and Supranational Governance* (OUP, New York, 1998).

C SCHLOEMANN and S OHLOFF, '"Constitutionalisation" and Dispute Settlement in the WTO: National Security as an Issue of Competence' (1999) 93 *American Journal of International Law* 424.

U SCHMALZ, 'The Amsterdam Provisions on External Coherence: Bridging the Union's Foreign Policy Dualism?' (1998) 3 *European Foreign Affairs Review* 421.

B SCHMIDT-BLEIBTREU, 'Artikel 12 a' in B Schmidt-Bleibtreu and F Klein, (eds), *Kommentar zum Grundgesetz,* 9th edn, (Luchterhand, Neuwied, 1999) Rdnr 10.

B SCHMITT, *European Armaments Cooperation: Core Documents,* Chaillot Paper No 59, (Institute for Security Studies of the European Union, Paris, 2003).

R SCHOLZ, 'Artikel 12 a' in T Maunz, *et al,* (eds), *Grundgesetz-Kommentar, Band II—* Art *12 a-37 GG* (CH Beck-Verlag, Munich, 1989).

J SCHWARZE, *European Administrative Law* (Sweet & Maxwell, London, 1992).

I SEIDNER, *Der freiwillige Dienst von Frauen in der Bundeswehr mit der Waffe als Gleichheitsproblem. Zum verfassungsrechtlichen Kontext von* Art *12a IV S 2 GG* (Shaker Verlag, Tübingen,1997).

V J SHRUBSALL, 'Protection Practices and the Equal Treatment Directive' (1987) 19 *Industrial Law Journal* 118.

B SIMMA, *et al*, *The Charter of the United Nations: A Commentary, Volume I*, 2nd edn, (OUP, Oxford, 2002).

V SLUPIK, 'Bewaffneter Dienst von Frauen in der "Bundeswehr"' (1990) 31 *Zeitschrift für Rechtspolitik* 305.

J SNELL, *Goods and Services in EC Law* (OUP, Oxford, 2002).

E SÖNKS, *et al*, *SIPRI Yearbook 2001: Armaments Disarmament and International Security* (OUP, Oxford, 2001).

——, *SIPRI Yearbook 2003: Armaments Disarmament and International Security* (OUP, Oxford, 2003).

TM SPRANGER, 'Die Entscheidungen "Sidar" und "Kreil" des EuGH–Diskriminierung oder Gleichberechtigung de luxe?' (2000) 42 *Neue Zeitschrift für Wehrrecht* 117.

C STEFANOU and H XANTHAKI, *A Legal and Political Interpretation of Articles 224 and 225 of the Treaty of Rome: The Former Yugoslav Republic of Macedonia Cases* (Aldershot, Dartmouth, 1997).

J STEINER and L WOODS, *EC Law*, 8th edn, (Blackstone, London, 2003).

A STEINKAMM, 'Der "Ernstfall für die Gleichberechtigung" ist in Sicht"' (1994) 36 *Neue Zeitschrift für Wehrrecht* 133.

J STOETZEL, 'The Evolution of French Opinion' in D Lerner and R Aron, (eds), *France Defeats EDC* (Praeger, New York, 1957) 72.

CW STOLLER, 'Europa nach Maastricht: Die Gemeinsame Außen—und Sicherheitspolitik' (1992) 33 *Neue Zeischrift für Wehrrecht* 221.

P SYRPIS, 'Smoke Without Fire: The Social Policy Agenda and the Internal Market' (2001) 30 *Industrial Law Journal* 271.

D THYM, 'Reforming Europe's Common Foreign and Security Policy' (2004) 10 *European Law Journal* 5.

C TIETJE, 'The Concept of Coherence in the Treaty on European Union and the CFSP' (1997) 2 *European Foreign Affairs Review* 211.

L TINDEMANNS IN A DROWN, *A Single European Arms Industry? European Defence Industries in the 1990s* (Brassey's, London, 1990).

P TREPTE, *Public Procurement in the EC* (CCH, Cheltenham, 1994).

C TRÜE, *Zur Verleihung von Rechtspersönlichkeit an die Europäischen Union und Verschmelzung zu einer einzigen Organisation—deklaratorisch oder konstitutiv?* (Vorträge, Reden und Berichte aus dem Europa-Institut, No 357, Universität des Saarlandes, 1997).

M TRYBUS, 'The Changes Facing the European Defence-Related Industry—Commission Communication COM (96) 08' (1996) 5 *Public Procurement Law Review* CS98.

——, 'National Models for the Regulation of the Acquisition of Armaments: Towards a European Defence Procurement Code?' in S Arrowsmith and A Davies, (eds), *Public Procurement: Global Revolution* (Kluwer, London, 1998).

——, 'European Defence Procurement: Towards a Comprehensive Approach' (1998) 4 *European Public Law* 111.

——, 'Developing a Model for the Regulation of European Defence Procurement' (1999) 11 *European Review of Public Law* 115.

——, *European Defence Procurement Law: International and National Procurement Systems as Models for a Liberalised Defence Procurement Market in Europe* (Kluwer, The Hague, 1999).

——, 'On the Application of the EC-Treaty to Armaments' (2000) 25 *European Law Review* 633.

——, 'The Recent Judgment in *Commission v Spain* and the Procurement of Hard Defence Material' (2000) 9 *Public Procurement Law Review* NA99.

——, 'Procurement for the Armed Forces: Balancing Security and the Internal Market' (2002) 27 *European Law Review* 692.

——, 'The EC Treaty as an Instrument of European Defence Integration: Judicial Scrutiny of Defence and Security Exceptions' (2002) 39 *Common Market Law Review* 1347.

——, 'On the List according to Article 296 EC Treaty' (2003) 12 *Public Procurement Law Review* NA15.

——, 'Sisters in Arms: European Community Law and Sex Equality in the Armed Forces' (2003) 9 *European Law Journal* 631.

——, annotations in (2003) 40 *Common Market Law Review* 1269.

——, 'At the Borderline between Community and Member State Competence: the Triple-Exceptional Character of Article 297 EC' in T Tridimas and P Nebbia, (eds), *European Union Law for the 21st Century: Defining the New Legal Order* (Hart Publishing, Oxford, 2004) 137.

——, 'European Community Competence to Regulate Defence Law' (2004) 9 *European Foreign Affairs Review* 189.

D URWIN, *The Community of Europe: a History of European Integration,* 2nd edn, (Longman, London, 1995).

A UTLEY, 'Army Struggles to Integrate Women', *The Times Higher Education Supplement*, 7 February 2003, 5.

J VERHOEVEN, in Constantinesco, *et al*, (eds), *Commentaire du Traité instituant la CEE,* (Economica, Paris, 1992).

A VON BOGDANDY and M NETTESHEIM, 'Ex pluribus unum: The Fusion of the European Communities into the European Union' (1996) 1 *European Law Journal* 267.

O VON DER GABLENTZ, 'Luxembourg Revisited or the Importance of European Political Cooperation' (1979) 16 *Common Market Law Review* 685.

——, 'Wege zu einer europäischen Außenpolitik' in H Schneider and W Wessels, (eds), *Auf dem Wege zur Europäischen Union* (Bonn, 1977) 85.

WÄGBAUR, in H von der Groeben, v Boeckh, Thiesing, Ehlermann, Kommentar zum EWG Vertrag, 3rd edn, (Nomos, Baden-Baden, 1983).

S WALKER and P GUMMMET, *Nationalism, Internationalism and the European Defence Market*, Chaillot Paper No 9, (Institute for Security Studies of the Western European Union, Paris, 1993).

W WALKER and S WILLET, 'Restructuring the European Defence Industrial Base' [1993] *Journal of Defence Economics* 141.

Index

R WALLACE, 'Free Movement for Workers and Social Security: Remedies for Foul Play' (1988) 13 *European Law Review* 267.

B WALTER, 'Frauen im BGS–Präzedenzfall für die Bundeswehr' (1992) 34 *Neue Zeitschrift für Wehrrecht* 89.

S WEATHERILL and P BEAUMONT, *EC Law*, 3rd edn, (Sweet & Maxwell, London, 1999).

JHH WEILER, 'The Transformation of Europe' (1991) 100 *Yale Law Journal* 2403.

——, 'From Dassonville to Keck and Beyond: an Evolutionary Reflection on the Text and Context of the Free Movement of Goods' in P Craig and G de Búrca, (eds), *The Evolution of EU Law* (OUP, Oxford, 1999) ch 10.

——, *The Constitution of Europe: 'Do the New Clothes Have an Emperor?' and other Essays on European Integration* (CUP, Cambridge, 2002).

F WEISS and F WOOLDRIDGE, *Free Movement of Persons within the European Community* (Kluwer, The Hague, 2002).

RA WESSEL, 'The International Legal Status of the European Union' (1997) 2 *European Foreign Affairs Review* 109.

——, *The Foreign and Security Policy of the European Union: A Legal Institutional Perspective* (Kluwer, The Hague, 1999).

——, 'Revisiting the International Legal Status of the European Union' (2003) 5 *European Foreign Affairs Review* 507.

——, 'The EU as Black Widow: Devouring the WEU to Give Birth to a European Security and Defence Policy' in: V Kronenberger, (ed), *The European Union and the International Legal Order—Discord or Harmony?* (TMC Asser Press, The Hague, 2001) 405.

——, 'The State of Affairs in EC Security and Defence Policy: The Breakthrough in the Treaty of Nice' (2003) 8 *Journal of Conflict and Security Law* 265.

W WESSELS, 'A "Saut Constitutionnel" out of an Intergovernmetnal Trap? the Provisions of the Constitutional Treaty for the Common Foreign, Security and Defence Policy' in JHH Weiler and CL Eisgruber, (eds), *Altneuland: The EU Constitution in a Contextual Perspective*, (Jean Monnet Working Paper 5/04, New York University School of Law and Woodrow Wilson School of Public and International Affairs at Princeton University 2004).

JB WHEATON, 'Defence Procurement and the European Community: The Legal Provisions' (1992) 1 *Public Procurement Law Review* 432.

P WILLAERT and C MARQUÉS-RUIZ, 'Vers une politique étrangère et de sécurité commun: état des lieux' (1995) *Revue du Marché Unique Européen* 35.

R WISH, *Competition Law*, 4th edn, (Butterworths, London, 2001).

T WOBBE, 'From Protecting to Promoting: Evolving EU Sex Equality Norms in an Organisational Field' (2003) 9 *European Law Journal* 88.

DS YOST, 'The NATO Capabilities Gap and the European Union' (2000) 42 *Survival* 97.

M ZULEEG, 'Frauen in die Bundeswehr' (1997) 50 *Die Öffentliche Verwaltung* 1017.

www.ingramcontent.com/pod-product-compliance
Ingram Content Group UK Ltd.
Pitfield, Milton Keynes, MK11 3LW, UK
UKHW020257051026
15470UKWH00020B/403

9 781841 1344